Presented through

The Haddonfield Friends

of The Library

Jack & Barbara Tarditi

Buildings, Landscapes, and Memory

PRECEDING PAGE
3.1. View of the University of Virginia from Lewis Mountain. Edward Sachse, painter, 1856. Casimir Bohn, lithographer. UVA Special Collections Library.

2.1. Marquis de Lafayette, 1824–1825. Painted by Samuel F. B. Morse, 1824–1825. Art Commission of the City of New York.

FACING PAGE TOP
3.30. East Wing of Campbell Hall, University of Virginia, addition built 2006–2008, W.G. Clark, architect. The elegant visual connections into studio review galleries dramatically frame the life of the School for people approaching the building. Photograph by Scott F. Smith, 2008. Courtesy of Scott F. Smith.

FACING PAGE BOTTOM
5.15. Foss & Conklin stone-crushing plant along the Palisades at Hook Mountain in Rockland Lake, New York. Photograph, c. 1900. Palisades Interstate Park Commission.

Stone Crusher, Rockland Lake, N. Y.

6.4. St. Louis riverfront plan proposing
a massive clearance project and construction of an elevated plaza, over a parking
garage. Harland Bartholomew, planner,
1928. Later site of the St. Louis Gateway
Arch and Jefferson National Expansion
Memorial. From A Plan for the Central
River Front, St. Louis, Missouri
St. Louis: City Plan Commission, 1928.

FACING PAGE
9.1. Charlottesville Courthouse Square.
Albemarle County Courthouse at center,
Clerk's Office at left. Building directly
behind the Clerk's office renovated for
court use in 2009 with addition of classical portico. Brick sidewalks and street
and colonial lantern lights added as
part of the early-21st-century improvement project. Confederate Memorial in
foreground. Thomas "Stonewall" Jackson
equestrian statue at left edge. Photograph
by author, 2010.

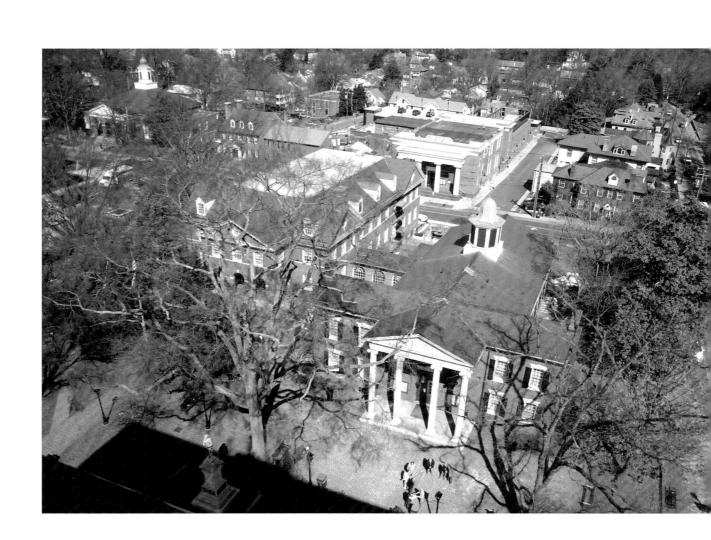

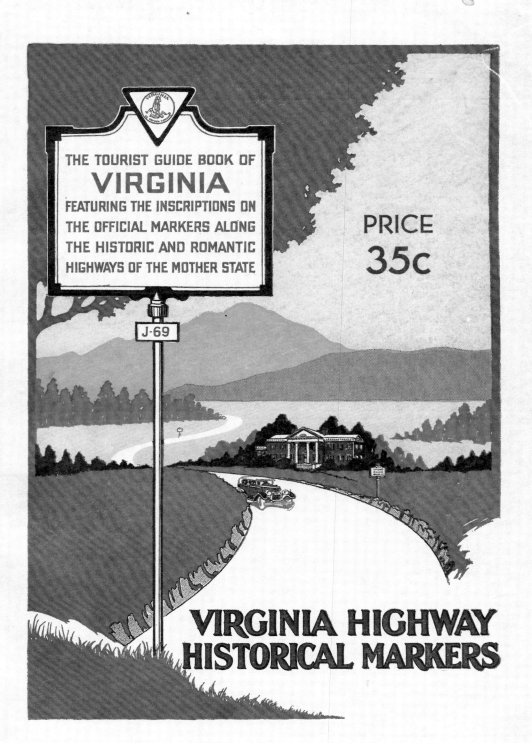

THE TOURIST GUIDE BOOK OF
VIRGINIA
FEATURING THE INSCRIPTIONS ON
THE OFFICIAL MARKERS ALONG
THE HISTORIC AND ROMANTIC
HIGHWAYS OF THE MOTHER STATE

J-69

PRICE
35c

VIRGINIA HIGHWAY HISTORICAL MARKERS

10.4. Cover illustration of road guide.
Virginia Highway Historical Markers, 4th edition, 1931.

*11.1. Fresno Sanitary Landfill, a mound
of 7.9 million cubic yards of garbage built
between 1937 and 1987 and designated
a National Historic Landmark in 2001.*
Photograph by author, 2010.

*11.6. Central Chemical Company EPA
Superfund site, Hagerstown, Maryland.*
Photographs 2003. UVA School of Architecture.

Buildings, Landscapes, and Memory

CASE STUDIES IN HISTORIC PRESERVATION

DANIEL BLUESTONE

W. W Norton & Company
New York • London

For

Barbara Clark Smith

builder of memories in our common landscape

For information about permission to reproduce selections
from this book, write to
Permissions, W. W. Norton & Company, Inc.,
500 Fifth Avenue, New York, NY 10110

For information about special discounts for bulk purchases,
please contact W. W. Norton
Special Sales at specialsales@wwnorton.com or 800-233-4830

Manufacturing by Friesens
Book design by Abigail Sturges
Production manager: Leeann Graham
Electronic production: Joe Lops

Library of Congress Cataloging-in-Publication Data
Bluestone, Daniel
  Buildings, landscapes, and memory : case studies in historic
preservation / Daniel Bluestone. — 1st ed.
      p. cm.
  Includes bibliographical references and index.
  ISBN 978-0-393-73318-1 (hardcover)
1. Architecture—Conservation and restoration—United
States—Case studies. 2. Historic preservation—United
States—Case studies. I. Title. II. Title: Case studies in
historic preservation.
  NA106.B59 2011
  363.6'90973—dc22
                                2010019094

ISBN: 978-0-393-73318-1

W. W. Norton & Company, Inc., 500 Fifth Avenue,
New York, N.Y. 10110
www.wwnorton.com
W. W. Norton & Company Ltd., Castle House,
75/76 Wells Street, London W1T 3QT

0 9 8 7 6 5 4 3 2 1

Sections of chapters 7, 8, and 11 were previously published:

"Chicago's Mecca Flat Blues," *Journal of the Society of
Architectural Historians*, 57 (December 1998): 382-403.

"Preservation and Renewal in Post-World War II Chicago,"
Journal of Architectural Education, 47 (May 1994): 210-23.

"Toxic Sites as Places of Culture and Memory: Adaptive
Management for Citizenship," chapter in *Reclaiming the Land:
Rethinking Superfund Institutions, Methods, and Practices,*
Gregg Macey & Jon Cannon, editors, (Amsterdam: Springer,
2007), 245–65.

Contents

Acknowledgments

This book project engaged parts of the decades on either side of the millennium. I owe heartfelt thanks to many, many people. I want to thank Robert A. M. Stern for encouraging me to start writing the book. I want to thank Ned Kaufman for encouraging me to finish it and for illuminating the way. Richard Longstreth read everything between the beginning and the end and was more generous and helpful with his time and critical commentary than I could have ever hoped for. None of these three will accept responsibility for, nor agree with, all that is here, but all three have a special knack for sharpening the analysis by taking their stands, clearly.

Philip S. Krone and I began collaborating on Chicago historic preservation projects over twenty-five years ago. Phil has a brilliant way of making connections between people and places and ideas. While the case studies in this book are from Chicago and the United States, Phil, a whirlwind traveler of the world, always counseled the importance of learning from the international context. He guided the way between continents from Barcelona and Bilboa, to Tangier and Marrakesh, from Buenos Aires and Machu Picchu to Prigi and Borobudur.

These travels and this book have had constant companions in Barbara Clark Smith, Hattie Bluestone, and Henry Bluestone Smith. At times the travel days seemed long. At times the research and writing seemed to distract from more pressing matters. Still, they have the gift of humor that has filled the places we have shared with laughter, joy, and extraordinary memories. This book is theirs in more ways than I can say. They have my love and gratitude.

Colleagues and students at the University of Virginia and others, both in the academy and in the historic preservation field, have sustained this project with ideas and insights too numerous to account but inspiring nonetheless. I want especially to thank: Julie Bargmann, John Beardsley, Betsy Blackmar, Casey Blake, Lydia Brandt, Tico Braun, Robert Bruegmann, Jon Cannon, Richard Collins, Sheila Crane, Robin Dripps, Eric Field, Emily Gee, Virginia Germino, David Glassberg, Laurin Goad, Neil Harris, Ted Hild, Peter Holsten, Mike Jackson, Gregg Macey, Randall Mason, Martin Melosi, Judy Metro, Beth Meyer, Vince Michael, Fernando Opere, Max Page, Joan Powell, Reuben Rainey, Janet Ray, the late Roy Rosenzweig, Tim Samuelson, Chuck Shanabruck, Bill Sherman, Howard Singerman, Peter Waldman, Mike Wallace, Carroll William Westfall, Chris Wilson, Richard Guy Wilson, and Aaron Wunsch.

I thank all the keepers of memory in the archives and collections upon which this book relied, especially at the Special Collections and Facilities Management Resource Center at the University of Virginia, the Albemarle-Charlottesville Historical Society, the Library of Virginia, the National Archives, the Library of Congress, the Chicago History Museum, the Brooklyn Historical Society, the New York Public Library, Avery Library and the Columbia University Archives.

Several institutions have provided important support for this publication including the Sesquicentennial Fellowship Program at the University of Virginia, the National Endowment for the Humanities, and the Graham Foundation for Advanced Studies in the Fine Arts.

The editors at W.W. Norton have been a pleasure to work with. Nancy Green reads with deep insight and edits with clarity, patience and purpose. Fred Wiemer's copy-editing eyes have saved me from more blushing than one could imagine. Libby Burton has kept us all on track.

CHAPTER ONE

Introduction

Buildings, Landscapes, and Memory

In 1986 architect Philip Johnson called preservation a "phony movement."[1] Preservationists had strenuously opposed recent Johnson buildings that they insisted compromised the historic character of New York's Times Square and Boston's Back Bay neighborhood.[2] Johnson's counterattack suggested a surprising about-face, for a quarter of a century earlier Johnson had stood with preservationists, even walking a picket line, to protest the proposed demolition of McKim, Mead & White's monumental Pennsylvania Station in New York City. Johnson thought the building compared well with "the great cathedrals of Europe."[3] Outrage over the 1963 demolition of Pennsylvania Station provided momentum for the modern preservation movement in the United States; it contributed directly to the 1965 founding of the New York City Landmarks Preservation Commission, the passage of the 1966 National Historic Preservation Act, and the 1978 ruling of the United States Supreme Court that upheld the regulatory power of public officials to protect architectural, historical, and cultural landmarks. By the 1980s, Johnson felt that preservation had sprawled far beyond the bounds he had earlier envisioned: "Preservation is a double-edged sword. It gets too broad, and every lady in tennis shoes feels that everything should be preserved. There is no judgment." Johnson's comment revealed not only his sexism—a view he shared with many contemporary opponents of preservation—but also his elitism. In Johnson's view the preservation movement needed to be based on "architectural quality" and aesthetics, "checkable with authorities" and limited to the most architecturally significant buildings.[4] What ordinary people thought—indeed, what nonarchitects thought—was unimportant. Preservation based on attachments to place, sentiment, or historical association struck Johnson as subjective, emotional, and irresponsible.[5]

What Johnson failed to acknowledge was that in the United States preservation had roots in people's attachments to place quite apart from connoisseurship or architectural appreciation.[6] What people see, or fail to see, in historic places varies broadly. Understanding preservation involves coming to terms with the ways cultural, economic, political, and historical values are bound up in the fate of historic buildings and landscapes.[7] Indeed, despite Johnson's desire for a different sort of preservation movement, historic preservation in the United States is not now and never has been just about architectural values. Engaging the debates concerning preservation and destruction at ten different sites, this book explores core values that have shaped historic preservation in the past and have relevance for its future. These ten places range from the Palisades along the Hudson River north of New York City to the grounds of the Jefferson National Expansion Memorial along the Mississippi River in St. Louis, from the Mecca Flat Apartments in Chicago, Illinois, to Courthouse Square in Charlottesville, Virginia. Preservationists are not always very articulate about why they feel certain places merit preservation: their assumptions about why history, heritage, and place should matter are important but often remain unstated. Yet the principles that have guided both preservationists and their opponents can be unpacked and scrutinized. Fundamentally, both preservationists and their opponents agree in focusing on clearly delimited places: buildings that stand within precise property lines, like Pennsylvania Station; districts or neighborhoods that stand out from the broader cityscape or townscape, like Boston's Back Bay; or bounded landscapes of special significance, such as Asheville's Biltmore Gardens, the Gettysburg Civil War battlefield, or the Grand Canyon. All of these places have in common a palpable, tangible, physical character that is valued by preservationists and devalued by their opponents. In this book I generally do not consider preservation in the context of abstract discourses about, for example, the imperatives of historic memory or the prerogatives of private property;[8] like preservation itself, this book addresses actual places, using them to frame a broader set of ideas and values rather than the other way around.

Preservation often involves an effort to retain the familiar lines of a historic place; yet, as a discipline, preservation is anything but static. The understanding of what constitutes a reasonable object of preservation desire has changed drastically through time. Assumptions about the proper use of private and public power in preservation have also changed.[9] Most important, beliefs about what benefits preservation confers upon an individual, group, or society have shifted with time and place. This book starts with a discussion of the commemoration of place in the Marquis de Lafayette's triumphal tour of the United States in 1824–1825 and concludes with a discussion of the political import of interpreting history on Superfund toxic waste sites. These two themes, seemingly so fundamentally different in time and place, chart the continuing relationship between preservation of place and the politics of citizenship. Lafayette's tour occurred a generation before what is often assumed to be the start of historic preservation in the United States.[10] The chapter looks at the way in which Lafayette visited sites associated with his earlier participation in the American Revolution that were assumed to have special power to both recall history and to channel the ongoing currents of American civic life. The reverent sensibility with which Lafayette approached historic places later framed patriotic efforts to preserve places viewed as relevant in the narrative of the formation of the American nation. A more reverent approach to the history and preservation of place on toxic Superfund sites stands to help us shape the contours of a new ecologically grounded citizenship vital to survival in an age of environmental degradation and global warming. People stand to gain a great deal by reflecting upon human actions that create and then clean up toxic sites. Both Lafayette and the interpreters of history on toxic sites have engaged in serious-minded preservation efforts that stand well outside of Philip Johnson's aesthetically determined preservation frame. These cases and others in this book chart the rich variety of ways people have grappled with the significance of place and history in their landscape.

By the end of 1986, Johnson had balanced his dismissive criticism of preservation by a noteworthy gesture, the donation of his country estate in New Canaan, Connecticut, to the National Trust for Historic Preservation.[11] Yet, if anything, the donation served to reinforce Johnson's one-sided view of preservation. The estate, in which Johnson retained life tenure, included Johnson's famous Modernist Glass House (1949), which stood with Mies van der Rohe's Farnsworth House and Frank Lloyd Wright's Fallingwater as one of the notable American monuments of Modern style domestic architecture. Johnson's donation buttressed his vision of a preservation movement devoted to what were considered aesthetically notable buildings. Indeed, the house's design, with its plate-glass walls, its highly visible, unpartitioned, and sparsely furnished interior, was widely assumed by observers to have privileged aesthetics over domestic comfort and livability.[12] It was built as a work of art and could now be preserved as a work of art, perhaps capable of artfully inspiring future generations of architects and clients. Nevertheless, sentiment and the consideration of tax breaks for the donation did not entirely escape Johnson's calculations. Johnson declared, "Perhaps I'm flattering myself that it's historical but I want the International Style to be seen as historical before it's old fashioned."[13] Johnson resolved to use the power of architecture, the power of his private financial fortune, and the power of preservation to ensure his own architectural legacy. Sentiment stood at the center of this effort. He insisted that "all architects want to live beyond their death. There's room for 12 houses on the land—I'd rather preserve it than have a ticky tacky subdivision built. And I'd like to build up a national trust."[14] The donation might also have reduced tension between Johnson and preservationists, including those with whom Johnson had served during his term as a trustee of the National Trust.

Philip Johnson died in 2005, and the National Trust opened the New Canaan estate and the Glass House to the public in 2007. Part of Johnson's legacy on the site, as preserved, aimed to forcefully insist, all evidence to the contrary, that architectural aesthetics should provide the worthy core for the preservation movement and for National Trust stewardship. Although aesthetics enter into the preservation debates taken up in this book, they do not constitute its central focus. The chapter on the late-nineteenth- and early-twentieth-century campaign to preserve the Hudson River Palisades north of New York City, for example, necessarily engages directly the arguments that insisted upon the utmost importance of preserving scenic beauty and the geological spectacle of the Palisades. Perhaps more important, it delves into a time and a case when historic preservation and scenic conservation efforts were viewed as complementary; the American Scenic and Historic Preservation Society, founded in New York in 1895, one of the leading organizations advocating the preservation of the Palisades, actually encompassed both preservation and conservation in its institutional mission. If aesthetics entered into the consideration of organization members, it almost always had to do with natural beauty and rarely with historic preservation. The Palisades campaign also nicely frames the tensions that arise when people value sites that are owned privately by others who are more committed to their destruction than their preservation. Along the Palisades the contemplative eyes admiring scenic beauty took on the destructive hands of stone quarry operators.

Philip Johnson saw preservation as a double-edged sword because of what he saw as sentiment-driven preservation campaigns; however, there are also clear cases where aesthetics-driven preservation has produced its own pitfalls. In Chicago after World War II, the center of gravity in preservation shifted from sites valued for historical association to aesthetically notable buildings, especially those connected with the rise of what historians were increasingly describing as a Chicago School of Architecture. As the chapter on Chicago argues, this shift in focus meant that preservation came to encompass only a handful of sites with buildings by Louis Sullivan, Frank Lloyd Wright, and Burnham & Root while abandoning huge swaths of the nineteenth-century city; the fact that this took place during what proved to be the most destructive period in Chicago history since the disastrous 1871 Chicago fire made it a preservation catastrophe for the city. In fact, preservationists, whether focused on aesthetics or association or various other rationales, ironically contributed not only to preservation but also to destruction. In Chicago in the 1950s and 1960s, entire residential neighborhoods and blocks in the downtown, full of what in another time would be viewed as significant buildings, were demolished for urban renewal and highway projects. Here buildings seemingly stood and then fell beyond the reach of preservation because the most organized preservationists ignored the entreaties of community activists and local historians committed to places that did not neatly fit the conception of a Chicago School.

Thinking critically about preservation requires also thinking critically about its opposite—destruction. We have a good deal to learn about historic preservation by tracing the values that promote destruction.[15] Both preservation and destruction involve people framing narratives and stories about existing places that promote the process of holding on or letting go of those places. In Chicago and other major American cities, for example, settling upon broad urban renewal programs involved a process of "inventing blight," and promoting a narrative about the dire conditions in certain buildings and neighborhoods, particularly in the years around World War II.[16] I have charted this development in microcosm in the chapter dealing with the preservation campaign to save Chicago's famous 1892 Mecca Flat Apartments. In the Mecca, despite its notable precedents in architectural design, preservation arguments turned on a different set of issues related to housing supply, social equity, and an effort to preserve African-American cultural and domestic space. In the chapter on the disap-

pearance of Dutch homesteads in the Flatbush section of Brooklyn, I have traced the key routes toward the devaluation of traditional Dutch vernacular architecture in the face of the urbanization of the Borough of Brooklyn. To the extent that people succeeded in preserving the heritage of Dutch homesteads in Brooklyn, they did it by literally moving houses out of the everyday landscape and into a local park and museum. The houses were collected as outsized examples of decorative arts detached from the landscape they had historically defined. Preservation often requires individuals or communities to come to terms with places in a way that pushes back against the powerful natural forces and cultural narratives that contribute to destruction.[17] Here, charting the routes toward destruction in Chicago and Flatbush provides sobering accounts of the relative powerlessness of preservationists in the face of what is often portrayed as the benign process of building up the future, unfettered by the past.

Preserving and demolishing buildings and landscapes involves much more than simple thumbs-up or thumbs-down decisions about particular places. Since preservationists generally assume that the physical character of place is crucial in linking present and future generations to valued aspects of history, they have established a broad range of conservation principles and policies about how best to maintain, use, and adapt historic buildings, landscapes, and their immediate environs so as to preserve the "integrity" of historic places.[18] In the twentieth century, preservation organizations have developed detailed policies to control the nature of changes and additions made to historic sites. Between 1975 and 2008 the National Park Service, for example, published forty-seven Preservation Briefs to guide the preservation, rehabilitation, restoration, and additions to historic buildings and landscapes. The series assumes that without guidelines and regulations the meaning, significance, and legibility of preserved historic places can easily be compromised. While such guidelines often focus on the historic resources themselves, they also attempt to regulate the form and nature of new buildings and landscapes built in the vicinity of historic sites. In my chapter on preservation and design at the University of Virginia, a place designed originally by Thomas Jefferson and added to the coveted United Nations Educational, Scientific, and Cultural Organization's World Heritage list in 1987, I focus in particular on the changing influence of a historic site itself on the form and character of new buildings added to the growing university. Guided by strong preservation ideals and sentiments, the university has often approached new construction above all as a threat to the legibility and meaning of the Jeffersonian architectural legacy. The result has been a tradition of new architecture inspired less by the excellence of Jefferson's original design and more by gestures of fitting in that all too often shade off into mediocrity and banality. At Jefferson's university and in many places regulated to preserve historic "character" and historic "integrity," the resulting pervasive mediocrity flows directly from a belief that we need to closely control the environs of historic sites, privileging the past over the present and future. Preservationists need to critically reflect on the extent to which their vision of history as bound up in the material form of buildings and landscapes sometimes fosters new places that will never themselves be valued as historic or particularly notable.

The case of the University of Virginia is a compelling one because it straddles preservation categories. Preservation at the university has involved an effort to maintain an extraordinary architectural ensemble, one that Philip Johnson undoubtedly would have admired. It has also aimed to maintain a tangible and particularly illuminating link to Thomas Jefferson himself, the founder of the university. Preservation constitutes only one way of presenting or preserving history. There are also written histories, oral traditions, and historical productions—including theater, movies, and museum exhibitions. Preserved buildings and landscapes actually rarely have the ability to narrate their own histories; they often rely on some manner of historical interpretation derived from people, things, and historical narratives that stand very much outside of the preserved place itself. Lafayette's history in the Revolution was preserved both in commemorative historic places and also in numerous written histories, paintings, and sculptures. There are dozens of American cities, townships, counties, and geographical features that preserve his memory by taking on his name. Place names have the power to link us to the past. Chapter 10 discusses the efforts of Virginians to develop a system for evoking local history in the landscape through one of the earliest and most extensive installations of historic highway markers. To scrutinize historic preservation practice in the context of other efforts to frame narratives of history in the landscape, I have also explored the construction of historical monuments in which the power of tangible architectural form assists in inspiring reflection upon history. Lafayette's tour involved cornerstone-laying ceremonies for key Revolutionary War monuments, like the one on Bunker Hill. Chapter 6, on St. Louis's Jefferson National Expansion Memorial arch, includes an extended discussion of the debates that played out on the Mississippi riverfront between monument builders and historic preservationists. Monument builders aimed to demolish an extended territory including historic buildings to provide a site for the proposed national monument. Some preservationists saw the demolition as inconsistent with the underlying strategy of recognizing and celebrating history. Chapter 9, on the preservation campaigns in and

around Court Square in Charlottesville, Virginia, focuses on a similar tension between the demolition of historic buildings and the construction of historic memorials; here a park and an equestrian statue of Civil War hero Thomas "Stonewall" Jackson replaced several of the oldest buildings in the city. On Charlottesville's Court Square, as in Chicago's Mecca Flats, race and identity framed the debates over history and commemoration. Considering these commemorative monuments in their urban and political context opens important vistas on historic preservation. Both monuments and historic preservation share considerable common ground when it comes to public and popular presentations of history. Monuments tend to cast a new light on the tenacious efforts to preserve the historic "integrity" of historic buildings and landscapes when it seems quite clear that the monumental landscape successfully conveys history quite apart from site integrity or place authenticity.

Monument building and demolition in St. Louis and in Charlottesville privileged national and regional events while eclipsing narratives of local import. In these and other places it is apparent that historic preservation, like other forms of commemoration in the landscape, involves considerable editing and selective historical recall. The process whereby individuals, institutions, and communities choose to wield both private and public power to highlight certain histories, and to ignore or render invisible others, is a critical dimension of historic preservation and public history.[19]

In the places scrutinized in this book I have sought to understand something of the process involved in remembering history as it stands in the landscape. I have also explored locales in which forgetting and the failure to appreciate historic narrative were implicated in the demolition of historic places. Like preservation practice, the book is grounded in its particular places. *Buildings, Landscapes, and Memory* is not a comprehensive survey of the methods and practice of historic preservation. It is neither particularly geographically nor chronologically expansive. It does not treat thoroughly all of the social, cultural, or economic issues that have guided historic preservation through time. In its cases it does directly challenge the narrowness of Philip Johnson's vision of preservation as exclusively devoted to architectural appreciation. Preservation has been and ought to continue to be fundamentally about constituting a politics of place and a place-centered citizenship in which buildings and landscapes provide the grounds for us to critically understand and thoughtfully negotiate the relationship between the past and the future. Beauty is surely part of this calculus. This book's histories highlight a much broader usable past for historic preservation wherein people have defined themselves and their communities by grappling with the place of history, culture, and economy both in their landscape and in their lives.

CHAPTER TWO

Patriotism in Place

Lafayette's Triumphal Tour of the United States, 1824–1825

Historic preservation engages history through the palpable character of place. It aims to preserve and interpret histories that are profoundly bound up with specific buildings and landscapes. In this respect preservation occupies an unusual place among the broad set of forms that chronicle history. That constellation ranges from private storytelling to public orations, from amateur genealogical charts to scholarly history monographs, from portrait painting to commemorative monument construction, from museum exhibitions to movie productions. In contrast to these forms, the practice of preservation gets much of its evocative power from tangible qualities of place. That physical anchor often lends credibility to historical accounts; it helps bear witness by drawing upon the full range of our human senses; it also strengthens the social, political, and cultural role of preservation by making narratives of past history accessible and meaningful to present and future generations.

In the decades after the American Revolution, preservation in the United States was not common; in fact, much public discourse and many civic pursuits in the early republic were devoid of substantial engagements with history of any sort. The nation's relatively shallow historic record, a diverse population gathered from distant places to share new beginnings, unburdened by the past, and a public critique of Europe with its monarchies and the dead hand of history—all encouraged apathy, if not hostility, toward history. Most scholarly accounts of preservation history bypass this era and locate the origin of America's preservation movement a full generation later.[1] Nevertheless, during this period some Americans sought to promote civic order by preserving

buildings and landscapes that could shape national memory, history, and politics.[2] The triumphal tour of America in 1824–1825 by the Marquis de Lafayette (fig. 2.1), former major general in the Continental Army and French hero of the American Revolution, provided a national venue for thinking about the American past and exploring modes of preserving its memory. The extraordinary thirteen-month tour focused the attention of diverse groups of Americans on specific places connected to the history of the Revolution, places that some viewed as vessels of history worthy of celebration and preservation. Such views of preservation possibilities anticipated central elements of the later historic preservation movement. The tour spurred preservation of a number of specific Revolutionary historic sites. Moreover, planners of and participants in Lafayette's tour considered various ways historic preservation might draw upon and enrich a much broader commemorative universe, for the tour gave rise to portable historic relics, art, portraiture, souvenir production, and temporary and permanent civic monuments. It gave those concerned with retaining public memory of the Revolution the impetus to think about the usefulness and impact of such forms. This chapter examines Lafayette's historic tour as it reflected and influenced contemporaries' emerging preservation sentiments. The Lafayette celebrations reveal that reverence for historic forms and desire for modern improvements stood in complex and at times tense relationship in this period. The vibrant commemorative culture of the tour also shows Americans examining the relevance of their past to their future. As they came to terms with history and place, they helped build the foundation for the historic preservation movement.

*2.1. Marquis de Lafayette, 1824–
1825. Painted by Samuel F. B.
Morse, 1824–1825.* Art Commission
of the City of New York.

Lafayette:
Politics and Preservation

In August 1824 the Marquis de Lafayette proposed a toast at a Boston banquet held to honor his return to America. He toasted "the City of Boston, the Cradle of Liberty—May Faneuil Hall ever stand a monument to teach the world that resistance to oppression is a duty, and will, under true republican institutions, become a blessing."[3] Besides Faneuil Hall, Lafayette's tour also inspired efforts to preserve Philadelphia's Independence Hall, numerous battlefields, and many artifacts of the Revolution. Lafayette believed, as later preservationists would, that specific historic places in the American landscape could help frame key narratives of American history and politics. Preserving and recognizing that history could foster patriotic nationalism, lend coherence and unity to a growing nation roiled by political and regional conflict, and give continuing relevance to the Revolution's ideals both in the United States and around the world.[4] This convergence of legacy, lesson, and landscape clearly distinguishes preservation from most

other forms of national historic memory. Lafayette was ahead of his time in identifying a significant political and social role for historic buildings and landscapes. In 1805, for example, Boston officials had commissioned architect Charles Bulfinch to design a massive expansion of Faneuil Hall, which had become too small to accommodate both growing town meetings and the public market. Bulfinch's plan doubled the width, added a third floor, and tripled the interior space (fig. 2.2). Although Bulfinch set out to "conform to the original style of the building," the cradle now seemed more like a four-poster bed, significant less for its historic form than for its practical accommodations.[5] In Philadelphia in 1816, Pennsylvania officials considered demolishing Independence Hall and selling the land for private development.[6] Lafayette's concept of the power of historic places countered such advocates of change and destruction.

An 1824 invitation from President James Monroe and the United States Congress initiated the visit that turned into one of the most notable civic spectacles of nineteenth-century America.[7] During 1824 and 1825, as the jubilee of the Revolution approached, Lafayette visited

2.2. Faneuil Hall, built in 1742 and substantially enlarged in 1806. Addition by Charles Bulfinch, architect. Photograph, c. 1906. Library of Congress.

2.3. Reception of Lafayette. French lithograph,
c. 1825. Blancheteau Collection, Cornell University.

all twenty-four states and spurred huge celebrations. In major cities crowds estimated in the tens of thousands turned out to greet the "Nation's Guest" as he made his way along parade routes to elaborate banquets, balls, and receptions (fig. 2.3). Traveling to Bunker Hill, Yorktown, and other battlefields, visiting Washington's tomb, and stopping at landmarks of his earlier American travels, Lafayette explored the historic resonances of particular American places. Structured as a pilgrimage, the tour cultivated the essential link between historic remembrance and place that later infused the American preservation movement. Indeed, the tour came at a time when direct historic memory of the Revolution had begun to wane. By 1824, Lafayette was the last living general of the Continental Army. As such, he played the role of narrator of the historic landscape. He conveyed lessons of patriotic duty, sacrifice, unity, and triumph as he revisited historic sites. Such narration could keep alive historic memory, but fifty years after the Revolution many people worried that this direct recounting of history was about to disappear along with beloved figures like Lafayette. This concern brought historic buildings and landscapes into an interesting tension with other forms of historic recall, including monuments, portraits, and sculpture. True,

historic sites seemed to carry some authority of their own: thus, the palpable physical qualities of the buildings and landscapes that Lafayette visited seemingly lent veracity and bore witness to the general's historic accounts. Yet personal, eyewitness narratives, like those that pervaded the tour, would now increasingly need to be replaced by forms that could provoke critical civic inquiry by successive generations about what had happened in those places. In this context leaders began to scrutinize the emerging relationship between historic places and broader commemorative undertakings.

The places of interest in the Lafayette tour were vessels for a rich associational history. Lafayette's interest in Faneuil Hall had everything to do with associations and nothing to do with aesthetics. Associational histories of place, as opposed to the aesthetic history of form, dominated Lafayette's interest, and Lafayette's tour involved an elaborate choreography of commemoration. Nearly every major state and locality appointed committees of arrangement, hosting delegations, and escorts that organized events of the visit, accommodations, and decoration and embellishment of celebration sites. Although the tour demonstrated great commemorative variation, dominant patterns emerged. Lafayette and the planners of the tour

2.4. English earthenware Lafayette pitcher. R. Hall, designer, c. 1825.
Courtesy of Skillman Library, Lafayette College.

considered particular sites significant solely for their associational history, and such associational histories of place would provide the central focus for American preservation until the very end of the nineteenth century. Equally important, Lafayette and his hosts engaged locality in two divergent ways. They noted familiar historic places, but they also viewed with hearty approbation new places of obvious progress and improvement. Simultaneous admiration for these very different kinds of landscapes captured elements of the complexity and occasional contradiction of nineteenth-century preservation visions. After all, zeal for improvement often threatened the very existence of historic buildings and landscapes. Monuments built to commemorate the Revolution hovered between these two classes of admired landscapes. Such monuments were simultaneously about history while also representing prosperity and improvement. To understand the move toward preserving historic places in an around the Lafayette tour, it is important to explore the use of these landscapes in relationship to other leading commemorative forms that flourished during the visit. These commemorations included banquet toasts and veterans' reunions; parades; the exhibition of historic artifacts; the creation, display, and sale of portraits, statues, and other artworks and souvenirs (fig. 2.4); and finally, the creation of both temporary and permanent monuments. In one way or another, all of these disparate efforts to promote historic memory aimed to help citizens make the lessons of the Revolution part of their ongoing civic life.

The Body as Political Space and Relic

Places and props aided the commemoration of Lafayette and the Revolution in the 1824 tour, but in the most immediate sense Lafayette himself provoked historic memory. In Kentucky a student at Transylvania University gave interesting verse to this embodiment; he declared Lafayette ". . . a PRECIOUS RELICK in our sight / Of ancient worthies, still in MEMORY bright."[8] In Alabama, Lafayette's hosts declared, "Your presence, General, awakens the fond and cherished remembrance of those early scenes in the history of our country, when young in years and feeble in resources, she assumed the bold and commanding attitude of resistance and defense against the arbitrary assumption of tyranny and oppression."[9] A Connecticut newspaper also described the general's presence as a vehicle for remembrance: "Looking through the vista of more than forty years, the memory breaking from its slumbers, calls into rapid review 'the times that tried men's souls.'—The noise of battle, the shouts of victory and the terrors of defeat . . . rush upon the mind. . . . These are the images and reflections, which uncalled for present themselves, on seeing before us the Hero, who . . . flew to our succor."[10] Observers differed over whether memories were bright or slumbering, but Lafayette's simple, dignified physical presence clearly moved people to reflect on the past.

At the center of the Lafayette spectacle stood the vexed question of whether the citizens of a democratic republic could remember and show gratitude toward their supporters and benefactors. Did the turbulence of popular rule foreclose possibilities both for memory and gratitude as the democratic people confined their interests narrowly to the present?[11] Lafayette's hosts worked strenuously to counter the charge of republican ingratitude. People throughout the country received Lafayette warmly and entertained him lavishly. The Congress provided him with $200,000 in stock and a township of public land. More symbolic and social displays of gratitude to Lafayette and his generation were more common. At one dinner in New York among the nearly fifty separate toasts were ones to Lafayette, "our distinguished guest," "the Memory of George Washington," "the memory of General Warren, whose blood has watered the tree of liberty," "the 19th of October 1781: Capture of Cornwallis at Yorktown," to many other battles and their heroes, "the Constitution of the United States; as it was ordained, so may it always be administered, for the good of the whole," and also a toast, "May our Republic be admired by future ages, for her gratitude to illustrious benefactors, as well as for the free principles of her government."[12] Similar toasts were proposed over and over again in public celebrations. They provided pithy but eloquent lessons about history, patriotism, and gratitude. Toasts circulated with good cheer in the banquet, were published in the newspapers, then lasted in individual and social memory.

Even more dramatic embodiments of the Revolution came when Lafayette encountered surviving comrades or their families. In August 1824, as he moved in front of an "immense concourse of spectators" at the State House in Providence, Rhode Island, Lafayette was approached by the veteran Captain Stephen Olney, who had served under the French general and participated with him in the battlefield victory at Yorktown. According to the newspaper, Lafayette "instantly recognized" Olney and "embraced and kissed him in the most earnest and affectionate manner. A thrill went through the whole assembly, and scarcely a dry eye was to be found among the spectators, while the shouts of the multitude, at first suppressed, and then uttered in a manner tempered by the scene, evinced the deep feeling and proud associations it had excited."[13] In many places on his tour Lafayette met with old veterans; their reunions and stories personified the "proud associations" and historical and patriotic narratives that were celebrated in banquet toasts. And newspaper accounts celebrated as particularly poignant these moments and acts of recognition between old comrades; this is what the newspapers were doing themselves and promoting for Americans in general, even those who hadn't been there.

The Arts and Relics of Commemoration

In contrast to fleeting commemorations embodied in toasts and reunions, portrait painting and sculpture lent a powerful additional dimension to historical recall. Portraiture itself represented an important means of acknowledging the deeds and contributions of historical figures. Indeed, historian Marc Miller argues that portraits of Lafayette and other Revolutionary heroes began to be commissioned in the late eighteenth century as a sign of gratitude and an effort to acknowledge the courage, valor, and accomplishments of the leaders of the Revolution. To be asked to sit for a portrait was a high honor. The portraits also sought to convey patriotic lessons for present and future generations. Portraiture and historical painting served as important props in the staging of Lafayette's tour. In 1824 when Lafayette visited the Buchanan's house on Monument Square in Baltimore, he found marble busts of Washington and Hamilton, Charles Willson Peale's 1784 painting of the surrender of Yorktown, and full-length portraits of Washington and himself. In the library of Yale's Lyceum he viewed a full-length portrait of Washington painted by John Trumbull. At Boston's Exchange Coffee House he dined with portraits of Hancock, Adams, and other Revolutionary patriots nearby. In 1824 when he attended a ball at New York's Castle Garden, Lafayette encountered a bust of Hamilton. In city after city, Lafayette and the people gathered by the tour's spectacle communed through the artists' medium with departed comrades and past events. Illuminated transparencies reunited Washington and Lafayette and transported them back to various scenes of their triumph. Anticipating Lafayette's final departure from America, many state and local governments, including those of New York City, Philadelphia, Kentucky, and New York State, commissioned portraits of the elderly general. Ary Scheffer's portrait of Lafayette assumed a place of honor in the Rotunda of the United States Capitol. These artistic renderings of Lafayette and other heroes of the Revolution provided an important means of focusing public gratitude and memory around the nationalist civic pageantry of the tour.[14] Yet, while aspects of the tour expressed veneration of historic places, the use of portraiture as a vehicle to constitute historical memory was not bound to specific sites. It thus enjoyed some of the same flexibility that toasts and veterans' reunions did in fostering links to and lessons from the past.

Portraiture and the imaginative conception of Lafayette as a "relick" suggested an underlying public faith in the power of material things to encourage historical reflection and patriotic belief. Portraits and historical paintings were generally created in the aftermath of the glories they recorded. By contrast, in actual artifacts of Revolutionary times the planners of the Lafayette celebrations cultivated a quite different form of material connection to the past—a connection that drew its claim to public recognition from its supposed material authenticity. At various points along the tour, the undoubted power of Lafayette's person came into contact with keepsakes of his earlier service. When Lafayette visited the "brilliantly decorated" New York State Capitol, the banner carried by Brigadier General Peter Gansevoort's regiment of New York militia at Yorktown was displayed and attracted "universal attention." Local newspapers forged a clear connection between Lafayette and the Revolutionary artifact: "It was a relic of days gone by and like the man whom it was brought forth to honor, carried back our minds to scenes of toil and bloodshed in the sacred cause of liberty."[15] Similarly, Lafayette seemed especially pleased with a Connecticut display of a flag taken from the British in battle and an exhibition of Count Pulaski's regimental banner in Maryland.[16] Artillery pieces said to have survived from Saratoga, Yorktown, and other Revolutionary battles similarly embellished the tour, and some were even fired in salute at public celebrations. At the Pennsylvania State House, Lafayette sat in a chair occupied earlier by John Hancock.[17] All these artifacts powerfully "carried back" people's minds.

George Washington's tent from his Continental Army campaigns was perhaps the most notable relic of the Revolution displayed during Lafayette's tour. George Washington Parke Custis, Washington's adopted grandson, provided the "venerable" tent for use in the Lafayette receptions in Baltimore, in front of the Capitol in Washington, D.C., and on the Yorktown battlefield. In subsequent years, Custis used the tent during July 4th celebrations on his Potomac River estate.[18] For a generation of Americans who carried no memories of the Revolution, Lafayette's visit and relics such as Washington's tent could provide important means of focusing civic attention and shaping historical memory and nationalism; they helped materialize the past in people's minds. For his part Lafayette displayed a keen interest in relics as well as some curatorial acumen. In Concord, when he was shown the gun that killed the first British regu-

lar in the Revolution, "the alarm gun to . . . the whole world," Lafayette "suggested the expediency of perpetuating its identity, by inserting a plate on the stock, with an inscription containing the particulars of the event."[19] This proposal, like the display of the Revolutionary souvenirs themselves, anticipated forgetfulness even as it promoted memory; it assumed that time would erode the capacity for telling stories and thus raise doubt about their veracity.

On some occasions during the tour, relics of the Revolution were juxtaposed with historic places. Lafayette viewed the Concord gun at the site of the Concord battle. Nevertheless, like portraits and statues, the relics were moved from place to place without much compromise of their evocative power. Washington's tent was pitched where it had never stood before, but it still attracted civic veneration. Yet, when Lafayette and his hosts celebrated individual places, they recognized the landscape itself as a special and immovable relic, a repository of history and interpretation. One newspaper reported that, in Concord, Lafayette "made very particular inquiries about the precise spot where the first gun was fired by our men."[20] In Lexington, Lafayette visited the "memorable spot" of "hallowed ground, consecrated by the blood of the first martyrs to liberty." Lafayette declared that he especially appreciated being able to visit "scenes so memorable."[21] The presence of fourteen surviving Minutemen enhanced the visit to Lexington, but veterans, like relics, often moved about without losing their narrative power. Places recognized as historic were different. They, of course, could not be moved. But more important, historic places were suffused with a sense of a specific narrative—something happened there that seemed to have affected the course of history. The fact that so many places memorable from the Revolution were places where soldiers had died worked to increase their power and significance. Portraits and written history of the Revolution placed the figure of the artist or author unmistakably at the center of remembrance. A similar act of narration or interpretation was essential to convey the significance of historic places. The historic buildings and landscapes that Lafayette visited did not tell their own stories. However, unlike portraits or written history, the narrator of places stood not at the center but at the edge of remembrance. The power of the account seemed to flow from the place itself, as if place itself could be sufficient witness to the important events that had occurred there.[22] With fewer and fewer people capable of representing the Revolution through their own person, the tour helped dramatically shift the burden of historical narrative from people to places. Lafayette took up an interesting transitional role: he toured

2.5. *Lafayette laying the cornerstone of the Bunker Hill Monument, June 1825. French lithograph, c. 1825.* Courtesy of Skillman Library, Lafayette College.

as a pilgrim to key places; at the same time he himself and the places he visited became the objects of civic pilgrimages by the curious and patriotic. Just as he worried about the Concord gun and posterity, Lafayette framed the terms of reverence for place.

Monuments:
Marking Place, Setting Memory

Beyond highlighting Faneuil Hall, Lexington, and Concord, Lafayette's visit to Boston involved a special procession to and celebration on Bunker Hill. For many years Bunker Hill had enjoyed local reverence and recognition, recalling, for all who visited, Boston's pivotal role in the early years of the Revolution. In 1817, President James Monroe, a Virginian, had paid homage at the site, saying "the blood spilt here roused the whole American people, and united them in a common cause in defense of their rights."[23] When Lafayette visited Bunker Hill, Dr. A. R. Thompson insisted that the visit "revive[d] high national feelings and recollections." Thompson assumed that people in Boston shared the "thrill of delight" at Lafayette's visit with others around the country; however, he asserted that there was "peculiar emotion" that could not be suppressed in receiving Lafayette "on the memorable heights of Bunker," on the "holy ground, immortalized by the deeds, and sacred to the manes of Revolutionary Heroes." Lafayette responded with his own celebration of historic place: "With profound reverence, Sir, I tread this holy ground, where the blood of American patriots—the blood of WARREN and his

companions, early and gloriously spilled, aroused the energy of three millions, and secured the happiness of ten millions, and of many other millions of men in times to come."[24]

Lafayette's interest in Bunker Hill reinforced the efforts of Daniel Webster, Edward Everett, William Tudor, and a group of other civic and business leaders in Boston to preserve Bunker Hill and erect a permanent monument commemorating the battle there. Despite some people's vision of the site as "holy ground," there appeared to be little guarantee in the 1820s that the site would not be subdivided and developed by private owners. Webster worried that "the apathy of the generation" might let "this field of honor . . . be thus violated and for ever obscured."[25] True, in 1797, Boston's Masons had built a monument with a brick pedestal 8 feet square and 10 feet high supporting an 18-foot wood column of the Tuscan order, topped with a gilt urn bearing the inscription J.W., AGED 35 to memorialize Dr. Joseph Warren, the martyr of the Battle of Bunker Hill. However, in 1822 the owner of the open site of the battle, including the Warren monument, announced plans to sell the land at auction. This action inspired Webster, Everett, Tudor, and others to found the Bunker Hill Monument Association in an effort to protect the site and to preserve its history. Members of the association hoped that Lafayette would boost their project. They orchestrated his visit to the site in 1824 and had Lafayette place his name at the head of the subscriber list for the monument. They also won the general's commitment to return to Charlestown in 1825 to celebrate the fiftieth anniversary of the battle and lay a cornerstone for a new Bunker Hill monument.[26]

The planned return to Bunker Hill determined the pace and direction of Lafayette's western tour in the winter and spring of 1825. When he arrived back in Boston, Lafayette laid a cornerstone for a monument that was anticipated but not actually designed (fig. 2.5). After an open architectural competition, the Bunker Hill Monument Association decided to raise a 220-foot obelisk to commemorate the battle on its original site. The obelisk form was lauded as the most appropriate classical form because of its funerary associations. Robert Mills, who had designed a 160-foot triumphal column in Baltimore as a monument to Washington, insisted that columns in commemorative architecture best represented victory and arches stood as a symbol of triumph.[27] With such a catalog of form and meaning, it is perhaps not surprising that all of these forms became associated with Lafayette's tour.

The particular history of the Bunker Hill project reveals tension between places venerated for their history and places celebrated for their improvements. In 1824 and 1825 the Bunker Hill Monument Association purchased the 15-acre battlefield site. The state endorsed the project by granting the association eminent domain powers in order to deal with landowners who refused to sell their part of the battlefield. This purchase effectively saved the site for the education and veneration of future generations. Nevertheless, simple preservation was not the end of the project. Members of the association felt that the mere power of a historic place might not be adequate to keep the narrative of the Revolution in the minds and eyes of future citizens. Accordingly, the association embarked on an ambitious campaign to build a monument that would powerfully mark the battlefield on Boston's skyline and in the imagination of future generations, who would lack a firsthand knowledge of the events that had unfolded on the site.[28] Horatio Greenough, who submitted the winning design entry to the Bunker Hill Monument Association, called for a 227-foot obelisk. Greenough later insisted on the power of the form to invite reflection on the meaning and significance of place. He wrote, "The obelisk has to my eye a singular aptitude in its form and character to call attention to a spot memorable in history. It says but one word, but it speaks loud. If I understand its voice, it says, Here! It says no more."[29] The "here" that Greenough heard referred to the "memorable" spot, the actual landscape of the battle. The obelisk certainly raised the profile and the significance of the site—monumentalizing the historic place's powerful narrative.

Yet, despite an auspicious beginning and the presence and support of Lafayette, monumental aspirations soon outran resources. Lafayette laid the cornerstone in

June 1825, but actual digging of the foundation did not proceed until March 1827, supervised by Boston architect Solomon Willard. Lack of funds halted construction in 1829, with the monument standing at 37 feet of its planned 220 feet. Work did not resume for five years and then stopped again a year later for want of money. The project then languished for six more years and was finally completed in July 1842, seventeen years after it began (fig. 2.6). Most important, financial difficulties led the association to compromise their original preservation vision. In order to raise a building fund to resume construction in 1834, the association sold off 10 acres of its 15-acre battlefield site for the same kind of urban development against which the members had initially rallied. In the end, the monument rose on a site that measured 400 by 417 feet, falling short of the project's earlier goal of preserving the place of the battle itself.[30]

Those associated with the Bunker Hill project clearly felt a high regard for history. Their concern for preserving narratives of the Revolution distinguished them from those developers who aimed to transform the battlefield into streets, row houses, and commercial space. Nevertheless, in 1843 one of the chroniclers of the monument outlined two starkly different opinions that swirled around the project: "To perpetuate the memory of such localities, and to secure them against the dubious haze with which the lapse of time invests them, is perhaps the best argument which can be adduced for the erection of costly monuments. Still, there will be, as there now is, a great difference of opinion as to the expediency of such structures. The open battlefield, undisturbed and unaltered through all time, would be for many far preferable to any monument."[31] Thus, people disagreed whether new monuments added to or subtracted from the historical landscape. Members of the Bunker Hill Monument Association acted as both preservers and improvers; even as they raised their monument, they sold off the ground that constituted the substance of a competing and far simpler preservation vision.

For some, simple preservation of the battlefield would not have spoken as eloquently to the values and ideals of their own generation. Removing the site from the modern operations of the real estate market would surely have testified to the values of the preservers and their reverence for embedded narratives of the Revolution. But it did not mark contemporary commitments as vividly as a monument. Daniel Webster, a leader in the association and the patriotic orator at ceremonies celebrating both the start and finish of the project, addressed this issue in his remarks. Webster initially questioned whether monuments themselves were the most effective means of civic memory. He argued, "We

2.6. Bunker Hill Monument, cornerstone laid by Lafayette in 1825, completed 1842. Photograph, c. 1899. Library of Congress.

know, indeed, that the record of illustrious actions is most safely deposited in the universal remembrance of mankind. We know, that if we could cause this structure to ascend, not only till it reached the skies, but till it pierced them, its broad surfaces could still contain but part of that which, in an age of knowledge, hath already been spread over the earth, and which history charges itself with making known to all future times." A monument, in this view, was inadequate to the events of 1776. Yet, for Webster the importance of the monument lay in what it said about the present as well as the past. He said, "Our object is, by this edifice, to show our own deep sense of the value and importance of the achievements of our ancestors; and, by presenting this work of gratitude to the eye, to keep alive similar sentiments, and to foster a constant regard for the principles of the Revo-

lution." Webster thus hoped that future visitors would remember the patriots of '76 and the commemorators of 1825. In his formulation the monument testified to contemporary aspirations and achievement. Webster highlighted the building of the monument as both an act of gratitude and a work of development. He rallied his listeners around contemporary standards of improvement while adding preservation as a duty: "There remains to us a great duty of defence and preservation; and there is opened to us, also, a noble pursuit, to which the spirit of the times strongly invites us. Our proper business is improvement. Let our age be the age of improvement. . . . Let us develop the resources of our land, call forth its powers, build up its institutions, promote all its great interests, and see whether we also, in our day and generation, may not perform something worthy to be remembered."[32] As the nineteenth century's "age of improvement" advanced, the forces of progress proved less easily reconciled with the forces of commemoration and preservation than had been the case at Bunker Hill. Historic buildings and landscapes were sold not to provide funds for historic monuments but rather to serve current interests in commerce and utility.

The Marquis de Lafayette visited the Yorktown battlefield on the anniversary of Lord Cornwallis's surrender. The visit paralleled the celebrations at Bunker Hill but involved the added significance that Lafayette had participated in the Yorktown campaign. The victory at Yorktown and the surrender of the British army were subjects of many toasts during the tour; however, as the anniversary pilgrimage to the battlefield approached, toasts posited the importance of the battlefield site itself in both personal and civic memory. In Alexandria, Virginia, for example, General Samuel Smith offered a toast to Virginia and the "classic fields" of Yorktown, "destined soon to recall to the recollections of our guest the morning of his glory, and to impress upon the hearts of ten millions of freemen, the achievement won here."[33] When Lafayette reached Yorktown, his hosts were indeed particularly proud and interested in the lessons of place. B. W. Leigh greeted him and declared everyone's happiness to "renew there the glorious recollections of the past. . . . On that spot, sir, we are most proud to receive you. . . . We greet you as the bosom friend of Washington. We greet you as one of the fathers of the Republic."[34]

Even before the dust had cleared from the 1781 Yorktown battle, people had stepped forward to insist that the landscape be specially marked for posterity. The Continental Congress passed a series of resolutions thanking the military leaders of the armies and the navy involved in the victory. Congress also recognized the evocative power of material artifacts from the battle site. They resolved that two pieces of field ordnance, taken from the British army at Yorktown, be presented to Count de Rochambeau and that there "be engraved thereon a short memorandum, that Congress were induced to present them from considerations of the illustrious part which he bore in effectuating the surrender."[35] Finally, Congress acknowledged the significance of the battlefield site itself. They resolved to erect at Yorktown a "marble column, adorned with emblems of the alliance between the United States and his Most Christian Majesty [the King of France]; and inscribed with a succinct narrative of the surrender of Earl Cornwallis."[36] Thus, within two weeks of the historic event itself, Congress affirmed the importance of marking the historic landscape to preserve memory, show gratitude, and convey the Yorktown history to future generations. Despite that,

in the end it took a century to raise a national monument on the site; however, when Lafayette returned to Yorktown in 1824, his visit demonstrated a continuing belief in the power of historic places to evoke narrative, reflection, inspiration, and patriotism.

Indeed, the general's visit dramatically tied past to present. Lafayette stayed in the Nelson House, used in 1781 as the Yorktown headquarters for Lord Cornwallis, which still bore bullet holes and other scars from the battle. Auguste Levasseur, Lafayette's secretary, noted that the conditions at Yorktown were "very appropriate to mark the fete." The town had "never recovered from the disasters of the Revolutionary War because its dangerous location could not attract new inhabitants." As a result, the scene remained reminiscent of battle, with "some houses in ruin, blackened by fires, or riddled with bullets; the land covered with remnants of arms, bomb blasts and overturned gun carriages."[37] A cherished authenticity of place carried the day; General Robert Taylor, addressing the Yorktown gathering, wondered rhetorically: "can we be here and forget . . . the movement of that moral power which was destined to give a new direction and character to political institutions?"[38] While making preparations to receive Lafayette in the Cornwallis headquarters house, the hosts made an astonishing discovery. In the basement they found a heavy box of candles that they determined had been among Cornwallis's provisions forty-three years earlier. The festivities in Yorktown then proceeded with a nighttime ball illuminated by Cornwallis's candles. These candles, relics of the past, fittingly illuminated remembrance, highlighting the drama of historic place that pervaded Lafayette's entire visit.[39] Participants could reflect that, at Yorktown at least, memory shone bright and the flame of liberty yet burned.

Lafayette himself expressed special gratitude for being received on the historic site and on the anniversary of the battle. Lafayette's secretary also reported that his own excitement "to traverse and visit the terrain on which American independence was assured by a brilliant victory . . . did not permit me to stay in the arms of sleep for long." Despite local efforts to cultivate gardens and to pursue agriculture, Levasseur was able to easily locate the wall of the town and remains of fortifications. While pursuing his "research," Levasseur encountered a man "immersed in deep thought." As it turned out, the man was a veteran of the Yorktown battle, who worked a small farm near Yorktown. The man had traveled every year to the Yorktown battlefield on the anniversary of the battle "to pay tribute" to the history and memory of the Revolution. Noting Levasseur's keen interest in the place, the veteran offered to recount and explain the battle: "Let us ascend together to the part of the fort that has remained standing in the midst of so many ruins; from there, we will be able to take in with a glance the plan of operations, and I will be able to make myself understood." This meeting between the secretary and the old soldier surely represented the ideal interaction between the generations, a coming together of historic landscape and historic witness. In this event the landscape itself lent significance and authority to historic remembrance; Levasseur wrote that he "had not dared to interrupt a single time during his account, with so much interest was I listening."[40] The seeming veracity that percolated in the Yorktown landscape was precisely the constellation of historic meaning that the Continental Congress had hoped to foster by calling for a marble column carrying a succinct narrative located on the battlefield.

At Yorktown, Lafayette's hosts did not rely solely on the power of historic places to foster memory and patriotic sentiments. Indeed, they erected temporary monuments on the battlefield to underscore the history. An "elegant triumphal arch" marked Point Rock, where Lafayette had successfully stormed a British position. A 5- or 6-foot-high carved eagle surmounted the 45-foot-high Roman triumphal arch. The arch opening itself was 24 feet high and was formed by thirteen keystones, denoting the original thirteen states. An artist named Warrell worked with an architect named Swain to design the temporary arch built of wood and painted to imitate marble. Beyond the arch stood two 26-foot obelisks, one marking the spot where Baron de Viomenil had stormed a second British redoubt and the other marking the spot where Cornwallis's sword was surrendered.[41] Yet at least one orator effectively dismissed such embellishments as inessential to the power of the original site. General Taylor spoke to Lafayette and the assembled crowd about the commemorative power of the battlefield.

> Here, around us, everything speaks to us of the past and awakens our memories. These plains, on which the plow of peace has not yet effaced the works of war, these ramparts half knocked over, this village in ruins in the middle of which one still recognizes the pits hollowed out by bombs, reminds us how long, cruel and uncertain was the struggle. . . . There, on this little rise, the last scene of this bloody drama ended in the taking of an entire army, and our liberty was assured forever. In the presence of such memories, how do we contain our gratitude for the hero whose courage assured us the benefits of liberty? The soil we tread upon was then a fortification occupied by the enemy, and our vivid imagination recalls to us at once the young chief whose valor rendered us masters of it![42]

Taylor contrasted the authenticity at Yorktown with the pageantry of "novelty" and "dazzle" that greeted Lafayette in some other places. He clearly placed a premium on the traces of the historic battle landscape over against the temporary monumental flourishes made by triumphal arches and obelisks marking the battlefield. "On behalf of my comrades, I bid you welcome," he told Lafayette. "They come to greet you, with no pageantry, intended to surprise by its novelty, or dazzle by its splendour: But they bring you, General, an offering which wealth could not purchase, nor power constrain. On this day, associated with so many thrilling recollections; on this spot, consecrated by successful valour, they come to offer you this willing homage of their hearts."[43]

As Taylor had suggested, the fact that Yorktown had languished as a community following the Revolution meant that development did not threaten to eradicate the history evident in the landscape. In 1838 a congressional committee argued that the monument should be built because the Continental Congress "knew how to appreciate the importance of an event that terminated the struggle of our fathers for liberty and independence, and because no other event in our history is more worthy of commemoration . . . this monument should be erected by the government . . . in a style corresponding with the importance of the event, the benefits derived from it, with the characters of the principal actors in the achievement, and comporting with the pride, patriotism, and dignity of this nation."[44] Calls for the monument continued intermittently but failed to produce results. Yorktown became a site of battle during the Civil War, further complicating the legibility of colonial history and the possibility of unified support for the monument. In 1879, as the centennial of the Yorktown battle approached, Congress did appoint a study group to revisit the matter. Voices from around the county insisted that Congress fulfill its hundred-year-old commitment to mark the battlefield. In 1880, Congress appropriated $100,000 and the secretary of war commissioned architects Richard Morris Hunt and Henry Van Brunt and sculptor John Quincy Adams Ward to design the Yorktown Victory Monument. When completed, a marble column sat on a broad base and carried a sculpted figure of "Liberty." The "succinct narrative" of the siege, the alliance with France, and the resulting peace treaty with England were all inscribed on the base along with representations of nationality, war, alliance, and peace. Masons laid the monument's cornerstone on the centennial anniversary, and the *Liberty* statue was set at the top of the monument in 1884.[45] The 6-acre site of the monument still stands within what had been Cornwallis's line of defense, commanding a vista over the surrounding landscape. In 1930, as the sesquicentennial of the York- town battle approached, Congress and President Herbert Hoover adopted new plans for Yorktown, aiming to increase the commemorative and interpretative impact of the site. Yorktown became a section of the Colonial National Historical Park, as the federal government purchased nearly 2,000 acres of the battlefield for preservation, commemoration, and education.[46] What was most notable about the 150-year-long vision of Yorktown commemoration was the consistent value placed by generation after generation of public officials and citizens upon gathering and channeling the power of place assumed to be embedded in the Yorktown landscape. It shared in the response to the landscape that Lafayette and his hosts engaged while visiting the site in 1824.

The Importance of Place

Like Boston and Yorktown officials, leaders in other localities used their own historic sites as a means of both securing and highlighting a visit from Lafayette. In 1824 a deputation of New Jersey citizens invited Lafayette to "view the ground" of the battle he had fought in June 1778 in Monmouth. Similarly, Princeton residents called special attention to the place where General Hugh Mercer had died in battle.[47] In Philadelphia, residents made Independence Hall central to the sites that Lafayette visited. The triumphal procession into the city ended at Independence Hall (fig. 2.7), and it was here that Lafayette received important delegations. The event effectively reversed a tendency to discount the significance of the hall. In recent decades, with the federal government moved to Washington and the state government to Harrisburg, Independence Hall had languished in some disrepair. In 1781 the prominent steeple on the tower had been removed. In 1802, Charles Willson Peale's extensive collections of natural history and painting became the primary tenant, and the museum remained in the building up to (and beyond) the time of Lafayette's visit. In 1816, Pennsylvania officials even considered demolishing the hall in order to sell the site and its adjacent public square for private development to fund a new state capitol building in Harrisburg. In the late eighteenth and early nineteenth centuries, officials demolished the building's east and west wings and removed the paneling of the first floor Assembly Room where the Continental Congress had met, modernizing the room with plaster and paint. The original doorway on Chestnut Street was removed and replaced with a more stylish entrance.

Thus, the building had hardly been treated as a venerated historic shrine. Lafayette's tour changed that. It inspired cosmetic repairs and, more important, helped inaugurate a sustained interest in the preservation and rehabilitation of the Hall. The mayor of Philadelphia claimed that the "hallowed Hall," meeting place of the second Continental Congress, the place where Independence was declared, and where the Articles of Confederation were drawn up, qualified as the "Birthplace of Independence." Lafayette expressed his own special acknowledgment of the "sacred walls" that had housed the "council of wise and devoted patriots."[48] In 1828 architect William Strickland provided the design for a new steeple that was modified to meet public demands for a restoration of the original building. In 1831 architect John Haviland drew up plans for the building with "a view of reinstating it with its original embellishments." Haviland's actual designs for the restoration of the Assembly Room involved considerable conjecture, and his changes were subsequently removed in the more research-intensive National Park Service restoration. However, it is clear that Lafayette's visit focused public attention on the evocative power of the building and contributed to the enshrinement of place. Preservation ideals and fidelity to Independence Hall's 1770s form provided the rhetorical and practical basis for maintaining and restoring the building.[49]

The recognition of place during the tour ranged from passing historical curiosities to moments of great evocative power and civic poignancy. In Williamsburg, Lafayette viewed with interest the former home of Peyton Randolph, the first president of the Continental Congress.[50] In Halifax, North Carolina, his hosts thought it a "gratifying circumstance" that they could receive him in "the birthplace of freedom of North Carolina"—the building where North Carolina had adopted its first state constitution and local representatives had voted resources to aid the Revolution.[51] Yet few scenes along the tour matched the emotion of Lafayette's descent into Washington's tomb. Here, Lafayette paid respects to the memory of his friend and comrade and renewed the public's identification of the two great men, played out in artwork and at many stops along the tour. The tomb itself (fig. 2.8), of course, did not qualify as a place previously visited by Lafayette. Nonetheless, the landscape through which the general traveled to reach the tomb contained many sites where he and George Washington had traveled together. In Bergen, New Jersey, Lafayette received a cane carved from the wood of an apple tree that had shaded him and Washington during a meal they shared in 1779. The tree had blown over in 1821. The cane offered a portable relic of place.[52] In Annapolis, the

2.7. Linen handkerchief depicting Lafayette arriving at Philadelphia's Independence Hall and at New York City in 1824. Manufactured by the Germantown Print Works, 1824–1825. Henry Francis du Pont Winterthur Museum.

old State House stood as a more fixed relic. Here Washington had resigned his commission in the Continental Army and Washington and Lafayette had parted for the last time in 1784; the historic site stood intact. Washington's voluntary surrender of his power as head of the army held a special place in the history of American republicanism. The mayor of Annapolis declared that Lafayette stood "on the very spot where" Washington resigned his commission—"an act which stands alone among the recorded annals of the world." Lafayette himself described Washington's act as one of "unshaken and unalloyed republicanism." He then testified to the power of the Annapolis site in affecting his own personal mem-

ory. "Amidst those solemn recollections," said Lafayette, "there are personal remembrances endearing and honorable, which the view of this city, of this State House most particularly impress upon my mind, and which mingle with the sense of my actual obligations."[53] The sight of the city and the State House helped both Lafayette and his listeners to draw out the meaning of things and the lessons of place.

Many hosts viewed the resonances of past places as more important than present accomplishments and non-sacred sites. Lafayette heard this sentiment expressed at countless points on his tour. In Fredericksburg, Virginia, for example, the mayor admitted directly that his town's

*2.8. Lafayette at Washington's Tomb.
Lithograph by N. Currier, 1845.* Courtesy
of Skillman Library, Lafayette College.

limited population would "not admit of the pageantry
of a splendid reception," nor could the town "vie with
our sister cities in the erection of triumphal arches, the
display of military parade, and other magnificent exhibition." But Fredericksburg was Washington's childhood
home, the home of General Mercer, and the place where
General George Weedon died. The people who lived in
such a place would give no quarter to other towns in the
extent of their civic pride or the "unmingled gratitude and
love" they held for Lafayette. Fredericksburg, according
to Lafayette, "recalls to our recollection several among
the most honorable names of the revolutionary war" and
thus stood as an equal to other places wealthier in current resources but less well endowed historically.[54] The
residents of Camden, South Carolina, felt the same contrast between their rich historic sites and their relative
economic modesty. On the general's arrival in Camden,
Lafayette's hosts rested their claim to attention on the
"classic ground," the places "consecrated by the shades
of heroes," the spots "honored by their dust." One of
the residents who greeted Lafayette in Camden felt that
the historic places compensated for the town's limited
economic prosperity; he declared "General, your visit

to Camden, excites sublime emotions; we live over in
fancy the scenes of its early history though no splendid
edifices—no gorgeous temples—no 'cloud capt' turrets
meet your eye; still, there are associations connected
with it, more imposing than them all."[55] Lafayette did,
however, help dedicate a modest monument in Camden to Baron Johann de Kalb, the German soldier who
fought and died in the service of the Continental Army
(fig. 2.9). In the absence of booming nineteenth-century
growth, towns like Fredericksburg and Camden proved
more than anxious to receive Lafayette while resting on
their historic laurels and sacred ground.

Modern Improvements as Legacy

As Lafayette toured America, he and his hosts expressed
a reverence for place in many communities that lacked
rich revolutionary histories. The tour's overarching
interest in historic places, of course, implicitly endorsed
preservation ideals. Nevertheless, in traveling to every
state, many in areas hardly settled at the time of the
Revolution, Lafayette took the measure of many locales
that lacked a connection to the war for independence.
Lafayette's enthusiasm for the improvements he found
in new and old places alike bespoke another aspect of
his interest in place. In town after town Lafayette drew
on his memory and his absence of forty years to assess
the economic and social development of the country.
Memory was invoked here less to instill historic patriotism and more to praise achievements of the present
and prospects of the future. In the twentieth century,
some preservationists argued for preserving the scale
and form of certain places as counterpoints to modernity. By contrast, nobody connected with Lafayette's
tour expressed any interest in that sort of preservation; in most cases, they heartily cheered the eclipse
of earlier everyday landscapes by all forms of modern
improvements.

The tour's pageantry of place thus involved preservation and something akin to its opposite—the celebration
of improvement, albeit improvements that were viewed
as evidence of the beneficent possibilities of democracy
and republican government. When Lafayette visited
Frederick, Maryland, William Ross candidly declared
that the town had "no hallowed spot to bring to your recollections some gallant achievement. No fort that was
stormed; no redoubt taken; no field stained with your
blood." But Frederick residents could display "the practical results of these rational and elevated principles of
liberty that led you to our shores . . . a population of
forty thousand, spread over this peaceful valley, all who

2.9. *De Kalb Monument in Camden, South Carolina,*
where Lafayette laid the cornerstone in 1825.
Monument designed by Robert Mills. James Hill,
engraver, 1827. New York Public Library.

are cultivating their own fields, reaping their own harvests, and in the full enjoyment of all the blessings of that independence which you contributed so gallantly to achieve."[56] The absence of any direct connection to the Revolution presented residents of the newer territories and states an even more challenging job of associating themselves with the world of Lafayette. In Shawneetown, Illinois, Judge James Hall noted that European-American settlers had not established the town at the time of the Revolution. Hall acknowledged the shallowness of local history by referencing the historic places and monuments that existed in the more settled East. "Around us are none of the monuments of departed despotism, nor any of the trophies of that valor which wrought the deliverance of our country," he said. "There is no sensible object here to recall your deeds to memory—but they dwell in our bosoms—they are imprinted upon monuments more durable than brass. We enjoy the fruits of your courage, the lesson of your example. We are the descendants of those who fought by your side—we have imbibed their love of freedom—we inherit their affection for La Fayette."[57] For hosts in places like Frederick and Shawneetown, there was an obvious degree of expe-

dience in linking the present to the past through ideology as opposed to place; however, these proud tributes to the present underscored some of the limitations on engagement with history and preservation through the agency of the landscape.

At one of his receptions in Washington, D.C., Lafayette stood in front of the new Capitol building and next to George Washington's military tent and praised the modern changes he witnessed in the country. He declared that "every step of my happy visit to the United States could not but enhance the inexpressible delight I have enjoyed at the sight of the immense [and] wonderful improvements, so far beyond even the fondest anticipations of a warm American heart."[58] He attributed these developments to the superiority of "popular institutions and self government" over the inferior polities of other countries. Similarly, when he admired the "great improvements" at Harvard College, he interpreted them as evidence "of the tendency of liberal political institutions to promote the progress of civilization and learning."[59] In Poughkeepsie, Lafayette expressed his admiration for the "great and astonishing changes" he witnessed in the village."[60] He also told a delegation from

Utica that it would give him "high satisfaction" to return to that area because when he had visited Fort Schuyler in 1784 it stood in "a wilderness." He now understood that "a flourishing and populous town" had developed.[61]

Many of the hosts for Lafayette's tour shared Lafayette's own enthusiasm for improvements and his sense of their political meaning. One newspaper wrote, "At every step he will meet with some object familiar to his memory; objects which must awaken in his ardent mind the most grateful feelings, and fill his soul with the purest enjoyment. He left us weak, unorganized, and tottering with the infancy; he returns to us, and finds our shores smiling with cultivation, our waters white with the sails of every nation, our cities enlarged, flourishing and wealthy, and our free government, for whose establishment he himself suffered, perfected in beauty, union, and experience."[62] At Baltimore one of Lafayette's hosts said: "You are about, general, to enter the city of Baltimore which you have known in other days. In her growth and embellishment you will behold a symbol of our national prosperity, under popular institutions and a purely representative government."[63]

Although improvements were perhaps most notable in towns like Baltimore, rich agricultural areas also had the power to suggest progress and cultivation. In North Carolina a justice of the state supreme court pointed out that areas that had been "trackless forest" when Lafayette last visited were now "cultivated fields" worked by "a nation of farmers, unobtrusively cherishing the domestic virtues."[64] In Mississippi, "a comparative desert" at the time of the Revolution, "obstacles of nature" had been surmounted and "boundless forests . . . converted into a fruitful garden."[65] In Pennsylvania, Lafayette's hosts peopled the wilderness with images of "Indian barbarity" and portrayed the demise of indigenous inhabitants as yet further evidence of progress— "Where the roving son of the forest pursued the chase, towns and villages have arisen—agriculture and arts are cultivated—and instead of the calumet and wampum, the symbols of savage amity, we are this day enabled to offer you the sincere greetings of a social and civilized people, enjoying in peace the blessings of a free government and just laws."[66] In places not familiar to Lafayette, an imagined wilderness could easily substitute for actual memory in setting the stage for the appreciation of modern developments. Again, as in the case of most of the towns, nobody connected with the tour proposed the preservation of wilderness areas as a means for future generations to evaluate the improvements in the landscape. The places that Lafayette and his hosts admired and venerated on the tour were either improved places or spots with the resonances of national history. In this context of progressive development, preservation of places with associational meaning actually levied relatively modest demands on the landscape.

Classical Monuments: Revolutionary Heritage as Improvements

As Lafayette toured the United States, he found some Americans ambitiously exploring a third kind of veneration for place. Some of his hosts constructed a commemorative landscape that, as at Bunker Hill, would combine straightforward veneration of historic places with the celebration of modern development. They raised temporary and permanent monuments that commemorated the people and events of the Revolution, often using the monumental forms of Europe, and particularly of Rome. Such monumental forms were erected not only at historic sites but also at spots with no direct connection to the Revolution. They thereby raised the important possibility that Americans might rely on the power of landscape to convey lessons of history quite apart from the history of the locale where the monument stood. In Savannah, Georgia, for example, Lafayette laid the cornerstones for two sepulchre monuments for General Nathanael Greene and General Count Pulaski. The monuments were built on public squares unrelated to the biographies of the heroes buried there. Nevertheless, their sites and their meanings, like those of many historic places visited by Lafayette, were thought to have great importance in distilling patriotic pedagogy. The Savannah newspaper reported, "Monuments erected by contemporaries or posterity, in commemoration of great events, or as tributes to individual excellence, furnish moral lessons to future generations whilst they stand as mementos of the gratitude of those who rear the structures."[67] That premise suggested that monuments could also be deployed to increase the power of a place already celebrated for its historic associations. In fact, since historic buildings and landscapes did not automatically convey their own stories, monuments could help focus inquiry and attention on the historic events of a locality; they might provide the empathic "here" that Horatio Greenough anticipated for the Bunker Hill obelisk. Monuments deployed their power by celebrating venerated people and events with forms that fit comfortably into the landscape of improvement, admired by Lafayette.

For Lafayette's visit to Philadelphia, residents energetically cultivated the combined power of historic sites and a monumentalized commemorative landscape. The atmosphere of nationalism surrounding the tour did little to temper the strenuous competition

ABOVE
2.10. Temporary arch along Lafayette's Philadelphia parade route, 1824. Samuel Honeyman Kneass, watercolor painter, 1824. Independence National Historical Park, National Park Service.

BELOW
2.11. Grand Civic Arch honoring Lafayette in front of Philadelphia's Independence Hall. Wood engraving, 1824. Courtesy of Skillman Library, Lafayette College.

between individual cities over the grandeur of their civic embellishment. Philadelphia, a city that had lost its earlier economic and political dominance to New York City and Washington, pursued the preparations for Lafayette's arrival with great zeal. Like other places, the city cultivated both local memory and invented tradition. The old Pennsylvania State House, built in the 1730s and later called Independence Hall, provided the focal point for the Lafayette reception. Lafayette's procession to the old State House on the first day of his visit juxtaposed the sites and people of historic Philadelphia with the images of Rome. The procession numbered over 20,000 marchers and included uniformed militia troops, Revolutionary War veterans, elected representatives and distinguished individuals, as well as contingents representing the city's various trades— printers, shipbuilders, rope makers, coopers, butchers, cartmen, and others—and farmers from the surrounding countryside. The procession recalled Rome as it traversed thirteen civic arches (fig. 2.10) modeled on ancient arches. The final arch standing in front of Independence Hall was the most elaborate. The architect William Strickland wrote that he based his design on

the Arch of Septimius Severus at Rome. Canvas painted to appear like stone and sculpture covered a framework of wood. The arch, 45 feet wide, 12 feet deep, and 35 feet high, was topped by wooden sculptures of Wisdom and Justice, designed by sculptor William Rush, and Philadelphia's coat of arms, painted by Thomas Sully[68] (fig. 2.11).

The contrast between the arch and Independence Hall could not have been greater—the historical reality of Georgian provinciality faced the painted illusion of Roman grandeur. The fact that the committee overseeing the celebration commissioned Strickland's arches suggested that they felt that the resonances of their historic sites could be usefully buttressed by commemorative monuments based on European monumentality. The newspapers of Philadelphia helped define the significance of the arch. Its "imposing appearance" stood as a tribute to the "taste and liberality" of Philadelphia. It presented "a most affecting view, one that the pen is inadequate to describe." Adequate or not, the newspaper described the arch in terms of its relation to its city of origin—"The whole of it is, and will be, during the time it is intended to stand, worthy of Rome in her 'most high and palmy state.'"[69] Republican simplicity was obviously set aside for the moment.

American communities orchestrated Lafayette's movement through their streets with varying degrees of grandeur. New Orleans followed Philadelphia's Roman model. Scene painters J. B. Fogliardi and Joseph Pilie constructed a massive, temporary Roman triumphal arch. In Trenton people reerected the arch under which Washington had passed in 1789 on his way to meet the Congress in New York. The columns and arms and framework of the arch, which had been "carefully preserved from the dilapidations of [the] years,"[70] were now covered with natural and artificial flowers and evergreen wreaths. At Trenton the organizers of Lafayette's reception juxtaposed an American interest in commemorative monuments with a compelling relic from the Revolutionary generation. Some communities did not raise Roman arches but relied instead on simple vernacular arches made of pine bowers and flowers. But even these designs could take on rich iconographic significance. At Newark, New Jersey, for example, a circular temple, 35 feet in diameter, was constructed as a floral masterpiece with thirteen 15-foot-high arches, representing the original states, and surmounted by an eagle and a dome of olive branches.[71] Similarly, the temporary Roman triumphal arch built on the Yorktown battlefield had used classical form to punctuate and ennoble the Revolutionary narrative embedded in the local landscape.

Beyond marking a narrative of the Revolution, the spectacle of classical and Roman architecture in America marked a constructed narrative of the place of the United States in world history. Rome had influenced American architects and planners for decades. In 1791, Thomas Jefferson had pointed to classicism as the only proper form for the Capitol of the new American republic. He wrote to Pierre L'Enfant, "Whenever it is proposed to prepare plans for the Capitol I should prefer the adoption of some one of the models of antiquity which have had the approbation of thousands of years."[72] American neoclassicism extended beyond the civic landscape to shape elements of American religious, commercial, and residential architecture. Nevertheless, public buildings and civic designs generally adhered more closely to classical models than did other forms of late-eighteenth- and early-nineteenth-century American architecture. Civic and political ideology in the United States stirred interest in the architecture of ancient republics. As a modern experiment in republican government, the United States, with its shallow history, cultivated the "approbation of thousands of years" and constructed a narrative of human history that envisioned the new nation as the political successor of the ancient republics and the heir to their architecture. At Independence Hall, Yorktown, and numerous other places on the tour, classical architecture marked places of triumph of the American republic. There was considerably more involved here than imitation of European high-style monumentality; tour planners and their artists were fundamentally involved in a project of appropriation and transformation that confidently located the United States in genealogical relation to earlier republics. In this context civic architecture and commemorative monuments, even temporary ones, reinforced the patriotic and nationalist lessons of the historic sites visited and venerated by Lafayette.

Aspirations Toward Permanence: In Places and Monuments

The temporary designs put in place for Lafayette celebrations suggested that American resources fell short of some people's architectural ambitions for civic grandeur and commemoration. The position of the nation was comparable to the position of the various localities that addressed the modesty of their resources by directing attention to their rich endowment of "sacred" places. Classical commemorative monuments, both temporary and permanent, positioned the United States as the triumphant young heir to ancient republican history. The tour juxtaposed remembrance of the Revolution, embedded in specific places in the American landscape, with a deeper republican history manifested in classical architectural form. Summoning a republican lineage stretching back long before the Revolution, the monuments also represented modern aspiration toward civic elegance, grandeur, and, above all, improvement. Yet those aspirations also threatened the tide of preservation. Indeed, contemporary enthusiasm for improvements, expressed

2.12. *Ceramic platter depicting Lafayette landing at New York's Castle Garden in August 1824. Manufactured c. 1825–1830.* National Museum of American History, Smithsonian Institution.

by Lafayette on many occasions, combined with the idea that modern monuments could diffuse the lessons of the Revolution, eventually undermined the rationale for preserving specific historic sites. Monuments representing both history and improvement had none of the inconvenience of actual historic places, which all too often stood in the way of improvements and that could not be conveniently moved about as could portraits, statues, or smaller historic artifacts. When the Bunker Hill Monument Association divided and sold the battlefield for streets and building lots, it certainly underscored the potential conflict between preserving historic places and celebrating improvement.

Lafayette's tour inspired people to look beyond temporary forays into civic grandeur. As soon as the civic arches were removed from Philadelphia's streets, local residents began to crusade for more permanent civic monuments. A delegation of Philadelphians had in fact told Lafayette that they planned permanent memorials to the Revolution and to George Washington.[73] Still, in 1830 Benjamin Silliman's *American Journal of Science*

and Arts bemoaned the fact that no "tangible memorial" of Lafayette's tour itself existed that could continue to stir civic reverence, veneration, and "love of country" for generations to come. In the face of American commercial character, with its "individuality," "restlessness," and susceptibility to the "pressure of business," the *Journal* insisted that Americans needed something "to turn the mighty energies of our nation, or portions of it, into one channel; to give us some common objects of pursuit and pleasure, or regret and praise; . . . something to make us more a people of one heart and one mind." This "something"—both in the *Journal* and in the rhetoric of many designers of the civic landscape—included civic spectacles like Lafayette's tour as well as the construction of public monuments, buildings, and spaces that might permanently encourage similar spectacles. With such places around him or her, a citizen would feel "warmed, expanded, refined and ennobled," lifted above "selfish and contracted views."[74] The spectacle of Lafayette's tour, with its expressions of gratitude, remembrance, proposals

2.13. *Invitation to Cincinnati ball honoring Lafayette, 1825. Engraved on silk, 1825.* Cornell University.

for monuments, and indeed the entire privileging of history, suggested a transcendence of the market and the present. The *Journal*'s editors clearly hoped to promote that transcendence in contemporary culture. Of course, these acts of historical transcendence could rather easily be turned to market advantage. Cities that built great monuments to history tended to be places where the age of improvement had brought sufficient prosperity to support monumental ambitions. To the extent that monuments made such prosperity manifest, they enhanced the city's ability to attract population and wealth, turning monuments into a form of market advertising and attraction. This same process unfolded at the level of personal consumption, where Lafayette's tour spawned a vast market in souvenirs. Everything from handkerchiefs and gloves with Lafayette's por-

trait to chinaware, hip flasks, paintings, and engravings permitted citizens to appropriate something of the tour. Purchasers recognized the power of things to invoke history in the form of commoditized remembrance (figs. 2.12, 2.13).[75] Historian Sarah Purcell has argued that this souvenir trade and the "commercialization of memory" provided a substantial basis for women acting as consumers to raise their profiles as citizens.[76]

The commercial aspects of monument building and souvenir buying at times tempered their ability to help citizens, communities, and the nation to rise above "selfish and contracted views." In fact, one of the reasons for delays in completing the Bunker Hill Monument was that the Monument Association felt that the project needed to be funded as a Massachusetts and New England initiative alone, so that it would highlight the region's, as opposed to the nation's, contributions to the Revolution.[77] Moreover, the expansive market in Lafayette souvenirs and artworks united people in commemoration even as it divided them by their varied abilities to purchase goods. These tensions worked against the vision of national civic unity conjured up in 1830 by the *American Journal of Science and Arts*. Interestingly, the *Journal* failed to recognize the preservation of historic buildings and landscapes as a "tangible memorial" of Lafayette's tour. And yet among the tour's most significant legacies was its expansive sense of the power of historic places "to turn the mighty energies of our nation, or portions of it, into one channel."[78] On the Revolutionary War sites that Lafayette visited, historic events of great social and political import had transpired. Acknowledgment and preservation of these places had great potential for stirring civic reflection and promoting political unity, despite growing divisions in American society. Unlike monuments and souvenirs, these historic places seemed less susceptible to a narrow market calculus; frequently, the preservation of these sites actually frustrated the ordinary operations of a market for improvement. The preservation movement's view of historic places as the cornerstone of a tourist economy came much later. This view lacked credence in Lafayette's time. What the tour crystallized was the power of historic buildings and landscapes to lend continuing meaning and authenticity to the American Revolution. Significant events had transpired in particular places, and citizens were invited to reflect upon their meaning, thereby focusing on a shared nationalism as a powerful basis for unity. Lafayette's tour thus highlighted civic possibilities and directly fed into the nascent preservation movement in the United States. Places mattered, and their veneration and preservation were among the most important legacies of Lafayette's triumphal tour.

CHAPTER THREE

Captured by Context

Architectural Innovation and Banality at Thomas Jefferson's University

In the first third of the twentieth century, stewards of historic places moved from well-established efforts to protect individual landmarks to more expansive efforts to control development surrounding those historic sites. As their society built on a new scale and economic changes transformed much of the nation, many preservationists worried that discordant development of adjacent land threatened people's ability to connect with historic places and the cultural heritage those places embodied. To secure that crucial connection preservation turned its attention to the broader context in which their valued landmarks stood. Thus, in 1899, following the restoration of Charles Bulfinch's 1798 Massachusetts State House, Boston officials moved to protect the views of this civic landmark by limiting the heights of buildings on nearby blocks of Beacon Hill.[1] In 1931, worried that gas stations and other modern forms would compromise the character of its historic eighteenth- and early-nineteenth-century residences, Charleston, South Carolina, established a board of architectural review to oversee the "Old and Historic District."[2] In Santa Fe, meanwhile, an informal consensus had developed in the 1910s that new construction should blend in with local historic buildings by adopting a regionally derived Pueblo-Spanish style. And in 1926, John D. Rockefeller's restoration at Williamsburg, Virginia, removed 720 buildings constructed after 1790 to make way for an uninterrupted gathering of 341 reconstructed Colonial buildings.[3] These ambitious efforts to regulate the context of historic sites laid a foundation upon which preservation design guidelines and boards of architectural review proliferated in the later twentieth century.

In advocating compatibility between historic sites and their contexts, preservation shared common ground with contemporary efforts to establish harmonious urban ensembles. Private legal covenants for residential subdivisions, City Beautiful Movement civic centers, and early-twentieth-century zoning fostered urban order by clustering compatible urban uses and building types.[4] In preservation, a series of national and international charters has sought to codify various local efforts to create harmony with history by establishing principles for additions and new construction around historic sites. In 1931 the Athens Charter, drawn up at the First International Congress of Architects and Technicians of Historic Monuments, recommended that "in the construction of buildings, the character and external aspects of the cities in which they are to be erected should be respected, especially in the neighborhood of ancient monuments, where the surroundings should be given special consideration."[5] Subsequently, this same organization's 1964 Venice Charter and the United States Secretary of the Interior's 1977 Standards for Rehabilitation reaffirmed these basic principles. In 1979 the Burra Charter of the Australia National Committee of the International Council of Monuments and Sites addressed the conservation of sites of cultural significance. Here, too, a principle of deference prevailed: "Conservation is based on a respect for the existing fabric, use, associations and meanings. It requires a cautious approach of changing as much as necessary but as little as possible." In relation to the context of historic properties, the Burra Charter declared, "conservation requires the reten-

3.1. View of the University of Virginia from Lewis Mountain. Edward Sachse, painter, 1856, Casimir Bohn, lithograph. UVA Special Collections Library.

tion of an appropriate visual setting and other relationships that contribute to the cultural significance of the place. New construction, demolition, intrusions or other changes which would adversely affect the setting or relationships are not appropriate."[6] As the context surrounding historic sites entered the purview of historic preservation, history took precedence; but the guidelines also generated novel and unforeseen architectural and urban forms. These forms now constitute part of historic preservation's modern legacy, and they pose a problem of their own. Defined as "context" and assumed to be secondary to more valued products of the past, buildings designed to be unobtrusive and harmonious can eschew the ambition of being stunning, visionary, or even noteworthy in their own right. Does historic preservation bear any responsibility for the mediocre buildings that often flow from promoting designs intended, above all, to simply not distract people as they engage nearby historic sites? If so, preservationists might need to revisit the matter of the proper relationship between historic sites and adjacent development.

University of Virginia: Jefferson and Heritage

This chapter explores these questions in the case of one extraordinarily rich historic site: the University of Virginia, founded and designed by Thomas Jefferson and opened in 1825 (fig. 3.1). Jefferson's brilliant original design created a legacy and a challenge for university administrators. Through the years, it has led many to value architectural and landscape preservation as an important means of connecting the latest generation of faculty and students back to the institution's founder. Moreover, in many cases university officials expressed a belief that preserving Jefferson's campus has required more than simple architectural preservation; it has also meant deploying Jeffersonian classicism when adding new buildings to the university. Yet the scale of growth and expansion—and the intrusive reality of social, economic, and cultural change—have challenged the effort to maintain a narrative of simple or easy continuity. As designed by Jefferson, the university accommodated 10 professors and 220 students. Over the next century

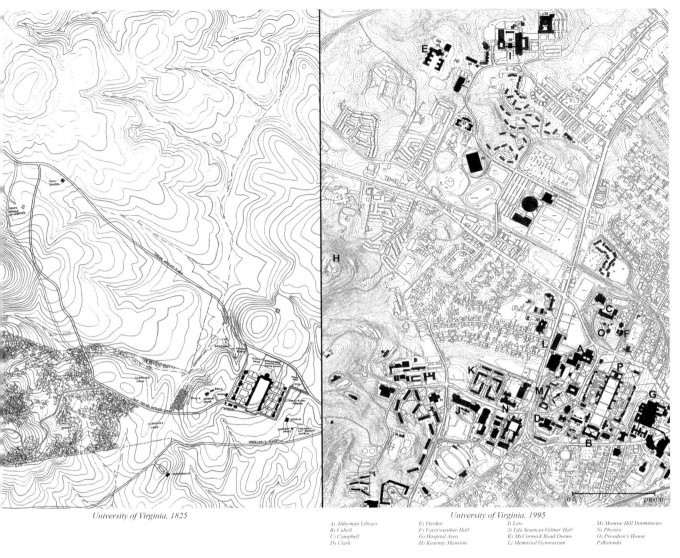

University of Virginia, 1825

University of Virginia, 1995

3.2. University of Virginia growth between 1825 and 1995. Cultural Landscape Survey, UVA Office of the Architect. Adapted by Laurin Goad and Eric Field.

and three-quarters the faculty grew to number 1,800 and the student body expanded to over 20,000. University officials and their architects faced the vexing question of how to determine and maintain the "proper" architectural, historical, and cultural relationship between buildings and landscapes recognized for their aesthetic brilliance and deep historical resonances on the one hand, and substantial and necessary modern additions on the other (fig. 3.2). The depth of Jefferson hagiography at Virginia prompted vigorous debates over the issue. These debates were very much in evidence in the closing decade of the nineteenth century, well in advance of their articulation in the modern preservation movement. The ways in which the university negoti-

ated the relationship between new buildings and its storied architecture and landscape thus suggest both the possibilities and the pitfalls of what are now generally accepted approaches to design in the vicinity of historic landmarks.

In surveying the 185-year history of the university, it is clear that ideas about tradition held by university administrators, faculty, and alumni have intersected with the broader currents of architectural production in complex ways. This account of the university's architectural, institutional, and planning ideals begins in the late nineteenth century and carries through to the early twenty-first century. By looking at key building projects, the chapter provides a sweeping view of the tenacious hold of a particular version of tradition, the shifting ground of preservation practice, and the rise of efforts to have historic form control new design. Because of changes in architectural fashion, efforts to preserve tradition at the university have at times stood with the architectural mainstream; at other times the university has seemed to strenuously resist prevailing currents of architectural production.

The long-term success of the university's preservation efforts was partially recognized in 1987 when the United Nations Educational, Scientific, and Cultural Organization (UNESCO) added the University of Virginia to its coveted World Heritage List. The listing, which also included Jefferson's nearby home Monticello, became the 442nd site recognized worldwide for cultural or natural significance of "outstanding universal value." In the view of UNESCO, Thomas Jefferson's design for the University of Virginia architecturally embodied his Enlightenment philosophy and democratic political ideals.[7] In analyzing how university officials and their architects have zealously guarded the Jeffersonian architectural heritage, it is important to keep in mind that Jefferson himself constantly negotiated his own relationship to architectural precedent. The university's main Rotunda (fig. 3.3), located at the head of the Lawn, was modeled at half-scale upon the ancient Roman Pantheon from 126 A.D. The Pavilions that housed the university's professors and classrooms attended closely to sixteenth-century Renaissance design theories and architectural elements of Italian architect Andrea Palladio, who himself had freely adapted Roman classical architecture. Jefferson also adeptly united his buildings with their site, opening them to garden views close at hand as well as to vistas of surrounding countryside and hills.[8] The overall design provided a compelling image of what Jefferson called the "Academical Village," powerfully capturing a sense of *in loco parentis*, with the professors residing in two-story Pavilions connected around a Lawn by a colonnade fronting one-story student rooms. The Rotunda, housing the university's library, dominated the plan. Dining halls occupied the Hotel buildings, part of the two dormitory Ranges that flanked the Lawn. Public and private gardens connected the Pavilions and Lawn rooms, and the Hotels and Range rooms. As recognized by UNESCO's World Heritage List, the University of Virginia constituted an extraordinary accomplishment in architecture and history.

That accomplishment allowed later architects and university officials to interpret their connection to tradition in quite divergent ways. They could view Jefferson's work as an inspiration for continued and evolving architectural excellence. In other words, they might

have explored new design, new material possibilities, new technologies, and new programs to produce buildings that strived for an architectural and cultural artfulness that rivaled and complemented Jefferson's. Alternatively, architects could work to create an architecture that did not attract attention—that seamlessly blended in, almost obsequiously, with Jefferson's original work. Such an approach was perhaps codified in the demand for respect of historic character as outlined in the Athens Charter and subsequent historic preservation design guidelines. Well before those guidelines, however, Virginia had adopted a particular view of Jeffersonian tradition and a strategy of what I call "tiptoe contextualism." From the 1890s the university consistently fostered quiet, hushed, unobtrusive designs that hesitated to distract from (let alone rival) Jefferson's work. Architectural traditionalism at the University of Virginia has often taken the form of red brick, white trim, and the classical Georgian details characteristic of Jefferson. This approach dominated architectural and campus planning strategy until the late 1950s. A relatively brief period ensued that brought modest experiments with modern architecture, but these initiatives were abruptly terminated by a renewed national

3.3. Rotunda, University of Virginia, built 1822–1826. Photograph by Tyson & Perry, c. 1880. UVA Special Collections Library.

enthusiasm for tradition surrounding the United States Bicentennial and the rising popularity of Postmodern architecture. Once reasserted, the university's particular interpretation of tradition remained the imperative at Virginia, long after the architectural mainstream turned to other ideas and different sources of architectural form and expression.

Trauma and Tradition

In designing new buildings, university officials have kept their eyes fixed on alumni sensibility, deep attachments to tradition and to Jefferson, stylistically considered. Before taking up individual building design, it is important to recognize the broader cultural framework in which traditional architecture developed at the university. That architecture did not flow entirely from cultural confidence, from a seamless institutional continuity, from simple force of habit, or even from a strong commitment to historic preservation. Rather, it aimed to use Jeffersonian elements to parry the effects of a rather stunning series of social and cultural traumas. Virginia drew on the commonly supposed ability of historic preservation to help people and communities deal with unsettling change by preserving old buildings and designing new ones that appeared old.

Growth itself involved some measure of trauma, as the university approached new building warily, not as an opportunity for inspired architectural excellence but as a grave threat to architectural and institutional traditions. Yet, the long practice of traditional architecture that began in the 1890s was in part rooted in two significant nineteenth-century community traumas, one general and one specific. First was the profound trauma of the Civil War, which had depressed the fortunes and disrupted the socioeconomic system of the university and of the Commonwealth of Virginia. Although the university remained in operation during the war, enrollment plummeted from over 600 to just a few hundred.[9] Twenty-five hundred University of Virginia students and alumni fought for the Confederate cause; over 500 died. In March 1865, when Union troops briefly marched into Charlottesville, a white handkerchief attached to a walking stick and the direct intervention of Union officer George Armstrong Custer saved the university's buildings from destruction.[10]

After the surrender of the Confederate Army at Appomattox in April 1865, university enrollment jumped briefly but then receded for decades to between a third and a half of pre–Civil War levels. The library was initially opened only two hours a day. Main-

tenance on buildings was deferred past the point of safety and prudence.[11] With its agricultural economy in shambles, Virginia's government was unable to pay even the interest on its public debt. It was not until 1899 that university enrollment returned to 1850s levels. The university's poverty following the Civil War meant that little building was done for three decades. The provocation of competing architectural aesthetics and eclectic designs that filled many other college and university campus landscapes hardly materialized at all at the University of Virginia, forced to make do with the forms passed down from a more prosperous time. In 1926 architect and museum director Fiske Kimball insisted that "few colleges came unspoiled through the 'dark ages' of Victorianism. The poverty of Reconstruction in the South saved The University of Virginia. Since then the artistic ideals and spirit of Jefferson have again presided, and the new buildings have conformed to them."[12]

Beyond the preservation agenda forced on the university by its constricted circumstances, the existing architecture took on new meaning in the context of the Commonwealth of Virginia's post-Reconstruction reemergence on the national scene. Architecture from the Colonial and early national eras played an important role in buttressing Virginia's claim for a central place in national narratives. At Chicago's 1892 World's Columbian Exposition, for example, the Virginia Building was a replica of Mount Vernon. Historic architecture and re-creating Mt. Vernon at the Columbian Exposition involved a cultural and political strategy of reminding the nation of the commonwealth's role in the founding of the republic, back on the other side of the Civil War.[13]

Virginia's representation in Chicago was significant because the state had refused to participate in the 1876 Centennial Exposition at Philadelphia. In the years just prior to the Centennial, Virginia Governor James Kemper had urged the legislature to appropriate $10,000 for a state pavilion that would represent Virginia's history and resources to visitors at Philadelphia. Governor Kemper was a Confederate veteran of the First and Second Battles of Bull Run and Antietam and had been severely wounded and captured in Pickett's charge at Gettysburg. In addressing the Virginia legislature, Kemper acknowledged that the opponents of Virginia's participation in the Centennial deserved "respectful consideration." The governor agreed that, in the course of the Civil War, Virginia "had been scourged, stripped, desolated and trampled by more than a million . . . armed men."[14] He described the war and Reconstruction as an era of "prolonged mental suffering" and "cruel humili-

3.4. Rotunda and Lawn after 1895 fire.
Photograph by Wampler Excelsior Art Gallery, 1895.
UVA Special Collections Library.

ation" "without parallel within the limits of Christian civilization" for white Virginians who considered themselves the natural and proper rulers of their society. He then succinctly summed up the opposition: "So long as the sections stand in the relation of conqueror and conquered; so long as the laws are in force which treat the one as inferior in right to the other, or one portion of the people as less worthy than another, the representatives of all cannot honestly unite in the common rejoicings of a national festival."[15]

Although he understood opposition to Centennial rejoicing, Kemper still felt that Virginia's resources and people should be represented. A simple reading of history suggested to Kemper that Virginia above all others deserved a prominent place at the Centennial.

> What part of the country has higher claim to be greeted at Philadelphia than the commonwealth whose sons gave that city the grandest of its historic glories? What state of the old thirteen has the better right to stand in the front of this centennial celebration? . . . Does any other state present a roll of superior names? George Washington, father of the country—Thomas Jefferson, author of the declaration of independence; James Madison, father of the constitution—George Mason and Edmund Randolph, architects of American law, and John Marshall, its foremost expounder.[16]

Historic sites, replicas, and traditional architecture, including Jefferson's, could all play a role in buttressing these claims for Virginia's national recognition; they could provide a palpable link between the inglorious postbellum world and earlier glories—before the trauma of secession, war, and surrender. Nevertheless, in 1875 the legislature refused to provide any support for Virginia's participation in the Centennial.[17] There was no easy consensus on how or even whether to take part in national traditions or a narrative of national greatness.

Twenty years later a more specific trauma heightened the reverence for Jefferson's architecture; on October 27, 1895, a "great calamity" and "grievous disaster" befell the university. A fire engulfed the Rotunda, leaving in ruins the most prominent of Jefferson's buildings at the university (fig. 3.4). Seeing the university's main building destroyed, with the dome and floors collapsed, provoked almost immediate demands that the building be rebuilt as Jefferson had designed it. Within days of the fire, the faculty called on the Board of Visitors, the university's governors, to hire an architect to draw up plans for "restoration of the Rotunda" in which the "original proportions of this central building should be religiously observed."[18] A few days later the faculty could cite alumni and others as standing in agreement. "The faculty share in the well-nigh universal sentiment the Rotunda should be restored as nearly as possible, inside as well as outside, to the appearance it presented before the late fire."[19] Here, in the face of destruction, the clear insistence was to reinstate "religiously" the familiar forms that had been lost. These feelings were not limited to people with a direct or sentimental connection to the university. New York architect William Mead of McKim, Mead & White, answered a letter from a university official in the aftermath of the fire: "We all regret the calamity which has befallen the University in the loss of a building that was one of the architectural monuments of the country—and our hope [is] that its reconstruction has fallen into reverent hands. It would indeed be a misfortune if some one tries to be original and improve on what has gone before."[20] Lest disaster beget disaster, the attention of officials at the university turned to restoration, while attempting to hold at bay modern architecture.

The Architecture of "Harmonious Combination"

The sense of loss over Jefferson's central building and interest in its immediate restoration also prompted members of the faculty to insist that six proposed new buildings adhere to the style that Jefferson had established three-quarters of a century earlier. In the view of the chairman of the faculty, the new buildings should be located so as to "constitute an integral part of [Jefferson's] beautiful composition, . . . adhere strictly to classical proportions, . . . so arranged as to heighten the effect of the original . . . group."[21] The faculty reported that it was "deeply impressed with the propriety of following in these new buildings classical types of designs and of locating them so as to create a harmonious combination with the original Jeffersonian group. As we examine the additions made to this system by Jefferson's successors, we are forced to confess with a certain shame that not one of them has added in the least degree to the harmony and beauty and magnificence of the original composition."[22] The consideration of university architecture prompted by the fire led the faculty to cast a critical eye upon the additions to the university between Jefferson's death in 1826 and the Rotunda fire in 1895. To their eyes the view was less than flattering. The faculty demanded that Robert Mills's 1850s Annex to the Rotunda, where the fire had originated, be cleared from the site entirely rather than reconstructed. The Annex (see fig. 3.1) had arguably marred the "majestic loveliness of Mr. Jefferson's Rotunda" and amounted to "a monstrous tail projecting into the space behind and only ending apparently when the bricks gave out."[23] The Rotunda fire helped forge a single vision uniting preservation, restoration, and Jeffersonian revivalism.

For faculty and university officials there was literal currency in simultaneously restoring the Rotunda and constructing new buildings that adhered to original Jeffersonian lines. As it linked the university to a national narrative, that architecture seemed the key to attracting donations from charitable and patriotic-minded individuals around the country, including Americans with no previous connection to the university. Although the national appeal for funds included money slated for new buildings located beyond the Jefferson core, the university titled its fundraising brochure *The University of Virginia. A Plea for Its Restoration*. The tract insisted that the university was a national treasure. "The history of this University, its special features, and unique plan, are all indissolubly linked with the great name of its father, Thomas Jefferson, the statesman of our Revolutionary era." It noted that the Civil War had brought "desolation" to the university. As "the country was stripped of all accumulated wealth, it found itself without resources and with less than a third of its number of students. . . . The resources of the State of Virginia, charged as she is with heavy public burdens, are inadequate to do more for the University than she is now doing." After visiting sectional and regional issues, the appeal for funds returned to matters of the nation, mediated, not surprisingly, by Jefferson's architecture: "At once the crowning work and child of the greatest American statesman . . . [the University was] bequeathed by him as a sacred trust to his people. It is not believed that the pride of this great nation will suffer this trust to fail and this great work to cease from lack of their generous support in this hour of its adversity."[24] Crafted in the wake of the Rotunda fire, the argument linking preservation, Jeffersonian architectural tradition, and fundraising continued to frame discussions about the practice of university architecture for the next century.

Continuity and Change:
The Rotunda Inside and Outside

Despite initial calls for restoring the Rotunda to its original form, the rebuilding actually introduced important changes. A north-facing portico took the place of Mills's earlier Rotunda Annex, acknowledging the emerging pattern of streets and residential settlement north of the university grounds. More important, where the original Rotunda had two main floors, the restoration by McKim, Mead & White threw those floors into a single monumental space (fig. 3.5). This plan permitted a clearer orga-

3.5. Rotunda interior after Stanford White's postfire remodeling, which created a single monumental space in the place of separate Rotunda floors. Holsinger Studio, 1912. UVA Special Collections Library.

nization for the university library, which had outgrown its original accommodations on the upper floor of the Rotunda. The central space of the Rotunda received colossal-order Corinthian columns, grander than any of the earlier Jeffersonian classical elements. These alterations of the Rotunda interior brought the building somewhat closer to its Roman Pantheon model. They also inspired an early effort on the part of university architects to justify designs by intuiting Jefferson's endorsement; in 1898, Stanford White pointed to his design for a new monumental interior and declared, "In restoring the Rotunda . . . only one deviation from the original plan has been made, but this is one which Jefferson would unquestionably have adopted himself had he been able to do so when the Rotunda was built, and one which he would have himself insisted upon still more could he have directed the restoration."[25] In White's view, the utilitarian need for providing diverse accommodations in the Rotunda had forced Jefferson to depart from the Pantheon model and introduce separate floors. Still, even at this juncture, some students

and alumni vigorously objected to the change. They were being asked to contribute to the rebuilding but not consulted about the loss of the Rotunda's oval lecture rooms, "endeared to them by all the memories which bind the college man to his Alma Mater . . . [and] to the scene of their occurrences."[26] In strongly associating memory with landmarks of their formative college years, alumni hinted at the ongoing allure of traditional Jeffersonian architecture.

The reverent restoration of the Rotunda exterior and the advocacy of new buildings that were harmoniously related to the "original Jeffersonian group" were not solely inspired by the trauma that came with the burning of the Rotunda or the subsequent necessity of making national appeals for a restoration fund. The particular upheaval of the Rotunda fire overlapped neatly with emerging trends in architectural production that favored a Jeffersonian restoration. In fact, the years just prior to the Rotunda fire heard notable voices raised against the handful of nineteenth-century buildings constructed at the University of Virginia that had strayed from the classical style. In 1893, for example, William Mynn Thornton, chairman of the faculty, advocated hiring an architect or landscape gardener to provide a general plan for enlarging the university in ways that would avoid the "grave aesthetic and sanitary blunders" of past additions.[27] Thornton, while condemning post-Jefferson buildings at the university, praised the design of Fayerweather Gymnasium (fig. 3.6), just completed in 1893, as "carrying on worthily the Jeffersonian scheme of architecture at the University."[28] Indeed, Thornton specially praised John Kevan Peebles, an alumnus, whose firm designed Fayerweather, and who seemed a worthy exemplar of the Jeffersonian scheme. For his part, Peebles used an 1894 article in the university's *Alumni Bulletin* to insist that readers ask why Jefferson's "architectural scheme has been so desecrated?" Peebles praised Jefferson's recourse to the "most monumental of all architectural styles, the classic," and observed that the architectural success of the World's Columbian Exposition flowed from the decision to work in the classical style.[29]

Brooks Museum:
Victorian Form, Classical Critique

Peebles linked his own advocacy of "Jeffersonian" building to the current enthusiasm for the American Renaissance and Beaux-Arts classicism, exemplified by the monumen-

tal Columbian Exposition's Court of Honor—adjacent to Virginia's Mount Vernon replica. It also reflected emerging ideals of the City Beautiful Movement, which increasingly placed a premium on harmony and classical order in civic buildings, buildings ideally grouped together in spatially unified civic centers. Peebles then proceeded to criticize Mills's Annex to the Rotunda, utilitarian buildings like the Medical and Chemical Laboratory, and the Gothic-style Chapel, designed by Charles Emmet Cassell, 1884–1890. He took special exception to the Second Empire Victorian–style Brooks Museum (1876–1877), designed by John Rochester Thomas, "the first building" "to make an irreparable break" with Jeffersonian tradition (fig. 3.7). In Peebles's view, "The architects who planned it, either failed to visit the University before doing so, or were possessed of a greater share of iconoclasm than falls to most mortals."[30]

This criticism of the Brooks Museum took on particular importance in the effort to revivify Jeffersonian classicism in the late nineteenth century. The Brooks Museum was one of the few buildings constructed during the decades of poverty that gripped the university following the Civil War. The building was the gift of Lewis Brooks of Rochester, New York, who professed an interest in both Thomas Jefferson and the teaching of natural sciences.[31] Brooks died before the building was completed, but he was remembered as one who set out to heal the Civil War's regional rift, which he saw as "inflamed and exasperated" by the "the worst

3.6. Fayerweather Gymnasium, built 1892–1893.
Carpenter & Peebles, architects. Holsinger Studio,
c. 1920. UVA Special Collections Library.

3.7. Brooks Museum, built 1876–1878. John Rochester Thomas, architect. Lacking classical form, and roundly criticized within fifteen years of its completion, Brooks was nearly demolished in the late 1970s because of its anomalous appearance. Holsinger Studio, 1914. UVA Special Collections Library.

passions of our nature." In the view of the rector of the university, the donation involved the "extraordinary spectacle" of someone "rising above the infirmities of human nature, and animated by that spirit of Christian charity."[32] Upon its completion the building was hailed as "an ornament to the University grounds."[33] Given this contribution to healing after the war, there is no small irony in the fact that the Brooks Museum was later criticized as an aesthetic aberration, constituting an "irreparable break" from university tradition. Planned before the official end of the Reconstruction era, its later critical reception at the university perhaps bespeaks the continuation of regional hostility. Even dedication speeches for the Brooks Museum in 1878 included an interesting rhetorical turn that directed attention away from the northern donor and his architect and back to local luminaries. The university rector presiding over the dedication pointed out that even the "proudest structures" of "human hands" "must soon crumble beneath the touch of time's effacing finger." The real work of the building would be to inspire "a noble intellectual contribution to the store of human knowledge." In that intellectual contribution those attending the dedication were asked to acknowledge a different "architect" of the building, neither Brooks nor his architect but rather those who constructed "human knowledge" within its walls:

In casting about for an architect competent to plan and erect this intellectual monument, more stately than the proudest column, and more durable than the pyramids of Egypt, it was readily perceived that he should be a native of Virginia, intimately acquainted with Virginian character, and deeply imbued with Virginia feeling, so that he might give suitable expression to the sentiment of Virginia. It was proper, in the next place, that he should be an alumnus of the University, with a heart filled with filial love to his alma mater, and a mind trained to letters, and scientific investigation, by her admirable system of intellectual culture.[34]

With that introduction James C. Southall—lawyer, newspaper editor, and graduate of the university—delivered the main Brooks Museum dedication address. Within fifteen years, as American architecture moved toward Renaissance and classical revivalism, people associated with the university proved increasingly critical of the Brooks Museum's unfortunate departure from local tradition. For his part, Peebles concluded his trenchant critique of newer university architecture by praising his own design for Fayerweather Gymnasium, where the Board of Visitors "exercised a controlling voice" in a building that "follows the lines laid down by Jefferson, being classic in feeling and in detail."[35]

3.8. *Fraternity houses and boardinghouses along the Madison Bowl. The building at the far right was built in 1904 to house fraternities by Professor William E. Peters following the style of Pavilions on the Lawn.* Holsinger Studio, 1914. UVA Special Collections Library.

Fraternity House Design: "In Keeping with the Other Buildings"

The university was moving toward an orthodox "Jeffersonian" style even as aspects of university life seemed to depart substantially from the founder's ideals or intentions. Thus, in 1853 the faculty had refused to consent to the establishment of an early fraternity because the covert nature of the organization's bylaws and activities might be "open to grave abuses," social "iniquities," and the regrettable "tendency among the members of the conventional fraternities to withdraw from every branch of social life" beyond a narrow circle of members.[36] The Board of Visitors later accepted fraternities on campus, and in 1892 it used its "controlling voice" to outline the conditions upon which fraternities could build chapter houses on lands owned by the university. Emphasizing architectural conformity to the Jeffersonian tradition, the board declared that such houses would have to "present in durability, safety, and style, an appearance in keeping with the other buildings of the University . . . such buildings shall be of brick, covered with metal or slate, and of such dimensions, style, and according to plans and specifications . . . accepted by the Board."[37] This architectural policy helped finesse long-simmering tensions in university governance related to the secret nature, and at times riotous behavior, of fraternities. Architecturally, the fraternity chapters did their part to reassure the university by embracing

Jeffersonian architectural forms, suggesting a seamless identity of purpose between fraternities and the broader university. When one fraternity purchased a lot on Madison Lane for a chapter house, the landowner attempted to promote a corresponding degree of social control with deed language that insisted that "at no time shall there be sold . . . any intoxicating liquor," and that the "conduct of the premises shall at all times be quite as unobjectionable as though the said lot was the private residence of a gentleman and his family."[38] An early example of fraternity appropriation of the Jeffersonian model came in 1904 when William E. Peters, a retired professor of Latin, built a house on Madison Lane for rental as a fraternity (fig. 3.8). Peters, who had earlier resided on the Lawn, used the Lawn pavilion as a model for his rental property. He thus reassigned the temple-front faculty Pavilion form to new use in student accommodations, making an intriguing departure from Jefferson's low one-story colonnaded dormitories. In these instances, conformity to what was becoming an orthodox "Jeffersonian" style masked substantial change.

Continuity and Change: On the Lawn and Over the Hill

University officials and their architect, McKim, Mead & White, took on postfire rebuilding by reverently preserving and restoring the Rotunda. They also added three new buildings—Cabell, Cocke, and Rouss halls—in which they deployed a palette of Jeffersonian classicism that would harmonize aesthetically with Jefferson's original design. Here fidelity with tradition existed largely in the realm of building material and architectural style. In these new buildings McKim, Mead & White effectively deployed elements of Jeffersonian classicism, even though in Cabell Hall (fig. 3.9) they worked at a scale that greatly exceeded that of previous buildings. The red brick, white classical columns, porticoes, and pediments that they employed were all elements of the common vernacular of Jefferson's university. The firm also paid particular attention to the size, color, and pattern of brick in the new buildings. The architects insisted that the brick needed to be "made the size of those in the Rotunda, of the roughness and color of those in the buildings on the lawn," as well as laid up in the same Flemish bond. When Stanford White saw brick arriving from a brickyard in Lynchburg, his displeasure with the resulting contrasts of color and texture led him to argue successfully that the face brick for the new buildings needed to be made on the university grounds, using the same clay used for the original buildings.[39]

By contrast, when it came to the broader landscape character of the historic site, university officials failed to see or to preserve the spatial structure of Jefferson's original design. The founder had designed the south end of the Lawn to be open, with views to distant mountains, yet the university placed its new buildings at the south end of the Lawn, and closed off these views. Although the McKim firm has often received criticism for this closing,[40] they had actually advised against the plan when they discussed expansion options with university officials. In February 1896, Stanford White recommended a more modest placement of new buildings at the sides of the Lawn; although closing the Lawn would give the "most natural and architectural finish of the group," he argued, "we feel that the second site at the side would be the most practical; and we should regret blocking the beautiful vista at the end of the present campus."[41] Perhaps White would have been more convincing if he had grounded his argument not in the mere beauty of the south vista but in terms of the reverent preservation of its Jeffersonian character. Ignoring his advice, university officials decided to close the vista.

If McKim, Mead & White did not prevail when it came to preserving the landscape character of the original university, their sensitivity to the landscape setting, particularly the hilly topography around the Lawn, did help them buttress the architectural dominance of original Jefferson buildings. In 1896 the firm described a key

3.9. Cabell Hall, built 1896–1898. McKim, Mead & White, architects. Cabell enclosed the south end of the Lawn, which had previously been open to views of the region's mountains. Holsinger Studio, 1914. UVA Special Collections Library.

3.10. Cabell Hall, built 1896–1898. McKim, Mead & White, architects. View shows major portions of the building constructed well below the level of the Lawn. Photograph, c. 1920. UVA Special Collections Library.

element of the site for the new buildings. "The character of the land, falling away on the southern side of the road, allows . . . buildings to appear as only one story in height, whereas on account of the steep grade they actually count for practical use as two. The charm of the present Close and the domination of the Rotunda are therefore preserved."[42] This view, that additions to the university should be visually understated, represented an early expression of tiptoe contextualism that, depending upon one's perspective, could either appear respectful or timid. Nevertheless, the approach was unambiguous, as the architects contemplated a somewhat unarchitectural ideal to campus planning—they aimed to add space by partially hiding buildings (fig. 3.10). This approach of minimizing the visibility of new building became a hallmark of subsequent planning at the university.

Expanding:
Jefferson, Manning, and Bradbury

Although they spoke to the broader landscape context of their designs, McKim, Mead & White worked exclusively on individual building commissions for the University of Virginia. In 1908 the university retained landscape architect Warren H. Manning to develop an overall plan for expansion. Like McKim, Mead & White before him, Manning advocated stylistic harmony between existing and future buildings. He favored buildings that followed "closely that of the Georgian period of colonial architecture, in which Jefferson's structures were such a dominant factor."[43] Manning argued that future building needed to be "based on a study of the original plan of the University as laid down on the ground by Jefferson." He searched Jefferson's letters and plans for hints of how Jefferson envisioned the expansion of the university. He decided to expand the grounds west of the West Range by creating

another great "quadrangle" that would "visually" have its terminus at McKim, Mead & White's recently completed President's House, which Manning "fixed on the main axes of the quadrangle."[44] The house, earlier described by its architects as "somewhat patriarchal in character and very close in its general style to that of the old University buildings," seemed a suitable terminal element for the new quadrangle.[45] On this axis Manning proposed a new formal entrance to the university. He also urged officials not to "depart from the Jefferson plan" with its preference for small-scale student accommodations.

Manning's systematic approach to the university landscape, his ideal of stylistic harmony between new and old, and his vision of formal axes using new buildings as terminal features aimed to give coherence to the expansion while also permitting the continued dominance of Jefferson's original plan. In essence, Manning planned for both reverent preservation and harmonious expansion. His plan carefully orchestrated the monumentality of the Jefferson design. New additions to the university took their place in a spatial system that was organized from the center outward, from Jefferson to more recent additions. Significantly, this systematic spatial hierarchy, favoring the Jeffersonian core, also galvanized Manning's leading design ideas for an important private residential commission adjacent to the university. In 1909, Manning collaborated with architect Eugene Bradbury on an estate for John Watts Kearney on the top of Lewis Mountain, the highest promontory in the immediate vicinity of the university. Kearney owned a 152-acre tract on the sides and top of the mountain. Bradbury designed the house itself, while Manning advised on the selection of a site and the laying out of its grounds. Manning clearly visualized the Kearney design as an aspect of the larger university landscape. He used his trip to meet with Kearney to consult on the university's expansion plans. The fact that some visitors to Charlottesville continue to mistake Kearney's house for Jefferson's Monticello suggests the extent to which the house became an integral feature of the university's composition. Indeed, Kearney's land offered many potential building sites. In the end, Kearney, Manning, and Bradbury agreed to locate the building on the easternmost edge of the Lewis Mountain summit, on a spot crowning the steep final rise to the mountaintop. This site had the strongest possibility for visual connection to the university, located one mile to the east on a ridge that stood 300 feet below the summit of Lewis Mountain.

In an unmistakable form of architectural address, Bradbury gave the Kearney house a tetrastyle portico with a tympanum lunette in the pediment on the elevation facing the university. In this way Bradbury deployed a historicist, classical, and contextual strategy for rooting the house in its locality. The design of the university below provided a center of architectural gravity of some consequence. Indeed, the house terminated an axis stretching west from the Rotunda very much in the way that Manning viewed the President's House on Carr's

Hill terminating the new entrance axis. In this expanded sense of the university, Jefferson's Rotunda now dominated more than the rooms, pavilions, and colonnades along the Lawn; it now seemed to set up classical architectural lines that radiated out over the countryside to the top of Lewis Mountain. Although differing in scale, the façades of both Kearney's house and the President's House, with their four-column porticoes and pediments, incorporated a classical motif similar to five of the ten Jefferson-designed Pavilions on the Lawn.

In a more private realm, less visible from the university, Bradbury eschewed Jeffersonian red brick in favor of a more picturesque character, and a very different sort of contextual engagement. There was not much of the Jeffersonian or "Virginia Colonial" in the hand-cut stone exterior of the Kearney house, stone quarried on Lewis Mountain itself (fig. 3.11). Instead, there was an emphatic response to scenery, setting, and the geology of place that was Jeffersonian in a broader sense. This aspect of Jefferson is sometimes lost in narratives of his stylistic classicism, and yet it is precisely such engage-

3.11. *John Watts Kearney House, built 1909–1910. Eugene Bradbury, architect; Warren Manning, landscape architect. The design incorporated the classical elements of the adjacent university but also forged a powerful connection to the geology and topography of the site.* Holsinger Studio, 1912. UVA Special Collections Library.

ment with topography and place that gives Jefferson's architecture much of its power and brilliance. One need only think of the terracing of the Lawn, the variation of the number of student rooms between the Pavilions in order to manipulate the sense of perspective and increase the university's apparent monumentality in the landscape, the integral accommodation of gardens in the design for Pavilions and student rooms, the orientation of both the university and Monticello toward views of distant mountains, and the embedded service dependencies at Monticello that represent such an ingenious response in architectural plan and section to the social and topographic realities of the site. Jefferson's 1782 *Notes on the State of Virginia* also underscored his deep understanding of the Virginia landscape. Jefferson had a landscape agenda that was as profound as his agenda for classical architecture and, in many cases, even more successfully developed. Consonant with that element of Jeffersonianism, the driveway to the Kearney house circled the summit two and a half times before reaching the door, spiraling up through rock outcrops and retaining walls and gardens and terraces that seemed to be incorporated directly into the main walls of the house itself.

In the Kearney design, then, Manning and Bradbury worked with a sense of experiment in their treatment of both the house and the surrounding landscape. These design qualities often eluded architects employed on university commissions, including Bradbury himself, who designed the Entrance Building in 1912–1914 (fig. 3.12). The Entrance Building, which housed a bookstore, tearoom, and university offices, appropriated the arcaded motif of the Ranges, the projecting portico common on the Pavilions, the alternating mass of one- and two-story sections, the Chinese Chippendale balustrades familiar on the Lawn, and the traditional Flemish bond brick pattern and white trim. The building thus adhered to the architectural recommendation made earlier by Manning that new buildings follow the lines laid down by Jefferson. Reflecting the historic buildings at the core, the Entrance Building lacked the innovative approach to material and site that characterized the Kearney mansion; there was no carefully articulated connection to the landscape and no artfully orchestrated sense of movement around or into the building. The building captured the idea of "Entrance" rhetorically but not in its actual design, plan, or site. While appearing in its details to be more Jeffersonian than the Kearney mansion, the Entrance Building failed to explore the deeper aspects of Jeffersonian design that pervaded the Kearney project.

3.12. *University of Virginia Entrance Building, built 1912–1914. Eugene Bradbury designed the building drawing on the classical style, materials palette, and massing of the nearby Jefferson-designed Lawn and Ranges.* Holsinger Studio, 1915. UVA Special Collections Library.

3.13. *Dawson's Row, built 1859. William Abbott Pratt, architect. The one-story classical porticoes were added in 1911–1912 to help reconcile the six buildings to the classicism of the University's Lawn and Ranges. Ludlow & Peabody, architects.* Postcard photograph, c. 1915. UVA Special Collections Library.

Tempering Competing Aesthetics

In the 1890s, when Professor Thornton and architect Peebles criticized the post-Jefferson development of the university landscape, they did not single out particularly the 1850s work of university architect William Abbott Pratt. Pratt, a Richmond architect, had worked as superintendent of buildings and grounds at the University of Virginia between 1858 and 1865. However, their general, dismissive comments on architecture following Jefferson made it clear that Pratt's work was an object of disdain. In the midst of pervasive classicism at the university, Pratt explored a competing nineteenth-century design aesthetic; he sited new buildings using a more picturesque sensibility that contrasted sharply with the regular and symmetrical geometries of Jefferson's work. When Pratt designed an infirmary in the area south of the Lawn, for example, he rotated the axis of the building so that it related more directly to its hilly site than to the classical lines of the nearby Academical Village. In the late 1850s, Pratt also designed six dormitories that accommodated approximately one hundred students on the south edge of the Lawn. Known as Dawson's Row, the project increased the number of students accommo-

dated at the university by nearly 50 percent. The small scale of the two-story brick buildings, each with eight rooms, certainly adhered to the intimate scale of the original student dormitories. However, rather than organizing them in a geometrical pattern, Pratt laid out the dormitories in a sweeping arc, stepping up Monroe Hill. The plan drew attention to the informal character of hilly topography while eschewing the university's classical lines. During this same time Pratt designed a new, turreted, Gothic-style front for Charlottesville's Albemarle County Courthouse. Pratt's plans at the university and the courthouse provided an aesthetic contrast to local classical architectural traditions.[46]

Pratt's picturesque aesthetic contrasts did not survive long once the university and its architects began to advocate reverent preservation of Jefferson buildings and adoption of Jeffersonian classicism for new buildings. In 1910, university president Edwin Alderman commissioned architects William Orr Ludlow and Charles Samuel Peabody to design a new "colonial façade" for each of Pratt's six Dawson's Row dormitories (fig. 3.13). The new plan would "make the Row in keeping with the prevailing architecture." In particular, in an effort to "improve and beautify" the university, each building on Dawson's

Row received a classical portico "after the same style seen on the lawn and ranges." An unexecuted part of the plan also called for a colonnade linking all six buildings on Dawson's Row with one-story student rooms opening onto the colonnade and filling the space between the individual two-story dormitories. This plan would give the row "an appearance very much like that of the lawn, with a nearly semicircular contour."[47] Thus, the policy promoting architectural harmony for new buildings also influenced changes made in existing buildings.

"Sons of Virginia": Proper Design Through Proper Schooling

Over time, having alumni architects take on work at the university tended to reinforce these nascent ideals of traditionalism. In the 1920s, the officials decided to economize on architectural services by asking several alumni architects, including John Kevan Peebles, Walter Dabney Blair, and Robert E. Lee Taylor, to serve on a commission of architectural advisors who would design university buildings while members of the architectural faculty and university staff assumed responsibility for producing working drawings and superintending construction. The Board of Visitors' Buildings and Grounds Committee assumed that such a plan offered the "fullest guarantee of preserving our architectural traditions."[48] In President Alderman's words, they all felt that gathering "sons of Virginia," "a group of men homogeneous in feeling about the University," would "be a very handsome thing to do."[49] This approach was later codified into law when the state legislature mandated that Virginia architects be employed on state building projects, including those at the university.

Walter Dabney Blair, who felt that his previous university work should have earned him direct commissions, intensely objected to serving on the proposed architectural commission. He wrote to the president,

> When we today look at the [Brooks] Museum or the Randall Building, we wonder how the University authorities could permit such structures, so devoid of any architectural merit, to be built. We ask ourselves how it was possible to be so insensible to architectural beauty. . . . apparently to your Committee, a building [is] a building, nothing more, which any architect with or without experience could design equally well. It has not occurred to your Committee that that high quality of design, that emotional content which is revealed in great buildings, is the product of individual genius.[50]

Blair outlined his objection further in a letter to William A. Lambeth, superintendent of buildings and grounds: "At the time when other eastern Universities are employing the most talented architects to carry on their building operations, resulting in the creation of monuments of superb beauty, it is profoundly disheartening to know that your committee thinks that it can achieve architecture excellence, which by its nature must always be personally created, by means of a Commission. The results would inevitably fall far short of the best."[51] To some extent the question hovering over this sharp disagreement was whether working in the university's well-defined tradition required "individual genius" or not. Or perhaps the issue was whether the "most talented architects" then building at other eastern universities were superfluous—or outright unwelcome—in the particular case of Virginia. The university surely had already felt the hand of an individual architectural genius. Was it sacrilege or an honor to the founder's legacy to encourage continued creativity at Jefferson's university?

Preservation Through Topography: Hiding Books, Beds, and a Gym

Blair eventually gave up his campaign for individual genius and joined the Architectural Advisory Commission to design Memorial Gymnasium and then many other buildings at the university (fig. 3.14). The sheer size and ambition of the gymnasium project had the potential of raising a competing aesthetic with the Jefferson buildings, but the commission followed the precedent of McKim, Mead & White, adding a new building but also hiding it. Memorial Gymnasium ended up on a site at the edge of the grounds, on land standing at a substantially lower elevation than that of the historic Rotunda, Lawn, and Ranges.

Purposefully creating less visible new architecture became a well-worn strategy. When the university had their architectural commission design a major expansion of student housing on campus, President Alderman briefly objected to the relatively obscure site selected on the west side of Monroe Hill, largely blocked from the Lawn and Ranges, which would put them "rather out of sight."[52] Fiske Kimball proposed an interesting alternative that would bring the Memorial Gymnasium into a tighter composition with the rest of the campus—four dormitory buildings would fill in the ground between the gym and the plaza on the north side of the Rotunda. The plan would place the buildings symmetrically in two rows that climbed the hill toward the Rotunda.[53] One of Kimball's other proposals was for a dormitory cluster on

3.14. Memorial Gymnasium, built 1924. University's Architectural Commission, architect. The building's massiveness was tempered by its construction well below the ridgetop site of the university's Jefferson-designed buildings. Holsinger Studio, c. 1930. UVA Special Collections Library.

the athletic field and tennis court area immediately north of Madison Hall. Here the plan called for "another lawn flanked by colonnades and pavilions not unlike the main lawn of the University, but all used for dormitory purposes. . . . The fundamental thought was to preserve the unique and special architectural character of the University, namely, to have low rows of dormitories punctuated by pavilions."[54] Neither plan was followed as the dorms went into hiding on the west side of Monroe Hill.

Yet growth itself increased the pressure for the university to utilize sites near Jefferson's original core. In the 1930s the land between the gym and the Rotunda plaza that Kimball had recommended for dormitory construction became the site for Alderman Library. Alderman, the new main library, was built when the university's book collection numbered 250,000 volumes, or 150,000 more books than could be housed in the Rotunda.[55] In the view of officials the main recommendation for the site was that it would be possible to hide books below the grade of central grounds. In 1932, explaining the preference for this site, university librarian Harry Clemons

wrote, "If the building is to correspond in architecture with the prevailing 'Jeffersonian' style, much elevation above the ground will be impossible." The Library Committee especially favored the new site because it could provide for "two floors above the average level and three floors below. . . . The entrance to the Memorial Hall would therefore be on the ground level. The architect would have a pretty problem to save the high rear of the structure from resembling a factory. But that high rear would face only a huge gymnasium while the lower front would complete a low quadrangle."[56] The completed library building had the character that Clemons predicted. On the level of the quadrangle the central section of the library comprised a colonnade of eight colossal-order Doric columns framing seven arched openings for two-story windows and a central door giving access to a monumental double-height lobby (fig. 3.15). The building had only two stories facing the quadrangle. The architects further reduced the mass of the building by giving it two wings that flanked the central volume, with a connection that was recessed from the front plane of

3.15. Alderman Library, built 1936–1938. University's Architectural Commission, architect. The west elevation of the Anatomical Amphitheater is visible at the right; it was demolished in 1939 to open up the quadrangle in front of the library. Photograph, c. 1938. UVA Special Collections Library.

the main elevation. At the sides and rear of the library, the architectural embellishment of the top two floors, the colossal-order piers and columns, the arched opening, the heavy cornice with its dentil molding, and the dominant window frames continued. Below these floors, however, down the hills below the quadrangle, there were three floors of relatively unembellished brick elevation that did indeed take on the factory-like character that Clemons had anticipated (fig. 3.16); only simple brick jack arches marked the window openings.

The strategy evident in Alderman Library and indeed in Cabell Hall and the Monroe Hill dormitories before it, of using the sides of the main ridge that the university occupied to mask newer and larger buildings also informed later additions to the library system. The Architects' Collaborative designed an undergraduate reading library (1979–1982) named after Harry Clemons, with only a single story at the level of the main grounds but with three stories and the vast majority of the book shelving and library space tucked into the side of the ridge below the level of the main campus. The strategy was apparently important enough to influence the choice of architect for the undergraduate library. Indeed, the university had originally hired New York architect Ulrich

Franzen to design the building, but dismissed Franzen over his apparent disregard for the strategy of hiding the library building and its books. His initial designs called for eliminating Miller Hall, the building on the west side of the Alderman Library quadrangle. University officials preferred the "comfortable" scale of Miller Hall, wanted a library with only one story at the level of the quadrangle, and rejected Franzen's design that would have obstructed the western vista toward Lewis Mountain and the Kearney mansion.[57] In contrast, the Architects' Collaborative design addressed all of these concerns. Miller Hall remained in place, helping to obscure the modest modern lines of a one-story section of Clemons Library from Jefferson's core.

Miller Hall was later demolished to make way for the Hartman-Cox designed Albert and Shirley Small Special Collections Library (2002–2004) (fig. 3.17), built adjacent to Clemons and Alderman libraries. The Hartman-Cox design provided what earlier planners may well have considered a "comfortable" scale, but its inept historicist elements deprived the building of both elegance and dignity.[58] What Hartman-Cox did achieve with the building was the continuation of the post-Jefferson tradition of hiding library buildings and books. The

ABOVE
3.16. *Alderman Library, built 1936–1938. The top two floors share the ridge top of the Lawn and Ranges while the lower three floors stand below the crest of the ridge, out of sight of the university's original buildings and gardens.* Photograph, c. 1938. UVA Special Collections Library.

BELOW
3.17. *Small Special Collections Library, built 2002–2004. Hartman-Cox, architects. Eighty percent of the building is underground, illuminated in part by the skylights in the foreground.* Photograph by author, 2007.

3.18. Anatomical Theater, built 1825–1826. Thomas Jefferson, architect. Built to accommodate the dissection of cadavers by medical students. Photographed with the medical school class of 1873. Building demolished in 1939.
Photograph, 1873. UVA Special Collections Library.

new building provided 72,700 square feet of space, 80 percent of it underground, including the Special Collections reading room, exhibit space, and the shelving for the entire collection of 300,000 rare books and 16 million manuscripts.

Moreover, the Small Special Collections Library design stands as part of a seventy-five-year effort to discreetly tuck away or hide the university's library buildings and collections with the aim of harmonizing these much larger buildings with the Jeffersonian character and scale of the original university. Ironically, this architectural strategy of tiptoe contextualism ignored a central aspect of the ideological power of Jefferson's design. When Jefferson chose to locate the library in the Rotunda, he aimed to place secular knowledge and the book as opposed to religion at the monumental core of the Academical Village. Indeed, at a time when

many national universities continued to have religious foundations, Jefferson did not design a space in his university for religious services. The centrality and monumentality of the library represented the Enlightenment basis of the university, as did the Anatomical Amphitheater. In moving to go small, to go over the hill, to go underground in housing the library, the university respected Jefferson, architecturally considered, while perhaps losing touch with ideals that Jefferson cherished even more highly than architecture—or, at the least, considered inseparable from it. The truly Jeffersonian thing to do may have been to monumentalize the libraries so that they dominated the expanded university landscape in the same way that the Rotunda dominated the original plan. To monumentalize the library would have given continuing relevance to Jefferson's vision of the absolute centrality of books as a basis for education and the university's broader Enlightenment endeavors.

Indeed, libraries hidden away from view testify to the shallowness with which many supposedly "Jeffersonian" buildings engage with the founder and his world. In designing the Small Special Collections Library, Hartman-Cox engaged locality by incorporating semilunette windows like those on Jefferson's earlier Anatomical Amphitheater into their design. The Anatomical Amphitheater (fig. 3.18), the only Jefferson-designed building demolished at the university, had stood immediately adjacent to the Small Library site and had been removed in 1939 to make way for the new Alderman Library quadrangle. The amphitheater had been central to training in anatomy and the adoption of empirical methods in training medical doctors. Controversy surrounded the use of the earlier building, as the cadavers studied in the Anatomical Amphitheater had at times been stolen from African-American graves. The irony of the architectural recall of the building was that the substantial foundations of the Anatomical Amphitheater (fig. 3.19) stood within a few feet of the underground section of the new special collections library. Leaving those foundations out of the library plan bypassed an opportunity to literally engage locality, interpret the site's rich history, and add a memorable artifact to the special collections. Awkwardly incorporating semilunette windows highlights the superficiality of historic engagement represented by many recent designs at the University of Virginia.

After War:
Modern Ways in a Traditional Context

The university undertook a massive post–World War II expansion after building had largely ceased during the Depression and the war. As modern architecture began to fill the landscape of American cities and towns, architectural advisors to the university reaffirmed the importance of extending the Georgian and Jeffersonian traditions. There was also a sense that local architects and university graduates could use their familiarity with Jeffersonian architecture as a wedge against outsiders who might want to undertake university work. Robert E. Lee Taylor, who had worked since the 1920s as part of the university's architectural commission, confided in a Board of Visitors member in 1944: "It would be little short of criminal to let the University get into incompetent or unsympathetic hands and future generations would never forgive us."[59] One of the first major projects in the postwar period was the provision of dormitory space for 1,200 students. The project was so large that architects

immediately began to consider the relationship between the new buildings and the earlier architecture. In 1947, New York architect Lewis A. Coffin, Jr., wrote to university professor Robert Gooch, "Tradition, while temporarily going somewhat out of date, seems very important in the long run."[60] In the hopes of getting a commission for university work, Coffin also wrote to President Colgate Darden and reported having "steeped" himself "for many years in Georgian and Virginian architecture."[61] Coffin didn't get the commission for the dormitory project, which went instead to the New York firm of Eggers & Higgins. In 1951, ten three-story dormitories were constructed around a series of quadrangles on McCormick Road. The design stressed economy. Concrete frames provided the structural system, but this was completely obscured by historicist brick façades. Rooftop pediments marking the entrances, classical door surrounds, eight-over-eight windowpane configurations, prominent chimneys, red brick and white trim all located the large dormitory complex in the university's Jeffersonian mold (fig. 3.20).

For a number of reasons, however, the seamlessness of the Georgian and Colonial stretching out as far as the eye could see in the post–World War II building boom did provoke dissenting voices. Where Jeffersonian tradition might arguably complement domestic spaces, it seemed to some inadequate to buildings that housed the latest, progressive disciplines of natural science. Criticism initially focused on plans for a new physics building with a radioactive laboratory. After all, physics represented

3.19. Anatomical Theater south wall partially uncovered during the 1997 archeological dig done in connection with the construction of the Small Special Collections Library.
UVA Special Collections Library.

3.20. *Aerial View of University West Grounds. In foreground,*
Thornton Hall, built for the Engineering School, 1930–1935,
University's Architectural Commission, architects. In middle
ground, Physics Building, built 1952–1954, Eggers & Higgins,
architects. In background, McCormick Road dormitories, built
1946–1951, Eggers & Higgins, architects. Photograph, c. 1955.
UVA Special Collections Library.

an especially powerful and significant discipline in the modern university. Physics had played a central role in the war by harnessing the power of the atom for use in atomic bombs. Now the physics faculty anticipated considerable growth in the department, which included Frank Hereford, one of the research scientists involved in the Manhattan Project. The department needed new accommodations, and in 1951, Professor Jesse Beams argued, "The School of Physics is rapidly approaching a cross roads where it must either take the road to a position of low grade mediocrity or it can go on to help the University take its proper place in our educational system."[62] Initially, the university's architect designed a building for a site adjacent to Rouss Hall, one of the three McKim, Mead & White buildings added to the south end of the Lawn in the post-Rotunda fire expan-

sion. Yet the proposed site was restricted in size, and the desire to forge a stronger link between physics and engineering prompted selection of a new building site on McCormick Road, across the street from the Engineering Building and adjacent to the new student dormitory complex. The traditional stylistic palette adopted for the Physics Building (fig. 3.21) echoed the lines of the adjacent McCormick Road dormitories. The traditional design caused consternation among members of the Virginia Art Commission, who had to approve all designs for university buildings. The commission complained to President Darden that it viewed the design of the McCormick Road dormitories as a "lost" opportunity to build contemporary architecture at the university. They also worried that proceeding with the current Physics Building design would seal the aesthetic fate of

McCormick Road, a primary area envisioned for expansion. The Art Commission minutes lay out the essence of the debate:

> The Commission members stated . . . that they were in unanimous agreement that a real opportunity to change to a contemporary type of structure now exists. If the Physics Building, as now located, were built, this opportunity would possibly be lost. A contemporary type allows the Architect a far greater use of his talents in space design relative to use, space relationship, traffic flow and adaptation to the site. This when properly done, results in a building with meaning and expression. This type of structure also allows the Architect to use simple forms, to eliminate costly cornices and ornament and the use of more maintenance free materials such as stone, glass block and aluminum sash.[63]

In other words, modern physics seemed to call for a modern building.

President Darden invited members of the Art Commission to meet with the Board of Visitors on April 11, 1952, to discuss the issue of contemporary architecture at the university. Art Commission chairman Edwin Kendrew, an architect from Williamsburg noted for his extensive experience in restoration at Colonial Williamsburg, reiterated all the reasons the Art Commission felt that the university should adopt a contemporary style in the Physics Building. He stated, "It was the feeling of the Commission that if the University were ever to change from its classical design, now was the time to make the break; it was the sense of the Art Commission that the University should make this fundamental change in design." Board of Visitors member Thomas Benjamin Gay, a Richmond lawyer, asked the Art Commission members how they would act if they were members of the Board of Visitors and were "asked to make a change from the classical architecture which had been followed here for more than one hundred and twenty-five years." Edwin Kendrew replied that "he realized it was a difficult decision but he thought that in the long run the University would benefit greatly from the change and that was why the Commission was recommending it." The Board of Visitors minutes of the meeting then reported that "the President thanked the members of the Art Commission for taking time to come here and appear before the Board, whereupon they were excused." The board voted to retain the existing traditional design for the building.[64] It was a significant moment: fifty-seven years after the fire, despite major changes in the scale and uses of university buildings, the Board insisted that its new laboratory and classrooms devoted to modern physics and radioactive research and efforts to harness the energy of atoms should be cloaked in Jeffersonian garb—pediments at the rooftop, classical door surrounds, and colonial-style divided light windows. The elevation of the three-story brick Physics Building stretched 286 feet along McCormick Road, nearly half the distance covered by the entire original Lawn.

3.21. *Physics Building, built 1952–1954. Eggers & Higgins, architects.* Photograph, c. 1955. UVA Special Collections Library.

3.22. *Gilmer Hall, Life Sciences Building, built 1959–1963. Louis Ballou, architect.* Photograph by Ed Roseberry, 1964. UVA Special Collections Library.

The Physics Building's architect, Theodore Young, quickly countered the suggestion that he himself had objected to a contemporary design. To correct the record Young wrote President Darden that his firm had followed the "tradition of Jeffersonian Architecture" only because they felt that university design policy was "completely fixed" on this style.

> Our view is that we would welcome a contemporary style of architecture, of conservative characteristics, and that it could be made to blend harmoniously with the old structures, though it would not come in close contact with the Jefferson Lawn. Buildings devoted to scientific teaching and research seem particularly out of place housed in the style of the older buildings on the campus. It is difficult for the Architect to offer the advantages of modern techniques in planning and building if restricted by the styles of previous eras.

Young concluded, however, that it was not his responsibility to change the architectural policy of the university.[65]

The debate over the Physics Building did not change its design, but it did, perhaps, lay the groundwork for subsequent tentative forays into contemporary design. In 1959, Louis W. Ballou, a Richmond architect, graduate of the University of Virginia, and member of the Virginia Art Commission, provided a contemporary design for the Life Sciences Building (Gilmer Hall) (fig. 3.22) for a site on McCormick Road. The scale of the building was reduced by separating a two-story laboratory wing from a three-story classroom and office wing, linked by a one-story auditorium that bulged out

toward the street with a solid serpentine brick wall, loosely modeled on the serpentine walls in the Pavilion gardens. At one point in the design process the Art Commission reviewed plans to replace the auditorium's serpentine wall with a plain curved wall. The members declared their unanimous support for the gesture toward tradition and the serpentine exterior remained.[66] The main elevations were dominated by a simple concrete frame, in-filled with concrete breeze-block grilles of the sort that had stirred controversy in 1956 when architect Edward Durell Stone added one to his townhouse in New York City. It turned out that the earlier assumption that the Physics Building would seal the design fate of McCormick Road was not true. In explaining his design to his colleagues on the Art Commission, Louis Ballou declared that,

> although it was felt advisable to use a contemporary architectural style for this building, the choice of materials and colors has been based on a harmonious relationship with the materials of the traditional buildings on the campus. Furthermore, the large mass of the building has been broken up in an attempt to develop a scale, which would not be too contrasting with that of existing buildings. The introduction of architectural screens in front of the windows is proposed to provide flexibility in fenestration and to camouflage the many required louvers, vents, etc., on the facades of the building, and to give a lightness in the general appearance of the building.[67]

The auditorium, which in the case of the Physics Building had been constrained within the building mass, now became a modern and dynamic element, pushing out beyond the main elevation. Nevertheless, this modern aesthetic based on the element of function was tempered with its serpentine configuration. Ballou insisted that the project receive preliminary approvals based on $1/16$-1 scale rather than $1/8$-1 renderings because he felt that by giving "as little information as possible" he would be "allowed more freedom in design."[68]

A Question of Chemistry: The Hiring and Firing of Louis Kahn

The difficulties faced by designers who sought to introduce Modernism in buildings that housed scientific research and learning became more apparent in 1961 when the university started planning a major new building to house the chemistry department on a site immediately east of Gilmer Hall. The recently established Architectural Advisory Committee, made up of faculty members and university planning staff and charged with recommending architects for university projects, endorsed the selection of noted modern architect Louis Kahn to design the Chemistry Building. The chemistry department, with the support of President Edgar Shannon, hoped to heighten its national reputation. A modern building created by a leading architect seemed an appropriate expression of the aspirations held by the university for the future of the chemistry department. As the chairman of the department wrote, "the building plan means the fulfillment of life-long hopes of a group of fifteen members of the Chemistry Faculty, the chance that we may be able to hold on our faculty some of our younger brilliant members, and that our plans for expansion and participation in the chemical growth of the

major American universities is dependent on the fulfillment of their promise." In his view, "the University of Virginia, led by President Shannon, has staked its reputation on building up this Department."[69]

Yet the university's relationship with Kahn proved difficult. Kahn attended to the project only in spurts of intense work—frequently changing the design drastically. As his work ran behind schedule, it threatened existing state appropriations, even as it exceeded the budget provided. After two years of tension and frustration the university fired Kahn.[70] Historian Stephen James, surveying this history, attributes the failure of the building project largely to the strained working relationship between architect and university.[71] However, the archives are full of letters that take direct aim at the aesthetic character of Kahn's various proposals, rather than the design process that generated them. In 1962, for example, President Shannon wrote a long letter to Kahn complaining about the design and highlighting the difficulty of working in the shadow of Jefferson even as the university moved toward a modern building:

I must say frankly that I am quite disappointed in the design. . . . As you know so well, Thomas Jefferson succeeded in providing the University with certain physical qualities that we all cherish. As I recall, you said when we first discussed your undertaking the design of this building that the "Lawn" inspired you to attempt to interpret these qualities in the so-called modern idiom. I do not see an attainment of this aim in your design. The building appears too massive, and rather cold and forbidding. I am reminded of a Norman Castle with its formidable towers. I am particularly concerned over the design of the auditorium. It seems too large for its location and its turrets seem to me to detract from its appearance.

3.23. Model of Chemistry Building, designed 1961–1963 but not built. Louis Kahn, architect. Photograph by Michael J. Bednar. UVA Special Collections Library.

Shannon was not far off in his characterization of the design as Norman. Kahn's fascination with castles was apparent in the design for an auditorium that broke free of the building and filled an open courtyard facing McCormick Road (fig. 3.23). In a sense, Kahn had mirrored Ballou's adjacent Gilmer Hall design, where the auditorium became an independent figure in the elevation. Yet, Ballou tied the modern expression of the auditorium to the tradition of brick serpentine walls at the university. Kahn had abstracted formal sources from much further afield and found his clients unreceptive. President Shannon urged movement "toward the achievement of the distinguished building that you and I are equally desirous of attaining. As you can well understand it is of utmost importance that our initial contemporary building be as successful as possible."[72] Kahn insisted that he would try to respond to the criticism, but added, "I have the feeling that what is wanted is a 'red and white' building"—the sort of traditional building in which he had little interest.[73] University officials later complained that their concern over "design brutality" had not been addressed and the final design was "totally unsatisfactory in appearance and . . . not appropriate as a visual form to the spirit of the architecture of the University." After Kahn was fired in 1963,[74] the next architects, Anderson, Beckwith & Haible, produced a building that went even further over budget than the estimates that had been made for Kahn's design.

Campbell Hall:
Master Planning and the Invisible Modern

Kahn's Chemistry Building design reflected the effort of the university to raise the national reputation of the chemistry department and especially of its research and graduate programs. Modern architecture could potentially serve those aspirations well. Indeed, as one surveys the grounds of the university, Modern architecture was most readily embraced by research-driven science and by graduate and professional education, in short by programs that had especially stood to gain with an image of pushing new frontiers. Despite the debacle over Kahn's design, the enthusiasm for Modern architecture among these departments corresponded with new design ideals adopted in the master planning of the university. The Jeffersonian core would be preserved and wherever possible protected from the contaminating presence of Modern architecture—while more distant sites on the expanding edges of the university would be open to freer interpretations of the Jeffersonian legacy, or even to Modernism. In

1965 the Sasaki, Dawson & DeMay master plan called for specific design guidelines at the core and a loose effort to "achieve harmony in development" between the regulated core and the periphery.[75]

Designer Richard Dober, working with Sasaki, wrote, "A major problem facing the University is how to meld the new and old architecture in a fashion that is neither a compromise with contemporary requirements in building design nor a desecration of the architectural values of the older buildings. The genuine delight of the historic parts of the campus comes about through a careful handling of site composition. The scale of the buildings is matched by the scale of the open spaces and their planting. The building materials selected by Jefferson are delightfully appropriate to the region. We believe these special design characteristics can be used in other sectors of the Charlottesville campus. Imitation is not desirable because facsimiles detract from the original." Here the idea was that in areas outside of the core the university and its architects could explore divergent modern aesthetics, reflecting a "more permissive approach to development on the basis of functional requirements."[76]

This work led to some important experiments. We have seen that, earlier in the century, the university prized efforts to hide new buildings from the Jeffersonian core. In the 1960s, during ambitious modern expansion for the sciences and the professional schools, officials began to contemplate or tolerate new styles and forms of building—but the same rules prevailed, and the buildings needed to be hidden on sites somewhat distant from the central grounds. Campbell Hall, the building constructed to house the School of Architecture, represented a case in point. Designed by Pietro Belluschi, the dean of the MIT School of Architecture, and Kenneth DeMay of Sasaki, Dawson & DeMay, the building adopted a fairly modern, novel palette. President Shannon tested the waters for contemporary design by engaging the Virginia Art Commission in a very early discussion of the project. In 1965 he argued that the "difficult topography" on the hilly site on the north side of Carr's Hill suggested that a contemporary style of architecture would "permit greater freedom" in designing the building and integrating it with other buildings in the Fine Arts Center. President Shannon acknowledged that there were "differences of opinion" regarding this matter on the Board of Visitors. The Art Commission endorsed Shannon's views and pointed out that "the abrupt change in styles from traditional to contemporary would not result in a clash of design relationships, because the site provided not only a visual barrier between the two, but also prevents simultaneous views of the different groups." They then concluded their unanimous resolution, "that every effort will be made to achieve the finest and most attractive buildings possible in a modern style, so that they will reflect as much credit to the progress of the University as previous buildings."[77] The message was clear. The university could proceed with contemporary design if the buildings were at least partly invisible from the historic core. There were severe limits even to this development. In 1971, when architects with Sasaki, Dawson & DeMay proposed a twelve-story high-rise dormitory for a site on Lambeth Field, immediately north of Carr's Hill, members of the Board of Visitors objected to "any high rise structures" at all and also opposed the demolition of the old Lambeth Colonnades.[78] The high-rise would be invisible from the Lawn, but this aspect of contemporary design was completely eliminated from the Lambeth project. Instead, Lambeth featured low-rise dormitory apartments integrated with the classical colonnade of the old football stadium.

Despite the protection that Carr's Hill afforded the architecture school site, Belluschi made efforts to closely attend to the formal character of the Jeffersonian core and incorporate key elements of that core in his design. Like Stanford White before him, he paid special attention to the character of the brickwork, in order to harmonize his walls with those of the original parts of the university. He carefully inspected "matters of brick color, mortar color, and the tooling of the joints." He also adopted the large-size bricks used in earlier buildings. At a level above the brick, Belluschi and his colleagues sought to achieve an "archi-tectural character sympathetic with the richness of Mr. Jefferson's architecture." They "abstracted from the existing architecture those essential elements which contributed to the unique visual serenity of the grounds, mainly: red brick of proper scale and color, visual impression of white roof fascias and columns, the fine detailing along windows, and lastly, the weathered patina of copper roofs." What can be seen in this project was a new approach to design at the university—one in which new materials, such as exposed concrete frames, in some cases carefully finished with sandblasting, related themselves to the formal character of the old architecture while accommodating new forms, new programs, and a new and much larger scale. Campbell Hall was unmistakably modern; it was a relatively large building dominated by large expanses of glass and framed by exposed concrete (fig. 3.24). However, the materials palette offered continuity between the old and the new. Belluschi aimed at a "very sensitive subtle treatment" with "simplicity of construction and interesting juxtaposition of building masses" rather than "flamboyant and spectacular designs."[79] At one point in the design process the plan for copper-clad monitor skylights was called into question. Architecture Dean Joseph Bosserman (fig. 3.25) quickly objected to any changes at all—arguing that the design was intended to flood the deep studio space with light and, perhaps more important, provide a "strong statement esthetically helping to define the upper levels of the building as studio space."[80] The skylights remained. Thus, on Carr's Hill in the 1960s,

3.24. Campbell Hall under construction, combining modern concrete slab construction and plate glass with traditional brick, built for Architecture School 1965–1970. Pietro Belluschi and Sasaki, Dawson & DeMay, architects. Photograph, c. 1969. UVA Special Collections Library.

an architectural aesthetic based on revelation of function and structure, among the defining premises of Modern architecture, complemented a more familiar and traditional approach to architectural expression.

Law and Darden:
The Satellite Modern in Red Brick

The ongoing effort to avoid having new architecture and development impinge upon the Jeffersonian core of the university intensified the suburbanization of the campus that accompanied growing enrollment. In the 1970s, the graduate schools of business and law relocated to Copeley Hill, over a mile and a half from their former sites adjacent to the Lawn (see fig. 3.2). The move underscored the way in which preserving historic architecture actually disrupted valued social and institutional patterns. In 1967, Board of Visitors member Frank W. Rogers toured the vicinity of the university. "Unless the University is to become a fragmented institution of magnificent distances," he reported, "we must find more land in or near the 'old' University. . . . We can readily see what that would mean, not only in cost but in keeping these two important schools as integral parts of the hard core of the University."[81] Despite this concern about economic and institutional costs associated with outward sprawl, the university proceeded to radically detach the business and law schools from the institution's historic center.

It did so in part because the Copeley Hill site would permit future expansion and a degree of monumentality that was seemingly barred at the law school's former Clark Hall location. Law School dean Hardy Dillard declared: "Naturally we . . . are very enthusi-

3.25. Campbell Hall and the transparency of modern materials in the office of Dean Joseph N, Bosserman.
Photograph, 1970. UVA Special Collections Library.

astic at the prospect of beginning from scratch instead of adding on to our present building in light of the restricted space available. We also applaud the notion of planning for a really superb complex instead of one that is acceptable but undistinctive."[82] Around the core of the university there was ample precedent for the addition of acceptable but uninteresting buildings. There was also a history of growing concern that "further congestion" around the Lawn would compromise the aesthetic character of the area even when buildings were built without being visible from the Lawn.[83] Dillard understood that the law school stood to lose something valuable as the university approached what Frank Rogers envisioned as a "fragmented institution of magnificent distances." Dillard wrote, "We have in mind recapturing the notion of Mr. Jefferson's 'academical village' in the spirit of the Inns of Court."[84] Missing from Dillard's idea was an appreciation that Jefferson's Academical Village was not a specialized community like the Inns of Court; rather, it was an interdisciplinary community. Removing lawyers and law classes—or graduate business people and business courses—from the center of the university notably dissipated the historical richness of the traditional arrangements, even while preserving in some manner the richness of the university's historical architecture. Frank Rogers apparently also saw the problem more fully as it extended to issues of architecture. In 1966 he had promised to attend a meeting of the Buildings and Grounds Committee and to mildly "grimace if there should be proposed any other building that would jar the bones of Mr. Jefferson."[85]

The university chose Modern architect Hugh Stubbins in April 1967 to prepare designs for the law and business schools.[86] Stubbins helped select a final site for the schools from the 590-acre Duke tract, which included Copeley Hill, purchased by the university in 1963 for $390,000. Stubbins selected the tract's high ground for his site, an area that also happened to be the section of the land that stood farthest from the center of the university. Stubbins referred to the building complex as a "satellite campus."[87] The designs for the law and business schools were Modern in the way that Belluschi's architecture school was Modern. Prominent concrete frames reflected the fascia of the buildings that Jefferson designed; freestanding concrete posts marked the entrances like an abstracted line of columns. In 1968, President Shannon (fig. 3.26) had advised Stubbins "to use brick in some manner where possible in view of the Board of Visitors preference for brick."[88] The recommendation paralleled the advice given by university bursar Vincent Shea, who the previous year encouraged

3.26. *School of Law under construction, built 1968–1974. Hugh Stubbins & Associates, architects. Colgate W. Darden, Jr., at right, with President Edgar F. Shannon, Jr., at left; modern concrete construction system visible in rear.* Photograph by Dave Skinner, c. 1973. UVA Special Collections Library.

the architects of the School of Education building to incorporate "Jefferson flavor" in their design to suit the preference of the Board of Visitors and the Art Commission for designs that "blend in with the styles associated with the Lawn."[89] Stubbins honored Shannon's request, and brick shared the façade with large expanses of glass and concrete. Still, when the law school building opened in 1974, the upper floor was cantilevered out over the lower floors, concrete dominated the material palette, and the scale of the building contributed to its unmistakably Modern style. This architecture was as distantly related to Jefferson's architecture as the "satellite campus" was to the Lawn and central grounds. The temporal and geographical space had provided Stubbins and the law and business school officials with the grounds and the license for embracing Modern architecture at the university.

The design of new buildings for architecture, business, and law followed by a few years the early 1960s construction of Alderman Road dormitories. Here, too, exposed concrete and brick dominated the elevations. Designed by Johnson, Craven & Gibson, the most architecturally striking elements in the new dormitories were exterior balconies, cantilevered from the building elevations and providing circulation to the student rooms. In the initial designs this strikingly modern device of the cantilever was muted by the presence of columns in front of the balconies. When the Virginia Art Commission considered a revised plan that eliminated the columns, "there was considerable sentiment in favor of

retaining" them. Nevertheless, Floyd Johnson, one of the building's architects, and also a member of the Art Commission, prevailed on his colleagues to approve the omission of the columns.[90] Stripped of their columns, the modernity of the buildings became manifest for all to see. Not merely reserved for professional schools, in the new dorms Modernism would mark the undergraduate experience itself.

Coeducation and the Reassertion of Architectural Tradition

Yet, the undergraduate experience was about to shift dramatically, with one result being a retrenchment in architectural style. Indeed, despite its successes in the Modern buildings for architecture, law, and business in the 1960s and '70s, the university's era of tentative experimentation with Modern architecture did not last very long. A return to more traditional designs occurred as broader currents in architectural production, most notably the rise of Postmodern architecture, intersected with a particularly poignant period of institutional trauma, involving the challenge to the tradition of educating only men in Virginia's undergraduate program. Officials had rejected coeducation at several points in the course of the twentieth century. What prompted a reconsideration was congressional passage of the 1964 Civil Rights Act, which barred discrimination based on gender as well as race. In the spring of 1965, President Shannon asked the

Committee on the Future of the University to explore coeducation. In December 1966 the committee recommended full coeducation.[91]

Some members of the university community saw coeducation as a threat to cherished traditions and ideals. The Board of Visitors found broad support for coeducation among the faculty; current students seemed divided on the issue; and, as expected, many, many alumni found the idea completely abhorrent. Alumni opposing the admission of women often framed their opposition as a defense of cherished tradition, a defense of Jeffersonian ideals, and a defense against the inroads of mediocrity—the rise of "State Uism" at the university. Richmond lawyer and Virginia alumnus W. Davidson Call wrote to the board: "The idea of women in the College of Arts and Sciences is appalling to me.... The whole affair brings to mind a letter written by Mr. Jefferson to James Madison on January 30, 1787, in which he wrote, 'A little rebellion now and then is a good thing.' However, I seriously doubt that Mr. Jefferson envisioned mini-skirted young ladies scurrying down the Lawn to Cabell Hall. Yes, I know that times have changed. I also realize that the growth of the University is imminent. But if it must grow, let it grow within the framework pictured by its founder."[92] In this letter, Call managed to both acknowledge and deny Jefferson's own revolutionary history and outlook, in theory accepting "rebellion" but in practice rejecting mere miniskirts. Call's argument from the supposed intention of the founder echoed sentiments long voiced in relation to university architecture. Others expressed concerns that coeducation would strike at the very heart of "tradition." Bill Lyle, a 1948 graduate of the college, objected that the "valuable traditional characteristics of the University would be diluted with 'rinky-dink' female modifications. A sickening thought."[93] Others worried that the cherished student-run Honor Code would be compromised: "Sexual encounter is often filled with deceit . . . [and will] eventually turn the Honor Board into a scandalous Jr. divorce court."[94] In the late 1960s there was an entire range of traditions and conventions under siege in American society. Many University of Virginia alumni obviously felt strongly that the university was one traditional, masculine cultural space that they hoped to defend.

There was little that was distinctive about this. Other colleges and universities faced much the same pressures to admit women in these decades; many schools surely heard from disgruntled alumni, expressing a similar sense of disruption and intrusion and summoning similarly scattered and—in retrospect—seemingly overblown objections. Yet the University of Virginia could and did respond to sweeping change by tightening its grip on material, architectural, and landscape traditions. What was distinctive at Virginia, in other words, was its significant historic architecture, so closely identified with the founder as designer and a visible marker of Virginia "tradition." Links between architectural and social traditions had been made earlier. In the 1950s, for example, Board of Visitors member Thomas Benjamin Gay had insisted on "classical architecture" for the Physics Building while also going on record as being "unalterably opposed" to coeducation.[95] Now it seemed possible—some thought necessary—to reassert loyalty to an established building aesthetic even while expanding and transforming the institution.

Significantly, just at the moment in the 1960s when at least some university tradition seemed to be disintegrating in the face of women's aspirations for admission, the administration set out to restore the Rotunda in a high-profile affirmation of Jeffersonian tradition. The university decided to scrape the traces of Stanford White's single great room out of the Rotunda and restore the building to what it assumed to be its original Jeffersonian form, rebuilding two floors in the place of one. The idea of restoring the Rotunda "to its original Jeffersonian appearance" was not new. Frederick Doveton Nichols, a professor of art and architecture, had proposed the project as early as the mid 1950s.[96] Nichols had supervised several smaller projects in the early 1950s to restore various pavilions and their gardens to their Jeffersonian appearance and arrangement. His proposal for the Rotunda far exceeded the magnitude of any previous restoration. Nichols insisted that Jefferson's last visit and final attention to the university had been dedicated to the selection of books for the library and supervision of construction details on the Rotunda—"the crowning glory of the university."[97]

In January 1955, the Board of Visitors' Building and Grounds Committee met with Nichols to review his Rotunda proposal. When the full board heard a presentation from Nichols, board member and federal judge Alfred Barksdale responded, "Young man, I have served on this board for eleven years, and every time that we have done something particularly outrageous, the Alumni have all said that the next thing we would do would be to tear down the Rotunda. Do I understand correctly that this is what you now intend?"[98] The next month President Darden, a committee of the Board of Visitors, and Professor Nichols met with the Virginia Art Commission to explore in a "preliminary and confidential manner" the idea of restoring the Rotunda. Nichols asserted that next to the U.S. Capitol, the Rotunda was the best-documented early public building in the United

3.27. *Queen Elizabeth on the steps of the Rotunda after its Bicentennial interior restoration, 1973–1976. The queen's presence nicely linked the university, Jefferson, and the Revolution back to England. Her presence also underscored the arrival of women as undergraduates in 1970.*
Photograph, 1976. UVA Special Collections Library.

States. The Art Commission "approved heartily . . . a faithful restoration."[99] Professor Nichols then got Fiske Kimball to endorse the plan and reported that Kimball considered Jefferson "a greater architect than Stanford White."[100] In 1957 the board approved the general idea of the Rotunda restoration but insisted that the plan be pursued only with private funds. The plan lay fallow for several years. It wasn't until September 1965 that President Shannon appointed a Rotunda restoration committee. The appointment of the restoration committee came several months after the Committee on the Future of the University was charged with studying the admission of women. Past and future seemed to be tugging in different directions, with university traditions and architecture hanging in the balance.

In 1966, despite strictures against public funding for the Rotunda restoration project, the university prevailed upon the state to redirect a $55,000 appropriation for replacing the Rotunda roof toward the planning of the restoration of the Rotunda to its original Jeffersonian form.[101] A few years later the Cary D. Langhorne Trust agreed to match money collected for the restora-

tion, and the United States Department of Housing and Urban Development, against a backdrop of mounting criticism concerning the destructiveness of its urban renewal program, contributed nearly $1.1 million to the project as part of a federal celebration of the Bicentennial. Under the direction of Richmond architects Ballou and Justice, the Rotunda was stripped down to the exterior walls, much as it had been after the 1895 fire, and entirely rebuilt. Work began in 1973 and was completed in 1976. Queen Elizabeth helped dedicate the restored Rotunda (fig. 3.27). The queen's participation was fitting. She evoked a general Anglo-American cultural tradition. But she did this even as her presence ignored or minimized the revolutionary political rupture that was so vital to Jefferson. As a woman, the queen perhaps symbolized the gathering number of women who began enrolling as undergraduates in 1970, a modern presence amid tradition.

The Rotunda restoration was not without its critics. Wolf Von Eckardt, architecture critic of the *Washington Post*, criticized the planned restoration; for the purpose of the review, he assumed the persona of Jefferson, speaking from the dead, and declared his "fear" that restoration would "produce a fakery."[102] Paul Goldberger, the *New York Times* architecture critic, pointed to the many "conjectural" aspects of the restoration, where work was guided by little or no real evidence of the Rotunda's earlier form. The university had made its choice, he concluded, "not between White and Jefferson, but between real White and not entirely real Jefferson." In this act of preservation, "by going back in time to celebrate one part of its history, the University of Virginia has necessarily obscured another part of it."[103] These critiques had little impact. The restoration led many people at the university to conclude that it would now be possible to re-create Jefferson in entirely new buildings. This sense of possibility corresponded with broader currents in architectural and urban design and pushed the university's long-held commitment to traditional architecture and to its tiptoe contextualism back to the forefront.

Stuck on Postmodernism: Familiar Forms in an Unprecedented Age

In the two decades between the first proposal for the restoration of the Rotunda and its Bicentennial dedication, entrenched national commitments to Modern architecture and urbanism waned. Increasingly, leading designers appropriated key elements of preservation discourse and practice. They called for greater openness toward historic and urban contexts, renewed historicism and stylistic diversity in design, and closer attention to American architectural heritage. This reorientation proved particularly encouraging for preservationists, who saw the new architecture and urbanism as evidence of the vitality and relevance of their own discipline's guiding principles. Vincent Scully, the Yale architectural historian, for example, insisted that preservation had "gone hand in hand with the new seeing and the vernacular and classical revivals." According to Scully, preservation was "without question, the most powerful popular movement in architecture of the past two hundred years."[104] He praised the work of such architects as Robert Venturi, Andrés Duany and Elizabeth Plater-Zyberk, and Robert A. M. Stern, whose Postmodern designs, historicist palette, and proposals for New Urbanism drew heavily upon preservation's commitment to fostering historic continuity and tradition in the built world. It was as if the key concerns that were now shaping late-twentieth-century design were premised upon the ideas that had been explored and refined at the University of Virginia since the 1890s.

As the main currents of architectural practice shifted into new channels during the 1960s and '70s, the university and its architects redoubled their efforts to cultivate Jeffersonian tradition. During these two decades both architects and critics began to aggressively attack Modern architecture and its estrangement from history and tradition. Numerous architects proposed drastic changes in contemporary approaches to design. Architectural design assumed a new palette that was at once more historicist in outlook and more eclectic and contextual in its expression. Preservation concerns moved from the margins of contemporary design production to a more central position. What was most notable was the extent to which a relationship to tradition and heritage that had pervaded questions of preservation and design at the university now entered the mainstream discourse of architecture. Architect and educator Robert A. M. Stern, one of the more articulate advocates of the new position, wrote in 1977, "In devoting themselves to pure form and the mystique of the machine, the architects of the modern movement banished any reference to the familiar surrounds of everyday life. . . . The postmodernist . . . is eclectic."[105] According to Stern, Postmodern architects sought, among other things, to overcome the "smug hostility to the preexisting environment which had for so long stood between modern architecture and its urbanistic responsibilities."[106] The aim was to establish designs that would more seamlessly integrate historic and contemporary design, to fit into rather than to contrast with the existing context. These prescriptions for architecture could easily have been modeled on the deeply rooted practice at the university, where generations of architects had attempted to follow "lines laid down by Jefferson."[107]

With the Bicentennial, restoration of the Rotunda, and the new credibility given to tradition by the broad currents of postmodernism, architecture at the university comfortably resettled on traditional architectural grounds. In 1986, Benjamin Forgey, architectural critic for the *Washington Post* visited the campus and dismissed as "dreary . . . disasters" Gilmer Hall, the Alderman Road dormitories, the architecture school, the law school, and the business school. It seemed to him that "anti-ornament, anti-classical modernists . . . lacked the tools" for working well at Jefferson's university. Forgey applauded the turn to Postmodernism at Virginia and the ability of Jaquelin Robertson, then the architecture school dean, to inspire "thoughtful respect for Jefferson's accomplishments" and to attract architects to the university who were "sympathetic with its environment." Forgey's article featured Robert A. M. Stern's 1984 addition to the Observatory Hill Dining Hall (fig. 3.28) as exemplary of the better recent work. Stern had

3.28. Pavilions added to the Observatory Hill Dining Hall, addition built 1984. Robert A. M. Stern, architect. Photograph, c. 1995. UVA Special Collections Library.

taken on a Modern-style dining building that seemed "mindless at Jefferson's University" and added two wings, each made up of four pavilions with hipped roofs and skylit cupolas, framed by Tuscan columns. Stern's distinguished Postmodern addition performed a similar function to the porticoes added onto the Dawson's Row buildings in 1911 that pulled architecturally wayward structures back into the familiar idiom of the surrounding campus. Forgey also commended the "spare and elegant" addition to Gilmer Hall done by the firm of Kliment & Halsband (1984–1986).[108] The addition had a two-story brick hemicycle with an abstracted Palladian window that cleverly terminated one of the quadrangles of the postwar McCormick Road dormitory complex. The addition attended to the Rotunda terminating the Lawn as a precedent for the addition.

The Postmodern projects that Benjamin Forgey admired shared a modesty of scale and an intricacy of detail that enhanced their appeal. Having settled back into its earlier traditionalism, the university generally stayed put even as the scale of new projects increased and the broader architectural world moved beyond Postmod-

ernism. In 1997 the Board of Visitors rejected a modern addition to the architecture school designed by Steven Holl because "it was not in keeping with the Jeffersonian architecture."[109] Constructing buildings worth well over a billion dollars, the university complemented the distinguished work that Forgey noted with more than its share of mediocre designs, where the easy application of red brick, white trim, and columns seemingly substituted for architectural rigor and excellence. Stern, after winning well-deserved praise for the Observatory Hill Dining Hall design, received a commission for a huge new Postmodern complex for the Darden School of Business (figs. 3.29 and 3.30). The design appropriated Jeffersonian motifs while rather thoroughly misapprehending the broader principles of Jeffersonian design. At Darden a large central building with a four-column portico and a cupola lantern skylight sits at the head of a landscaped court. Eight projecting pavilion-like wings, connected to two major buildings frame the court. Jefferson understood his pavilions as essentially providing a rich diversity of classical forms; no two Pavilions on the Lawn are the same. At Darden no two Pavilions were different; a single design loosely based on Jefferson's Pavilion IX was simply repeated eight times over. Whereas Jefferson used the Lawn and Pavilions to gently step down the landscape and to frame distant views, at Darden the replication of the Lawn failed to work with either landscape or views. The Darden lawn terminated in a mound of dirt piled up from leveling the building site. It looked obliquely at a huge retirement complex in the middle distance. The Lawn orchestrates a notable cosmopolitanism by having all residents and visitors move to and

3.29. *Robert A. M. Stern and Darden School, built 1992–1996. Robert A. M. Stern, architect.* Photograph by Mark Rosenberg, 1996. UVA Special Collections Library.

from their buildings and rooms along the Lawn colonnade. Their comings and goings enliven the space and build a sense of community. At Darden the colonnades are in place, but massive interior corridors provide the major circulation in the complex, draining the colonnades of their purpose and life, abandoning something essential in the meaning of the precedent. This failure stood in stark contrast to Michael Graves's Postmodern design for Bryan Hall (1990–1995), where the most successful element of the building was a colonnade that, despite its awkward handling of the classical language, did provide a major circulation path between Monroe Hill and the Lawn. In the Darden complex the Ayers/Saint/Gross–designed parking garage borrowed architectural motifs from student dormitory rooms on the Range (fig. 3.31), suggesting an unfortunate equation between students and automobiles. Less than twenty years after being placed on the far edge of the university, the Darden School and its architect engaged in a rather stunning act of architectural hubris; they attempted to recreate the Jeffersonian core on the edge; the problem is that beyond the red brick, white trim, and classical details they consistently botched and trivialized the lessons of Jefferson.

3.30. *Darden School, built 1992–1996. Robert A. M. Stern, architect. With its pavilions, colonnades, red brick and white trim, and massive scale, Darden represents the university's most notable expression of Postmodern design.* Photograph by author, 2010.

In Darden and in many other recent additions to the university, private donors and alumni have taken over the responsibility for paying for new buildings at Jefferson's public university. This change in the funding has involved some recourse to architectural tradition as a means of tapping sentimental enthusiasm among donors who want to nobly build up Jefferson's university. Architectural traditionalism has been one powerful means of drawing together current private dollars, future public buildings, and a venerated past. The effort at times devolves into silliness, as it surely did at the Darden School and in the case of the John Paul Jones Arena (2001–2006) designed by VMDO Architects with Ellerbe Becket. What exactly should a 16,000-seat Jeffersonian basketball arena look like? As one journalist put the problem: "Imagine the pressure associated with designing the new John Paul Jones Arena on the campus that Thomas Jefferson built? Yet architects at Ellerbe Becket and VMDO rose to the challenge, delivering an arena that combines the best of the Jeffersonian era with the modern amenities today's sports and concert patrons want."[110] The best of the Jeffersonian era must be the colossal white columns supporting the huge pergola at the front entrance plus the ample quantity of brick enclosing the steel and concrete-block structure. The arena is ten times the enclosed floor space of the entire Jeffersonian core of the university; despite the change in scale, the Jeffersonian arena bravely, but rather ineptly, trafficked in Jeffersonian classical details. The headline in the *Washington Post* used this author's own words to describe the result: "Jefferson on Steroids."[111] Architecturally, the building leaves much to be desired. Here is a huge expenditure of money with little to commend it aesthetically or architecturally; it seems fitting that the John Paul Jones Arena has garnered the "Best New Major Concert Venue" from Pollstar Concert Industry Awards as well as the "Facility of Merit Award" from *Athletic Business* magazine. The awards for architectural design do not seem to be forthcoming.

The issue of out-of-scale buildings with Jeffersonian details that caused particular problems with Darden and the John Paul Jones Arena also affected other projects. In 2003 the university set out to expand space for arts and sciences on a site south of Cabell Hall. After cycling through a number of architects, officials settled on California architects Moore Ruble Yudell to lead the architec-

3.31. *Darden School parking garage, built 2001–2001. Ayers/Saint/Gross, architects. The Jeffersonian parking garage was designed to be compatible with Robert A. M. Stern's earlier historicist design for the Darden School.* Photograph by author, 2010.

tural work for the $110 million South Lawn Project. With John Ruble, a Virginia alumus, the university seemingly returned to the comforting notion of the 1920s that Virginia graduates could provide special insight about adding to the grounds. But the Moore Ruble Yudell design seems to have taken its main inspiration from Stern's Darden School. They have broken up the apparent size of two large buildings by creating a series of projecting and receding masses that approximate pavilions gathered around a lawn with seemingly separate roofs; because of the area circulation patterns, this lawn is likely to be even more barren than Darden's. The material palette goes from thin brick veneer to modern metal but only as part of a strategy to make the top floor less prominent. A massive hemicycle with an auditorium sits atop this new miniature lawn and replicates simultaneously the Rotunda and nearby Cabell Hall's auditorium volume. A clumsily detailed glass curtain wall encloses one of the least visible sections of the hemicycle, in a half-hearted gesture to twentieth-century Modernism. The university will invest millions of dollars to build an elevated grass-covered bridge to connect the historic Jeffersonian core with its new offspring on the south side of Jefferson Park Avenue, a major city arterial route. The impression created with the name of the project and by the incredibly ambitious landscaped bridge is that the university feels more comfortable building lawns than building buildings. It carries on as if the project, accommodating thousands, is a simple addition to the Lawn that accommodated an original community of about 230 students and faculty. Given the complexity of the original Lawn, with its combination of students and faculty accommodations, classrooms and library space, it is notable that the South Lawn Project miscomprehended the richness of the historical precedent and failed to provide even a single student or faculty residential space, despite severe shortages of both at the university. Still, the university seemed content to drink from the fountain of a derivative traditionalism rather than to think more deeply about precedent or to actually cultivate architectural excellence.

Campbell Hall Expanded:
Models for Moving Forward

In the early stages of the South Lawn Project, the university retained and then dismissed the distinguished New York architect James Stewart Polshek. Polshek had a reputation for making sensitive modern additions to traditional buildings and complexes. The unhappy parting of ways in 2005 resembled earlier aesthetic tensions between the university and Louis Kahn. As Polshek was dismissed and Moore Ruble Yudell retained, long-simmering disagreements between the administration and members of the School of Architecture faculty burst into the open. The architecture school had long been the most highly rated unit of the university. In September 2005 the faculty wrote an open letter to the University of Virginia community suggesting that people survey the university grounds and `ask why Jefferson's innovation in architecture and design has "been allowed to degenerate into a rigid set of stylistic prescriptions? . . . a faux Jeffersonian architecture . . . obsessive in its references to history, and incapable of responding to the profound social, political, and ecological discoveries of the last century?" The letter wondered aloud, "Is the University committed to architectural excellence? . . . Is there not a difference between buildings that merely look Jeffersonian as opposed to the infinitely more difficult task of being Jeffersonian? Is stylistic simulation the sincerest form of respect, or does it devalue the authenticity of the truly historic?"[112]

The letter provoked some good discussion, some evasiveness on the part of the president and the Board of Visitors, and a torrent of criticism from the vanguard of neotraditionalists—including a second open letter labeling the architecture school faculty as part of the "modernist architectural establishment" and declaring that "though open dialogue about the University's architecture is essential, the University community should not defer to the architecture school's modernists about what is and is not suitable on Grounds." Architect Andrés Duany stood out among those who signed this counterletter. Architectural historian Carroll William Westfall also signed the counterletter. Westfall, too, was unhappy with much of the recent architecture at the University of Virginia, which he considered, at best, "inept essays in Jeffersonianism." In Westfall's view "deficiencies" in education, the failure of architecture schools to teach classicism, is at the root of inept work by VMDO, Hartman-Cox, and Michael Graves.[113]

For their part, the architecture faculty, while not hostile to traditional architecture, clearly feel that changes in the scale of university buildings, and new technologies and materials, demand an openness to forms beyond the "lines laid down by Jefferson." Moreover, recent architectural and civic concerns with ecology, hydrology, and sustainable building practices suggest the importance of more innovative and flexible forms of building and architectural expression. They feel strongly that Jefferson would stand with them and innovation. They also feel that completely disparate architectural forms could fill sites around the university and pose no threat whatsoever to the character, history, or integrity of their World Heritage

3.32. East Wing of Campbell Hall, addition built 2006–2008. W. G. Clark, architect. The elegant visual connections into the studio review galleries dramatically frame the life of the school for people approaching the building. Photograph by Scott F. Smith, 2008. Courtesy of Scott F. Smith.

Site. The architecture faculty responded in part by designing two additions to their own Campbell Hall that reflected a deeper understanding of Jefferson and of architectural excellence than anything produced by the neotraditionalists. Architects W. G. Clark and William Sherman and landscape architects Warren Byrd and Thomas Woltz, all members of the faculty, designed elegant modern additions that reflected new sensibilities about community, environment, and resources that exemplify the ethical forging of a link between the past and the future. New studio review spaces where the work of the school is displayed and debated now framed the main approach to Campbell Hall with a brilliant transparency and clarity that would be nearly impossible to achieve relying only on Jeffersonian forms (fig. 3.32). New faculty offices were designed around shared outdoor porches heated by the sun. Similarly, classrooms were designed with accessible exterior spaces while framing distant views toward Lewis Mountain and the Blue Ridge. Rainwater was channeled to tumble through a rain garden rather than into the closest sewer. These distinct parts established a powerful reciprocity between buildings and landscape and community that got closer to the core of Jefferson than the more common, and narrower, view of him as primarily a classicist. The Campbell Hall project tiptoed not around design context but around the hostility of the Board of Visitors toward untraditional architecture that earlier forced the dismissal of Steven Holl from the same project.

Learning from the University

Preservationists and other stewards of historic sites need to reflect deeply on the conundrum presented by the University of Virginia. It is hard to accept that our reverence for and preservation of past history and architecture should somehow translate into a legacy of mediocrity going forward. In the last decade the university has spent in excess of $1 billion on its building projects, and yet it has not apparently aspired to create architecture or even places that will be revered two centuries from now. Hopefully, grappling with the ways in which social and institutional trauma, preservation ideals, and a sense of design contextualism have contributed to this legacy of architectural banality can help us begin to build our way out— toward excellence. This is not a problem limited to the university; the university is, perhaps, just a place that has deeper roots than many other places we now revere and protect. It is a site that does suggest the need for greater rigor and imagination as we approach the challenge of building in the face of valued places and traditions. Excellence should, in the end, inspire excellence.

CHAPTER FOUR

Dutch Homesteads in Modern Brooklyn

The Unused Past

Buildings are among the largest and most expensive objects produced by humans. Human use and wear, the actions of weather, the second law of thermodynamics, faltering regimes of maintenance and memory, and various forms of obsolescence all militate against preservation. The surest route to preservation is for individuals, communities, or institutions to actively cultivate a place for continuing use, for history and memory, within their own culture. Even this does not guarantee success. Preservation requires both insight and resources; the process is part cultural, part physical, part political, and part economic. Culturally rapid and unsettling changes to familiar places can spur preservation campaigns. Geographer David Lowenthal has noted that the "impulse to preserve" can grow out of a "reaction" to change; he argues, "In the face of massive change we cling to the remaining familiar vestiges. And we compensate for what is gone with an interest in its history."[1] Similarly, historian Michael Kammen points out that in the late nineteenth and early twentieth centuries, American "resistance to change actually provided a powerful impetus for the preservation movement."[2] Exploring New York City's chaotic late-nineteenth- and early-twentieth-century growth, preservation planner and historian Randall Mason argues that beyond resistance, preservation actually eased the transition to urban modernity by "fusing celebrations of the past with optimism about the future."[3] Whether preservation resists or facilitates change, it clearly needs to resonate with some cultural, social, or economic vision. Preservation does not happen by itself; familiar and valued landmarks often stand at considerable peril in the face of simple physical deterioration or broader shifts in values.

This chapter focuses on the Flatbush section of Brooklyn, New York, during a period of dramatic change in the late nineteenth and early twentieth centuries. Flatbush, a largely rural agricultural area settled initially by Dutch immigrants who built architecturally distinct frame houses, grew from 6,000 residents in 1880 to well over 200,000 in the 1920s. Following the 1878 completion of a rail line between Flatbush and downtown Brooklyn, later extended to Manhattan, developers gave the town's rural agricultural landscape an increasingly suburban and even urban form. The town of Flatbush was annexed to Brooklyn in 1894 and then consolidated into New York City in 1898.[4] In the midst of such extraordinary transformation, one might expect the emergence of a vital preservation movement focused on the area's numerous Dutch homesteads. However, between the 1880s and 1920s, over fifty prominent Dutch-American farmhouses, dating from the eighteenth to the early nineteenth centuries, were demolished, leaving a landscape largely devoid of the architectural traces of a quarter millennium of local settlement and history. The story of Flatbush helps highlight the formidable obstacles to preservation and the destructive influence of changing patterns of social, cultural, and economic endeavor. In Flatbush, and indeed in many developing landscapes, isolated acts of preservation were often less striking than the sheer relentless devaluation of all vestiges of the preceding architectural, landscape, and economic order. Understanding historic preservation's past and anticipating its future comes not simply from narrating preservation success stories but from understanding the devaluation and destruction of cultural heritage.

Even amid the change and nostalgia that Lowenthal

4.1. *Lefferts homestead, built c. 1785. Preservationists removed the nineteenth-century wing, at the left, before moving the house to Prospect Park in 1918.* Photograph, c. 1895. Courtesy Prospect Park Archives.

and Kammen have identified as fertile ground for preservation, most preservation efforts in Flatbush either never really got started or quickly floundered. Longtime Flatbush residents and the hordes of newcomers did not see the tangible remains of local history and memory as essential, or even particularly relevant, aspects of their modern world. Despite exhortations from preservationists, most Flatbush residents did little to preserve history in the form of old buildings. Lafayette's 1824–1825 tour had helped frame both local and national narratives that became central to the civic and political dramas of their time. This gave motive power to preservation and commemorative efforts. In Flatbush, a fundamentally different relationship to the past unfolded. People who settled in the detached wood-frame houses built in the new affluent suburban enclaves of Flatbush showed relatively little interest in the area's Dutch past. For these new suburban residents and for the people of more modest means who occupied the brick apartment houses and mixed-use commercial buildings fronting Flatbush Avenue, the claims of the present had obviously outweighed the social importance of a palpable history, manifested in the traditional architecture and landscape of the locality.

To place Flatbush preservation efforts in context, this chapter will first explore four key routes toward devalu-

ation of the local historic landscape. First, changing bourgeois ideals of fashion, convenience, and high-style architecture undercut existing architectural tradition. Second, the decline of local agriculture disrupted the intricate network of familial relations that had centered on Dutch homesteads. In Flatbush many of the same people and families who advocated preservation of their heritage also had a hand in destroying it. Third, turning homesteads over to new social groups and different economic uses hastened their social and architectural devaluation in the eyes of those people most interested in their preservation. Finally, the area's older architecture and preservationists' attempts to cultivate historical memory appeared peripheral to the pervasive goal of constructing a middle-class suburban neighborhood. Flatbush preservationists necessarily confronted the apathy of their neighbors and members of their own families as the community traveled these routes toward the devaluation of historic architecture. Although these routes to devaluation are in many ways particular to Flatbush, they underscore the broader cultural and economic challenges confronting preservation efforts.

After tracing devaluation of the Dutch-American architectural heritage, the chapter focuses upon two Dutch homestead preservation campaigns. An effort to preserve the Vanderveer homestead failed in September 1911. Then in January 1918, the Old Dutch House Preservation Committee successfully moved the Lefferts homestead four blocks from its original site on Flatbush Avenue to Brooklyn's Prospect Park. For a brief time, as streetcars stopped in their tracks and workers winched the house along the avenue, the eighteenth century appeared to dominate the twentieth. Nevertheless, conversion of the homestead (fig. 4.1) from a house to a relic had much more to do with pressing twentieth-century concerns than with eighteenth-century history. In 1909 one Flatbush preservationist noted the "rapid and startling evolution" of the community and protested that "buildings and landmarks in evidence today are next week wiped out of existence." He asserted that "every trace and suggestion of this Old Dutch settlement so rich with legends and anecdotes, quaint and historical . . . will in a very short time be obliterated and forgotten unless action is taken now to perpetuate their memories."[5] How did this perception of dislocation translate into the action that ensured that the Lefferts homestead would still be standing today, nearly a century later? What actions or inactions accounted for the rather stark difference between the survival of the Lefferts house and the destruction of the Vanderveer homestead and nearly every other Flatbush Dutch homestead? A very different social and institutional context surrounded the Lefferts homestead preservation and contrasted with the surrounding pattern of homestead destruction. The chapter concludes with a consideration of the preservation protections that have settled upon the residential houses and neighborhoods that took the place of the earlier Dutch homesteads.

Fashion and the Devaluing of Heritage

Early-twentieth-century chroniclers of Flatbush often portrayed the forces changing the community as coming from outside. They thought that people apathetic to the importance of local history and memory arrived along rail lines as new suburban settlers. However, major architectural changes originated earlier, within the community, among the families that traced their lineage to seventeenth-century Dutch immigrant farmers. Members of these families played a central role in devaluing the community's distinct architecture; they were the first builders in the community to cross the crucial threshold from traditional Dutch-American residential forms to fashionable forms of eclectic and high-style architecture. In doing so they signaled the inadequacy of the local architecture for their own

accommodation and its growing cultural obsolescence. Early nineteenth-century historians of Flatbush readily perceived this community pattern unfolding. In 1839, Benjamin Thompson's *History of Long Island* recognized the features that had dominated Flatbush historically—the productive and highly cultivated soil. Beyond its agriculture, Flatbush seemed "hardly excelled" as a place of residence. A "spirit of improvement" was apparent, "several splendid private residences have been erected, bearing all the insignia of taste and opulence."[6] Standing outside of the dominant agricultural identity of the community, these architectural and landscape "improvements" pointed toward a drastic reconfiguration of the community.

Nobody ever laid the charge of taste and opulence at the door of Dutch-American houses. On the contrary, residents and chroniclers of Flatbush often insisted that a moral and aesthetic simplicity characterized both the houses and their builders. The simple one-and-a-half-story wood-frame houses with overshot, double-pitched roofs, low exposed post-and-beam-work interiors, large open fireplaces, multiple-use rooms, wall beds, and sprawling additions connoted, in the words of Dutch Reformed minister and early Flatbush historian Thomas Strong, "frugality, economy and industry." Strong admired the apparent cohesion and social continuity of resident Dutch families in the village with their "simple, unaffected, economical habits."[7]

These admired traditional Dutch-American forms had undergone major changes and innovations in the seventeenth and eighteenth centuries. Indeed, they had started out with innovation by incorporating, for example, Anglo-American wood-frame techniques in the place of the dominant brick construction and anchor-bent wood-frame techniques of Holland. A characteristic medieval pattern of unspecialized room use, which had often combined eating, sleeping, cooking, and entertaining in the same main hall of a two-room first floor, had given way to more differentiated room uses. The introduction of a central hall that separated circulation and created four newly specialized first-floor rooms fundamentally transformed the traditional Dutch house plan. In the Lefferts homestead the characteristic overshot roof and low rambling plan were combined with a central hallway framed by arches built in fashionable late-eighteenth-century style. Generations of farmers in Flatbush obviously had adopted elements of innovation and fashion and constructed larger, more balanced, and symmetrical houses. They developed a hybrid framing system that was quite distinct from the forms initially introduced from Holland. Nevertheless, they had generally adhered to a traditional idiom, and they continued to do so in the late eighteenth and early nineteenth centuries as many of them built new houses in the place of pre-Revolutionary ones; however, many Flatbush residents who left farming and joined more cosmopolitan circles boldly adopted newly fashionable high-style house forms, forms that emphatically undercut the conservative elements of local architectural tradition.[8]

For all his obvious reverence for the past, Reverend Strong concluded his history of Flatbush with an enthusiastic chapter entitled "Modern Changes and Improvements." Strong identified change primarily in landscape and architectural terms. Village residents had recently built "noble," "stately," "magnificent," and "commodious" mansions and "palaces," many with "Grecian" fronts. Despite his interest in earlier architectural and social forms, Strong did not condemn these significant departures from the Dutch-American forms of the neighborhood. In fact, he looked forward to the emergence of the village as the "pride and beauty of Long-Island."[9]

In the early 1840s, when Reverend Strong surveyed

Flatbush improvements, the efforts of Matthew Clarkson attracted his attention. Clarkson had impressively added the imprint of the villa suburb to the village's dominant agricultural identity. In 1836, Clarkson built a fashionable Greek Revival wood-frame house with hexastyle Corinthian porticoes at the front and back (fig. 4.2).[10] To some extent Clarkson arrived as the sort of Flatbush outsider who later commentators viewed as pivotal in the transformation of the village. Son of a Revolutionary War leader and prominent New York City merchant, Clarkson grew up not in Flatbush but in a house on Whitehall Street, Manhattan, and he later attended Princeton. Clarkson prospered as a Manhattan merchant and broker and in 1821 joined Flatbush society when he married his second cousin, Catherine Clarkson. Catherine's father's family had settled in Flatbush before the Revolution; her mother was a Vanderbilt and traced her lineage back to the town's earliest Dutch settlers. Indeed, the 80 acres that Clarkson settled came from Catherine's family in 1828. Clarkson had bought out Catherine's two broth-

4.2. Matthew Clarkson House, built 1836. House and landscape setting, c. 1880. Brooklyn Museum.

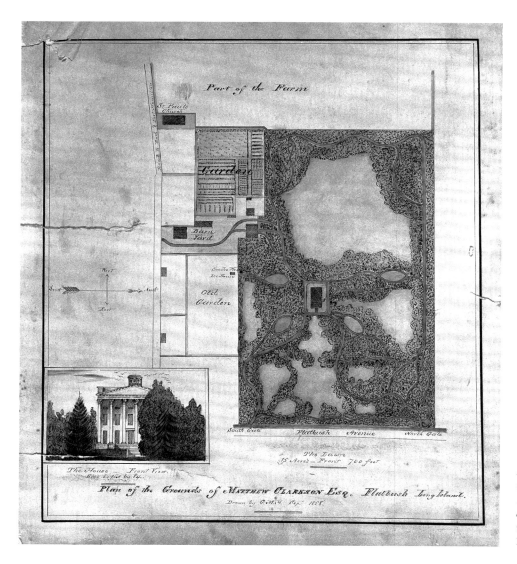

4.3. Plan of Matthew Clarkson estate, 1858, showing gardens in the immediate vicinity of the house. Brooklyn Museum.

ers' share of their deceased parents' land for $40,000.[11] In contrast to the dominant Dutch Reformed religious practice, Clarkson brought Episcopal worship to Flatbush. He paid nearly three-quarters of the cost of constructing St. Paul's Episcopal Church, the first church built in Flatbush outside the Dutch Reformed denomination. Still, with his marriage to Catherine, Matthew Clarkson joined a long-established Flatbush family, and the house that he and his wife constructed was rooted in the local landscape as much through insider genealogy as through outsider purchase.

When Matthew Clarkson settled his tract in the 1830s, the pattern of its cultivation changed; his spouse's brother continued to work the farm and resided in the mansion with his sister and brother-in-law. Clarkson developed the front part of the farm tract as a garden and residential park, complete with a 1-acre planted labyrinth. In the place of productive agriculture he cultivated

the area as an ornamental setting for his residence, with "one of the most beautiful lawns in the state."[12] Matthew Clarkson subsequently highlighted his preference for lawns over fields when he reduced his land holdings to a 12-acre estate (fig. 4.3).[13] The ornamental possibilities of the site were enhanced by setting the house 360 feet back from the main Flatbush road, departing from the traditional Flatbush pattern, which sited houses immediately adjacent to the road. Despite this setting back, Clarkson also undertook the improvement of the road itself. He spent a considerable sum leveling and graveling the walk in front of his property. Other residents later followed Clarkson's first serious definition of separate walks in the village, and eventually sidewalks became village-wide improvements. Similarly, before the Revolution the Flatbush branch of the Clarkson family had inaugurated the construction of picket fences in the place of field enclosures made of stone and earth piles

4.4. Vanderbilt House, built 1846. Alexander Jackson Davis, architect. Photograph c. 1900. Brooklyn Historical Society.

planted with primrose. The picket fences, sidewalks, and growing stock of fashionable houses imparted a more decidedly suburban aspect to Flatbush's agricultural landscape.[14]

In 1846, a decade after Matthew and Catherine Clarkson built their mansion, John Vanderbilt and his spouse Gertrude Lefferts built their own mansion and joined the Clarksons in the front ranks of Flatbush architectural improvers. Unlike their neighbors, Vanderbilt and Lefferts were both born and raised in Flatbush. Like Matthew Clarkson, John Vanderbilt gained his education, wealth, and wide prominence outside of the village. Valedictorian of his Columbia College class, and later a county judge, Vanderbilt had grown wealthy at the bar and enjoyed a fine reputation in Democratic Party political circles both in Kings County and throughout the state.[15] Distancing themselves from the agricultural occupations and vernacular forms of the village, the Vanderbilts, like the Clarksons before them, built their fashionable house on an expansive landscaped tract. Vanderbilt and Lefferts were the children and the descendants of long lines of Flatbush farmers. Lefferts had grown up in the Dutch vernacular Lefferts homestead (see fig. 4.1) that stood directly opposite the site of her new house on the main Flatbush road. Vanderbilt was raised in the house his grandfather built about 1800, which showed some affinity for early pattern-book carpenter designs; it had two and a half stories and a centrally placed Palladian window; nevertheless, wood clapboarding, a steeply pitched roof and dormers, the wood frame, and its location on the edge of the Flatbush Road complemented the forms of the area's older farmhouses.

No such link existed between the neighborhood and the house that Vanderbilt and Lefferts commissioned in 1846. Alexander Jackson Davis, one of New York's most prominent architects, designed their villa. Built as an adaptation of the Perpendicular Gothic pointed style, the house promoted reciprocity between the building and the surrounding landscape (fig. 4.4). When landscape designer Andrew Jackson Downing published a similar Davis design, he asserted that such a house should not stand on a "common-place, contracted, or mean site." Proposing a "cultivated landscape" like a "well-kept park or pleasure-ground," Downing and Davis conceived of the house as but one element in a broader composition. At 12 acres the Vanderbilt site could easily accommodate such a vision.[16] With its porches, bay windows, and balconies the house also reinforced contemporary architectural expressions of an ascendant middle-class ideology of cozy domesticity.[17] Where habit and traditional prac-

tice had dominated house building in Flatbush for two centuries, a powerful system of fashion and taste now began to influence decisions about house design. Downing and Davis fostered genteel contemplation of the aesthetic character of land over more utilitarian aspects of the agricultural landscape.[18] Within the growing middle and upper classes, fashion and goods increasingly defined the self and mediated social relations between people; in this context the house with its setting stood out as one of the most expensive and prominent of goods.

Although a villa in the pointed style was not a farmhouse and ornamental horticulture was not farming, John Vanderbilt and Gertrude Lefferts engaged directly the local history that their house seemingly eclipsed. Architecturally, they did not build a straightforward Gothic villa; they built one with Dutch stepped gables. This historicist feature addressed the Dutch history of Flatbush in an abstract, cosmopolitan, and playful way. Stepped gables were not elements in the Dutch-American farmhouses of Flatbush; instead, they appeared among the Dutch townhouses of Manhattan, where Alexander Jackson Davis had recorded them in youthful sketches. Moreover, Davis probably referenced a cultivated literary and architectural source for his design. The picturesque juxtaposition of stepped gable, projecting bays, and landscaped site echoed the design of Washington Irving's Hudson River residence Sunnyside in Tarrytown, New York. Built in 1835–1837, the author's residence incorporated a modest Dutch farmhouse at its core while introducing dramatic new Dutch architectural elements, like the stepped gable.[19]

Gertrude Lefferts Vanderbilt later settled upon an even more direct way to engage the history of her village. She took up her pen as an historian. In 1880 she published *The Social History of Flatbush*. She conceived of her project as a way of constructing and reinforcing memory in the face of "great changes." She outlined the project in her introduction: "Our Dutch ancestors were slow to accept innovations. It is probable that before the beginning of this century their manners and habits had remained for generations the same. Such is no longer the case. We need only go back a few years to find customs which have now ceased to exist. . . . Nearly every trace of Dutch descent has been swept away." By writing about the early Dutch settlement, the architecture and material culture of the community and its social, economic, and institutional life, Gertrude Lefferts Vanderbilt hoped to foster cohesion among the "large family circle" of Dutch descendants who were losing their cultural distinction and connection.[20]

4.5. *John Ditmas homestead, built c. 1800. Addition made in 1835 at left. Main section of the house, at right, was extensively remodeled in the 1880s.* Photograph by John Ditmas, 1911. Brooklyn Historical Society.

Vanderbilt wrote wistfully about the past; however, like Strong before her, she did not develop a critique of modern changes of the sort that her villa certainly exemplified. Organizing part of her 1881 narrative around a contemporary walk along the main Flatbush road (called Flatbush Street during part of the nineteenth century), and using a map from 1842 published in Strong's history as a guide, Vanderbilt complimented as "handsome" many of the modern houses built in Flatbush, even when their construction had involved pulling down an old homestead. She paid close attention to modern manifestations of taste and applauded the signs of genteel refinement evident in displays of ornamental horticulture surrounding many of the newer houses. Reflecting her own earlier step across the architectural threshold to fashion, Vanderbilt noted, "The young couple just starting in life do not build after the pattern of the old homestead, . . . [which is] not suited to the change in our mode of living. . . . we require different arrangements now." With modern heating there was no reason for low ceilings; manufactured yarns displaced the need for a garret storage space for spinning wheels; a decline in patterns of neighboring and increased traffic on local streets rendered house sites "directly upon the street"[21] less desirable.

At times, farmers' children showed enthusiasm for modern fashion over tradition by remodeling their traditional homesteads rather than by undertaking new construction. John H. Ditmas grew up in a house built by his grandfather on the Flatbush road in 1795. The house replaced an earlier family homestead standing since the late seventeenth century. Ditmas remembered such elements as a large open fireplace, a brick oven, and divided upper and lower doors that lit the central hallway. He also eliminated many of these features in an 1880s remodeling. When Ditmas, who was born in 1830, became a banker and got married, he continued to live with his father and mother, who had farmed the land behind their Dutch-vernacular-style house. After his father died in the 1880s, Ditmas substantially remodeled the house. He raised the roof, added a second floor, extended the broad front porch, and added a projecting dormer bay and balcony on the second story. Intricate millwork embellished the additions. In 1916, as the Ditmas house was being demolished, one newspaper reported that a Dutch door was about all that "escaped the restoration of this old Dutch colonial farmhouse . . .

when its style of architecture was completely changed to Queen Anne."[22] In fact, a side wing added to the house in 1835 more faithfully exemplified the traditional style than did the house itself (fig. 4.5).

Besides Vanderbilt, Lefferts, and Ditmas, numerous other Dutch descendants maintained residencies in Flatbush while vocationally and culturally forsaking the Dutch agricultural history and material culture of the community. As they adopted modern and high-style forms and endorsed cosmopolitan notions of fashion, they devalued the older architecture of the community and opened the way for its eventual destruction. Judge John A. Lott, John Vanderbilt's law partner, for example, had replaced the "gloomy looking, but time honored house of Barent Van Deventer" with his own "commodious," columned residence.[23] In the early nineteenth century Gerrit Martense, a lawyer son of a farmer, had torn down his family homestead and built his own "stately" Greek Revival edifice; by 1878 his only grandchild married merchant John Wilbur, and they built a fashionable Stick Style house nearby. A similar development had played out in the family of Charles A. Ditmas. A descendant of one of the original Dutch settlers in Brooklyn and a distant cousin of John Ditmas, Charles Ditmas became a leading advocate of Flatbush preservation in the early twentieth century. Born in 1887, he lived his entire life in a large, modern two-and-a-half-story suburban eclectic frame house built by his parents at 60 Amersfort Place, immediately south of Flatbush. Ditmas had an excellent example of the Dutch vernacular very close at hand. At 150 Amersfort Place stood a modest one-and-a-half-story Dutch-American frame house, built in 1827, where Ditmas's mother, Margaret Ditmars Van Brunt, had grown up. Moreover, Ditmas's father and mother had also lived together in this house before building their own house. Ditmas's uncle, Albert Van Brunt, who grew up in the house, built one of the largest suburban houses in the neighborhood; standing at Amersfort Place and Avenue G, the impressive two-and-a-half-story frame house had a massive corner turret and a prominent wrap-around porch.[24] The Ditmases and the Van Brunts could literally survey the transition in residential forms by looking down on the traditional architecture of their youth from the windows of their modern eclectic suburban mansions. Many close relatives of the stately villa and mansion builders, those family members who remained in farming, found continued utility in the old farmhouses. But starting in the 1830s and 1840s and accelerating in the late nineteenth and early twentieth centuries, residents of Flatbush who participated in what Gertrude Lefferts Vanderbilt called the "differ-

ent arrangements" of a broader social, political, and economic world increasingly adopted new architectural forms and fashions. They could have remained in the old houses or built using the traditional forms of their locality; instead, they turned to new forms and, in doing so, even if some later advocated preservation, they devalued the traditional architecture and contributed to its obsolescence. This process precipitated the sort of preservation crisis that arises when people who have the resources no longer have the desire to use and maintain older buildings.

Changing Familial Bonds and the Devaluing of Homesteads

The suburbanization of Flatbush devalued the area's historic architecture by deploying fashion against tradition. The passing of the agricultural homestead provided a second route toward devaluation. Suburban villas and houses did not generally serve as the hub of family economic life as was typically the case with earlier homesteads. Instead, male heads of households usually traveled away from their villas and outside the community to engage in business. Thus, the newer houses generally lacked the more intricate family relations that characterized Dutch homesteads. Even before he expressed architecturally his separation from the world of his father and father-in-law, John Vanderbilt, for example, came to occupy a class by himself within his family. His father's 1842 last will and testament left wife Sarah her clothes, household furniture, silver, china, and earthenware, $7,000, and a life interest as a widow in his farm and estate. Under Sarah's control the farming of the homestead passed into the hands of her son Jeremiah and Irish farmworkers who boarded in her house.[25] Furthermore, in his will John's father insisted that in the eventual distribution of his estate to his children, John would receive $2,000 less than the others on account of his having "received a liberal education and for other considerations."[26] Thirty years earlier John Vanderbilt's grandfather had made no such distinction among his sons in his will. He simply divided the "farming utensils and implements of husbandry of every sort" equally between them. He had conceived of his house as the center of a complex set of familial relations—the brothers were instructed to pay their sisters for use of the farm, and the unmarried sisters were willed the "use and possession of the two upper front rooms in the second floor" of the farmhouse, along with "the fruit and other productions of the orchard and garden."[27] By contrast, when it came to

4.6. John Vanderveer homestead, built 1787. Nineteenth-century additions are visible at the left and the right.
Photograph, c. 1900. Brooklyn Historical Society.

making out his will, John Vanderbilt's father exempted his liberally educated lawyer son from such a pattern of mutual dependence.

At one point Gertrude Lefferts Vanderbilt had felt a set of familial bonds that bridged the vernacular and high-style forms separating her childhood homestead from her adulthood villa. Writing to her brother's children, who had grown up in the homestead where she was raised, she reported her memory of childhood: "We seemed like one family in two houses, so constant was the intercourse between us. We were all devoted to each other's interests, and there was never any jarring or any strife between us."[28] Despite this vision of coexistence, the landscape that Vanderbilt surveyed in 1880 revealed numerous homesteads "out of repair and fast falling to decay" and others that had been pulled down and replaced by fashionable modern houses. When Gertrude died in 1902, her will directed her executors to sell her Flatbush property. Despite the fact that she had lived in the house for years with her son's widow (for whom she provided a substantial bequest), she assumed that after her own death familial social and economic interdependence and patterns of continuity would not revolve around the house as they had around earlier farm homesteads.[29] Vanderbilt's executors found

no expressions of sentiment concerning the land. For all her concern about the Dutch "family circle," Vanderbilt left legacies for the children of her brother's first wife but not his second. If her house had been part of a generations-old farm that was to be handed down through the family, rather than a suburban villa in a garden, the fate of the house would likely have involved a complex calculus of interdependence among farming heirs. This was the case with the Vanderveer homestead. The family had constructed the simple lines of their wood-frame Dutch-American–style house in 1787. The house included a prominent double-pitched over-shot roof and asymmetrically placed side additions, and it was built with its gable end adjacent to the Flatbush road (fig. 4.6). On over 100 acres of fields the Vanderveers raised potatoes, wheat, corn, rye, oats, and meat cattle, milk cows, horses, and hogs. As in the case of other local farm families, the house served as the focal point of familial and economic relations. When John C. Vanderveer died in 1845, his will directed that his spouse Elizabeth retain all the plate, household goods, and furniture and be permitted to live in "the westerly part" of the house. The will obligated the two sons who inherited the farm to provide Elizabeth and their unmarried sister "with Bread stuff, Beef and Pork and vegetables for her family's use and also fire wood ready cut at the door sufficient for two fireplaces." A third son had left farming for medicine and occupied a substantial house nearby; the will simply relieved him of financial debts he owed to his father.[30]

John Vanderveer's sons and grandsons continued to work the farm into the 1890s. The patterns of familial interdependence housed by the homestead itself began to decline in 1892, when John Vanderveer's heirs sold two-thirds of the farmland to Henry A. Meyer's Germania Real Estate & Improvement Company. Meyer profited handsomely as he developed Vanderveer Park—a restricted residential subdivision.[31] Within a decade Peter Vanderveer, who still occupied the farmhouse with members of his extended family, left farming to take up real estate development himself. He featured the homestead in advertisements for Vanderveer Place's "336 Eligible Building Lots." Vanderveer invoked the historic qualities of the homestead as a selling point: "The Property has been in the possession of the Vanderveer family since 1652 and is now offered for the sale by the heirs of John Vanderveer."[32] Dutch homesteads in Flatbush had historically provided the physical locus of intricate familial social webs; as selling "eligible building lots" took over from plowing fields, the homesteads were significantly devalued. The question that hovered over this transition was whether the old farmhouses could find a place in the new suburban landscape.

Surveying the suburban transformation of Flatbush more from the perspective of the farm field than from the perspective of Dutch vernacular houses, historians Marc Linder and Lawrence S. Zacharias have noted a parallel movement toward devaluation. Charting the process of "deagriculturalization" in Flatbush, and more generally in Kings County, Linder and Zacharias note that the increasing market orientation of Dutch farmers encouraged them to let go of the fields that their families had worked for generations. Before the 1820s many of the farms produced grains and focused generally on subsistence forms of agriculture, aided in part by slave labor. In 1790 two-thirds of Flatbush households had slaves. By the 1880s many of the farmers had set aside grain production for more intensive forms of market gardening. They produced fresh vegetables that could be easily shipped to, and quickly consumed in, the densely settled sections of Brooklyn and New York City. Indeed, the horse manure from those urban neighborhoods provided the fertilizer that permitted intensive gardening, without having to take fields out of production to lie fallow. As market gardening expanded, many Dutch-descended farm families actually stopped working the land and rented their fields to immigrant Irish and German tenant farmers. For the descendants of Dutch farmers, renting their fields became just one of many venues for the investment of individual and familial assets; they bided their time till the demand for land for housing raised land prices to a point where "no cabbage crop could be more lucrative than the coupon-clipping made possible by a mass sell-off of the farms." In this sense the growing treatment of land as a mere commodity, capable of being cashed out for "a solid annuity" and divorced from sentimental and ideological connections to local traditions, undercut the need and desire to preserve Dutch ancestral homes.[33] In 1910 the *New York Times* surveyed the Flatbush landscape and reported that traces of Dutch settlers had largely been "forced to succumb to the march of new improvements. . . . Although gardening on a small scale may still be indulged in, the great territory known as Flatbush is distinctly a residential section, the broad acres of farming days being occupied by thousands of homes."[34]

Discrepant Uses, Broken Bloodlines, and Devalued Homesteads

A third major route to the devaluation of historic Flatbush buildings arose from the social perception that discrepant present uses and ownership patterns diminished the value of particular buildings in the currency of local preservation. The major twentieth-century preservation campaigns in Flatbush, those to preserve the Lefferts and the Vanderveer homesteads, focused on buildings that occupied land controlled by the same families since the seventeenth century. Yet, as people valued these sites and homesteads, they neglected numerous similar buildings that either lacked clear bloodlines between the present and the Dutch Colonial or agricultural past or that had been substantially altered in their use through time. Since preservationists often asserted the importance of architecture as a reminder of the past, as a link in a chain of historic memory, then contemporary use and ownership status should not have been particularly relevant. Nevertheless, local preservationists attended closely to such issues, and in the face of working-class use or commercial redevelopment of homesteads, they often declined the challenge of their own preservation ideals.

Conversion of the Martense residence into an apartment house in the 1890s, for example, apparently pushed that building beyond the pale of preservation

4.7. Birdsall homestead, built c. 1800. The barn at the left was adapted into a carpentry shop in the 1880s. The business later expanded into the house itself. Photograph, c. 1915. Brooklyn Historical Society.

interest. Constructed in the late eighteenth or early nineteenth century, the farmhouse fit the common pattern of local wood-frame buildings that stood with their gable ends facing the Flatbush road; like the house that John Vanderbilt grew up in, it had two and a half stories. In the 1840s when Susan Catin willed the land to her daughter, Margaret, she sought to protect the house and land from the pitfalls of the modern commercial enterprises of Philip S. Crooke, her daughter's lawyer spouse. Catin gave her daughter the property for "her sole use and benefit and not to be subject or liable to the control of her husband and subject to or liable for any of his debts or any claim of his creditors."[35] A 96-acre farm, the Martense land produced turnips, potatoes, wheat, corn, rye, oats, and livestock that included neat cattle, milk cows, horses, and hogs. Philip Crooke did not work the farm himself, and his children eventually turned to cultivating real estate values rather than grain. By 1880 the Crookes had sold off 88 acres; then in 1890 they sold the house as well. Five years later Martin Lahn, a German immigrant, converted the residence into the first apartment building in Flatbush. Lahn lived in one of the six units; in 1900, his tenants included a family headed by a broker, another headed by a dry-goods dealer, and three families headed by clerks. The change was dramatic: in 1850 the Crooke house had accommodated twelve people, including family members and servants; in 1900, having "give[n] way for the march of improvement,"[36] the same house accommodated twenty-seven people. When it was demolished and replaced by a modern brick apartment building, no one called for its preservation.

The Birdsall house was similarly divested of historic interest in the late nineteenth century by a new use. The Birdsall family constructed the wood-frame, two-and-a-half-story, double-pitched-roof farmhouse with its gable end facing the Flatbush road in 1800. Its fall from grace began, perhaps, as early as 1845, when the house and the farm passed to an Irish immigrant farmer named Thomas Murphy. Murphy's family raised buckwheat, potatoes, wheat, corn, and oats, and quartered a small number of cattle, milk cows, horses, and hogs on an 80-acre farm.[37] In the late 1860s and 1870s, Murphy and his heirs sold off parts of the farm. In the following decade, an Irish immigrant carpenter named John McElvery converted the barn into a woodworking shop. For a time, McElvery's family resided in the farmhouse, and eventually the woodworking shop expanded into the ground story of the house itself. In 1880, Gertrude Lefferts Vanderbilt observed, the house was "out of repair and fast falling to decay. . . . Passing through the hands of various owners, it has not for many years been occupied by descendants of the family by whom it was first held."[38] Thirty-five years later the *Brooklyn Daily Eagle* reported that the once-impressive house was "fast going to ruin" because of its years of providing for the "baser uses" of a carpentry shop (fig. 4.7). Furthermore, the question of the present owner was "a matter of mystery." In the end, the place was dismissed lightly: "Doubtless it will soon give way to the

4.8. Jeremiah Vanderbilt homestead, built
1800, remodeled as a gas station in the 1910s.
Photograph, c. 1920. Brooklyn Historical Society.

march of improvement. There is little of interest about it except its age."[39] The building survived another ten years, but no one proposed it as the object of preservation or veneration.

In 1800, Jeremiah Vanderbilt constructed a new farmhouse on the Flatbush road. Like the adjacent Birdsall house, changing patterns of ownership and commercial use of the building in the late nineteenth and early twentieth centuries pushed the Vanderbilt homestead beyond preservation interest. It did so even though the wood-frame house, with its double-pitched overshot roof, approximated the exterior forms of the earlier Dutch vernacular houses. In 1880, looking back at the house her spouse's grandfather constructed, Gertrude Lefferts Vanderbilt commented, "It has gone out of the possession of its first owners, has not been kept in repair, and it is at present scarcely habitable."[40] When Jeremiah Vanderbilt, the son of the builder, had died in the 1850s, his children were not old enough to take over the farm, and the executors sold the homestead and the land. Later owners split the Vanderbilt homestead off from the farm, and an English immigrant hardware dealer, a Swedish machinist, and an American printer and advertiser resided in the house.[41] In 1908, Peter J. Collins purchased the property with plans to build row houses behind the house and apartments and stores on Flatbush Avenue (formerly Flatbush Street) in the place of the house itself. In 1911 the homestead felt "the touch of progress and development" as Collins sold off old doors, mantels, and fittings to an antiques dealer.[42] Still, Collins did not tear down the Dutch vernacular

house; instead, he propped billboards in the yard and on the roof advertising his adjacent residential development and later rented the house as a gas station (fig. 4.8). The place attracted no preservation campaign, even though it stood into the 1920s, a rare survivor long after the demolition of most other local homesteads.

Commercial redevelopment tended to block preservation interest in individual buildings. Flatbush Avenue, the oldest road through the village and the site of most of the Dutch homestead houses, developed as the community's primary commercial and transportation artery during suburbanization. As it commercialized, Flatbush Avenue provided a less venerable context for remaining homesteads and further disrupted the continuity of remaining Dutch families. John Ditmas, who had remodeled his homestead in the fashionable Queen Anne style in the 1880s, found Flatbush Avenue a less and less tenable place of residence at the turn of the century. In 1904, for example, across the avenue from Ditmas's house a builder constructed two four-story apartment buildings that housed eight families each. These buildings provided higher-density accommodations for people of more modest means than those who had taken up single-family houses off of the avenue in the Ditmas Park subdivision, carved out of John's father's farm. In 1905, John Ditmas, his wife Maria Convene, his forty-year-old daughter Mary, and their three Irish servants, Mary Carroll, Mary Mason, and James Hackett, moved out of the house that Ditmas had occupied for seventy-five years.[43] They did not move very far, about 220 feet; but they left Flatbush Avenue for the residential splendor of Ditmas Avenue and a substantial two-and-a-half-story modern suburban house with a corner turret tower and a wraparound porch. Veneration or no veneration, the character of the Ditmas homestead had changed along with that of Flatbush Avenue. In 1914, Ditmas rented his house to George S. Durand, a butcher by profession, who lived with his spouse, his fourteen-year-old son who attended school, and his eighteen-year-old daughter who worked as a dry-goods clerk. As was increasingly the case for the growing numbers of residents along Flatbush Avenue, the Durands had no live-in servants.[44]

The Durands were the last occupants of the Ditmas homestead. In 1914, just before he died, John H. Ditmas entered a contract with Farmers Realty Associates to sell the homestead and its adjacent ground for $51,750. The site would soon accommodate a building that combined stores and modest rental apartments. In reflecting upon the impending demise of the Ditmas "paternal acres," a newspaper apologist for Flatbush development observed that "to retain these acres would probably be a task of the antiquarian doubled with one of a millionaire, and more sentimental than feasible, in the growth of Brooklyn, so the house will have to go."[45] Similarly, the *Brooklyn Daily Eagle* reviewed the pattern of development that led to the destruction of the Ditmas homestead. Dismantling the old house, said the paper, was "the first step in the retreat before that ruthless foe of things old and established, the march of progress."[46] The ruthless foe had, of course, found an ally in John Ditmas, who since the 1880s house remodeling had shown himself more comfortable with fashion, progress, and an unsentimental farming of real estate values than with veneration of the past or attachment to his ancestral homestead and paternal acres.[47] In the face of these commercialized relations to land, buildings, and their settings, few preservationists asserted any claim upon what they viewed as the sullied history of such places.

As Flatbush Avenue changed from a rural route to a

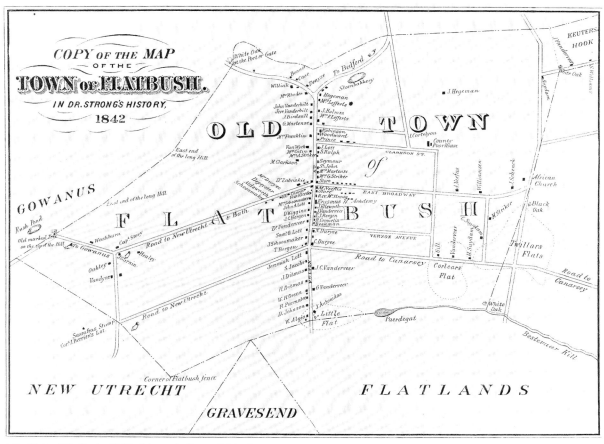

4.9. *Map of Flatbush, 1842. Linear pattern of historic settlement visible along what later became Flatbush Avenue.*
Map published in Gertrude Lefferts Vanderbilt, *The Social History of Flatbush* (1881).

4.10. Flatbush Avenue, c. 1930. Dutch Reformed Church, built 1785, at right. The two- and three-story hybrid buildings, mixing commercial and residential space, dominated early twentieth-century development on this street. Brooklyn Historical Society

commercialized landscape serving the exclusive residential neighborhoods built off of the avenue, the devaluation of historic residences turned upon changing views of the individual buildings and the cultural perceptions of the broader setting. What had been built up historically as the most civilized space in the village now appeared to accommodate the flotsam and jetsam of a modern suburban landscape, including service, transportation, and commercial spaces. In 1651 the Dutch had established a concentrated linear settlement along Flatbush Avenue. They built their distinctive Dutch vernacular houses on both sides of an established Native American path with farm fields extending behind their houses. Dutch governor Peter Stuyvesant had envisioned that such a plan would promote neighboring and cooperation when he laid out the town's land grants, "enabling the Inhabitants in general, when necessary, the more readily and effectually to assist each other."[48] Subsequent street and transportation improvements reinforced the dominance of this road as the only convenient direct route

through the neighborhood (fig. 4.9). In the late nineteenth and early twentieth centuries, as developers laid out farmland for "highly restricted" middle- and upper-middle-class subdivisions, they promoted redevelopment of Flatbush Avenue as "the future Broadway of Flatbush."[49] Between 1900 and 1930, landowners, builders, and architects constructed a continuous line of commercial storefronts, monumental banks and movie palaces, and multifamily housing for working-class residents along the "Broadway" of Flatbush Avenue.[50] Toward the end of this period an ardent preservationist surveyed the community and noted that nearly all the landmarks had disappeared. The exceptions were two late-eighteenth-century institutional buildings—Erasmus Hall Academy and the Dutch Reformed Church—and two houses—the Lefferts and the Vanderbilt homesteads (fig. 4.10).[51] It is possible that if Stuyvesant had established a more dispersed pattern of residence the displacement of Dutch vernacular houses in the nineteenth and early twentieth centuries would not have been as extensive; commercial pressure to redevelop both sides of Flatbush Avenue was very intense indeed.

Suburban Valuing and Devaluing of Dutch Homesteads

As new suburban and urban residents swelled the population of Flatbush, their ambivalence and apathy toward the physical vestiges of Dutch heritage represented a fourth major route toward the devaluation of Dutch homesteads. To the extent that preservation asserted the significance of genealogy, of historic place and the "family circle" of Dutch settlers over other groups, it did not as easily galvanize newer residents caught up in efforts to construct a stable middle-class suburban neighborhood. The simple vision of history and memory that focused most readily on a dwindling number of homesteads with unbroken bloodlines, those untainted by connections with divergent social groups and economic uses, suggested a narrow ethnic base of Flatbush preservation. Nevertheless, the major preservation campaigns in early-twentieth-century Flatbush, those to save the Vanderveer and Lefferts homesteads, did transcend parochialism; indeed, the valuing of Dutch homesteads now significantly reinforced the dominant domestic ideology of suburban women while buttressing the moral and sentimental identity of Flatbush's new suburban neighborhoods. In these limited cases, preservation seemed relevant to the modern life of the community. Homesteads that came into the twentieth century through inheritance rather than through commercial exchange assumed an importance beyond ethnic associations; they now resonated with efforts to define a domestic realm apart from the aggressive commercialism that destroyed landmarks, memory, and sentiment. Their importance stemmed from preservationists' and homeowners' overlapping interest in a noncommercial set of values. At the same time, the failure of the Vanderveer campaign in 1911 revealed the very real limitations of such an alliance of interests.

The John Vanderveer homestead combined continuous ownership from the seventeenth century with a contemporary perception of its architectural purity. In 1908, Charles A. Ditmas, one of the leading Flatbush preservationists, wrote a brief overview of "the near perfect structure" of the Vanderveer homestead (see fig. 4.6). Perhaps reflecting critically on the improvements carried out by John H. Ditmas, he noted that "few descendants have had the wisdom to leave the buildings alone which their ancestors had constructed, but have made them ludicrous by changing their contour and adding monstrosities of jig-saw work, instead of adding modern improvements and leaving the simple lines that are so dear to the architect of a well-balanced mind, which the original designer intended."[52] These words bespoke a generational change in attitudes toward Dutch heritage.

Starting in the 1890s, after the Vanderveer heirs sold off the farm fields for residential development, their farmhouse became the focus of preservation interest. Initially, the Daughters of the American Revolution (DAR) sought to preserve the homestead by purchasing it from the family. Although they failed in this effort, they later served as the institutional custodian for the Lefferts homestead. The involvement of the Daughters in Flatbush preservation points to significant developments in the national preservation movement that increasingly impinged upon local efforts. Despite the strong interest of the DAR itself and their work decorating the graves of Revolutionary war soldiers and marking historic battlegrounds and sites,[53] what is notable about preservation in Flatbush is the marginal status afforded the history of the war. In 1776 the British army had easily rolled over resistance in Flatbush in the Battle of Long Island. Flatbush residents lived out the war under the occupation of, and in some cases in collaboration with, the British. In the nineteenth century, interest focused on the stories of war destruction; however, preservationists did not envision their work as a means of connecting future generations to a somewhat inglorious political and military history stemming from the Revolution. On the contrary, the interest in Flatbush preservation focused on domestic history and matters of colonial customs and material styles.

The emergence of preservation interest in Flatbush coincided with a shift in the focus of the national preservation movement. Sites associated with political figures and military engagement had formed the basis of nineteenth-century preservation work. At the turn of the century, preservation expanded its purview to take in buildings valued primarily for their aesthetic character and their associations with everyday domestic life and activities of the past.[54] This change brought women more forthrightly into engagements with local history. Gertrude Lefferts Vanderbilt's literary efforts at Dutch preservation asserted as much. Although she admired Reverend Strong's historical work, she wrote Flatbush history "from a different standpoint. As a woman, I have inclined to the social side of life, and have endeavored to record the changes which time has made among the people in their homes and at the fireside."[55] Writing in the 1890s, Mrs. John King Van Rensselaer surveyed Dutch colonial history from the same standpoint. She asserted that "history is generally written by men, who dwell on politics, wars, and the exploits of their sex. Household affairs, women's influence, social customs and manners, are seldom chronicled. . . . The life of the 'Goede Vrouw of Manaha-ta' was written between the lines of contemporaneous history; I have merely taken the liberty of placing her in the foreground, with the men of the day in shadow as her background . . . instead of (as is usually done) reversing the process." Dutch house preservation campaigns extended this narrative strategy by insisting that historical memory could be cultivated by looking at the domestic sphere of women's work, apart from the male aspects of farming. The entry of the DAR into preservation and their curatorial stewardship of numerous historic houses was built upon a rethinking of what was important in history. That rethinking cast women as notable characters in the narrative and, in turn, in the presentation of history.[56]

The focus of homestead preservation interest on the domestic, the familial, the female, and the everyday proved particularly important in the expansion of the movement beyond the Dutch family circle. After the DAR failed to gain control of the Vanderveer homestead, the Flatbush Taxpayers' Association mounted a preservation campaign of its own. With a membership of over 800, the association served as a civic lobbying and neighborhood association that directed most of its energy and resources to ensuring the successful redevelopment of the neighborhood as a comfortable, accessible, middle-and upper-middle-class residential suburb. Standing committees worked on railroads and transportation; streets, lights, and sewers; schools and libraries; health and sanitation; public affairs; tunnels and bridges; legislation and city ordinances. This orientation to the present and future had in many ways provided the pretext for the wholesale destruction of Flatbush's historic architecture and agricultural landscape. However, the fact that Dutch homestead preservation emphasized the domestic and familial meant that it neatly coincided with the central community-building concerns of the Taxpayers' Association.[57]

Subdividers and developers built modern Flatbush on a foundation of a bourgeois ideology of separate spheres that located middle- and upper-class men in a downtown commercial realm spatially separated from an idealized, stable, domestic realm where women supervised the moral and intellectual education of children.[58] The Taxpayers' Association could realize its goals by promoting the emergence of the Flatbush neighborhood as a perfect domestic realm, conducive among other things to the sentimental moral education of children. Some preservationists envisioned Dutch homesteads as "a glorious . . . object lesson in history for the children."[59] The homesteads seemed to carry important lessons for those growing up in a materialistic world. They provided a delightful Dutch backdrop for a morality tale concerning people who thrived amid "simple refined conditions," with "personal integrity" and "love of community."[60]

Beyond moral education, the preservation of Dutch homesteads could be counterpoised to the commercial world and thus reinforce the culturally desirable and economically profitable images of Flatbush's suburban identity. Preservation could benignly point to the cultural and moral priorities of the community, which had turned aside from the march of progress to save history and landmarks. In 1906 the vice president of the Taxpayers' Association complained that without some action the evidence of their "quaint Dutch country village" will have "passed completely from view and in another generation be forgotten." Pointing to the neighborhood's modern developments and improvements, he declared, "We want them all and as quickly as possible. But in our progress should sentiment be entirely ignored?"[61] This insistence on the place of sentiment in the face of commerce complemented the values of morality and domesticity supposedly instilled in the specialized residential community. Some viewed the homesteads as a sobering "lesson to our modernism." In 1908, Charles A. Ditmas conceived of the Lefferts homestead as reinforcing the suburban landscape's separate spheres ideology. He wrote: "Situated at the gateway of Flatbush, the tired man of business, wearily riding home at dusk, sees first, as he enters Flatbush, this beautiful old Dutch house, nestling low down in a group of grand old maples, and his tired mind finds refreshing thoughts of the suburban home to which he is going, of the quaint old town, . . . with its society as old as New York's Knickerbocker stock."[62] This chronicle of domesticity could create a reassuring history for people who had only recently settled in the community hoping to buttress their own sense of community and place.

In 1909 the Flatbush Taxpayers' Association prevailed upon the Vanderveer heirs to give them custody of the homestead with the understanding that the association would move the house off the Vanderveer's valuable property fronting on Flatbush Avenue. John J. Snyder, president of the association, viewed the house as a "lasting monument," one that had "witnessed the development of sleepy Midwout into a bustling section of our great city." Since 1906 the preservation of the Vanderveer homestead had become a favored project of President Snyder. Although he had spent his entire life in Flatbush, the Dutch of Flatbush did not form branches in Snyder's family tree. In fact, Snyder's father was a German immigrant who, after a modest start in 1871, prospered by building a thriving hardware business. It was reported that when he settled in Flatbush, Snyder's father was the only German in the community; he built up his trade through extensive advertising, calling himself "Snyder of Flatbush." John Snyder extended this genteel gesture of assimilation when he entered the family business; he enthusiastically joined the ranks of local Flatbush historians and civic leaders.[63] Like other members of the Taxpayers' Association, Snyder actively promoted Flatbush's modern real estate and commercial interests. He published the *Midwout Magazine*, which combined nostalgic accounts of old Flatbush with pages of advertising for "Snyder of Flatbush." Nor did Snyder choose to live in a Dutch homestead. He preferred instead a modern two-and-a-half-story detached house on East 18th Street, a house typical of those lining the new residential streets in Flatbush.

Although Snyder and members of the Taxpayers' Association viewed the Vanderveer homestead as a "relic" in and of itself, they hoped to turn it into a historical museum capable of housing a broad range of other relics. Snyder imagined that if the Vanderveer house opened as a museum, then family heirlooms, antique furniture, pictures, and historical documents would soon overflow the place.[64] One of Snyder's associates, Charles A. Ditmas, viewed the house as a potential "shrine of patriotism."[65] The association needed about $5,000 to purchase several empty lots located off of Flatbush Avenue. It also aggressively pursued the possibility of convincing the city park department to purchase neighborhood land for a homestead park. When this failed, Snyder turned to the Brooklyn Institute of Arts and Sciences in the hope that a site could be obtained in the new Brooklyn Botanic Garden. However, Olmsted Brothers, the landscape architects for the Botanic Garden, balked at the suggestion because they felt that the homestead would be "so wholly different in character and treatment" from the rest of the garden that it would require too much space to develop an adequate landscape shield.[66]

A Vanderveer Homestead Committee coordinated plans for funding and moving the house, and editorialists directed their appeals to local banking, real estate, and commercial interests, arguing that the project would "greatly enhance the property of dear old Flatbush."[67] Nevertheless, in the end, the preservation campaign failed to raise the needed $5,000. In September 1911 the homestead was demolished. The site then stood empty until 1915 when the owner built a 25-by-11-foot billboard on the lot. Buildings did not fill the site until 1921, when Harry Schwartz commissioned architect Benjamin Cohn to build a two-story structure with stores on the ground level and a billiard hall and residences above.[68]

Some observers blamed the "apathy of some of the old Dutch families themselves" for the failure of the Vanderveer campaign.[69] There was, in fact, a rather stark contrast between the hundreds of thousands of dollars generated by selling old farms and real estate in Flatbush and the inability to raise a $5,000 preservation fund. The historic pattern of destruction in the area suggested that preservationists had failed to convince developers and residents that social cohesion and community identity somehow depended upon keeping the neighborhood's older farmhouses. In fact, alternative means of defining a community of interests among the newer suburban residents already seemed in place. In 1902, Edmund D. Fisher's *Flatbush: Past & Present* embraced the present at the expense of the past; the "rapid stride of improvement" had "outstripped the Past" and created "something very much better, a section of comfortable, commodious, artistic and happy homes."[70] Herbert F. Gunnison's 1908 *Flatbush of To-Day: The Realm of Light and Air* did not override as lightly an interest in the past. He found a useful theme of "enterprise" that linked the Dutch settlers to the modern suburbanites. However, the layout of the book's illustrations highlighted a certain superficiality in its approach to history. Single pages simulating the random organization of a scrapbook reproduced pictures of Flatbush homesteads. This design contrasted sharply with the straightforward documentary photographs of Flatbush's suburban homes and streets. Thus, homesteads provided a historic pastiche for the real resources of the neighborhood—modern suburban houses with their expensive accommodation of suburban domesticity.[71] Within this community, the book implied, there were more powerful and direct agents of social identity and cohesion than those offered by history or preservation.

Covenants on deeds and private restrictions on development in Flatbush had strongly shaped the identity of the emerging suburban community. Since the early 1890s the Lefferts family, for example, had slowly sold off their farm fields for closely regulated building development; their entire section was "restricted: only the highest class modern dwellings will be allowed."[72] The restrictions barred commerce and industry from residential blocks. They established a minimum height of two stories for the houses. They restricted the building materials to brick or stone. They established a building line set 14 feet back from the property line, and they prescribed a minimum of $5,000 for the construction cost of what were limited to single-family houses.[73] A replica of the Lefferts homestead could not have occupied a lot in the residential community that developed on the land formerly farmed by the Lefferts.

Furthermore, the continued presence of farmhouses on Flatbush Avenue contradicted the logic of the restricted landscape. In the face of restricted residential subdivisions, multifamily commercial buildings settled along the transit corridor of Flatbush Avenue. The apartment buildings and stores that surrounded the detached farmhouses on Flatbush Avenue presented precisely the unflattering picture of inharmonious commercial intrusion on the domestic realm that builders sought to avoid in their subdivisions. An economically profitable and visually harmonious order prevailed when the Lefferts homestead was moved to Prospect Park, and opened the way for a further extension of the Flatbush Avenue pattern of multifamily housing and commercial businesses. In 1925 the Lefferts heirs sold the homestead site, a piece of land 205 feet by 110 feet, for $100,000. Two six-story buildings that cost $500,000 and housed one hundred apartments and retail space on the ground floor soon filled the site. The development would have had a very different character had it been built around the Lefferts house. Indeed, there were some large subdivisions on the suburban fringes of New York City where early-twentieth-century builders retained "colonial" farmhouses, preserving "old age beauty," "great charm," and the "graceful lines" of Dutch vernacular. With dormers and bathrooms added, kitchens extended, and partitions moved, the houses received modern conveniences while they "retained the old-time characteristics."[74] Flatbush generally, and Flatbush Avenue specifically, seemed decidedly less conducive to such a pattern of preservation and adaptation.

The Flatbush Avenue land on which John and Gertrude Lefferts Vanderbilt had constructed their 1840s suburban villa and garden shared the same fate as the land under the Lefferts homestead. It, too, was densely developed for apartment houses. Vanderbilt's executors found no expressions of sentiment concerning the land, and they, in turn, exercised no sentiment in carrying out their work. They advertised the land as a simple commodity: "The Vanderbilt Estate for Sale . . . Will Positively Double in Value Within Five Years. . . . One of the most desirable locations in the greater city for *Modern Apartments* or an *Apartment Hotel*."[75] When they sold the land for $110,000, they anticipated a transformation of the neighborhood nearly as striking as the change represented by the earlier construction of Vanderbilt's fashionable suburban villa in the midst of a Dutch vernacular landscape; the new owners would "begin immediately the erection of apartment houses on the property. The location is believed to warrant development of high character as it is close to Prospect Park and a point from which all the transit lines of the section radiate."[76] Major changes did indeed come quickly. By 1915 the four major blocks encompassing the Vander-

bilt's property, bounded by Lincoln, Flatbush, Parkside, and Ocean avenues, housed 442 residents; in 1925 the same area accommodated 1,290 people.[77]

Covenants with Neighbors vs. Covenants with History

The pressing concerns of Flatbush residents and real estate interests alike in the late nineteenth and early twentieth centuries coalesced much more readily around the standard of middle- and upper-class domesticity than around the standard of history. The Dutch Reformed congregation, which continued to occupy a late-eighteenth-century church at the corner of Flatbush and Church avenues, offered a source of social and religious community to a declining percentage of neighborhood residents. New and old neighborhood residents rallied much more readily to civic organizations like the Flatbush Taxpayers' Association. Here they showed more unanimity on issues of transportation and school improvements than on issues of history and preservation. When President Snyder asked the association to endorse the Vanderveer project, just over half of the people attending the meeting supported his plan.[78] As a more diverse population settled in Flatbush, they increasingly shared an identity with their neighbors that focused on the covenants and restrictions that bound them and their properties together. They took on identities related to their particular residential subdivision, enthusiastically promoted and described by local boosters.

The Midwood Club represented another neighborhood institution that was self-consciously conceived as a way of encouraging cohesion among neighborhood residents. The club, like the social needs it served, originated in local real estate developments. Founded in 1889, the club grew out of the Flatbush Park Association, a real estate concern created to subdivide the Matthew Clarkson estate grounds. The association decided to preserve the Clarkson mansion as a clubhouse while developing its surrounding lawns and gardens for residences. The directors viewed the club as a place where "the older residents of the town can gather together and become acquainted with the new-comers, who are flocking there in greater and greater number each year."[79] Lectures, amateur theatricals, fairs, receptions, balls, and a number of outdoor sports would provide the attractions. Midwood Club plans for a museum of relics and mementos from the early history of Kings County never developed, however. Equally important, as a preservation project the Clarkson mansion itself shifted historical interest away from Dutch colonists and agriculture and

4.11. Prospect Park South, a Flatbush residential subdivision, rose from former farmland. The steeple of the Dutch Reformed Church is at right; the rise of land in the distance at the left is Observatory Hill in Prospect Park.
Photograph, c. 1900. Brooklyn Historical Society

onto merchants, remarkable wealth, and the roots of the contemporary villa suburb. Club members did not take refuge in the history of the place; instead, they built a log room in the basement with a raccoon-skin entrance and walls lined with hunting trophies. Here they exchanged "words of good cheer" around an open fire—a modern vision of the family circle that drew out social connection from a fantasy of "primitive character" rather than from history and memory. Nevertheless, in 1908, Herbert Gunnison reported that the club was "one of the striking examples of the successful blending of the old with the new, so difficult of accomplishment . . . in a growing community."[80] Numerous Dutch descendants joined the Midwood Club; yet, a common contemporary pattern of leisure and a shared vision of domesticity more readily provided common bonds than did historic relics.

Despite the pervasive displacement of old Flatbush by new, efforts at blending old and new in the local architecture did emerge. This did not come primarily through preservation. Rather it came through a proliferation of historicist residential designs—designs that lightly referred to a local history and design tradition. The stepped gables on the Vanderbilt house had initiated this development. In the late nineteenth and early twentieth centuries, as architects built an eclectic array

of new residences in Flatbush, they often introduced such historic elements as gambrel roofs, stepped gables, rooflines that swept from above the third story to just above the first floor, broad shingle surfaces, and gables oriented to the street (fig. 4.11). Below these exterior forms stood the modern improvements characteristic of the middle-class house—gas and electricity, central heating systems, higher ceilings, bigger windows for more lighting and ventilation, and a general move toward much larger scale and more interior space. People who attempted to introduce modern space and amenities to older Dutch vernacular forms encountered considerably more trouble. They found it impossible to maintain the "beauty and quaintness" of the exterior while seeking all the "comfort and convenience" of modern dwellings. Experts concluded that such a project was best left in the hands of the few "sentimentalists" who were "lover[s] of low ceilings."[81] Few of Flatbush's more recent residents fit this profile; they built and bought big houses loaded with modern comforts and conveniences, topped off by an almost whimsical historicism.

In the early 1910s, when Peter J. Collins started designing and building houses in Flatbush, he showed some affinity for architectural historicism but little affection for the existing historic buildings of the area. Collins presided over the demolition of both the Jeremiah Vanderbilt and the J. Birdsall homesteads. In his effort to sell "Easy House Keeping One Family Houses," Collins could not discover any useful connection between the historic houses on the site and the new buildings he had to sell. In fact, he found the historicist inspiration for his new Tudor-style rowhouses built on Chester Court not in Flatbush but rather in Chester, England. After seeing similar houses during a summer trip in 1911, Collins adapted the form for his own development in Flatbush.[82]

Possessed of two of the more prominent historic buildings in Flatbush, Collins might have promoted his development and a broad sense of a social community by preserving the homesteads he owned. Such a link between preservation and development was not all that unusual. In 1917, for example, Charles A. Ditmas encouraged one landowner to permit the Colonial Dames to take control of Schenck House on Mill Island; he insisted that it would benefit the development of the surrounding property because large crowds would visit the site and newspaper accounts would "advertise the locality in a way that would cost a promoter thousands upon thousands of dollars."[83] Still, Collins opted instead for demolition and the restrictive covenants that characterized the adjacent Lefferts development. Collins had been born in Brooklyn in the 1860s, the son of Irish immigrants. He worked as an architect and builder and served at the turn of the century as Brooklyn's superintendent of buildings. While planning his Chester Court development Collins lived in a substantial two-and-a-half story suburban house, with a dominant half-timbered gable and a broad front porch, located at 135 Westminster Road in Flatbush's Prospect Park South subdivision. There was little in his background, his profession, or his private residence that suggested any great interest in the historic forms of the Dutch vernacular landscape that he was demolishing and redeveloping.[84] His row houses were three stories high. Built of brick, they cost $5,000 and they were limited to single-family occupancy. Like Collins, home purchasers on Chester Court had never occupied the Dutch family circle. In 1915 the residents of Chester Court's eighteen row houses represented a diverse gathering of middle-class, largely white-collar, professional families headed by clerks in brokerage offices, lawyers, salesmen, an engineer, a lumber merchant and his stenographer daughter, an employee of a millinery importer, managers of a plumbing works and an electric fixture company, and a searcher for a title company.[85]

Families moving into Collins's subdivision, like many other recent settlers in Flatbush, came from socially, ethnically, and geographically diverse backgrounds. Few of them grew up in Flatbush or came from Dutch ancestry. Most paths to either valuing or devaluing local architec-

tural heritage did not run through their particular family lines. The crossing of the fashionable threshold from Dutch-American houses to high-style residences, the disintegration of the intricate family networks that had characterized Dutch agricultural homesteads, and the lapse of preservation interest in houses that had been taken over for new uses by different people, all influenced primarily the views and actions of Dutch descendants. Flatbush preservation undoubtedly would have enjoyed greater success had it resonated more deeply with the people selling and buying suburban lots. Properly developed, and properly understood, Flatbush's past could have been powerfully associated with the community's suburban future. Governor Stuyvesant's image of a community of mutual assistance, Gertrude Lefferts Vanderbilt's notion of an expansive "family circle," and the vision of "quaint" domestic forms could all have been tapped in shaping and promoting a new neighborhood identity for Flatbush. Preservation often has the greatest chance of succeeding when people whose minds are firmly set on the present and the future decide to devote their own resources to making buildings and landscapes from the past a vital part of their contemporary world. This rarely happened in Flatbush. What Collins and his fellow developers built and marketed for their suburban buyers was less a common history than a modern residential form suited to a middle-class ideology of domesticity. It proved a more inclusive, and perhaps more salable, basis for connection than a narrowly conceived link to a Dutch colonial history. In the context of a transient and aggressively commercial world, the covenants of a restricted community provided a more compelling means for establishing oneself among neighbors than a reverence for a remote ethnic heritage and the modest architectural fragments of a rural and agricultural world.[86] Only the tenuous links concerning historic patterns of domesticity provided real common ground between a Dutch past and a middle-class present; in 1911 the tenuousness of those links, and the failure of the preservationists to more persuasively articulate the relevance of Flatbush's past to its present and future, stymied the campaign to preserve the Vanderveer homestead.

For the Vanderveer preservation effort to succeed would not necessarily have required some tidy fit between historic narrative and community vision. Some committed individual could have preserved the building quite apart from community sentiment. The Vanderveer heirs could have sold all of their property except the historic house and the parcel of land it stood on. They would likely have received less money from the developers who purchased the land, but family members certainly had both the power and the resources to preserve the building. Alternatively, an individual developer, or

4.12. *Lefferts homestead being moved across the Brooklyn Botanic Garden on the way to its new site in Prospect Park. Brooklyn Museum in the background at the left.* Photograph by Louis Buhle, 1918. Courtesy Brooklyn Botanic Garden Library.

for that matter any private individual, could have preserved the house by purchasing it and moving it to one of the innumerable empty suburban lots that stood close at hand. Community ideals need not have come into play; with adequate resources preservation can be done individually or even idiosyncratically. While continuing to live in their historic house, the elderly members of the Vanderveer family had operated, in a sense, as individual preservationists. They stayed long after they commanded the financial resources to live elsewhere, in a more modern residence. Eventually, this preservation line ended. After their deaths other members of their family did not jump at the opportunity to move into the homestead and continue to maintain it. In this way individuals, families, and the broader community were all, in some measure, implicated in the growing destruction of the Dutch vernacular homesteads.

Preserving the Lefferts Homestead, Collecting Decorative Arts

In 1918 when the Lefferts homestead was hoisted up (fig. 4.12) and moved into Prospect Park, the campaign received crucial support from the Lefferts family and from residents of the Flatbush community. However, the successful preservation of the Lefferts homestead came less from family or community support and more from institutional support firmly tied to the broader Brooklyn community, well beyond Flatbush. Finally, in the Lefferts campaign a serious-minded preservation effort attracted the financial resources necessary to reverse all the movement along the well-established paths toward devaluation of the Dutch vernacular architectural heritage.

In some measure the failure to preserve the Vanderveer house indirectly contributed to the preservation of the Lefferts homestead. It helped intensify both local historical and preservation work. For example, it spurred Charles A. Ditmas's 1911 founding of the Kings County Historical Society. The society ambitiously set out to raise $100,000 for the preservation of at least one homestead in each of the initial Dutch settlements in Kings County. Although this initiative failed, the society also aimed to encourage original research; disseminate knowledge of early history in Flatbush and Kings County through lectures, exhibits, and publications; mark historic spots; and collect relics and other items of historical interest.[87]

In its early years the society directly engaged Dutch material culture through its annual antique loan exhibitions. In 1911, for example, the society organized a two-day fair to commemorate the 275th anniversary of the first purchase of land on Long Island by European settlers. People loaned the exhibition an eclectic array of goods: pewter, wedding veils, mahogany chairs, four-poster beds, fireplace bellows, spinning wheels, candlesticks, Old Dutch Bibles, and the door knocker from the Vanderveer homestead. The sheer volume of stuff available for display underscored the fact that local families had preserved and extended memories of Dutch culture by holding on to small artifacts easily transported across the threshold separating vernacular homesteads from modern residences. Clarkson, Lefferts, Vanderbilt, and Ditmas, for example, had undoubtedly placed Old Dutch antiques into the radically different houses they built in the nineteenth century. These goods fit well the picturesque eclecticism of Victorian domestic consumption and later stood as exemplars in the emerging Arts and Crafts Movement, with its promotion of aesthetically simple craft and design. In both cases such furnishings were acceptable according to prevailing market visions for provisioning the domestic sphere.[88]

Interest in decorative arts and colonial relics actually played a pivotal role in the institutional support for the preservation of the Lefferts homestead. In many ways the Vanderveer and Lefferts campaigns were quite similar. They started soon after the death of a longtime Dutch-descended homestead resident. A member of the "Snyder of Flatbush" clan, represented in the Lefferts campaign by lumber merchant and banker Alex C. Snyder, promoted the preservation effort.[89] Charles A. Ditmas played an important role in both efforts, and James Lefferts, the last resident of the Lefferts homestead, had earlier served on the preservation committee for the Vanderveer homestead; after he died, his heirs sought the preservation of his homestead, a tribute to the role James had played in trying to save the Vanderveer house. In both cases, too, preservation advocates approached the Brooklyn Institute of Arts and Sciences for help. Earlier, the institute's decision not to provide a site in its botanic garden for the Vanderveer homestead contributed indirectly to its demolition. Now the institute's institutional backing helped ensure the success of the Lefferts campaign. Interestingly, the institute's support derived less from visions of local history and preservation in Flatbush and more from its newfound commitment to collecting and displaying American decorative arts. The Lefferts homestead simply became the largest of the American artifacts collected as part of a new curatorial program.

The institute got involved in the Lefferts campaign in 1916; Louise Lefferts Downs asked institute board member Alfred T. White to cooperate in the plan to relocate the homestead to Prospect Park and to consider it as a setting for displaying artifacts drawn from the institute's new American decorative arts collection. The proposal was quite timely and drew White's enthusiastic cooperation.[90] In 1911, as the Vanderveer campaign floundered, a miniature historical diorama of a Dutch homestead on view in the children's section represented the institute's only engagement with Dutch-American material culture.[91] Furthermore, the institute did not own any pieces of American decorative arts. This all changed in 1914 when Luke Vincent Lockwood, a wealthy lawyer and antiques collector, joined the institute board. Author of *Colonial Furniture in America* (1901), Lockwood had helped organize, and loaned furniture to, the influential display of American decorative arts at the Metropolitan Museum's 1909 Hudson-Fulton Celebration exhibition.[92] The exhibition's critical and popular success had led the Metropolitan to make its first purchases of American decorative arts;[93] a month after Lockwood joined the board, the institute followed the Metropolitan and approved the start of acquisitions of "Early Americana." The first purchases included a doorway, a Dutch kas (a large storage cupboard), and three chairs, all in Dutch style. Over the next five years the institute spent nearly $14,000 purchasing American furniture. The institute also collected many American period rooms; however, limitations on space at the central museum did not permit the installation of the rooms or the adequate display of the furniture.[94] Within this institutional context the preservation of the Lefferts homestead opened important possibilities to the institute, ones that were not as readily apparent when the Vanderveer preservation advocates had approached the institute in 1911, before Lockwood's arrival. On a familial level, the Lefferts heirs were also honoring their family and genealogy; when Louise Lefferts Downs was engaged in 1905, the social notice pointed out that she and her parents still lived in the "historic house pointing back to the days when Flatbush was a Dutch town."[95] When the marriage ceremony was performed at the homestead, the *New York Times* reported that it was the spot where "five generations of Lefferts in succession have been married."[96]

When the twenty-one-member Old Dutch House Preservation Committee was formed in 1917, its membership overlapped with that of the Brooklyn Institute's board. A. Augustus Healy, a leather merchant, president of the board, and a member of the decorative arts committee, occupied a prominent place on the Preservation Committee. Other board members, including Luke Vincent Lockwood, merchant Alfred T. White, and lawyer Walter H. Crittenden also joined the Old Dutch House Preservation Committee. Frederic B. Pratt served on the committee; Pratt, the brother of the institute's first vice president, had given the institute its first piece of American furniture, a 1720 six-legged highboy. These men enthusiastically supported the Lefferts project as a means of obtaining a period setting for the display of objects from the institute's collection.[97] When it came to raising the $14,500 dollars needed to move and restore the Lefferts house, the Brooklyn Institute people led the way; White and Pratt started the campaign off by donating $3,000 each. Familial interests led the Lefferts heirs to contribute $2,325 and the house itself.[98]

Notably, the participation of the Brooklyn Institute board members projected the preservation campaign beyond Flatbush and its direct link to Dutch-American identity. Neighborhood residents did, of course, serve on the Old Dutch House Preservation Committee. F. A. M. Burrell, a Pennsylvania native, a wealthy manufacturer of leather belting, and a resident of the new upper-middle-class Flatbush neighborhood of Prospect Park South, led the group. The committee also included other manufacturers and real estate promoters, including the developer of Vanderveer Park, Henry A. Meyer. Herbert F. Gunnison, one of Flatbush's leading boosters and the business manager of the *Brooklyn Daily Eagle*, also joined. Nevertheless, none of the institute board members who served on the committee lived in Flatbush. The entire committee did live in Brooklyn, and with the editorial support of papers like the *Eagle*, parties interested in Dutch homesteads framed their preservation as a question of Brooklyn civic pride and competition. In 1916 the Dyckman family had restored their family homestead in Manhattan and presented it to the city as a house museum and park. Brooklyn residents then turned to the Lefferts campaign to match Manhattan, to promote local civic patriotism, express gratitude to past generations, and help teach history by tangible illustration, giving inspiration and guidance to future generations.[99] Accepting the homestead from the Old Dutch House Preservation Committee, the parks commissioner declared it "of great value to the people of Brooklyn."[100] The Parks Commission then leased the building to the Brooklyn Institute, which in turn subleased it to the Fort Greene Chapter of the Daughters of the American Revolution. The institute immediately placed on display a Hepplewhite dining room set including a sideboard, donated to the institute by Frederic B. Pratt; a dining room table and six chairs, donated by George D. Pratt; and a mirror. Along with an early-nineteenth-century card table, all of the items placed on display had been

acquired by the institute in 1915 and 1916 and stood in a "little exhibited room" at the central museum.[101] The broader civic and institutional base, represented by the Brooklyn institute, the DAR, and the involvement of non-Flatbush residents, had clearly propelled the success of the Lefferts homestead preservation campaign.

The coordination of the Lefferts preservation campaign with the Brooklyn Institute's initiative in collecting American decorative arts and period rooms provided crucial impetus, rationale, and support for the preservation effort. The Lefferts campaign also appropriated the social urgency found in appeals to patriotism, nationalism, and Americanization that marked the rise of the Colonial Revival in the United States in the late nineteenth and early twentieth centuries. Unsettled by the massive influx of foreign immigrants to the country, and especially to large cities like New York and Brooklyn, political and social leaders struggled both to assert the primacy of their own heritage and to articulate the values that they felt immigrants needed to acquire as part of the process of becoming Americans. The values of simplicity, honesty, hard work, and modesty that had long framed local images of Flatbush's "quaint" Dutch vernacular architecture took on a new life; indeed, these character traits seemed to stand at the core of the American values that leaders thought needed to be recognized, celebrated, and taught to recent immigrants. In 1915 the vice-regent of the New York State Daughters of the American Revolution pointed to the "last Dutch house" in Manhattan and argued that it was essential to "bolster up the civic pride and to preserve the fast-diminishing landmarks that tell the story of our forefathers' lives." The threats seemed clear enough: the "rush of foreigners to our country and the accession to office of many who have absolutely no regard for our traditions" suggested that ideals of community, civic pride, and tradition, along with the landmarks of history, would be "relegated to the scrapheap" by "newly imported citizens."[102] At the turn of the century, social commentators like *Ladies' Home Journal* editor Edward Bok began crafting arguments insisting that Holland had played a central role in the formation of American values. Bok, borrowing from American historian Douglas Campbell, traced a free press, free elections, free public education, and the freedom of religion directly back to Holland.[103] This broader vision of the significance of Dutch heritage for New York City and for the United States could now provide the influential context for the personal and institutional preservation of Flatbush's Dutch vernacular heritage. Earlier individual, familial, and community resources had failed to protect threatened homesteads; a changed conception of the meaning and importance of

Dutch heritage briefly altered the prevailing pattern of devaluation and demolition.

Despite the successful combination of individual, community, and institutional support, there is little evidence that the preservation of the Lefferts homestead buttressed social cohesion among Dutch descendants or civic patriotism and community identity within Flatbush. When preservationists moved the Lefferts homestead to Prospect Park, they revered its history by segregating it from the pervasive suburban "Realm of Light and Air." The park provided the Lefferts house with a new setting insulated from the jarring yet powerful contrasts with the modern developments along Flatbush Avenue. Indeed, in this respect the park resembled a cemetery: contemporary observers suggestively designated Prospect Park as "the final resting place" of the Lefferts homestead.[104] As a result, in Prospect Park and in the hands of the institute, the Lefferts homestead fostered historical memory in a place, and on a site, that did not encourage visitors to grapple in any immediate or tangible way with the historical relationship between rural Dutch vernacular and Flatbush's modern suburban landscape. Indeed, as the house moved, it shed a large two-story wing constructed in the 1850s by John Lefferts, an addition that in the view of preservationists had compromised its "pure Dutch type of architecture." However, keeping the wing could have permitted visitors to measure the changing standards of domestic space between the seventeenth and twentieth centuries and helped them see how people had earlier adapted historic houses for changing needs.[105] Despite its limitations, preservation through radical discontinuity seemingly offered one of the only alternatives to the pervasive destruction of Flatbush's architectural heritage. In his essay "The Necessity for Ruins," cultural landscape essayist J. B. Jackson insightfully explored the civic limitations of a preservation practice that posits a discontinuous "golden age" and tends to truncate critical reflection on the relationship between past and present. With a focus on "harmonious beginnings," the past is, according to Jackson, "brought back in all its richness. There is no lesson to learn, no covenant to honor; we are charmed into a state of innocence and become part of the environment. History ceases to exist."[106] Prospect Park introduced a strain of discontinuity between the Lefferts homestead and its place in Flatbush history.

After years of advocating for the preservation of Dutch homesteads, with only the most limited success, Charles A. Ditmas undoubtedly took some measure of pride in the outcome of the Lefferts campaign. He may never have appreciated the historical and civic compromises involved in relocating the homestead from Flatbush Avenue to Prospect Park. It undoubtedly looked like a rare and notable preservation success to him. Yet in a slightly different context he voiced strong opposition to the juxtaposition of historic commemoration and Prospect Park. In 1932, Ditmas rallied members of the Kings County Historical Society against the proposed construction of a replica of Mt. Vernon in the park in connection with the bicentennial of George Washington's birth. Ditmas asserted that "you can't take a replica and make it into a shrine. This is rather a curiosity, a piece of showmanship. A shrine must be a site or the building itself."[107] Ditmas and his associates suggested an alternative to the replica, the restoration of the eighteenth-century Gowanus House that stood in ruins on Brooklyn's Fifth Avenue. They argued that General Washington had stood near the stone house during the Revolution's Battle of Long Island. Ditmas also recommended that the Lefferts house be opened for extended hours during the Washington celebration. Despite these suggestions, the New York Bicentennial Commission and the New York City Parks Department went ahead with the replica, and in June 1932 Ditmas accompanied the United States First Lady, Lou Henry Hoover, on her tour of the park and the Mt. Vernon replica.[108]

Charles A. Ditmas's critique of the Mt. Vernon replica highlighted both the essential core and the troubling limitations of his own preservation vision. Ditmas had great faith in what he assumed to be the power of authentic built remains to capture the imagination, command civic reverence, foster historical understanding, and motivate preservation. This faith in the authenticity of preserved places usually exists as a guiding but clearly malleable tenet of preservation practice. Replicas posed a threat to the assumed power of historic places. If replicas could assume the status of historical shrines, then the need to preserve historic places could be diminished. Replicas could also raise troubling issues for preservation practice. At what point did preservation begin to take on the qualities of a replica? Did this happen when buildings were picked up and moved away from their historic settings, when additions were pulled off, when restoration was done to give the building purer lines, and when the interior was filled with an eclectic assortment of decorative arts? Though Charles Ditmas never acknowledged it, in Prospect Park the reviled Mt. Vernon replica and the Lefferts homestead shared more than mere physical proximity.

In the 1970s and '80s, Flatbush preservation broadened as New York City designated large areas as local historic districts, regulated by the Landmarks Preservation Commission. Facing rapid demographic change and a threatened spiral of economic decline, the latter-day preservationists campaigned to preserve the architectural forms and the economic viability of Flatbush's turn-of-the-century suburban landscape; this architecture had been built by people, and for people, who had never given much credence to the importance of preserving Flatbush's older historic buildings. In the late twentieth century the suburban domestic architecture that filled Flatbush still enjoyed broad popular understanding and appreciation on its own terms. It appealed to people who could deploy considerable resources in maintaining and preserving the stock of substantial older houses. Key aspects of the suburban ideology that had initially shaped the neighborhood held continuing meaning for both longtime residents and recent newcomers. This cultural continuum meant that preservationists found much more fertile ground in Flatbush's suburban landscape at the end of the twentieth century than their predecessors had found at the beginning of that century while attempting to preserve the traces of Flatbush's traditional Dutch-American homesteads. The later preservationists worked with historic narratives and architectural forms that easily moved them from Flatbush's suburban beginnings, through the intervening decades, and right onto the front lawns and front porches of the contemporary neighborhood. For the advocates of Flatbush's traditional Dutch-American homesteads, the route between the past and the present had never been so straight.

CHAPTER FIVE

Conservation on the Hudson

Saving the Palisades

At first glance, the federal government's 1872 creation of Yellowstone National Park did not share much common ground with the Mount Vernon Ladies' Association's 1850s preservation of George Washington's home. Yellowstone was revered for its natural scenic beauty. In contrast, Mount Vernon exemplified national narratives of American history. Geological time held sway at Yellowstone, while historical time dominated Mount Vernon. Nevertheless, making Yellowstone the first national park and opening Mount Vernon as an early historic shrine aimed fundamentally at the same idea: the preservation of place for future generations. To view scenic conservation as somehow distinct from historic preservation overlooks their common ideals. Expanding dramatically in the late nineteenth and early twentieth centuries, historic preservation and conservation both aimed to protect valued resources from the unfettered and often destructive prerogatives of a market economy. Supporters of both movements claimed that social refinement, cultivation, and enjoyment would flow from engagements with their hallowed places.

The tendency to view wilderness as the opposite of or antidote to human culture and history often militates against our ability to recognize the interconnectedness of historic preservation and conservation. Treating historic preservation and natural conservation as separate endeavors tends to distort their history. It ignores organizations like the Trustees of Reservations, founded in Massachusetts in 1891, and the American Scenic and Historic Preservation Society, founded in New York in 1895, which combined historic preservation and scenic conservation within a unified institutional mission.[1] It

overlooks the fact that the landmark federal Antiquities Act of 1906 gave the president the power to establish "national monuments" on public lands that had "historic landmarks, historic and prehistoric structures, and other objects of historic or scientific interest." In the hands of President Theodore Roosevelt, the act quickly facilitated the creation of the Petrified Forest and the Grand Canyon national monuments, best known for their stunning scenery.[2] It similarly fails to engage the complex vision set out in the National Parks Act of 1916 for an agency to "conserve the scenery and the natural and historic objects and the wild life therein and to provide for the enjoyment of the same in such a manner and by such means as will leave them unimpaired for the enjoyment of future generations."[3] Here history and scenery stood as parts of a single vision.

Environmental historian William Cronon helps us push beyond the simple duality of wilderness and civilization and to see them as interrelated cultural strains. Cronon argues that rather than seeing wilderness as an antidote to culture, we should recognize "how invented and how constructed, the American wilderness really is. . . . There is nothing natural about the concept of wilderness. It is entirely a creation of culture that holds it dear, a product of the very history it seeks to deny."[4] The same culture that constructs the importance of wilderness also constructs the significance of historic sites. We develop a more complex understanding of historic preservation by exploring its associations with efforts to conserve scenery and natural areas. In the United States the rise of conservation following the Civil War involved a movement away from previous land policies that supported unregulated development and economic exploi-

*5.1. Palisades Cliff and Hudson River, with talus slope
of broken stone, quarry buildings, and vegetation below.*
Photograph by Rotograph Company, 1900. The Nyack Library.

tation of the environment. New technologies employed for clear-cutting the forest, mining the mountains, and impounding water devastated landscapes on an unprecedented scale, while the railroads brought growing numbers of people either to participate in or to witness the destruction. Environmental reformers eventually succeeded in their efforts to set aside certain landscapes for the aesthetic and cultural enjoyment of the public.[5] In doing so they drew upon historic preservation models while vastly broadening the scope of preservation itself.

This chapter discusses the conservation of the Hudson River Palisades, the spectacular walls of stone that rise to over 500 feet along fourteen miles of the west bank of the Hudson River immediately north of New York City (fig. 5.1). Formed when molten rock intruded into a sandstone layer, the Palisades later developed distinctive striations from Ice Age glacial action. In the closing decades of the nineteenth century, trap rock quarrymen were energetically destroying the Palisades. They blasted the cliffs, crushed the stone, and shipped it to New York City and other towns as aggregate for macadam roads and concrete building foundations. This chapter will scrutinize the different perspectives and values brought to bear in the struggle over the Palisades. The most obvious conflict existed between the aesthetic ideals and contemplative eyes of the preservationists and the commercial calculations of the quarrymen.

Beyond this rather stark opposition stood an important conflict within the Palisades conservation movement itself. Would the exercise of public power or private purchase best advance preservation? Many preservationists assumed that their only hope of success would come from a public process of building a broad activist coalition and demanding regulatory action and public financing from political leaders. This approach differed drastically from a more curatorial view that advocated simple purchase, preferably private purchase, to stop the quarrymen's destruction. Potentially, either approach could preserve the Palisades. However, private purchase could preserve the Palisades while contributing relatively little to forging a more vital preservation and conservation movement in the region and in the nation. In the end, the destruction of the Palisades ceased with the cobbling together of both public powers and private resources. The interplay between public and private that characterized Palisades conservation proved central to developing notions of historic preservation in the United States.

Blasting the Palisades

On March 4, 1898, Alice Haggerty, "a pretty slip of an Irish girl" from Coytesville, New Jersey, easily attracted

5.2. Hugh Reilly, the Carpenter Brothers' "boss-blaster," at their Palisades quarry. This newspaper photograph of Reilly's working-class attire provided a stark contrast to the "grandeur" of the destroyed scenery. From New-York Daily Tribune, May 31, 1899.

5.3. Palisades sightseer. Keystone View Company, c. 1920. New York Public Library.

the attention of a crowd gathered near Fort Lee, New Jersey, along the Hudson River Palisades. Haggerty, the niece of the Catholic bishop of Buffalo, had won an "animated contest" for the privilege of demolishing a section of the Palisades by detonating 7,000 pounds of dynamite. The dynamite would hurl the prominent rock formation known as Indian Head from the Palisades cliff down to the Carpenter Brothers stone crushing plant at the river's edge. It dislodged 350,000 tons of traprock, enough stone to keep the crushers employed for several months. After viewing the blast, George Carpenter and Aaron Carpenter came ashore from the safety of their boat and congratulated Hugh Reilly (fig. 5.2), their "boss blaster." According to one newspaper account, Italian quarry workers "swarmed down, looked over the wreck, got together, and cheered hoarsely."[6]

As the quarry owners and their workers celebrated, others condemned the "detestable vandalism," the "abominable spoliation of one of Nature's noblest monuments," the crime "perpetrated against the human race."[7] These denunciations provided a rhetorical foundation for the campaign that aimed to silence the blasts, preserve the scenery, and drive the Irish and Italian quarry workers, with all their cheering, away from the Palisades. The preservationists sought a landscape of refined contemplation (fig. 5.3) over against a landscape of rugged work. They favored the cultivated eye over the "hand of the vandal"[8]—be it Alice Haggerty's hand,

which had "dabbed coquettishly" at the plunger, or the hand connected to Hugh Reilly's "brawny arm," which gave the plunger a "quick, vicious thrust" when setting off dynamite charges.[9]

After 1900, preservationists cheered and quarrymen protested. They did so as the legislatures of New York and New Jersey established the joint Palisades Interstate Park Commission. The commission combined private and public resources to establish a park and, in the words of the legislation, "preserve the scenery of the Palisades;"[10] this natural landmark, preserved by the commission, was indeed central to the aesthetic character of the lower Hudson Valley (fig. 5.4). For their part, quarry interests largely viewed the Palisades Park and its subsequent extensions as a "flimsy scheme," a land grab by rich people who had "suddenly become hysterical because of the 'vandalism' exhibited in the grinding up of the valueless rocks." In the face of park plans, quarry workers asserted, "We cannot live on scenery."[11]

As an object of preservationist desire, the Palisades maintained a rather complex relationship with more traditional sites of historic preservation. Advocates of historic buildings and places often argued that these places possessed the power to make a particular historic narrative more palpable, more memorable. By contrast, most preservationists valued the Palisades more for their spectacular geological form than for any specific connection with human history (fig. 5.6). There was also a significant difference in scale between a rock formation that reached 500 feet high and stretched for miles along the Hudson and the more familiar historic buildings or sites that preservationists often sought to protect. Despite these differences, there were significant ways in which the campaign to save the Palisades drew upon existing forms of historic preservation. To begin with preservationists identified a common evil threatening both the Palisades and many other historic sites. They also felt that the Palisades, like other historic sites, could provide a significant sense of stability to counteract feelings of dislocation that people experienced in New York's rapidly changing urban landscape. The shared sense of threat and the shared sense of purpose behind scenic and historic preservation even led preservation advocates to argue that the Palisades were indeed historic and significantly linked to central narratives of American history, nationalism, and identity.

In underscoring the shared threat to both scenic and historic sites, preservationists pointed directly to the destructive imperatives of the modern economy. In 1894 the *Tribune* reported, "The spirit which prompts the demolition of old buildings whose associations are historic in order to make room for great commercial towers, which throws the glare of an electric lamp on the altar and along the aisles of ancient churches . . . has laid its hand on the Palisades and threatens to obliterate the giant wall."[12] Zealous commitment to shallow pursuit of dollars seemed to increasingly threaten both

sites of scenic beauty and sites of historic significance. Destroying such places seemed to put in serious jeopardy the social refinement that was assumed to flow from respecting and being bound by history and also from admiring scenes of natural beauty. The agents of modern destruction attended to present concerns, usually commercially defined; many preservationists supported an alternative set of values committed to culture, aesthetics, and history aligned against narrow commercial commitments.[13]

The apparent opposition between preservation and the modern market needs some qualification; many of the people who loomed especially large in the Palisades preservation movement also dominated the modern world of business and finance. There is little evidence that men like J. P. Morgan, John D. Rockefeller, George W. Perkins, and Edward Henry Harriman viewed their support of Palisades preservation as significantly undercutting the logic of their private business pursuits. Rather, they seem to have approached the world of scenic and historic preservation as a cultured and civilized realm that could actually help justify and add meaning to lives and landscapes devoted largely to business. Many of them assumed that the measure and meaning of their lives flowed partly from the proper use of their wealth to promote a more refined and cultivated world. In their shaping of the modern market world, they did not find it inconsistent to also include history and scenery and art and culture as key elements. Indeed, the substantial

5.4. Palisades and the steamer Homer Ramsdell. National Railway News Company, c. 1910. Postcard in author's collection.

private contributions made to Palisades preservation rather neatly dovetailed with the "gospel of wealth" as laid out by Andrew Carnegie in the late 1880s. Carnegie argued that surplus wealth concentrated in a few hands needed to be treated as a trust, administered by the wealthy to produce the "most beneficial results for the community." In his view, rich men had it in their power to organize "benefactions from which the masses of their fellows will derive lasting advantage, and thus dignify their own lives."[14] Without any sense of contradiction, wealthy contributors to Palisades preservation occupied, and in some cases built, modern commercial towers while at the same time admiring and preserving scenic and historic places.[15]

When the *Tribune* pointed to the commercial tower as implicated in the destruction of historic buildings, it evoked a familiar image of urban novelty, innovation, and dislocation. Historic buildings and scenic places had the ability to provide some sense of familiarity and stability in a New York landscape characterized by rapid and dramatic change. Arguably, since the character of many historic buildings was profoundly changed and compromised when the surrounding context was transformed through new construction, Palisades preservation would have even greater power to provide stability amid urban transformations. For people buffeted by the rapidity of modern change, there was undoubtedly something reassuring about looking northwest from the city and seeing a familiar and unchanging landscape made up of

a river bounded by rather impressive cliffs—seemingly immune from human settlement or modification. More than the streets, blocks, and buildings of the city, the natural scenery that bounded the city seemed to have the greatest potential for providing a familiar sense of place. Indeed, although pervaded by the artifice of the landscape artist and the engineer, Central Park derived a significant part of its power from its apparent immunity to the dramatic urban and architectural changes that surrounded the park on all sides. When the *New York Times* reported on the 1898 destruction of the Indian Head on the Palisades, it highlighted the loss of a familiar, venerable, and stable landscape:

> Indian Head,' one of the finest and most impressive points of the Hudson Palisades, the shadow of which has fallen upon the broad waters of the river for uncounted centuries, the towering majesty of which impressed Hendrik Hudson when he first explored the silent stream, and has delighted millions of people during two hundred years, was yesterday blown to pieces by 7,000 pounds of dynamite. . . . It [had] seemed to proclaim to the puny men and their little machines passing by that it had been there before men began to crawl upon the earth, had looked upon the passing of innumerable generations of them, and would remain after the last of them had gone, and all the crowded, aspiring structures they had built over the river [in New York City] had crumbled.[16]

When Indian Head was dynamited, more than rock shattered; the experience and even the expectation of a stable and familiar landscape seemingly shattered as well. People clearly experienced a similar sense of loss when their historic buildings and places disappeared.

Advocates of preservation proved quite adept at arguing that beyond the scenic significance of the Palisades, within geological time, the Palisades contributed to narratives of human history and American nationalism. In this way the campaign to save the Palisades corresponded more closely to the familiar strategies used in advocating the preservation of historic buildings and places. The suggestion in the *Times* that Henry Hudson had been impressed by the Palisades involved a modest effort to graft some narrative of human history onto a site valued primarily for its scenic quality. In this context Indian Head was as much historical apparition as solid rock. Preservationists also pointed out that the Palisades included a number of sites made famous during the Revolutionary War. Beyond these associations stood a deeper cultural perspective that recognized the significance of American scenery as an important proxy for a more storied historic landscape; this concept provided

5.5. Palisades sightseer.
Photograph by William M. Chase, c. 1875. New York Public Library.

5.6. *Palisades above Fort Lee, New Jersey.* E. & H. T. Anthony, c. 1880. New York Public Library.

something of a foundation for historic visions of American nationalism grounded in part in American scenery. Thomas Cole had explored these themes over a half-century before the start of efforts to preserve the Palisades. In his 1836 "Essay on American Scenery," Cole contrasted American scenery with European scenery and argued that people should not dismiss the value of American scenery because it seemed "destitute of those vestiges of antiquity, . . . for though American scenery is destitute of many of those circumstances that give value to the European, still it has features, and glorious ones, unknown to Europe." In Cole's view the "want of associations" with human history was not especially problematic; great things undoubtedly stood in the future. As Cole surveyed American scenery, he did express his sorrow that "the beauty of such landscapes are quickly passing away—the ravages of the axe are daily increasing—the most noble scenes are made desolate, and oftentimes with a wantonness and barbarism scarcely credible in a civilized nation." But he viewed this as the road that any society had to travel and predicted that it "may lead to refinement in the end." For Cole, American scenery was very much part of the story of the American nation.[17] Cole's essay implied that the wanton destruction of scenery could result in an American landscape that lacked both history and beauty.

The criticism of the quarrymen's destruction of the Palisades certainly echoed Cole's earlier concerns over the destruction of American scenery. Indeed, there was a growing urgency about this matter in the late nineteenth century as Americans came to terms with the sobering assessment of human destructiveness toward nature; this notion had been captured in the enormously influential 1864 book *Man and Nature* published by the conservationist and diplomat George Perkins Marsh.[18] Marsh persuasively argued that humans were actually interfering with the balance and harmony of nature and that they could continue to do so only at their own peril. He warned that deforestation modified the earth's ecology and was doing great damage to elements of nature upon which human life depended. Marsh wrote that "the ravages committed by man subvert the relations and destroy the balance which nature had established between her organized and her inorganic creations; and she avenges herself upon the intruder, by letting loose upon her defaced provinces destructive energies hitherto kept in check by organic forces to be his best auxiliaries, but which he has unwisely dispersed and driven from the field of action."[19] Where Cole had surveyed mountains, lakes, waterfalls, rivers, forests, and the sky, Marsh paid particular attention to the woods, the water, and sand. The revulsion and resistance that greeted the highly visible destruction of the Palisades clearly drew upon the aesthetic perspective, represented by Cole, as well as the growing environmental and ecological perspective, represented by Marsh. For his part, Marsh had endorsed the efforts to preserve in their "primitive condition" parts of the Adirondack forest as "a museum for the instruction of the student, a garden for the recreation of the lover of nature, and an asylum where indigenous tree, and humble plant" could be afforded some protection.[20] The creation of the Adirondack State Park did not take place until 1892, but it complemented the earlier establishment of special preserves in the landscape that aimed to protect American scenery.[21] This important act was followed in 1894 by a provision in the new state constitution that required that state forest preserves be "forever kept as wild forest lands," totally protected from any logging whatsoever.[22] The creation of the Niagara Falls Reservation in 1885 and the 1872 founding of Yellowstone National Park had anticipated this approach. Both aesthetic and ecological views of these landscapes acknowledged the special link between nature and American identity and nationalism. They helped define the context in which people demanded special protection for the Palisades.

The Palisades preservation movement has been chronicled against a celebratory backdrop of inevitability—"the need for public action was dramatically apparent" so that sentiment "began to crystallize in opposition to the destruction of the Palisades."[23] In his history of

changing attitudes toward scenery of the Hudson River Valley, Raymond O'Brien argues that the "ire" of various citizens groups "prompted remedial action."[24] Nevertheless, the movement, once started, was not assured of success. Large-scale quarrying had taken place relatively unfettered for decades—as a matter of legal private-property right. In 1899 the *Tribune,* a strong editorial supporter of preservation, reported that "the plain fact is that interest in the preservation of the Palisades is not general and strong enough to accomplish the object on which a minority is, and long has been, seriously intent." Many people, in fact, strongly resisted the notion that public tax money should be spent for preserving the scenery (fig. 5.7).[25] In order to understand how a supposed minority view won success requires scrutiny of the social, political, and ideological position of the preservationists.

Nuisance in the Neighborhood

The people in the Hudson River's residential neighborhoods, more than anyone else, led the campaign to preserve the Palisades scenery and to end the quarry "nuisance." The tremendous popularity of the Palisades Park as a place of public recreation has tended to obscure the narrower, more private interests of early preservationists in Palisades scenery. For much of the nineteenth century, quarry operators and people interested in scenic beauty had simultaneously pursued their divergent interests in the Palisades. In the 1890s their

different views of the Palisades clashed sharply, in part because changes in quarry practice represented more of a threat to the scenery. Quarrying in the early nineteenth century had been largely confined to the talus slope of broken stone at the foot of the cliffs. In the 1880s and '90s growing use of trap rock, the introduction of steam drills, the use of high-grade explosives, and the rising investment in fixed crushing plants prompted quarry operators to work beyond the talus slope and to begin quarrying up the face of the Palisades cliffs. In the 1890s active quarry operations occupied only a few thousand feet of the Palisades. However, these areas, stripped of all vegetation, formed, in the view of preservationists, "torn unsightly blotch[es]," "ugly heaps of broken stone, topped by niches of loosened earth" (fig. 5.8). At the water's edge stood the "dingy, dusty, clanging, roaring crushers always belching forth clouds of white dust."[26] Many people began to envision the "ultimate destruction" of the Palisades.

In the face of Palisades quarry expansion, residents along the Hudson promoted a number of schemes for preservation. In 1894, for example, large property owners near Englewood, New Jersey, sought to form a village improvement association in an effort to preserve the Palisades. The association was to include landowners on the Palisades bluff and at the river's edge as well as subscribers for a projected commuter railroad running along the bluff. The association would seek to regulate development along lines consistent with the preservation of the area's most important scenic amenity. Furthermore, the planners hoped to provide a preservation model to residents and communities all along the Palisades.[27]

The village improvement association never organized beyond the planning stages and thus did not effect Palisades preservation. Nevertheless, the idea highlighted the tendency of residential property owners in the 1890s to identify their own interests with Palisades preservation and against stone quarrying. This alliance paralleled broader patterns of nineteenth-century suburbanization; newer suburban residents, increasingly committed to idealized notions of a separate domestic sphere, aligned themselves against the industries and "nuisances" that had earlier occupied extensive sections of the metropolitan fringe.[28]

Across the Hudson from the New Jersey suburbs, the wealthy residents of estates in the Riverdale section of New York City also sought to buttress the refined domestic sensibilities of their community by eliminating the Palisades quarries. New York publisher and Riverdale resident William H. Appleton complained bitterly of the "dreadful affliction to which we & our families have been exposed" by the quarry operations across the river.[29] In 1894 he lent his name to the call for founding the Palisades Protective Association. Appleton's neighbor, metal merchant and copper magnate William E. Dodge, complained that the "terrible reverberations of these dynamite explosions" made his summer home at Riverdale and "many miles of the most valuable property now included in the City of New York . . . useless for residence."[30] Dodge's copper and coal operations used their share of dynamite and crushing machinery; however, mines in Arizona and New Mexico stood out of earshot of Hudson River estates. Here the preservationist engaged in a form of relativism. They supported the preservation of nature in some locales but not in others. Indeed, Dodge felt so attached to local scenery that the Hudson River and the Palisades cliffs were prominently featured in his 1896 portrait, painted by Daniel Huntington (fig. 5.9). James G. Hasking, a New Jersey banker, insisted, "If commerce must have trap rock . . . there are plenty of places from which it will not be missed." He pointed out that the western side of the Palisades ridge could be quarried, but he predicted that the quarrymen would resist paying the additional expense of transporting the stone to the river for shipping.[31]

The Protective Association moved on several fronts, going in different directions simultaneously, seeking both private remedies and public solutions. The association hoped to test the private legal rights of those "injured" by the quarrying—that is, the rights of people who felt their quiet possession of Hudson River homes and Palisades views had been intruded upon by the Car-

5.8. Section of Carpenter Brothers' Palisades quarry at Fort Lee stripped of vegetation and reduced to rubble high into the cliff formation. Photograph, c. 1897. Palisades Interstate Park Commission.

penter Brothers and other quarry operators. If a court found that the quarry operators were trespassing upon the private property rights of their neighbors, then they could potentially shut the quarries down without any broader commitment or participation on the part of the public. But the Protective Association also aimed to rally public support and to "arouse a proper American sentiment for the preservation of the beauty of the Palisades."[32] William Dodge consulted Harvard professor Charles Eliot Norton and landscape architect Frederick Law Olmsted, both of whom had played important roles in preserving Niagara Falls. Dodge also laid plans to enlist the support of various "local parties and editors."[33] Norton, Olmsted, and the editors would likely propose a more public course of action. Indeed, when landscape architect Calvert Vaux and Olmsted, his former partner, considered the Palisades preservation issue, they viewed it in many of the same ways that they had viewed Central Park forty years earlier. They felt that the growth of the city more than justified taking the Palisades and reserving them as a park for the "free access" of the public. Olmsted insisted that a major scenic area such as the Palisades, with its close proximity to New York City, should not be privately owned.[34]

Olmsted's suggestion for a public park obviously went beyond the needs of many estate owners, who could envision holding onto their scenery through a series of private purchases and court decisions. Indeed, William Dodge had already explored this direction. When the Brown & Fleming Company started operating a stone quarry and crushing plant across the river from William Dodge's Riverdale home, Dodge responded by purchasing tracts of Palisades land surrounding the quarry onto which Brown & Fleming had hoped to expand their operation. When the company exhausted the stone on their tract, they had to close their plant.[35] Dodge did not stand alone in pursuing such "private way" preservation. During the 1890s many wealthy owners of residential land on the Palisades bluff had purchased the face and the foot of the cliff in "self-protection" from the possible development of quarries.[36] Some observers insisted that this was the way to proceed, and, in their view, it seemed far preferable to "holding indignation meetings or trying to secure legislation to prevent their present owners from making money."[37]

The New Jersey legislature had itself attempted to prevent the destruction of Palisades scenery without a park; in 1874 the legislature barred advertising signs and notices of any kind from the Palisades. In 1895 the legislature attempted to more aggressively preserve Palisades scenery not by regulating or taking private property nor by creating a park, but rather by restricting the use of public riparian lands. The legislature directed

5.9. *William E. Dodge at his home in Riverdale, New York, portrait with the Hudson River Palisades in the background. Daniel Huntington, painter, 1896.* Chamber of Commerce of the State of New York.

the state's Riparian Commission, which controlled New Jersey's underwater lands, to bar people engaged in "injurious or destructive work or operations against the Palisades" from use of the riparian land. The law sought to "preserve unbroken the uniformity and continuity of the Palisades."[38] The legislation would also prevent the shipping of crushed stone on the Hudson River over state-controlled waters.

Members of the Riparian Commission asked the legislature to extend protection to the trees, shrubs, and piles of broken stone on the talus slope below the Palisades because of its beauty; however, the legislature declined to do so.[39] Still, preservationists hoped the law would end quarry development along the river.[40] The Carpenter Brothers managed to avoid the regulations by taking out a perpetual riparian lease on the underwater land adjacent to their quarries just before the enactment of the law. The company received the lease on January 31, 1895, four days after the New Jersey Senate passed their restrictive bill and only two weeks before the Assembly and the governor concurred and made it law. The company may have used some ingenuity to get in under the wire; it is at least suggestive that one of five riparian commissioners who issued the lease, Hudson County lawyer Willard C. Fisk, served as limited partner and secretary of the firm when the Carpenter Brothers incorporated three years later.[41]

State Legislatures, Congress, and Public Park Proposals

In the mid-1890s, when New York and New Jersey officials explored the possibilities of a public park on the Palisades, they looked most hopefully to the federal government. Between 1895 and 1898, members of New York's and New Jersey's congressional delegations and their constituents petitioned the Committee on Military Affairs to have the federal government take over the Palisades. In 1895 the New York and New Jersey legislatures established Palisades commissions to explore the military park idea and recommend legislation; in early 1896 both legislatures passed laws ceding Palisades land to the federal government for use as a military park. In 1895, when the New Jersey State Senate debated the Palisades question, leading senators explicitly rejected Senator Henry Winton's claim that the state had assumed the role of a "guardian" of the Palisades and thus should act to "beautify" the property with a series of "handsome parks . . . for the pleasure and benefit of the public."[42]

The focus of both private and legislative action in the mid-1890s continued to be on the preservation of scenery; however, some astute participants felt that their arguments needed to be refined in order to appeal to federal officials. John James Robertson Croes helped articulate a case for shifting the preservation rationale for the Palisades. Croes, who worked as a civil engineer, with extensive expertise on water supply, waterpower, sewerage and irrigation systems, lived opposite the Palisades in Yonkers, New York. In the 1870s, Croes had collaborated with Frederick Law Olmsted on the street plan for the Bronx that aimed, among other things, to set aside the dominant city grid in favor of a plan patterned more closely on the topography of the area. Croes and Olmsted paid special attention to the possibilities of promoting Riverdale's development as an exclusive residential area.[43] As a member of the New York commission that developed the plans for ceding the Palisades to the federal government, Croes felt strongly that only government action would save the Palisades. He considered it "utterly fallacious" that "public spirited citizens of wealth" could successfully accomplish the preservation of the Palisades.[44]

In 1896, Croes outlined to William Dodge his strategy for enlisting the federal government in the purchase of 2,000 acres to preserve the Palisades. He reported, "The prime motive is unquestionably the sentimental and aesthetic one, but as beauty and the gratification of the senses are not recognized in the Constitution of the United States, the argument must be made on the grounds of public policy alone." Croes moved the argument toward public education and, more important, toward public security. For Croes that public policy would involve "keeping alive the spirit of patriotism by preserving memorials of the struggle for independence." Further, it also included a "visible manifestation" of the federal police power sufficient to "keep in awe that turbulent element of foreign anarchists and socialists" gathered in New York City and seemingly waiting for "some local demoralization" to proceed to the "overturning of all law and order."[45] Here, Croes demonstrated a willingness to substantially adapt political claims in order to promote preservation goals. This strategic repositioning of the argument anticipated many future preservation battles in which individuals and communities deployed preservation arguments and regulations to fend off various forms of supposedly undesirable new development.

Despite the efforts of Croes and his commission colleagues, and despite the tentative support of the secretary of the navy, few people took seriously the security claims made by the proponents of a Palisades military park. The Congress's House Committee on Military Affairs appeared "rather indifferent" to a Palisades military park. The secretary of war did not endorse the idea.[46] The deepening economic crisis of the late 1890s also undoubtedly dampened interest in the proposals. The military park idea also sparked a coalition between people who usually worked as adversaries in debates over the Palisades. The quarry operation joined large landowners who occupied the crest of the Palisades in working to defeat the idea. If the 2,000-acre military park included a tract on top of the cliffs, then quarry owners, residents, and residential developers along the Palisades all stood to lose their land. Some people attempted to work out a compromise whereby the government would take only the Palisades themselves and the narrow strip of land at the foot of the cliffs. This compromise seemingly undercut the military park idea by failing to command the high ground over New York City.[47]

The proposed jurisdiction of the federal government would have helped overcome the anticipated difficulty of reconciling the greater interest of New York residents in the preservation of lands located in an adjacent state. William Dodge had alluded to this tension when he wrote to Frederick Law Olmsted seeking his advice and support for the preservation cause. He wrote that "unfortunately the Palisades are on the edge of New Jersey and subject to its laws but are never seen or thought of by the people of that State, so we are at a disadvantage."[48] The argument contained some exaggeration, but nevertheless it did underscore the premium placed upon the Palisades as a scenic amenity quite apart from any notion of its potential as a park.

Preservation Crusaders

In the late 1890s, as hopes for effective private preservation and for a federal military park dimmed, preservationists explored the possibility of establishing an interstate park commission. The commission idea would follow in the steps of the New Jersey and New York legislative study commissions that had initially settled on the advocacy of a military park. It would also move the notion for public preservation from the federal government to state governments. Here the preservation movement gained formidable personal and institutional support that went well beyond the immediate Palisades area. Two civic organizations, the New Jersey State Federation of Women's Clubs and the New York–based American Scenic and Historic Preservation Society, seized the preservation cause and lobbied quite effectively for public support of Palisades preservation in the New Jersey and New York state legislatures. They attempted to push beyond the idea voiced in 1895 by New Jersey legislators that there was no need for a public state park to preserve the Palisades.

The Palisades campaign reinforced the literary, educational, and welfare agenda of the Federation of Women's Clubs. The federation was established in 1894 to encourage communication, acquaintance, and "mutual helpfulness" among the disparate women's clubs and associations throughout New Jersey. The early work of the federation included the promotion of town improvements, public libraries, school kindergartens, and other educational reforms. The federation also campaigned for a "safe and sane" Fourth of July, with patriotic pageants taking the place of fireworks displays. In the early years of the twentieth century the federation supported prohibition, women's suffrage, motion picture censorship, and a variety of Americanization campaigns. At certain points the federation worked to expand the boundaries of what middle-class women could take up in public life; however, their work generally followed prevailing assumptions concerning woman's role as the steward of ethical, moral, and aesthetic values defined apart from and, in many cases, in opposition to, the commercial pursuits of men engaged in the market.

The federation pursued its Palisades work with "purely aesthetic motives."[49] On the face of it, preservation pitted the ideal of natural beauty and domestic tranquility against the imperatives of the market. Women were drawn into the conservation campaign in part because the Palisades stood within a metropolitan area and because the quarry operations intruded upon domestic sensibilities. The absence of women in other major late-nineteenth-century conservation campaigns ranging from Yosemite to Yellowstone to Niagara Falls made their presence in the ranks of Palisades crusaders all the more notable. In these other places, and particularly in the West, the proponents of wilderness conservation saw men as the primary beneficiaries. In the case of the Palisades the arguments were different. Here, because of the ease of access, women stood a much better chance of benefiting from conservation.

Initially the federation simply joined other individuals and organizations in petitioning Congress to preserve the Palisades by establishing a military park.[50] As that plan languished, members of the federation rallied support for preservation within New Jersey. Papers on Palisades preservation were presented at a federation meeting in March 1896. In May 1897, in Englewood, just above the cliff, the federation considered the Palisades issue for a full day. It followed this up in September 1897 with a yacht trip inspection running along the Hudson River from Jersey City to Haverstraw Bay. According to federation president Cecelia Gaines, the organization hoped to preserve the Palisades from "desecration; it abhors the thought of selling the magnificent ramparts of the Hudson to pave streets with. As women we are barred from legislating; but we can agitate."[51] Their agitation helped lay the public foundation for Palisades preservation in New Jersey.

In New York a good deal of the credit for successful promotion of Palisades preservation went to the American Scenic and Historic Preservation Society. The society was founded in 1895 under the leadership of Andrew H. Green, a lawyer, former commissioner of Central Park, former comptroller of New York City, a commissioner of the Niagara Falls Reservation, a leading proponent of the consolidation of Greater New York, and the legal partner and political protégé of former New York governor Samuel Tilden. Originally called the Society for the Preservation of Scenic and Historic Places, the Scenic Society pursued a diverse and ambitious agenda—its work was "preservative, creative and educational." It aimed "to preserve from disfigurement beautiful features of the natural landscape, and to save from obliteration or destruction names, places and objects identified with local, state and national history."[52] The society served as the institutional custodian of several scenic areas and historic places that included the Stony Point Battlefield Reservation on the Hudson River, Letchworth Park on the Genessee River, Philipse Manor Hall in Yonkers, and the Hamilton Grange in New York City (fig. 5.10). The society aimed to cultivate a national agenda but worked most effectively in the New York State region.

For the Scenic Society, perhaps more so than for the Federation of Women's Clubs, the palpable material

5.10. Hamilton Grange, built 1802, John McComb Jr.,
architect. Preserved in a campaign organized by the
American Scenic and Historic Preservation Society.
Photograph, c. 1889. Library of Congress.

quality of a scenic or historic landmark assumed utmost
importance. The society held great faith in the power
of things, properly interpreted, to teach and cultivate
people. In 1902, A. D. F. Hamlin, professor of architecture at Columbia University, delivered a lecture to the
Scenic Society that addressed the material basis of its
work. Hamlin insisted that "sentiment, which is the
moving power of human action, always leans on material
symbols. In all ages it has been stirred to new life by the
appeal through the eye and the ear, when the calm whis-
per of reason was powerless to arouse it. . . . Historic sites
and buildings . . . enshrine the memories and exhale the
subtle influences which refresh patriotism, civic virtue,
piety and love. A historic edifice is an unceasing teacher
of history and of all that history teaches, . . . a perennial
fountain of inspiration."[53]

The preservationists' faith in the power of things to
promote historic memory, continuity, and stability under-
lay much of the Scenic Society's preservation work. In
1905, for example, the society sought to convince New
York's First Presbyterian Church not to abandon its
1840s building—a "notable barrier to the dull monotony
of secular architecture" which was "encroaching" on
lower Fifth Avenue. Edward Hagaman Hall, secretary
of the society, wrote that "in this ever changing city,
we must look to our churches and cognate institutions

for our landmarks and evidences of stability. Business
structures and apartment houses rise and disappear in
a generation under the exigencies of the city's growth.
There is little of permanence upon which to fasten our
memories, our affections and our historical traditions.
We need just such piles as the beautiful First Church to
give us some idea of firmness and stability in contrast
to the fleeting changes around."[54] The society seized
upon the Palisades as a significant site that could foster
a sense of stability as a memorable object of topography—a landmark in every sense of the word.

The members of the Scenic Society and the Federation of Women's Clubs sought something more fundamental than to mediate the relationship between past
and present. They sought to build a vital civic community
founded upon cultivated pursuits and standing in opposition to the "encroachments of commercial enterprise,"[55]
embodied by the likes of the Palisades trap rock industry. The Scenic Society sought to preserve buildings like
the First Church "as monuments of the best and noblest
human effort and to serve as visible bonds to bind
together generations and centuries of high endeavor."[56]
In the case of the Palisades, the preservationists cast
their cause in generational terms; they worked from an
"obligation to posterity," from a sense that their "remot-
est descendants will never forgive us" if the cliffs were

destroyed.[57] They considered preservation as the "high endeavor" of a cultivated community.

In promoting the "bonds" between individuals, landmarks, and the past, the preservationists also forged bonds among themselves, quite apart from the material objects of interest. The Women's Federation promoted a much broader community among New Jersey women by affording them the opportunity to develop civic connections beyond the parochial interests of their own clubs and communities. The Scenic Society promoted a civic public through the assertion of shared history and aesthetics. As in the case of the federation, the society's preservation process itself built community; people who campaigned for preservation felt that they occupied a vanguard position in promoting a "step forward in the advance of civilization."[58] For all the discussion of generational connections, the sense of civic virtue and community prevailed most clearly among the preservationists themselves through shared efforts on behalf of preservation. In the case of the Palisades a vital and informed preservation community of this sort clearly stood less chance of developing if the preservationists had settled upon the more private efforts of court litigation or simple private purchase of quarry sites.

The strong community that developed within the Women's Federation, the Scenic Society, and among the residents along the Hudson River provided a promising foundation for taking the Palisades campaign to a broader public. Most fundamentally, the campaign won over the members of the New Jersey and New York legislatures. In 1899 the governors of New Jersey and New York, with legislative approval, appointed new Palisades commissions to draft new preservation plans. New Jersey governor Foster M. Voorhees, said to have told federation members that the cause was "hopeless," did respond to lobbying by the federation and appointed the new five-person commission; it included federation president Cecelia Gaines and Elizabeth B. Vermilye, the head of the federation's Palisades subcommittee. Women's prominence in preservation itself became an issue. When the commission's proposals were cast in the form of legislation, one New Jersey senator declared that "one of the principal things that condemns this bill, is that the women are in favor of it, my wife among the rest." Proponents of the bill slammed the remark as a "slur upon the noble women" of New Jersey.[59] In New York, Governor Theodore Roosevelt filled his commission with people recommended by the Scenic Society.

The 1899 study commission contributed to Palisades preservation by conceiving of the mechanism of an interstate commission with overlapping membership appointed and confirmed by the governors of New Jersey and New York. The interstate commission idea, in the view of Governor Roosevelt and others, helped overcome the obstacle posed by the strong interest of New York residents in land on the New Jersey side of the Hudson.[60] Despite the history of contest and political inaction over the Palisades, the late 1890s preservation campaign eased the way for members of the state legislatures to support preservation. The work of the Federation of Women's Clubs and the American Scenic and Historic Preservation Society successfully broadened

5.11. Cartoon promoting the coordination of legislative efforts by New York and New Jersey to preserve the Palisades (depicted here as female). From New-York Daily Tribune, March 24, 1901.

IT'S UP TO NEW-YORK TO COMPLETE THE RELEASE OF THE PALISADES the constituency for the Palisades beyond the people and the legislative representatives who lived adjacent to the Palisades. In March 1900 the act to establish a park "to preserve the scenery of the Palisades" passed unanimously in the New York legislature and attracted only one dissenting vote in New Jersey. This broad support did not guarantee preservation success (fig. 5.11). The New Jersey legislation provided only $5,000 and New York appropriated $10,000, amounts that would cover little more than administrative expenses of an interstate park commission.

Palisades Interstate Park Commission: Quiet Acquisitions

The creation of the permanent Palisades commission brought with it an important reconfiguration of the ideological and political contours of Palisades preservation. Before 1900 the Palisades preservation campaign had combined intermittent "private way" initiatives with the increasingly effective community-building campaigns of the Federation of Women's Clubs and the American Scenic and Historic Preservation Society. After 1900, Palisades preservation turned away from the its growing community base and adopted a second powerful strain in preservation—simple private curatorial acquisition. There was no small irony in the fact that just as the Palisades preservation movement acquired one of the most public of powers, public condemnation of land,[61] it veered away from the institutional support that could have fostered preservation far beyond the Palisades issue. With the rise, or more correctly the reemergence, of a private curatorial sensibility in Palisades preservation, the market that had appeared as the destroyer of the Palisades emerged as the preserver.

The appointments to the permanent Palisades commission in 1900 signaled the transition from civic activism to curatorial acquisition. Only two of the five members of the 1899 New Jersey study commission became members of the new Palisades Interstate Park Commission, and those two were not the pair of federation women. In New York, Governor Roosevelt did not carry over a single member of the 1899 commission and did not include any members of the Scenic Society on the permanent commission. This caused no small annoyance in the Scenic Society. Some preservationists did feel that appointing a permanent commission made up of people genuinely interested in the beauty of the Palisades with a background in business would prove more effective than having activists who had "axes of their own to grind." In this sense, the exclusion of the

5.12. *George Walbridge Perkins.* Photograph by Harris & Ewing, 1911. Library of Congress.

federation and the Scenic Society seemed carefully calculated to change the nature of the debate over the Palisades.[62]

George Walbridge Perkins (fig. 5.12), the first president of the new commission, personified the changed approach to Palisades preservation. Perkins, the empire-building vice president of the New York Life Insurance Company and a future partner of J. P. Morgan, knew the Palisades well. His three-story house in Riverdale had a wraparound porch that looked directly across the river to the cliffs. In 1900, at age thirty-eight, Perkins shared many comforts in Riverdale with his wife Evelina and his young daughter and son. A house staff of nine people made up primarily of Swedish immigrants attended to Perkins and his family. Still, the quarrying of the Palisades intruded upon the joys of their home. In 1894, Perkins had joined his neighbor William E. Dodge in seeking a legal end to the quarrying and blasting; he complained that the work awakened his two-year-old daughter from her naps.[63] Nevertheless, Perkins had never gotten involved in the more organized efforts to save the Palisades. His approach to Palisades preservation stood in rather striking contrast to previous efforts. He put little stock in public campaigns. Perkins approached the Palisades as a problem of consolidation, not unlike his work as a Morgan partner in putting together the International Harvester, United States Steel Corporation, and Northern Securities Company trusts. The parallel was clear enough; the Palisades Park plan called for a single corporate entity, the commission, to consolidate 175 independent land holdings over fourteen miles of the Hudson into a public park. The differences were clear enough as well. Business trust negotiations were generally carried out in great secrecy. The preservation of the Palisades had heretofore been urged with great publicity.

Perkins's initial "plan of operation" included little effort to strengthen or work with the existing preservation coalition. He simply sought to get a list of Palisades landowners together, to approach them concerning their willingness to donate land to the commission or, barring that, to determine the price at which they would sell their land. These plans expanded upon earlier private efforts at preservation and assumed that many landowners would now recognize their shared interest in the commission's efforts. As mentioned earlier, some large residential landowners above the Palisades had purchased the cliffs and the land along the Hudson shore in "self-protection" against the quarry industry. With the advent of a "practical and responsible" commission, many landowners looked forward to cooperating in the creation of a park.[64] In Perkins's plan the commission would capitalize on this history of private interest and private preservation; it initially planned to sell $250,000 to $500,000 worth of $100 certificates to interested individuals to support commission land purchases.[65] The certificate plan could possibly draw upon the earlier supporters of Palisades preservation; however, Perkins found it quite problematic that the old base of preservation support demanded publicity. Their public methods ran counter to his hope that the commission would "make no attempt to impress upon the public, through newspapers, that we are doing anything or meeting with success. As it is generally supposed that we are impotent we can get lower figures from owners for their property."[66]

In pursuing his quiet approach Perkins generally ignored the advice that he forge a coalition of civic associations. Frederick S. Lamb, a member of the Scenic Society, for example, urged Perkins to put together a coalition including the Federation of Women's Clubs, the New England Society of New Jersey, the New-York Historical Society, the Reform Club of New York, the Architectural League of New York, the National Sculpture Society of New York, and the National Arts Club of New York. Even though Perkins would find it difficult to get the "co-operation" of the slighted Scenic Society, Lamb urged Perkins to write a "diplomatic" letter asking for the Scenic Society's assistance. In an effort to improve the "more or less antagonistic" relations, Lamb also got Perkins quickly elected as a trustee of the Scenic Society. Perkins accepted the election, but when the society asked him for a briefing on the commission's

progress, he refused; he insisted that "the Commission is unanimous in feeling that it has made better progress up to date by keeping very quiet, saying little but working a great deal." Perkins maintained the policy despite the fact the press speculated openly on whether the commission was "alive" or not.[67]

The commission's quiet plan of proceeding also rankled the Federation of Women's Clubs. Rather than setting aside their work on the Palisades after the creation of the permanent commission, the women pushed on. The three members of the 1899 New Jersey study commission who were not appointed to the permanent commission, including the two federation women, established the League for the Preservation of the Palisades. They anticipated that the league would continue to build civic sentiment for preservation and raise money for purchasing land for a Palisades park. The Palisades had provided a good mobilizing issue for the federation, and the women did not wish to stand aside. The league president quickly objected when Perkins wanted to make private fundraising an object for the commission and for a private auxiliary he had planned to form. Elizabeth B. Vermilye, who served as the league's first president, insisted that Perkins designate the league as its auxiliary. When Perkins hesitated, Vermilye declared that the commission's existence was "principally due to the persistent efforts of the women" and that their work merited "a recognized status as co-operative with your Commission." Vermilye concluded her appeal by writing, "Pardon me for my apparent intrusion, but I have given years of thought, effort and time to this matter and truly desire success for your work, and ours."[68] Perkins responded that he wished to proceed in "the most harmonious manner possible;" nevertheless, he refused the league any formal role.[69]

The contrast between the women's public appeals to sentiment and Perkins's private curatorial approach quickly emerged. In one of its first efforts the league drafted a Palisades fundraising appeal. It outlined the "romantic beauty" evident in the "great convulsions of nature." It condemned "the sordid claim of selfish interests" represented by the quarries. It declared that "love of country," "the highest type of patriotism," and "nationalism" made it "of gravest importance to preserve inviolate those conspicuous features of natural scenery . . . which engender a just pride in our native land." Perkins wrote that the draft contained "rather too flowery language and . . . does not keep close enough to the earth, deal strictly enough with the facts that confront your league or our Commission." He thought that "it would not pay" to send the letter out.[70]

The critique of the language and tone of the league's

5.13. *Carpenter Brothers' Palisades quarry and stone-crushing plant, c. 1901.* From *American Monthly Review of Reviews*, July 1901.

letter struck, in part, at the civic rhetoric aimed at galvanizing a broad public to action—a style that the curatorial appeal generally eschewed. As he did with the Scenic Society, Perkins also turned aside the efforts of the league to enlist him in rallying public sentiment. In 1901, Vermilye asked Perkins to address the annual meeting of the league. She aimed to have a "large and enthusiastic meeting" that would help in "rousing public opinion." Perkins hesitated to join the effort, responding that "all our work has been rather quietly done." Vermilye did not see the merit in such a strategy, particularly when the Palisades commission sought further action from the legislature. She wrote Perkins that "the quiet method may do in New York, it will not do I fear in New Jersey. The only thing which carried our Bill . . . was an expression of public sentiment."[71] The triumph of the "quiet method" was underscored when the league gave up its efforts to raise a fund to buy Palisades land. Vermilye wrote to Perkins that "the women of New Jersey have done far more . . . than you would know of. . . . The women have been creating public sentiment for years throughout the State and that has certainly helped in New Jersey. Now I do not want all this hard work to go entirely unrecorded." What Vermilye sought was to have a site along the Palisades designated to commemo-

rate the work of the women. In the end, money raised by the league was devoted to the construction of just such a memorial.[72]

The early successes of the commission furthered the eclipse of the women. Despite Perkins's insistence that the commission pursue a quiet approach to preservation, he set a course that would dramatically impress public opinion. He sought to quickly stop all blasting along the Palisades. He succeeded in this by reaching an agreement to close down the Carpenter Brothers' Quarry. Even with only limited resources available, the commission used the $10,000 appropriated by New York State to take an option on the Carpenter Brothers property and then to solicit private funds for the purchase itself.

More than other quarry operators, the Carpenter Brothers had received the enmity of Palisades preservationists; they were often castigated by name in newspaper accounts of the destruction of the Palisades. They operated the largest of the Palisades quarries; they employed about 150 workers and sold over 100,000 cubic yards of traprock annually. George Carpenter and Aaron Carpenter, who had earlier worked as road contractors, started their Palisades quarry operation (fig. 5.13) in 1891 on land they leased from William O. Allison for $1,500 a year. Allison had owned large tracts of land suitable for

5.14. *John Pierpont Morgan, Jr., disembarking from his yacht in Manhattan.* Photograph, c. 1914. Library of Congress.

residences and made some effort to protect the beauty of the Palisades. His lease stipulated that the Carpenters were to "work the quarry so that the Palisade wall is left perpendicular and so far as practicable, preserving a straight surface horizontally."[73] These restrictions ceased and more extensive quarrying started in 1894 when the Carpenter Brothers purchased the tract outright for $25,000. In 1898, when the Carpenter Brothers incorporated their business with $100,000 in capital, the Bradstreet credit report stated that the plant and quarry were worth well over $100,000 and that the Carpenters managed their business well for "good profit"; as business operators, they were held in "excellent personal repute."[74]

In 1900 when George Perkins entered negotiations for the Carpenter Brothers quarry, there was little, other than their business interests, that set George and Aaron Carpenter apart from the relatively wealthy preservationists who had taken up the Palisades preservation cause. George age fifty five, and Aaron, age fifty, were both born in New York of parents who had been born in New York. They lived with their families in substantial houses, staffed by immigrant servants, on King Street in Port Chester, New York.[75]

After some dealings with Perkins the Carpenters professed to be as interested in Palisades preservation as those who had excoriated them during the 1890s. George Carpenter wrote to Perkins that "the directors are entirely in sympathy" with the effort to preserve the Palisades and wished to assist the commission "in so far as they can do so without injustice to the stockholders." The Carpenters itemized their investments in land, docks, buildings, bins, engines, boilers, gravity, cable, and horse railways, stone crushers, elevators, derricks, steam drills, belting, and other tools. Taking into consideration their superior competitive advantage made possible by the 1895 riparian exclusion of other quarry operators from the Palisades, the Carpenter Brothers offered to join the ranks of preservationists for $200,000.[76] In October 1900, Perkins wrote to Carpenter: "I am red hot after your option. Am working on it every spare moment I have."[77] After some negotiations the Carpenters insisted that "they couldn't possibly take less than $200,000 for the property, but they were so anxious to see the Palisades saved that they would contribute $25,000 out of their own pockets."[78] They ended up agreeing to sell the quarry for $132,500; with a $10,000 down payment they agreed to stop quarrying by December 24, 1900, giving the commission five months to raise the balance of the purchase price. Furthermore, the Carpenters agreed to refrain forever from quarrying, blasting, or removing stone along the Hudson River, "especially" in the area of the Palisades.[79]

By the time the Carpenter Brothers agreed to give the commission a purchase option and to stop quarrying the Palisades, Perkins had already made substantial progress toward gathering the necessary funds from private sources. Here curatorial acquisition came in the form of a commitment from J. Pierpont Morgan. According to an oft-repeated account, when Perkins approached him for money to buy the Carpenter Brothers quarry, Morgan immediately agreed to give $25,000. He then added that if Perkins would become a partner in J. P. Morgan he would donate the entire $122,500 necessary for the purchase. Perkins initially refused the offer of partnership; before he joined Morgan as a partner in March 1901, Morgan had already agreed to pay the balance of the Carpenter price.

For Morgan, the great collector of art and literature, the Palisades provided a scenic landmark along the route of his frequent yacht trips between New York City and Cragston, his Hudson River estate located in Orange County near West Point (fig. 5.14). Morgan had purchased the estate in 1872 and had developed it into a model gentlemen's farm of 675 acres, with spectacular views of the river. The estate included fruit trees, vineyards, flower gardens, a dairy, and herds of blooded cattle. Morgan enjoyed carrying fresh produce and dairy products from his farm to friends in New York City. In 1900, Morgan's three-story house surrounded by porches and gardens was staffed by eleven cooks, maids, and butlers. The comforts of Cragston stood out of earshot of the quarry blasting along the Palisades; however, Morgan enjoyed the scenery and felt a certain sympathy for his neighbors to the south.[80]

The flair and power of Morgan's other acts of acquisition, which ranged from rare art and literature to railroads and banks, also marked his purchase of the Carpenter Brothers quarry. His simple purchase contrasted sharply with the years of public campaigning to end the quarrying. For some observers Morgan's purchase vindicated the agents of business and the market. A landscape threatened by base commercialism had been rescued by someone who personified modern finance and capitalism. After the agreement to sell the quarry was worked out, Perkins himself tried to cast the plan as a simple business matter. He declared, "The principal firm of quarrymen, generally regarded by New Yorkers as arch fiends, I found to be straightforward, businesslike men, ready to meet us half way, as is shown by the fact that they have sold their property to us at a reasonable figure." One of the newspapers that reported Perkins's view editorialized even further in the interest of business: "The stone contractors engaged in blasting away these beauties of nature could hardly be approached as aesthetes and the way to handle them was not to abuse them as common, commercial brutes and scenic vandals. . . . Blasting on the Palisades could have been stopped long ago—need never have been begun—had business men at the outset been charged with the task of securing the preservation of the cliffs."[81] This version of events, of course, obscured the earlier preservation efforts of Riverdale's men of business and put aside the negotiating edge that the public power of eminent domain gave to Perkins and the commission when they approached the Carpenters. Nevertheless, private money had clearly furthered Palisades preservation.

Perkins and the commission used the opening provided by the Morgan purchase to leverage substantial public funds for Palisades preservation. He approached the New York and New Jersey legislatures with the news that the blasting and quarrying had stopped and that Morgan's money would bring the Carpenter tract under the commission's jurisdiction. Then he reported a condition for Morgan's purchase. Morgan would only buy the tract if the legislatures made an appropriation sufficient to guarantee the acquisition of all the remaining tracts envisioned as part of the park. Governor Benjamin Odell urged that the legislature follow the lead of the "public spirited gentleman" who had offered to buy the quarry as a "practical and business-like solution of the question of the preservation of the Palisades."[82] The New York legislature unanimously appropriated $400,000 for the commission, while New Jersey appropriated $50,000. Nevertheless, Perkins gave the credit for the development to Morgan—"Your munificent gift . . . made all the legislation we have secured possible, and thus saved the Palisades."[83]

Morgan's purchase of the Carpenter tract established a significant role for private contributions in Palisades preservation. The activist and more public work of the Federation of Women's Clubs and the Scenic Society now stood at the margins of the preservation movement. The Scenic Society's 1905 election of Morgan as the organization's honorary president reasserted its links to Palisades preservation but did little to foster the broader civic vision that informed the society's earlier Palisades work.[84] In important ways the Morgan contribution changed the nature of the debate over the commission's work. In particular, it opened the movement to direct charges that rich people engaged in a self-interested land grab, a "flimsy scheme," stood behind Palisades preservation. The contest grew particularly sharp between 1902 and 1906 when the commission and the New York legislature debated extending the park farther north along the Hudson and especially over Hook Mountain in the village of Upper Nyack.

When the commission considered expansion to Hook Mountain, it met with none of the "business-like" agreeableness that had characterized relations with the Carpenter Brothers. Wilson P. Foss, a leading traprock quarry owner on Hook Mountain (fig. 5.15), heaped scorn and ridicule on the commission.[85] In the case of Hook Mountain, preservationists contended less with the apathy and the need for building a preservation constituency and more with an open contest over preservation values and ideals. Morgan's prominent support for Palisades preservation opened the way for opponents of Hook Mountain preservation to cast their disagreement as a conflict between the aesthetic interests of millionaires and the economic interests of quarry workers and their communities.

Contentiousness had greeted the arrival of large-scale quarrying on Hook Mountain in the 1890s. The shifting editorial position of the *Nyack Evening Journal* on the utility of quarrying highlighted the main lines of the emerging debate. When a large quarry operation prepared to open on a 37-acre tract on Hook Mountain, the *Journal* enthusiastically greeted the prospect of a large new area payroll and the "welcome hum of industry."[86] After two weeks of reflection the paper declared that the new quarry would "badly scar the fair face of nature" and cause great nuisance and annoyance with no compensation. Furthermore, the growth in working population that the paper had initially looked forward to would "certainly not enhance the value of neighboring property, for the new settlement will be a dirty and undesirable one."[87]

When the *Nyack Evening Journal* reported indignation "among the people of this entire community" over the quarry, it exaggerated the unanimity of local opinion. Around Upper Nyack and in particular in the community of Rockland Lake, large numbers of immigrant laborers and stoneworkers eagerly anticipated the quarry. They came from many countries, but Italians, Slovenians, and Hungarians stood out in the ranks of the stoneworkers. When the *Journal* reported that the quarry would force "residents" to move away and prevent others from coming, it simply did not count stoneworkers as residents. Supporters of the traprock quarries asserted that preservation of Hook Mountain would hurt precisely these inhabitants; the opponents dismissed the argument by insisting that the stoneworkers were foreigners, "unable to speak English."[88] Thus, in the preservation campaign the stoneworkers shared a curious status of being both visible, as agents of destruction, and invisible in terms of their ability to levy claims on community tolerance of their work. When it came to debating the quarry issue, no one, for example, heard from Salvatore Mazza, a thirty-one-year-old Italian stoneworker. After immigrating in 1899, Mazza rented a house on Crusher Road in Upper Nyack. He lived there with his wife Giovanna, his daughter Nino, and seventeen Italian lodgers who all worked as quarry laborers.[89] In the preservation debate the quarry owners argued with the people who looked to the Palisades and now Hook Mountain not for trap but for scenery.

Arthur C. Tucker and James P. McQuaide, the owners of the estates immediately adjacent to the new Hook Mountain quarry site, launched the first challenge to Hook Mountain quarrying in 1899. They sought to have the courts enjoin the Mack Paving Company of New York from opening a quarry and stone-crushing plant on Hook Mountain. They stated their concerns quite clearly. They both felt that dust, dirt, smoke, and the noise of quarry blasting and stone crushers would destroy their enjoyment of their estates. Tucker, who was thirty-nine years old, lived with his mother, his spouse, five children, and four Irish servants. His large, expensive house stood on about 20 acres of land, improved with greenhouses, conservatories, shade trees, shrubbery, and flowers. He had owned the house since the mid-1880s. McQuaide, age thirty-eight, an executive in the National Conduit & Cable Company, was a more recent resident. He purchased his home in 1895 and lived there with his spouse, his three children, his spouse's parents, and four servants. McQuaide's estate, Larchdell Farm, included an attractive residence, surrounded by 50 acres of beautiful grounds, and was noted for its "celebrated" Bartlett pears that grew on its nearly 600 trees. To this world of

5.15. Foss & Conklin stone-crushing plant along the Palisades at Hook Mountain in Rockland Lake, New York.
Photograph, c. 1900. Palisades Interstate Park Commission.

family life and enjoyment of nature, the quarry would mean, according to Tucker and McQuaide, "great and irreparable injury and damage." In the local court Tucker and McQuaide prevailed; the New York Supreme Court barred the opening of the quarry. However, in 1901 the Appellate Division of the Supreme Court overturned the decision. It declared that to bar the opening of the quarry would deprive the quarry owners of their right to "enjoy" the use of their land. Tucker and McQuaide's attorneys did not encourage them to litigate further.[90]

When Tucker and McQuaide's problems began, the permanent Palisades Commission did not yet exist. When their suit faltered, however, they looked with great interest to the commission's early successes. In particular, they hoped that a bill expanding the geographical jurisdiction of the commission could force the closing of the Hook Mountain quarries. In 1902, Senator Louis Goodsell introduced a bill in the New York legislature to permit the commission to obtain land for a boulevard and park strip between the Palisades and the state park reservation at Stony Point, nine miles north of Hook Mountain. The boulevard would ease the transit north along the river, create a handsome drive, and provide the basis for saving other scenic points along the Hudson River, including Hook Mountain.[91] Pointing to the court defeat of Tucker and McQuaide, "who have money in carloads," those favoring local quarry interests

declared that "the rich men's lawyers knew the law was against them; hence the boulevard scheme by which it is proposed to get rid of the 'nuisance' on the mountain. . . . it is just possible that now that the game is being scented, the 'plot' to have the state grab private lands for the benefit of 'shoetown's' millionaires, will be nipped in the bud."[92]

James McQuaide actively organized support for the bill to extend the jurisdiction of the commission. In particular, he sought to interest people living on the east side of the Hudson River in working to get the legislation passed. He found his most important ally in John D. Rockefeller, Jr., whose family estate at Pocantico Hills (fig. 5.16) stood opposite Hook Mountain. McQuaide asked Rockefeller to organize the "influential men" on the east side of the river to contact their "friends" in Albany to secure passage of the Goodsell bill. The quarry blasting had annoyed Rockefeller for years. Rockefeller pressed his case for the bill with New York's lieutenant governor, Timothy L. Woodruff. Woodruff proved quite sympathetic to Goodsell's bill. Earlier he had served as a Brooklyn parks commissioner and, as Theodore Roosevelt's lieutenant governor, actively advocated keeping forest preserves forever "wild" in the Adirondacks and the Catskills. Woodruff promoted a permanent Palisades commission and took a lead in the Association for the Protection of the Adirondacks, established in 1901.

Although Roosevelt's successor, Governor Benjamin Odell, had signed the $400,000 appropriation for the Palisades commission in 1901, he appeared more equivocal concerning the move to expand the jurisdiction. According to Woodruff, support of the Goodsell bill would need to be "re-enforced by whatever influence" Rockefeller could bring to bear.[93]

The legislature did pass the Goodsell bill, as the Assembly supported the expansion of the jurisdiction unanimously; in the Senate the bill passed on a vote of 27 for and 7 against. The bill did not include any appropriation, however, and again the figure of the millionaire loomed large—rumors circulated that Rockefeller or Morgan stood ready to purchase the additional land.[94] The Scenic Society had supported the bill, and the Upper Nyack village board passed resolutions favoring the project. Nevertheless, McQuaide directed his "sincerest thanks" to Rockefeller and wrote that he and his neighbors in Nyack felt that the passage of the legislation was "entirely due to your influence."[95]

The preservationists quickly discovered the limits of their influence. Despite the broad legislative support for the Goodsell bill, Governor Odell decided to hold a special hearing to listen to the arguments for and against his signing the bill into law. Governor Odell had built his Orange County business and political fortune in the ice business and shared much in common with the quarry owners and ice producers at Hook Mountain and Rockland Lake. After listening to the preservationists' defense of their "public-spirited" cause and arguments concerning the economic interests of quarry owners, workers, and their communities, Odell vetoed the bill. He insisted that without an appropriation to purchase the area, the Goodsell bill would cloud the titles and operations of local businesses.[96]

Both sides in the Hook Mountain debate cast the veto in terms of private interest versus public interest. The preservationists adopted the rhetoric of opposition to the market and portrayed the veto as a defeat of public interest in nature by private greed. The "mutilation of the scenery" would now continue because the governor "was not brave enough to brook the displeasure of a clique of grasping monopolists."[97] However, the emergence of Morgan and Rockefeller, of Tucker and McQuaide, in the vanguard of the preservation movement permitted the quarrymen and their allies to raise their own charges of self-interest. The *Rockland County Times* reported Odell's veto under the headline "Governor Vetoes Bill. Hook Mountain Grab Was Permanently Knocked in Head, It Was a Flimsy Scheme, Had It Passed It Would Have Ruined Many Property Owners and Made Many Idle Hands." The paper cheered the governor for

turning aside the plans of those individuals who hoped to "make the people pay for their private scenery."[98] The Hudson River estate owners asserted the interest of a broader traveling public in an attempt to dislodge charges of self-interest. Quarry owners answered back in a similar manner; they asserted the interest of their employees and of economic progress.

The confusion about public versus private interest in Palisades preservation continued. In 1906, John D. Rockefeller, Jr., "and other rich New Yorkers owning mansions along the Hudson," supported legislation to extend the jurisdiction of the Palisades commission from Piermont north to Stony Point. The *New York Times* reported, "Mr. Rockefeller, it is said, objects as much to the blasting as he does to the defacement of the scenery." Nevertheless, he and his neighbors stood ready "to pay any additional expense incurred by the commission"[99] in extending the park northward. Public power would blend with private money. This raised the question of whether the park was public or a private initiative. Was the park promoting primarily public or private ends? In connection with Rockefeller's 1930s donation of a large tract of land for the Palisades Parkway project, valued at $5 million, former New York governor Alfred E. Smith declared that the Rockefeller contribution had the "somewhat unique value of making possible the carrying out of a great public project without the expenditure of public funds."[100] In 1908, for example, addressing President Roosevelt's White House conference on conservation, George F. Kunz, the president of the Scenic Society, outlined the economic value of beauty. He rejected the notion of an irreconcilable conflict between "so-called sentimentalism" and "utilitarianism," the opposition that often framed debates about scenic preservation. Scenic preservation would pay in terms of tourism, taxes, and happier, more efficient citizens. Citing the case of the Palisades, Kunz insisted that continued quarrying would have produced relatively modest economic returns in contrast with the lowering of New York property values by an estimated $10 million had the river landscape been further despoiled. Kunz then provided a surprising narrative of Palisades preservation; the Palisades were saved "through the initial step taken by one of our foremost citizens, Mr. J. Pierpont Morgan, who has always been ready to save an object of beauty, whether the product of nature, of art, a painting, a mineral collection, or anything of public interest."[101] Here Kunz's obvious interest in giving Palisades preservation a market framework, embodied by Morgan's participation, involved slighting the sentimental and civic impetus given to the preservation movement by his own Scenic Society.

5.16. Kykuit, John D. Rockefeller estate at Pocantico Hills, New York, overlooking the Hudson River and the Palisades, completed 1913. Delano & Aldrich, architects. Photograph by Michael Brooks, c. 1992. Library of Congress.

One of Rockefeller's representatives rejected such private logic. In 1906, New York Governor Frank Higgins, who had declared his interest in preserving scenic and historic places, sought written guarantees that his signing of a new Hook Mountain park expansion bill would prompt private parties to buy the scenic lands. Rockefeller's assistant objected. "It is not a private measure, nor in private interests," he wrote. "The beauty of the Hudson River is one of the great scenic attractions of the eastern part of the United States; . . . the movement to preserve it is of the same public character as the movement to preserve the [Niagara] Falls, or the Yellowstone Park, or the Yosemite Valley." Even with the assertion of public character, the bill for expanded jurisdiction again carried no public appropriation, and many preservationists assumed that the private support of "public-spirited citizens"[102] would in fact save Hook Mountain with "the State lending its power of eminent domain."[103]

Beyond Scenery:
A Public Park and Public Constituencies

Preservationists generally did not invoke history as part of their argument for saving the Palisades. They asserted the importance of beauty, permanence, and continuity in their landscape, and of the value, economic and otherwise, of Hudson River scenery. Interest in the Palisades was as much connected to the absence of a palpable history as to its presence. In nineteenth-century America many writers did argue that natural wonders carried with them nationalistic values comparable to the historic human landscape found in the Old World. Landscape painting won equal praise and filled the niche that history painting did in Europe.[104] Thus, advocates placed scenic preservation in the context of national purpose; but Palisades scenic preservation did not initially address historical narratives. Although the Palisades movement started and made considerable progress under the sway of aesthetic ideals rooted in leisure and domestic sensibility, the commission did reinforce its work with appeals to history.

J. DuPratt White, the Palisades commission's secretary, outlined the conscious turn to history in 1903. He was inspired by magazine publisher John Brisben Walker's call in the pages of *Cosmopolitan* magazine for a fitting celebration of the tercentenary of Henry Hudson's arrival at the Hudson River. White, a highly regarded lawyer who became deeply involved in the commission's work, wrote to Perkins that the commission would do well to "anticipate the public interest in the matter and place itself in a position where its interests will, as a matter of course fall into the general plan of the construction of public improvements to commemorate the occasion." He continued that "up to the present time the Commission has, in my opinion, made a rather remarkable record. . . . It would seem to me that if this Commission can force itself to a conspicuous place in such a movement, it will fare far better by being able to take advantage of the combined force of many other interests, than it would by, unaided, attempting to promote a proposition of the magnitude in contemplation."[105]

Dedicated to history, the Hudson commemoration also embraced economic and civic boosterism when it expanded to include a celebration of Fulton's application of steam to navigation. White saw great potential in the Hudson-Fulton celebration's ability to generate additional public and private enthusiasm for the Palisades project. Perkins aimed to have the Palisades land purchase completed in time to permit the park to be dedicated as one of the Hudson-Fulton events. He increasingly presented the Palisades Park as a "permanent monument to the discovery of the river."[106] Perkins, White, and other members of the commission thus joined the cause of scenery with the power of historical memory. The turn to history testified to a certain leverage that history exerted in public life—a leverage that could significantly complement the dominant interest in Palisades scenery.

The 1909 Hudson-Fulton celebration took place between September 25 and October 9, and included marine flotillas, dedication of monuments to Henry Hudson, and numerous institutional and educational events, including the Metropolitan Museum's Hudson-Fulton loan exhibition that presented the first serious museum effort to display American colonial decorative arts. The planners adopted a certain nationalistic vision of Americanization that came to pervade their efforts.[107] After years of quiet work, joining the Palisades Park dedication to the Hudson–Fulton celebration prompted

the reemergence of the broader civic vision and rhetoric reminiscent of the early preservation work of the Federation of Women's Clubs and the Scenic Society. The September 27, 1909, dedication of the Palisades Park bore ample evidence of these changes; after traveling up the river on yachts and other boats, accompanied by United States warships, participants in the dedication arrived at the place thought to be Cornwallis's headquarters for a time during the Revolution (fig. 5.17). Here the governors of New York and New Jersey celebrated the completion of the original park plan. George Kunz envisioned the development of a sort of historical sculpture park filled with monuments and tablets memorializing Native Americans, Henry Hudson, Revolutionary War soldiers, and the leading figures who promoted "advancing civilization" through the preservation of the Palisades. The raising of the United States flag, a gun salute from the warships in the river, band music, and a ceremonial dance by a group of Iroquois Indians underscored these historical themes.[108]

The greater prominence of history in the view of the Palisades and all of the attendant didactic possibilities helped the commission conclude its initial work and carried the work well beyond the wealthy neighbors and contributors along the river. For these people, including Perkins's own family, the preservation movement had already succeeded when the quarrying ended and the threat to scenery ceased. This project did not require historicizing the place or developing a park along the Palisades. Nevertheless, in writing Theodore Roosevelt, Perkins acknowledged a broader constituency; he had come to understand, in a way he had previously not, "what a great thing it is for the entire country to preserve for all time the entire face of the Palisades." Furthermore, Perkins now looked beyond land acquisition to park development. At the dedication Perkins declared, "Now that the task of saving and acquiring the Palisades has been accomplished the commissioners intend to devote their efforts . . . to a fuller development of the park."[109]

More than the rising interest in history and the celebratory dedication of the park prompted Perkins to recognize the growing importance of public park use, considered apart from park acquisition. Interestingly, a private donation, comparable to Morgan's, dramatically signaled the changing nature of the Palisades project. Just a week before the dedication Hamilton McKown Twombly and his spouse Florence Vanderbilt donated 60 acres of land and over 3,000 feet of riparian rights to the commission. Valued at $125,000, the tract stood out among the 175 parcels that constituted the original park area. The gift of the land equaled Morgan's earlier

5.17. Palisades and the Cornwallis Headquarters, built c. 1761, purchased by the Palisades Interstate Park Commission in 1907. Photograph by R. Merritt Lacey, 1936. Library of Congress.

gift and framed the beginning and end of Palisades Park development with private philanthropy. Twombly, who managed the New York Central Railroad for his Vanderbilt in-laws, owned a 1,000-acre estate and model farm in Madison, New Jersey. Here he experimented with scientific agriculture, raised Guernsey cattle, and kept extensive gardens and greenhouses, where he cultivated his prize-winning orchids and chrysanthemums. Believing in the civilizing possibilities of outdoor recreation and leisure, the Twomblys had, since the 1890s, sponsored summer excursions to their Palisades tract for people too poor to afford a country outing. At the time the Twomblys donated their property to the commission, they had sponsored an estimated 365,000 people on the boat trips and day visits to the Palisades. The Twomblys' philanthropic project anticipated the development of the Palisades as a public park; in fact, they insisted that their dock and land remain available for similar uses by institutions and individuals as part of park operations.[110]

The effort to complement the aesthetic use of the Palisades with new historical and recreational uses assumed the involvement of a broad public audience. The quiet methods and private support that Perkins pursued had clearly eclipsed the broader public participation that characterized earlier Palisades preservation. The park dedication seemed to promise a transition in the park and preservation constituency, at least as far as the commission was concerned. However, the privatism that characterized the acquisition did not abate. In fact, it grew in prominence. Since the legislature authorized the expansion of the park to Hook Mountain and Stony Point, no public or private money had been appropriated or donated to accomplish this goal. However, within months of the park dedication this inaction abruptly ended. Private philanthropy again dominated in the Palisades developments.

The death of railroad financier Edward Henry Harriman, in September 1909, helped spur a major new expansion of Palisades Park. Harriman, who had controlled the massive railroad network of the Union Pacific and Southern Pacific and helped direct the Illinois Central and other railroads, owned about 40,000 acres of land around his country home, Arden, in the Hudson River Highlands. Harriman had started to assemble this tract in the mid-1880s and did so with an eye toward building an estate and protecting the local scenery from local lumbermen. Harriman also supported other conservation and scientific projects. In 1899, for example, when his doctor urged the necessity of a long vacation, he sponsored an Alaskan expedition to Kodiak Island; representatives of major scientific institutions along with John Muir and other naturalists joined the Harrimans on

the trip. After his death Harriman's spouse, Mary Williamson, decided to donate 10,000 acres and $1 million to support the expansion of the Palisades Park.[111]

The Harrimans knew George Perkins quite well. In 1901, Perkins helped establish the Northern Securities Company, a consolidation of the Harriman and James Hill railroad interests; although the U.S. Supreme Court ruled against the railroad trust in 1904, the divestiture netted Harriman a profit estimated at $80 million. With Perkins acting as an intermediary, Mary Harriman, like Morgan before her, set conditions on the gift that were intended to leverage other financial support for the park. She insisted that her donation be matched by $1.5 million in private funds and $2.5 million in state funds. There were other conditions as well. Harriman insisted that the state stop the construction of a prison in the Highlands near the Arden estate, a development greeted with the same distaste as trap quarries. Perkins quickly laid out a plan to use the new park funds to complete the northward expansion to Stony Point and create a park and boulevard strip west from the river to the new Highlands property.

It took Perkins and the commission less than six weeks to raise the $1.5 million from private parties. Morgan reentered the picture; this time donating $500,000. John D. Rockefeller, who had followed Palisades matters closely, matched Morgan's gift. Then Rockefeller and Perkins solicited $25,000 and $50,000 contributions from friends, neighbors, and associates, many of whom maintained their own Hudson River estates. Helen M. Gould, for example, owned the Lyndhurst estate on the river in Tarrytown and answered Rockefeller's appeal with $25,000. Moving beyond appeals to neighbors, Rockefeller wrote to Andrew Carnegie that the preservation campaign was "not local, nor can it be considered as of interest solely to the State,—it is really national in its importance for the Hudson River is the gateway to this country." Carnegie found in his $5.5 million gift to New York City libraries reason not to give; however, Rockefeller and Perkins did not have much trouble raising the private fund.[112]

In May 1910 the New York legislature played its part when it overwhelmingly approved relocation of the state prison and voted for a referendum on $2.5 million in park bonds. The voters then approved the bonds in the November 1910 election. This hybrid funding of Palisades improvements continued in 1916 when another $5-million fund was established, half from public bonds and half from private sources, again with Rockefeller and Morgan in the lead.

As the park developed, the pattern of privatism tended to obscure the commitment of public money and power to Palisades preservation. Some newspapers not only gave exclusive credit to private individuals for the park but saw the park as vindication of private accumulation. In 1910, pointing to the "princely" Harriman gift, one paper declared: "Here is wealth lavishly pouring its treasures into the lap of the people. Instead of hoarding, of extravagant spending . . . these generous and public-spirited citizens offer earth, air and water, the primal elements from which we came and to which we return, and on which all life is sustained. The red flag and all that masquerades under it, the notions of the equal distribution of property or that all property is robbery, have never received more emphatic contradiction."[113] Here private individuals were credited with the park's creation; accordingly, the notion that a broad public could define and assert preservation ideals in the landscape tended to disappear from public discourse.

When Perkins and Rockefeller raised money for Palisades preservation, they forged a community of private wealth as the base for Palisades preservation. In the view of Perkins and his contemporaries, private funds advanced the cause of preservation. Although the development of the park could have encouraged an expansive public preservation sentiment, Perkins and the Palisades Commission did little to promote preservation beyond the park. The pithy annual reports of the commission stood in striking contrast to the lengthy letters detailing park developments that Perkins sent to private contributors.

Perkins kept private contributors informed about park affairs in part because he hoped they would "contribute in the future even larger sums of money than they have in the past, . . . to carry the work still further."[114] He also needed to keep in touch with contributors because some of them began to demand to know what the commission had done for them lately. In 1911, for example, an assistant to John D. Rockefeller, Jr., reported to Perkins that "the family at Pocantico Hills have noticed considerable blasting on the opposite side of the river, and I am instructed to ask if anything has been accomplished toward securing the Hook Mountain property for the Palisades Park Commission."[115] Perkins responded that the commission was "having an endless amount of serious difficulty" in getting hold of the Hook Mountain quarries. In 1912, Rockefeller again inquired about the quarry question; this time he wrote that "I ask this information not only for myself, but for other subscribers, who are neighbors of ours along the Hudson and who are feeling that the object which they very naturally had primarily in mind in making their subscriptions is not being accomplished." Perkins apologized for the delay and assured the contributors that condemnation proceedings were moving ahead and that their money was not being used for other park purposes.[116]

The spirit of "business-like" cooperation that the commission encountered along the Palisades was entirely lacking at Hook Mountain. The higher profile of the private donors in the preservation effort sparked resentment among the quarrymen. In 1912, J. DuPratt White reported one of his efforts to negotiate a land purchase with one of the quarrymen, Albert Hagar. White told Hagar that, since he had rejected the commissioners' $250,000 offer for his property, they were considering bringing condemnation proceedings. But since the action would cost time and money, the commissioners were willing to raise the offer to $300,000. White presented the offer in the "most pleasant manner" possible. The result, White wrote to Perkins, was an "outburst of a torrent of abuse and insult to the Commission such as took my breath away. The burden of it was that that was a cowardly position for the Commission to take; that they were all cowards; that that was a regular Wall Street trick; that it was just the way the Standard Oil ground the little fellow; that he recognized the Standard Oil trick in the suggestion; that it emanated entirely from Perkins; that that was just the way Perkins would do such a thing, etc. etc., until I thought he would never stop." White reported that for himself he was pleased that he kept his own temper. But this fact failed to bring a quick end to ongoing quarrying and blasting.[117]

Wilson P. Foss led the quarrymen opponents of Hook Mountain preservation. He declared that Hook Mountain could never be used as a park because it was so steep one could hardly climb it. He rejected the aesthetic complaints that quarries rendered landscapes hideous: "'Why,' said he, 'that beautiful bronze color now given to the mountain adds to the variety and beauty of that scenery, and I can see no objection to it whatsoever.'" The idea that one needed a road to connect the Palisades to the "park" at Stony Point was laughable: "'Why you can't even get a sandwich there or even a drink. . . . Not even a sarsaparilla.'"[118]

Foss did not share the prevailing disdain for quarry blasting. He had moved to New York from Maine in 1882 as the sales representative of an explosives manufacturer anxious to make sales in connection with the Haverstraw, New York, railroad tunnel. Foss then founded the Clinton Dynamite Company and started manufacturing explosives himself. Working off of this base in explosive manufacturing, Foss formed a partnership to quarry traprock on Hook Mountain. Between 1896 and 1903 he served as the mayor of the working-class quarrying, shipping, and brick-making center of Haverstraw. He

5.18. Automobiles negotiating the Englewood Approach
section of the Henry Hudson Drive in the Palisades
Interstate Park, Englewood Cliffs, New Jersey, built 1916.
Photograph, c. 1920. Library of Congress.

much preferred billiards to Hudson River scenery; for three years he held the United States amateur billiard championship and even competed internationally. When the legislation to expand the jurisdiction of Hook Mountain was enacted, Foss continued to run his quarry and to resist all purchase offers with deft legal maneuvers.[119] Hudson River estate owners probably took no comfort from the fact that as he continued to quarry Hook Mountain, Foss moved from Haverstraw to a sprawling river estate in Upper Nyack, just 2,500 feet down the river from the Tucker and McQuaide estates. Finally, in 1917, the commission took Foss's quarry for a court condemnation price of $2 million.[120]

Wilson Foss and the other Hook Mountain quarry owners and workers were only the most vocal and litigious opponents of the Palisades Park. As the commission started condemning property between the river and the Harrimans' Highlands tract, it displaced many longtime residents. Such displacements had already taken place along the Palisades. The narrow strip between the river and the cliff had accommodated people who lived at both the geographical and the economic margin. Along the Palisades there were residen-

tial clusters of Italian quarry workers, African-American domestic workers, and long-established settlements of families who fished the river. Some people paid modest rents for their space; others had simply squatted on the land. All were moved off by the commission's park development. In 1914, Reverend Mytton Maury, the rector of St. John's Church in Hastings-on-Hudson, took up the cause of the several hundred people who lived on, and in many cases farmed, the future parkland between the river and the Highlands. He objected to the condemnation that drove them from their homes and deprived them of the "means of living," particularly the elderly residents. Maury rejected the commission's argument that the park was for the benefit of the people. He insisted that "the people of the entire State are hoodwinked by the palpable untruth that this park is for the benefit of the poor." Perkins rejected numerous pleas from people who wished to remain in their homes until they died; if full value was paid for their land, then the commission had done "absolutely the fair thing by them." A few exceptions to this policy displacement were made to keep from offending people of "standing" in the community.[121]

Maury and others who would resist the Palisades Park plans clearly had to fight the rising tide of popularity of the park with its public, hoodwinked or not. By the 1910s hundreds of thousands of people visited the park every year—arriving by foot, boat, and car (fig. 5.18), spending the day or camping out for longer periods. The sense of the park as a scheme by rich people to protect their interests waned in discussions of the park except among property owners and workers threatened with displacement. The popularity of the park itself overshadowed its shifting place as an object of desire among conflicting factions along the river.

For people taking a day in the country the intrigues of who paid for the land and who benefited from it beyond themselves probably did not matter very much. For preservationists and their potential allies these questions were vitally important. The Palisades campaign had succeeded far beyond the most sanguine early expectations; preserved land now stretched along the Hudson to Hook Mountain and Stony Point and on into the Highlands. Moreover, following his work in the Palisades, John D. Rockefeller, Jr., dramatically expanded his private work in conservation and historic preservation; he spent approximately $100 million on scenic conservation and historic restoration projects,

including Acadia National Park in Maine, Fort Tryon Park in New York City, Jackson Hole Preserve, and the Grand Teton National Park in Wyoming, Yosemite National Park in California, Virgin Islands National Park, and saving redwood trees in California. Starting in 1926, historic restoration of Colonial Williamsburg in Virginia loomed especially large among Rockefeller's philanthropic initiatives.[122] At the same time, to the extent that Rockefeller came to personify the preservation of the Palisades, others did not. The fact that the Women's Federation and the Scenic Society and the governors and the legislatures blended into the background didn't leave much room for the cultivation of an ongoing, pervasive, and publicly committed preservation movement.

The private curatorial route had its advantages. It gained impetus through simple purchase. There is little evidence that the legislatures of New York and New Jersey would have been willing to take the initiative, cooperate, and commit public money to save the Palisades on their own. Private contributions to Palisades preservation consistently paved the way for the commitment of public money. However, quiet acquisition itself did little to foster the preservation of scenic and historic places beyond the landscape at hand or beyond the hand of the wealthy. Palisades preservation, like other preservation, embodied the authority of a particular narrative or a particular way of seeing. The extraordinary subsequent popularity of Palisades Park underscores the fact that places, once preserved, can and often do acquire new meanings beyond the views and intentions of the original preservationists. This, indeed, represents the benign outcome of Palisades preservation. Yet, subsequent broadening of the public benefits of the Palisades should not obscure the very real limitations of private curatorial preservation. If groups like the Federation of Women's Clubs and the Scenic Society, with their public institutional base, had managed to assert and win their noisy claims, they could have supported a much more vibrant and dynamic public preservation movement—one with a broader palette and a wider range. As marginal participants, the federation, the Scenic Society, and the public itself stood as spectators of a system that attended narrowly and somewhat idiosyncratically to scenic and historic preservation. The Palisades had indeed been impressively preserved (fig. 5.19); however, the preservation movement's reliance on a relatively narrow group of wealthy individuals meant that countless historic places and scenic sites would subsequently disappear without advocates, agitation, or an effective appeal to public memory or public values.

5.19. New Jersey section of the Palisades photographed from the Mountain House, the Englewood Cliffs hotel perched on the cliff, 375 feet above the Hudson River. Photograph, c. 1880. New York Public Library.

CHAPTER SIX

The Arch and the Neighborhood

Marking Westward Expansion in St. Louis

The power of narrative is central to historic preservation. First, narrative does much of preservation's cultural work. Historic preservation gathers its influence from the palpable physical character of its preserved places. History can usually be conveyed with greater ease and less expense by simply telling it or writing it down. But people work to save buildings and landscapes because narratives embedded in places appeal to more of our human senses than oral or written histories do. History preserved in place often attracts broader public engagement. Even though historic places are, by themselves, fairly inexpressive and rarely tell their own stories, the narratives associated with them make them worthy of preservation. Second, in terms of the process of historic preservation, narratives of place are what prompt individuals, communities, and institutions to direct resources, both private and public, into preservation. True, there are solid preservation rationales that stand somewhat outside of the bounds of historic narrative. Places are preserved through simple continuing use. Environmental arguments can favor continued use, or adaptive reuse, of older places quite apart from any associated history. Some places are preserved for their impressive beauty or comforting familiarity. But despite such examples, in historic preservation narrative generally dominates. To understand preservation successes and preservation failures it is important to explore why in certain cases the narratives associated with place inspired preservation and why, in other cases, they failed to do so. It is also useful to understand that there are forms with a palpable physical character that can convey historical narrative, with little or no connection to preservation. The most obvious examples of this are monuments and memorials. With his tour of America in 1824–1825, Lafayette laid the cornerstone of the Bunker Hill Monument built to complement the power of the historic battlefield. Even when not juxtaposed directly with historic places, monuments can impressively promote engagement with history through the medium of space, built form, and artistic expression. In fact, monuments often get more precisely at history's meaning and interpretation than preserved buildings and landscapes. Understanding the relative narrative powers of historic buildings and landscapes and of monuments and memorials helps clarify historic preservation's civic possibilities.

This chapter explores narrative, historic preservation, and monument building in relation to the Jefferson National Expansion Memorial in St. Louis (fig. 6.1). In the 1930s, President Franklin D. Roosevelt, members of Congress, and St. Louis political, business, and civic leaders advocated the clearance of thirty-seven blocks on the Mississippi riverfront for the memorial. The decaying riverfront district offered important commemorative possibilities. A French fur-trading post, the European foundation of modern St. Louis, had been established in this area in 1764. A flag ceremony on the site had finalized the official transfer of territory from France to the United States under the terms of the Louisiana Purchase in 1804. Building on these events, the proposed memorial would celebrate Thomas Jefferson, the Louisiana Purchase, and the national drama of westward expansion. Later preservationists would consider the sweeping demolition of the site's buildings, carried out in the name of historic commemoration, as an enigmatic or even cynical first use of the 1935 Historic Sites Act.[1] They

*6.1. St. Louis Gateway Arch, Jefferson National Expansion
Memorial, built 1961–1966. Eero Saarinen, architect.*
Photograph by Jack Boucher, 1986. Library of Congress.

6.2. *Aerial view of the section of the riverfront designated as the site for the Jefferson National Expansion Memorial, looking south.* Photograph, 1933. Jefferson National Expansion Memorial

wondered how so much destruction could be carried out under the provisions of a law that declared it a "national policy to preserve for public use historic sites, buildings, and objects of national significance for the inspiration and benefit of the people of the United States."[2] Thus, in St. Louis, preservation advocates and monument builders pursued two very different approaches toward engaging history on the same site. Yet, criticism of the planned monument often failed to recognize the common ground between historic preservation and monument building. In St. Louis, Eero Saarinen's sweeping 630-foot-high stainless-steel arch has powerfully shaped national memory and identity. The arch raises the possibility that in some cases new monuments can more effectively convey history than old buildings can. The failure of preservation on St. Louis's riverfront involved a failure of historic narrative and imagination. Preservation advocates in the 1930s thought too narrowly about the significance of riverfront buildings. Their constricted approach to architectural history proved infertile ground

for appealing to the stewards of the site and the monument builders. The debates involving public officials and private citizens in St. Louis took place during a formative period for the national preservation movement; for that reason the disparate visions for the Jefferson National Expansion Memorial site merit close examination.

History, Aesthetics, and Obsolescence on the Mississippi Riverfront

Charles B. Hosmer, Jr., a historian of the preservation movement, has argued that the Jefferson National Expansion Memorial "was an urban renewal project with a veneer of history used to coat an expenditure for unemployment relief."[3] Some people associated with the project in the 1930s expressed similar ideas. In 1937 individual members of the National Park Service's own Advisory Board complained that the memorial "appeared to be, in the first instance, a slum clearance project" (figs.

6.3. *Aerial view of the riverfront area after clearance, looking north. Photograph, c. 1945.*
Jefferson National Expansion Memorial.

6.2, 6.3), which involved a questionable use of the Historic Sites Act.[4] Such conclusions represent an oversimplification of the interests brought to bear on the memorial project; however, this critique found plausibility in the fact that civic and business leaders had supported the renewal of the riverfront area for decades quite apart from any strong commitment to historical narrative. In the second half of the nineteenth century St. Louis's population growth, the opening of the Eads Bridge, development of rail and transit lines, and specialization of the commercial landscape all helped push the business section of the city westward, away from the riverfront. As a result, the area along the Mississippi River, largely dating to the rebuilding following the great St. Louis Fire of 1849, took on a more marginal economic role as a center of light industry, warehousing, and working-class housing.

In the first decades of the twentieth century, St. Louis leaders had indeed developed several plans to renew the riverfront district in the hope of improving the for-

tunes of the downtown business district. However, these efforts were not incompatible with a major 1930s project aimed at historic commemoration. The aspects of American history settled upon for commemoration on the St. Louis riverfront undoubtedly resonated deeply with Americans confronting the trauma of the national economic depression in the 1930s. A memorial to Jefferson's initiative in the Louisiana Purchase amounted to a celebration of presidential leadership at a time when many Americans were looking hopefully for bold presidential action to move the country out of depression. At the same time, the celebration of westward migration and the hearty pioneers who were assumed to have triumphed amid adversity in staking out the continent offered a useful narrative. The pioneers provided a model of people who seemingly confronted the physical and social dislocations that came of new and unfamiliar circumstances. The fact that the St. Louis project linked executive action, millions of hours of public work for the unemployed, and massive urban redevelopment did not negate or compromise the efforts to explore history on the site.[5] Unlike the preservationists, the monument builders deployed historical imagination in ways that reached to the core of the relationship between past and present.

The debates over the clearance of the site in St. Louis underscored important changes in twentieth-century preservation. The preservationists in that debate generally did not look to buildings and landscapes as keys to a narrative of local or national history. Rather, they showed greatest interest in the formal aesthetic and structural character of the buildings, preserved and interpreted primarily as part of a more academic conception of the forms and styles of architectural history. Here preservation took leave of its roots in historical association. In favoring preservation based on the aesthetic and technological aspects of architecture, St. Louis preservationists drastically narrowed the historical ground that they could potentially share with the monument builders. Preservationists valued buildings highly as potential elements in a three-dimensional encyclopedia of building forms. Within this framework, a building's historic importance derived from its ability to exemplify a style or type, the work of a particular builder or architect, or some other related aspect of architectural production. These preservation priorities, which grew increasingly central to twentieth-century preservation work, had little in common with the national commemorative vision of the leading proponents of the Jefferson National Expansion Memorial.

The growing interest in aesthetic preservation had several important sources. The professionalization of architecture itself, with its university-based system of training, its local standards and certifications, and its national professional associations, prompted greater interest in the history of American architecture. Furthermore, architectural history, developed as a branch of the teaching of fine arts, emerged as a vital part of the growing codification of academic history and instruction.[6] The late-nineteenth- and early-twentieth-century interest in Colonial Revival architecture and American decorative arts and antiques, displayed in period room and museum settings, also encouraged scholars, collectors, and a curious public to scrutinize more closely the formal aesthetic history of early American architecture.

This interest in historic things, aesthetically considered, increasingly overshadowed preservation associated with other narratives of local and national history. The National Park Service's inauguration of the Historic American Buildings Survey in 1933, a program designed to aid unemployed architects, codified the growing aesthetic priorities of historic preservation in the United States. Surveyors chronicled the formal character of buildings while slighting historical questions of how buildings and places related to the society and culture of people who built and used them. Charles E. Peterson, a National Park Service architect who helped establish the Historic American Buildings Survey and later became a leading advocate of preserving buildings on the St. Louis riverfront, developed thorough guidelines for documenting historic buildings with photographs and measured drawings; by contrast, he believed that historical data could be limited to "only the briefest resume of facts" gathered from local and state institutions, without employing project historians.[7]

The interest in aesthetic preservation in St. Louis did not guarantee success. In fact, in this instance preservation proposals based on the architecture's formal character failed to modify a memorial project inspired by the historic associations of a site, apart from its buildings. Thus, in St. Louis, historical associations of a site actually dominated the newer interest in aesthetics. Despite its popularity in preservation circles, the aesthetic model did not put preservation on the strongest footing. The St. Louis case suggests some of the very real limitations of staking preservation claims mainly on prevailing standards architectural taste and beauty.

Plans for historic commemoration on a redeveloped riverfront had circulated for years before the entry of the federal government. A plan was floated in 1887 for a riverfront statue of Jefferson. In 1898 members of the centennial planning committee for the Louisiana Purchase Exposition discussed the construction of a pioneer village on the riverfront.[8] A 1907 plan offered by the Civic League of St. Louis envisioned City Beautiful grandeur taking the place of riverfront squalor. The Civic League, a group of college-educated business and professional people who promoted numerous progressive reforms, considered the riverfront the "natural gateway to the city" and deplored its "unsightly appearance" and "shabby and dilapidated buildings." What seemed true of the buildings also seemed true of the area's people; parts of the riverfront had "become to such an extent the rendezvous of the vicious and depraved that respectable citizens hesitate to pass through these quarters on their way to the boats on the river." League planners hoped that a massive riverfront promenade with trees, fountains, commemorative statues and "stately" office buildings would replace the district's existing structures. The plans reflected contemporary City Beautiful ideas with their monumental civic spaces. The riverfront promenade would be elevated above the level of the river and mask both rail and transit lines and the small freight storage areas located below and in the basements of

6.4. *Riverfront plan proposing a massive clearance project and construction of an elevated plaza raised over a parking garage. Harland Bartholomew, planner, 1928.* From *A Plan for the Central River Front, St. Louis, Missouri* (St. Louis: City Plan Commission, 1928)

more elegant office structures that would line the promenade level. Overall, the plan sought to combine a new "attractiveness and dignity" on the riverfront with the area's continuing "usefulness to traffic and commerce."[9] Like the plan's parks and parkways, the promenade masked or rendered tidier the images of work in the city. Envisioned as the "gateway" to the whole city, it also provided a gateway to the largely middle-class, white-collar landscape of the downtown area.[10]

Other plans similar to the Civic League proposal appeared under the auspices of the City Plan Commission in 1913 and the Chamber of Commerce in 1922. In 1928, Harland Bartholomew, a leading American city planner, studied the riverfront and echoed earlier calls for sweeping renewal (fig. 6.4). He hoped that such action would stop what business leaders perceived as the movement of riverfront blight westward into the main business district. Like Civic League planners twenty years earlier, Bartholomew proposed an elevated riverfront plaza. The lower level would now accommodate transit lines as well as express roadways and a massive parking garage. The 350-foot by 1,400-foot plaza would reverse the historic neglect of the riverfront area and give the city a "truly creditable front yard" where residents and visitors

could look out at the Mississippi River "amid pleasing surroundings." Bartholomew attended more closely to history than the previous planners. He sought to have the plaza focus on the Old St. Louis County Courthouse, a mid-nineteenth-century domed civic building considered "one of the finest pieces of architecture west of the Mississippi River." On the plaza's river edge, on axis with the courthouse, Bartholomew proposed "a memorial of surpassing beauty" dedicated to the founders of the city, who were thought to have landed in the vicinity. In embellishing the connection between the downtown and the riverfront and in infusing the area with new vitality, Bartholomew thought he had settled upon a practical way to establish a historic "bond with the days when St. Louis found the Mississippi River its source of life and prosperity." As with subsequent plans for the Jefferson memorial, Bartholomew's interest in riverfront history or historical celebration did not extend to many buildings beyond the courthouse and the early-nineteenth-century St. Louis Cathedral that he proposed relocating outside of the clearance area.[11] Bartholomew's plan combined contemporary concerns regarding traffic and economic vitality with the earlier interest in fostering images of the City Beautiful.

In 1907, Luther Ely Smith, a thirty-four-year-old St. Louis lawyer active in many civic improvement and social welfare projects, helped develop the Civic League's city plan. In subsequent years Smith, more than any other single individual, led the movement to build the Jefferson Memorial on the St. Louis riverfront. What is perhaps most striking about Smith's decades of civic engagements was the seamlessness of the links he forged between urban reform, urban development, and historical commemoration. His biography challenges the characterization of the Jefferson National Expansion Memorial as urban renewal disguised by a "thin veneer of history." Smith had initially established himself in planning and welfare circles through helping to found St. Louis's playground movement, a project he pursued under the auspices of the Civic League. The playground movement aimed to provide children in the congested neighborhoods of St. Louis with places of recreation and open air. The league hoped that after demonstrating the value and popularity of its model playgrounds the city would then take on playgrounds as a regular part of municipal responsibility. The league sought to use organized play to teach poor and immigrant children "the fundamental virtue of honesty, fair play, and a thorough respect for themselves and for others," thus undercutting "crime and lawlessness."[12] Smith also helped frame St. Louis's early zoning and city improvement statutes and as a member of the league crusaded against the "grotesque forms of civic ugliness" presented by billboard advertising.[13]

For Smith and other Civic League members, City Beautiful and Progressive Era campaigns were shaped by a reform agenda rooted firmly in the present while looking solicitously to the future. Nevertheless, Smith and the Civic League felt that understanding history was an essential ingredient in reform and in good citizenship. In 1906 the Civic League's Historic Sites Committee proposed a program to mark several historic sites in St. Louis. The committee's first plaque, commemorating the memory of explorer William Clark, was unveiled in September 1906 on the one hundredth anniversary of the Lewis and Clark expedition's return to St. Louis. The plaque was placed on a bank building that occupied the ground where William Clark had lived for many years. The committee also planned to mark sites associated with the early European settlement of St. Louis, the Louisiana Purchase, and the Civil War.[14]

In the context of the Civic League's overall program, the marking of historic sites offered the possibility that history could affect civic coalescence and usefully promote the league's civic improvement plans. This link envisioned between historic celebration and civic improvement received its most dramatic expression in the Pageant and Masque of St. Louis, presented in 1914. As executive secretary of the St. Louis Pageant Drama Association, Luther Ely Smith directed one of the most ambitious historical pageants of the early twentieth century. The pageant, which took place on five nights in May and June 1914, involved 7,000 actors and an audience of over 400,000 people in a dramatic chronicle of St. Louis history. Many of the people who joined Smith in organizing the pageant had worked with him in earlier campaigns for municipal reform. In fact, Civic League progressives hoped that civic patriotism stirred by the pageant might encourage St. Louis residents to support improvement bonds at the polls and progressive reforms in their neighborhoods. In aiming to create civic coalescence, pageant planners left out of the pageant a chronicle of the more contentious aspects of local history, such as labor and class strife. Nevertheless, Smith, a dedicated member of the Missouri Historical Society, took his engagement with local history very seriously.[15]

Luther Ely Smith felt that with the pageant St. Louis became "history-conscious." Civic leaders like Smith came to feel that the city had "a wealth of historic material, a wealth of consecrated memories on the shores of the Mississippi River." Smith and his colleagues found support for their growing interest in local history among United States historians who followed Frederick Jackson Turner's interest in frontier history. As Smith declared in 1934: "There has grown up a new school of history in this country, which has turned its eyes away from the exclusive attention that was formerly given to the Atlantic Seaboard and has realized that the character of America was made not on the costal plain of this great country, but was forged in the frontier as the pioneers went out to grapple with the conditions which confronted them; . . . Let us vindicate ourselves, let us pay back the debt we owe to the American pioneers who gave us the American nation and gave us the American character."[16] Like the temporary form of the pageant, the permanent form of the Jefferson memorial could celebrate St. Louis's part in this major reorientation of the project of American history and nationalism.

Beyond his engagement with St. Louis history and various city improvements, Luther Ely Smith brought to the Jefferson National Expansion Memorial project experience with the construction of an earlier national historic monument. In 1928, President Calvin Coolidge appointed Smith, a friend from his student years at Amherst College, to serve on the George Rogers Clark Federal Sesquicentennial Commission, a commission appointed by Congress to build a monument in Vincennes, Indiana, commemorating the 1779 capture of

*6.5. George Rogers Clark Memorial, built 1931–
1936, Vincennes, Indiana. Frederic C. Hirons,
architect.* Postcard in author's collection.

Fort Sackville by General George Rogers Clark and his troops. Important parallels existed between the monument at Vincennes and the one Smith later envisioned for St. Louis. In both places the memorial site had few buildings or landscape features connecting the present with the history commemorated by the monument. No traces of Fort Sackville survived. As in the case of St. Louis, local residents supporting the project saw the monument as an integral part of a broader municipal improvement project. The Clark memorial would ornament the approach to a new interstate Wabash River bridge connecting Illinois and Indiana and provide a gateway to a new riverside boulevard system. The clearance of the memorial site involved the purchase and demolition of a warehouse, an 80,000-bushel grain elevator, a feed mill, an auto repair shop, and several working-class boardinghouses.[17] As in St. Louis, the monument planners initially hoped to reconstruct the historic buildings that had stood on the site; however, after New York architect Frederic C. Hirons won the 1930 architectural competition for the monument, a round classical temple rather than a re-created Fort Sackville rose on the banks of the Wabash.[18] It is notable that in September 1933 Smith's commission colleague Frank Culbertson presided over the bridge dedication, while Smith presided over the ceremonial sealing of the historical documents in the cornerstone of the memorial.[19]

Memorializing Thomas Jefferson and the Louisiana Purchase

When Smith watched President Roosevelt dedicate the Clark Memorial at Vincennes (fig. 6.5) in June 1936, he had already won Roosevelt's support for an even more ambitious historical memorial along the Mississippi at St. Louis. In December 1933, working with the newly elected mayor of St. Louis, Bernard Dickmann, Smith assumed the leadership of a civic committee formed to seek support for a federal memorial to Thomas Jefferson, the Louisiana Purchase, and the exploration and settlement of the west by Euro-Americans. The committee was incorporated as the Jefferson National Expansion Memorial Association in April 1934, with Smith as president. By June 1934 the association had prevailed upon Congress to create the United States Territorial Expansion Memorial Commission. The commission had fifteen members—the president of the Senate, the speaker of the House, and the president of the United States each appointed three members, and the Jefferson National Expansion Memorial Association appointed six members, including Luther Ely Smith. Congress directed the commission to consider and make plans for a permanent memorial on the banks of the Mississippi River near the site of Old St. Louis to honor the memory of "the men who made possible the territorial expansion of the United States, particularly President Thomas Jefferson and his aides, Livingston and Monroe, who negotiated the Louisiana Purchase, and to the great explorers, Lewis and Clark, and the hardy hunters, trappers, frontiersmen, pioneers, and others who contributed to the territorial expansion and development of the United States of America."[20]

In the resolution of Congress, in the discussions of the United States Commission, and eventually in the presidential executive order approving construction of the memorial, the rationale for the memorial stayed fixed on historical commemoration. The participants in the memorial project tended to leave aside local issues related to urban renewal. Political expediency might have suggested such a course. The memorial project required a national constituency, and thus boosters emphasized national history and commemoration. President Roosevelt, Secretary of the Interior Harold Ickes, Public Works Administrator Harry Hopkins, and residents and voters in St. Louis showed great interest in the effect the project might have on local unemployment, but more often than not they cast their support for the Jefferson Memorial in historical terms. Indeed, the memorial stood among a series of projects that saw the government taking increasing responsibility for celebrating, marking, and preserving American history. The National Park Service in the 1930s became the vital center of these activities as it increasingly complemented its work in conservation and scenic preservation with initiatives in historical commemoration and public education.[21]

The strength of the rhetoric affirming historical commitments in discussions of the Jefferson monument contradicts the characterization of the project as a thin veneer of history applied to an urban renewal project. In 1933 the membership of the American Historical Association had endorsed the memorial. Members of the Territorial Expansion Memorial Commission, at their first meeting in December 1934, articulated deep patriotic and nationalist interests in the project. President Roosevelt telegraphed the commission that he wished them the best in their efforts "to recall and perpetuate the ideals, faith and courage of the pioneers who developed the great West." Like Roosevelt, Senator Alben W. Barkley of Kentucky, who was elected chair of the commission, failed to mention urban renewal in his expansive statements on the importance of the commission's work. He declared, "I have, all my life, been a great admirer of Jefferson, and I think it is almost a national disgrace that no outstanding monument has been erected to his memory or to his achievements. . . . I share the sentiment that this great monument . . . shall be a monument to the

countless unnamed men and women who gave voice and power and determination to the vision of men like Jefferson and of George Rogers Clark, John C. Frémont, and of Joliet and Marquette. . . . There will be a monument to the Unknown Pioneer no less than to the Unknown Soldier." Barkley then affirmed crucial connections between the history commemorated and the contemporary depression experience: "It is our duty to catch the torch that is handed down to us from our forefathers, and to throw it into the hands of those who come after us because in the complexity of our lives, in the multiplicity of our problems, the pioneering is not over with. . . . they must still march out on untried fields and take chances for the benefit of mankind." Similarly, Charles Merriam of the University of Chicago, vice chair of the commission, declared that he viewed the memorial "as a rededication to the spirit of democracy, which is not dead. I should regard it as a rededication to democratic statesmanship, which is not dead. I should regard it as a rededication to the tactics and policies of American democratic statesmanship, which in my judgment, are not dead. . . . Make it a fitting memorial to one of the greatest deeds of one of the greatest democrats, greatest philosophers, greatest statesmen, greatest tacticians of all times."[22] One person after another, who like Merriam and Barkley stood outside the orbit of St. Louis booster and civic interests, made it clear that their commitment to the historical aspects of the project ran deep.

The initial architectural conception of the Jefferson Memorial fit the expansiveness of the monument builders' vision. In 1934 the Memorial Association retained St. Louis architect Louis LaBeaume to draw up initial sketches. LaBeaume and his collaborators in the association proposed a series of buildings built on the Third Street plateau with memorial gardens and stairs descending to the river. The memorial complex would cover much of the original eighteenth-century town site. A central building on the axis with the old courthouse would house a "Jeffersonian shrine." Flanking buildings would be divided into sections that celebrated the individual contributions of the various states to westward expansion. The project would rely on museum displays, extensive mural and sculptural projects, and monumental elements including an obelisk celebrating the Santa Fe Trail and another one devoted to the Oregon Trail. LaBeaume reported that the memorial was conceived "as a sort of Pantheon to all our explorers, pioneers and statesmen, who made the territorial integrity of the United States . . . possible. . . . Every American in every section of the country will find here something reflecting the contribution of his own section of the country toward the present greatness of the United States. . . .

The idea is so grandiose and so inspiring that here indeed will be a summing up of all the historical achievements of the nation, and it will be a visual and enduring page of history."[23]

In 1935 the Territorial Commission argued that the construction of the memorial was the "nation's responsibility." The commission based its conclusion upon its review of what it considered the site's important history, including such highlights as the Louisiana Purchase transfer ceremony, the residence of William Clark, the site of the lower-court trial of Dred Scott, and places visited temporarily by President Lincoln, Generals Lee and Grant, and Mark Twain. It recommended a national architectural competition to determine the design and estimated the cost of the project at $30,000,000, with 23,000,000 hours of labor to be used over a period of three years.[24] In September 1935, St. Louis voters approved $7,500,000 in bonds for the memorial. Local leaders hoped that the bonds would help win both support and financial aid for the project from Congress. In the St. Louis election civic and political leaders succeeded in the bond election by appealing to patriotism, history, the self-interest of the unemployed, and promises of civic uplift that would flow from the monumental development of the river.

As interest in the memorial grew, the National Park Service sent John L. Nagle, a Park Service engineer, to review the project. Nagle reported to the Park Service director that the events to be memorialized were of sufficient importance in United States history to "warrant Federal participation." He considered the project "entirely feasible from all practical standpoints" and suggested that the Park Service build and administer the monument. Reviewing the early plans for memorial structures and for a park along the entire riverfront of the memorial site, Nagle demonstrated great sympathy with the general outlines of the project. He also supported the project's urban renewal potential; echoing the earlier proposals of the Civic League and other local planners, Nagle insisted, "It is certain that the clearing out and the demolition of the dilapidated structures . . . and the improvement resulting from the completion of this memorial project, will redirect a considerable amount of civic interest to this blighted section of the City."[25] In June 1936, when Nagle became superintendent of the memorial, his own sense of the site's national historic importance and his willingness to contemplate the clearance of the site quickly brought him into conflict with those who sought to preserve the area's older buildings.

In December 1935, with advice from Secretary of the Interior Harold Ickes, President Roosevelt signed Executive Order 7253 directing the interior secretary to develop a memorial on the St. Louis site because it possessed "exceptional value as commemorating or illustrating the history of the United States." Funds were to come initially from $2,250,000 in St. Louis improvement bonds and $6,750,000 in federal Public Works Administration funds. Roosevelt's executive order itemized the historic value of the site, including the locations of the Louisiana Purchase flag ceremony, the establishment of the first civil government west of the Mississippi, the visit of Lafayette in 1824, the point of embarkation for the Santa Fe and Oregon trails and the Lewis and Clark expedition, and the site of Dred Scott's local trial. Roosevelt's order also made passing reference to the importance of work relief and the need for increased employment in St. Louis.[26]

The ordinances affirming the local St. Louis bond referendum and Roosevelt's executive order unleashed the first in a long series of court cases concerning the legality of the proposed memorial. A strikingly different group of preservationists from the ones who later argued the aesthetic and architectural importance of the buildings supported these court challenges. Companies, building owners, and workers who faced displacement from the area sought to redress their grievances through the Citizens Non-Partisan Committee and the courts. A telegram sent to Secretary Ickes just before the signing of the executive order summed up the arguments of the district's representatives. William F. Pfeiffer wrote, I PROTEST JEFFERSON MEMORIAL. URGE YOU REFUSE CONSENT. IT WILL DRIVE MANY GOING CONCERNS OUT OF ST. LOUIS AND OUT OF BUSINESS AND HUNDREDS OUT OF JOBS. IT WILL BE A TOMBSTONE AS WELL AS A MEMORIAL. ST. LOUIS NEEDS ACTIVITY NOT COLD STONE ON HER RIVERFRONT. PLEASE REFUSE SIGNATURE. Paul O. Peters, the leader of the committee, declared the project "pure political pork" and insisted that "citizens of St. Louis who cry for bread will not accept a stone in the form of a real estate purchase on our river front." Many landowners felt that their condemnation awards would bring only deflated depression prices, far below the prices they had paid for their land. They felt as well that their losses would represent gains for other area real estate owners, whose property would be improved by construction of the monument.[27] These people sued to preserve business and real estate holdings without arguing a case based on the history of their buildings or their community. The series of cases went on appeal to the United States Supreme Court, which in June 1937 let stand a lower-court finding that the government could proceed with condemnation of land and construction of the memorial.[28] The cases slowed but did not stop the memorial. Equally important, the interests represented in these cases shared few concerns with the people who later argued the historical importance of particular buildings that stood on the memorial site.

National History, Local Buildings, and an Architecture Museum

Despite the national historic framework for the Jefferson Memorial, some interest in aesthetic preservation came in 1936 from people within the National Park Service. Charles E. Peterson stood out among those who advocated the architectural value of existing buildings. Trained as an undergraduate in architecture at the University of Minnesota, Peterson occupied the position of senior landscape architect on the Park Service's Jefferson Memorial team. He had distinguished himself in 1933 by helping to establish the Park Service's Historic American Buildings Survey; the program's effort to record American architecture based on the formal categories of architectural "period, type and locality" had represented a clear departure from the Park Service's devotion to national associational history. Peterson pursued similar ideas in his work at the Jefferson Memorial site. He initially developed a prospectus for the construction of a Museum of American Architecture to be included in the Jefferson memorial. The plan originated with the simple assertion that Thomas Jefferson had exercised "a greater influence on American architecture than any other single man."[29] The architecture museum would serve as a living memorial to Jefferson and complement a second museum planned to chronicle the history of the fur trade and western settlement.

Peterson thus hoped to use Jefferson's memorial as the departure point for further expanding the Park Service's commitment to the study of "the builder's art." The museum would chronicle Jefferson's work and also possibly display structural and ornamental fragments salvaged during the clearance of the memorial site. However, Peterson's plan went far beyond the site's buildings. Drawing loosely on Rockefeller's Williamsburg, Ford's Greenfield Village, and the Metropolitan Museum's American Wing, Peterson looked forward to collecting entire buildings, building fragments, models, and drawings. He pictured contemporary craftsmen "working materials in the ancient tradition" in order to "present to the public the story of the development of architectural design in this country from the earliest times to the present and . . . create a physical plant for the storage and exhibition of important specimens."[30] In Peterson's view "the meeting house of New England, the plantation mansion of the South, the log cabin of

6.6. *Old St. Louis Cathedral, built 1831–1834. Morton & Laveille, architects. One of the few buildings preserved on the site of the Jefferson National Expansion Memorial.* Photograph by Alexander Piaget, 1934. Library of Congress.

the Western pioneer, the hacienda of the Southwest and the log fort of Alaska tell a more forceful story than any arrangement of words." All these elements would find their way into the museum that Peterson hoped would be more diverse than the high-style collections found at the Metropolitan Museum and the local collections of outdoor museums like that at Williamsburg. Subject matter would range from the history of the log cabin to the history of the skyscraper.[31] The museum would, in Peterson's view, also serve as a center to advise on the conservation and restoration of buildings throughout the Park Service system. It could, for example, assist with the restoration of buildings related to the early history of St. Louis. While Peterson did not want the museum to focus on collecting historic buildings for the site, he hoped that the museum could step in to rescue buildings from around the country threatened with demolition. Furthermore, the buildings on the memorial site that were considered "ugly" might be salvaged in part to "show the general confusion and decay of architectural design immediately following the Civil War."[32]

Peterson rallied support for these museum proposals within the American architectural community. He looked immediately to the American Institute of Architects, which had earlier joined the Park Service in sponsoring the Historic American Buildings Survey. Peterson also enlisted the help of Chicago architect and historian Thomas E. Tallmadge to write newspaper articles supporting the museum proposal. When Tallmadge toured the memorial site in 1936, he spoke to the Park Service and local newspapers about the importance of preserving individual buildings on the memorial site. He spoke highly of the St. Louis courthouse and cathedral (fig. 6.6). But he also broadened his preservation advocacy to include a number of "rich examples of early architecture," most notably buildings adorned with early cast-iron facades. He insisted that it was important to preserve "everything of real artistic merit." Tallmadge thus became one of a line of architectural historians to declare the importance of the existing buildings on the site. Henry Russell-Hitchcock soon followed. Sigfried Giedion lauded St. Louis's cast-iron architecture (fig. 6.7) and included the subject in his book *Space, Time, and Architecture*. As for the buildings of lesser importance, Tallmadge looked hopefully to the possibility that fragments of the demolished structures could be housed in the museum of architecture.[33]

Tallmadge's visit provoked the first opposition to the plan of fostering American architectural history as a central theme of the Jefferson Memorial. Although John L. Nagle had supported Tallmadge's visit to the memorial, he wrote that he was "disturbed" by the effort to "justify or defend" various proposals for developing the site.[34] After Nagle voiced objections, Tallmadge retreated from his more expansive preservation ideal. He provided Nagle with a site report that declared that since none of the area's buildings was "outstanding," their destruction, with the exception of the cathedral, would not pose a serious loss to St. Louis or the nation. While the age of some of the buildings endowed them with considerable interest, he thought that only future generations could appreciate them as an example of a business district of the second half of the nineteenth century. Lack of appreciation by contemporaries made immediate preservation difficult. According to Tallmadge, such a preservation scheme would be practically impossible "even if advisable, which in my opinion, it is not."[35]

Beyond tempering Tallmadge's call for preservation, Nagle quickly limited the scope of Peterson's museum plan. He asked the director of the National Park Service to head off Peterson's effort to have the board of the American Institute of Architects pass a resolution supporting his museum plan. After considerable reflection, Nagle had begun to "fear that such [a] museum would lead into purely academic fields of architecture and [that the] results could not be squared with fundamental conceptions of the epic qualities to be memorialized . . . the Museum of Architecture [is] suitable and appropriate if and only if given proper weight in relation to other features and distinctly from [the] Louisiana Purchase."[36] Ned J. Burns, with the Park Service's Museum Division, concurred with Nagle's objections. Departing from the history selected for national commemoration, he felt, would make the museum seem to be placed in St. Louis by "chance" and thus threaten the entire plan.[37] This resistance from within the National Park Service was not premised on any political commitment to St. Louis urban renewal; it flowed from the perception that the local development of cast-iron architecture seemed outside of the historical purview of Thomas Jefferson, the Louisiana Purchase, and even westward expansion. Moreover, preserving mid-nineteenth-century commercial architecture stood outside the bounds of architectural preservation in the 1930s.

The differences that arose between Nagle and Peterson and their various allies thus measured the distance between a history based on a narrative of people and

6.7. *Cast-iron-front building at 119–121 North Main Street in the riverfront area. Similar buildings attracted preservation interest during planning for the Jefferson National Expansion Memorial. Built c. 1875.* Photograph by Theodore La Vack, 1936. Library of Congress.

6.8. Detail of Bird's Eye view of St. Louis in Mississippi riverfront area later cleared for the Jefferson National Expansion Memorial. Drawn by Parsons & Atwater, published by Currier & Ives, 1874. Library of Congress.

events and a history focusing on the changes in the form, material, and aesthetics of architectural design. In surveying this history, Charles B. Hosmer, Jr., dismisses Nagle's position as that of an engineer committed to a "mammoth program that was to involve the purchase and demolition of entire city blocks." Hosmer casts Peterson, by contrast, as a champion of historical appreciation, "fresh from his triumphs in founding the Historic American Buildings Survey."[38] Yet the contrast was not so simple. Starting with these early debates and continuing over the years of his work as superintendent, Nagle defended the primacy of commemorating the "epic" qualities of a narrative history against the values of a less well-established form of preservation based largely on architectural aesthetics, studied at some remove from national history.

Peterson had sought to address the perceived gap between architectural history and national history when he sought Thomas Tallmadge's help in outlining possible connections between the memorial's national narrative and the architecture standing on the site and the fragments planned for exhibition in the museum. He suggested that Tallmadge write an essay entitled "Architecture as a Graphic Expression of History."[39] Peterson's initial museum plan had generally eschewed such links in arguing the importance of presenting a chronicle

of the formal development of American architecture. Tallmadge never wrote the essay, and Peterson failed to cultivate the idea on his own. Given the fact that the memorial plans conflicted so directly with architectural preservation, Peterson and his allies made surprisingly few efforts to reconcile the paths to history that might flow from monuments and what might be available coming from historic preservation on the St. Louis riverfront. Part of St. Louis's role in westward expansion involved the warehousing and transshipment of goods between the East and the western interior of the United States. The existing riverfront landscape, with its dense pattern of warehouses and tight network of streets, was the architectural legacy of St. Louis's historical role in westward expansion (fig. 6.8). Indeed, the scale and width of the streets and blocks were vestiges of the eighteenth-century platting of the city; they directly connected the historic settlement to the present day. However, Peterson did not develop the narrative that might have reconciled the historic urban and architectural form of the site with the larger national narratives of the monument builders. Instead, Peterson focused his energies on what turned out to be an unconvincing project for a museum narrating the "builder's art."

Superintendent Nagle continued to support the national historical narrative affirmed by Congress, the president, the Interior Department, and the National Park Service in their statements on the Jefferson memorial. In 1938, in a speech to a St. Louis Kiwanis club, broadcast over local radio, Nagle sketched his vision of the memorial. Leaving aside the history of bloody relations between native people and European and American settlers, Nagle wanted the memorial to commemorate the Louisiana Purchase and the supposedly peaceable assembly of empire to provide an inspiring lesson for future generations that "war is not the only path to glory." Although no buildings contemporary to the Louisiana Purchase survived, the fact that the sites of buildings important in this narrative could be fixed with some precision led Nagle to look forward with great optimism to the memorial's ability to preserve the area's historic "identity." Since the time of the ancient Romans, Nagle argued, monuments had provided "that touch of common history to the generations which follow that is so necessary to cement a people together into a nation . . . and urge them on to greater national accomplishments." Members of the Jefferson National Expansion Memorial Association generally endorsed the plan to cultivate citizenship around a chronicle of national history. In a prospectus for an architectural competition drawn up in 1935, the association declared that the memorial would consist of buildings or other memorial features of "a monumental nature" that would "beautifully and majestically" commemorate territorial consolidation and "the courage, vision, and statesmanship of an impressive group of national heroes." Such a memorial would provide the means of "influencing better citizenship."[40] For his part Nagle titled his address to the Kiwanis club "The Essentially National Aspects of the Jefferson National Expansion Memorial."[41] In a commemorative effort framed around an "essentially national" narrative, Peterson and other preservationists stumbled badly in failing to articulate a link between the local objects of their preservation desire and the broader national story. The problem wasn't that such a link was impossible; the problem was that Peterson was too committed to his own stylistic basis for engaging architectural history to recognize and foreground the links to the national story.

Although some members of the Advisory Board on National Parks criticized the memorial project as a slum clearance plan, other members strongly supported the nationalism articulated by Nagle and members of the Memorial Association. They all sought to combine an inspiring monument with buildings, displays, and interpretive programs to convey a national narrative. A subcommittee of the Advisory Board led by Hermon C. Bumpus hoped that the memorial's program would

survey all of the factors related to expansion and the creation of the nation, with every state and territory represented. Bumpus, a zoologist and retired museum and university president, had helped the National Park Service establish park museums at Yosemite, Yellowstone, and the Grand Canyon. Not surprisingly, then, an emphasis on interpretation and on conveying a national tradition surfaced in the Bumpus committee's ideas for the memorial. With its ambitions toward a survey of national history, the committee looked forward, "figuratively speaking," to a project that "would become an inspiring volume rather than a highly interesting chapter."[42] Bumpus even saw this "volume" reflected in the architecture of the memorial itself. A building devoted to chronicling the natural resources of the West would mirror a building devoted to interpreting the results of national expansion. These buildings would flank a broad open space representing the western frontier. The landscape for the site would suggest the converging interests of the East, meeting at the gateway of St. Louis, then following "diverging paths into the vast regions of the west."[43] Nagle expressed enthusiasm for Bumpus's vision of the memorial. Such a system might sort out the "confused mass of apparently unrelated historical happenings" on the site. Peterson and other members of the project team had prepared a map locating precisely the sites of various historical events, while omitting from the survey buildings he considered architecturally interesting. Nagle hoped that the events could be "disentangled and correlated" in the interest of interpretative clarity and "inspirational value."[44]

With their shared focus on national history, Nagle, Bumpus, and other advocates of the memorial did not see how the existing buildings on the memorial site would clarify the "confused mass" of events or help present a comprehensible and usable history. In fact, their interest in a specific historical line even undercut some of the monumental ambitions of initial plans for the memorial. The memorial site took in an area three city blocks wide; however, the initial boundaries linked the domed St. Louis courthouse (fig. 6.9) with the memorial proper by expanding the site between Market and Chestnut streets to a width of six blocks. St. Louis then offered the federal government possession of the courthouse as part of the memorial. In 1939, Hermon Bumpus and the Advisory Board urged the Park Service to leave the courthouse outside of the memorial; the board felt that the building lacked the historic interest or the architectural pretensions to warrant its inclusion in the site. Of the over 400 structures standing on the thirty-seven-block riverfront site, the board felt that only the 1834 cathedral and the Old Rock House (fig. 6.10), a warehouse thought to date to 1818, merited preservation. Nagle, who considered the issue of the courthouse moot because President Roosevelt had already endorsed its inclusion in the memorial, did support preservation of the cathedral and the Rock House. He reported to the director of the Park Service that "no other buildings should be left standing unless the demand therefore, as yet not proved to my satisfaction, shall be clearly demonstrated."[45] Charles B. Hosmer, Jr., has characterized the Advisory Board's failure to endorse the preservation of the courthouse as "one of the strangest" decisions made by the National Park Service Advisory Board.[46] However, the board's established interest in commemorating a narrative of national history and the general absence of arguments demonstrating how the St. Louis courthouse might have furthered this ambition gives their conclusion a measure of credence. Enthusiasm for the courthouse has undoubtedly grown stronger over time as it became an integral element in Saarinen's evocative design for the memorial. From the perspective of those who sought a coherent historical narrative, however, the Court House seemed inessential.

The general unwillingness of Nagle and various Park Service officials to endorse a broader preservation program did not end debates over preservation. The 1852 federal building at Third and Olive streets (fig. 6.11), called the "old Custom House," had greater potential than most local buildings to assimilate itself to the national focus of the memorial's commemorative intent. Built as part of a massive federal building program in the 1850s, the building housed the federal court, the post office, and the customs service.[47] Although it did not date from the time of the Louisiana Purchase, it certainly represented the role of the national government in local public life better than other local buildings did. However, in a manner characteristic of the divide between aesthetic and associational preservation, most people calling for the preservation of the building did not attempt to reconcile their interests with those of the memorial builders. Perry T. Rathbone, the director

6.9. Old St. Louis Courthouse, built 1839–1861. Preserved as a terminal feature in the Jefferson National Expansion Memorial area. Henry Singleton, Robert S. Mitchell, and William Rumbold, architects. Photograph by Alexander Piaget, 1934. Library of Congress

6.10. Old Rock House, riverfront warehouse, built c. 1818. Initially preserved on the site of the Jefferson National Expansion Memorial and incorporated into Saarinen's plans for the Gateway Arch. Preservation plans were later scrapped and the building was dismantled. Photograph by Alexander Piaget, 1934. Library of Congress.

of the St. Louis City Art Museum, for example, argued that the Custom House was a "substantial monument to St. Louis's past;" a building with "considerable beauty and distinction" that stood as "a splendid example of civic architecture of the mid-nineteenth century." Rathbone, who helped lead the "movement to preserve this fine monument to our past," reported that he was "dismayed" by the planned demolition because he had felt that St. Louis was capable of distinguishing itself from other American cities, like Detroit, with their "appalling disregard for what few fine examples of architecture still remain from the nineteenth century."[48]

Laura Inglis, a resident of Webster Groves, Missouri, joined Rathbone in urging aesthetic preservation: "This one should be saved to show the type of that period," she wrote. Missouri Supreme Court Judge James M. Douglas, president of the Missouri Historical Society, similarly insisted that "it is a very handsome building and I heartily agree that it should be saved." William Booth Papin, local real estate executive and an officer of the City Art Museum, declared that the building was "the finest of the Vignolesque classical type ever erected in St. Louis," and a potential "ornament to the memorial."[49] These kinds of arguments for aesthetic preservation did not resonate much with those who viewed their role as commemorating Jefferson and the Louisiana Purchase.

Another pool of sentiment favoring the preservation of the Custom House did turn, at least in part, on a different sense of the past. The Custom House had served as something of a landmark in the public life of the com-

6.11. St. Louis Federal Building and Custom House, built 1852 and demolished 1941. Photograph by Alexander Piaget, 1934. Library of Congress.

147

*6.12. Building demolition on Jefferson National
Expansion Memorial site.* Photograph c. 1941.
Jefferson National Expansion Memorial.

munity, quite apart from its form and style. But preservationists did not define very clearly this conception of the
building's role in crystallizing civic meaning and memory.
Julius Polk, Jr., wrote to Secretary of the Interior Ickes
that the building was both a "fine example of architecture"
and had "many historic associations, and is very dear to
the hearts of many St. Louisians." In arguing the case for
preservation the postmaster of St. Louis insisted that no
other building standing in St. Louis carried more "historical significance, as bearing on the relationship between
the United States government and the City of St. Louis,
than this noble old building." Beyond this important relationship between national and local life, the postmaster
declared on behalf of all his employees that "the postal
service would be deprived of one of its oldest tangible traditions" if the building were destroyed.[50] The conception
of the building as a tangible connection between postal
workers and their history clearly resonated less with the
memorial builders than what Nagle and others viewed as
the "epic" qualities of the site.

The letters of protest over the planned demolition of
the Custom House and editorial support for preservation from the *St. Louis Post-Dispatch* did give Park Service officials cause for pause from December 1940 into
January 1941. Over the years, the Park Service had been
somewhat equivocal concerning the Custom House. In
1936, Park Service personnel had envisioned parts of
the building's façade, along with surviving original drawings, as the basis for "a particularly interesting" exhibition in the proposed museum of American architecture.
Some Park Service staff argued that the building's fine
architecture, its status as the first major federal building built west of the Mississippi, and its importance in
the contentious days of the Civil War suggested that
the entire façade of the building should be saved and
reerected on the interior of one of the memorial buildings. In a long memorandum of August 1940, Charles E.
Peterson outlined "good arguments both for retaining
and removing" the building. Local planners felt that a
project to widen Third Street for traffic necessitated the
building's removal. According to Peterson, "others, who
may represent the vanguard of progressive thought in
such matters, and who seem a part of the rather recent
but important growth of interest in American archaeol-

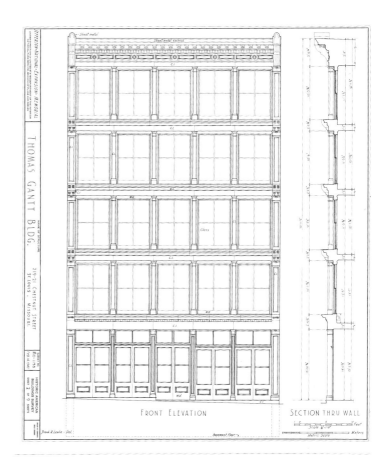

6.13. *Cast-iron façade of Thomas Gantt Building, 219–221 Chestnut Street, St. Louis, built 1877 and demolished c. 1940 in the clearance for the Jefferson National Expansion Memorial. Elevation drawn by Frank R. Leslie, 1940.* Library of Congress.

ogy and social history, regret each removal of an architectural unit of the old 'riverfront atmosphere' and feel it contrary to the spirit of the enabling legislation." Peterson did not identify personally with this vanguard. Rather, he sought a compromise; he suggested that the façade be preserved and reerected later in a new building in order to ensure "the continued existence of the building in an important sense yet allowing the unimpeded development of Third Street."[51]

This "sense" of history gained from architectural fragments undercut the more progressive preservation position while giving new possibilities to the somewhat dormant plans for an architectural museum. The idea that the building could be preserved by saving its façade was consistent with the view that patterns of form, as opposed to patterns of use, constituted the essence of architecture. Indeed, Park Service staff had earlier concluded that the Custom House interior, the area of greatest public use, was "not worth saving." Even so, growing public interest in preservation led Peterson to modify his position from one of favoring demolition to one of studying the problem in greater detail. Peterson hoped

that, as the memorial site was cleared and a "good view" of all sides of the Custom House became visible, Park Service advisors might urge the preservation of the building based on its "good design."[52]

The debate over the future of the Custom House ended up in the hands of Newton B. Drury, director of the National Park Service. He noted that among his staff advisors only Charles Peterson favored preservation of the building. Drury rejected the logic of Peterson's arguments. If the Custom House was saved based on its formal stylistic character, because it was "interesting as representing the architecture of a past era," or "typical of the architecture of early St. Louis," then the Park Service could not reasonably justify demolishing many of the other buildings in the memorial site. Drury pointed to the money that the Park Service had committed to rehabilitating the St. Louis County Courthouse, a building he considered historically more important, and suggested that this represented a large enough commitment to preservation. Noting plans for widening Third Street and concerns over how the Custom House would fit into final plans for the memorial, the Park Service concluded that the building did not possess "sufficient national and historical significance to justify the high cost of restoration." After being rather cool toward the idea of an architecture museum, government officials now found that the possibility that details salvaged from the Custom House façade might later be exhibited actually made it easier to proceed with the controversial demolition plan.[53] The Park Service saved three cast-iron details of the main stair, a Corinthian pilaster capital, a cast-iron interior column that combined structure with heating elements, carved stone window consoles, modillion courses, a pair of decorated iron doors, and the Corinthian capitals from the columns on the main façade.[54] They placed these fragments in storage along with other architecturally interesting material salvaged from the memorial site.

That material grew as demolition proceeded. In 1939, after overcoming the legal challenges to the memorial project, the government had condemned the memorial site and begun to take control of the land, paying landowners over time $5,970,000 for 484 separate parcels of land.[55] On October 9, 1939, Mayor Dickmann gave the demolition project a ceremonial start when he used a wrecking bar to dislodge bricks from a building on Market Street. In clearing the memorial land (fig. 6.12), the Park Service collected and stored the entire façades of four cast-iron buildings. The cast-iron collection included the five-story façade of the Gantt Building (fig. 6.13), a building that Sigfried Giedion had especially admired. The fragment collection also included column capitals, pillars, arches, window arcades, doors, stairways, ornamental panels and grilles, and other architectural details made of iron, wood, plaster, and stone.[56] Peterson and other Park Service staff had looked forward to using these elements in some form of architectural exhibition on the memorial site.

World War II and subsequent funding problems slowed development of the Jefferson National Expansion Memorial. As various people struggled to keep the project afloat, the architectural museum concept, always a peripheral part of the memorial plan, languished further. Although a museum of architecture appeared in the program for the memorial's 1947 architectural competition, it lacked the support of key Park Service staff. In 1957, before final funding for the memorial was obtained, the Park Service's chief historian concluded that the museum of architecture was not feasible. He considered many of the artifacts too big for easy display. The national focus of the memorial continued to undercut the seeming utility of architectural displays. The St. Louis fragment collection appeared too limited, "only a small part of architecture in western expansion," and

nobody seemed especially interested in building the collection further.[57] In 1958 the Park Service abandoned the architecture museum and distributed the fragments collection to the Missouri Historical Society, the Smithsonian, other interested institutions, and the garbage.

The Limits of Valuing Architecture as Architecture

Setting aside the architecture museum highlighted the Park Service's broader decision to omit historic architecture from its interpretative program. Long-debated plans to reconstruct buildings typical of St. Louis at the time of the Louisiana Purchase were dropped from the memorial plans in the 1950s. The Park Service also refused to provide space on the memorial grounds for relocating historic structures threatened with demolition. For example, in 1947 preservationists, including Perry Rathbone and Charles Peterson, sought a site on the memorial grounds for the Jean Baptiste Roy house. Built about 1829 and occupying a threatened site adjacent to the memorial, the Roy house stood chronologically closer to the privileged history of the Louisiana Purchase. Many people in St. Louis also valued the building because they believed that a sausage shop located in the Roy house in the 1870s produced the first hot dogs. Members of the Memorial Association and the Park Service resisted the plan for relocation, and the owner proceeded to demolish the building.[58] In 1958, Barnard College English professor and historian John A. Kouwenhoven suggested that the memorial site would be a great place to move a "splendid Greek revival mansion" faced with demolition on its original site a short distance away. Kouwenhoven admired the building's "dignified proportions, its beautifully laid brick, its lovely cast-iron balcony, and its handsome columns and cornices." The building, the "only example" of its type in St. Louis, seemed a suitable addition to a historical monument. In rejecting the plan the Park Service declared its belief that historic structures lost much of their historic value when they were relocated. It also feared that the memorial ground might become a "happy hunting ground" for people anxious to move their historic buildings to safe ground, which would "jeopardize" the overall plans for the memorial and saddle the Park Service with the expense of operating something akin to Henry Ford's Greenfield Village.[59] Thus, over a period of nearly twenty-five years, preservationists and historians had sought in a variety of ways, all unsuccessful, to make historic architecture a part of the memorial's commemorative landscape. Their interests and vision, their passion for architectural history and beauty, did not convincingly complement national commemorative ideals.

The architectural formalism of the preservationists, their strong interest in the internal dynamics of architectural style, form, structural systems, and type, impeded their efforts to define a commemorative role for the old buildings on the St. Louis memorial site. Beyond the preservationists, the embrace of architectural formalism by the boosters and builders of the memorial itself precluded the exploration of the potential power of historic buildings and landscapes to convey history. Early in the planning process, Secretary of the Interior Ickes articulated what became a dominant view of the formal design relation between the memorial and the city's older buildings and landscapes. Ickes wrote,

> Grounds upon which important memorial edifices are to be constructed should be spacious enough to provide the necessary landscape setting and to shield the structure from all detracting influences of the surrounding buildings. When this principle is violated, a crowding effect results and a large part, if not all, of the dignity and impressiveness of the Memorial, is sacrificed. The principle applies with special emphasis to the St. Louis project, where the . . . nature of the surroundings is such that ample open space is required for the essential isolating effects.[60]

This vision of the monument standing in a detached and glorious isolation, separated from the city, was firmly rooted in contemporary canons of monumentality. A monument, by prevailing definitions, stood out from its context; however, nothing in this definition necessitated the physical divorce from the historic city that people envisioned for St. Louis. The effort to build such a memorial reflected, in part, a perceived clash between the monument's celebratory chronicle of the march toward empire and the clear evidence of urban decay and economic decline along the Mississippi riverfront. In fact, the "blighted riverfront business buildings" stood as a metaphor for uncertainty over St. Louis's future urban status. People who had supported clearance of the riverfront for decades were more concerned about the future than about the past; they wanted to demolish the "ghost town—the shabby, crumbling shell of the commercial St. Louis of the bustling steamboat days."[61] They wanted to replace it with a piece of modern city building presenting a more sanguine lesson from history. History coursed through both the streets and the old buildings on the riverfront; however, formalism and monumentality, combined with a certain aversion to the evidence of historic decline, led the monument builders to value most highly the historic associations of place quite apart

from existing buildings. Thus, the riverfront demolitions themselves were cast as a means of connecting people with history; as one newspaper reported, "slowly but surely, wrecking crews are uncovering the land on which the first settlers in St. Louis built their homes and later their businesses."[62]

"Pure" Monuments, Saarinen's Arch, and Historic Narrative

By May 1942 the concerns that older buildings might crowd or compromise the effect of the Jefferson Memorial abated as demolition left only the St. Louis Cathedral, the Courthouse and the Old Rock House standing. As history in the form of the old buildings on the site no longer threatened the canons of monumentality, the monument builders' concerns over the relationship between the history and the memorial shifted in important ways. Professionals within the Park Service expressed growing fears that the memorial might overwhelm their presentation and interpretation of national history. They carefully distinguished between the symbolic and the didactic roles of the memorial. Such a distinction was not new. All of the early plans for the memorial had envisioned history and museum displays as complements to the monumental features of the memorial. In 1938, Harold C. Bryant, assistant director of the Park Service, toured the memorial site and declared to a local newspaper that "we want to see the finest monument possible arise on the riverfront here. But we want to be sure that it will tell the story of the growth of the country adequately and beautifully."[63] In 1944, while outlining the "purpose and theme" of the St. Louis project, National Park Service historian Charles W. Porter sharply differentiated between its intended role as a memorial and its use and operation as a historic site. He declared that a "symbolical memorial in stone or bronze, or a memorial building with murals, no matter how large it may be, cannot tell the story as effectively as a good museum program."[64] This distinction emerged as the Park Service executed its initial plans for museum displays, quite apart from the broader efforts of the Jefferson National Expansion Memorial Association to promote a memorial.

The distinction between the Park Service and the Memorial Association, between plans to commemorate history and to build monuments, went beyond the simple issue of institutional interests. It bore heavily on how the site would actually be shaped and presented to the public. As Charles Porter pointed out, the treatment of the riverfront as a historic site required that "existing historical remains of outstanding importance should be preserved." Once the site was cleared, this point was largely moot; however, historians in the Park Service did argue that the designers for the memorial should preserve the still-extant pattern of historic streets. These streets would provide the frame for a network of historic markers, tablets, and guided tours. The historians felt that removing the streets would make it impossible to present their interpretive programs with "intellectual honesty." Insisting that the memorial design work around the existing streets and established markers represented one effort to ensure the clarity of a memorial program in the face of monumental ambitions. Surveying the welter of interests focusing on the riverfront, ranging from municipal concerns with traffic and parking to aspirations for "a smartly rendered project according to the latest cult of architectural design," to the enthusiasm for a Williamsburg-style restoration of colonial houses, some Park Service historians sought to "stand firm" for the "standards that should obtain in this sort of an undertaking."[65] In 1945, as the Memorial Association planned its prospectus for the design competition, historians in the Park Service grew more emphatic about their responsibility to mark history. Park Service director Newton Drury wrote, "I have tried to divert the thought and energies of the sincere sponsors of various schemes for the development of the project away from the symbolic architectural memorial . . . toward the simpler treatment that would be appropriate to the preservation of the physical remains and evidences of early human associations as a national historic site." In Drury's view "the development of an artistic symbolic memorial on a grand architectural scale would . . . be a departure from established Service policy." Drury also indicated that the Park Service felt especially strongly that the association's plans for a memorial should develop the theme of westward expansion, including a museum, and remove the site's elevated railroad tracks in order to reestablish the visual connection between the river and the memorial site. Drury's ideas and demands, made in the 1940s, further highlighted ongoing efforts of the National Park Service to develop the site in a historically rigorous fashion completely apart from local interest in embellishing the riverfront area.[66]

Recognizing the potential for conflict between the historical and monumental aspects of the Jefferson Memorial, the Park Service committed itself to interpretive exhibits. In 1938, John L. Nagle identified the effort to "commemorate the westward expansion of the United States with emphasis on the Louisiana Purchase," as the "major purpose" of the planning for the memorial. The Park Service's interpretive plan would rely on exhibits

with dioramas, murals, large-scale maps, and other displays "memorializing, illustrating, and dramatizing the conditions and events prior to the Louisiana Purchase, as well as the historical factors of the westward expansion which were outstanding in their importance and results."[67] Part of the challenge for Park Service historians was that the historical narrative asserted in the executive order approving the Jefferson Memorial contained "half truths based on technicalities." To argue, as the executive order did, that St. Louis was the site of "the first civil government west of the Mississippi" overlooked the earlier Spanish civil governments in Texas and the Southwest. St. Louis's position as the beginning point of the Santa Fe and Oregon trails ignored the more accurate claims to that distinction of an area along the Missouri River near Kansas City. St. Louis as the origin of the Lewis and Clark expedition needed some qualification since the pre-expedition camp actually stood on the east bank of the Mississippi River. St. Louis as the location of the Dred Scott Trial emphasized the site of the less significant lower-court case rather than the Supreme Court case.[68]

Correcting the executive order's historical narrative led to a more precise portrait but did not drastically reorient the priority placed on territorial acquisition and expansion. The Park Service placed its first interpretive displays on view in April 1942 in the St. Louis County Courthouse. The exhibits explored the "basic theme of the Memorial"—national expansion.

The exhibition's first panel, "The Story of National Expansion" declared: "This is the story of those hardy and courageous people who transformed thirteen disunited, dependent, colonies on the Eastern Coast into one great independent nation extending across the continent." Park Service historians devoted cases in the exhibition halls to the European origins of American settlement, the natural environment, English colonial culture, the ethnic composition of the colonial frontier, a diorama of the French settlement at Ste. Genevieve, French exploration of the Mississippi River valley, life on the frontier with interpretative quotes from historian Frederick Jackson Turner, the political process and chronology of statehood, Jefferson, the Louisiana Purchase, and "the peaceable acquisition of empire," Lewis and Clark's expedition, "the Winning of the West," migration, settlement and economic development, the expansion to Oregon, California, and Texas, the Homestead Act, and a final summary of territorial expansion. The exhibition concluded with a panel that aimed to further cultivate nationalism; it suggested that despite the closing of the frontier, people could still participate in the "drama of American development."[69]

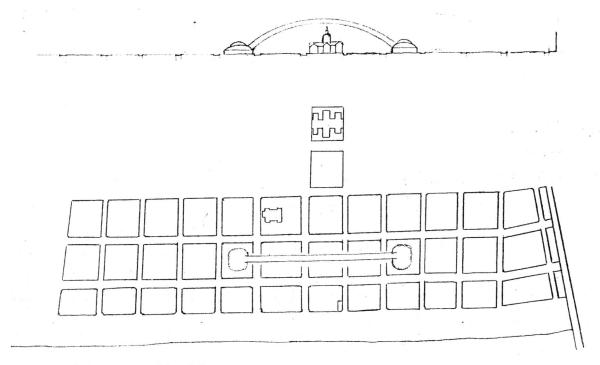

6.14. *Julian C. Spotts's proposal for a Jefferson National Expansion Memorial, February 1945. This sketch for a 1,200-foot-long arch on the riverfront preceded Saarinen's proposal for a Gateway Arch by two years.* National Archives.

The renovated St. Louis County Courthouse provided a dignified civic setting for the exhibition of national history. The addition of suitably marked historic sites around the memorial grounds might well have fulfilled the Park Service's responsibility for the place under the Historic Sites Act. Nevertheless, Luther Ely Smith and his colleagues in the Memorial Association still saw real advantages in the addition of the long-anticipated monument. While referring to history, the monument could boost the civic and economic fortunes of St. Louis. People in the association certainly understood the contemporary use of a monument that could affect the long-sought renewal of the riverfront and would also reflect well on the cultivated commitment to civic life of the local residents who devoted both time and resources to commemorating the past. Julian C. Spotts, the man who succeeded John L. Nagle as superintendent of the memorial in 1940, saw the monument as an integral part of the historic site. He firmly believed that a monument would powerfully diffuse historical lessons. In 1945, with an eye to the potential audience, Spotts reported on his own sense of the use of a monument on the memorial grounds; he wrote, "many visitors to our parks are vacationists bent upon recreation and sight seeing. Others go beyond the sight seeing state and breathe in the

inspiration and absorb the educational and interpretive features. History is dull to many people unless made interesting. . . . An inspirational memorial could well be the mecca which would attract people who would unconsciously come in contact with our interpretative work and through mere power of suggestion absorb our national history."[70]

Spotts's sense of the power of a monument to boost awareness of national history led him to urge the Park Service to cooperate fully in the Memorial Association's sponsorship of an architectural competition for the design of the memorial. Nevertheless, in February 1945, Spotts's ideal of a truly monumental memorial led him to sketch his own vision of a suitable design. In a conception he thought might be "too bold," he outlined a "Gateway to the West," a concrete memorial arch spanning 1,200 feet and rising to a height of 240 feet, connected directly with two buildings used for museum and interpretive purposes (fig. 6.14). Electric cars and a pedestrian path would follow the curve of the arch and permit visitors to survey the surrounding countryside while passing by murals, maps, dioramas, and exhibits related to the pertinent history of the site and westward expansion. The proposed arch nicely fit Spotts's vision of drawing vacationers interested in recreation and sightseeing into a memorable engagement with history. He presented the arch as "nothing more than a stunt." But he had a broad definition of monumental stunts. He insisted that memorials such as the Washington Monument, the Statue of Liberty, and Mount Rushmore "are in themselves hardly more than stunts, but stunts if successful in time become landmarks and ripen into traditions." Spotts pointed to the arch as "practical and feasible" and "an inspirational and appropriate memorial . . . representative of the Gateway to the West; . . . a symbol of strength, progress and expansion . . . representative of the arts, architecture, et cetera." Although Spotts declared that he would not publicly advocate or promote such an idea, he did admit to having "considerable fun in delving into the possibilities" and argued that if such a plan was "forced" on the Park Service he felt that it could be taken "seriously." Spotts's colleague Ned J. Burns, chief of the Park Service's Museum Division, responded that, "a glorified beer garden under the largest arch in the world will appeal to many elements in the Corn Belt."[71]

There is no evidence that the proposal Spotts outlined in 1945 for a grand arch influenced the design of the winning entry in the Memorial Association's national competition for the Jefferson Memorial. Nevertheless, Eero Saarinen's 1947–1948 design for a colossal stainless-steel arch clearly appealed to those judging the competition; those who hailed from the Corn Belt joined those who did not in giving Saarinen's design their unanimous support. The noted Philadelphia modern architect George Howe, designer of the International Style PSFS Building in that city, served as professional advisor for the architectural competition sponsored by the Jefferson National Expansion Memorial Association.[72] The association raised $225,000 in private contributions to support the competition but could not guarantee those entering the competition that the government would actually build the memorial. The competition prospectus, several drafts of which the Park Service commented on, subtly tipped the thinking and designs for the Jefferson Memorial back toward monumentality. The purpose of the memorial touched the interests of those concerned with both the past and the present. The prospectus declared that the memorial was "not only to commemorate the past but also, and especially, to keep alive in the present and in the future the daring and untrammeled spirit that inspired Thomas Jefferson and his aides to offer men of all nations new opportunities under democracy by consummating the Louisiana Purchase."[73] The jury for the competition included Herbert Hare, Fiske Kimball, Louis LaBeaume, Charles Nagel, Jr., Richard Neutra, Roland Wank, and William Wurster. Their selection of

Saarinen's plan was unanimous and put the National Park Service on course as the client of an "audacious," monumental, modern design, built to celebrate history.[74]

To the extent that framers of the competition sought to boost "new opportunities," they were willing to countenance departures from the Park Service's more curatorial attitude toward the site's historical remains. Competition rules required preservation of the old courthouse and cathedral. However, the preservation of the Old Rock House, although considered "desirable," was not made mandatory. Similarly, historic markers, existing streets, and the topography itself could be modified or eliminated as competitors saw fit. If they wished to provide a Williamsburg-like site for the reerection or reproduction of a group of five buildings, typical of early St. Louis, they could do so. The competition prospectus also called for an educational complex, dedicated to "interpreting the historical significance of the site of Old St. Louis, the Louisiana Purchase, and westward expansion, as well as an area displaying architectural remains. Beyond these requirements and their own actual memorial designs, competitors were encouraged to offer ideas and plans for activity programs that would help recall and interpret the past as a "living Memorial" to Jefferson.[75]

In outlining his monumental intentions for the St. Louis memorial, Eero Saarinen and his critical proponents argued the case for "the pure monument" as opposed to a more "utilitarian" living memorial. Saarinen felt that structures like the Lincoln and Washington monuments in Washington, D.C. and his proposed monument for St. Louis possessed tremendous possibilities for "reminding us of the great past, which is so important in relation to looking toward the future."[76] The monument, with its technical audacity and display of modern materials, captured by design some of the aspirations of St. Louis boosters for the present and future as well as for the commemoration of the past. The *St. Louis Star-Times* viewed the architecture as akin to frozen music, "a trumpet blast, sharp and simply dramatic . . . calling St. Louis to a new, unfettered advance. . . . Through the gateway St. Louis can, if it will, go on to a better future." In the Saarinen memorial plan "old and new [would] become clearly one."[77]

The presentation and critical reception of Saarinen's design assumed a place in contemporary debates over the place of monuments and Modernism, over the claims of pure versus living memorials.[78] Saarinen's interest in the power of his "pure" monument to do the work of commemoration revealed an architectural formalism and drew upon what historian William Graebner has termed the "politics and aesthetics of demolition" shared by many architects in the 1930s and 1940s. Nev-

6.15. St. Louis Gateway Arch, Jefferson National Expansion Memorial, built 1961–1966. Eero Saarinen, architect. Photograph by Jack Boucher, 1986. Library of Congress.

ertheless, the design's formalism shared a good deal in common with ideas of earlier St. Louis preservation advocates who aimed to preserve isolated buildings and building fragments on the memorial site based on their aesthetic and technical form as opposed to their associational character. Even so, Saarinen's arch was not "pure" or isolated in its commemorative power (fig. 6.15). Its physical and iconographic context helped bridge architectural purity and political ideology. The design resonated with the familiar associations of tradi-

tional commemorative arches; it derived further public and commemorative meaning from its axial framing of the conventional civic forms of the old courthouse, and its civic "stunt," as Spotts would have pointed out, relied upon an expansive museum complex to construct and confer the meaning of St. Louis history, now reinforced by the appellation of the "Gateway to the West." Some of that case was already made by the exhibitions on display in the courthouse. In fact, these displays carried the burden of history and interpretation on the St. Louis river-

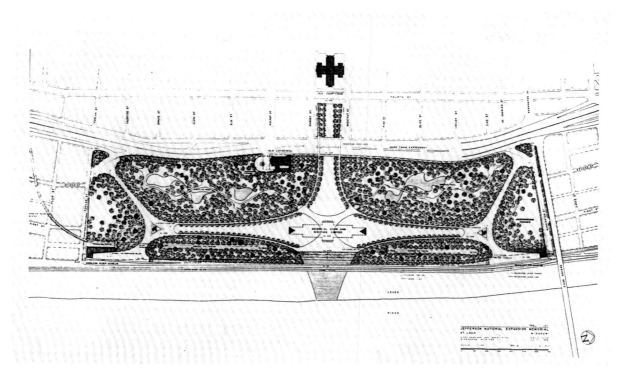

6.16. *Final site plan for Gateway Arch. Dan Kiley,*
landscape architect; Eero Saarinen, architect, 1957.
Jefferson National Expansion Memorial.

front during a decade of delay, while proponents settled a dispute over the removal of an elevated train line on the site and convinced Congress and the president to fund construction of the Jefferson Memorial according to Saarinen's plans. Further funding and construction delays put off the completion of the arch until 1968. As was befitting of its basically nationalist intentions, the Museum of Westward Expansion opened in 1976 at the height of the enthusiasm for both local and national history occasioned by the Bicentennial celebration.

Far from being a "pure" monument, the Jefferson National Expansion Memorial relied, as had always been the plan, on buttressing from a narrative of national history. Saarinen's initial plan, worked out in close collaboration with landscape architect Dan Kiley, sought to open a view between the memorial and the Mississippi River, to clarify the significance of the river system in westward expansion. Kiley's initial landscape plan also set aside the historic street grid in favor of a forested park. Here, Kiley sought to poetically link visitors with the historical experience of pioneers moving across a forest zone in a western prairie landscape (fig. 6.16).[79] The extraordinary popularity of the monumental arch strongly reinforced the historical narrative that had remained quite constant over the more than four decades between the conception and the completion of

the memorial. Few people who have visited the Jefferson Memorial would argue that the history of territorial acquisition and westward expansion could have been evoked much more creditably if several cast-iron commercial buildings, or the 1850s federal building, or an entire nineteenth-century industrial and commercial district stood in the place of the Saarinen arch. Saarinen's original plan included the Old Rock House as an entrance to the arch's internal transport system. It also provided space for a colonial village and a museum of architecture. Such displays of traditional architectural elements were expected to heighten the historical interpretation. Beyond these elements it is possible in retrospect to see that all the structures proposed for preservation could have stood in the Saarinen plan without compromising the design's monumental intentions; these structures could not have easily "crowded" the 630-foot-high arch. Nevertheless, as the project moved toward construction, the colonial village and the museum of architecture were dropped, and relocation of the elevated riverfront railroad track into a tunnel, running across the memorial site, led to the dismantling of the Old Rock House. Still, people learned history, or at least one version of it, on the grounds of the memorial. The success of Saarinen's design in playing a vital part in this national narrative represented both a confirmation of and a challenge to the preservationists' belief in the power of architecture to convey history. Looking back nearly six decades, Charles E. Peterson concluded: "The end result was an almost total defeat for the cause of historic preservation. However, on the positive side, Saarinen's arch is not only one of the most recognized monuments in the country; it is listed in the National Register of Historic Places."[80] As he had admired earlier cast-iron structures for their form and structure, Peterson seemed especially moved by these aspects of Saarinen's design. Nevertheless, the monument also confirmed the power of architecture to dramatize and make more memorable the resonance of history attendant to the place. The monument challenged preservation ideals because in St. Louis the architecture that reinforced the historic vision of the memorial's builders was not historic architecture. The fact that claims for preservation based on aesthetic and structural character had proved so ineffective should perhaps have stirred more critical debate among preservationists about what histories the movement could usefully invoke to put the preservation of the historic landscape on a stronger foundation. However, the development of such a national debate required a gestation period nearly as long as that needed for the realization of the Jefferson National Expansion Memorial itself.

The Monument as an Object of Preservation

It is now clear that the Jefferson National Expansion Memorial has both successfully commemorated national history and become a treasured local icon shaping St. Louis's urban identity and its modern economy. Despite its relative youth, in 1987 the arch became the thirty-second Missouri site entered on the National Historic Landmarks list.[81] In 2008 as the arch turned forty, an old debate again flared around the question of protecting historic architectural character within the bounds of the memorial site. Some prominent St. Louis residents, led by the former United States senator, diplomat, and philanthropist John Danforth, sought to transform the riverfront into a "world-class destination," introducing a "major new destination attraction to complement the Arch, such as a museum or cultural facility."[82] Willing to dedicate tens of millions of dollars of his family fortune toward the project, Danforth hoped to change what he viewed as the "disgraceful" condition of the memorial grounds. Danforth turned on its head the logic that had guided those earlier monument builders, who had viewed the absence of buildings on the site as an important means of giving the memorial a dignified monumental isolation

from the rest of the city; Danforth argued that "you cannot have this great treasure—that's the Arch—and surround it by junk. The highway is junk. The riverfront is junk. The grounds of the Arch are zilch. There is nothing there." Danforth and his allies now want to enrich the experience of people visiting St. Louis and the Jefferson National Expansion Memorial by adding a major new building and, in doing so, lengthening the time that tourists and visitors spend in St. Louis.[83] The National Park Service has responded to these proposals by insisting on its responsibility to protect the significant, and now historic, architectural and landscape character of the monument and its grounds. The Park Service views the Kiley landscape as an integral part of the Saarinen design. The Park Service's determination to protect the historic integrity of the arch and the grounds parallels its earlier focus on national narratives. What is different is that now the design of the arch is itself considered a treasured element in a national narrative that has formal architectural qualities at its center. Charles Peterson's preservation advocacy, steeped in the formal and aesthetic character of local architecture, has now gained a credence that may help determine Park Service policy on its St. Louis site.

John Danforth sees the grounds as a forlorn, vacant, and desolate landscape that should be developed and improved. Hovering in the background of this recent preservation debate is the earlier concern for how the riverfront area could boost the fortunes of St. Louis. The ground for this common perspective shifted substantially between the 1930s and 2008. In 1930, St. Louis's population was 821,960. In 2000 after massive suburbanization, deindustrialization, and regional dispersal, St. Louis's population was only 348,189. Complaints about the openness, desolation, and lack of vitality of the memorial site echoed the assessment of the character of many other sections of St. Louis's commercial and residential landscape. Once again St. Louis leaders turned back to the site of St. Louis's founding to chart a course forward in difficult times. The advocates of the destination attraction have even come up with a political strategy for relieving the National Park Service of its stewardship commitment and seeming intransigence. Danforth would like to approach the United States Congress and have them remove the monument grounds from Park Service control, placing it in the hands of a local nonprofit entity that would likely be more willing to go along with development plans. Complex and competing ideas concerning the relationship between historic preservation, the future of the riverfront city, politics, and the control of land have again defined the terms of debate over development in this neighborhood.

CHAPTER SEVEN

Preservation and Destruction in Chicago

Narrating History While Building a City

Historic preservation represents a negotiation between the past and the future. If we occupied a stable and well-maintained world, without growth, development, or change, such negotiation would be unlikely. Historic preservation would be pervasive as an ethic and unnecessary as an actual practice. During the nineteenth and twentieth centuries, the United States provided a prospect of seemingly endless architectural and landscape change. Preservation came to mediate between existing buildings and landscapes and competing visions for those same places. This was particularly the case in rapidly developing cities. Individuals, communities, and institutions had to grapple with what history, what buildings and landscapes would be preserved? What role would these places and their histories play in the ongoing development of the city? At the same time, preservationists confronted the skeptical question of why they wanted to preserve anything at all? At times historic preservation seemed to frustrate new development. At other times preservation seemingly eased the way toward modern transformations by saving a familiar and comforting token of the past in the context of relentless forward movement. In either case historic preservation assumed a role in the ongoing structuring of the urban landscape. As preservation's ideals and practices shifted, key aspects of city form changed. This chapter explores historic preservation in Chicago, a city where phenomenal growth repeatedly and poignantly forced questions of preservation and destruction into public consciousness. Chicago developed a fairly sophisticated architectural culture that merged history, preservation, modern architecture, and modern urbanism together in complex and at times unexpected ways.

Between 1840 and 1860 the population of Chicago increased from 4,470 to 112,172 (fig. 7.1). The city leapt from ninety-second place to ninth place among the largest cities in the United States. Change proved to be one of the few constants for the city's architecture, landscape, and economy. Residents and boosters felt they were participating in the making of a place destined for greatness; in 1890, Chicago's 1 million residents made the city the second-largest in the United States. Present possibilities and future prospects dominated public attention. Indeed, it struck some observers as a bit strange when in 1856 leading citizens established the Chicago Historical Society, committed to "the preservation of the early history" of a city that was barely twenty-five years old; a "safe depository" for historical materials would help ensure the "memory" of "pioneer history."[1] Besides the history that might flow from the archives, some people believed that old buildings and landscapes could also preserve memory, helping to link the past and the future. A century after the founding of the Historical Society, the Chicago City Council established the Commission on Chicago Architectural Landmarks, providing the institutional foundation for Chicago's modern preservation movement. Over the course of that century residents had often grappled with the potential of buildings to capture aspects of Chicago history as part of its modern development.

Such efforts marked the two decades following World War II, the decades in which Chicago leaders explored the public legal basis for historic preservation. At this time an extraordinary coalition between two unlikely partners supported Chicago preservation. Preservationists, committed to preserving a sense of place, received

CHICAGO IN 1845, FROM THE WEST.

*7.1. View of Chicago skyline in 1845. Moss
Engraving Company, 1884.* From Alfred T.
Andreas, *History of Chicago, from the Earliest Period
to the Present Time* (Chicago, 1884–1886).

support from Modern architects and civic leaders committed to a massive rebuilding of the city, with all of its
attendant destruction. The work of this coalition does
not conform to the standard surveys of the history of
historic preservation, which portray modern historic
preservation as emerging in direct opposition to federal urban renewal programs with their "widespread
obliteration of visual landmarks."[2] With preservation
and renewal often working in partnership, the Chicago
case suggests the need for a more nuanced reading of
preservation history.[3] In Chicago, engagements with
the past moved from sites associated with particular
social and cultural histories to sites reflecting particular
architectural aesthetics. At the heart of this transformation stood the academic and popular construction of the
Chicago School of Architecture narrative that served as
the basis for a coalition between preservationists and
modern developers. The Chicago School construct supported only a modest preservation program, limited to
scattered buildings on individual lots, in what turned out
to be the most destructive period in Chicago since the
1871 fire.[4] The narrow focus on monuments comporting
with the Chicago School narrative was later eclipsed by
a more diverse preservation ethic reflecting the priorities of a host of neighborhood residents and activists.

Old Landmarks, New Buildings,
and the Aesthetics of Eclipse

In 1855, the year before the founding of the Chicago Historical Society, the *Chicago Tribune* noted the passing of

"one of the old landmarks of Chicago in its infancy—*a
log house*." Replaced by a "fine block" of LaSalle Street
stores, the log house, perhaps twenty-five years old, had
kept alive a history of "early life when 'roughing it' was
the order of the day." In losing a valuable "memento of
olden time, and of the unparalleled growth of the Garden
City," Chicago residents and visitors might lose touch
with the city's history. Having "held its own manfully
against the airs and pretensions of its yearly increasing neighbors, with their new fangled architectural and
city notions," the log house was now gone.[5] The sense
of loss seemed twofold and not entirely consistent. On
the one hand, there was wistful nostalgia for a simpler
and less pretentious time. On the other hand, the *Tribune* bemoaned lost evidence of Chicago's "unparalleled
growth." That concern had nothing to do with nostalgia.
It had everything to do with losing a symbol capable
of inspiring confidence in potential settlers and inves-
tors—people who would be impressed to see that the
city had grown so quickly, and so prosperously, that log
houses that had seemed adequate only a few decades
earlier now stood next to fine stores. Similarly, in 1906
the *Tribune* noted the disappearance of 1870s downtown
business blocks. These "interesting landmarks" were
notable not only because of the "history which attaches
to them" but also because "they mark in a striking manner the remarkable evolution which Chicago has undergone."[6] This juxtaposition of old and new constituted
something of an aesthetic of eclipse, encouraging further investment in modern development. Old buildings
became the foil for new or proposed buildings.

In the late 1860s some Chicagoans worried that in

"rapidly outgrowing her youth" Chicago's landmarks, although only thirty-five years old, were being "obliterated and forgotten."[7] The crisis seemed more pressing after the 1871 fire destroyed a huge swath of Chicago, including almost the entire downtown. This was apparent with the 1875 destruction of a large 1840s frame building on the West Side that had variously served as a hotel for people driving stock to the city stockyard, a boardinghouse, and as a sanatorium for treating alcoholics. Upon its demolition, the *Tribune* reported, "there is an impressive dignity about an old house. . . . Antiquity excites our veneration. . . . It is a landmark of the city's progress . . . and furnishes a starting-point, as it were, from which to measure the growth it has attained. . . . They are a relief from contemplation of everlasting change, and the ruddy, staring newness of everything; and the mind that turns to them is refreshed." The ambiguous role of the landmark persisted. It simultaneously inspired critical reflection on the shallowness of modern speculation and materialism while also providing a starting point for proudly measuring, and perhaps contributing to, the upbuilding of the city.[8]

People understood early in Chicago's history that landmarks could literally narrate stories, linking the past and the present to the future. Still, they worried that the city's zealousness in business could actually tear asunder any sense of connection to, or community with, the past. In the year after the 1871 Chicago fire, city officials expanded Lincoln Park by removing the remains of 10,000 people from the old City Cemetery. The *Tribune* noted that "the remnants of the old city" were disappearing. "One by one the old landmarks fall under the sacrilegious hand of progress, and are obliterated from the mind and vision." Removing graves was especially unsettling because they provided "one of the few remaining links connecting the early history of the city with the Chicago of to-day . . . . There are memories clustered around this old spot too sacred to be disturbed by the hand of the invader . . . . But idealism, in the present day, must make way for materialism."[9] Old buildings and landscapes did reflect "memories"; the question remained what would happen when landmarks disappeared. Generations of Chicagoans confronted this issue as the city developed.

From Bemoaning Loss to Preserving Landmarks: The Water Tower and the Treaty Elm

In Chicago nineteenth- and early-twentieth-century concern over the disappearance of landmarks rarely prompted calls for the actual preservation of buildings. This was especially the case when preservation would have frustrated private plans for modern development. A 1906 article noting the passing of downtown's postfire buildings had the headline "Landmarks Yield to Skyscrapers."[10] Commerce, materialism, and the prerogatives of private property seemingly carried the day. However, when it came to some publicly owned landmarks, turn-of-the-century Chicagoans did actively campaign for preservation. Perhaps the most sustained early preservation crusade centered on the Water Tower and Pumping Station at Michigan Avenue and Chicago Avenue. Designed in the late 1860s by William W. Boyington, the 154-foot castellated Victorian Gothic–style Water Tower monumentalized the innovative engineering system that brought water from Lake Michigan and distributed it to households and businesses (fig. 7.2). Despite massive neighborhood destruction, the Water Tower and the walls of the Pumping Station survived the 1871 fire.[11]

In the first decade of the twentieth century, the city installed new pumps in the Chicago Avenue plant. The

7.2. *Chicago Water Tower and Pumping Station, built 1866–1869. William W. Boyington, architect.* Photograph, c. 1964. Library of Congress.

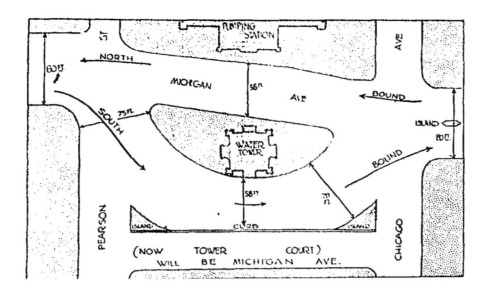

Water Tower lost its historic function of equalizing water pressure. Moving in new equipment would involve the demolition of one of the main façades of the Pumping Station. City engineers announced plans to replace the Victorian Gothic façade with a new exterior of modern design. They also proposed the demolition of the obsolete Water Tower. These plans provoked public outrage. Members of the Chicago Historical Society launched "long and emphatic" protests. This was, after all, one of the most prominent buildings to survive the Great Chicago Fire. Here, Chicago residents and visitors throughout the late nineteenth century climbed the narrow stairs and took in extended views of the city and the lake. The *Chicago Tribune* editorialized in favor of preserving the forty-year-old structure, "the most distinctive and the most venerable landmark remaining in the city." The paper insisted that "about this tower have clustered many associations. . . . The old water tower is picturesque, esthetically worthy, and associated strikingly in our memories with our thought of home." For the *Tribune* more was at stake here than simple comfort or nostalgia. The *Tribune* challenged the city engineers' notion that the tower was not "useful." Part of Chicago's claim to greatness as "a center of civilization" now turned not simply on its wealth or growth but on its ability to transcend such narrow concerns and to cultivate memory and history and beauty.[12] With preservationists clamoring for a different course, Chicago embarked on an ambitious preservation project. In 1910 the stones of the Pumping Station were numbered and removed one by one; after improvements were completed, the façade was reconstructed according to its original form. In 1911 the threat to the Water Tower ended when the City

Council made a substantial appropriation to stabilize and preserve it. This commitment continued for decades. For example, in 1926 the city rejected calls to remove the traffic "bottleneck" posed by the Water Tower. The city instead widened Michigan Avenue, locating the automobile lanes on either side of the water tower, surrendering the park areas adjacent to the tower and the old pumping station but carefully preserving the structures (fig. 7.3).[13]

In 1928 preservationists again confronted Chicago engineers and advocated for landmarks over municipal efficiency. The object of interest was an old elm tree occupying the intersection of Rogers, Caldwell, and Kilbourn avenues (fig. 7.4). Oral tradition suggested that the tree marked the northwest corner of the Fort Dearborn Reservation, ceded to the United States in 1816. The elm was also thought to be the place where Billy Caldwell (Chief Sauganash) gathered with members of the Potawatomi tribe after the ratification of the 1833 Treaty of Chicago. Having ceded the last of their tribal land in Illinois, Wisconsin, and Michigan, they set out for Council Bluffs, Iowa, and lands west of the Mississippi. Reporting on improvement plans, the *Tribune* declared, "The crew of pavers will come with their axes and their tar wagons. A hundred strokes of the ax, a crash—and good-by Treaty Elm forever." Preservationists called the Treaty Elm "Chicago's most vivid memento of its beginning" and the "stateliest of its historic treasures." The City Council barred the destruction of the tree. The Illinois Federation of Women's Clubs offered to donate an ornamental fence. Palmer School students made a special pilgrimage to the tree. Tree surgeons worked to extend the tree's life.[14]

7.4. *Treaty Elm located in the intersection of Rogers, Caldwell, and Kilbourn avenues, Chicago. Photograph, c. 1928.* Reprinted with permission of the *Chicago Tribune*, copyright *Chicago Tribune*; all rights reserved.

play advertisements promoting Sauganash: "If you will drive out to Sauganash . . . you can accomplish two things. You can see Chicago's most historic tree and inspect the city's most beautiful home development. When you look at the wooded lots of Sauganash, you will readily understand why the Indians under Chief Sauganash in 1835 were loath to push farther westward. Where stood the tepees of the red men 100 years ago now rise beautiful homes of wood, of brick and of stone surrounded by scenes of natural beauty." The advertisement's image captured the contemporary version of the aesthetic of eclipse; Native Americans sat under the elm with tepees close at hand while the image of a 1920s suburban home floated above in the smoke rising from the campfire (fig. 7.5). The supposed simplicity of earlier life, the harmony

The *Rock Island Argus* editorialized that the campaign to save the Treaty Elm would reveal whether "Chicago, supposedly given over to materialism, cares enough for its past to save this memento."[15] This case, however, was not so neatly parsed out between commerce and culture. People visiting the Treaty Elm, with its connections to historic land transactions, could, in the 1920s, hardly overlook a more modern form of land transaction. In 1924, on a site adjacent to the Treaty Elm, developers Koester & Zander started a 250-acre "high class" neighborhood of "distinctive residences" named "Sauganash in the Woods." It included a model street where eighteen different architects designed thirty-two different houses. The developers told prospective buyers that they didn't "have to live in humdrum, common place looking houses, similar in nearly every respect to their neighbors homes."[16] The Treaty Elm permitted the developers to buttress the premium placed upon distinction by capitalizing on a unique historic feature in the neighborhood. George F. Koester, Jr., became the leading advocate for protecting the Treaty Elm.[17]

In the midst of the campaign to preserve the Treaty Elm, George Koester began to feature the tree in his dis-

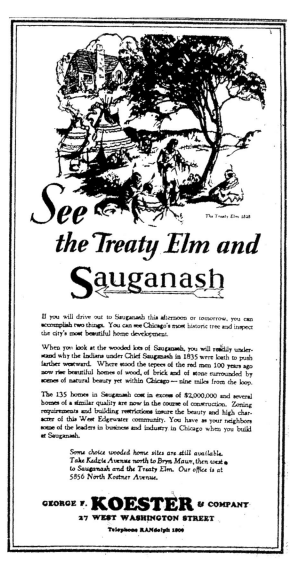

7.5. *Treaty Elm featured in Koester & Company real estate advertisement for Sauganash. Advertisement, c. 1928.* Library of Congress.

of living in nature, the refinement of attending to history, were all pressed into the service of a powerful commercial image of modern suburban living.[18] As Sauganash grew, the Treaty Elm slowly died, despite the efforts of tree surgeons to prolong its life (fig. 7.6); city crews cut down the dead tree in April 1935.[19]

Marking History:
Bronze Textbooks and Centennial Pageants

The Treaty Elm again entered civic discourse in Chicago in 1937. As part of Chicago's 1937 Charter Jubilee celebration, the Treaty Elm site received a bronze historical marker. The Jubilee celebrated the centennial of the incorporation of the City of Chicago by the state legislature. Historic recognitions loomed large during centennial events. As Mayor Edward J. Kelly declared, "the youngest of the great cities of the world, Chicago is nevertheless rich in sites where stirring historical events took place. . . . [T]hese historic sites should be identified and fixed for posterity with suitable plaques and markers. . . . A veritable textbook in bronze, . . . and a permanent memento of this eventful Centennial year."[20] The Jubilee landmarks stand in striking contrast with the landmarks that historic preservation advocates focused upon after World War II. As in the case of other earlier recognitions of local landmarks, the Charter Jubilee combined reflection on Chicago history with an effort to build and develop the city. In 1936, in the depths of the Depression, Mayor Kelly proposed the celebration hoping to spur both "civic patriotism" and "commercial benefits."[21] Lasting from March 4 to October 9, 1937, the Jubilee included a Melting Pot Pageant that attracted over 20,000 people to Chicago Stadium to watch as 1,000 people enacted the drama of different races and nationalities moving to Chicago and becoming Chicagoans. The opening pageant and other Jubilee activities were meant to capture Chicago's spirit of "I Will" and "It Can Be Done." Among its events the Jubilee included a grand homecoming celebration, a major exhibition at the Chicago Historical Society covering one hundred years of Chicago fashion, the dedication of Chicago's Outer Drive Bridge by President Roosevelt, and a great dramatic spectacle, "Light of Ages," staged by the Chicago Civic Opera. The city designated nineteen different weeks for weeklong neighborhood celebrations, with local parades, carnivals, athletic contests, festivals, civic celebrations, and dramatic entertainments.[22]

The Charter Jubilee inspired a fair amount of historical reflection on the events of Chicago history. Charles B. Pike, president of the Chicago Historical Society, headed

7.6. *Tree surgeons working to save the Treaty Elm from disease.* Photograph, 1929. Reprinted with permission of the *Chicago Tribune*, copyright *Chicago Tribune*; all rights reserved.

the Jubilee Historical Committee and refined the list of sites to receive bronze plaques. This project expanded upon earlier efforts by the Historical Society to emulate London and other European cities by marking historic sites. Historical Society officials viewed their markers as a way to inspire a deeper love of the city, to educate residents, to create "a valuable auxiliary" of historical society and museum collections, and, most important, to "popularize the history and bring it home to the greatest number." By 1899 the society had already participated in marking the sites of Fort Dearborn, the "massacre" of early settlers by Native Americans, and the site where the 1871 Chicago Fire began. It also aimed at that time to mark the home site of John Kinzie, an early settler, the Sauganash Tavern, and the northern limits of the Chicago fire.[23] The marking of these sites actually awaited the Charter Jubilee.

The Charter Jubilee Historical Committee thought primarily along the lines of associational history. Beyond the hope of inspiring civic patriotism, planners hoped that a system of well-marked historic sites would encourage visitors to spend more time and money in Chicago.[24] The Jubilee Historical Committee failed to identify architecture, in and of itself, as part of its "enduring record" of Chicago history. They placed historical markers at the locations of the first Chicago churches

7.7. Henry B. Clarke House, built 1836, said to be the oldest surviving building in Chicago. Photograph by Albert J. DeLong, 1935. Library of Congress.

of various religious denominations, of early taverns, roads, bridges, hotels, schools, post offices, theaters, and homes of early settlers, the first cattle market and the Union Stock Yards, the first places associated with Lincoln's family, and at the site of Mrs. O'Leary's barn, where the 1871 Chicago fire started. Marking seventy-three historic sites in all, the designation program relied strongly upon the historic resonances of place, since in most cases the original structures had been demolished or destroyed in the 1871 fire. Places recognized for their architecture were in most cases buttressed by historical associations. The 1836 Henry B. Clarke House was designated as the oldest surviving house in Chicago (fig. 7.7). In a city that had enjoyed a reputation as an early pioneer in skyscraper construction, the historical committee referred to skyscrapers only once, in the designation of the Lind Block, a 90-foot-tall building constructed in the 1860s, "one of Chicago's first 'Skyscrapers,'" but the plaque text noted the additional significance that the Lind Block was one of the few buildings in downtown Chicago to survive the fire. Similarly, the Chicago Avenue Water Tower was marked. A plaque identifying the block where the home of the first mayor of Chicago was located informed the curious that the house was the first one in the city designed by an architect; however, the plaque failed to record for posterity the architect's name. Three sites related to Billy Caldwell (Chief Sauganash) were marked; they included the Treaty Elm, the site of Caldwell's home, and the site of one of Chicago's earliest hotels, named the Sauganash.[25]

"On this site" was the most common opening for the Charter Jubilee markers. Mayor Kelly's "textbook in

bronze" provided site narratives for a storied landscape that generally lacked actual physical traces of the history being recalled. In this sense the textbook lacked illustrations. On March 4, 1937, when Mayor Kelly opened the Charter Jubilee celebration, he gaveled the assembly to order using the gavel of Mayor William B. Ogden, Chicago's first mayor to serve under the charter form of government. The gavel represented just the sort of important physical connection to the past that was missing from so many of the sites given bronze markers. The markers offered a particularly convenient way to have both history and unfettered modern redevelopment. At the opening assembly of the Jubilee, Mayor Kelly declared, "As we honor the past, we think of the future."[26] In the years leading up to the ambitious celebration of Chicago history in the Charter Jubilee, the *Tribune* observed that

> only from the roots of the past come the flower and fruitage of the future." Anticipating the rhetorical claims of the Jubilee, the editors insisted that, although still young, Chicago had a history that "has touched the imagination of the world. . . . Out of this memory and this consciousness of its heritage a community creates personality, civil character, and unity of purpose; creates, in short, something stronger and higher than a mere aggregation of people and individual activities, becomes a city.[27]

This sense of the possibilities and limitations of a storied landscape changed rather drastically as a narrative of architectural history came increasingly to define Chicago landmarks after World War II.

"Chicago School" in Architecture and Preservation

After World War II the focus of Chicago historic preservation shifted from the historic associations of sites to the architectural aesthetics of particular buildings. In this transition the critical and historiographical concept of the Chicago School of Architecture assumed great significance. It provided a common ground between preservationists and Modernists. To chart the development of Chicago historic preservation in the decades following the 1937 Charter Jubilee, it is necessary to come to terms with the development and popularization of the idea of a Chicago School, considering in particular the power and utility it offered in the face of post–World War II urban challenges. Beyond that we will survey the ways in which commitments to particular visions of historic significance framed key preservation campaigns after World War II.

In scrutinizing these developments it is important to understand that historians have recently expressed skepticism about whether a unified and definable "Chicago School" of architecture actually existed.[28] There is little evidence that the architects of late-nineteenth-century Chicago skyscrapers conceived of themselves or worked as a school self-consciously attempting to create a modern, structurally expressive style that eschewed formal connections to the traditions of architectural expression. One of the earliest chroniclers of their work, the anonymous editors of *Industrial Chicago*, argued that the "commercial style" was "largely technic." They wrote, "A gigantic skeleton or box structure of steel is ornamented with columns, pilasters, piers, capitals, band-courses, arches, panellings, gables, moldings, etc., gathered from every nation of the earth and from every chronological cycle." In the 1890s many critics clearly considered the style eclectic. Skeleton construction and predominant height more than a shared style characterized the early Chicago skyscrapers.[29] Yet despite the elusiveness and imprecision of the overall concept, the idea of a distinct Chicago School did gain some currency among historians and provided the foundation of a new preservation vision.

The term "Chicago School" first appeared around the turn of the century in reference to literature. In 1925, H. L. Mencken noted the city's literary ferment even as he marked the "passing of the Chicago school. . . . At least half of the new authors of any genuine force and originality who appeared between 1895 and 1920 had some sort of relation to the Gomorrah on the lake. . . . The town attracted revolutionists in all the arts and it somehow helped them to realize their dreams."[30] "Chi-

cago School" as applied to economics, particularly the advocacy of unregulated markets and limited government, did not emerge until the 1940s and 1950s, tied in particular to economic training at the University of Chicago.[31] People who applied "Chicago School" to architecture used it with imprecision, often in relation to domestic architecture. They did maintain some notion that the architectural work, like the literary work, was the product of artistic radicals. Thus, in 1912 when the poet, architectural writer, and biographer of John W. Root, Harriet Monroe, commended Walter Burley Griffin's first prize in the competition for a plan for a new capital city in Australia, she insisted that Griffin had "scored a point for the 'Chicago school' of architecture." Noting the relationship between Griffin, Wright, and Sullivan, Monroe wrote that for these men "the historic schools and classic order of architecture are not responsive to modern need or expressive of the modern art impulse, [and they] have abandoned all the old lines and ornaments."[32] In 1914 architect George W. Maher felt that residential architecture may well prove to be the foundation of a "distinctive Chicago school of architecture. . . . It will be indigenous to the extent that it will be truly American."[33] In 1938, Maher and his modern colleagues were viewed as "radicals who seceded vigorously from the imitative traditions, and . . . borrowed nothing from ancient European models. They were 'the Chicago school.'"[34] The vision of a "Chicago School" gained power in the 1920s and 1930s with growing interest in Modern architecture. University lectures, critical and scholarly writing, and museum exhibitions fostered the idea.[35] The idea gained broader currency outside of the academy when business leaders, politicians, and preservationists seized upon it as a useful history in the troubled years after World War II.

The Museum of Modern Art's 1933 display of thirty three photographs, in an exhibition titled "Early Modern Architecture, Chicago 1870–1910," laid the groundwork for the canonization of the Chicago School concept in the 1930s. The Modern's typescript catalog and the text on each photograph narrowed the interpretation of significant Chicago architecture to focus primarily on skyscrapers. The catalog surveyed the technical and aesthetic development of the skyscraper, then set out a Chicago School trajectory that linked Richardson to Sullivan to Wright, creating a "free non-traditional architecture" that ended in 1910, as the revivalism of the "World's Fair of 1893, vitiated its force."[36] This narrative also played locally when in 1933 the Museum of Modern Art exhibition opened at the furniture galleries of Chicago's Marshall Field & Company.[37]

The Museum of Modern Art exhibition suggested not

*7.8. The domed Pulitzer Building, built 1890.
George B. Post, architect. New York City Hall
stands in the foreground.* Photograph, c. 1900.
Postcard in author's collection.

only that there was a school but also that there was a
"Chicago formula of skyscraper design." To underscore
the point the exhibition included George B. Post's domed
Pulitzer skyscraper (fig. 7.8) in New York (1889)—"progressive neither in structure or design." In contrasting
Chicago with the East, the "Early Modern" exhibition
distorted Chicago skyscraper history in which little
consensus on style or ornament or form existed except
in the production of single firms. Indeed, even at the
scholarly center of work on the Chicago School, considerable tentativeness persisted through the 1930s. Hugh
Morrison's 1935 book *Louis Sullivan, Prophet of Modern
Architecture*, insisted that "until the work of the Chicago
School is better known than it is at present . . . it will
be impossible to estimate correctly the real force and
character of Sullivan's direct practical influence in this
country."[38] Such hedging disappeared in the work of historians Sigfried Giedion and Carl Condit.[39] Their work in
turn provided "real force" when it came to deciding the
fate of Chicago's older buildings.

In the context of postwar urbanism, the Chicago
School construct operated both as a polemic concerning style and history and, perhaps more important, as

an ideology supporting the definition of the city and
its redevelopment. Although preservationists focused
more on the definition of the city and architects were
primarily concerned with redevelopment, both groups
shared a civic boosterism surrounding the idea of a
distinct Chicago architecture, existing in the past and
providing the basis for future building. Following World
War II, building interests confronted a socially and
economically troubled city. Aging buildings occupied
a landscape that had stagnated through a decade of
depression and a decade of war and dislocation. Despite
the full employment and prosperity of the war years, the
Chicago economy appeared threatened by decentraliza-
tion, suburbanization, and growing cities in the southern
and western United States. In 1950, Chicago's population reached its historical high of 3,620,962. In the next
two decades the population declined for the first time
ever, with the loss of more than a quarter of a million
residents by 1970. The city's industrial and commercial
preeminence slipped as well. Meatpacking, for example,
declined precipitously in the 1950s. In 1957, 3.6 million
animals were slaughtered in Chicago as opposed to 14.5
million in 1919. In 1959 when both Swift and Armour

announced the closing of their Chicago plants, *Newsweek* reported this development under the headline "The Shrinking Giant."[40]

The aspirations of nineteenth-century Chicago leaders toward primacy within the United States urban system disappeared in the twentieth century. After World War II the future seemed fraught with more dangers of decline than with boundless possibilities for growth. Adopting a racist urban vision, political and business leaders lamented the city's changing demography. The massive suburbanization of white residents was never balanced by the in-migration of poor African-Americans from the South attracted to the city's industrial jobs. Chicago's African-American population climbed from 278,000 in 1940 to 682,000 in 1956, from 8 percent of the population to 18 percent.[41]

Planning and redevelopment literature portrayed the residential neighborhoods where African-American residents came to reside, almost by definition, as slums. More troubling for Chicago leaders than the existence of slums was that they impinged on the downtown area (fig. 7.9). In an article titled "An Encroaching Menace," *Life* magazine reported, "The slums of Chicago each year have pushed closer to the heart of the city. Some of the worst come only six blocks from the glittering skyscrapers. . . . [E]very month, new slums are being born."[42] Moreover, the downtown remained stagnant in the years immediately following World War II. In 1962, *Architectural Forum* reported that the "major reason why Chicago seemed not to be doing any building after World War II was that there was almost no activity in its aging central business area." The downtown area, which formerly projected images of boom times seemed "asleep" after World War II, "as dead as prohibition." Chicago's leaders appeared "especially defensive" as the city lagged far behind its traditional urban revival, New York City, in new postwar office construction.[43]

In the face of such difficulties, history and the Chicago School narrative seemed especially reassuring; by looking back, many builders in Chicago discovered hope for a more promising future. Earlier skyscrapers had seemingly testified to the city's commercial vitality. In the mid-1950s, as the city's leaders organized the Chicago Central Area Committee to promote massive redevelopment of the downtown, they invoked the name of the Chicago School to give them a sense of historic mission and even destiny.

Similarly, in 1957, history and boosterism pervaded the introduction of the new journal published by the Chicago Chapter of the American Institute of Architects. Titled *Inland Architect,* the journal assumed the name of the nineteenth-century Chicago journal that had

chronicled early skyscraper development. The journal explored the utility of invoking a Chicago School in the architectural and planning discourse of the 1950s. The cover of the first issue showed an etching of the portal of Sullivan's Transportation Building at the Columbian Exposition and a photograph of Harry Weese's apartment building at 227 Walton Street with its Chicago windows. "Chicago Builds 1893 and Today," read the caption. The journal's introduction recalled the "strength and stature," the "pioneering" work, and the "bold brash builders of the Chicago School." Deploying history in favor of present concerns, the journal continued, "We are always building and rebuilding a new city, a new region. . . . There is much more to do, to see, to create. And it is our heritage, our business, and our hope in ourselves to build and build better."[44] Invoking Sullivan, Burnham, Jenney, Root, and Adler, the editors offered more than reverie in past glories because they were looking to the future: "The spirit of the Chicago School was a powerful potential never yet wholly realized."[45]

Architects were not alone in having a lot to gain from a historically inspired effort at a postwar building boom. Nor did they stand alone in their enthusiasm for harnessing the Chicago School construct to help promote future building. One of the important crystallizing points for such an effort came in 1957 during Chicago Dynamic

7.9. *Cartoon depicting the perceived threat to downtown prosperity represented by Chicago's slums. Jacob Burck, cartoonist, 1953.* Chicago Sun-Times

Week, an event sponsored by U.S. Steel and other business groups. Mayor Daley proclaimed Chicago Dynamic week in August 1957, only a few weeks after clashes between blacks and whites in Calumet Park sparked one of the city's worst race riots in many years. Mayor Daley's proclamation further underscored the migration of the Chicago School narrative from academic and professional discourse into the public and political realm where preservation and development debates took place:

> WHEREAS, Chicago is the birthplace of American architecture, the curtain wall building, which ushered in the age of the skyscraper; and WHEREAS, Chicago today is concerned with the continued use of the newest building forms, materials and techniques to make Chicago a better place in which to live and work; and WHEREAS, the Chicago Dynamic Committee comprising our community's business and civic leaders has been organized to honor the sound building and far-sighted planning of Chicago, the world's most dynamic city . . . I Richard J. Daley, Mayor of the City of Chicago, do hereby proclaim the week of October 27 through November 2, as 'Chicago Dynamic Week.'

Edward C. Logelin, a vice president of the U.S. Steel Corporation and chair of the Chicago Dynamic Committee, insisted that the week would bring together people capable of recognizing the "possibilities" of the city, leaders capable of giving form and direction to the city's "billion-dollar rebuilding." Pointing to Chicago's "great architectural and building tradition," Logelin sought a continuum between past and present: "We have enormous talent, unused power, and we must begin to use

7.10. Frank Lloyd Wright (left) debates urban form and culture with Carl Sandburg (right) in a televised Chicago Dynamic Week event moderated by Alistair Cooke. Photograph, 1957. Chicago Sun-Times.

it now. We must think about our city building problems, about our creative, life-enriching, unknown art known as architecture, and keep doing something about it. For, as Sullivan said, 'Chicago can pull itself down and rebuild itself in a generation.'"[46]

When Chicago Dynamic Week arrived, reveling in history was more than rhetorical. The seventy-nine-year-old Carl Sandburg returned to chronicle Chicago's renaissance. Sandburg's earlier poetry had portrayed a tough, sprawling commercial and industrial city; in 1957 he obliged his sponsors by updating his earlier work. Chicago, said Sandburg, "has elements of toil, combat, risk taking chances, departing from the known into the unknown. In this spirit during an earlier Chicago Dynamic the skyscraper was born. Today's Chicago Dynamic has cut loose from old traditions and begun to make new ones. Yesterday's skyscrapers are overtowered by steel clad structures rising far taller and with ease and grace."[47] During the Chicago Dynamic Week, Frank Lloyd Wright debated Sandburg on issues ranging from the political character of Lincoln and Jefferson, to Sputnik, to skyscrapers and urban form (fig. 7.10). To the obvious discomfort of his hosts, Wright declared that skyscraper construction was "pushing the city to its end. They have no business in the city—they belong in the country where they can cast shadows on their own ground. Decentralize the entire affair and send people back to scenery."[48] He also ventured the opinion that "steel buildings are now dying of arthritis at the joints" and that "in another 15 years this city will be on its way out."[49] As if to rebuff Wright, participants in Chicago Dynamic week took part in a workshop on curtain-wall construction, placed Carl Sandburg's writing on Chicago in the cornerstone of the new, Modern-style Mutual Trust Building designed by Perkins & Will, and held a conference on the question "Can Good Architecture 'Pay Off'?"[50]

For Chicago's architects of Modern curtain-wall buildings, the Chicago Dynamic emphasis on local architectural heritage could steer new commissions to a circle of local firms, effectively barring competition from firms based in other cities. In Chicago, architects jockeyed for the mantle of the Chicago School. Historians and critics proved quite willing to construct a connection between local architects and the origins of Modernism. They established a clear lineage between the First and Second Chicago schools; they anointed Mies van der Rohe the proper heir of the Chicago School legacy. In 1963, architect George Danforth reported, "It seems natural that Mies should be asked to come here, because in his every work is the essence of the spirit of the Chicago School of architecture so long gone unrealized."[51]

7.11. Frederick C. Robie House, built 1908–1910. Frank Lloyd Wright, architect. The house was nearly demolished in 1957 to provide a site for a Chicago Theological Seminary dorm. Photograph by Cervin Robinson, 1963. Library of Congress.

Preserving the Robie House, Renewing Hyde Park, Listing Landmarks

In March 1957, prior to his participation in Chicago Dynamic Week, Frank Lloyd Wright had used a visit to Chicago to preserve and promote his own claim as the leader of Chicago Modernism. In doing so he fueled one of the first major preservation battles in 1950s Chicago. This came when the Chicago Theological Seminary, located in the Hyde Park neighborhood on the South Side of Chicago, announced plans to demolish Wright's 1908–1910 Frederick C. Robie House (fig. 7.11) to make way for a student dormitory. Wright visited the house and denounced the plans to the local press. He argued that the Robie was "a cornerstone of American architecture" and that "to wreck it would be like destroying a fine piece of sculpture or a beautiful painting."[52]

Wright found ready allies among local architects and residents of Hyde Park. A core of supporters came from a small group of people who had participated in some preliminary discussion of the "preservation of architecture wonders in Chicago" during 1956.[53] These people included Hyde Park resident Thomas B. Stauffer, a writer and a history and philosophy teacher in the city

college system, the Hyde Park independent alderman Leon Despres, and Chicago architects Leo Weissenborn and Earl Reed. Reed, chair of the national American Institute of Architects' Committee for the Preservation of Historic Buildings, argued that, as Wright's finest domestic design, the Robie's destruction would be a "great loss" to Chicago.[54] Chicago Modern architect and Hyde Park resident George Fred Keck also joined the campaign. Those advocating preservation did not seem mollified by the seminary's assertion that "an outstanding example" of contemporary architecture, designed by Holabird & Root, would take the place of the Robie house.[55] Initially, those interested in preservation aimed to move the house after the seminary offered to donate it to anyone who would take it. Despite the intervention of the National Trust for Historic Preservation, in its first campaign to save a twentieth-century structure, the Robie was nearly demolished in July. Various fundraising efforts lagged, and the future looked bleak until developer William Zeckendorf purchased the building and the lot for $125,000. Zeckendorf's firm of Webb & Knapp had recently joined the city in an ambitious urban renewal of the Hyde Park neighborhood, occupied in part by the Robie house and the University of Chicago.

Here, according to Zeckendorf, Chicago could have its history and its renewal, too. Zeckendorf's newspaper advertisement of its purchase put the issues succinctly, "Our Christmas Gift to Hyde Park, to Chicago, to Posterity: Robie House, Hyde Park's World Famous Monument. The Heritage of the Past. The Headquarters of the Future. Acting as Guardian of Great Architecture Webb & Knapp is purchasing Robie House to be used for their headquarters during the development of Hyde Park A and B."[56] The deal between Zeckendorf and the seminary hinged upon the willingness of the city to rezone a nearby parcel for the seminary to build its dormitory.[57]

A certain irony pervaded the embrace of history in the context of a local urban renewal project that involved the demolition of over 880 buildings in the Robie house neighborhood. But Zeckendorf's sense of history was shared a by large number of local residents. The Hyde Park–Kenwood Community Conference, a local citizens' group that had sought a major urban renewal program for the area, had in fact conducted a historical survey of all the buildings charted for demolition. It identified forty-three structures worth photographing, and with the help of the urban renewal agency it salvaged interior and exterior ornaments from about fifteen of them. The conference's survey committee could not identify any targeted structure worth preserving. The conference even endorsed the removal of "good" buildings because without such action "any urban renewal planning would be defeated."[58] The broader planning effort aimed to "preserve" the university's community as a viable middle-class housing area by demolishing the buildings

that housed poor, working-class, and largely African-American residents. The city planners, the University of Chicago, and the university's citizen allies in the conference supported Zeckendorf's plans in part because of his interest in using new low-rise construction to knit new and old together in a way uncharacteristic of other clean-sweep proposals like that of Herbert Greenwald, who had worked with Mies on earlier projects, and who envisioned Hyde Park redeveloped with high-rise structures surrounded by large open spaces.[59] In his rental brochure for the University Apartments, designed by I. M. Pei, Zeckendorf promised tenants that they would "discover the exciting architecture that has been created to provide an unusually sensitive blending of functional residential design within the traditional charm of Hyde Park."[60]

In Hyde Park there were large multiblock tracts and entire streetscapes demolished, yet in a departure from the urban renewal destruction of other neighborhoods, the Hyde Park plan conserved expansive sections of nineteenth- and early-twentieth-century urban fabric. The "patch work" of preserved blocks was carefully knit together with new construction. People in Hyde Park would be able to have "a kind of old world charm in a modern home" built in the midst of a neighborhood that "has decided to arrange itself for the future in a manner which does not deny the past."[61] The Robie house easily fit this pattern; however, the concern with the future of Hyde Park conspired to submerge most local histories. Viewing the landscape through a prism of class and race contributed to the devaluing of major sections of the neighborhood's architectural history. *Segments of the Past*, the conference's booklet on its survey project, addressed this sense of a departed history. It asserted that a "once gracious old mansion which has long since been converted into living quarters for thirty families . . . and which has not been maintained is no longer an asset, and usually has to be removed."[62] The idea that some history was no longer historic or worthy of chronicling or saving was common in Chicago. Considering the potential of Chicago landmarks in 1965, Ruth Moore, architecture critic for the *Chicago Sun-Times*, reported that "changing times, changing neighborhoods" had "all but destroyed the usefulness" of many landmarks.[63] Present use and changed neighborhoods should not necessarily block historic engagement with a structure, but in Chicago, in neighborhood after neighborhood, demographic change somehow pushed buildings beyond the reach and interest of many preservationists. In 1956 the Historic American Buildings Survey inventory form for Louis Sullivan's own house, located two blocks north of Hyde Park–Kenwood, reported under "Historical Signif-

7.12. Carson Pirie Scott department store, originally Schlesinger & Mayer, built 1899–1906. Louis H. Sullivan, original architect, with additions at the right by D. H. Burnham & Company and Holabird & Root. Photograph, c. 1915. Library of Congress.

7.13. *Inland Steel Building, built 1954–1958. Skidmore, Owings & Merrill, architects. The modern lines contrasted sharply with the Majestic Building to the right, built 1905.* Photograph by Hedrich Blessing, 1958. Chicago History Museum, HB-21235-B.

icance and Description" that the house had been subdivided and that the "neighborhood is now predominated by colored occupants."[64] Just as the recording wandered from the architectural and historical facts, preservation interest wavered. The Chicago chapter of the American Institute of Architects called the building a Chicago landmark. But the building stood vacant for years, unable to attract the interest or support that flowed to the Robie house. In 1964, Thomas Stauffer called the condition of the Sullivan house "a scandal." He insisted that the house was "constructed by the best craftsman of the day and designed by the best designer. Other cities have preserved much lesser buildings as memorials to much lesser men."[65] Photographer Richard Nickel, one of the most devoted preservationists committed to the Chicago School narrative, gave up his plans to purchase the house when family, friends, and local police convinced him that the neighborhood was too dangerous.[66] A plan to restore the house as a neighborhood youth center languished.[67] The house was eventually abandoned, picked

clean of its ornament, and demolished. Around Hyde Park, history came in fragments, "segmented" or separated from the community.

Beyond the 1957 Robie house campaign and Wright and Sandburg's personification of history during Chicago Dynamic Week, the first formal public recognition of Chicago landmarks came in 1957. In January the City Council unanimously passed an ordinance sponsored by Alderman Despres establishing the Commission on Chicago Architectural Landmarks. The ordinance called attention to Chicago's "internationally important monuments of architectural engineering and style" and cited six buildings as examples—Richardson's Glessner House; Sullivan's residence, the Carson Pirie Scott store (fig. 7.12), and Auditorium Theater; Wright's Robie house; and Burnham & Root's Monadnock Building. The ordinance also called attention to the need for landmark preservation by pointing to the earlier demolition of Richardson's Marshall Field Wholesale Store and Wright's Midway Gardens. It then charged the commission with designating Chicago's architectural landmarks, identifying and marking them, educating the public about their importance, and developing policies for their preservation.

Like the juxtaposition of heritage and contemporary visions for architecture and city building that characterized Chicago Dynamic programs, the first official list of architectural landmarks included both historic and contemporary structures. The six major Chicago School monuments featured on a special architectural tour during Chicago Dynamic week—the Rookery, Monadnock, Leiter, Auditorium, Carson Pirie Scott, and the Reliance—were among the fourteen structures singled out for special recognition on the commission's initial list of thirty-nine landmark buildings. The list, drawn up by a committee of architectural historians, architects, and commission members, included numerous structures by Adler & Sullivan and Burnham & Root and other buildings considered to have a role in the local Modernist genealogy. Then, to complete the links to the present, the commission designated such buildings as George and William Keck's University Avenue residence (1937), Mies's Illinois Institute of Technology campus (1947) and Lake Shore Drive Apartments (1951), and Skidmore, Owings & Merrill's Inland Steel Building (1957) (fig. 7.13). The commission's designation offered no protection but elaborated the narrative links between historical and contemporary architectural production. Architectural "merit," "structure," and "planning" were singled out as the landmark criteria. People committed to the Chicago School narrative developed the criteria and drew up the lists for designation.

Old Town Charm:
Preserving the "Unarchitectural"

Unlike the historical associations that dominated the marking of Charter Jubilee landmarks, a much narrower standard of significance guided the Commission on Chicago Architectural Landmarks. The popularization of the Chicago School construct in the decades following the Charter Jubilee had clearly inspired a rather fundamental rethinking of which Chicago sites merited public attention and designation. In fact, as Thomas Stauffer, Leon Despres, and others sought to establish a landmarks commission in the mid-1950s, they aimed to exclude historical and cultural sites from designation. For Stauffer the interest in the "monuments" of architectural engineering and style was "an intrinsic and artistic one, distinct from the accidental interest of historical association, of the 'Lincoln slept here' kind, nor merely antiquarian. . . . These buildings are not only one of Chicago's great claims to fame, but treasures which our people should hold in trust for the entire nation."[68] In the 1930s, Chicago's history and fame had clearly lain in very different venues.

Despite the growing interest in architectural aesthetics as the basis for preservation, the residents of Chicago's Old Town found themselves struggling against the narrowness of the Chicago School construct. They lived in a neighborhood developed in the late nineteenth century by middle-class and working-class German immigrants. In the years after World War II the area's "old world charm" seemed to offer a vital alternative to middle-class suburban communities. Although located inland from the Lake Michigan shore, the site of North Side fashionable residence, the neighborhood had easy access to Chicago's downtown business and cultural institutions, located two miles south. Moreover, it stood just west of Lincoln Park, which did face Lake Michigan, and it possessed what residents and visitors considered architectural and urban character. In preserving their neighborhood, residents of Old Town appreciated the day-to-day value of the location, the utility, quality, and age of the housing stock, and the historic atmosphere of the neighborhood. These qualities led Old Town residents to compare their neighborhood somewhat imprecisely with gentrified urban neighborhoods elsewhere such as Beacon Hill, Georgetown, and the French Quarter. However, in the context of contemporary taste and the growing popularization of Chicago School Modernism, the preservationists in Old Town found it difficult to place their eclectic buildings in some broader narrative of architectural value or importance. Even architect Earl H. Reed, an Old Town resident, could not easily articulate

the historic value of Old Town's architecture (fig. 7.14). In 1953, Reed wrote in his neighborhood "architectural portrait" that "the Triangle's close-packed architecture is jumbled, completely Chicagoesque, and endures as an unsurpassed relic of Old Town. Built mostly by modest citizens, often of foreign origin, it is compounded of the accidental and the expedient, reflecting various successive designs." Given current taste, Reed noted with some sense of regret that there was "no hint of the International style of architecture." He then concluded his portrait by declaring: "The 'Triangle Look' is diverse, actually unarchitectural, and sometimes crude. Yet its charm is undeniable and merits jealous preservation. It is undefined—unmentioned even—in the book on architecture, but go out and discover it for yourself. We guarantee that you'll feel well rewarded."[69] Academic and critical discussions of architecture provided little guidance to residents interested in asserting the value of neighborhood's architectural heritage.

In the late 1940s the neighborhood assumed a new name—Old Town. The people who formed the Old Town Triangle Association in 1948 coined the name. Their association promoted better garbage collection and the enforcement of building codes and encouraged public and private improvements aimed at halting the conversion of single-family dwellings into apartments in the triangular area bounded by North, Clark, and Ogden avenues. In 1950 the association sponsored the first of its annual Old Town Holidays. The fair offered for sale the arts and crafts of local artists and boosted the community to tens of thousands of visitors.[70] Taking on the competition of suburban lawns, and inspiring private improvements, the annual Old Town arts fair also sponsored a judged garden contest with prizes in several categories: window box, porch or roof gardens, backyard gardens, vegetable gardens, enclosed patio gardens, and front-yard gardens.[71]

Earl H. Reed proved to be one of the more complex boosters of Old Town architecture. At various points in his career he had both advocated Modern architecture and promoted preservation. The professional route from Modern architecture to "jealous preservation" in Old Town was not direct. Born in Chicago in 1884, Reed had studied architecture at the Massachusetts Institute of Technology. He directed the architecture department of the Armour Institute of Technology between 1924 and 1936 and frequently expressed his enthusiasm for Modern architecture. Mies van der Rohe took over the leadership of the school in 1936. In a debate over Modern architecture at the 1930 annual convention of the American Institute of Architects, Reed talked about Chicago architecture in terms that echoed the critical

*7.14. House on North Orleans Street in Old Town
purchased by architect Earl Reed in 1942, built c. 1885.*
Photograph by Barbara Koenen, 2010. Courtesy of Barbara Koenen.

1942, Reed moved with his two older children, Marion, and their young daughter to 1835 North Orleans Street (fig. 7.14) in the middle of what later would become Old Town. Gone was the spacious yard of Reed's Evanston residence. The house they moved into was a two-story 1880s brick worker's cottage with rusticated stone hood-molds over the windows and doors and an ornate cornice. Here Earl and Marion Reed fit the model of the artistic people who increasingly settled in Old Town, defining its "Bohemian character."[75] Marion Tufts Reed helped organize the early art fairs that promoted Old Town while Earl Reed chronicled the neighborhood's "unarchitectural" character.

Over the next decade Old Town residents and writers attempted to come to terms with Old Town's historic and architectural value. This effort was certainly aided when researchers discovered four row houses designed by Adler & Sullivan. But such a find could not support the broader interest in the neighborhood, especially one with so many houses that failed to emulate Sullivan's work. In 1954, Roger Ingalls and his family found themselves admiring the decidedly un–Chicago School Victorian gingerbread woodwork of a house at 225 Eugenie Street, with its Rococo ceiling on the interior.[76] Increasingly in the 1960s, local chroniclers came to celebrate the work of Old Town's "humble and honest" anonymous architects and builders as an antidote to urban Modernism: "Their genuine naiveté gave a scale that seems human, not the lifeless expression of a machined art. Certainly in this human scale we can find a raison d'etre for Old Town's current popularity and a heartening message for our own day."[77] Surveying the same history, architect John A. Holabird, Jr., wrote in 1964, "Victorian, which was a dirty word in architecture for fifty years, synonymous with stiffness and eclecticism has come back into its own and Old Town is its Leader."[78]

Just as expressions of Chicago School aesthetics bypassed Old Town, so too did older notions of associational significance. National history and even Chicago history as celebrated in textbooks and in earlier programs of historic markers seemed to bear little relation to Old Town. In a 1959 essay "A Sense of History, More or Less," Herman Kogan, a resident of Old Town and a member of the *Tribune* editorial staff, reflected on the neighborhood's supposed obscurity: "If any of the professional historical-site outfits has designated Old Town a likely area for plaques and markers, then I have not heard of it. . . . In purely objective moments, we may be compelled to admit that the official affixers of historical monuments have a point, technically speaking, but we have our own treasuries of historical fact, lore and memorabilia (and some trivia), and we cherish

passion of Louis Sullivan. He declared that the 1893 Columbian Exposition with its "coldly classical" forms had "laid upon us the withering hand of dead ages" with all of its "insipid historical detail."[72] Reed also criticized Chicago's nineteenth-century architecture that had been "blemished by Victorianism."[73] The Depression helped move Reed from Modern architecture to architectural history. For two years he served as the Northern Illinois district officer for the Historic American Buildings Survey, a Depression-relief project to employ architects and draftsmen to produce measured drawings and documentation of historic buildings; in this position Reed made an effort to record "the important architectural remains of pioneer culture which flourished in the Midwest up to the time of the Civic War."[74]

Reed's personal route to settling in Old Town was hardly direct either; however, he came to represent the early wave of suburbanites reclaiming city residence in Old Town. In 1917, Reed married musician Edith Lobdell and initially lived in a mansion on Chicago's Prairie Avenue with Edith's parents. In 1920, he moved to a suburban residence on Ridge Court in Evanston to raise a family. Edith died in 1934. In 1939, Reed married Marion Tufts, a sculptor and an Art Institute instructor. In them all, however unimportant they may seem to the site-pickers."[79] With history valued from the top down, as a chronicle of famous people and events, local traditions and the invention of Old Town itself did not provide residents with a historical link between themselves and their neighborhood or a broader public. In 1960 neighborhood boosters wrote, "Old Town is essentially a state of mind, preferably of an artistic bent. . . . What it is not is a historical entity. Its foothold in Chicago history is . . . precarious."[80] The recourse to promoting Old Town as a diverse community of artists and backyard gardeners provided a more direct route to preserving the neighborhood from threats posed by deterioration and clean-sweep urban renewal.

Even as the Old Town Triangle Association did its work of "groping for neighborhood identification as a rallying point for preserving old values,"[81] it worked to hold at bay the more destructive practices of urban renewal. Association members viewed their work as one of urban conservation rather than architectural preservation. Conservation officially gained credence in Chicago in 1953 when both city and state agencies sought to temper more destructive forms of urban renewal. Starting in 1947 and continuing into the 1960s, Chicago urban renewal officials cleared nearly 1,000 acres of urban land for redevelopment projects ranging from Sandburg Village on the north, to Lake Meadows on the south, to the University of Illinois at Chicago Circle on the west. Chicago's community conservation boards recognized the value of improving existing housing stock by engaging in a more selective urban renewal program. Conservation did not address historical value; it simply acknowledged the high cost of clearance projects and their limited effectiveness in arresting the deterioration of housing throughout the city. The nonprofit Lincoln Park Conservation Association received its state charter in 1954 and set about ensuring that the neighborhood did not deteriorate into "slum" conditions and coordinating neighborhood participation in the public and private planning for the area. Although history was not a center-piece of the effort, conservation did look at old buildings as a neighborhood resource rather than as a neighborhood threat; under the auspices of the Conservation Association news articles appeared with headlines such as "Old Buildings Don't Have to Be Slums" and "Spruce-Up Renews Charm of Old Home." An alternative to prevailing city planning practice now seemed possible.[82]

The conservation approach relied on code enforcement, improved building maintenance, selective demolitions, and new infill development to stabilize and improve neighborhoods. Conservation, in particular, tried to stem overcrowding and the conversion of single-family houses into apartments, and apartments into rooming houses, which they felt accelerated the deterioration of residential property and neighborhood character. Conservation proponents celebrated when the late-nineteenth-century six-flat building at 2111–2115 North Cleveland was rehabilitated, removing thirty-one single-room units and putting eight apartments in the same space.[83] After being incorporated in the Lincoln Park conservation area in 1954, the Triangle Association and other Lincoln Park groups developed renewal plans for the area. In 1961 the Triangle Association clearly articulated its views concerning urban renewal: "We are for urban renewal. The many abuses and blunders of such programs in Chicago and elsewhere do not furnish sufficient reason for opposition to urban renewal as a whole: we are simply against the repetition of abuses and blunders." In 1964 the association declared: "We will fight to maintain the present character of the neighborhood. . . . We are firmly against clearance of any rehabilitable structure. We are unreservedly opposed to high-rise buildings in the interior of the Triangle."[84]

Working with the Conservation Board, the community sought to define guidelines for new construction and rehabilitation that would be "true to the history" of the community. In doing so it rejected many of the cherished ideals of Modern urbanism. One Lincoln Park conservation group declared: "Our residents seek the exchange and diversity of the city, and reject the distance and isolation of the suburbs. . . . Most of us find considerable charm in this style, and many residents have restored their homes to resemble more closely the original form. . . . This search for roots in the past, this attempt to preserve traditions, is not a rejection of progress; it is an attempt to maintain an atmosphere which will give stability and form to life in the 'faceless' city."[85] In the 1,008 acres of the Lincoln Park conservation area, there were 7,444 structures, and the conservation plan called for the demolition of 2,097. The largest concentration of structures planned for demolition stood along the diagonal commercial strip of Ogden Avenue. Here, the Cambridge, Massachusetts, landscape architecture and planning firm Sasaki, Walker Associates developed an innovative plan that advocated the closing of Ogden Avenue and the reknitting of the renewal sites into the dominant neighborhood grid, providing parks, community facilities, pedestrian paths, and sites for new contextually sensitive private housing.[86]

The conservation strategy in Old Town mirrored some of the federal government's experiments with preservation in the late 1950s and early 1960s. In 1963, for example, distancing itself somewhat from its years of clean-sweep renewal, the federal Urban Renewal Administration declared that "in a number of cities urban renewal has made possible the preservation of historic or architecturally significant structures by providing the means whereby the deleterious surroundings have been removed and the historic building or place has had a chance to survive."[87] The agency released a 1963 report titled *Historic Preservation Through Urban Renewal*. *Antiques* magazine then published a roundtable exploring "Preservation and Urban Renewal: Is Coexistence Possible?" Federal urban renewal commissioner William Slayton answered with an "emphatic yes," insisting that it was "unthinkable" that urban renewal could not "save the best of the past—and give significant buildings and areas a brighter future."[88] Slayton highlighted the 1959 project in Providence, Rhode Island, *College Hill: A Demonstration Study of Historic Area Renewal*, with its system for evaluating local "architectural achievements." Laying the groundwork for selective demolition and aesthetic preservation within federal urban renewal policy, the study declared that "cities are the museums of buildings and the people are their curators."[89]

Beyond demolition the renewal agencies began to establish plans and architectural guidelines that aimed to prevent "disharmonious and unsuitable developments" in historic areas. These guidelines went beyond the incompatibility of high-rises to focus on building mass and materials, fenestration patterns, setbacks from lot lines, and related architectonic issues.[90] In Chicago many preservationists thought that historic and architectural significance pervaded certain buildings and places, but not in Old Town. Under conservation planning, Old Town's fidelity to historic forms proved less important. Within general rules that controlled scale and material, people actually cultivated striking contrasts between, for example, historic brick exteriors and "ultra-modern" interiors. Here the aesthetic of eclipse found another venue, not at the scale of the city of the block but rather at the scale of the residence. The traditional exterior could provide a dramatic foil for the modern interior.[91]

Surrounded by Demolitions: The Garrick and Beyond

In the 1950s and 1960s, Chicago's Old Town and Lincoln Park were more the exceptions than the rule. Most other neighborhoods fared less well. The neighborhood just one block south of Old Town, with its similar architectural pattern but with a larger poor and African-American population, was demolished. In its place developers constructed a high-rise, middle-class housing development named Sandburg Village, after Chicago's

7.15. *Pullman Building, built 1883–1884. Solon S. Beman, architect. The building accommodated business offices and residential apartments. Demolished in 1956 for the construction of the twenty-story enamel-porcelain-clad Borg-Warner Building, designed by A. Epstein & Sons.* Photograph by J. W. Taylor, c. 1890. Faculty of Architecture, University of Melbourne.

poet laureate. The plans for Sandburg Village received enthusiastic support in Old Town. The unevenness of the sway of history in the neighborhoods paralleled developments in the city center. Here working with the imprecise notion of a Chicago School raised preservation interest in the case of only a handful of structures while many other buildings were destroyed. In 1956, Earl H. Reed wrote, "Our historic structures melt away like snow in the summer sun."[92] Reed wrote this in the wake of the 1956 demolition of Solon S. Beman's 1882 Pullman Building (fig. 7.15), where George Pullman had carried his fetish for the sleeping arrangements of Americans off of his sleeping cars, out of his company town, and into the skyscraper. The building combined office space for Pullman employees and apartment space intended for Pullman's middle managers. Stylistically, the building, with its prominent corner turret, its rusticated base, and its deeply modeled window surrounds and entrance arches, did not fit the structurally expressive model of the Chicago School. The building was destroyed in 1956 almost naturally and without surprise or protest. No one argued for its preservation, and a local newspaper

7.16. *Columbus Memorial Building, built 1891–1893. William W. Boyington, architect. Demolished in 1959 for the construction of a seven-story addition to the Chas. Stevens department store.* Photograph, 1895. Chicago History Museum, ICHI 22331.

simply assured people that the buildings like this would "remain as legends in the pages of the city's history."[93]

The lack of a narrative of architectural production apart from the Chicago School line of Modern unornamented, structurally expressive designs, made the understanding, appreciation, and preservation of many Chicago buildings extremely difficult. One can sense the problem in reading the federal government's Historic American Buildings Survey inventory cards from the 1950s. Paragraphs on structural expression filled the forms. But when surveyors confronted a building like William W. Boyington's 1892 Columbus Memorial Building (fig. 7.16), they could only manage a pithy entry on significance. "It commemorates the World's Columbian Exposition; Notable features: Bronze Statue of Columbus and use of ornamental metal in its structure." The building had indeed appropriated civic life as part of its monumental expression, incorporating what contemporaries appreciated as some of the most dramatic ornamental iron and mosaic work in Chicago. Yet the building was demolished in 1959 without public protest. One of the few concessions to history came in the preservation of the 9-foot statue of Columbus, sculpted by Moses Eze-

kiel, which occupied a niche above the main entrance. After being donated to the Municipal Art League and removed with great fanfare, the statue languished year after year in a local lumberyard. A 1965 campaign to return the statue to public view culminated in its 1966 installation in Vernon Park.[94]

In the 1950s and 1960s, concerns over stagnation clearly held in check many claims of history and memory. In 1961, for example, a manager in Arthur Rubloff's real estate development company reacted hotly to a sympathetic article on landmarks preservation written by *Chicago Daily News* reporter Georgie Anne Geyer. Rubloff's manager wrote: "It is all well and good for various artistic, esthetic and cultural groups in this country and in Europe to mourn the passing of these relics of the past. . . . I shed no tears for the passing of these uneconomical blocks of brick, stone, and steel. They have served their purpose and their era has ended. The City of Chicago would soon be a most old-fashioned and undesirable place to do business if the heart of the city—the Downtown—consisted of a scatter of new buildings set among these many outworn and outmoded antiques."[95] Often what developers aggressively proposed was the opposite—a "scatter" of old buildings set within a completely modern downtown. At times even that seemed too much.

The picketing, lobbying, public debates, and court challenges that greeted the 1960 plan to demolish Adler & Sullivan's 1891 Schiller Building/Garrick Theater (fig. 7.17) contrasted sharply with the uncontested demolition of the Pullman, Columbus Memorial, and other Loop buildings.[96] The owners of the Balaban & Katz theater chain wanted to replace the Garrick with a parking garage. Sullivan and the Garrick occupied a dominant position both in the Chicago School canon and on the Commission on Chicago Architectural Landmarks list; the demolition plans provoked considerable fury. The Garrick campaign, which ended in demolition in 1961, derived its greatest support from the critical and professional circles supporting Modern architecture. People associated with the Illinois Institute of Technology (IIT), where Mies was a teacher and where the education followed the lines of the Bauhaus, provided a strong core of support. Students and faculty revered Louis Sullivan and his buildings as providing the antecedents for their own Modern ideals and forms. When Richard Nickel, a photography graduate of IIT's Institute of Design, where he had written a thesis on Louis Sullivan, formed a picket line (fig. 7.18), students, former students, and professors from IIT dominated the group.[97] John Vinci, an IIT graduate, left his drafting table at Skidmore, Owings & Merrill to join IIT students on the picket line. Mies, who was said to be ill and unable to join the picket line, sent word that he was "'100 per cent' for saving the Garrick." When Le Corbusier wrote to Mayor Daley on behalf of the Garrick, he helped authenticate the genealogical links to Modernism asserted as part of the movement. He explained the "birth of machinism" to Daley and called it a "sacrilege" that the Garrick might be demolished. He concluded, "The buildings of Sullivan and his School must be saved, even if it means that some streets must be turned aside."[98]

The *Sun-Times* reported the protest under the headline "Culture Walks the Picket Line." Cultural historian Hugh Duncan presented a picket-line brief for preservation that affirmed both history and progress: "I'm imbued with a deep belief in the future of this city. We have such a reputation for gangsterism. But this city is one of the few in the world's history to have created a whole order of architecture, like Gothic or classic, not just a style but an order. . . . The three great American architects of the 20th century are all Chicagoans—Frank Lloyd Wright, Sullivan, and Ludwig Mies van der Rohe. Do we care?" The preservationists staked their claim entirely on the Chicago School canon. In doing so, they set architectural heritage and the claims of memory in opposition to popular engagements with the memory of Chicago gangsters.[99] The Garrick's architectural landmark designation underscored the importance of the building and of their cause. Richard Nickel scoffed at assertions of the building's obsolescence: "The truth is that the Garrick, as great architecture, can never be old-fashioned."[100]

Opponents of preservation labeled the campaign an "egghead protest." One letter to the editor urged the preservationists to give up on the Garrick and to save the Art Institute—"These so-called abstract paintings are monstrosities." High culture did undoubtedly raise the stakes in the Garrick campaign. Numerous arts groups joined the preservation coalition in the hopes that the building could be converted into an arts center. Cultural politics turned to electoral politics when Alderman Leon Despres declared his support for preserving the Garrick. At the same time, Alderman Paddy Bauler opposed the movement, declaring, "Tear it down! Tear it down before it falls down!" Editorialists at the *Sun-Times* suggested that Alderman Bauler might be an authority on "the durability of a head on a glass of beer" but that

7.17. *Schiller Building/Garrick Theater, built 1891–1892. Adler & Sullivan, architects. The building combined a theater n the lower floors and offices above. Demolished in 1961 to provide a site for a parking garage.* Photograph, c. 1900. Library of Congress.

7.18. *Richard Nickel leading the picket line protesting the proposed demolition plans of Adler & Sullivan's Schiller Building/Garrick Theater, June 1960.* Photograph by Ralph Walters, 1960. *Chicago Sun-Times.*

he'd best defer to the experts in matters of the Garrick's structural integrity. The politicians and the courts could hold up the demolition by refusing to issue a demolition permit.[101] The Chicago court initially found that beauty and architectural heritage provided a substantial basis for preventing the demolition. In this finding the court seemed to endorse the argument of IIT professor Alfred Caldwell, hired by Mies in 1944 to teach landscape architecture, that the Garrick was "part of the cultural inheritance of the nation and does not belong to individuals to destroy."[102] However, the courts also came to insist that if the city or other parties wished to preserve the building they would have to buy it.[103]

Mayor Daley proved equivocal in his support. He appointed a committee to study the problem, and preservationists increasingly pinned their hopes for the Garrick on the possibility that the city would modify plans for an adjacent civic center to include the Garrick. Daley finally rejected this solution and decided not to pursue further legal action when the Illinois appeals court unanimously overturned the lower court decision and ordered the city to issue a demolition permit. The appeals court affirmed the owners' private property rights, declaring, "It is laudable to attempt to preserve a landmark; however, it becomes unconscionable when an unwilling private party is required to bear the expense."[104] The preservation campaign quickly shifted from saving the building to savings its fragments. With $10,000 contributed by the Garrick owners as well as other private funds, Richard Nickel, architecture student David Norris, and John Vinci salvaged ornament from the building and distributed it—along with the fame of the Chicago School—to museums, universities, and individual collectors around the world. This work started to institutionalize the ongoing private efforts of Richard Nickel, who had devoted considerable time to both photographing and salvaging ornament from Louis Sullivan's buildings.[105] In comparison to fully preserved buildings, collected fragments provided a severely constricted link to the architectural past. In the case of Chicago buildings they also presented something of a conundrum; buildings revered as central to the Chicago School narrative of structural expression and stylistic modernity were now preserved for posterity with collections of ornament. Fragments left the private real estate market unfettered. The city could both remember and build.

In 1960, Mayor Daley actually endorsed fragment salvage as a part of the city's urban renewal policy. Daley ordered the rescue of "significant architectural art" and its "reuse in the future city." More specifically, he proposed that the ornament be incorporated in the design of parks, schools, shopping centers, and playgrounds in renewal areas. Proposed by the commissioner of the community conservation agency, the policy aimed to give neighborhoods "a sense of continuity." Ira Bach, the city's planning commissioner, looked upon the idea as an important means of giving residents an idea of the Chicago's architectural heritage.[106] There was ample Chicago precedent for such an approach. In 1922 architect Thomas Tallmadge worked to salvage the entrance portal of H. H. Richardson's Franklin McVeagh House, "one of the architectural gems of the county," and to put it on display at the Armour Institute. The policy, which won the praise of many planners, architects, and preservationists, led to some public collecting, but the city's fragments did not often get displayed publicly. The collecting of building fragments proved a prominent enough occupation in the city that in 1966 Chicago magazine offered a "handbook" to aid readers interested in salvaging "a piece of the past" from the ruins of older buildings.[107] Decades later, fragments went on display in the vacant lots within the Prairie Avenue historic district and in the permanent architectural galleries of the Art Institute.[108]

The Garrick campaign highlighted some of the obvious tension within the coalition between Modernists and preservationists. There was simply no question that the preservationists' efforts to define and preserve a sense of place based on historic buildings was hampered by the calls of Modernists for rebuilding the city. Although Modernists felt they could discern the qualitative difference between the designs of Mies and Skidmore, Owings & Merrill and less distinguished forms of contemporary architecture and urbanism, it was difficult to both embrace and reject massive projects of urban redevelopment. In 1962, radio and television commentator and newspaper columnist Norman Ross emphasized the need for Chicago preservation by objecting to the forms of the Modern cityscape, "What one wishes for, in the rising jungle of sterile steel, glass and concrete, of stark, straight lines are a few rambling, extravagant old buildings that seem to have roots in the soil on which they are built."[109] Steel, glass, and concrete were the precious materials of Modern rebuilding. The Modernists' interest in a local Modern lineage that reached back to the nineteenth century offered the possibility of making Modernism seem rooted in Chicago. However, even the narrowest of Chicago School constructions could not hide from view the obvious fracture lines developing between preservationists and developers.

The Garrick campaign did foster "a new appreciative interest in . . . architectural heritage."[110] A loose coalition of historians, architects, and preservationists, led by Tom Stauffer, Leon Despres, Richard Nickel, Hugh

7.19. *Republic Building, built 1905–1909.*
Holabird & Roche, architects. Demolished in
1961 to accommodate the sixteen-story Home
Federal Savings & Loan Association in a modern
glass-curtain-wall building designed by Skidmore,
Owings & Merrill. Photograph by Richard
Nickel,1960. Library of Congress.

Duncan, and architect Benjamin Weese, veterans of the Robie house campaign, founded the Chicago Heritage Committee in the midst of the Garrick campaign. The committee energetically, if somewhat selectively, pressed preservation claims.[111] It met monthly and sponsored lectures by interested parties. Members orchestrated campaigns to preserve Chicago School buildings. The aesthetic bias was clear. When Stauffer objected to the demolition of Holabird & Roche's "noble" 1905 Republic Building (fig. 7.19), he insisted that the building was "one of the latest examples of the distinctive Chicago style, erected just before a wave of confused eclectic taste buried the native genius of the American cities for a generation." He objected that the building would now "be lost to the patrimony of the city." Stauffer proposed removing other "blighted structures" on the same block so that a new tower could stand beside the Republic and "show at once the native roots and the continuing vitality of Chicago's architectural genius."[112] The Chicago Heritage Committee had a Frank Lloyd Wright subcommittee that conducted tours of Wright's buildings, some-

times raising money for their restoration.[113] Playing the role of "gadfly,"[114] they engaged in other civic crusades: promoting a Chicago preservation ordinance, working to preserve Chicago's parks and the Indiana dunes, and advocating for the public sculpture program under Benjamin Ferguson's 1905 charitable bequest.

The wide publicity generated by the Chicago Heritage Committee over the demolition of the Garrick undoubtedly spurred greater vigilance concerning the buildings within the Chicago School canon. The campaign to preserve and restore Adler & Sullivan's Auditorium Theater, for example, gained momentum from the climate of urgency surrounding the destruction of the Garrick and other Sullivan buildings. Nevertheless, many buildings proposed for demolition in the center of Chicago unfortunately fell beyond the purview of Chicago School concern. The case of Henry Ives Cobb's domed, Corinthian-order, Federal Building (fig. 7.20), built between 1896 and 1905, offers a good illustration. One plan after another in the postwar period anticipated the demolition of the Federal Building. Plans called for government not only to rebuild but also to do so along Modernist lines with tall modern buildings sited on wide-open plazas. Government could thus boldly renew an aging, cluttered, and stagnant downtown. The Central Area Plan looked to these plans as cornerstones for inspiring private rebuilding—the Federal Center would "open up downtown Chicago, providing greenery, a striking urban scene, a place to sit and enjoy the city." According to the reviews of the plans, "plazas and skyscrapers would replace 19th century 'eyesores' and . . . open landscaped areas would 'let the sun into the Loop.'" Some people believed that the Federal Building possessed a "certain solidity and classical charm," but it covered its entire lot and together with various buildings on the adjacent land the effect was one of "overcrowding, of dirtiness, and . . . of an urban backwater."[115]

No small irony accompanied the plans for demolishing the Federal Building and replacing it with a skyscraper. When the project was undertaken in the 1890s, some people had called for the construction of a skyscraper. Rejecting the proposal, the Treasury Department's supervising architect declared: "It would not be dignified to erect a steel-frame building. The government puts up heavy masonry structures and puts them up to stay."[116] Now, as people contemplated the building's demolition, few of those who campaigned to save the Garrick came forward to join the small group of people who proposed preserving the Federal Building. If the building had been built as a structurally expressive skyscraper, it might have enjoyed a different fate in the mid-1960s. But Mies van der Rohe led the design team on the

7.20. The dome in the foreground is the Chicago Federal Building, built 1896–1905. Henry Ives Cobb, architect. In the background is the thirty-story Dirksen Federal Courthouse, built 1961–1964. Ludwig Mies van der Rohe, architect. Photograph by Hedrich Blessing,, c. 1964. Chicago History Museum, HB-27043-0.

new Federal Center, with its skyscrapers and plaza, and the preservationists, both Modernists and historians alike, did not plan on having "classical charm" get in the way of a bold new structuring of urban space.

Thomas Stauffer did not think that the Federal Building was "historic" or "distinguished architecture"; however, he privately favored its preservation as "a fully stated expression of the style of the time" and evidence of the "rich texture of stages in the growth" of the city and its architecture. Stauffer's colleagues on the Chicago Heritage Committee roundly rejected getting involved in saving the Federal Building. David Norris, who had salvaged ornament from the Garrick, wrote that he thought the building was "juck (a new word)" and promised to "make a big stink" if Stauffer got the committee involved; the building "lacked sufficient merit or interest to deserve a fuss." They also thought that the modern plaza proposed for part of the site would provide "a most

valuable amenity for the whole Loop area."[117] In 1965 the Federal Building was demolished (fig. 7.21); fragments were saved for placement in other federal buildings while people carried off other pieces of the building as part of a private, non–Chicago School recall of a public building.

In 1968, members of the Chicago Heritage Committee were also divided when it came to debating the fate of Shepley, Rutan & Coolidge's 1897 main branch building of the Chicago Public Library. The Renaissance Revival limestone and granite exterior and the embellished marble and mosaic interior enjoyed considerable civic prominence but did not fit into the Chicago School canon. Nonetheless, Chicago Heritage Committee member Charles G. Staples formed a library building subcommittee and pushed for years for the preservation of the library, insisting on the importance of invoking the recently enacted landmarks ordinance to protect the building from destruction. Other Chicago residents joined Staples, urging the importance of preserving the building for "future generations" and imploring city officials to "preserve one building of beauty in this city of modern monstrosities."[118] The interest in the building worked in concert with a scholarly interest in and popular appreciation of American architectural history in the 1960s.[119] It captured a shift from viewing Chicago buildings merely as exemplars of Modernism to seeing them as part of a much broader cultural and architectural narrative. City officials finally determined to preserve the building as a cultural center—eventually moving the main branch of the library into a new downtown building.

Many people in Chicago's civic and political community called for preserving Jane Addams's Hull House complex in the West Side clearance project that provided the University of Illinois a new campus. Favoring an extensive preservation of the Hull House buildings, United States Senator Paul Douglas insisted that "symbols and the embodiments of the noble past help to call

forth the best in men and women, and they need to be cherished and not ruthlessly destroyed."[120] Members of the Chicago Heritage Committee offered some support for Hull House preservation even though they did not consider the complex "a great work of art" (fig. 7.22). Thomas Stauffer wrote to Mayor Daley urging preservation as a memorial to Jane Addams and her coworkers and "to their selfless service to the City." Forging a rare link, for the committee, between associational and aesthetic preservation, Stauffer wrote, "The fame of Louis Sullivan and Dankmar Adler, and of Jane Addams is secure in the world, whether Chicago honors them or not; we owe the preservation of these shrines not to them but to our City, ourselves, and our children." Stauffer and the committee were also interested in the city-building problem presented by Hull House—that of integrating old and new architecture. Committee member and architect Ben Weese hoped that "a nobly begun experiment can still prove its usefulness in a changing environment." Despite these pleas, and despite the fact that Hull House occupied an edge of the proposed cam-

7.21. *Demolition of the Chicago Federal Building, built 1896–1905. Henry Ives Cobb, architect. The federal government constructed a post office and a federal building on the site.* Photograph, 1965. National Archives.

Hull House, Chicago, Ill.   42

*7.22. Hull House buildings, built 1895–1909. Pond & Pond,
architects. Demolished in 1963 in connection with construction of the University of Illinois at Chicago Circle.* Photograph
by Kaufmann-Fabry, c. 1945. Postcard in author's collection.

pus, the comprehensive planning of the university's modern megastructure by Skidmore, Owings & Merrill only
accommodated the reconstructed Hull mansion, while
the sprawling Hull House complex was demolished. The
house itself was restored to an earlier period than Jane
Addams's associations with it, failing to capture its social
and historical significance. Chicagoans now seemed ill
prepared to press architectural appeals outside of the
Chicago School narrative and even less equipped to
argue for associational preservation.[121]

The Chicago School lineage, of course, assumed a pattern of harmony between the architecture of the past and
the present. However, as the government spurred redevelopment of the downtown, growing numbers of early
skyscrapers were replaced. Carl Sandburg even noted
this in his Chicago Dynamic Week poem: "When one tall
skyscraper is torn down To make room for a taller one to
go up, Who takes down and puts up those skyscrapers?
Man—the little two-legged joker . . . Man."[122] Historian
Carl Condit hoped that building owners and the city's
planning, landmarks, and land clearance agencies would
cooperate so that "new buildings can be erected on sites
now occupied by ugly and obsolete structures while the
fine work of the Chicago School is preserved."[123] In the
midst of his own impassioned effort to save the Republic Building, Ben Weese proposed a similar solution—

declare the entire downtown an urban renewal district
so that "low buildings pre-dating the Chicago School"
and considered of "minimal cultural value" could be
demolished to provide sites for a harmonious Modernism. This proposal appeared in a section of Weese's
essay entitled "History Is Important."[124]

History is indeed important; however, what buildings
come to represent history is very much dependent on
the historical narratives that preservationists bring to
their consideration of the built environment. Beyond
their highly selective views on preservation, the Chicago Heritage Committee sought to limit public education concerning architectural and historical landmarks
outside of the Chicago School canon. This effort became
particularly evident when the committee debated the
proposed contents of the Commission on Chicago Architectural Landmarks' first guidebook. The architectural
and urban guides of Chicago from this period tended to
codify and popularize the Chicago School interpretation
of local architecture.[125]

Some members of the Heritage Committee
expressed a sense of betrayal when they discovered
that the commission's guide would include a broader
range of structures than those represented on the official landmarks list. Richard Nickel was "dismayed"
by the selections for the guide. He insisted that in its

"singular interest with architecture as art, the [Commission on Chicago Architectural Landmarks] was unique." The appearance of "sentimental," "historical," and new buildings like Marina City and O'Hare Airport that did not serve as Modern models of the Chicago School struck at the supposed integrity of the landmarks movement. For Thomas Stauffer the commission's responsibility was to designate and publish only those structures with "universal recognition as masterpieces." He urged the need for "very careful and objective considerations." Stauffer complained to Carl Condit that the more expansive guide would "diminish the importance" of the official landmarks.[126] Published in 1965, the guide had some interesting points of intersections with the Jubilee buildings marked in 1937. The Commission's guide included, for example, the Greek Revival–style Clarke House, the Lind Block, the Water Tower, and several religious structures. The guide also signaled the importance of preservation by including entries on recently demolished buildings, including, for example, the Garrick Theater. Despite the gesture toward other forms of landmarks, aesthetic judgments of "architectural merit" dominated the guide, titled *Chicago's Famous Buildings*.

Expanding Beyond the Chicago School Base

The Chicago School's account of local architecture provided a basis for the cohesion of Modernists and preservationists during the 1950s and 1960s. For Modernists, preserving this narrow slice of Chicago architectural production reinforced contemporary interest in modern city building. Moreover, narrowly conceived preservation did not pose a threat to the plans for a massive public and private rebuilding of the city. As renewal and preservation proceeded, the historic city came to look increasingly like the Chicago School narrative; the diversity of the city's nineteenth-century architectural production was either destroyed with rebuilding or overlooked by those who relied on architectural designations to gather their sense of history. The absolute priority given to aesthetic over associational landmarks in the 1950s and beyond further restricted the use that citizens could make of history. Recognizing the importance of other buildings and histories glimpsed in *Chicago's Famous Buildings* and explored by the residents of neighborhoods like Old Town would at every hand have opened up the urban renewal process to the challenges of histories embedded in the city's other buildings and landscapes.

Despite these difficulties, in the 1960s, beyond the increasingly eclectic palette of the guidebooks, there was other evidence of growing interest in more diverse architectural forms. In 1964, Reed presided over a further Historic American Buildings Survey of Chicago-area structures. The surveyors recorded in photographs and drawings twenty-nine buildings. Many of the buildings fit comfortably in the Chicago School canon, including Sullivan's Charnley house, and the Carson Pirie Scott store, Burnham's Reliance Building, and Wright's Winslow house. But the sites also included Boyington's Water Tower, and Cobb's Federal Building, McKim, Mead & White's Colonial Revival Bryan Lathrop House, Cudell & Hercz's German Baroque Francis J. Dewes Mansion, and Toussaint Menard's Second Empire–style St. Ignatius College, designed in 1869. Reed insisted that the buildings were selected because they boasted a "unique feature" or represented "a significant development in design."[127] Interest in architectural production beyond the Chicago School moved out of neighborhood preservation and helped define a broader scope for urban preservation.

Preservation served city building well in the peak years of post–World War II renewal. However, the mounting challenge to urban renewal and Modernism from the mid-1960s onward was paralleled by a general broadening of the basis for recognizing and preserving Chicago landmarks. Founded to serve certain particular interest, the modern preservation movement in Chicago proved quite capable of flexibly adapting itself to changing historical times and aesthetic tastes. Old Town's years of struggle to define itself historically and architecturally culminated with its official designation on the local and federal landmarks registers in 1977 and 1984 respectively. When preservationists sought to preserve Richardson's Glessner house in the 1960s, they formed the Chicago School of Architecture Foundation. In 1977 the name changed to Chicago Architecture Foundation. Today the foundation presides over a broad program of architectural tours, exhibitions, and lectures that range far beyond its Chicago School cornerstone. The foundation guides people on tours of working-class neighborhoods and apartment districts; they have built upon the work of the city's Historic Chicago Bungalow Initiative and the Greystone Initiative. Today, as in the 1950s, preservation is only as useful as the narratives it tells through the historic landscape. The Chicago case strongly suggests that preservationists need to more self-consciously consider the link between the histories they choose to tell, or not tell, and the ongoing structuring of the contemporary city, both in fact and in memory.

CHAPTER EIGHT

Chicago's Mecca Flat Blues

Architecture, Music, and Race in the Politics of Place

The connections between historic preservation practice and historical scholarship are not always straightforward. Architectural historians tend to focus on the tidy nexus of meaning between original patrons and designers, architectural forms, and the immediate cultural context. In contrast, preservationists often value places in ways that original patrons and designers could never have envisioned. This is certainly the case for sites preserved for associational histories that occurred long after the original clients and designers departed. Moreover, preservation itself fundamentally changes the history of the places it preserves. In the history of architecture and landscape, preservation often constitutes the most recent chapter. It stands on the opposite end of the arc of history from where architectural historians concentrate their energies. While sometimes drawing upon the insights of scholars, the passion and advocacy of the preservationists also tends to run counter to the methods of architectural historians, who assume a stance of studied detachment. Historians think of themselves as interpreting history, they generally don't see themselves as making history. As preservationists take measure of the change from original form and intent to current meaning and significance, they can potentially enlarge the standard canvas of architectural history. Preservationists may seek to halt changes to form and to fix historical meaning, but their work helps us understand that a building's or a landscape's meaning is rarely fixed. Individuals and segments of society invent and reinvent meaning, value and devalue and value again their buildings and landscapes. Historical narratives are invoked as a part of this process, as people build, use, change, and pre-serve or discard their buildings and landscapes. These latter activities in the history of place are crucial for preservationists and should assume a place in architectural history.[1]

This chapter explores a single place, the Mecca (fig. 8.1), one of Chicago's largest nineteenth-century apartment houses. We will start, in the manner of architectural history, with a close analysis of the form and meaning of the original design. Over time at the Mecca, changing patterns of race intersected with urban space to drastically alter the building's meaning and history. This fragmented public perceptions of the Mecca. The analysis will focus on this rich later history of the Mecca, particularly on its emergence in the 1910s as a notable site of Chicago African-American culture and politics. The building inspired music, poetry, art, and literature. This culture and the Mecca's distinct sense of place stood at the center of a decade-long preservation struggle that began in the 1940s. Although architectural form was implicated in the cultural productions and political presence of the building on Chicago's South Side, the Mecca preservation campaign emphasized housing, neighborhood, and cultural space over design. In 1943, Mecca residents won a nearly unanimous vote of the Illinois legislature on a bill preventing the demolition of the building. By overlooking a narrower aesthetic rationale for preservation, the Mecca campaign provides a very different model of the way preservation can highlight and defend a community's vital attachment to place. The determined foes of Mecca preservation deployed their own narratives and understandings of history to defend their demolition plans. Analyzing these opposing constructions of Mecca history enriches our understanding

8.1. The Mecca, built 1891–1892. Edbrooke & Burnham, architects. The Mecca provided hotel accommodations during the Columbian Exposition. Detail from 1893 advertisement. Chicago History Museum, ICHi-29342.

of American architecture and urbanism and the dynamics of historic preservation.

The Mecca: The Architecture and Culture of Apartment Density

Architects Willoughby J. Edbrooke and Franklin Pierce Burnham designed the Mecca Apartments in 1891. Rising as one of Chicago's largest apartment houses, the Mecca reflected much broader architectural and urban developments. Edbrooke & Burnham's design incorporated natural light and landscape into a building that innovatively accommodated the city's increasing density. The Mecca, like many apartment buildings, differed from other urban structures in its unusually cosmopolitan combination of spatial and social elements. Chicago's late-nineteenth-century apartment buildings helped to dramatically transform the urban landscape while providing homes for tens of thousands of residents. Nevertheless, architectural historians have more readily focused on other Chicago subjects, including the down-

town skyscrapers and an alluring group of stylistically notable single-family houses dotting the suburban prairie.[2] In contrast to these structures, neatly categorized as either commercial or residential, the city's apartment houses represent an uneasy combination of public space and private realm, commerce and residence. These early apartment houses formed something of a hinge between the skyscraper and the single-family house, adopting skyscraper models for accommodating people at high density while navigating strong ideological commitments to the single-family residence. By their hybrid nature, they confounded the order that some observers believed appropriate to turn-of-the-century urban social life.

Apartment living vexed many late-nineteenth-century Chicagoans. In 1891 the astute editors of *Industrial Chicago* argued that the economic depression of the 1870s had "banished the idea of a permanent home from many hearts." Apartment buildings took the place of small homes by grouping between ten and forty units under one roof. Reflecting contemporary cultural concerns, the editors inquired, "What if the flat would destroy home

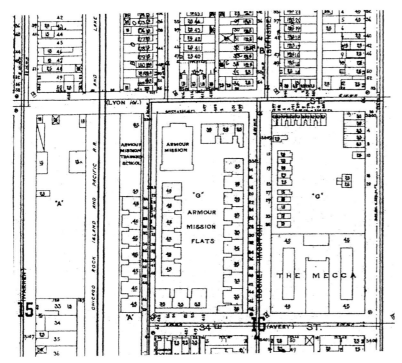

8.2. *Map plan of the Mecca and its context. The street at right is State Street; Dearborn Street at left (marked Boone). The five-story Armour Mission Training School was the first building of the Armour Institute, later renamed the Illinois Institute of Technology.* From Greeley-Carlson Company, *Second Atlas of the City of Chicago, Volume Two* (Chicago, 1892)

life?"[3] Similar questions dogged apartment designers and profoundly shaped building design. Architectural historian Carroll William Westfall has summed up the problem confronting Chicago residents: "Although the house became less practicable for the lives they found themselves living, they continued to equate the house with home. The result was a conundrum: civil manners forbade what utility required."[4]

The romanticized image of middle-class, nuclear-family domesticity hovered over apartment-house debates. A 1905 *Chicago Tribune* editorial, capturing the tone of contemporary critiques, reported that physicians in London had found that the "monotony" of apartment living was "driving an alarming number of women mad. . . . Her husband leaves for business early in the morning and usually doesn't return until evening. Between the janitor and the maid she has little housework to do. . . . The greater the number of the people living in the building with her the fewer she knows. . . . Race suicide or the rules of the flat deprive her of the luxury of children." Though the editors identified "avenues of escape," including reading, art, charitable work, and even business occupations, the editorial gave credence to the fear that apartment living would lead Anglo-American couples to stop raising large families, further tipping the demographic balance toward immigrants.[5] To the extent that women were charged with the moral stewardship of the family and the nation, the notion of the deterioration of their privacy and their possible jettisoning of family

altogether troubled some social commentators. This critique framed apartment-house design at the turn of the twentieth century.[6]

The Mecca's size and the originality of its design captured considerable attention in the 1890s. Projected as a Mecca for "flat-seekers," the building would require a large population, since the $600,000 structure included ninety-eight flats and occupied a site that cost $200,000. Built four miles south of downtown, the four-story building stretched 234 feet along State Street and 266 feet west along 34th Street to Dearborn. The Mecca's simple Romanesque-style elevations, with their arched entrances and round-arched top-floor windows, rippled with projecting window bays and the play of shadows cast by the cornice and stringcourses. The style and composition reflected the popular forms of numerous commercial and residential structures built by leading Chicago architects during the 1880s. What struck reporters as unusual was that each floor covered nearly 1.5 acres. The Mecca's density contrasted sharply with the more familiar patterns of organizing domestic space in the growing city. The *Chicago Tribune* reported that the anticipated population of nearly 500 residents would approach that of a "fair-sized village. Ninety-eight cottages would cover each lot in two five-acre blocks, and with twelve stores [the Mecca] would outrank many a rising suburb."[7]

Many late-nineteenth-century Chicago architects actually fostered associations with the suburbs and dis-

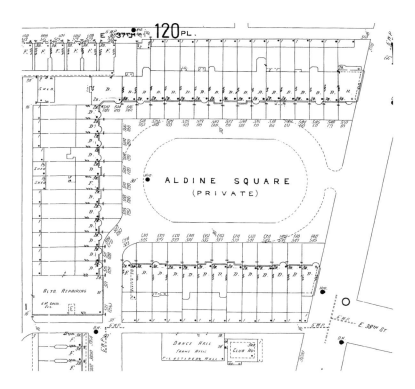

8.3. *Aldine Square, Chicago, built 1876, demolished c. 1935. Single-family row houses faced a landscaped park.* From Sanborn Map Company, *Insurance Maps of Chicago, Volume 4* (New York, 1912).

guised flats as houses in order to diffuse the hostility toward apartment living. In multifamily dwellings with from two to six units, architects could give apartments the appearance of single mansions. In larger buildings varied fenestration patterns, pitched gables, ornamental details, and choice building materials helped blend apartments into the broader residential landscape. When the size of apartment buildings stretched beyond that of the house or mansion, architects appropriated hotel and club models to maintain domestic associations.[8] Although homeowners in single-family neighborhoods often complained of the "flat invasion," apartment-house builders in these areas proudly pointed to the exclusive character of the neighborhood.[9]

Beyond formal stylistic strategies for blunting the prejudice against flats, architects developed site plans that incorporated the cherished images of single-family suburbs. Landscaped courtyards proved central to the effort. When the *Tribune* calculated that the Mecca's ninety-eight units would require 10 acres of land if configured as suburban cottages, it implied that nearly 8.5 acres of trees, yards, and gardens would be jettisoned in the transit from suburb to Mecca. Some apartment buildings actually stood back from their lot line in order to incorporate a modest landscaped setting. The Mecca did not do this. Instead, Edbrooke & Burnham gave the Mecca an unusual U-shaped plan centered on a landscaped courtyard that opened south onto 34th Street. On the way into the Mecca's main entrance, residents and visitors traversed the apartment equivalent of a suburban lawn, a "miniature park" measuring 66 by 152 feet (figs. 8.1, 8.2).[10]

The Mecca's exterior courtyard, with its handsome fountain, provided the first local example of the low-rise courtyard apartment building that proliferated in Chicago and its suburbs from 1900 through the 1920s.[11] In Chicago small residential parks had earlier provided a focus for single-family row-house developments like Aldine Square, built in 1876 at Vincennes Avenue between 37th and 39th streets (fig. 8.3). Beyond the landscaped court, the Mecca's plan also provided a bay window in nearly every parlor, increasing light and air circulation through the apartments. In subsequent Chicago courtyard designs the concern for natural light expanded to include sunrooms, balconies, and individual porches. For a given-sized lot, the courtyard configuration created a much longer embellished front façade than was possible in a building massed on the front lot line. In the Mecca, walls of high-quality Roman brick lined the courtyard and the three street façades. Cruder common red brick appeared only on the rear alley wall. In contrast to apartments built around interior light wells, these designs also opened a greater percentage of interior spaces to prime prospects over landscaped courts and to the street.[12] These elements compressed suburban forms for apartment tenants.

Courtyards also addressed another critical issue in the debate over apartment houses—that of domestic privacy.

Large apartment buildings that relied upon central stairs and elevators concentrated building residents and visitors at single main entrances, in lobbies, around stairs and elevators, and in common corridors linked to the circulation core. In contrast, courtyards diffused the building's density before people actually entered. As the courtyard form developed in Chicago, numerous entrances opened onto the courtyard. Each entrance gave access to a stair that generally reached only two apartments on each landing (fig. 8.4). Thus only six to eight families, as opposed to all of the building's tenants, used each entrance. Architectural critic Herbert Croly argued that Chicago courtyard buildings could "wear a domestic aspect," "obtain a certain amount of propriety," and "suggest the privacies and seclusion of Anglo-Saxon domestic life."[13]

The Mecca Atria
Density and Social Spectacle

Yet unlike Chicago courtyard apartments constructed later, the Mecca turned both outward toward its exterior courtyard and, most unusually, inward toward extraordinary interior atria. Edbrooke & Burnham planned each of the two primary wings of the Mecca around an enormous interior skylit atrium, each one measuring 33 by 170 feet (figs. 8.2, 8.5). In each wing a ground-story lobby, stairs, and heavily foliated ornamental balconies that cantilevered from the atrium's walls provided access to the individual apartments. Each apartment's interior rooms had windows opening onto the atria courts and received natural light from the gabled skylights. The atria provided the Mecca with two expansive interior spaces flooded with light that expressed in monumental form a pervasive cultural concern for light and air. Although suburban landscapes reflected this same desire for light, they rarely captured it in the monumental architectural forms that emerged as middle-class residents started living and working at much higher densities.

The Mecca's exterior courtyard helped establish a Chicago precedent for courtyard buildings; however, the atria distinguished it in important ways from subsequent courtyard buildings. The Mecca had two entrances on State, two on Dearborn, three in the courtyard, and one on the rear alley. The multiple entrances conformed to the general pattern of later courtyard buildings that discreetly diffused the building's density. Yet the Mecca's atria made a spectacle of the comings and goings of resi-

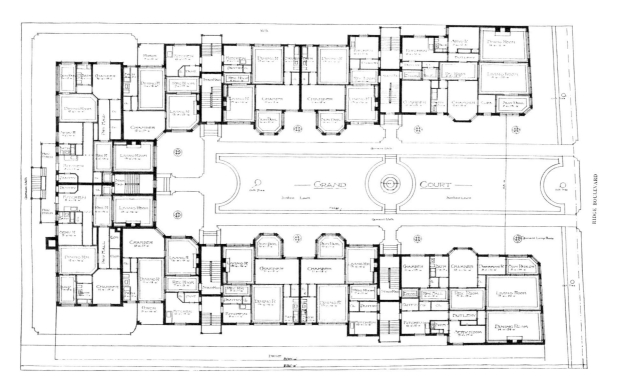

8.4. *Courtyard apartment plan with five separate entrances diffusing circulation. Oak Ridge Apartments, Evanston, Illinois, built 1914. Andrew Sandegren, architect.* Plan from A. J. Pardridge and Harold Bradley, *Directory to Apartments of the Better Class Along the North Side of Chicago* (Chicago, 1917).

8.5. The Mecca, 1891–1892. The interior atrium served as a "Ladies Parlor" when the Mecca provided hotel accommodations for the Columbian Exposition. Detail from 1893 advertisement. Chicago History Museum, ICHi-29342.

dents, of the concourse of daily human life. In the atria, on the balconies, at interior doors and windows, the massing of people in the Mecca clearly manifested itself. With their "promenade balconies," the atria developed as public places where people would see and be seen.[14] The atria thereby negated the potential for privacy made possible with courtyard entrances. Thus, the Mecca design contained two rich but contrary tendencies. One tendency, captured in the exterior courtyard and separate entrances, responded to entrenched fear over the compromise of single-family living and familial privacy; the other tendency, represented in the skylit atria, cultivated the possibilities of a gregarious and cosmopolitan gathering of 500 people under a single roof. It took only a few years for the more private model to completely rout the cosmopolitan one in the work of Chicago apartment architects.

The Mecca's novel courtyard followed the general logic evident in the downtown commercial landscape, where architects had learned to sacrifice space for light, "leaving out of doors everything that cannot be perfectly lighted."[15] Successful commercial architects warned that dark rooms would not be rented and should not be built.

8.6. The Mecca, built 1891–1892. Interior atrium with detail of foliated metalwork along the promenade balcony rail. Photograph by Wallace Kirkland, 1951. Chicago History Museum, ICHi-29352.

8.7. Chamber of Commerce Building, built 1888–1890. Baumann & Huehl, architects. View of balconies and interior skylit atrium where the developer and architect of the Mecca had offices. Avery Library, Columbia University.

8.8. Chicago, Burlington & Quincy Railroad Building, built 1881–1882, Burnham & Root, architects. Perspective of interior skylit atrium and balconies. From *New York Daily Graphic*, February 26, 1883.

The Mecca atria (fig. 8.6) had local precedents among some of Chicago's notable skyscrapers. The *Chicago Tribune* compared the Mecca's atria to the prominent skylit atrium in Baumann & Huehl's thirteen-story Chamber of Commerce Building, constructed in 1888. That building incorporated a 35-by-108-foot skylit atrium rimmed by galleries and ornate balustrades that provided access to the offices on every floor (fig. 8.7). Describing the Mecca plan in terms of the Chamber of Commerce Building, the *Tribune* settled on a model known for its prominent 200-foot-high atrium. Moreover, it singled out a building that the Mecca's architects knew well; Edbrooke & Burnham maintained their architectural offices at the very top of the Chamber of Commerce atrium.[16] George W. Henry, the Mecca's developer, had a real estate office opening onto the atrium two floors below Edbrooke & Burnham.

Beginning in the 1870s, many leading Chicago architects had developed great architectural effect by flooding the interiors of their increasingly massive buildings with natural light. In the 1880s the modern light-court atrium became an integral and monumental part of skyscraper architecture. In 1881, for example, Burnham & Root designed the six-story Chicago, Burlington & Quincy Railroad's office building around an atrium measuring over 100 by 50 feet. Iron galleries encircled the light

court, giving access to the offices (fig. 8.8). Burnham & Root's 1893 Masonic Temple Building contained a central light court that ran 302 feet to a rooftop skylight. Other Chicago office buildings incorporated central light courts without fully developing such dramatic architectural effects. Burnham & Root's 1885 Rookery Building, for example, enclosed a central light court at the level of its two-story lobby rather than at the top of the building and relied upon an internal double-loaded corridor system rather than galleries for access to offices.[17]

Chicago's skylit commercial and residential interiors drew upon a broad nineteenth-century building tradition. Technological developments in the manufacture of both glass and metal permitted the expansive lighting of interior spaces, which proved especially important given the increasing size and complexity of nineteenth-century buildings. Skylit retail arcades, with shop-lined pedestrian corridors, opened in major cities throughout Europe and the United States. The arcades, with central skylights and multistoried galleries, included key features of the atria system at the Mecca. Art galleries, train stations, conservatories, prisons and asylums, department stores, and office buildings all used skylights to great effect. Buildings like J. B. Bunning's Coal Exchange, London (1846–1849), had offices open onto galleries around a circular court topped by a glass and

8.9. The Yale, built 1892–1893. John T. Long, architect.
Photograph by C. R. Childs, c. 1909. Collection of LeRoy Blommaert.

8.10. The Yale, built 1892–1893. View of interior skylit atrium, stairs, and elevator core. Photograph by Mildred Mead, 1953. Chicago History Museum, ICHi-24351.

metal skylight. Many retail arcades provided housing on the floors above the shops.

The purely residential application of the arcade found formative expression in early-nineteenth-century utopian plans for phalansteries made by French social reformer Charles Fourier. It is notable that Fourier's vision of collective housing communities of 2,000 residents incorporated an interior "street gallery" to give access to apartments on several floors. It also included enclosed skylit passages between different parts of the community. The architecture of the phalanstery highlights the gregarious and collective basis of the residential atrium with its gallery corridor system. The preferences for domestic privacy in Chicago contrasted sharply with Fourier's own encouragement of community as well as with the use of atria by prison designers who sought better supervision of inmates. The Chicago structures extended the disparate uses of the building type.[18]

The Mecca's atria also reflected aspects of a broader European and American tradition of central-courtyard apartment buildings. Central courtyards provided a semipublic space with possibilities for weaving the fabric of community. In some notable model tenements, such as Alfred Treadway White's 1890 Riverside Apartments in Brooklyn, designers established courtyards as protected areas of leisure for both children and adults.

Courtyards also undoubtedly accommodated informal patterns of social life. Making a cultivated virtue out of the need to provide light to interior rooms, some developers planned handsome courtyard gardens, lawns, and carriage driveways. Nevertheless, most central courtyards functioned in the same way that exterior courtyards did; they distributed tenants into separate stairways and elevators located inside the walls of the building, giving access to only a few apartments per floor. Placing the entire circulation system outside in the courtyard space was far more unusual. The Ashfield Cottages, built in 1871 by the Liverpool Labourers' Dwelling Company, included exterior stairs and continuous balconies to reach apartments on the three upper stories. In 1895, Frank Lloyd Wright's two-story Chicago model tenement, Francisco Terrace, provided access to second-story units along a continuous balcony ringing a central courtyard. These unusual designs shared with the Mecca a level of spectacle and gregariousness lacking in more common courtyard buildings. In the United States, in general, domestic ideology deterred developers of central courtyard buildings from promoting or exploiting their potential for collective activity.[19]

The Mecca rose as the first Chicago residential building to appropriate the atrium. In 1892 local architects constructed two other Chicago apartment buildings

8.11. *The Brewster, built 1892–1896.*
Enoch Hill Turnock, architect.
Photograph by C. R. Childs, c. 1909.
Collection of LeRoy Blommaert.

around skylit atria. John T. Long designed the Yale, an apartment building at the corner of Yale Avenue and 66th Street. The seven-story Romanesque-style building had a six-story skylit and galleried atrium measuring 25 by 82 feet (figs. 8.9, 8.10).[20] Like the Mecca, the Yale's fifty-four apartments had interior rooms with windows opening onto the atrium. Built on its lot line, the Yale stood as a striking anomaly in its suburban neighborhood of Englewood, where two-story wood-frame houses set on landscaped lots dominated the local streetscape. Nevertheless, the flood of light entering the Yale's atrium evidenced a shared concern for light and air that characterized the area's development. In 1892, in a somewhat denser urban neighborhood on Chicago's North Side, Enock Hill Turnock designed the city's third skylit-atrium residential building. The eight-story Brewster Apartments at the corner of Diversey Boulevard and Pine Grove Avenue was initially planned in 1892, but it was not completed for several years (figs. 8.11, 8.12). The Brewster's central light court was narrower than the courts in the Mecca and the Yale. Glass-decked bridges extended across the center of the interior court on each

8.12. *The Brewster, built 1892–1896.*
View of interior skylit atrium, glass-block
hallway bridges, stairs, and elevator
core. Photograph by Bob Thall, 1982.
Commission on Chicago Landmarks.

floor, while short gangways extended to the doors of the building's forty-eight units.[21]

Developers constructed the Mecca, the Yale, and the Brewster during the building boom spurred by the World's Columbian Exposition. In 1894 the boom yielded to a deep depression that lasted until the turn of the century. When apartment building resumed, developers attended quite selectively to the precedents embodied in the Mecca. At the turn of the century developers constructed more than ten thousand apartment units in Chicago every single year. The number was usually four to five times higher than the number of single dwellings.[22] Looking back to the period of intense experimentation with building plans, developers built hundreds of apartment buildings with exterior courtyards like the one at the Mecca. They built no buildings with skylit, galleried atria; the interior skylight turned out to be a road not taken in Chicago residential design. Instead of atria, high-rise apartment buildings that concentrated tenants and visitors at main entrances and around elevators often included quite ornate lobbies that similarly provided grand interior public spaces. These elevator apartment buildings tended to cluster in a narrow geographical strip along the Lake Michigan shore. The effort to take advantage of the lake's scenic and recreational resources pushed land values higher and encouraged designers to orient floors toward prime views. In these high-rise areas, developers appeared less willing to make the generous allotments of space required for an interior light court when the real amenity of the location existed in exterior views of the lakeshore. Cultivation of views in high-rises and continuing efforts to foster images of domestic and suburban privacy in low-rises spurred alternative apartment arrangements at the turn of the century.

Changes in the Neighborhood

In the absence of architectural emulation, continued public and historical recognition of the Mecca's grand atria and innovative plan was more dependent on the fate of the building itself than on the structures it inspired. The Mecca's history thus became bound up with the dynamics of urban change that drastically altered both public

8.13. Armour Mission, built 1886. Burnham & Root, architects. From Irene Macauley, *The Heritage of Illinois Institute of Technology.*

8.14. *Armour Flats, built 1886–1890. Patton & Fisher, architects. Armour Flats at the right; the Mecca stands in the left background. The modest character of the wood-frame row houses was typical of the surrounding neighborhood. View taken c. 1909.* Collection of LeRoy Blommaert.

and private perceptions of the building. In the mid-nineteenth century few people had built or settled in the area around the future South Side site of the Mecca. When the railroads extended lines through the area in the 1850s, they brought in their wake various factory operations and block after block of working-class residences. The Mecca's site stood just a block east of the Chicago, Rock Island & Pacific Railroad. A major industrial belt developed on the far side of the track, where the sprawling Union Stock Yard opened in 1865. In the area east of the Mecca's future site, Senator Stephen A. Douglas established a 70-acre suburban lakeshore subdivision in the early 1850s and provided land there for the campus of the first University of Chicago. Between the suburban residences to the east and the stockyards to the west rose a large neighborhood of modest working-class homes—one- and two-story wood-frame and brick houses standing on 25-foot-wide lots.[23]

Situated on an emerging commercial artery and surrounded by rather modest homes, the lot at the corner of State and 34th streets did not seem to provide fertile ground for investing hundreds of thousands of dollars in a building intended for middle-class residents. The construction of monumental buildings in the 1880s and early 1890s on the single block immediately west of the Mecca's site undoubtedly encouraged the Mecca's developers. On this block the meatpacking Armour family made a substantial philanthropic investment in middle-class domesticity. In 1886, with a fund of over $200,000, the Plymouth Congregational Church opened its Armour Mission. Occupying a handsome Romanesque-style building designed by Burnham & Root, the mission provided spiritual, educational, and recreational programs for the neighborhood's poorer residents (fig. 8.13). In 1886, in an effort to establish a system of perpetual support for the mission, Philip D. Armour constructed the Armour Flats, 29 three- and four-story buildings with 194 large middle-class apartments. The profits from rentals would support the mission. Patton & Fisher, architects of the Armour Flats, took advantage of the whole-block site to disguise the dense apartment development in the formal elements of single-family row houses. Rusticated Marquette sandstone fronts, with pressed brick and terra-cotta, conspicuous placement of chimney stacks and corner turrets, bay windows, varied massing, and variable design treatment of adjacent sections adopted the general forms of the city's recent single-family architecture (fig. 8.14).[24] Armour encouraged middle managers and other employees in his company to rent apartments in the Armour Flats.[25]

In 1891, Armour laid the cornerstone for a massive five-story building, designed by Patton & Fisher. Built to house the Armour Institute, chartered with $1 million from Armour, the impressive structure accommodated a college for training industrial technicians and engineers. The building added a final note of monumentality to the block it completed just west of the Mecca's site (fig. 8.15). By the time the institute opened its doors, the Mecca was nearing completion on State Street The connections between Armour and the Mecca intensified in the coming decades; simple geography and complex urban dynamics increasingly enmeshed their institutional and architectural histories.

When the Mecca opened, it provided apartments for Chicago residents; however, hoping to cash in on World's Columbian Exposition business, the owners rented hotel rooms. The Mecca stood midway between the fair and the downtown "business and amusement" area. State Street cable cars ran by the door; and the 33rd Street station of the recently completed South Side elevated train stood a block away. The Mecca Hotel offered special advantages to families, who could stay in five- to seven-room furnished suites with bathrooms. The hotel also rented single rooms for 75 cents to $2 per day, with corner and bay-window rooms costing slightly more. Patronage by visitors to the fair passed quickly and was followed by a deep national economic depression. The Mecca failed to establish a solidly middle-class tenant population. In fact, its initial owners lost the building in foreclosure. Paul J. Sorg, an industrialist from Middletown, Ohio, who had purchased and leased the Mecca's site to the developers for $12,000 a year, ended up owning both the land and the building. Sorg subdivided some of the flats; renters could obtain two- to seven-room apartments for between $10 and $35 per month. These rents were generally lower than those charged for middle-class South Side apartments located both east and south of the Mecca.[26]

When the United States government's census taker visited the Mecca in June 1900, he found 107 units occupied by 365 people. There were blue-collar and white-collar employees and relatively few middle-class professionals. The Mecca accommodated carpenters, electricians, house painters, dry-goods, railroad, and grocery clerks, as well as clerks in insurance and other business offices, traveling salesmen, egg inspectors, day laborers, several bartenders, waiters, cooks, tailors, bookkeepers, a typesetter, machinists, a butcher, a packinghouse foreman, an architect, a physician, an optician, a musician, locomotive engineers and firemen, railroad and elevator conductors, music teachers, a watchman, a postal clerk, a glass cutter, a freight checker, janitors, a real estate agent, a coachman, a teamster, a decorator, a retired capitalist, and a frog dealer. Some families made the rent by taking in boarders. No family had live-in servants. The vast majority of Mecca residents in 1900 were born in the United States; many had parents born in the United States. Some residents had Scottish-, Irish-, German-, Canadian-, or Polish-born parents. All of the Mecca's residents were white.[27]

The surrounding neighborhood was not nearly as uniform. During a time in which the black population of the city was expanding rapidly, poverty and racial exclusion in housing had spurred an increasingly concentrated black settlement pattern. South Side blacks settled in an area known as the Black Belt, a narrow strip of land along the railroad and industrial land just west of the Mecca, from the downtown southward. It extended east of the Mecca to Wabash Avenue, which after the early 1890s suffered from the blighting effects of the elevated transit line running down the alley between Wabash and State streets. In 1900, blacks occupied many houses in this area, stretching from the Loop south to 39th Street. They lived in some of the more modest houses on the

8.15. Armour Institute Main Building, built 1891–1893. Patton & Fisher, architects. From Irene Macauley, *The Heritage of Illinois Institute of Technology.*

north end of the block occupied by the Mecca, and they pursued many of the same occupations as their white neighbors in the Mecca—house painter, day laborer, cook, paperhanger, and porter. Set in an integrated neighborhood, the internalized atria in the Mecca constituted a more exclusively white realm.[28]

The racial disparity between the Mecca and its neighborhood increased over the next decade. In 1910 the Mecca's residents were still white, while blacks occupied many adjacent houses and apartments. Like the Mecca apartments, the Armour Flats continued to have only white tenants. In 1910 native-born Americans still predominated in the Mecca, though there were also German, Swedish, Austrian, Canadian, Irish, Scottish, English, and Russian immigrants living in the building. Russian-born Israel Goldman, for example, the fifty-year-old sexton of a local synagogue, lived in a Mecca unit with his wife, Golda, and three of his four children, including a son who worked as a tailor and a daughter who was a dressmaker. In 1910 the Mecca housed porters, cooks, waiters, hatmakers, actors, journalists, day laborers, piano movers, elevator operators, and many other people with occupations similar to those who had lived in the building in 1900.[29]

In 1911 the Sorg estate sold the Mecca for $400,000—half the amount it cost to build twenty years earlier. With a gross annual rent of $42,000 and a $170,000 mortgage at 5.5 percent, the Mecca investment looked attractive. In 1912, Franklin T. Pember, a banker, fur trader, and commission merchant, agricultural-implement manufacturer, and prominent naturalist and philanthropist in upstate New York, and his wife Ellen purchased the Mecca.[30] The Pembers' investment came just a few years before a massive migration of African-Americans from the rural South to Chicago industrial jobs, spurred by World War I production. As Chicago's black population more than doubled in the 1910s, from 44,103 to 109,458, the neighborhood around the Mecca received an influx of new residents. Real estate interests and many white Chicagoans greeted African-American residential expansion with alarm and hostility, ranging from threats and broken windows to house bombings. Racial violence encouraged a more concentrated settlement pattern among blacks than had previously existed. It also created both economic and social pressure for the conversion of white-occupied residential buildings within and adjacent to the already established Black Belt neighborhood.[31] In the months after their purchase of the Mecca, the Pembers' rental agent began to advertise in the *Chicago Defender* and to rent apartments to African Americans. The advertisements declared that the Mecca was for "first class people only." The twenty-year-old building

now stood as a monumental addition to Chicago's South Side Black Belt.[32]

In July 1919 racial tensions on Chicago's South Side burst into a full-scale riot. A group of whites stoned a black youth swimming in Lake Michigan, who drowned as a result. The incident sparked over a week of mob action that took a huge toll, including 38 people killed, 537 injured, and over 1,000 people displaced from their homes. Some of the most serious rioting occurred up and down State Street both north and south of the Mecca.[33] The building had completed its transition from white to black tenants before the riot.[34] In 1920 it was occupied by people with many of the same occupations as those who had previously lived in the building. There were porters, foundry molders, machinists, upholsterers, tanners, tailors, butchers, bakers, cooks, laundresses, janitors, maids, bellboys, hairdressers, manicurists, day laborers, switchmen, steelworkers, musicians, chauffeurs, postal clerks, shipping clerks, peddlers, and mattress, mantle, shade, dress, and cigar makers. Nearly all of the residents were born in the United States, and the majority were born outside of Illinois, largely in southern states. The census takers counted 148 occupied units with 510 residents. Many families took in boarders to help pay the rent. Mecca households were now large and complex. Thomas McClure, for example, a thirty-one-year-old native of Alabama, worked as a chauffeur for the Nash Motor Company and lived with his wife, Lula, a twenty-eight-year-old native of Tennessee, who was not employed outside of the home. The McClures accommodated a forty-eight-year-old uncle, Nobles Clark, a native of Tennessee, who worked as a packing-company butcher. Jesse Walker, a twenty-nine-year-old packing-house laborer from Alabama, and Mattie Pierson, a twenty-one-year-old waitress from South Carolina, also lived with the McClures.[35]

South Side Jazz Clubs and the "Mecca Flat Blues"

When the Mecca turned from white to black, the spectacle of public life that played out in the exterior courtyard and around the atria became more closely patterned after life in the immediate neighborhood (fig. 8.16). In the late 1910s the Mecca stood just a block north of what emerged as Chicago's African-American business and retail center. Around 35th and State streets, business buildings, many constructed by African Americans, housed banks, real estate and insurance offices, retail stores, fraternal lodges, and newspaper offices. In the 1910s and 1920s this area also

8.16. Keith Elementary School students crossing the intersection of 34th Street and Dearborn Street in front of the Mecca. Photograph by Wallace Kirkland, 1951. Chicago History Museum, ICHi-29353

accommodated a dynamic nightlife, including many Chicago's leading jazz clubs, featuring such musicians as King Oliver, Louis Armstrong, and Jelly Roll Morton. The Pekin Theater at 27th and State streets led the way when it opened in 1905; other clubs included the De Luxe, a block south of the Mecca; the Dreamland Café, two blocks south; and the Elite Club, three blocks north. The Royal Gardens and the Sunset Café on 35th Street shared local nightlife with other clubs such as High Life and the Entertainers.[36]

Links between the Mecca and jazz were immortalized when local bands began to play and record improvised blues tunes titled the "Mecca Flat Blues." In August 1924 pianist and composer James "Jimmy" Blythe recorded "Mecca Flat Blues" with jazz singer Priscilla Stewart. Two years later Blythe followed with a song titled "Lovin's Been Here and Gone to Mecca Flat." In 1939 pianist Albert Ammons also recorded "Mecca Flat Blues," and musicians have continued

to record versions of the music down to the present. Jimmy Blythe and Priscilla Stewart's version of the song gave dramatic personae to the "Mecca Flat Man" and the "Mecca Flat Woman," who led sensual and adulterous lives, causing no end of heartbreak to their partners. Local "extemporizing troubadours" continually added episodes to the "Mecca Flat Blues," charting the "trials, tribulations, and tragedies" of the residents. One observer speculated that if collected and printed the verses would "make a book."[37]

The musicians were doing more than simply punning on musical notations when they seized upon the Mecca "Flat." By referring to the local people and landmarks, they could root their blend of New Orleans, St. Louis, and other jazz expressions into a distinct Chicago idiom. Tales of heartbreak and adultery, the stuff of the blues, were perhaps more apparent at the Mecca because of the urban spectacle captured around the atria; these tales seemed to confirm the nineteenth-century critique of apart-ment-house living. Here, according to the songs, were concentrated the temptations and evils of high-density living and the obvious intrusions on familial privacy and domestic virtue. Nevertheless, the pub-lic space of the atria helped give the Mecca a sense of place and a comprehensible identity that few other "private" buildings enjoyed. The public permeability of the domestic realm that had made the design prob-lematic in its conception now contributed to its fame, or notoriety, in Chicago culture. In the 1960s, Chicago poet Gwendolyn Brooks expanded the Mecca canon in verse. Her work "In the Mecca" follows family members in search of a lost child, visiting flat after flat and making inquiries along the balconies. The poem nicely captures the cosmopolitanism of a build-ing with an array of alluring, fascinating, as well as repulsive characters.[38]

Armour Institute, the Black Belt, and the Mecca

Simple geography had always united the Mecca and the Armour Mission, Institute, and Flats. On the face of it, the shifting racial composition of the neighborhood should not have affected Armour, with its ecumenical and racially inclusive vision. The mission was estab-lished to be "broad and wholly non-sectarian, without any restrictions whatsoever as to race, creed, and color." Armour Institute was an integrated school since its founding in the 1890s. Nevertheless, Armour officials were troubled by the expansion of the Black Belt, as they found it increasingly difficult to persuade company employees and Armour Institute faculty to live in the Armour Flats. Mission and institute officials responded curiously to the housing crunch caused by the migration of African Americans to Chicago: they demolished the Armour Flats. Between 1917 and 1919, 131 of the 194 apartments were torn down, and many of the remaining units were converted to offices, laboratories, and class-rooms (fig. 8.17.)[39]

In demolishing the Armour Flats, the officials eliminated vestiges of the middle-class residential landscape that had provided the context for construc-tion of the Mecca. Despite creating a physical buffer between its academic buildings and the surround-ing residences, Armour actively tried to relocate the campus altogether. There had been some discussion as early as 1902 of becoming affiliated with the Uni-versity of Chicago. In 1920, J. Ogden Armour paid $1 million to purchase an 80-acre tract of land in South Shore, a growing suburban neighborhood of Chicago, five miles south of the institute. Subsequently expe-riencing financial difficulties, Armour sold the South Shore site in 1922, stating that it had grown too valu-able to hold while awaiting the resources to fund the institute's relocation.[40]

The Armour Institute persisted in efforts to raise an endowment and leave its historic campus. In the 1920s it attempted to affiliate with Northwestern University, and in the 1930s, Armour considered a move into an eleven-story building on Lake Shore Drive, north of downtown. The Depression heightened the distress with which institute officials viewed their location and at the same time diminished the possibility of amassing resources for relocation. In 1937 a committee of the institute's Board of Trustees intensively studied Armour's pros-pects. Board president James Cunningham insisted that the institute had a bright future as a leading school of scientific and engineering education, governed by a board of industrial leaders who "think straight," in one of the world's largest industrial centers.[41]

In 1937 the board clearly viewed the institute's fate as tied to its location. After spending months looking at sites in the Loop, on the North Side, on the West Side, as well as in suburban locations, a board committee advo-cated remaining at the existing location. Cunningham reported:

This will undoubtedly shock some of you out of your chairs. The present site, at Thirty-third and Federal, was, and I say "was" advisedly, in the heart of the Black Belt, but it got too dilapidated and run down for the Negroes so they have moved further south. They have left a totally devastated area in their wake, to be sure. It is axiomatic that when anything has gotten to the very bottom the only direction it can go is up, and this is just the conclu-sion of the Committee. The present Institute occupies a site of nine acres. It is proposed to purchase about thirty acres of property adjoining the nine acres. . . . Wrecking of the buildings in the entire area could be accomplished, I think, by a moderate wind storm, so dilapidated are the structures. . . . There is a possibility of having State Street boulevarded from the Loop south, which, of course, would greatly influence the trend of this entire district. Many students of real estate are definitely committed to the development of this area from the Loop south, as a so-called white collar community.[42]

The board then mapped out a strategy for quietly pur-chasing the necessary parcels, including the Mecca, to control the area from 31st Street south to 35th Street, from State west to the Rock Island tracks.

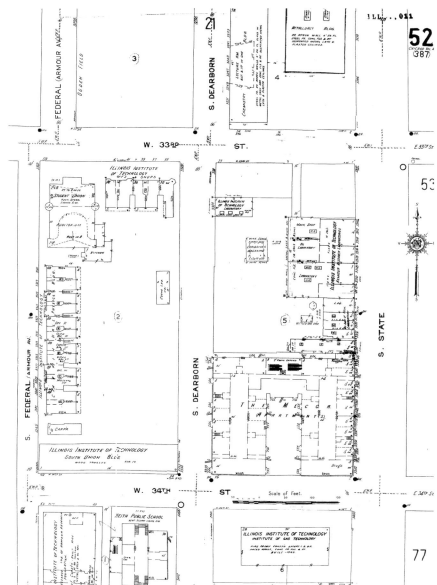

8.17. Map of the Mecca and the Illinois Institute of Technology, 1949. The vacant land along Dearborn was occupied by the Armour Flats before their demolition in 1917–1919. "Chapin Hall," fronting on Federal, adapted part of the Armour Flats as a physics laboratory. The Armour Mission has been converted into the Student Union. From Sanborn Map Company, *Insurance Maps of Chicago, Volume 4, 1912–1949*. Library of Congress.

The institute modeled its plans on slum clearance precedents of the 1930s. Federal legislation enacted in 1934 and 1937 supported massive assembly and clearance of urban tracts. Starting in the mid-1930s, planners proposed numerous South Side clearance projects. In 1934 the federal government selected a 47-acre tract at 37th Street and South Park Avenue for the Ida B. Wells Homes. Opened in 1941, the project provided 1,662 units of public housing on a site that had previously contained nineteenth-century brownstone row houses and single-family detached houses. Landlords had subdivided many of these buildings into more modest units, occupied primarily by African-American tenants.[43] These land clearance programs provided some institutions with an alternative to suburbanization; they might choose to stay in their historic locations, buffered from neighborhoods in decline by cleared land and renewed neighborhoods.

Departing from prevailing approaches to Chicago urban renewal, the institute initially adopted a plan for pursuing renewal through the private real estate market. Newton C. Farr, a Chicago realtor who directed the board's campaign to purchase property for the institute, reported that the Mecca, with 178 apartments, "occupied by colored," was one property that "has caused us some concern in the expansion." Farr thought that the building, with a gross annual income of $38,881 and a net income of $9,739, could be purchased for $85,000. In 1938 the board's secretary, Alfred L. Eustice, acting as a private citizen, bought the Mecca from Franklin Pember's estate for $85,000.[44] Meanwhile, the institute's land acquisition program secretly continued for several years and involved dozens of purchases.

Illinois Institute of Technology: Mies van der Rohe's Campus Plans and Neighborhood Resistance

People deliberating the Armour institute's future proved acutely sensitive to the landscape and racial character of the surrounding neighborhood. In 1940 the institute's president, Henry Townley Heald, wrote that it had been "beset" by the "increasing deterioration of its neighborhood."[45] The board saw the "morale" of both faculty and students decline. For years, through all of the various relocation plans, people openly worried that the institute's immediate urban context might frustrate its effort to rival national institutions such as the Massachusetts Institute of Technology and the California Institute of Technology.[46] These concerns intensified when Armour merged with the Lewis Institute to form the Illinois Institute of Technology in 1940. The next year the institute went public with its plans for a new campus, with modern buildings on a site cleared of its Black Belt identity. Even with the central site under control, the board continued to worry about the approaches to the campus; it had hoped for a boulevard from the Loop, but also wanted to control the frontage of all streets approaching the future campus.[47]

In 1941, when Alfred Eustice deeded the Mecca to the institute, the building quickly crystallized the racial and class calculus that governed the board's view of its neighborhood's people and buildings. By the early 1940s the Mecca accommodated more than a thousand residents. The combination of a decade of depression, the onset of further war-induced migration, and continuing white hostility to the expansion of black housing resulted in the Mecca's having far more residents than the building was designed to accommodate. The sheer density and visibility of the people who resided there had made the place an object of cultural interest in the 1920s. As the institute pursued its campus plans, that same density and visibility came to symbolize all that the board deplored about its location. By the same token, the fact that so many people called the Mecca home presented a problem for the institute's clearance plans. The board hoped that the mere act of purchase would let it

tidily clear a monument of neighborhood "blight" from one of its approaches. It soon became clear that local residents had not, in fact, moved farther south and that it would require more than a "moderate wind storm" to clear the site.[48]

When the institute took control of the Mecca in 1941, it aimed to demolish the structure as quickly as possible. Nevertheless, the board resolved to wait until Mecca leases expired in September 1942 to vacate the building. A sense of urgency hung over the Mecca deliberations because Chicago's Fire Prevention Bureau had brought suit against the institute to force it to install a fire sprinkler system required by the local building code.[49] The sprinkler for the Mecca was estimated to cost as much as $26,000. The institute stalled on the sprinkler litigation, hoping that either tenant leases would lapse or the court would order it to demolish the building immediately. By 1942, however, the war had exacerbated the housing crisis, and the proposed demolition took on a very different meaning. As the leases began to expire, the institute tried vacating the building. This stirred public debate, as the Metropolitan Housing Council, the Chicago Urban League, the Chicago Welfare Administration, and local politicians joined with Mecca's tenants to protest. The Metropolitan Housing Council professed no great affection for the Mecca, which it considered old, overcrowded, unsanitary, and a fire hazard; nonetheless, it reported: "There's a war on, and it looks as if there'll be little more new building, if any, in Chicago. And the Negro community is beyond the saturation point"[50]

In 1942, Newton Farr expressed some sympathy for the plight of Mecca tenants. As long as the war limited campus building, the $22,000 in net rental income seemed attractive as a means of funding institute real estate purchases. President Heald was unmoved by Farr's arguments. Ignoring the number of boarding families, he insisted that surely it would be possible to "absorb" 175 families "somewhere in the total colored population." Giving voice to entrenched distaste for the Mecca and the appearance of the institute's neighborhood, Heald concluded, "As long as it stands, it is a distinct handicap to our efforts to clean up our campus area and, even though it produces an income, I really believe that it is worth more to us torn down than in its present state."[51] Despite this view, the pressure of the civic organizations as well as a direct appeal from Alderman Arthur G. Lindell, chair of the Chicago City Council's Housing Committee, persuaded the institute to defer demolition of the building.

In 1943 the Mecca preservation battle moved to the Illinois House and Senate. State Senator Christopher

Wimbish, an African-American graduate of Northwestern University Law School, effectively galvanized a huge coalition against the Mecca's impending demolition. His bill barring the demolition passed in the House 114 to 2 and in the Senate 46 to 1. The legislative debate featured impassioned appeals to patriotism. Advocates of the bill pointed out that more than forty residents of the Mecca were fighting abroad "for democracy they did not enjoy at home," and yet the institute proposed to tear down the roof over the heads of their families. One delegate charged that the bill's interference with private property rights was "un-American." This claim met a harsh rejoinder from one of the bill's supporters: "You who refuse to vote to prevent the eviction of these women, children, and war workers, the lame and the sick, from the Mecca flats; you who vote 'No' on this roll call, you are un-American, you are vicious."[52] Beyond patriotism, the bill's supporters hoped to prevent "trouble" that could be expected when Mecca tenants searched for housing in adjacent white neighborhoods.[53] Despite broad support, Governor Dwight Green vetoed the Mecca bill as unconstitutional.[54]

After the governor's veto, Senator Wimbish pushed the battle forward in Chicago Municipal Court, where he represented tenants threatened with eviction. Wimbish argued that the case involved "property rights versus human rights." He pointed to the difficulties faced by blacks in finding housing in a city where "restrictive covenants and neighborhood clannishness prohibits normal expansion"; the tenants were "hemmed in by an American ghetto system." Institute lawyers had to admit that the site could not be rebuilt until after the war; but they argued that the building was unsafe and should be torn down immediately. In his ruling, Judge Samuel Heller barred the evictions and ordered the institute to abide by all municipal building and safety codes.[55] The institute hired a watchman rather than install sprinklers. It also sent a letter to tenants demanding that they move out, stating, "ALL PERSONS WHO CONTINUE TO REMAIN IN THE BUILDING DO SO ON THEIR OWN RESPONSIBILITY AND AT THEIR OWN RISK."[56] These developments added a dimension of political history to the building's significant architectural and cultural history.

Just a few months after failing in its effort to demolish the Mecca, IIT sought to put some distance between itself and the building. In July 1943 the United States War Department decided to sell the Stevens Hotel, purchased at the outset of World War II to serve as a training school and barracks. The twenty-five-story building on Michigan Avenue between Seventh and Eighth streets, designed between 1922 and 1927 by Holabird & Roche,

had 3,000 rooms, a myriad of public meeting spaces, a convention hall seating 4,000, and kitchen and dining facilities. With over 1.5 million square feet of space, the building could easily be converted to house the institute's dormitories, laboratories, offices, classrooms, library, auditorium, and gymnasium. When the board heard about the availability of the Stevens, it jumped at the chance to move from the "heart of the Black Belt" to the "heart of Chicago's cultural center." One board member insisted that the move would have a positive "psychological effect" on faculty and students.[57] The board reported that dormitory space with a view across Grant Park to Lake Michigan would help the institute cultivate "national importance." Proximity to the Art Institute, the Field Museum, the Planetarium, the Chicago Public Library, and other institutions would add a "humanistic-cultural background" to IIT's "scientific-technological education."[58]

The institute lost the Stevens with a cash bid that was $581,000 less than that of an investor who planned to reopen the building as a hotel.[59] IIT then revived earlier plans to clear a space for itself in and around its original campus. President Heald vigorously advocated clearance and redevelopment of broad tracts well beyond the institute's immediate bounds. In 1946, at a Chicago housing forum, Heald termed the existence of 15,000 acres of blighted land in Chicago "intolerable." "Blight is a deadly disease which attacks and destroys cities and devours the property and investments in them," he stated. He advocated eminent domain to assemble large tracts and subsidies to encourage developers to rebuild in urban areas rather than in expanding suburbs. He declared that institute officials "had only two choices—run away from the blight or to stand and fight. I submit that this is everybody's choice—and that behind the principle of 'Stand and Fight' is where we must all be counted."[60] After years of flirting with running away, the institute would stand. Fighting meant, among other things, fighting to demolish the Mecca. It also meant that the institute would become a key partner in the massive postwar South Side urban renewal program. In 1946, IIT and Michael Reese Hospital joined forces to establish the South Side Planning Board, a not-for-profit organization advocating a new vision for the area. The Planning Board, with Heald serving as its first chairman, focused on a large area from Roosevelt Road to 47th Street, the Rock Island tracks to Lake Michigan. It maintained that this seven-square-mile tract was the minimum planning area needed for successful redevelopment. The board advocated the South Expressway construction, which involved demolition of a huge area of very modest housing just west of the

8.18. Photo collage of a model for the Illinois Institute of
Technology's campus expansion and an aerial view of the
South Side of Chicago, Ludwig Mies van der Rohe, lead archi-
tect and planner for campus expansion. Photograph,
c. 1940. Courtesy Mies van der Rohe Archives, Museum of Modern
Art. Copyright Artists Rights Society.

campus. It also quickly identified 333 acres for public
clearance, including the entire neighborhood between
the institute and the lake.[61]

Despite advocating construction of private and public housing, IIT did not want low-income housing just
anywhere and continued its efforts to transform the
immediate campus area into a middle-class, white-collar
community. In 1944, when the institute's board learned
that the Chicago Housing Authority was planning a low-
income housing project just north of the campus, toward
the Loop, it lodged a strong protest. Heald had envisioned neighborhood housing for students and faculty
"unhampered by the construction of low-cost housing.
. . . We believe that with a great Center of Technology
as a stimulus, a large area of the South Side can be completely rehabilitated and once again become a really
important commercial, residential, and cultural area of
the City."[62] The institute failed to keep public housing

away. Just to its north, the Dearborn Homes, the first
high-rise public housing in the city, opened in 1950. With
sixteen elevator buildings, six and nine stories high and
including eight hundred units, the Dearborn Homes
took the form of Modernist towers spread across expansive greenswards.[63] Modernizing neighborhood form
and style, the building did not alter the area's racial or
class character.

As plans for South Side renewal and IIT's campus
developed, it became obvious that the Mecca represented more than a social and political challenge. The
building stood in stark contrast to the palette of Modern architecture envisioned as a key to a new urbanism and a changed neighborhood. The arrival in 1938
of Ludwig Mies van der Rohe to head the institute's
Department of Architecture boosted the vision of a
new architecture for the area. Mies used a number of
early studio classes to design a new campus and then

opened a private office to develop the plans more fully.[64] Proposing a radically different architectural expression, Mies's plan called for demolition of the Romanesque-style Armour Mission and Armour Institute. In their place Mies, who eventually designed twenty-two buildings for the institute, proposed strikingly Modern-styled buildings in brick, glass, and welded steel. Clean, abstract lines and carefully proportioned spaces resonated with the broader agenda of "cleaning up the neighborhood."

Mies's style also reinforced the vision of a radical break with the historic and, in the minds of IIT officials, the blighted character of the neighborhood. Photocollage techniques used to present the campus plan underscored the institute's effort to establish a unified stylistic and urban form. The visual representations effectively placed a photo of an architectural model of the proposed campus on top of an aerial photograph of the South Side. Order and harmony confronted the hodgepodge of high and low, wide and narrow, wood and brick, commercial and residential buildings (fig. 8.18). Since the campus plan aimed to demolish the adjacent neighborhood, it adopted a dominant low-rise, low-density form that sprawled across a landscaped site made up of cleared land and vacated alley and street right-of-ways of the earlier urban grid. In place of older buildings pressed to the lot line (fig. 8.19), the new campus would move buildings away from street fronts and surround them with grass (fig. 8.20). The Mecca, built on its lot line on both State and Dearborn streets, and including patches of terra-cotta ornament, obviously frustrated the stylistic and urban intentions of the early campus plans, disposed symmetrically around an axis running along 33rd Street (figs. 8.18,

8.19. The Mecca, built 1891–1892. View looking west along 34th Street with the Armour Flats visible in the background. The Mecca stands on its lot line. Two of the Mecca's State Street stores are visible. A large fence separates the exterior courtyard from the street in this view. Photograph, c. 1909. Collection of LeRoy Blommaert.

8.21). Planners also hoped that the campus would "have a harmonious relation to its environment," which they felt would be built up with "well planned housing developments surrounded by large park areas."[65] In fact, Skidmore, Owings & Merrill, Walter Gropius, Reginald Isaacs, and other noted Modernist designers who consulted on South Side planning shared Mies's commitment to a radical break with historic architectural and urban forms.[66] Modern urbanism generally eschewed historic patterns of retail spaces oriented to streets and pedestrians. These older patterns, exemplified by the Mecca's twelve stores fronting on State Street, ran counter to the single-use zoning and specialized patterns advocated by modern planners.

Campus plans and Mies's aesthetic ideals contained

8.20. At left is the Institute of Gas Technology Building, built 1947–1950. Ludwig Mies van der Rohe, architect. The building sits on a grass plot, away from the lot line. The Mecca is in the background, standing on its lot line. Photograph by Wallace Kirkland, 1951. Chicago History Museum, ICHi-29349.

8.21. *Illinois Institute of Technology Campus Model, Chicago, c. 1942. Ludwig Mies van der Rohe, architect. View includes faculty member James Clinton Peebles (left), Mies van der Rohe (center), Institute President Henry T. Heald (right).* From Irene Macauley, *The Heritage of Illinois Institute of Technology.*

little room for accomodation with the fifty-year-old Mecca. The rigid ideal of campus symmetry did eventually give way to incorporate the institute's earliest building, designed by Patton & Fisher, but the inclusion of this historic structure memorializing the institute's origin in philanthropic support undoubtedly proved easier than preserving neighborhood narratives associated with the Mecca. A more complicated form of campus planning that might have incorporated the Mecca and other existing buildings did not take place. Moreover, the institute never considered using the Mecca as a dormitory for students, even though its atria could have ideally accommodated the many students who reveled in the gregariousness of campus social life. Using the Mecca as a student residence hall would have compromised part of the institute's rationale for displacing the Mecca's black tenants—that the building had to be demolished because it failed to meet building codes.[67]

In the mid-1940s, Skidmore, Owings & Merrill made a plan for IIT student and faculty housing, reporting that, beyond a few old residences on Michigan Avenue that could be temporarily used as fraternity houses, none of the neighborhood buildings were suitable for housing.[68] Failing to view existing buildings, such as the Mecca, as a resource for campus expansion entailed steep costs. The institute's housing program adopted a high-rise model that led it to spend over $1 million apiece for ten-story apartment buildings, such as Gunsaulus Hall designed by Mies, that accommodated many

fewer residents than had lived in the Mecca in the 1890s. The institute and its planners saw little value in neighboring buildings. Leaders of the African-American community, including realtor Oscar C. Brown, president of the Chicago Negro Chamber of Commerce, advocated a planning approach that would identify the numerous dwellings that should be "left standing and integrated into the larger redevelopment program." More concerned with decent housing opportunities for African-Americans than with developing buffers between South Side institutions and their neighbors, Brown urged a less radical, more preservation-oriented vision of South Side renewal.[69] Yet, planners were determined to carve out a single-purpose academic campus where engineering students would be insulated from the very society they were being educated to serve.

After the war IIT started construction of its modern campus. In February 1950 the board noted an easing of South Side housing and renewed its push to demolish the Mecca.[70] President Heald again insisted that the building was unsafe.[71] Mecca tenants responded with mass protests (figs. 8.22, 8.23). Again Senator Wimbish advised them of possible legal and administrative remedies. Lillian Davis, a Mecca tenant, argued that it was "unconstitutional" to evict rent-paying tenants: "It's a law of life that a person has to have a place to live."[72] Ward aldermen filed proposals to bar issuance of wrecking permits until tenants had been legally evicted and a program initiated to alleviate their hardships. These proposals went to the City

8.22. Mecca
tenants organiz-
ing meeting.
Photograph by
Charles Stewart,
Jr., 1950. Chicago
History Museum,
ICHi-25338.

Council's Committee on Housing, which failed to take action.[73] Despite the echoes of earlier arguments, the dynamics of the preservation campaign had changed. Tenants did not argue against demolition so much as insist upon expedited assistance in locating alternative space in private or public housing.[74] The institute had sapped the energy of the preservation movement by continually lowering rents and filling the building with poorer and poorer people while refusing to put money into maintenance and repairs. The exterior courtyard deteriorated into an unkempt dirt patch, and graffiti covered interior walls. When the courts permitted relocations and evictions to proceed, squatters quickly moved into the Mecca apartments, furthering the building's reputation as "a prime example of the worst slum tenements."[75]

8.23. Mecca tenants filing legal motions in
the Illinois Institute of Technology's eviction
proceedings. Photograph by Charles Stewart, Jr.,
1950. Chicago History Museum, ICHi-24830

Mecca Myth:
Golden Age and Demolition

In the early 1950s these renewed efforts to demolish the Mecca were framed by a distorted historical narrative. A Mecca myth arose that embodied a classical story of a fall from grace. In this rendering of Mecca history the "last word in show apartments" had fallen into a "slum tenement," brought on by "deterioration" that originated when blacks moved into the building.[76] Built during "Chicago's golden age" for "fat cats" and the "rising

rich," the Mecca was once a "showplace because of its floors of Italian tile, its rising tiers of balconies overlooking enclosed courtyards where fountains played." Then "the rich tenants moved out; and the not-so-rich who replaced them gave up the Mecca's elegance to underprivileged Negroes"; the Mecca became "Chicago's most notorious . . . slum."[77]

Author John Bartlow Martin extended the Mecca myth in an extended essay on the building titled "The Strangest Place in Chicago," which was published in *Harper's Magazine* in 1950.[78] Martin developed the story of a "splendid palace," a "showplace" that had dazzled people as the "finest apartment building in Chicago if not in America." Then came the fall, providing a "showplace but of a very different sort . . . one of the most remarkable Negro slum exhibits in the world." Martin's article, illustrated by haunting line drawings by Ben Shahn, absolutely captured the building's gregarious life that centered on the interior atria (fig. 8.24). Here the disorder of the place appeared. Martin wrote of men and women spitting from the balconies to the floor below. The noises of the building's tenants always filled the atria. A toddler urinated from the balcony to the floor below. People reported the time when a pimp threw a prostitute from the balcony and when a man murdered the building's janitor in a struggle over a woman. Martin's essay recognized the same public massing of humanity around the atria that versions of the "Mecca Flat Blues" had captured. In the view of IIT and other South Side planners, the Mecca's fall from grace crystallized and rendered inescapable the logic of urban renewal and the need for inaugurating a new "golden age."

Martin's essay contrasted IIT's Modern campus of "sleek brick-and-glass buildings surrounded by new trees and new grass" with the Mecca, a "great gray hulk."[79] The conceptual tropes of traditional style and materials giving way to the Modern, of novelty gone stale, high gone low, white gone black, all supported the institute's demolition plan. The overall treatment of the Mecca presented it as a building unworthy of a longer life, a building that had slipped so far from its intended social station that it failed to stir a sense of historic veneration. Yet the tenants anticipated loss. Jesse Meals, who had lived in the Mecca for thirty-one years, told a

reporter "You watch, a lot of people who lived here, they gonna die from grief."[80]

A year after the *Harper's* essay appeared, *Life* magazine reworked Martin's narrative in captions for a photo essay by Wallace Kirkland titled "The Mecca, Chicago's Showiest Apartment Has Given Up All but the Ghost"[81] (fig. 8.25). The building's social standing had undoubtedly declined, but the decline was not nearly as precipitous as commentators suggested; the building had remained a largely working-class place throughout its entire history. The myth carried a note of truth only in relation to the Columbian Exposition promotion that had heralded the richness of the "elegantly furnished" rooms and fine dining available at the Mecca "Hotel." Nevertheless, this portrayal of decline into blight strengthened the case for demolition. In 1950, Jim Hurlbut presented a radio commentary on WMAQ that celebrated IIT's plans for demolition, stating, "Undoubtedly there are those in the city who will sigh regretfully over the passing of the once fabulous apartment house. . . . Even a few may be listening who lived in its richly appointed suites, when residence there was a sign of opulence and social position. Now, of course, residence at the Mecca is more a sign of desperate poverty." In Hurlbut's view demolition would help the institute develop "a beauty spot in the center of one of the city's worst slum areas. . . . It will be one of the city's most attractive sections."[82] For both planners and the institute, the demolition of the Mecca stood at the center of this vision.

IIT hired social workers to help relocate tenants and to coordinate the effort with housing agencies. It took nearly eighteen months to empty the building. In early January 1952 the Speedway Wrecking Company demolished the Mecca (fig. 8.26). The *Chicago Sun-Times*

8.24. Mecca tenants on balcony, drawing by Ben Shahn. From *Harper's* magazine, December 1950.

8.25. *The Mecca, built 1891–1892. Tenants in hats hanging out at balcony.* Photograph by Wallace Kirkland, 1951. Chicago History Museum, ICHi-29354.

8.26. *The Mecca, built 1891–1892, demolished January 1952.* Photograph by Bernice Davis, 1952. Chicago History Museum, ICHi-29350.

reported the event under the headline "Fabulous S. Side Slum Reaches End of Road." In what soon became a tradition in the culture of Chicago architecture, some people salvaged architectural bits of the Mecca. The distinctive foliated balcony panels that had lined the Mecca's atria proved popular among collectors of local architectural fragments. This method preserved forms and memories of the building while leaving the economic and social program of urban renewal advocates largely unfettered.

Nearly three years after the demolition of the Mecca, IIT's board, led by Cunningham, gathered on the Mecca's original site to break ground for a new building (fig. 8.27). Crown Hall, designed by Mies, would house the architecture department and at the same time assume the Mecca Apartments' old street address. In its program and formal elements, Crown Hall sharply contrasts with the Mecca. The roof is suspended from four exposed plate girders that project from the simple façade of plate glass and steel. Taking the form of a glass pavilion (figs. 8.28, 8.29), Crown Hall appears as a huge but relatively simple one-room glass box floating above the ground.[83] Mies used mod-

8.27. *Groundbreaking ceremony for Ludwig Mies van der Rohe, Crown Hall, Illinois Institute of Technology, December 2, 1954. Former site of the Mecca. Among those present: James D. Cunningham, first from left, and Henry Crown, fourth from left.* From Irene Macauley, *The Heritage of Illinois Institute of Technology.*

8.28. *Ludwig Mies van der Rohe, Crown Hall, Illinois Institute of Technology, built 1950–1956.* Photograph by Hedrich Blessing, c. 1955. Chicago History Museum, ICHi-18506-M3.

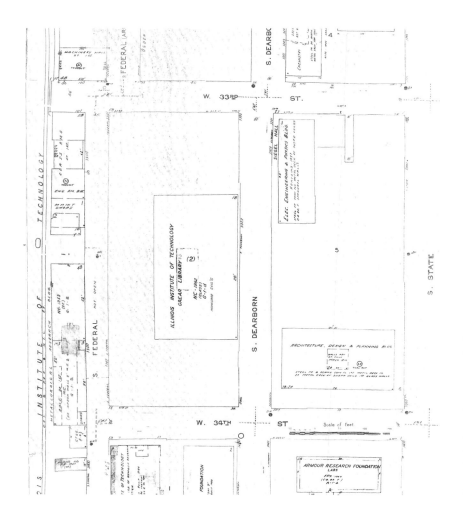

8.29. *Map plan of Illinois Institute of Technology, 1970. The Architecture, Design & Planning Building is Crown Hall and occupies the former site of the Mecca. The campus's large open spaces and low buildings are evident.* From Sanborn Map Company, *Insurance Maps of Chicago, Volume 4, 1912–1970.* Library of Congress.

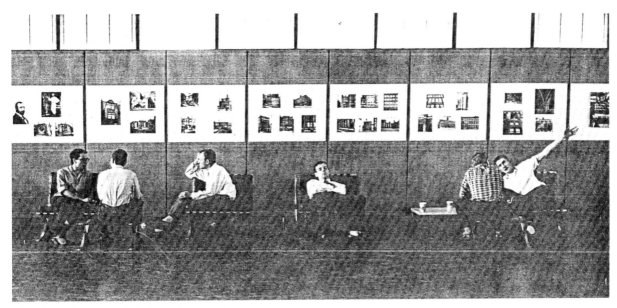

8.30. *Louis Sullivan architecture exhibit in Mies's Crown Hall, c. 1965.* Courtesy of Illinois Institute of Technology.

ern materials and forms to monumentalize an interior space, flooded with natural light and enlivened by the spectacle of people coming and going. Ironically, Edbrooke & Burnham had incorporated similar elements in the Mecca's atria.

Upon completion, Crown Hall was quickly assigned its own set of myths. Architect Eero Saarinen, who participated in the Crown Hall dedication ceremony, insisted that Mies's work established him as the third great Chicago architect after Louis Sullivan and Frank Lloyd Wright, ensuring the city's position as the "center of the universe in modern architecture." "This same bold spirit that created the Chicago architectural tradition [motivated] the creation of this campus. . . . Because Chicago is a place of courageous thinking, a slum gives way to a brand new campus—crisp and clean and beautiful and harmonious—a model of a total environment."[84] This connection between Sullivan and Mies (fig. 8.30) omitted, among other things, Sullivan's abundant and often foliated ornament, his sense of the vital connection between buildings and the street, and his knowledge of how to build urban density. These qualities are more akin to the Mecca than to Crown Hall. The institute's new buildings cultivated a myth of connection to Chicago's historic architecture even as they destroyed the physical basis for taking the measure of the architectural continuities and changes represented in Mies's designs.

In many ways the South Side "slum" created a lens

of race through which IIT officials had viewed the Mecca for decades, failing to see the building's architectural innovations. They failed to appreciate the tenants' efforts to preserve housing and to define a neighborly domestic realm in a market hedged by racism, violence, and a domestic ideology that spun on the axis of single-family housing. Moreover, the critical enthusiasm for Mies's teaching and his designs fostered a narrative of Chicago history and preservation that, on the face of it, viewed buildings like the Mecca as largely irrelevant.[85] Certainly, the Mecca's exterior courtyard represented a precedent of great relevance for Chicago domestic architecture. The extraordinary interior spaces, with their massing of tenants, failed to win broad emulation. In fact, the intensity of the institute's efforts to demolish the Mecca turned upon the visible massing, around the atria, at the windows, in the courtyards, of an African-American cultural presence. The cultural vitality evoked in the "Mecca Flat Blues" and the strength of the Mecca preservation campaign usefully underscore the value of an architecture and an urbanism that could embrace rather than jettison the possibilities of human density and public life in the city. Such spaces would undoubtedly enrich rather than detract from any "total environment." Capturing the richness of the Mecca's changing meaning and history necessarily involves following its story beyond the circumstances of its origin to those of its use and ultimate demolition.

CHAPTER NINE

A Virginia Courthouse Square

Reviving the Colonial

In preserved places the work of historic preservation never ends. Weather and human use make buildings and landscapes deteriorate. Preservation thus demands continuing conservation and maintenance undertaken with an eye to the way physical changes might alter historic meaning. Historic preservation also involves an ongoing responsibility for interpretation. It needs to assess changes in historical scholarship and scrutinize popular interpretations, or misinterpretations, of particular places. In doing so it can aim to encourage the most rigorous possible engagements with history and place. The new wine of interpretation should fill the old bottles of historic places. In the 1920s when Monticello was preserved as a national shrine to Thomas Jefferson, few people could have anticipated the site serving as a venue for scrutinizing slavery or Jefferson's sexual relationship with Sally Hemings, one of his slaves. But attention to the life of enslaved peoples has enriched the significance of this site. And in 1998 when DNA evidence linked Jefferson to Hemings's children, the new information made for a more complex interpretation of the site and its history.[1]

In order to marshal the civic power of its work, historic preservation also needs to constantly take on the popular myths that at times swirl around iconic American landscapes. The New England village with its central green highlights this point. It has often been viewed as a colonial landscape thought to express Puritan and democratic freedoms and patriotic ideals. In this way the New England town green with its white steeple-topped Congregational church has been consistently misrepresented and misunderstood, even as it has been preserved. Cultural landscape essayist J.

B. Jackson firmly challenged prevailing views when he wrote "no landscape has ever changed so profoundly. . . . So completely did the Colonial landscape vanish during the nineteenth century that aside from a few monuments nothing remains of it."[2] Geographer Joseph S. Wood has insisted that with the New England village what people revere is a product not of colonial times but of nineteenth-century village improvement societies, historic preservationists, and local historical society buffs. Wood thinks that preservationists need to come to terms with the ways in which the modern world "invents its past in its own image."[3] Grappling with myth and invented traditions has grown especially pressing since the 1980s, when historic preservation firmly seized upon heritage tourism as a way of demonstrating to increasingly conservative, free-market-oriented politicians and business leaders that historic preservation could literally pay dividends. In 1988, as President Ronald Reagan's chair of the National Endowment for the Humanities, Lynne Cheney provided a $300,000 matching grant to the National Trust for Historic Preservation to encourage projects in heritage tourism.[4] It is not clear that happy history and circulation of tourist dollars inspired by such efforts can dislodge myths about iconic landscapes and spur critical thinking among citizens.[5] Nevertheless, historic preservation ought to strive for accurate and rigorous engagements with history, including a clear understanding of what people see when they look at a historic place. Part of critical seeing, in this context, includes understanding which historic layers and narratives are missing, and which layers have survived through self-conscious constructions of history.[6]

9.1. *Charlottesville Court Square. Albemarle County Courthouse at center; Clerk's Office at left. The building directly behind the Clerk's Office was renovated for court use in 2009 with the addition of a classical portico. Brick sidewalks and street and colonial lantern lights were added as part of the early-twenty-first-century improvement project. Confederate Memorial in foreground. Thomas "Stonewall" Jackson equestrian statue at left edge.* Photograph by author, 2010.

This chapter explores critical seeing, the editing of historical layers, and heritage tourism within an iconic civic landscape, the Court Square in Charlottesville, Virginia (fig. 9.1). In 2004, Charlottesville spent over $3 million to "strengthen" the "historic character" of Court Square. The city buried utility wires, bricked the sidewalks and streets, raised a new brick wall around Court Square, and installed "colonial" lantern lights. Charlottesville had originated in 1762 when Albemarle County designated the area as the meeting place for the court. Court Square provided the nucleus of the town's earliest development. The twenty-first-century improvers recognized that Court Square had "changed over the past two centuries" but felt that "the colonial architectural theme is still intact and the urban character of a small town center is still coherent, both being worthy of preservation and enhancement."[7] For the planners Court Square exemplified the forms of "an early American town where three American Presidents, Thomas Jefferson, James Madison, and James Monroe, fre-

quently met."[8] What is most striking is that, contrary to the planners' visions, Court Square's architecture and landscape represented not colonial times, not even the nineteenth century, but rather the early twentieth century. In the twentieth century Court Square changed radically, becoming, for example, more of a rectangle than a square, and taking on Colonial Revival forms in the place of eclectic architecture and an accretive, layered, landscape. The north wing of the courthouse dates from 1803, but the building received an unusual Gothic Revival front in 1859 and didn't assume its current Colonial Revival form until 1938. The preserved landscape represents less about Jefferson, Madison, and Monroe and more about the political, spatial, and racial conceptions of the early twentieth century. This chapter will also explore those ideas as they influenced the broader civic landscape, particularly the 1930s construction of Charlottesville's main high school and the 1960s urban renewal destruction of African-American memory and community on Vinegar Hill.

Court Square's Confederate Memorials and Black Residents

In 1900 when planning began for a Confederate memorial in Charlottesville, Virginia, a vigorous debate ensued about the propriety of placing the monument on Court Square. Court Square had long stood out as a distinct landscape. The town's original 50 acres were divided into a simple grid of 28 one-acre blocks bounded by 33-foot-wide north-south streets and 66-foot-wide east-west streets. Court Square was different. It was two acres in extent, occupied the high ground at the northern edge of the original town, and was the only land in the original town plan designated for any particular use. The debate seemed unusual. By 1900, Confederate memorials had joined courthouses, jails, and court greens as standard elements of the iconic civic landscape of the southern county seats. The broader late-nineteenth- and early-twentieth-century City Beautiful Movement, with its monuments commemorating historic events and embellishing the public realm of American cities and towns, was clearly reflected in such Confederate memorial projects. City Beautiful advocates like Daniel H. Burnham and Charles Mulford Robinson saw in the architectural and aesthetic unity of Chicago's 1893 World's Columbian Exposition a model for bringing order to the American urban landscape.[9] The narrative dimensions of monuments and memorials nicely blended the making of a more beautiful civic landscape with the reform ideals of cultivating stronger and more informed citizenship, particularly among immigrants and new urban residents. Although somewhat immune from the dislocations and social chaos of major American cities, Charlottesville did participate in numerous City Beautiful initiatives. What is surprising is that groups supporting the construction of the Confederate memorial saw Court Square in radically different terms. The polarized views reflected something of the racial prejudices of the Civil War and its aftermath.

The Charlottesville Confederate memorial officially originated in 1900 when the Virginia legislature passed enabling legislation that permitted Charlottesville and Albemarle County officials to spend $2,000 in state funds for a memorial on Court Square. The memorial was intended to carry the names of all the Confederate soldiers from Charlottesville and Albemarle County killed during the war. The project lay fallow for several years. With costs rising for the memorial, the local chapter of the United Daughters of the Confederacy (UDC) joined the campaign. In the course of raising money for the memorial, these women were the first to question the propriety of locating the memorial on Court Square.

They felt that the memorial would "suffer in effect if given the cramped surroundings of the Court House Yard" and they insisted that the chapter would "not rest content to let so beautiful a monument be sacrificed to so unbecoming a setting as the courthouse square."[10] The critique of Court Square as a site for the Confederate memorial drew upon recent expressions of dissatisfaction with the courthouse itself. In 1907 the *Charlottesville Daily Progress* editorialized in favor of a new courthouse under the headline of "Our Great Desideratum." The editors declared, "our present court house is not only an eye sore in appearance, but it is absolutely inadequate to the proper and comfortable discharge of the public duties that appertain to it." After expansively enumerating all of Charlottesville's "exceptional inducements as a residential city," the editors concluded, "But it is all marred by our abominable court-house building"[11] (fig. 9.2). The local chapter of the Daughters of the Confederacy felt there were compelling reasons to look beyond the Court Square for a more dignified and impressive setting for the Charlottesville Confederate monument.

Beyond concerns about the architectural setting, people also worried that a memorial on Court Square would fail to get the attention that they hoped for. In 1908 they argued, "The courthouse yard is on a back street seldom visited by strangers and with nothing either in location or in surroundings to commend it as a proper site for a monument. . . . Monuments are supposed to be erected to be seen by the public. They pay little tribute to the dead and reflect but meager credit upon the living if placed in an obscure and undesirable locality."[12] To characterize the civic space of Court Square as "unbecoming" for a significant memorial reveals the existence of a starkly different view from the one that guided Court Square planners who drafted the enhancement plan in 2000. Indeed, the charm of the "urban character of a small town center" may have struck people in the early twentieth century with a different force. This then raises the question of how that view changed through time; the transformation in public perceptions had a great deal to do with what was built, and what was demolished, on Court Square after 1908.

In the course of the nineteenth century the center of Charlottesville's commercial development had moved away from Court Square, creating an intense pattern of party-wall urbanism along what became Main Street, two blocks south of Court Square. Residential development also moved to far-flung sections of the city. These changes made the area perhaps less prominent than it had been during the late eighteenth and early nineteenth centuries. Nevertheless, to understand the hostility to Court Square as a memorial site requires closer

scrutiny both of the architectural and the social configuration of Court Square and of the alternative memorial site supported by the United Daughters of the Confederacy, the Charlottesville City Council, a majority of the members of the Monument Committee, and a host of other local residents. Midway Park, a small triangular park located at the intersection of West Main Street and Ridge Street, was the leading alternative site proposed for the Confederate memorial. The park stood in front of the Midway School, Charlottesville's main public school for white children, built in 1894 (fig. 9.3). Standing in the middle of West Main Street, a monument on Midway Park (fig. 9.4) could serve as a terminal element for the street that ran along a straight course for nearly a mile connecting downtown Charlottesville with the University of Virginia. By contrast, the 5th Street axis leading to the most prominent potential memorial site on Court Square was only three blocks in length and rather modest in comparison. West Main Street was 60 feet wide, while 5th Street was only 33 feet wide. In 1908, Polk Miller, a Confederate veteran who helped the UDC raise money for the Confederate memorial, vigorously advocated the Midway Park site for the memorial. Polk's argument turned largely on issues of visibility and centrality; in connection with these claims he also invoked an interesting theory of urban growth: "The town is growing westward, as all towns do, and in a few years (if it is not already so) the bulk of your town people will be west of Midway Park. I contend that a Monument should be placed where the greatest number of people can see it, and without having to hunt for it, in order to see it."[13] Underscoring the monument's didactic civic value, the Midway Park advocates pointed out the "educational value" of placing the memorial in front of the school where nearly 2,000 children could receive "continual inspiration."[14]

Beyond issues of access and visibility the question of territory, both political and social, shaped perceptions

9.3. *Midway Park, looking east, at the site preferred by the Daughters of the Confederacy over Court Square for the construction of the Confederate Memorial. Midway School, built for white students, in background.* Holsinger Studio, 1917. UVA Special Collections Library.

about Court Square as an appropriate or inappropriate site for the Confederate memorial. Politically, Court Square belonged to Albemarle County even though it was entirely surrounded by land under the jurisdiction of the City of Charlottesville. Charlottesville, itself, was, in turn, entirely surrounded by the balance of Albemarle County's territory. Thus, a shared monument to Charlottesville and Albemarle County Confederate dead confronted the vagaries of political geography. As an object of civic pride and improvement, the Confederate memorial could stand on either city or county land and embellish either city or county buildings. In 1900 the Virginia state legislature had designated Court Square as the site for the memorial, thus resolving any geographical contest between the politically distinct city and county. In 1908 the Charlottesville City Council sought to switch the location to Midway Park, receiving the enthusiastic support of the UDC. A Midway Park memorial would embellish one of the city's prominent civic buildings, Midway School, and embellish one of the city's most important streets, West Main Street.

The most aggressive resistance to the Midway Park proposal came from the county representatives on the Monument Committee and most notably Micajah Woods, the committee chair, the commonwealth's attorney, and a Confederate veteran. Woods insisted that Court Square was a very special historic spot and the most appropriate site for the Confederate memorial. Supporters of this view argued, "The Court Green in Charlottesville and the Courthouse have been the place of assemblage for the people of Charlottesville and Albemarle County since the foundation of the town. It is ground that has become sacred and hallowed by the tread of the many great men of this County and of the ancestors of all the people of this region, and it is the spot that will be visited monthly and almost daily by the surviving Confederate Veterans and by their descendants for generations to come."[15] Even as the majority of members on the Monument Committee expressed their support for the Midway Park site, Woods insisted that the legislature's designation of the Court Square was binding, and he added, "I am glad to state that artists and experts who have inspected the loca-

9.4. Midway Park formed the terminal element for West Main Street, connecting downtown to the University of Virginia. Site proposed for the Confederate Memorial. Holsinger Studio, 1917. UVA Special Collections Library.

tion have expressed the opinion that it is the ideal place for such a monument." Such experts certainly had the weight of precedent on their side. Moreover, throughout the country outdoor monuments and memorials had become a leading City Beautiful fixture of the American civic landscape. In the end, Woods refused to entertain a motion from Monument Committee members to locate the memorial on Midway Park. The Albemarle Chapter of the Daughters of the Confederacy reported feeling that they were "overwhelmed by unfair and arbitrary methods" on the Monument Committee.[16] Albemarle County, which contributed nearly 50 percent more to the memorial fund than the City of Charlottesville and the UDC combined, prevailed in keeping Court Square as a site for the memorial.

The Charlottesville Confederate memorial was topped by a common infantry soldier "at ready" cast in bronze by the American Bronze Foundry Company of Chicago, Illinois (fig. 9.5). Art historian Kirk Savage has argued that the broad proliferation of this type of monument in the late nineteenth century helped Americans com-

9.5. Confederate Memorial, built 1909 by the American Bronze Foundry Company. Photograph by author, 2010.

memorate those killed in the war while at the same time appealing to veterans and reasserting the place of the citizen soldier as a model for civic virtue in American society.[17] The monuments tended to elevate the patriotism and sacrifice of ordinary people as the common coin of civic life. In Charlottesville, as in other communities, these monuments also fixed in stone certain preferred narratives of the Civil War. The Kyle Granite Company of Washington, D.C., provided the monument's pedestal and inscriptions, built of granite quarried in Barre, Vermont. The monument invoked the memory and instruction of a particular narrative of the Civil War; the north face of the pedestal carried a bronze medallion with the Virginia state seal and the motto SIC SEMPER TYRANNIS (THUS ALWAYS TO TYRANTS); the inscription on the north face read CONFEDERATE SOLDIERS DEFENDERS OF THE RIGHTS OF STATES. The pedestal's west side carried the inscription WARRIORS: YOUR VALOR; YOUR DEVOTION TO DUTY; YOUR FORTITUDE UNDER PRIVATIONS; TEACH US HOW TO SUFFER AND GROW STRONG; LEST WE FORGET. The east side of the monument identified the parties responsible for erecting the monument: TO COMMEMORATE THE HEROISM OF THE VOLUNTEERS OF CHARLOTTESVILLE AND ALBEMARLE COUNTY, LOVE MAKES MEMORY ETERNAL. The south face read 1861-VIRGINIA-1865 and had a battle flag of the Confederacy carved in stone over a bas-relief sculpture of cannons and cannonballs. There likely existed in Charlottesville and Albemarle County different memories and different conceptions of the Civil War. Certainly, local African Americans would have contested the "rights of states" interpretation of the conflict. Nevertheless, their views were not given interpretative or memorial credence on Court Square. Moreover, the figure represented on the Charlottesville monument followed the form of the common soldier memorial in all sections of the country—the citizen soldier, shouldering the responsibilities of citizenship, was portrayed as white. For a Confederate memorial the representation of whiteness enjoyed an easier rationale than it did in Union memorials where over 200,000 blacks had served as Union soldiers.[18] Nevertheless, the actual and representational presence to local African Americans quickly assumed much greater importance in the deliberations about the form of Court Square.

The May 5, 1909, dedication of the Confederate memorial involved thousands of community residents. City employees and students were given a holiday, and a major parade was organized leading from the University of Virginia to Court Square. The parade route carried the marchers, including members of the Daughters of the Confederacy, directly along the major axis of West Main Street past the Midway Park site that they had so vigorously advocated for the memorial. The parade

eventually turned up the minor axis of 5th Street where the memorial now formed the terminal element on the spot where the street ran into Court Square. The route likely seemed bittersweet to those marchers who could easily experience the difference between the monumental possibilities of the Midway site and the Court Square site. For those who supported Court Square, the dedication day undoubtedly provided evidence of an important step toward a more embellished civic landscape, toward the City Beautiful, and indeed a day on which Charlottesville finally assumed one of the iconic southern forms of civic commemoration—the juxtaposition of a Confederate memorial with the seat of government and justice.

The representation of the white infantry soldier on the Confederate memorial and the "rights of states" narrative set in stone left most local African Americans' history of slavery and emancipation out of the picture. Nevertheless, some local blacks were invited to participate in the dedication of the memorial. The official program elaborately choreographed the celebration, including the points along the parade route where different groups and officials could gather and join the procession, and at what points on Court Square they could sit. After all of this was laid out, the program extended an invitation to local blacks. It stated, "The colored men, who served faithfully as cooks and body servants during the war are invited to join in the procession and participate in the exercises, and they will report at 10 o'clock to Humphrey Shelton, in front of Midway School Building, and a place will be assigned to them."[19] Humphrey Shelton had been a slave who accompanied Major M. Green Peyton during the Civil War. According to a Confederate history in 1920, Shelton "cared for [Peyton's] wants as earnestly after emancipation as he had while a slave in his master's possession." Shelton then worked as a janitor at the University of Virginia for nearly fifty years.[20] His presence in the official program suggests that he likely participated in the dedication ceremony. What is perhaps more fascinating and even more important than the participation of cooks and body servants in the dedication of the Confederate memorial is the extent to which free African-American cooks, domestics, and laborers had come to form an important and highly visible part of the social and physical fabric of the Court Square neighborhood. Indeed, the fact that black households with a total of about thirty members occupied several buildings that directly fronted on the west side of Court Square very likely contributed to the earlier sense among some Charlottesville residents that the space was "unbecoming" as a setting for the Confederate memorial.[21] As subsequent City Beautiful initiatives for Court Square emerged, they appeared directed, in

9.6. McKee Block facing the Albemarle County Courthouse and including some of the oldest structures in Charlottesville. View looking north. Holsinger Studio, c. 1910. UVA Special Collections Library.

part, toward the complete removal of this black presence from the square.

In the years immediately following the dedication of the Confederate memorial, the number of black residents on the Court Square actually expanded. Residents included laborers Albert Brooks, Austin Brown, Robert Brown, Solomon Parker, and Porter Suesberry; laundresses Amanda Brown, Bettie Jones, and Lou Underwood; and domestics Lizzie Brown and Ida Robinson.[22] In the 1910s, after about twenty or twenty-five years of gradual racial transition, black renters came to occupy every building on the west side of Court Square (fig. 9.6). As this racial transition was completed, the Albemarle County Board of Supervisors began to contemplate improvement plans that envisioned the demolition of every one of these houses. On March 18, 1914, the County Board passed a resolution that ceded to the Charlottesville school board the street that ran between the Court Square and the block immediately to the west. The grant of the county-owned street was conditioned

on the city "pull[ing] down all of the buildings on the [west] block and erect[ing] a substantial and handsome school building for white pupils only somewhere on the block," enclosing the site with a "substantial and ornamental fence," raising the grade of the street to the level of the courthouse yard, covering it with turf, and using it as a school playground. The County Board stipulated that as soon as the site "ceases to be used as a public School Building for white pupils, the right to the use of said street for a playground shall cease and the County of Albemarle shall take possession of said street and make such use of it as it chooses."[23] Interestingly, the proposed plan would have brought about, after the fact, the juxtaposition of a school and the Confederate memorial that had earlier been cited as an advantage of the Midway Park site. Reporting on the proposal, the *Daily Progress* insisted that it would provide an "admirable location for a school but will also remove the old buildings that have long been an eye sore."[24] If the plan went forward, white schoolchildren would take the place of

9.7. *McKee Block, looking south and west across Court Square.* Photograph, c. 1900. Courtesy K. Edward Lay. UVA Special Collections Library.

black working-class residents as part of the aesthetic uplift on the square. The white civic landscape of Court Square would expand significantly and the black residential presence on Court Square would be entirely eliminated. In the end, the city decided that Court Square was not an appropriate site for a public school. The school plan did not reemerge, but within a matter of years an entirely new plan for the improvement of Court Square was undertaken, one that successfully swept away the buildings on the west side of the square, along with their black tenants.

In the course of the nineteenth century the block facing the west side of Court Square took on the name the McKee Block, after the name of a family that had lived on the square for generations, from the early nineteenth century into the early twentieth. In the early 1900s the block had five main buildings facing Court Square. Built of both wood and brick, the two-story buildings on the McKee Block included some of the older buildings in the city, built in the 1810s or even earlier (fig. 9.7). Indeed, half of the brick house at 301–307 McKee, at the corner of Jefferson, had been purchased in 1817 by Andrew McKee, a hatmaker, and passed to his son, Dr. Andrew Robert McKee, who lived there until his death in 1893. Many of the buildings housed both residences and businesses, including dry goods, a hotel, a tailor shop, a bank office, and a post office. In reviewing the history of the McKee Block, it is hard to separate out the

architectural and the social aspects of its early-twentieth-century characterization as an "eye sore." The brick buildings were substantial and well built. In fact, when the building at 315–317 McKee was finally demolished, the contractor found the construction so sound that he was unable to "throw" the walls built of 9-inch brick laid in a Flemish bond pattern; instead, he had to take the walls down brick by brick.[25] Moreover, at the same time that the buildings were condemned to demolition on the west side of Court Square, other buildings of approximately the same age on the south and east side were being preserved and adapted for new uses. Those buildings are still standing over eighty years later, helping to constitute Court Square's "historic visual character."

The racial transition of the McKee Block from white to black households took place over a period of about twenty years between the late 1880s and the early 1910s, and apparently advanced building by building from the north to the south end of the block. There were undoubtedly blacks residing on the block in the early nineteenth century, but they lived as servants in white households. In the late 1880s the entire building at 327–331 McKee Block, at the north end of the block, on the corner of High Street, was rented out to several black tenants. On August 4, 1894, John West, a Charlottesville barber and real estate developer, was the high bidder on the two-story frame double house at 319–321, sold at a public auction of the estate of A. R. McKee. West, who was born in

1849 to a mother who was a slave and was then adopted by a free black woman, parlayed his real estate investments into one of the largest fortunes in Charlottesville in the early twentieth century. The southernmost building on the block was the brick double house at the corner of Jefferson Street where the McKee family had lived from 1817. The building stayed in the family until it was sold in 1905 to J. J. Leterman, who initially rented his building to white tenants. Just after 1910 he began to rent to black tenants, making his building the last on the block to make the transition from white to black households.[26]

Paul Goodloe McIntire and Charlottesville's City Beautiful

During the years 1915 and 1916 the Charlottesville school board constructed the McGuffey School for white grade-school students on Second Street, four blocks west of Court Square. The new school seemingly foreclosed the possibility that the city would demolish the McKee Block for use as a school site. Within a few years the demolition of the McKee Block was again raised as part of an entirely new plan for beautifying the Court Square. In 1918, Paul Goodloe McIntire, a wealthy businessman and philanthropist who had spent his childhood in Charlottesville before making a fortune as a broker and investor in Chicago and New York, quietly purchased every building on the McKee Block. McIntire then had the buildings demolished to make a small public park featuring an equestrian statue of Thomas "Stonewall" Jackson, the revered Confederate general. The Board of Supervisors donated the street between Court Square and the McKee Block as part of the park plan. In this way the McKee site would actually become part of Court Square, making the square more of a rectangle than a square. In his gift to the city McIntire stipulated that the area be called Jackson Park and be held in perpetuity for use as a park with no buildings added to the area.

McIntire's gift of Jackson Park and the Jackson equestrian statue constituted one part of an ambitious City Beautiful program that he endowed for Charlottesville and the University of Virginia. In 1916 a community campaign to build a monument commemorating Albemarle County native sons Meriwether Lewis and William Clark initially inspired McIntire's efforts at local civic embellishment. John L. Livers, a street-railway and bank executive, led the movement for a Lewis and Clark monument. He seized upon the idea of placing the monument at Midway Park, the site that many people had favored for the Confederate memorial. Livers also approached Eugene Bradbury, Charlottesville's most

prominent local architect, for a design that would include granite slabs, bronze medallions of Lewis and Clark, and a drinking fountain for the Midway School children. The monument campaign required about $5,000 but floundered after collecting only about half that amount. Livers then attempted to push the campaign forward by associating it with a broader City Beautiful effort being promoted by the Charlottesville Chamber of Commerce. As reported in an editorial by the *Daily Progress*, the chamber sought to promote "the many local improvements which are needed to bring this community up to the high place and standard which it should occupy. Among other crying needs discussed was the almost shameful lack of beautification and adornment which is apparent on every hand." The newspaper editorialized in favor of the plans, declaring, "This monument should be erected and taken as a starting point in the beautification movement." Insisting that a land without monuments was a land without memories or history, the *Daily Progress* demanded, "Who will come forward and help this cause or give this money?"[27] Upon seeing this editorial, McIntire stepped forward to donate money for the Lewis and Clark monument. He also funded other City Beautiful projects, including those undertaken at Court Square.[28]

In participating in the Lewis and Clark project, McIntire's plan quickly eclipsed the vision of John L. Livers and the design of Eugene Bradbury. Setting aside the proposal for medallions and a fountain, McIntire commissioned New York sculptor Charles Keck to design a monument to Lewis and Clark costing $25,000. A renowned sculptor and member of the National Sculpture Society, Keck had studied at the American Academy in Rome and then spent five years as an apprentice to Augustus Saint-Gaudens. Dedicated in 1919, Keck's design featured Lewis and Clark, but also portrayed Sacajawea, the Indian guide who joined their expedition. The three-figure bronze group topped a carved granite pedestal that celebrated their expedition of discovery across the continent (fig. 9.8). In 1917, even before the model for the Lewis and Clark statue was finished and approved, McIntire moved ahead with plans for another park and commemorative sculpture. He donated land two blocks west of the Court Square as a site for a city park with an equestrian statue to Confederate General Robert E. Lee, given in memory of his parents. McIntire's plan for Lee Park was announced only about one week before thousands of people gained national attention as they gathered at the Gettysburg battlefield for the June 9, 1917, dedication of the Robert E. Lee equestrian monument.

Residents of Charlottesville found themselves amazed "at the swiftness with which Mr. McIntire work[ed] his miracles." It seemed that with "a wave of his hand" McIntire had put in place major projects of civic embellishment and promoted "artistic taste"; the newspaper surveyed McIntire's early efforts under the headline "City Awakes from Slumber, Long Nap Is Nearing Its Close."[29] Few people at the time comprehended the scope that McIntire's philanthropy would take. In June 1918, McIntire wrote to Edwin Alderman, president of the University of Virginia, and explained that the charitable and war relief work he had undertaken in France meant that he was unable to act on Alderman's suggestion that he commission and donate a monument to the memory of the Revolutionary War General George Rogers Clark. Nevertheless, McIntire made it clear that he had more projects in mind: "After the war I hope for several things that will interest Charlottesville & the University."[30] McIntire kept his promise; the Jackson Park plan was made public in December 1918. In March 1919,

McIntire announced his plan to build a public library building for white residents of Charlottesville, which was constructed on a lot overlooking Lee Park (fig. 9.9). McIntire hired Walter Dabney Blair, a New York architect, to design the library and also to develop a landscape plan for Jackson Park. Blair, who had been born in Amelia County, Virginia, graduated from the University of Virginia before studying architecture at the University of Pennsylvania and the École des Beaux-Arts. McIntire insisted that the library exterior "be an ornament to C'ville."[31] In 1919, as if to further promote the artistic side of life that he was working to cultivate in the Charlottesville landscape, McIntire donated $155,000 to the University of Virginia to establish a School of Fine Arts for the study of art, architecture, and music. In the case of art and architecture the university aimed not to actually train artists but to "interest the student body of the University in art and to increase their powers of art

9.8. Statue of Lewis and Clark and Sacagawea on Midway Park, dedicated 1919. Charles Keck, sculptor. The statue was used as the background for a photo of a new street-sweeping machine. Holsinger Studio, c. 1938. UVA Special Collections Library.

9.9. Lee Park. Public Library, building with semicircular portico, donated by Paul Goodloe McIntire to Charlottesville, built 1921. Walter Dabney Blair, architect. Library flanked by the Post Office and the First Baptist Church, both built 1904.
Holsinger Studio, c. 1923. UVA Special Collections Library

appreciation" by offering "academic courses covering the general history and appreciation of art illustrated by the best examples, in casts, photographs, paintings, and copies of masterpieces of the world's art."[32] At the same time, McIntire also contributed $60,000 to build an open-air Greek amphitheater at the university. McIntire then agreed to build the memorial to George Rogers Clark on a plot of university-owned land on West Main Street at the edge of the campus. In 1921 he endowed a new School of Commerce at the University of Virginia with $200,000.[33] People certainly understood what Edwin Alderman meant when he called McIntire a "lover of beauty" and "an artist in giving."[34]

Nationally, the City Beautiful Movement tended to focus its energies on the parts of the urban realm most easily controlled by interested reformers and city officials, on the civic landscape of streets, civic centers, and public buildings and monuments. City Beautiful tended to shy away from efforts to regulate the aesthetic dimensions of private property development. McIntire certainly

worked along familiar City Beautiful lines. Nevertheless, despite the urban and even urbane context of his early projects, he did cultivate another Charlottesville dimension of the City Beautiful, the part of the movement that drew upon earlier reform efforts to embellish cities and to improve the lives of residents by establishing large urban landscape parks. In Charlottesville in the 1920s, country lanes and natural scenes were still accessible on all sides of the city. Nevertheless, the city set out to appropriate another aspect of urban grandeur when it explored the possibility of establishing a large landscape park. Paul McIntire paid for the initial land for two parks in 1926, a 92-acre tract for what became known as McIntire Park, set aside for the white residents of Charlottesville. At the same time McIntire also purchased a 9-acre parcel, previously operated as a city quarantine facility and dump, for development as Washington Park, for use by the city's black residents; the headline in the *Daily Progress* announced: "McIntire Gives City Sites for Two Parks . . . Ninety-Two Acre Tract on Rugby Avenue Will

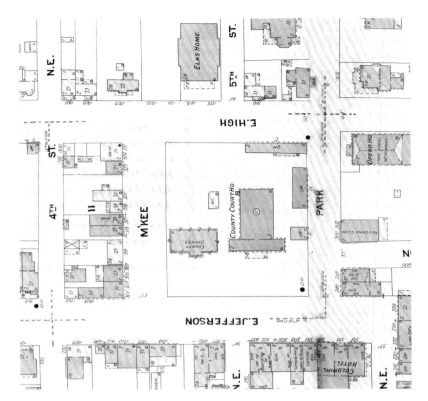

9.10. *Court Square in 1907; map showing McKee Block at the left and the private law offices built on the square to the right and behind the courthouse.* From *Sanborn Fire Insurance Company Atlas, 1907.* UVA Special Collections Library.

Be Converted into Playground for White People. Second Tract on Rose Hill for Colored."[35]

The broad scope of McIntire's city-building projects placed him firmly in the tradition of the American City Beautiful Movement. His residential, business, and leisure life brought him into close proximity with some of the most noteworthy sources for that movement. McIntire lived in Chicago during the 1893 World's Columbian Exposition; the temporary staff-and-plaster "White City" of the exposition grounds did not create the national movement for civic improvement, but it did provide a model of aesthetic harmony, order, and control on a grand urban scale. The participation of sculptors in creating the sense of grandeur and beauty helped push forward demands for permanent monuments and memorials in cities throughout the country. When McIntire purchased a seat on the New York Stock Exchange in 1901 and moved from Chicago to New York, he found a city that was in the midst of a great movement for the placement of monuments and memorials in public spaces and on public buildings. McIntire had an office first at 66 Broadway and then at 71 Broadway. Both stood just one block north of Cass Gilbert's monumental Beaux Arts—style United States Custom House, built between 1900 and 1907. With exterior sculptures by Daniel Chester French the Custom House was just one of numerous public buildings constructed in the early

twentieth century that included impressive allegorical sculptural programs. When McIntire walked around the corner from his office to the floor of the New York Stock Exchange, a glance to the north side of Wall Street would settle on John Quincy Adams Ward's 1883 statue of George Washington. Moving uptown, where McIntire lived for a time, he would see at the southeast corner of Central Park Augustus Saint-Gaudens's 1903 equestrian statue of Union general William Tecumseh Sherman. The statue of this hero in the Union pantheon went up more than twenty years after Saint-Gaudens's statue of Admiral Farragut in Madison Square Park.

Paul McIntire's personal equestrian interests likely contributed to his penchant for living on the suburban edge of Chicago and New York, and later Charlottesville, where he kept his horses. In his last years in Chicago he lived in the emerging suburban neighborhood of Buena Park. While working in New York, he lived briefly in the city, but he spent longer periods in Madison, New Jersey, and, for five years before returning to Charlottesville, in the Rockridge neighborhood of Greenwich, Connecticut, with its noted hunts and riding clubs. Greenwich was more on the scale of Charlottesville than of New York or Chicago. But it, too, had engaged in campaigns of civic embellishment. In 1890, Greenwich had dedicated its memorial "to her loyal sons who fought for the Union 1861–1865." Sculpted by Lazzari & Barton, the

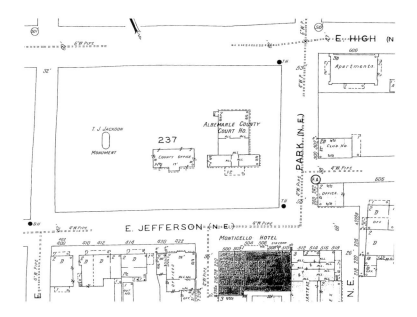

9.11. *Court Square in 1929 map after the demolition of the McKee Block and private law offices. Paul Goodloe McIntire donated the McKee land and the Jackson equestrian monument as part of an expanded Court Square.* From *Sanborn Fire Insurance Company Atlas, 1929.* UVA Special Collections Library.

monument was topped by a common soldier carrying the flag. Also, toward the end of McIntire's residence in Greenwich the community was caught up in a campaign to build and dedicate the prominent memorial statue to Colonel Raynal C. Bolling, a resident of Greenwich and a World War I aviator killed in action over Amiens, France. The campaigns for civic embellishment that McIntire encountered in Chicago and New York and Greenwich undoubtedly helped him visualize some of the civic and aesthetic possibilities of the City Beautiful adornments he sponsored in Charlottesville. Another important source for McIntire's urban vision derived from his extensive world travels. In 1920 a profile of McIntire published in the *Washington Herald* reported that "during much of the past 20 years he has spent much of his time in foreign travel. He has visited nearly every large country in the world. At one time he made his home in Italy, which reminded him of his native Virginia."[36] Just as they had for advocates of the City Beautiful, cities like Paris and Rome provided models for McIntire's plans of urban beautification. "Thrilled by what he had seen abroad, especially in Italy," and a "devotee of art in its best forms and highest estate," McIntire resolved to commit "his energies" toward a broad program of improvement in Charlottesville.[37]

In Charlottesville a City Beautiful aesthetic vision merged seamlessly with a dominant racial ideology, giv-

ing the City Beautiful plans their distinct local form. The pattern of racial separation in McIntire's provision of public parks, and the fact that his public library served white patrons only, lends some additional credence to the idea that improvements on Court Square supported white ideals of racial separation in the structure and embellishment of the civic landscape. The difference between improvements in the parks and on Court Square was that local blacks never had a separate courthouse. The demolition of black residences on Court Square pushed black residents away from that locale and from their physical and social proximity to an important local seat of civic authority and political power. Moreover, the commemorative space that filled the McKee Block site strengthened and monumentalized the Court Square's Confederate historical narrative established earlier with the 1909 memorial. The *Daily Progress* captured something of the transition: "Another exercise of Mr. McIntire's magic has removed the unsightly pile of buildings known as McKee Block, and there we shall see, in bronze, an expression of the austere dignity, the heroic spirit which made our Stonewall Jackson, the story of whose achievements has filled the earth with his fame, and engaged the pens of writers throughout the world"[38] (figs. 9.10, 9.11). The monument "filled the earth with his fame" in a quite local and literal sense, on the expanded Court Square. Resident blacks lost some-

*9.12. General Thomas "Stonewall"
Jackson statue on Court Square,
dedicated 1921. Charles Keck, sculptor.
It occupies the site of the McKee Block.*
Photograph by author, 2010.

The sculpture's evocative verisimilitude has won for it critical assessments that place it among the very best equestrian monuments in the United States. Two winged allegorical figures, a female figure of Faith and a male figure of Valor, stand at the front of the granite pedestal. The pedestal frieze lists Jackson's major battles: Manassas, the Valley Campaign, and Chancellorsville. Part of the power of the Jackson monument derived from the general's historic place in the Confederate pantheon, part from the monumental command of the newly configured space of Court Square. Part of the power came from a constituent element of equestrian statues—the power and control of the rider over the horse is viewed as a proxy for a broader power and control of the subject, over his men, his followers, and his adversaries.[41] The realism captured in the sculpting of Jackson in his full Confederate uniform riding his Little Sorrel effectively lent additional credence to the leadership qualities seen in Jackson himself. The realism of the horse was negotiated between Keck and a large group of horsemen in both New York and in Charlottesville who cast a critical eye on the emerging design. William Lambeth, Fiske Kimball, the first professor hired when McIntire's school of art and architecture opened at the University of Virginia, and a Mr. Cowden, "a Virginia gentleman," all expressed satisfaction with Keck's initial model of the horse. McIntire's representative, William Watson, forwarded less complimentary comments related to the height of the head, the position of the mouth and ears, the dilation of the nostrils, and the fullness and height of the rump, and the arch of the neck. Keck insisted that the poor quality of the photographs of the models accounted for the greater enthusiasm of people who personally saw the model, but he agreed to meet with his critics before finalizing his plan.[42] McIntire later personally resolved a debate about whether the name on the statue should read "Stonewall Jackson" or "Thomas Jonathan Jackson"; he opted for the latter name. McIntire also rejected the advice of William Lambeth and several "prominent citizens" who argued that the statue should face north toward the busier High Street. Such a position would have placed the back of the monument toward the main approach to the courthouse and clerk's office. McIntire insisted on having the statue face south, reflecting the dominant lines of the buildings around it.[43]

Paul McIntire did not attend the dedication ceremonies for the Jackson statue. Attracting thousands of people, the dedication took place on October 19, 1921, during a large reunion of Confederate veterans (fig. 9.13). A parade wound through the streets of the city; schoolchildren joined the marchers as the parade went by the Midway and McGuffey schools. The dedication

thing of their ability to easily "fill the earth" with a more complicated counternarrative related to black slavery, emancipation, and citizenship.

Charles Keck's early models for the Lewis and Clark memorial won the approbation of local residents, including William Lambeth, the University of Virginia's director of buildings and grounds. William O. Watson, McIntire's Charlottesville representative, trustee, and friend wrote to McIntire that Lambeth was "a man of good judgment & I am glad to have him interested."[39] The early acclaim that greeted Keck's work helped him win the commission for the $35,000 Jackson equestrian statue.

Keck's Jackson design captures the horse and rider in full trot, sharing an intense attentiveness to mission (fig. 9.12). At the time of the dedication critics easily recognized the portrayal of heroic bearing, seeing in the monument "impressive portraiture of the great soldier, expressing in feature and pose alert vigor, stern purpose and prompt forceful action, . . . pictured in face and figure. The monument informs the beholder that 'Stonewall' Jackson was a soldier who believed in action."[40]

9.13. *Dedication of the Jackson eques-*
trian statue during a Confederate soldiers
reunion in October 1921. Holsinger Studio,
1921. UVA Special Collections Library.

committee unanimously called upon Edwin Alderman
to represent McIntire in officially presenting the monument to the city and the county. Just as advisors had
worked with Keck to tweak the design elements of his
statue, Alderman used his dedication speech to tweak
the memory of the Civil War and to better frame the
meaning of the monument. The speech articulated the
core Confederate interpretation of the Civil War. He
declared:

Two generations ago a great war fell out in this land. No
war in human history was a sincerer conflict than this
war. It was a war between brothers fate driven to the
defense of two majestic ideas—the idea of local self-gov-
ernment and the idea of federal union. To call it rebellion
is to speak ignorantly; to call it treason is to add vicious-
ness to stupidity. It was a war of ideas, principles, political contentions, and of loyalty to ancient ideals of English
freedom. I am not in the mood, nor is the world in the
mood merely to praise war or to exalt force as an agent
of human discipline, but I may justly claim that out of the

flame and fire of this brothers' war issued some of the
noblest sanctities of human life and few undying names
which the world will forever cherish for the enrichment
of the spirit of mankind. We are gathered here in this central spot of an historic city, within the State which gave
him birth, to set in place an equestrian statue of Thomas
Jonathan Jackson, one of the greatest of these high stat-
ured men, . . . [who] passed without dispute, in the glory
of unconquerable youth, into the inner circle of the sol-
dier-saints and heroes of the English race.[44]

As was the case twelve years earlier with the dedication of the Confederate memorial, the Jackson dedication speeches and ceremonies did not grapple with black
slavery or emancipation or citizenship; such historic
issues did not easily comport with the vaunted efforts
to recognize "ancient ideals of English freedom." A key
difference existed between 1909 and 1921. In 1909 black
residents living in the McKee Block might have suggested, through their simple presence, some other interpretations of the events memorialized. In 1921, after the

demolition of the McKee Block, that simple presence did not exist on the west side of the square, or, for that matter, on any other side of the square.

Despite the radical change in the face of Court Square that came with Jackson Park and the Jackson monument, the City Beautiful efforts did not end in 1921. Indeed, McIntire's gift quickly inspired further demands for a City Beautiful program on Court Square. On March 25, 1921, even before the dedication of the Jackson statue, the board of directors of the Chamber of Commerce launched a new campaign of Court Square beautification. The chamber board pointed out the community benefits made possible through McIntire's "generosity" and then "respectfully" petitioned the County Board of Supervisors to "take such steps as may be necessary to clear up and improve the property belonging to the County adjacent to Jackson Park, and at this time to remove all buildings on the Courthouse Square except the Courthouse and clerk's offices."[45] The chamber's proposal went to the heart of a rather intriguing pattern of building on Court Square that stretched back three generations. Since at least 1855 several prominent attorneys had, with the permission from county officials, built and maintained law offices on the publicly owned property of Court Square, adjacent to the courthouse. The prominence of the attorneys was such that at times they served or came to serve as commonwealth attorneys or as circuit court judges; however, the buildings were generally used as private law offices and were passed down in families or were sold to other lawyers. The county collected a modest ground rent, designated the precise location

for the offices, regulated their "style and finish and appearance," requiring in some cases that they be built two stories in height, with brick walls and slates roofs. The county did not approve all the petitions to build offices on Court Square and also reserved the right to take hold of the buildings at any time, paying their owners the estimated value of the improvements.[46] In 1921 the chamber asked the county, in the interest of "cleaning up" Court Square, to exercise its rights to take the buildings and then to demolish them. As the County Board considered the matter R. T. W. Duke, Jr., the commonwealth attorney and legal advisor to the board, had to recuse himself from the deliberations because he owned parts of four of the buildings in question. In April 1921 the board asked the clerk to give notice to all lawyers with offices on the square that they should vacate their offices within six months (fig. 9.14).[47] They signaled their intention to extend the McIntire improvements by creating a more open and spacious setting for the historic courthouse. Their decision to clear Court Square came at the same time that Charlottesville inaugurated a "City Beautiful and Clean-Up Contest" built upon the theme that such a contest "effects environment and is a tremendous factor in the development of human character." The contest committee members asserted that "other things being equal, a child reared among trees, shrubs, flowers, cleanly surroundings, will be of a higher type than a child who grows up in an atmosphere of ugliness, shiftlessness, and careless indifference to beauty and sanitation."[48] Opening up the Court Square was one thing that could be done to put the municipal house in order.

9.14. Private law offices on Court Square in the course of the nineteenth century, often built by lawyers who served terms as the court clerk or as judges. Demolished in 1921–1922 as part of a civic beautification campaign. Photograph, c. 1900. Albemarle Charlottesville Historical Society.

9.15. *The south wing of the Albemarle County Courthouse, built 1859. The addition of the classical portico did not lead to the elimination of all of the earlier Gothic-style elements. The stucco cladding also survived.* Holsinger Studio photograph, 1912. UVA Special Collections Library.

Jeffersonian Character and the Courthouse

R. T. W. Duke withdrew from advising the county about its plan to clear Court Square; he did not withdraw from the public debate. He held out until August 1922, longer than any other law office owner, in settling with the county. Duke didn't accept the county's final offer of $1,600 for his property until just before the county determined to start legal condemnation proceedings. In April 1921, Duke offered a lengthy and complex retort to the Chamber of Commerce's proposal for removing the law offices. He pointed out that the private offices, located primarily on the east side of the courthouse, did not really intrude upon the emerging beauty of Jackson Park. Duke then proceeded to argue for an even more radical improvement scheme. He suggested tearing down every building standing on Court Square, including the clerk's office and the courthouse itself (fig. 9.15). He argued that the clerk's office was hopelessly overcrowded and was not even fireproof. As for the court, he chronicled his sixty-year-long memory of the building, including his time serving as a judge, and argued that "the present courtroom is really a menace to the health of the Judge, jurymen and all who are compelled to sit in it for hours. There is no sentiment connected with it in the decidedly senti-mental mind of the writer, except a sentiment of disgust at its present condition, and of amazement that he has practiced in it for forty-six years and survived to tell it." Duke sketched in broad outlines the long succession of additions and adaptations made in the courthouse. He objected to the fact that the courthouse portico and the building did not align with the 5th Street axis to Court Square, which to Duke suggested a lack of civic dignity.[49]

In recommending the demolition of the courthouse Duke attempted to reconcile his interest in modern convenience and beauty with his feelings of sentiment for the historic character of Court Square. Similar tensions over the claims of the past and the needs of the future had swirled about the courthouse for decades. Local newspaper editors had repeatedly called for a new courthouse because the existing building was "absolutely so uncomfortable and in all respects so far behind the times, . . . a positive discredit to the city and the county."[50] In the view of many the historic patina of the buildings on the Court Square had little to commend the place or the city. In 1907 the editors of the *Daily Progress* presented history as a detriment to the progress of the city. They editorialized, "Charlottesville's chief attraction is as a residential city; and it is of prime importance that our public square should be an attractive spectacle. This it can never be until a new and handsome court-house supersedes the

227

old timey and out-of-date building that now occupies the central place on that square."[51] At other moments people actually felt that the "old timey" character of the courthouse provided the rationale for its preservation. Only a year before insisting on the imperative of having a new courthouse, the *Daily Progress* editors had argued that the building had "historic interest and associations that should stay the hand of the destroyer and the modernizer." The editors felt that the older north portion of the courthouse "ought to be preserved" because it "carries the mind back almost to the Revolutionary era. It is . . . invested with rich historic interest. . . . Something, we say, must be spared to the historic spirit; something accorded to the sentiment of reverence."[52] Here the proposal called for preserving the 1803 north portion of the courthouse while providing space for enlargement by demolishing the 1860 south wing and extending the building farther toward the street.

By the 1920s, feelings of sentiment surrounding the courthouse had seemingly strengthened. The *Daily Progress* acknowledged that "a strong and sound public sentiment founded on reverence for the great men and the epochal periods of our history" made the demolition of the courthouse unthinkable; in the view of the editors "the historic associations which cling to Albemarle's temple of justice" barred the destruction of the "venerable structure."[53] Charlottesville perhaps had more to gain by preserving its storied court building than by demolishing it and building a modern building. R. T. W. Duke sought to undercut the rising preservation sentiments and reverence for the building by arguing that the succession of building additions and interior remodeling had completely deprived the building of its authentic historic character. What survived, in his view, was unworthy of reverence. Duke wrote,

> Some of our most highly respected citizens urge that the building ought to be kept for sentimental reasons—that Jefferson went to church there and great lawyers pleaded therein. . . . Of the old courtroom nothing but the bricks remain, and there will be about as much sentiment and historic value about them as about anything else. They can well be used in the new building for I doubt if any as good can now be found. To talk about preserving the 'old' Courthouse is well nigh absurd. There is nothing left but four brick walls—inconveniently situated.

What Duke proposed was a handsome, fireproof, Colonial-style courthouse, a "new portico like the present one if you will," with a better relationship to its new and historic surroundings "to bring out the beauties of the new park and . . . make the whole square an ornament to city and county alike, and thus show our appreciation of Mr. McIntire's generosity."[54]

Duke's interest in new buildings in a historic place, with Colonial elements, soon received monumental expression at Court Square, not in the form of a new courthouse but rather in the form of a "Jeffersonian" skyscraper hotel. With increasing clarity in the early decades of the twentieth century, Charlottesville business leaders recognized that the economic future of the city would be bound up with tourism and residential settlement tied in large part to the region's scenic and historical heritage. The 1924 decision to build the nine-story Monticello Hotel on the south side of Court Square was only the beginning of the effort to juxtapose history and the most modern form of accommodations. Guests visiting the skyscraper hotel could survey the area's scenic and historic resources both close at hand on Court Square and in sweeping views out over the landscape, to Monticello, the University of Virginia, and the Blue Ridge Mountains beyond. Part of the effort to juxtapose modern and historic form flowed from the understanding that tourists visiting Charlottesville were "the automobile tourist of the better class . . . demanding better hotel accommodations," who led modern lives, with modern expectations, coming to visit historic and scenic sites in modern cars that ran over modern highways.[55] For these automobile-borne tourists, skyscraper form likely seemed a guarantee of a fine hotel.

Stanhope S. Johnson and Ray O. Brannan of Lynchburg, Virginia, won the commission for the Monticello Hotel over New York architect William Van Alen, the architect who later designed the seventy-seven-story Chrysler Building, the Art Deco skyscraper that briefly held the record of the world's tallest building in 1930–1931.[56] Johnson & Brannan designed a skyscraper; however, acknowledging the tourists' interests in history and tradition, they aimed to soften the modern form of the building facing the courthouse by deploying familiar Jeffersonian architectural elements in a decidedly unfamiliar local building type: the skyscraper (fig. 9.16).[57] The reporting on the initial design captured this juxtaposition of modern form and traditional elements. The *Daily Progress* wrote that the hotel would be "a stately structure comparable with the finer hotels to be found in much larger and more ambitious cites than Charlottesville." It would be thoroughly modern and fit the skyscraper urbanism of larger cities in the United States. Nevertheless, the hotel would also take on key elements of the Charlottesville vernacular:

> The architectural treatment will be consonant with the architectural traditions handed down to us from the time of

9.16. *Monticello Hotel, built 1925–1926. Johnson & Brannan, architects. View looking south across Court Square, Jackson equestrian monument at the right; confederate memorial in the middle ground, Albemarle County Clerk's Office at the left.* Photograph, c. 1945. Collection of Dave Norris.

Jefferson. The dignified lines are the Colonialized Classic so endeared to the citizens of Charlottesville by the University buildings, Monticello, and other works inspired by the imperishable genius of Thomas Jefferson. This period will be typified in the lower stories of the building, the handsome brick shaft being set off by a graceful cornice, entablature of upper façade of an architectural character and value fully in keeping with the masterpiece of the great designer of an older day, whose memory it is our pleasure to keep green, and whose influence on our domestic art is frankly acknowledged.[58]

Upon completion, advertisements declared: "The Monticello Hotel 'All the Charm of Old Virginia' . . . with its Colonial atmosphere of beauty and charm."[59] People recognized that the building could be "seen and admired from afar . . . [and] harmonize with the prevailing tone of the old Colonial buildings among which it stands, . . . the perfect blending of the finest that has come down from old times with the most modern of hotel conveniences. Thus the Monticello is full of the atmosphere of old Albemarle, with its roots sunk deep in the days that are gone but yielding a fruitage of the industry and agriculture of

today."[60] The Monticello Hotel was owned and operated by the Jackson Park Hotel Company. It seems clear that this massive investment at Court Square was premised in no small measure upon the McKee Block demolition and the Jackson monument construction put in place by Paul Goodloe McIntire.

For its part Albemarle County never embraced Duke's idea for a modern courthouse designed in a historic style. It did quickly clear the Court Square of private law offices, including the ones owned by Duke. Like Duke, many people considered the buildings on Court Square "drab and dingy," incapable of eliciting reverence or demands for preservation. Some responded to this character by calling for the complete demolition of existing buildings. Others advocated remodeling and reconstruction of the buildings to make them appear more historic, and thus more worthy objects of veneration and preservation. Purged of competing aesthetics and stripped of historic layers, a new Court Square could perhaps accommodate modern needs while focusing public attention on the most historic features of the square. It was precisely this approach that was adopted during the 1930s when, at the urging of the Daughters

9.17. *View of the south wing of the Albemarle County Courthouse after its 1938 Jeffersonian "restoration," which gave the building a Flemish-bond brick veneer and classical door surrounds and jack arches that had not previously existed on the building.* Holsinger Studio, c. 1938. UVA Special Collections Library.

of the American Revolution and the Beautification Committee of the Chamber of Commerce, city and county officials set out to give the buildings on Court Square a more historic "Jeffersonian" or "colonial" appearance. The 1930s building campaigns entirely transformed the architecture of Court Square and established the "colonial architectural theme" that planners deemed "worthy of preservation" in the 2000 Court Square plan.

Once the private law offices were removed in the 1920s, there were two chief objects of concern—the south wing of the courthouse, which provided the main entrance to the court, and the adjacent building to the west that served as the clerk's office. The courthouse's south wing had a rather complicated and, for some, troubling architectural and aesthetic history. In 1859, William Abbott Pratt, a Richmond architect who worked as superintendent of buildings and grounds at the University of Virginia between 1858 and 1865, designed the two-story south wing in a picturesque Gothic Revival style. The main entrance was through a pointed arch with a projecting pointed hoodmold. A large Gothic-style lancet window rose above the front door. Two gable-topped towers that enclosed narrow spiral staircases

flanked the entrance. The windows on either side of the entrance bay were more conventional double-hung windows with a nine-over-nine pane configuration, but, like the main entrance, they had prominent projecting hoodmolds. The exterior of the wing was covered in stucco, and the older section of the courthouse was painted white to match the stucco. The Gothic forms stood in rather stark contrast to the regional palette of Jeffersonian classicism. Interestingly, William Pratt had explored other aspects of picturesque aesthetics in the late 1850s designs for the grounds of the University of Virginia. At the university Pratt's designs for a new infirmary and the series of student dorms forming Dawson's Row engaged the topography of their hillside site much more directly than the geometries of Jefferson's original campus plan. On Dawson's Row the six two-story dormitories formed a sweeping arc as they rose toward the top of Monroe Hill. Pratt's plan seemed calculated to provide an aesthetic contrast with the earlier campus. The Gothic-style courthouse likely presented a similarly striking note on Court Square in the 1860s. In 1871, Albemarle County officials substantially modified and toned down the picturesque lines of the courthouse.

They commissioned G. Wallace Spooner to redesign the courthouse front, removing the towers that flanked the entrance and building a new granite porch with a projecting classical portico supported by four Ionic-order columns. The stucco exterior and the Gothic pointed arches for the entrance and the window above remained as notable vestiges of the earlier design, balanced after 1871 by a more conventional classical expression of civic monumentality.[61]

In 1937 the Albemarle County officials attempted to spruce up the courthouse by ordering a fresh coat of paint to cover the peeling yellow paint on the stucco section of the building.[62] As plans for the courthouse were discussed, several local residents appealed to the Board of Supervisors to remove what amounted to the remaining vestiges of Pratt's 1859 picturesque design. In February 1938, Sallie R. Shaffer, the chair of the Albemarle Chapter of the Daughters of the American Revolution, and Nathaniel Burnley of the Beautification Committee of the Charlottesville-Albemarle Chamber of Commerce, joined other citizens in asking that brick replace the stucco on the front section of the courthouse and that the paint be stripped from the 1803 north wing to expose the original red brick. The board appointed two members of the DAR and two members of the Beautification Committee, including architect Milton Grigg, to meet with the county executive and develop a courthouse improvement plan. The committee endorsed the original suggestions for removing the stucco and replacing it with a brick veneer. They also proposed stripping paint from the rear section, replacing Gothic arched elements on the front of the building with classically derived jack arches and removing the octagonal piers that flanked the front door, the remains of the original picturesque towers.[63] Reporting back to her DAR chapter, Sallie Shaffer declared that "the restoration of the outside of the Courthouse will be of the Jeffersonian period."[64] The Flemish bond of the veneer and the jack arches applied over the windows all gave the "restoration" a Jeffersonian aspect that it had never had before, while unifying the architecture of the north and south sections of the building (fig. 9.17). The surface of the building and the new window treatment and the new entrance bay all blended more seamlessly with the classical portico that had been added to the building in 1871. The Daughters of the American Revolution were so pleased by the development that they passed a resolution commending the Board of Supervisors for its courthouse "restoration."[65]

The DAR also placed two markers in the courthouse wall on either side of the new entrance. One marker narrated the history of the establishment of Albemarle County. The other marker narrated the history of the courthouse itself and worked to fold the new addition and improvements seamlessly into the storied landscape. It reported, COURTHOUSE FIRST PORTION BUILT BETWEEN 1763 AND 1781. ADDED TO IN 1803 AND 1860. REMODELED AND RESTORED 1938.[66] The marker strained credulity. The eighteenth-century frame courthouse was long gone. The 1803 section stood as the rear section of the existing building, not as an addition to the building it had actually replaced. So the impression that visitors were viewing a Colonial building was false. Moreover, the 1938 work created a fundamentally new façade rather than a façade that was merely "remodeled and restored." The words of the marker aimed to do what new design itself aimed to do, "to carry people back" to an earlier time, even one that never quite existed.

Coinciding in time with the architectural transformation of the courthouse, a similar Jeffersonian conversion was taking place just two blocks east of Court Square. Here, at the northwest corner of High and 7th streets, F. Bradley Peyton, Jr., a Charlottesville automobile dealer, purchased the High Street Baptist Church and converted it into apartments. Built in 1901, and designed by architect Robert Carson Vandegrift, the High Street Baptist Church was a brick Gothic Revival building (fig. 9.18). A central gable facing the street was dominated by a large Gothic Revival–style tracery window and was flanked by two entrance towers. Buttresses projected from the front and side elevations. The High Street Baptist Church moved into a new building near the university in 1929, leaving a smaller congregation on High Street. In 1932 fire gutted much of the interior of the High Street building. Peyton purchased the building in 1936, and between 1937 and 1938, as he adapted the building for residential use, he gave it a simple Georgian Colonial Revival front (fig. 9.19). The small oculus window in the gable provided the only clear continuity between the façade of the church and that of Peyton's apartments.[67] Despite the buttresses left on the sidewalls of the High Street building, the trend was clear—Jeffersonian forms now extended from the Monticello Hotel skyscraper, to the courthouse, to smaller residential developments in the neighborhood.

In 1938, as the courthouse and the former High Street Baptist Church received their quasi-Jeffersonian exteriors, an even more important public project developed on Court Square. The multiplication of public business had pushed to the limit the storage and operating capacity of the 1891 Court Clerk's Office located just west of the courthouse. The one-story brick building had something of its own picturesque, nonclassical character and according to contemporary

9.18. High Street Baptist Church, built 1901. Robert C. Vandegrift, architect. The church stood two blocks east of Court Square. Holsinger Studio, 1912. UVA Special Collections Library.

9.19. The classical remodeling and residential conversion of the High Street Baptist Church, done in 1937–1938, left little more than the oculus window and engaged buttresses along the side elevation as vestiges of the earlier Gothic Revival design. The remodeling echoed stylistically the similar conversions undertaken nearby on Court Square. Photograph by author, 2010.

accounts was "long considered an eyesore because of its incongruous architecture."[68] Designed by Baltimore architect William F. Weber, the Clerk's Office had a steeply pitched front-facing gable that rose over the main entrance. Initially, the County Board planned simply to make an addition to the north side of the building. However, as plans developed and as funds became available from the federal government's Works Progress Administration, the board determined that "the proposed addition would be inadequate for the County's needs and that an entirely new building with sufficient space to provide for all County Offices should be constructed."[69] The board hired Charlottesville architect Elmer E. Burruss to design the addition, noting that he had previously furnished plans and estimates for the addition to the Clerk's Office without cost to the county. Although the scale of the two-story building

was larger than any of the Colonial or early-nineteenth-century precedents at hand, Burruss designed an arcaded temple-form building that drew inspiration from both pre-Revolutionary arcaded courthouses and post-Revolutionary temple-fronted Virginia civic buildings (fig. 9.20). This form was evident in several early-nineteenth-century Virginia courthouses and was also apparent in Thomas Jefferson's design for Pavilion VII at the University of Virginia. Burruss also designed a building that complemented the aesthetic initiatives taken on Court Square. He reported that "the structure will be of colonial architecture to conform with that of the recently renovated courthouse."[70] When the new building was completed and the old earlier building demolished, the Clerk's Office stood farther north on the Court Square and brought the Jackson statue more directly into the composition of the square, as seen

9.20. *Albemarle County Clerk's Office, Court Square, built 1938. Elmer Burruss, architect. The architecture is drawn directly from examples of Virginia's eighteenth- and early-nineteenth-century civic architecture.* Photograph by author, 2007.

from the main, Jefferson Avenue approach to the court-house. The Georgian Clerk's Office presented just the form that Duke had earlier envisioned when he proposed an entirely new courthouse for the square. This 1938 building also completed the twentieth-century form of the civic landscape that then became the object of desire among the twenty-first century's preservers of the "Colonial" architecture of the Court Square.

On Charlottesville's Court Square the 1930s construction of the new Clerk's Office building and the new brick veneer on the courthouse gave the city's civic landscape a more harmonious Georgian character. Achieving that aesthetic involved only limited preservation—for example, removing paint from the 1803 north wing of the courthouse—and a good deal of demolition, including the destruction of the 1891 Clerk's Office, the various nineteenth-century brick private law offices occupying the Court Square, and the removal of the remaining traces of William Pratt's 1859 Gothic-style court exterior. Substituting a narrower Jeffersonian character for the Court Square's architectural hodgepodge of historical layers reinforced the vision of Monticello serving as a Jefferson shrine after being opened to the public in 1923.[71] Moreover, a similar combination of preservation, demolition, and new historicizing construction had, since 1926, won for Williamsburg, Virginia, national prominence and furnished a concrete model of the Jeffersonian "restoration" on Court Square. The 1930s demand for Jeffersonian restoration in Charlottesville also coincided with the movement to establish the Jefferson Memorial on the Tidal Basin in Washington, D.C. Thus when the Daughters of the American Revolution encouraged Albemarle County

officials to adopt a Jeffersonian aesthetic for Court Square, they settled on an increasingly popular narrative of both local and national history.

The 1909 Confederate monument, along with the later addition of the Jackson equestrian statue, underscored the Civil War as a second significant local narrative that guided architectural efforts and civic expression on Court Square. The removal of the McKee Block's African-American residences to provide a grander setting for the Jackson monument provided a social parallel for the architectural and historical effort to narrow and focus, and in many ways distort, civic expression on Court Square. Working-class African-American families lining the west side of Court Square constituted a social and physical presence, an "eyesore," that seemingly ran counter to the celebratory images of the Confederacy or of Jefferson's promotion of liberty and independence. Cumulatively, the changes to Court Square provided both the physical and the social space for recognizing certain historic narratives while obscuring other aspects of both history and contemporary society. Architectural and social diversity declined in the face of efforts to provide cohesive narratives related to Thomas Jefferson and the Confederacy.

As Court Square Goes,
So Goes the City

In 1938, as Albemarle County officials were moving forward with Court Square improvements, Charlottesville's school board sought a grant from the federal Public

Works Administration for a new high school for the city's white children. The resulting building involved a monumental addition to Charlottesville's civic landscape. As in the case of the earlier plans for the Confederate and Jackson memorials on Court Square, a calculus of race and space intersected with and shaped the project in important ways. Racial issues were always present because of the city's segregated school system. The move to build a new high school was accompanied by plans for an addition onto the black high school. But more important, as different neighborhoods sought to have the high school built in their section of the city, city officials increasingly sought to find a site, which like the existing high school, was located adjacent to the downtown, equally accessible to the city's outlying neighborhoods. Such a choice would likely bring the school into closer proximity with the centrally located African-American residential section of the city. A prime choice for the new location was on the site of the existing high school, facing Midway Park. After the school board decided to rebuild on the Midway School site, state officials rejected the plan because the site lacked sufficient space for future additions and athletic grounds.

Selecting another central site for the new high school would in all likelihood involve selecting a more costly site occupied by existing buildings. The school board began seriously considering a site on Preston Avenue just west of downtown and at the edge of Charlottesville's largely African-American Vinegar Hill neighborhood. For proponents of putting the school in other sections of the city, it seemed easy enough to find fault with the Preston Avenue site. It was topographically lower than many other sites considered; it stood along the course of Schenck's Branch, the polluted stream that passed through the city gas works and through some of the poorest neighborhoods in the city, receiving chemical pollutants and raw sewage along the way. Fuel-oil tanks that stood near the proposed site also posed some potential danger. In opposing the Preston location, realtor Ernest Duff declared that the "school should be named Schenck's Branch Low School, rather than City High School."[72] Advocates of the Preston site insisted that it stood close to the center of the city's population and would prove much less costly to condemn because it was occupied by fairly modest African-American residences as opposed to homes and buildings in more expensive neighborhoods; the site also would potentially include a large tract of land owned by the railroad that could be used for athletics and future expansion in line with state requirements. As school officials moved toward selecting the Preston Avenue site, they seemed to be running the McKee Block and Court Square drama in reverse; they seemed poised to place a major civic building onto a site framed on one side primarily by African-American residences.

On September 20, 1938, Charlottesville voters went to the polls and approved the bonds for funding the 55 percent local share of the high school construction budget necessary to obtain the federal government's 45 percent contribution. The voters approved the bond issue. Judge Archibald D. Dabney used the corporation court's consideration of condemnation proceedings on the Preston Avenue site to again weigh arguments for and against the location. Judge Dabney rejected most of the arguments against the site. He believed that Schenck's Branch could be put into pipes and covered with dirt where it passed the site, that the site was not actually an "unhealthy hollow" but had a modest elevation, and that the nearby gasoline tanks did not pose a danger but could, in any case, easily be removed. He also declared that on Preston Avenue the city will have acquired a site "in the heart of the City at the direct center of the population for a value extremely low compared to the value of any other piece of land of that size in the heart of the City." Judge Dabney established the condemnation awards at $48,500 and argued that "of course, [a] better site for the school and the playground could be obtained by purchasing fourteen acres of land between the Court House and the McGuffey school, but this would cost at least a quarter of a million dollars. Nowhere can this amount of land be located as near the center of the City . . . . It would be totally unfair to the citizens living in either end or side of the City to have the school located in the opposite end or side, if a reasonably good site can be found accessible to all."[73]

In weighing the Preston location Judge Dabney did raise indirectly its problematic racial and economic context. Pointing to the south side of Preston Avenue, across from the proposed school, he declared, "A short distance away there is a slum section which should be cleared out. Such property can be bought very cheaply and the old houses removed. The good houses that the City has purchased could replace these and be sold at a good profit above what the slum clearance would cost." Thus Dabney envisioned eight of the condemned houses on the school site could be salvaged and moved across the street to provide a more suitable, less "slum"-like, residential frame for the high-school building. He didn't state whether he assumed that African-American or white residents would purchase the relocated houses, but with a monumental white high school rising on the north side of Preston Avenue, there was at least the possibility that white residents would settle on the newly "cleared out" "slum section."[74] By envisioning this possibility for the high school, Judge Dabney anticipated that

9.21. Aerial view looking north over Vinegar Hill, the commercial, civic, and residential heart of Charlottesville's African-American community. In the background is Lane High School, built for the city's white schoolchildren in 1938–1940. Pendleton S. Clark, architect. The 1949 municipal parking lot at the center represented an early expansion of downtown into Vinegar Hill. Photograph by Ralph Thompson, 1960. UVA, Special Collections.

this addition to Charlottesville's civic landscape would follow the model pursued outside his own courthouse where the Jackson equestrian took the place of the McKee Block and its African-American tenants.

Beyond the site, other controversies swirled around the early development of the high school. Some people objected to the fact that the bonds would raise their taxes. Judge Dabney addressed this issue in passing; he asked rhetorically, "What price education?" and then drew upon Jefferson's political philosophy to answer: "Jefferson's theory that knowledge is prerequisite to the survival of Democracy has been proven by modern history. Surely our people will not lose this golden opportunity of providing every facility possible to make our children better citizens."[75] People who did not object to the taxes did object to them being spent to support people from outside of the Charlottesville community. This was especially the case when the school board contracted with Pendleton S. Clark, a Lynchburg architect, to design the new high school. In a meeting presided over by Elmer E. Burruss, the architect hired to design the Court Clerk's Office, members of the local Kiwanis Club raised several objections to the hiring of an out-of-town architect. The *Daily Progress* editorialized against the outside architect, declaring, "The theory of P.W.A. distributions is to provide employment in those areas where allocations are made. Lynchburg can hardly be considered in the Charlottesville area." In the case of the architect, the paper endorsed the slogan of "Buy Charlottesville."[76] For his part Pendleton S. Clark declared his intension to hire engineers, draftsmen, and artists in Charlottesville to help with the commission.[77] Despite his status as an outsider, Clark's design for the new high school employed familiar monumental Georgian elements, with a classical portico, jack arches over the windows, and a tower and cupola topping the building. Given the contemporary sentiments favoring such forms on Court Square and given Judge Dabney's easy recourse to Jeffersonian ideals in justifying the building, the design seemed a fitting testament to local sensibilities. Clark's placement of what became Lane High School on its Preston Avenue site also seemed calculated to please official sensibilities. The houses condemned in the assembly of the high school site generally faced directly onto Preston Avenue. In fronting the avenue they also faced south, looking directly out upon the African-American Vinegar Hill neighborhood. Clark did not maintain this historical orientation to buildings and street with the new high school. Instead, he rotated the entire building away from Vinegar Hill and had it face more directly the downtown, where white-owned businesses and residences dominated and where a white elementary school and the county courthouse stood.

The neighborhood facing the new high school was not cleared of its slum housing as envisioned by Judge Dabney, at least not right away. The rotation of the high school building toward the downtown (fig. 9.21), with its attendant visual discontinuity with the Vinegar Hill neighborhood, did not, in the end, create a permanent barrier between Lane High School and Charlottesville's African-American community. In August 1956, United States Circuit Court judge John Paul ordered Charlottesville to integrate Venable Elementary School and Lane High School in accordance with the 1954 Supreme Court decision in *Brown v. Board of Education*. In September 1958, after numerous appeals of his earlier decision, Judge Paul ordered the enrollment of African-American students in both Venable and Lane. The response on the part of the Commonwealth of Virginia was "massive resistance" and the total closing of Lane High School from September 1958 to February 1959 as an alternative to following the court order to integrate. With continued legal challenges to segregation and with a change of political strategy on the part of Virginia's governor and legislature, Lane received its first African-American students in September 1959.[78]

Within months of the arrival of African-American students at Lane High School, Charlottesville residents and officials took on another community-wide public debate that was similarly framed around issues of race and space. They took up an issue raised twenty years earlier by Judge Dabney—the demolition of the Vinegar Hill neighborhood "slum." The scale of the proposed urban renewal project on Vinegar Hill far exceeded the scale of McIntire's earlier renewal project on Court Square. The project would involve the demolition of hundreds of buildings, including residences, commercial buildings, fraternal lodges, and churches in the historic core of Charlottesville's African-American community. Hundreds of working-class residents who worked at the University of Virginia, for the Charlottesville Public Works Department, in downtown hotels and businesses, would be displaced along with their families, some to new public housing projects far removed from Vinegar Hill. The debate over the Vinegar Hill urban renewal plan sharply divided the city. Many of the more conservative voices raised opposed the project as a further insinuation of federal programs into local affairs, beyond school integration. The idea of demolishing the neighborhood and accommodating some of the displaced residents in public housing seemed to sap private initiative, undercut the private real estate market, and pave the way for "socialism" in the provision of urban housing. Thus, the opposition to demolition was against a range of public initiatives rather than in favor of preservation. Nathaniel McG. Ewell wrote a letter to the editor of the *Daily Progress* denouncing the urban renewal plan; he demanded,

> Is it right to pauperize a group of people by encouraging them to live on a standard beyond their means? Is it morally right to have children grow up with the idea that the government owes them a living and will support them if they do not support themselves? . . . We must remember that people living in substandard housing—do not make "slums." "Slums" are substandard people wherever they might live. Truly public housing will open a Pandora's Box of evils—in exchange for what?—and certainly it is another step toward the socialist state.[79]

More moderate and progressive voices were raised in favor of the urban renewal, insisting that the community needed to "do something about the slums" and arguing that the private real estate market would not and could not solve the problem of providing decent housing with modern systems like indoor plumbing and hot water for the community's poorer residents.[80] In Vinegar Hill, residents could appreciate the prospect of improved housing; however, they also recognized that proposed demolitions would sweep away not only the most problematic housing but also more substantial residences and institutions and businesses that were integral to both community life and memory for Charlottesville's African-American community.[81]

A precipitating factor in the Vinegar Hill debate was that many of Charlottesville's business leaders viewed the presence of a poor African-American community in

9.22. Aerial view looking east toward downtown Charlottesville over Vinegar Hill after the neighborhood was cleared by urban renewal. Photograph, c. 1974. Halprin Archive, University of Pennsylvania Library.

such close proximity to the business center as detrimental to the long-term viability of downtown business. After a decade of depression and a decade of war, there was an open question in Charlottesville of how the downtown would now survive the challenges of private automobile transportation and residential suburbanization. In October 1959 the Barracks Road Shopping Center opened on the western edge of the city, advertising "Shop in Ease and Comfort in Our Arcade Connected Shops—ACRES OF FREE PARKING." Even before the city addressed urban renewal, it had already begun to redevelop some sections of Vinegar Hill for surface parking to accommodate the growing numbers of people who traveled to downtown in private automobiles. Many Charlottesville leaders framed the Vinegar Hill demolition as the best means to assure the renewal of the broader downtown. Addressing Charlottesville residents before the voter referendum on the Vinegar Hill urban renewal plan, Mayor Thomas J. Michie declared:

This vote will be on what might be called a double-barreled program—to provide decent housing for those who now live in slums, and at the same time to take the area in which the slums exist and make it into a vital, important, and attractive business area in extension of the existing downtown business area which is now hemmed in by slums and hills. We are fortunate that the worst slum area in the city lends itself so beautifully to plans for urban renewal. . . . From a financial point of view as well as from a social and cultural point of view, the substitution of a fine modern business section for the slum area now existing back of Vinegar Hill would be the most forward looking step that has been taken in Charlottesville in many, many years.[82]

When Charlottesville residents voted in June 1960 on the Vinegar Hill urban renewal referendum, they endorsed the program by the narrowest of margins, a majority of 23 votes in the 3,689 votes cast.[83] The City

*9.23. Zion Union Baptist Church during 1965
demolition in the Vinegar Hill urban renewal project.*
Photograph, 1965. Charlottesville Housing Authority.

Council then moved forward with the clean sweep of Vinegar Hill (fig. 9.22).

Charlottesville's "double-barreled" approach to urban renewal replicated the experience in many other American cities. An urban-renewal and public-housing program inaugurated to address blighted housing conditions was channeled into salvaging the fortunes of the post–World War II central business districts.[84] The Vinegar Hill program removed what many business leaders viewed as the blight on the edge of downtown while at the same time providing land for the expansion of downtown in its competition with suburban commercial development. In a sense, the Vinegar Hill project expanded the logic that guided public school officials when they selected the Preston Avenue site for Lane High School. The area provided inexpensive, centrally located land that could be seized through eminent domain to fulfill the vision of proper urban form advocated by many the civic and business leaders. It also expanded the logic that guided public officials and Paul Goodloe McIntire when African-American housing was demolished to provide a space for commemorating the Civil War and the

Stonewall Jackson narrative. Like Court Square's civic landscape in the 1920s, the overall downtown in the 1960s was viewed through a dominant lens of white prerogative and privilege. The right to memory and commemoration formed an important part of that privilege.

In the years around 2000 when Charlottesville planners and officials buttressed the fortunes of Court Square as a significant site of history and memory, they also began to grapple with ways the vacant Jefferson School, Charlottesville's historic African-American school, could be preserved and reused. Built in 1926, the Jefferson School still stood on the edge of the demolished Vinegar Hill neighborhood. By 2000, local residents and city officials envisioned the school as a possible site to commemorate black history in Charlottesville. Proposals abounded for the development of an African-American museum and cultural center in the vacant building. Clearly, the canvas of memory had broadened and the preservation priorities of the community had significantly changed. Nevertheless, the urgency of the Jefferson School preservation campaign played out against the backdrop of a historic

African-American landscape of memory that had been systematically disregarded and demolished. The Jefferson School loomed especially large because many other buildings that served as sites of local memory associated with the African-American community had disappeared in the Vinegar Hill urban renewal of the 1960s. The Old Jefferson School, built in 1894, on 4th Street; the nineteenth-century fraternal lodge at the southeast corner of Commerce and 4th Streets; the Zion Baptist Church on 4th Street (fig. 9.23), where generations of worshipers had been baptized, married their loved ones, mourned their dead, and prayed to their God; as well as many other shops and businesses of the local African-American community—all had been demolished on Vinegar Hill. The sense of displacement from sites of memory was undoubtedly private as well as public. For example, dressmaker Mary S. Jones and her husband, Charles N. Jones, a janitor for the *Daily Progress*, had taken on the rudiments of the American dream of homeownership in 1930–1931 when they built their own substantial house at 306 3rd Street. Charles died in 1951, and Mary continued to live in their home until 1963, when the Charlottesville Redevelopment and Housing Authority purchased and demolished her house. Less than thirty-five years old, Mary S. Jones's house couldn't be characterized as a slum.[85] Nevertheless, it was swept away with the rest of the neighborhood, removing a personal landmark of some note. In Charlottesville certain stories, certain histories, had been celebrated and monumentalized, while other stories were devalued or set aside. Acts of recent preservation at Jefferson School and elsewhere necessarily negotiated between the responsibility of remembering and celebrating and the legacy of forgetting and devaluing sites of a diverse local history.

Remembering and Forgetting on Court Square

When people visit the preserved historic Court Square, there is a great deal that they can learn about Charlottesville. They should perhaps see in Court Square's "colonial" landscape a reflection of early-twentieth-century design and culture as well as local commitments to Colonial Revivalism. Court Square improvements had long seized upon certain civic narratives as especially worthy of commemorating, monumentalizing, and preserving. Those narratives reached back to the Civil War and also cultivated links to Thomas Jefferson, the American Revolution, and American democracy. Fixing or preserving those narratives in their place on Court Square with architectural, landscape, and sculptured forms had involved gestures of remembrance as well as acts of social and architectural erasure. When the sculpted figures of Stonewall Jackson and his horse Little Sorrel emerged from the dust and demolition of the McKee Block, African-Americans had largely lost their place in the historic frame. The commemorative sculpture constituted a simpler but less accurate accounting of both history and current realities. This process in the 1910s and 1920s anticipated the much vaster scale of 1960s urban renewal whereby an expanded modern downtown emerged from the dust, demolition, and the blasted memory on Vinegar Hill. It would then take decades for Charlottesville in its proposed Jefferson School African-American Cultural Center to begin to seriously address some of the history that had been destroyed, lost, or forgotten. Very much beyond the imperatives of heritage tourism lies the imperative of encouraging local knowledge, critical engagements with history, and an enlightened citizenship for everyone who can look and see on Court Square.

CHAPTER TEN

Drive-by History

Virginia's Historic Highway Marker Program

People's encounters with historic sites have been shaped in important ways by changing forms of transportation. After World War I growing numbers of tourists in the United States moved from trains to private automobiles and began exploring scenic landscapes and historic sites on an expanding national highway network. Earlier tourists often had only fleeting glimpses of historic localities from the windows of moving trains. In contrast, automobiles actually placed a much larger number of tourists in storied landscapes where they enjoyed greater control over the timing and character of their engagements with history. The automobile also permitted tourists to range more broadly across the landscape, encountering many more sites connected to narratives of local and national history.[1] Railroad companies had long promoted scenic and historic locales as a way of building passenger traffic. Automobiles gave access to far-flung localities that both private entrepreneurs and public officials attempted to literally put on the map; they aimed to establish a new landscape and economy of tourism. How did this new transportation accommodate and change historic preservation practice and public presentations of history? How did the new automobile tourism influence the power of particular places to narrate history?

Declaring that the automobile could serve as a "Good History Teacher," a short *Los Angeles Times* article in 1923 underscored key issues surrounding the new automobile tourism. A Lafayette, a luxury touring car named in honor of the Marquis de Lafayette, pulled up to a hotel in downtown Los Angeles after visiting missions in the vicinity of Santa Barbara. Out stepped the young driver who took off his goggles and wiped his face with a handkerchief and declared to the passenger in the back seat, "'Mother, I thought I had gotten my fill of lessons in school but this automobile is a better teacher of history than any professor I ever met in college.'" The mother smiled and responded, "'Yes, son, if we had not had the car to take us to the scenes of stirring and romantic events, probably I never would have thought to call them out of memory and put them into words for you.'" Four things are striking about this report. First, the automobile was viewed as opening new perspectives on history. Second, these actual encounters with places seemed more effective in conveying history than classroom teaching and book learning. Third, the travelers were patronizing a Los Angeles hotel and thus contributing to the growing automotive tourist economy. Finally, for all the apparent power of the mission sites to teach the young man history, the mother's memory and narration on the tour appeared important. Hanging over the new automobile tourism were the same questions that hang over any encounter with historic places: how do people learn from the places they encounter? History derives partly from looking but also from understandings that people bring with them to sites, or that they learn on a site, or that a site provokes them to explore after a visit. How would this be done in the age of automobile tourism, when knowledgeable mothers were not always present, and when so many people were bound and determined to cultivate history for economic development, detached from any civic, political, or social implications?

Taking up issues of automobile tourism, historic sites and preservation, and historical narratives, this chapter

10.1. *Virginia highway historical markers on U.S. Route 60, in Henrico County. These markers related the area's June 1862 Civil War battles.* Photograph, c. 1938. Library of Virginia.

explores the early history of Virginia's pioneering historic highway marker program. In the late 1920s, Virginians took narratives of history long embedded in the landscape and displayed them on cast-metal signs along the state's main highways. In just three years the State Conservation and Development Commission set out over eight hundred historic markers on Virginia's roadsides (fig. 10.1). The work of late-nineteenth-century patriotic societies that placed commemorative plaques at historic sites inspired the commonwealth's effort; however, the magnitude of the highway program quickly eclipsed, both geographically and thematically, all earlier efforts to mark historic places. Aiming to promote tourism and economic development, the highway marker program made significant innovations in the popular presentations of history. The program deftly responded to the possibilities presented by automobile tourism. It framed the tourists' encounters with the past while subtly cultivating the state's present and future

development. In 1929 the official in charge of the highway marker program insisted that tourists could not encounter "romance and history" as rich as that found in the Virginia countryside in many other parts of the United States. He insisted that "the tourist crop is our best crop; it carries no overhead and distributes money so that it reaches everybody."[3] Although Mt. Vernon, Monticello, and Williamsburg loom large in assessments of Virginia's contribution to the national preservation and public history, the importance of the innovative highway marker program was recognized and quickly emulated by many other states.[4]

The connection forged in the historic highway marker program between heritage and tourism, between history and economy, distinguished the program from many earlier commemorative undertakings. The new economic calculation of Virginians concerning the possibilities of historic places gave the highway marker program its own particular form and character and set it apart from the work of groups like the Daughters of the American Revolution, the United Daughters of the Confederacy, and the Association for the Preservation of Virginia Antiquities. In Virginia, stewards of heritage and proprietors of historic sites had not traditionally viewed tourism and economics as central to their mission. Lafayette's extended pilgrimage through Virginia in 1824 explored the evocative power of particular historic sites but promoted patriotism and commemoration rather than tourism. The Mount Vernon Ladies' Association, which opened Washington's home as a national shrine in 1860, reacted ambivalently toward later proposals for electric streetcar service between Washington and Mount Vernon. They worried that the "wrong sort" of people would flood their property. Indeed, they felt that mass tourism as opposed to class tourism could compromise the diffusion of Washington's legacy.[5] Similarly, the patriotic societies often resisted the commercialization of history and, in fact, restricted their membership rolls; the DAR, for example, accepted into membership only lineal descendants of patriots of the American Revolution. The nurturing of social and political affinity within the patriotic organizations clearly predominated over any interest in tourism.

The advocates of tourism and development articulated a different sensibility concerning the uses and meaning of historic places. Governor Harry F. Byrd and his dynamic associate William E. Carson epitomized something of that new vision when they created the historic highway marker program. Still, the program often took on significance beyond economic development. Although overseen by administrators and historians in Richmond, the program tapped reservoirs of local enthusiasm among residents interested in building and reinforcing their sense of place by celebrating their connections to various histories. The changing dynamic between local chroniclers and professional administrators shaped the program while dramatizing the shifting ideals of public history and preservation in early-twentieth-century America.

Good Roads, Tourism, and the Marking of History

During the 1920s many Virginians were vitally interested in the subject of highways, or more properly, good roads. The question of roads, especially how quickly they could be improved and whether they should be paid for out of current tax revenue or through long-term bonds, proved an important issue in Harry F. Byrd's 1925 campaign for governor. A fifteen-year-old bronze historic plaque in Charlottesville led Byrd and his advisor William E. Carson to envision an interesting link between highways, history, and development. Placed on a site adjacent to the Albemarle County Courthouse in 1910 by the Association for the Preservation of Virginia Antiquities, that marker read SITE OF OLD SWAN TAVERN WHERE LIVED AND DIED JACK JOUETT WHOSE HISTORIC RIDE SAVED MR. JEFFERSON, THE GOVERNOR, AND THE VIRGINIA ASSEMBLY FROM CAPTURE BY TARLETON JUNE 1781. Virginia preservationists and historians had come to embrace Jack Jouett in an effort to gain the historical high ground on rival New England, with its Paul Revere story. At Charlottesville, Carson suggested to Byrd that similar markings of history along the state's highway would interest tourists and residents alike and promote the economic development of the state.[6]

Once the highway marker program was inaugurated, Jack Jouett's Ride was marked anew. Set in Louisa County, where Jouett's ride had commenced, rather than in Charlottesville, where the ride ended, the state marker recorded the same story in slightly more detail: JACK JOUETT, AT THE TAVERN HERE, SAW TARLETON'S BRITISH CAVALRY PASS IN THE NIGHT OF JUNE 3, 1781. SUSPECTING THAT THEY WERE GOING TO CHARLOTTESVILLE TO SEIZE GOVERNOR JEFFERSON AND THE LEGISLATURE, JOUETT RODE THERE BY ANOTHER WAY AND ARRIVED IN TIME TO GIVE WARNING. Despite the basic agreement on the facts of the history, the two markers emerged from strikingly different social and institutional arrangements. Under the auspices of the Association for the Preservation of Virginia Antiquities, marking historic sites had been one of the primary venues for the encouragement of a traditionalist view of Virginia history that celebrated the old order. Founded in 1889, the association had done important work to protect Jamestown Island, the Powder Horn in Williamsburg, the Mary Washington House in Fredericksburg, St. Luke's Church in Smithfield, and numerous other historic sites. The placement of historic markers inexpensively commemorated Virginia history without the costs of taking title to historic buildings or sites. Historian James Lindgren has argued that in preserving historic places, in marking historic sites, and in diffusing knowledge of early Virginia history through lectures and publications, members of the association sought to promote historic memory, reassert southern ways in the reunited nation, and defeat the forces of turn-of-the-century racial and economic readjustment in Virginia.[7] In sharp contrast to the later work of the state's highway marker program, the association used its landmarks to celebrate the past while constituting a society around a shared vision of the future and their own place in it.

The unveiling of the Jouett plaque in 1910 underscores something of the broader social context of the association's work. Largely forgotten in the course of the nineteenth century, Jouett and his story were revived at the turn of the twentieth century when R. T. W. Duke, Jr., a former Charlottesville judge, researched a passing reference to Jouett in Henry S. Randall's 1858 biography of Jefferson.[8] Duke then published an essay on Jouett's Ride in the *St. Nicholas* magazine in 1901 and encouraged the newly formed Monticello Chapter of the association to construct a marker to Jouett as one of its first projects. The marker was placed on the front wall of the building occupied by the elite Redland Club, of which Duke was president, and where he had established that Jouett's Swan Tavern had stood earlier. When the association unveiled its marker, it sanctified contemporary social space, the Redland Club, as well as historic space, the site of Swan Tavern. The unveiling took place on the 129th anniversary of Jouett's ride and marked historic time and place. The corresponding secretary of the association located Jack Jouett's grandsons in Kentucky and attempted to add genealogy to time and place in pursuing its objects. The grandchildren could not travel to Charlottesville but heartily thanked association members who "in the mad rush of the present, have the disposition . . . to look into the past and see that justice for its own sake is done to the memory of our worthy dead."[9] The association unveiled the tablet at five o'clock in the afternoon before a crowd of about two hundred, "mostly ladies;" Dr. William M. Randolph, a lineal descendant of Thomas Jefferson, stood in for the Jouett descendants and pulled the flag off of the plaque. The crowd listened to addresses by Judge Duke and by Professor R. Heath Dabney of the University of Virginia. After the unveiling "the ladies and gentlemen were invited into the club house to partake of elegant refreshments consisting of ice cream, cake, and punch."[10] Thus, the participants constituted current society even as they attended to history.

When the state's marker to Jack Jouett was erected over fifteen years later, there were no speeches, no anniversaries marked, no crowd of ladies or gentlemen, and no constituting of society through the agency of clubs, addresses, descendants, or elegant refreshments. Employees of the Virginia Highway Department placed the marker on its pole without fanfare. Despite the similarity of the Jouett chronicle on the association's commemorative marker and the historic highway marker, the meaning and purpose of the two memorials differed substantially.

The first $50,000 for highway historical markers came from the Virginia state advertising fund. Publicity, promotion, and development dominated the plan for dissem-

inating history with markers. Besides good roads Harry Byrd had campaigned on the promise to better promote the resources and the development of Virginia. On July 1, 1926, the State Conservation and Development Commission was established, with William E. Carson serving as chairman. The legislature gave the commission broad powers to develop and promote the natural and historic resources of the state. The commission could obtain scenic, recreational, and historic places through public purchase or, if necessary, through eminent domain. The sites would be thus "preserved and maintained for the use, observation, education, health and pleasure of the people of Virginia."[11] The legislature would have to appropriate the money for such acquisitions, but the legislation certainly countenanced history and historic sites as worthy of public support.

The state's vision of historic and scenic promotion mirrored that of the privately funded Virginia Historic Highway Association. Originating within the Lynchburg Lions Club, and founded in 1924, the association was a coalition of business and civic groups that sought to diffuse information throughout the United States about the "lavish historic and scenic attractions" of the state and to promote highway improvements and tourism; it published *Historic Places and Shrines of Virginia Accessible by the Virginia Historic Highway*, a guide to a 700-mile, weeklong travel itinerary through the heart of Virginia. The guide included concise descriptions of historic and scenic sites along the highway loop as well as candid descriptions of the varied highway conditions that a motorist would encounter along the way. In a sense, the format replicated the early maps and guides put out by tire and gasoline companies and by the American Automobile Association and other automobile clubs to promote automobile touring.[12] In the view of the association there was an "urgent need" for highway improvements to make accessible "the points which are of greatest national historical interest to the patriots, students, historians, and tourists of the United States."[13] In 1926 the Virginia legislature chartered the association even as it eclipsed its efforts with Conservation and Development Commission programs. Junius P. Fishburn, a Roanoke banker and newspaper publisher, and a noted world traveler, who served as president of the Historic Highway Association, became a charter member of the Conservation and Development Commission and helped put in place a far more ambitious program than anything contemplated by the association.[14] The commission quickly reached a consensus that the marker and shrine projects were "such important publicity agencies" that a large part of the commission's "advertising fund" would be spent on this work.[15]

The Virginia Historic Highway Association did not propose roadside markers. The guide and map would help tourists navigate the highway loop through Virginia. Their program represented something of a transition between the work of national and state patriotic initiatives and the full-fledged tourist promotion of the highway marker program. The Highway Association's vision of a narrated historic circuit spread out over hundreds of miles of landscape had already been explored earlier by various patriotic organizations. The association's interesting juxtaposition of history with modern automotive travel, road improvements, and tourist promotion clearly anticipated the central economic elements of the highway marker program.

The 1906 marking of the Santa Fe Trail by the Kansas Daughters of the American Revolution represented an early initiative by a patriotic organization to chart a historic circuit across an extended regional landscape. The Kansas Daughters lived in a state that, in the view of the state regent, had "few historical landmarks or places of historic interest," and yet they wanted to fulfill the national DAR commitment to marking and preserving historic places. In 1902, Fannie Geiger Thompson proposed setting out markers along the nearly 500-mile-long course of the Santa Fe Trail that had run through Kansas and provided one of the primary routes for the westward migration of European immigrants and Americans during the nineteenth century. In the late nineteenth and early twentieth centuries, the traces of the trail, which had been eclipsed by railroads in the 1870s, were being obliterated by modern development. The Daughters sought to mark what they viewed as the inspiring story of the westward push of "civilization" across the country. Drawing on historical maps and archives and old settler accounts, they campaigned to put in place ninety-six granite markers along the course of the trail. They selected significant campsites, forts, water holes, and places of memorable encounters, either in peace or in war, between settlers and travelers and native peoples. The expansive project drew upon and organized the people and resources of local chapters of the DAR and galvanized local communities with fundraising campaigns, essay contests, and patriotic speeches at the unveiling of the individual markers. There is little evidence that people in Kansas initially viewed the Santa Fe Trail project as connected to tourism or economic development. It was a civic, patriotic, and educational project. It recognized and celebrated a very particular view of national history within the Kansas landscape. The Santa Fe Trail marker work expanded into adjoining states and, in 1915, the DAR undertook a similar project to mark the course of the Oregon Trail across Nebraska.[16]

The trail-marking projects undertaken by the Daughters of the American Revolution encouraged some chapters of the organization to join coalitions promoting better roads in the United States. In the 1910s highway advocates harnessed patriotic sentiment and historical interests to advance the movement for road development. Organizations seeking transcontinental highway routes, like the National Old Trails Association and the Lincoln Highway Association, received support from various good roads committees of the DAR. These organizations linked highway development with the cultivation of national narratives of pioneer history, progress, and the celebration of historic figures. The identification of highways with national history undoubtedly strengthened road developers' claims on both public and private support for highway improvements. Historical interests provided some leverage for the development of modern highway infrastructure. The DAR hoped to see the national highway system incorporate major sections of the Santa Fe and Oregon trail routes that they had marked. History pervaded other highway projects as well; in 1913 the Lincoln Highway Association began promoting a transcontinental highway as a memorial to the sixteenth president. In the same year, the United Daughters of the Confederacy initiated the Jefferson Davis Highway linking Washington, D.C., and San Diego, California. Starting in 1927 and continuing for two decades, the UDC constructed sixteen substantial granite and bronze markers along the course of the Davis Highway in Virginia. In 1926 the federal Bureau of Public Roads began to standardize the marking and numbering of national highways. Much to the dismay of the various road and highway associations, the bureau refused to adopt the nomenclature of the existing roads, opting for uniform route numbers over named highways. Nevertheless, the bureau's effort to establish a federal road network was accompanied by the publication of a series of guides that identified the scenic and historic sites that travelers and tourists would encounter.[17] When Harry F. Byrd and William E. Carson simultaneously launched Virginia's new road improvements and the highway marker program, they gave novel form to the merging of highway and historical interests that had been intertwined for well over a decade.

The relative simplicity of the Virginia historic highway markers helped distinguish them from more monumental patriotic society markers as well as from more garish roadside advertising. In the early planning of the Virginia highway marker program, the highway commissioner, Henry G. Shirley, suggested the adoption of "simple and uniform" markers, perhaps metal tablets mounted on short concrete posts.[18] The uniformity of the markers would parallel the growing efforts to standardize the national highway landscape itself.[19] The standard metal historic markers generally measuring approximately 42 by 40 inches might have been conducive to safe and efficient travel, but they stood at odds with the particularity of historic places and the site-specific character of the commemorative monuments and markers raised by the patriotic societies. In the early years of its program the Conservation and Development Commission found itself carefully delineating the distinctions between "informational" and "monumental" markers. In 1928, Carson insisted that "we have no money whatever to erect monuments; the markers we are putting up are out of our advertising fund, and we feel we are thoroughly justified, from an advertising viewpoint."[20] The commission rejected the adoption of granite monuments, like those set out to mark the Santa Fe Trail by the DAR. Highway markers had to be highly legible and designed to be read in part form a moving car. Furthermore, through their design, they were intended to be quite distinct from roadside advertising.[21] Members of the commission in fact sought to enhance the visibility and didactic nature of their work by joining proponents of the regulation of roadside advertising.[22] The highway marker program aimed to advertise Virginia and to build the local economy; however, the refined appeals of heritage and culture set forth on tasteful and uniform signs seemed a world apart from the glaring commercialism of roadside advertising. In 1927, seeking to enlist Governor Byrd's support for legislation to "curb and control the evil" of outdoor advertising, the president of the Society for the Restriction of Outdoor Advertising in Virginia, insisted that Virginia was "spending many millions of dollars a year on the public highways, and is confidently looking forward to partial compensation for these large expenditures from the material advantages which will follow from the increase in the Tourist Movement in the State. . . . And yet a handful of out-door advertisers for their own private gain are permitted to mar every beautiful landscape and to defile the approaches to every sacred historic shrine in the State."[23] Virginia's standardized highway history markers provided a new form of roadside advertising, advertising that seemingly would reinforce rather than defile the state's scenic and historic shrines.

The Conservation Commission maintained the idea of "simple and uniform" markers even as it resolved to carry out the historic marker program without the funds from the Highway Department. The commission's advertising budget seemed a good way to put in place the historic project that Carson and Byrd had envisioned. In the view of the commission "points of historic inter-est attract people if they are accessible by good roads and identified by markers and tablets. The tourist leaves money in the State, and . . . becomes a walking advertisement."[24] One advisor to the state insisted that if historic markers and other historic resources were developed, "the world will come to Virginia's threshold to bow in reverence, leaving in its wake many millions of dollars each year."[25] Carson estimated that tourists and campers spent $3 billion annually in the United States, and he hoped to claim $250 million of the total for Virginia.[26] Although the commission felt that "the tourist crop is our best crop," it initially viewed money derived directly from tourism as secondary. The commission still viewed industrial development as its most important work; it hoped that tourists traveling along well-marked highways, having a good time in Virginia, would assume a broader role in the state's economic development. The commission actually conceived of history as a resource to be mined or harvested like other natural resources. William E. Carson argued, "The prosperity of the State is dependent upon the prosperity of her citizens, so it behooves the State to locate for her citizens or indicate to them where hidden wealth, such as is found in her minerals, her water resources, her parks, her forests, her history, her scenery, her climate, etc., exists . . . and to advertise to the world the advantages and values to be found within her borders."[27]

In 1927, in shaping Virginia's publicity program, the commission planned a "less direct but more effective means of reaching the persons whose steps and business we desire turned to Virginia." It decided that "the most effective method of making known the attractions and commercial possibilities of our State is by bringing people to Virginia as tourists and while they are here, bring to their attention the industrial, business and residential possibilities of the State. In other words, [we] have chosen the tourist appeal, with an industrial follow-up, instead of a direct commercial appeal, in our advertising copy." The task of convincing manufacturers to move to Virginia through direct advertising seemed rather ineffective or at best random. "On the other hand, the tourist appeal finds a very wide and receptive audience, and may be satisfied at a minimum of cost and effort to the tourist. In fact, it provides him with an objective in his recreational and educational wanderings. . . . Virginia has a wealth of attractions for the tourist, so that this type of appeal is available for our use." The commission cited programs in other states as well as the advice of the United States Chamber of Commerce as supporting the conclusion that the publicity program should be directed primarily to tourists.[28] Carson and Byrd thus conceived of a role for history, and more precisely for historic markers, in promoting the industrial and economic future of Virginia.

The Conservation and Development Commission and other promoters of economic development did not entirely eschew print advertising directed at business owners. In fact, the commission, in concert with local chambers of commerce, boasted of a historic past and an industrial future in a dynamic series of print advertisements during the late 1920s. The Alexandria chamber declared, "One of American's most historic cities welcomes the motorist to a score of noteworthy points

10.2. *Alexandria Chamber of Commerce ad highlighting historic attractions as well as industrial and aviation opportunities.* From *American Motorist*, April 1928.

of interest, but invites special attention to many unusual advantages for the manufacture of airplanes and aviation accessories, also for several other lines of industry"[29] (fig. 10.2). In 1928 the Norfolk-Portsmouth Chamber of Commerce ran an advertisement in *Scribner's* magazine alongside an article on Virginia written by Governor Byrd. The advertisement declared the region a "modern port of entry to historic Virginia. Norfolk-Portsmouth, center of Virginia's historic shrines, likewise is the embodiment of its modern facilities for rest and recreation, and the focal point of its rapidly growing industry and trade!" The images accompanying these advertisements juxtaposed etchings of eighteenth-century scenes with the electrical generating plants and bustling waterfronts and industrial districts of the imagined future (fig. 10.3).[30] The juxtaposition paralleled the connection made between modern highway development and historic exploration. Absent from the advertisements was any sense of the potential incompatibility of these images and the landscapes they conjured up. The popularity of tourism to historic places had for some time reflected the concerns of modern citizens troubled by the dislocations of the industrial world. But the advertising copy never reflected the fact that industrial and commercial development often posed a grave threat to the historic landscape.

Once it resolved to use publicity money for historic markers, the Conservation Commission hired a staff for the project. In December 1926, acting on the strong recommendation of Douglas S. Freeman, the editor of the *Richmond News Leader*, and a devoted historian of Virginia's Civil War history, the commission contracted with historian Hamilton James Eckenrode to develop its program. Eckenrode had received his Ph.D. from Johns Hopkins University in 1904 and had written his dissertation on Reconstruction-era government in Virginia. Eckenrode had worked with Freeman on the history of Richmond's Civil War battlefields and had helped Freeman chart a series of historic markers for the battlefields. Representing yet another link between the work of patriotic organizations and the commission's project, Freeman had earlier supported the landmark work of the association for the Preservation of Virginia Antiquities.

Eckenrode quickly demonstrated both his grasp of the advertising context of his work and some of the larger possibilities inherent in connecting narratives of history with tours through the Virginia landscape. Drawing upon personal and popular interest in Civil War history, Eckenrode envisioned the emergence of a series of historic markers along "Battle Highway" routes that would highlight the movement of troops engaged

10.3. Norfolk-Portsmouth Chamber of Commerce ad promoting modern port facilities, historic shrines, and scenic beauty. From *Scribner's* magazine, June 1928.

in particular wartime campaigns. Here tourists and visitors would actually follow unfolding historic narratives through space across the landscape: "Thus, the movements of armies, such as Lee's and Grant's armies from Spotsylvania to the vicinity of Richmond in 1864, can be easily followed by reading the markers."[31] Eckenrode recognized the existence of many more historic sites than could be researched, documented, and put into place immediately. At the outset he established rough

priorities. He felt strongly that roads that carried the greatest number of motorists into the state should be marked first and that here the commission would feature Civil War history: "It is believed that this route, well advertised, would attract many visitors. More than this, it might awaken such an interest in the battlefields of Virginia as would lead to the securing of money for battlefield parks."[32]

Beyond meeting popular views of history Eckenrode

put great stock in ensuring the accuracy of the history presented; he sought to distinguish the Conservation and Development Commission's own historical expertise from the commemorative work of the patriotic organizations. In fact, Eckenrode saw the policing of the accuracy of all markers in Virginia as a possible responsibility of the commission. In 1927 he proposed that the commission take up the task of correcting inaccuracies that existed in markers set up by Virginia's various private organizations; he hoped to explore whether the commission could have the power to "change or remove markers that are manifestly incorrect."[33] To further buttress its claim to accuracy and expertise, the commission established a panel of distinguished historians and educators. The commission staff planned to prepare draft inscriptions for the "criticism and verification" of a committee of "gentlemen" selected for their "preeminence in knowledge of the history of Virginia." The board included the presidents of Randolph-Macon, William and Mary, Hampden-Sydney, State Teachers College at East Radford, and historians at the University of Virginia and other state and local institutions. In subsequent years Eckenrode corresponded extensively with members of this advisory board concerning the content of the historical markers. In 1927, for example, one of Eckenrode's mentors, Douglas Freeman, reviewed the inscriptions for the Petersburg highway and wrote, "As far as I see, those relating to the war between the states are correct. I have no exact knowledge regarding those that concern the revolutionary period."[34]

The commission's work and the creation of its advisory board involved a fundamental shift in the gender dimensions of landmark work in Virginia. Where women had controlled many of the commemorative projects of the patriotic societies, and, for example, far outnumbered men at the 1910 unveiling of the Jack Jouett tablet, the commission now placed men in charge. In fact, the highway marker program eclipsed a state board established in 1922 and appointed by the governor to "place suitable monuments or markers on, at, or in places of historic interest located in the Commonwealth." One woman from each of the main patriotic organizations, including the Association for the Preservation of Virginia Antiquities, Colonial Dames, Daughters of the American Revolution, Daughters of 1812, and the United Daughters of the Confederacy, constituted this board.[35] The state provided little in the way of funds, and the board actually marked few spots before 1927, when the board's chair turned the state appropriation back to Governor Byrd in the belief that the Conservation Commission had taken in hand the board's work. Governor Byrd thanked her for her service and assured her that the commis-

sion would "be anxious to obtain your advice as to their work."[36] He then urged William Carson to communicate with members of the board and to "avail" himself of their "suggestions as far as practicable."[37] In fact, the commission kept the women's board together as a second advisory committee, but the women never played the substantial editorial role taken by the men.

From Commemorating the Past to Promoting the Future

The shift from women to men signaled something of the Conservation Commission's broader redefinition of landmarks from commemoration of the past to promotion of the future, from memory to economy. Still, commission members cultivated the women's patriotic organizations. They understood that these women most closely approximated an established constituency for its work. In 1927, Carson accepted an invitation to address the Colonial Dames on the subject of colonial roads in Virginia. In explaining his acceptance to Eckenrode, who had to prepare the address, Carson wrote, "I am very anxious to get these Ladies' Societies strongly back of our Commission, and think we ought to go to almost any amount of trouble to sell the work we are doing to the people of Virginia. . . . the women of the state are the only people who show real interest in this work." Eckenrode, for his part, agreed but made it plain that he aspired to cultivate more "general interest," meaning men (and women) who were not members of the women's organizations.[38] The support of women did not lead Carson and Eckenrode to take them very seriously as advisors. Eckenrode found their work historically inaccurate, and Carson enjoyed joking about the possibilities of Eckenrode finding a rich woman to marry among the members of the women's organizations.[39]

The commission's interest in economic development shifted the lead role in marking Virginia's historic sites work from women to men. It also fundamentally altered the geographical precision of historic commemorations. The power of landmarks, of marking history in the landscape, derived in large part from its site-specific character—something happened on this lot, in this house, on this hill or field, that shaped national or local history in some important way. The claim of a particular place on the attention of residents and tourists alike derived from the fact that the history celebrated did not happen somewhere else—it happened on the site actually marked for remembering. Americans interested in preservation and historic commemorations had cultivated this power of place from the early nineteenth century; Lafayette's tour in 1824–1825, for example, had provided an elaborate excavation of memory in place. Commemorative monuments sometimes lacked such precise connection to history, but tablets, plaques, and landmarks, almost by definition, encompassed a precise connection to site. That connection to place always operated as the link between the past event and the present observer. The commission's highway marker stretched and even burst the earlier spatial bounds of landmark designation.

Early in its work the commission came to terms with the dilemma brought on by its eagerness to mark only the busiest highways. In 1932, reviewing Virginia's marker program, an article in *The Highway Magazine* reported that "headliners in American history were unaccommodating when they selected out-of-the-way places to perform the deeds that made them famous. The Commonwealth of Virginia, realizing that it is physically impossible to accommodate the main highways to history and still keep them as direct as necessary, has moved her history to the highways."[40] This move disrupted the link between people, places, and history valued by earlier landmark efforts. In Richmond County the commission put up a marker declaring, NEAR HERE IS MENOKIN, HOME OF FRANCIS LIGHTFOOT LEE, SIGNER OF THE DECLARATION OF INDEPENDENCE. LEE WAS A MEMBER OF THE CONTINENTAL CONGRESS FROM 1775 TO 1779 AND DIED AT MENOKIN IN 1797. In King and Queen County a sign went up, saying, ABOUT TWELVE MILES EAST IS THE SITE OF THE ORIGINAL HOME OF THE FAMILY OF GEORGE ROGERS CLARK, CONQUEROR OF THE NORTHWEST. THE FAMILY MOVED FROM HERE TO ALBEMARLE COUNTY. The sign for Jefferson's Monticello went up not on the road at Monticello but near the Albemarle County courthouse in Charlottesville: MONTICELLO THREE MILES TO THE SOUTHEAST. THOMAS JEFFERSON BEGAN THE HOUSE IN 1770 AND FINISHED IT IN 1802. HE BROUGHT HIS BRIDE TO IT IN 1772. LAFAYETTE VISITED IT IN 1825. JEFFERSON SPENT HIS LAST YEARS THERE AND DIED THERE, JULY 4, 1826. HIS TOMB IS THERE. THE PLACE WAS RAIDED BY BRITISH CAVALRY, JUNE 4, 1781. In some cases people presumably might have been tempted to detour from the main highway to find the historic site, but often they would have little help in navigating: NEAR HERE WADE HAMPTON'S CONFEDERATE CAVALRY CAMPED THE NIGHT OF JUNE 10, 1864, JUST BEFORE THE BATTLE OF TREVILIAN. The markers thus fostered a "sense" of Virginia history, or an atmosphere, or even a miasma of history while foregoing the power and precision of more traditional commemorative landmarks.

The connection between historic sites and modern travelers grew even more attenuated when the commission grappled with the incompatibilities between driving an automobile and reading historic markers. The commission designed the markers for good visibility and placed them close to the road itself. It adopted a double-sided format, visible to automobilists traveling in both directions. After considering building turnoffs so that travelers could read the markers, the commission rejected the idea due to the great expenses involved. Still, members of the commission worried that the markers might prove a hazard if people stopped to read them while still on the roadway itself. In inserting history in the highway landscape the commission proved quite innovative. In 1929 it published a guidebook that included the full text of all of the existing markers (fig. 10.4). The preface advised:

> It is difficult to read anything when going at speed, and so the commission decided to supplement the inscriptions on the markers with a book giving the inscriptions and keyed to the road markers by means of their numbers. Thus the traveler supplied with this booklet has only to catch the number of a marker and to turn to that number in the booklet to find the inscription, which may be read without checking the speed of the car. . . . it is possible to get a good idea of the topography of Virginia history with an absolute minimum of reading. And in a busy age this is deemed to be a much desired convenience.[41]

Thus, in the highway marker program the commission not only dislodged the connection between site, history, and contemporary observers; it put in place a system that detached history further from its connection with any particular site, people would now "get the message of the marker when going at any rate of speed."[42] Directed toward selling the state to visitors on the basis of its past, the commission's work made the awareness of history more pervasive even as the historical power of any particular places seemingly diminished.

The detachment of history from specific and tangible places in the marker program stood in striking contrast to other commission efforts that cultivated the historic resonances of particular spots in the landscape. In 1928, William E. Carson and the commission promoted an idea, modeled upon Westminster Abbey, of gathering into a single "suitable center" the graves of Virginia's famous dead that were "scattered throughout the state," especially the graves of men who had served as presidents of the United States. In 1858, with great civic and patriotic ceremony, the remains of President James Monroe, which had been interred in New York for twenty-seven years, were moved to Virginia and buried in Richmond's Hollywood Cemetery. President John Tyler was later buried nearby. In 1903, again with the participation of civic and patriotic societies, the graves of President Monroe's wife and daughter were moved to Hollywood

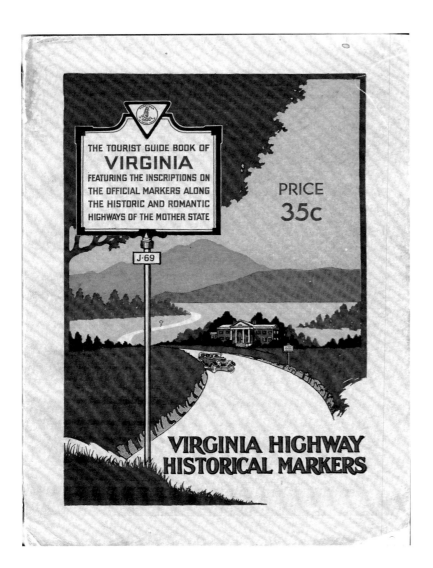

10.4. *Cover illustration of road guide.*
Virginia Highway Historical Markers,
4th ed., 1931.

Cemetery.[43] The gathering of graves would have created a single powerful place where Virginia residents and visitors could grasp something of Virginia's historical significance in the national narrative. The effort to promote Virginia through its presidential connections did not stop at deceased presidents, or even at Virginia's native sons. In 1929, William Carson enthusiastically guided President Hoover's selection of land along the Rapidan River as his personal outdoor recreation and fishing spot. Carson declared that he had obtained for the president "the best brook trout fishing ground in Virginia, or for that matter in the East. Streams full of falls, and shady pools, yet not steep, just ideal for brook trout." Carson focused on another sort of catch in outlining his project to Governor Byrd; he wrote, "Locating the President in Virginia is the best bit of advertising the State can develop. . . . I believe this is going to be a tremendous thing for the State. It will focus the eyes of the country on Virginia as a place for outdoor recreation."[44] In cultivating these

links between Virginia and the presidents, both past and present, their actual physical presence at specific points in the landscape played an essential part in fostering a sense of historical significance and authenticity. In the case of the highway historic marker program, which located historic narratives on the roadside, geographical precision was traded in for a geographically vague sense of historic atmosphere.

As the commission set out its markers of history along Virginia's highways, Civil War narratives clearly dominated. Virginia, the capital of the Confederacy and the focus of major military campaigns, included numerous sites considered worthy of marking. Prior to the commission's work, numerous civic and patriotic organizations had marked and commemorated the Civil War throughout Virginia. The cultural politics of the Lost Cause had sustained popular engagements with Civil War history in Virginia from the late nineteenth century into the early twentieth. The projects covered the political spectrum from ones sponsored by the embittered partisans of a Confederate revitalization movement to ones that acknowledged the war history but supported broader sectional and national reconciliation. In the course of the late nineteenth century, Civil War monuments erected in the South changed from a preponderance of funerary markers raised in cemeteries as part of bereavement to more celebratory civic memorials and markers placed on courthouse squares and battlefields. There was a growing celebration of the camaraderie and nobility of battle that blurred sectional tensions. White Virginians caught up in rapid social and economic changes, including the growth of towns, the rise of a market economy, the spread of industry, and the emergence of populist and radical politics, found in the celebration of the Confederacy a comforting engagement with a simpler, glorified, and romanticized past. The celebration of the Confederacy also dislodged the sense of dishonor associated with military loss. The Confederate reunions that attracted thousands, the growth of membership in Confederate organizations, the construction of monuments and memorials, the promotion of history writing and storytelling all reflected the continuing hold of the Civil War on broad sections of the population.[45]

By the 1920s some of the fervor had gone out of the celebration of the Confederacy. The number of veterans and contemporaries who still remembered the war had declined sharply. The rise of the New South and the continuing integration into national political and economic life eroded some of the insistence on a distinct sectional history. Moreover, the celebration of the Confederacy had grown increasingly commercial; manufacturers of everything from soap to caskets joined the proprietors of hotels and the operators of railroads in promoting a somewhat trivialized set of celebrations. Nevertheless, in the 1920s, interest still persisted in the Civil War on the part of residents and tourists alike. Eckenrode considered the Civil War a big "drawing card" for tourists.[46] He set out to satisfy people's interests and in the process to extend the commercialization of that interest from individual businesses to the selling of the state itself. With highway markers the commemoration of Civil War history completed its decades-long transition from cemetery, to battlefield, to public square, to roadside.

In 1927, just as the highway marker program was getting started, one enthusiast expressed something of the frustration of motoring to Civil War sites and failing to find reliable historic information; in a letter addressed to Governor Byrd, for example, Charles Johnson wrote: "For thirty years I have been a student of our great Civil War, and, to fulfill a twenty year expectation, I motored to the battlefield of the Wilderness, about a week ago.

What was my surprise to find not a single marker on the main highway, which would show a traveler—like myself—who was historically inclined—where some of the great events of history occurred. Had it not been for a blind farmer, who resided on the Plank Road, I could not have found a single point of interest." Johnson suggested actual text for several markers, but it lacked something of the editorial and political neutrality that the Conservation Commission later adopted. Johnson then concluded his letter to the governor, "Hundreds—nay thousands—of travelers are touring Virginia and the historic battlefields, and, even with guide books it is impossible to locate such points of historic interest as I have mentioned."[47] William Carson echoed these sentiments when he reported to Governor Byrd, "so much has been written about Virginia that tourists find a real disappointment when they come here, because they do not visualize the things they have heard and read about it." Carson hoped that with a planned 3,000 markers set up tourists would find themselves "in a land of romance" and slow down so as not be able to "skim through the State without at least spending one night."[48] As the highway marker program developed, the Civil War clearly provided, in the eyes of many, the kind of romance to slow people down.

As people slowed down to read highway markers, they engaged an interpretive treatment of the Civil War shaped by the promotional aspects of the development program. The tourists visiting Virginia and indeed the people with businesses and money to move to Virginia were primarily from the North. Eckenrode crafted markers dealing with the Civil War that avoided inflaming sectional rivalries. In fact, he hoped that the "elaborate marking of Union positions along the road would show the northern visitor the impartial nature of the work."[49] Such an approach was not evident in the earlier monument and marker campaigns of Virginia groups such as the United Daughters of the Confederacy. When it came to the highway program, the UDC strongly opposed any references to the Civil War as the "Civil War," demanding instead that the conflict be called the "War Between the States."[50] Eckenrode sidestepped this potentially troublesome nomenclature by not referring to the broader name of the conflict in the text of the markers. The markers bore numerous references to campaigns, retreats, battles, Union and Confederate sides, but none to the name of the war itself. This wielding of nomenclature permitted the commission to win a battle by losing a war. The commission also resisted placing markers directing motorists to historical monuments set up by other organizations. In this way the "impartial" presentation sought by the commission to accommodate northern visitors would not be undercut by the commemorative declarations of the organizations more concerned with the historical views and interpretations of Virginians.

Eckenrode did not prove as impartial when it came to advising Carson and the governor about whether the state or the federal government should own and control the various historic battlefields around Richmond. He was especially dismayed at the prospect of having the federal War Department control the land and interpretation of these battlefields. Eckenrode wrote to Carson: "It would be a pity to have the National Government right at Richmond, that it would make for bad feeling. Richmond is one place where we ought to be able to tell our story according to our own ideas and without the interference of the Washington authorities." He feared that if the War Department took over these sites their own work would be "completely thrown away." These views seemed to arise only around the exceptional case of Richmond, as the commission was at pains to appeal to outsiders with its stance of impartiality.[51]

Representing Particular Histories and Particular Places

Historical points of view aside, not all people greeted the proliferation of Civil War markers with enthusiasm. In fact, Eckenrode engaged in a long-running disagreement with a member of the commission's advisory committee over the predominance of Civil War history in the marker program. In 1927, Fairfax Harrison, the president of the Southern Railway and an amateur Virginia historian, reviewed the markers prepared for the Shenandoah Valley. He commenced the work but insisted that "undue emphasis is put on incidents of the War Between the States; or rather I may say that there is not sufficient emphasis put on the earlier history of the Valley. I note four items only of date prior to 1865, which, considering the history of the Valley, seems to lack proportion." Eckenrode defended the "numerosity of our Confederate markers" by claiming the commission was "pressed for time" and that it was easier to authenticate the Civil War markers that would be of "immediate interest to the traveling public." Earlier history often turned on the history of old houses that were hard to research precisely, but Eckenrode hoped that as the commission's staff moved forward it would "remedy our deficiencies and round out our historical information so as fully to include every period." In a later exchange with Harrison, Eckenrode further defended the predominance of Civil War markers but insisted that he himself entertained broader histori-

cal interests. He wrote, "Personally, I think that political history is much less important than economic and social history, but unfortunately our historians still give the first place to the performances of politicians, and the popular interest in the war conditions. The people think, as Thucydides declared, that war is about all there is to history. . . . I should like to give attention to such events as the establishment of important roads, the erection of iron furnaces, the opening of mines and other events of industrial development." For his part Harrison did not mind the marking of significant Civil War battle sites; what he objected to was the proliferation of markers that recorded every passing skirmish in areas that had "facts of greater interest to record in the same locality." After two full years of marker activity Harrison was still not satisfied, and he asked to have his name removed from the list of advisors. He viewed the problem as one of pandering to politicians who were measuring the popular response to the marker program. Harrison wrote, "much as I respect you and your problem at the hands of politicians, I feel strongly that many of these markers misrepresent the civilization of Virginia."[52]

The dominance of Civil War history came partly from the ease of authenticating the more recent history, but it also reflected the clear priorities of the commission and even the broader public. In the early stages of the program Eckenrode and the commission had decided that they would mark some colonial sites, particularly near Williamsburg, but would not attempt a comprehensive marking of colonial historic sites. Similarly, the commission would mark only a small selection of sites connected with Revolutionary War history. Markers dealing with individual historic figures would, for the most part, be left for a later date.[53] This left an abundance of Civil War markers along the main highways. What Harrison failed to appreciate was that a large number of the Civil War markers originated not with Eckenrode and his staff but with residents of particular localities who wanted to view the meaning of their place in terms of broader regional and national events and attract the patronage of outsiders and tourists. In 1929, for example, the vestry of St. Luke's Church in Isle of Wight, attempted to cast their particular parish history in broadly national terms. The vestry wanted the state to change or remove its sign that declared the church "one of the oldest in the United States." One brick in the structure bore the date 1632; however, the commission was not prepared to accept the vestry's assertion that this was the construction date and that it was the oldest standing Protestant church in America. For their part the vestry insisted that "we do not want all the glory for colonizing America, or for making it what it is, to go to Williamsburg and Plymouth Rock." In 1930, Robert Cabaniss, the president of the Petersburg Builders Supply Company, wrote to H. J. Eckenrode to press the case for a local historic marker recognizing the Civil War:

> Seeing a lot of markers along the different roads I think there certainly should be one on the White Oak Road at Five Forks, Dinwiddie County, Virginia. The Gilliam place there figured in . . . the War Between the States, as you know there was a two days battle there, which culminated in breaking the Confederate lines, and the tearing up of the Southside Railroad, which caused the retreat of the Confederate troops from Petersburg to Appomattox. At Five Forks General Warren was deprived of his commission by General Sheridan, which caused a court martial and a long investigation, which finally exonerated General Warren. Hoping you will see fit to investigate this matter, and locate a suitable marker at Five Forks.[54]

For his part Eckenrode rejected the request, citing the commission's policy of placing markers only on the main road where they could be seen by travelers. The fact that the White Oak Road was a dirt road traveled primarily by residents meant that a marker placed there would not attract the eye of tourists. Eckenrode did acknowledge that if the road was paved it would be appropriate to mark the Gilliam place, but in the meantime the marker referring to the Battle of Five Forks that stood on the highway six miles to the east would have to suffice. While Harrison was disturbed by the dominance of Civil War history in the Virginia program, a large number of individuals, like Cabaniss and institutions like the United Daughters of the Confederacy, pushed the state to clarify the connection between their locality and broader narratives of state and national history. For many, Civil War history was the most accessible history, the history that localities advocated, and the history that in the commission's push for production ended up dominating the highway markers in the early years.

Beyond public interest in particular places stood an equally strong insistence on the part of citizens that entire regions needed more extensive marking than they received in the early years of the program. In 1928, J. D. Eggleston, the president of Hampden-Sydney College and a member of the Conservation and Development Commission's historic advisory committee, objected to the failure of the commission to sufficiently recognize historic spots in Southside Virginia. Eggleston found this especially troubling, since he had served on a committee of the local Association for the Preservation of Virginia Antiquities that had identified numerous sites in Prince Edward County worthy of marking with his-

toric plaques—these included the site of the old Court House, the grave of a local captain in the Revolution, the site of a military encampment after the Yorktown surrender in the Revolution, the home of the father of an officer in the Revolution, and the site of an early Episcopal church. When Eckenrode reviewed Eggleston's work, he reported that he considered it a model piece of research that he hoped to be able to draw upon when the commission turned its attention to Prince Edward County.

Eggleston eventually got impatient and declared that he and other residents were "deeply disappointed" that the commission continued to "completely ignore several counties which have deep historical significance." This region included Eggleston's own Hampden-Sydney College, founded by Patrick Henry and James Madison. As he explained his feeling, Eggleston reflected, "I suppose we feel a bit touchy because it has been the custom—the habit—in times past for historians to take the attitude that there is no history southwest of Richmond. The truth is that Southside Virginia is amazingly fertile in early history—but the historians don't tell us about it." Eckenrode accepted the critique but turned it into a rationale for the commission's slowness in getting to work in the southwestern part of the state. He answered, "What you say about the Southside is perfectly true—the historians have neglected it. That is the reason that we have been delayed in reaching it; we had to take what we found ready at hand, and that information dealt chiefly with Northern Virginia. . . . as you know, it is much more difficult to work Southside history because of the meagerness of the data than it is to prepare for the vicinity of Richmond and Williamsburg." Rather than using the commission's program as a way to work against the accumulated imbalance in state history, Eckenrode felt bound to reinforce it because the advertising and tourism context of his work moved him to focus on "the most traveled" roads. He did insist that, as the program developed, "the Southside will be as well covered as any other portion of the State."[55] Eggleston and Harrison criticized the program because both found their own sense of Virginia history and place conflicted with the historical and geographical priorities developed by the commission to meet the market for tourism and promotion.

The leadership of the Virginia Historic Highway Association came from western and southern Virginia, from Lynchburg and Roanoke. The association likely established a 700-mile historic circuit in order to guide tourists from eastern Virginia to more remote parts of the state, using history as an attraction. The Conservation Commission continued this role of juxtaposing history and highways in the interest of economic development.

The commission's new emphasis on the eastern parts of Virginia understandably met with resistance from residents in other parts of the state. However, the commission fielded complaints that suggested that other interests, very much apart from economic development, framed public responses to the highway markers. In 1928, Eckenrode declared that it was "a matter of some honor to have the state erect a marker for a place."[56] As residents of different localities demanded highway markers for their community, they clearly sought recognition of their own particular place in the regional landscape. Celebrating history, the markers seemingly had the potential of increasing residents' pride of and attachment to the places in which they lived. They were obviously interested in enriching their sense of place culturally considered—quite apart from the possible economics of the program. In this way the form, meaning, and significance of the places recognized in the highway program were negotiated one marker at a time between the professionals, officials, and advisors of the Conservation Commission and local citizens throughout the state.

Highway Markers and the Direct Method of History Teaching

Eckenrode argued that even as the highway marker program boosted Virginia's economy it would also expand the historians' craft. He felt that he was engaged in pioneering historical work of great civic import. He also felt deeply disappointed by the initial response to the Virginia effort on the part of members of the historical profession. In 1927, Eckenrode attended the annual meeting of the American Historical Association, where he discussed the highway marker program. He confided to a colleague: "The historians seem to me to be an aggregation of dead ones. They do not seem to know what we [are] doing . . . I believe that our work, which is in most respects novel, will strike the historians after it has impressed the public. As a matter of fact, we are ahead of the time in what we are attempting to do. . . . If we gain public support I think that we shall do something great and unique, something that will attract the attention of the whole country."[57]

As the United States slid into the uncertain times of the Depression, Eckenrode felt that the highway marker program offered a good deal in the way of patriotic and civic education. In a 1930 essay, written for the Virginia Chapter of the Sons of the American Revolution, Eckenrode insisted that "it is of the utmost importance that American history be taught to children, and taught effectively, for never was there a greater need of stimulating

patriotism than at the present time. This is an age when the ideas and customs of the past are breaking down." In Eckenrode's view historians could assume a role in making society cohere by developing a "Direct Method of History Teaching," a method that would rely on books "but only in a secondary way." Historians would need to develop a "new and better way" to teach history, "an imagination stirring way."[58] Eckenrode's enthusiasm for John D. Rockefeller, Jr.'s Williamsburg restoration turned in part upon his sense that such work promised to become a powerful agent of civic education and social stability. In 1933 he confided to Rockefeller's Williamsburg associate, W. A. R. Goodwin,

> Numbers of books have been written on Colonial history and hundreds of scholars have worked in that period, but all of their labors amount to little in comparison with the Williamsburg Restoration when it comes to teaching history to the public. I consider the restoration the most unique project ever attempted in this country, and one of the most beneficent. . . . It teaches history in the most practical manner, and so adds to the stability of American institutions. It has awakened an interest in the past that nothing else could have done.[59]

Eckenrode believed that the highway markers, like Williamsburg and other historic sites intended to meet the needs of tourists who came to Virginia "in the search for historical atmosphere," could also fulfill the needs for educating local schoolchildren in history. He hoped that guides would be developed and children could learn history by visiting the scenes of historical events and receiving memorable instructions at the sites of those events. If the historical markers were "utilized as they might be, no school child of Virginia would go through the schools without having an adequate idea of the history of his state. It is easy to see the bearing of this on patriotism; there could be no better way to combat the poison of communism."[60]

The distinction that Eckenrode made between tourists experiencing "historical atmosphere" and schoolchildren learning history highlighted some very real limitations in the highway marker program. Eckenrode assumed that to really learn Virginia history people would need more than the very limited text available on highway markers; they would need guides and the power of buildings and landscapes and places, and books, used in a secondary way, and teachers. The highway markers trafficked in historical facts while actually skirting history. Long battle campaigns and numerous skirmishes could be marked, but the broader context or cause or meaning of the Civil War did not fit on a highway marker.

Recognizing all the other elements that needed to come into play in teaching students, even using Eckenrode's direct method of teaching, acknowledged the very real limitations of highway history. Eckenrode hoped to show northerners that Virginia was doing impartial history, providing as many facts about Union forces as about Confederate forces. He also assumed that "a simple marker is usually better, especially as it obviates controversy."[61] Of course, controversy and debate lends interest to history, but when history became part of tourist and economic promotion, controversy and debate were assiduously avoided. So the weakness of the marker program was its near-total dependence upon what people brought in the way of historical understanding to their reading of a particular marker. Its strength was perhaps in its ability to provoke people to explore history further, beyond the venue of the sign. But either way the simple, pithy, statements of fact did not seem designed to elicit the richest connection to history—they did little to explore or cultivate the interpretative ferment or context of historical events. In this way, just as history was becoming pervasive in the landscape, it seemed to be slipping from sight altogether. The triviality of the decontextualized, noncontroversial, simple facts that filled the highway markers obviously would fall far short of the grand civic and pedagogical vision that Eckenrode articulated. But the marker program continued to expand, growing from 1,000 markers to more than 2,220 markers today. Clearly, the interest in creating and celebrating a sense of historic place persisted, even though the history captured on the markers did little to get across the meaning or importance that places should hold for people.[62]

CHAPTER ELEVEN

Toxic Memory

Preservation on EPA Superfund Sites

In recent decades we have preserved places that stand well outside of traditional notions of sites valued for their historic or political associations or for their fine architecture. Preservation has flourished as older consensus notions of the historical canon unraveled in the academy and in public life. We have begun to look at the buildings and landscapes around us to see what they can contribute to a much broader, more diverse historical understanding of our world. This began amid the social movements of the 1960s, which inspired different approaches to history and a new interest in more varied narratives of historical experience. Social history, labor history, women's history, ethnic studies, and the history of vernacular architecture and everyday landscapes each flowed from an effort to move beyond the established canon of political history and the history of social and economic elites. In architectural history scholarly production took on subjects and sites well outside of the previous canon of high-style architecture. Historians grew increasingly adept at chronicling the history of everyday life, of working people, of people beyond the circles of privilege associated with the political, social, and economic establishment. Historic preservation has reflected these developments, preserving a much more diverse material culture. Part of the expansion has to do with simple political calculus. Since preservation demands public resources, attention, and regulatory support, it has sought to establish validity in a world increasingly attuned to diverse identities and varied experiences. Moreover, the local interest in building upon place identities for tourism and adaptive reuse has many localities scrutinizing their own resources, the ones that stand close at hand.

The preserved vestiges of the industrial landscape, in an increasingly deindustrialized world, provide abundant evidence of preservation's broadened vision. The federal government had started recording historic buildings in 1933 under the auspices of the National Park Service's Historic American Buildings Survey. In 1969 the Park Service established the Historic American Engineering Record to carry out the systematic documentation of engineering and industrial sites—including textile mills, bridges, dams, and other utilitarian structures. Industrial sites offered a new and very important perspective on American social and economic history. The Society for Industrial Archaeology was founded in 1971 to promote the study of industrial heritage. Preservationists also saw in vacant or underutilized industrial sites a substantial stock of buildings that could be adapted to new residential or commercial uses. Thousands of new units of housing, many for senior citizens, filled the long-vacant spaces of nineteenth- and early-twentieth-century New England textile mills and warehouses. The conversion of the Ghirardelli Chocolate Company's San Francisco factory in the early 1960s into shops and restaurants underscored a growing public interest in industrial history and buildings. The loft buildings of New York's cast-iron district in SoHo and many other urban warehouse districts assumed an entirely new meaning as trendy residential spaces. The unraveling of the consensus over the actions of political and economic elites in the 1960s was partly reflected in a parallel shift in the priorities of historians, preservationists, and the general public. The history of industrial sites and working-class life gained considerable prominence during the 1960s and '70s.[1]

This chapter focuses on the implications of this new

11.1. *Fresno Sanitary Landfill, a mound of 7.9 million cubic yards of garbage built between 1937 and 1987 and designated a National Historic Landmark in 2001.*
Photograph by author, 2010.

and expanded way of seeing. It explores twenty-first-century efforts to recognize the historical significance of a garbage dump in Fresno, California (fig. 11.1), and a chemical plant in Hagerstown, Maryland. Both sites have taken their place in historical imagination. They also stand as places of interest in our ecological imagination. They are on the Environmental Protection Agency's list of toxic Superfund cleanup sites. The urgent effort to clean and reclaim these blasted landscapes—EPA Superfund sites and other polluted brownfields—often involves an unfortunate exercise of cultural and historical amnesia. The sites are cleaned of their toxic substances, but they are also scrubbed of their history. This need not be the case. If former buildings and landscapes on Superfund sites were adapted to new uses and interpreted for the public, rather than being destroyed during redevelopment, we would retain an important material framework for better understanding both the sites themselves and their surrounding communities. Moreover, with tangible traces of former uses left in place, we would have an important venue for learning about the human use, abuse, and stewardship of the built and natural landscape. On Superfund and brownfield sites where traces of industrial use and pollution are removed entirely, the broader landscape makes less sense to residents and visitors. People whose lives and livelihoods were bound up with these places lose important landmarks from their local-

ity. My discussion takes up the implications of pursuing cleanup and redevelopment policies that fail to recognize the power and possibilities of the historical memories that hover over these sites. It also scrutinizes recent work on Superfund sites that reveals both the problems and possibilities of cultivating history and memory as part of the cleanup process.

Whether cleanup involves cap-and-cover methods where toxic materials are contained or neutralized on a site, or hog-and-haul methods in which pollutants are dug up and moved elsewhere (perhaps to become someone else's problem), the outcome is generally the same—sites are delivered for redevelopment devoid of any physical trace of their history, of their pollution, or even of their cleanup. These approaches to remediation ignore the potential of site interpretation to foster a more vital politics of place.[2] On blasted landscapes, a politics grounded in site history would facilitate fuller and more informed community participation in the remediation process as well as in the decisions about the future uses of reclaimed sites.

Toxic History and Amnesia

On a Superfund site, fostering public amnesia regarding site history may at first glance seem a prudent means to promote economic reuse or redevelopment. Some people with an understanding of these polluted sites might feel that over time, the less said, the less shown, the better. Nevertheless, such blindness to the past is problematic and ultimately undercuts the very work we are trying to accomplish in the remediation of polluted sites. People involved in the cleanup could make their efforts more comprehensible and decidedly less scary to the public if they could reveal how the flows of materials and pollutants on toxic sites had actually taken place. To see toxic sites as part of a broader industrial process with material inputs, products, and by-products that all worked their way through the buildings and the site would promote a kind of critical understanding of basic site processes that could in turn lay the groundwork for understanding something of the processes of site pollution, site reclamation, and site reuse. This general approach to industrial site history, although rarely applied to Superfund sites, has been honed by historians and industrial archeologists over the past three decades.

One of the great advantages of interpreting site history, pollution, and cleanup on toxic sites comes from foregrounding human agency and helping citizens reflect more critically on both the past and the present. Site histories, circulated in the form of brochures with illustrations and diagrams, on Web sites, and in public lectures at community meetings, can demystify the historical decisions whereby people interacted with each other, with the economy, and with the natural environment as they gave form to the human landscape, including its pollution and subsequent cleanup. Critically understanding history and plans for remediation on a polluted site helps us situate our own actions as linked in a profound way with the actions of citizens who came before us and who will come after us. In 1889, Harvard professor Charles Eliot Norton's essay "The Lack of Old Homes in America" recognized the ways in which architecture and landscape provided a palpable means for taking measure of human agency and values across the generations. Norton bemoaned the lack of old and hereditary residences in the United States. He worried about the social effects of transience on both public and private life. He wrote, "No human life is complete in itself; it is but a link . . . in a chain reaching back indefinitely into the past, reaching forward indefinitely into the future. Whatever weakens the sense of its linked relation is an evil."[3] It would be useful today to keep this insight in mind as we hone our approaches to managing Superfund cleanup.

The erasure of history on Superfund sites parallels the evil that Norton identified in the transience of people and families in the domestic landscape. Using a modern metaphor to push forward his analysis, Norton wrote, "To strengthen its connection in both directions, to quicken the electric current of conscious existence conveyed from the past through the present to the future, is to increase the vital power of the individual, his sense of dignity, and of responsibility. To the future every man owes the immeasurable debt for which he stands indebted to the past."[4] In grappling with the profound public health menaces on polluted sites, we, too, would benefit from a sense of the ways in which our actions are prescribed by people who came before us while defining the social, cultural, and economic possibilities of people in the future. The material remains of industrial processes and pollution, captured in existing buildings and landscape, provide a powerful venue for taking the measure of such histories. This historical understanding in turn creates a firmer basis for our own action as citizens and residents caught up in site remediation. With the site as the focal point, history shades into action and helps constitute an informed politics of place.

Local and everyday landscapes (like those we deal with on Superfund sites), because of their sheer familiarity and accessibility, are the places most capable of stirring an understanding of human agency and throwing into higher profile our own responsibilities as community members and citizens to the past and to the future.[5] These blasted landscapes can now again play a productive role in community by helping us constitute a politics attached to place that can help us take on the challenge of toxic sites and our own ecological relationship to the natural environment. It is precisely these local histories and landscapes that often resonate most deeply with people who are increasingly buffeted by the growing placelessness and homogenization of the modern world, a world that obfuscates human agency and trivializes citizen action.

The Fresno Sanitary Landfill

In the summer of 2001, controversy erupted in Washington, D.C., and Fresno, California, when Secretary of the Interior Gale Norton designated the Fresno Sanitary Landfill as a National Historic Landmark. A trash mound 4,200 feet long, 1,250 wide, and 45 to 60 feet high that was created between 1937 and 1987 joined Faneuil Hall, Boston's Old State House, and George Washington's Mount Vernon on a list of fewer than 2,500 American places with the coveted designation of a National Historic Landmark (see fig. 11.1).[6] These are the places that rise to special national status from the nearly 80,000 listings on the National Register of Historic Places. I want

11.2. Sketch of the Fresno Sanitary Landfill operation prepared for the 1939 meeting of the American Public Works Association. National Park Service.

11.3. Fresno Disposal Plant operation in 1935. Methods introduced here extended to the much larger Fresno Sanitary Landfill in 1937. National Park Service.

to briefly review the Fresno history because it underscores the challenge of recognizing and disseminating information about the everyday landscape.

It is notable that the designation of the Fresno dump would have been unthinkable in the 1960s when the National Historic Preservation Act passed congress. Like the study of the history of architecture and the built landscape, to which it is closely linked, historic preservation has expanded dramatically—increasingly surveying, documenting, designating, and interpreting the history and forms of everyday life. In this way, historic preservation has come to embody the popular and populist insights of social history and comple-

ments the earlier patriotic, nationalist, and aesthetic basis for historic preservation.[7] The Fresno Sanitary Landfill did not loom large in the political history of the United States, nor did it have an especially significant aesthetic aspect. Nevertheless, when it was established in 1937, it represented an innovative approach to the handling of municipal solid waste. Long trenches between 20 and 24 feet wide and 10 and 35 feet deep were dug out of the site. The trenches were then filled with garbage, leveled, compacted, and covered with dirt (figs. 11.2 and 11.3). The guiding idea promoted by Fresno municipal engineer Jean Vincenz was that the layering and compaction of dirt would help control rodent problems and reduce the volume of debris. This method eventually won broad favor over the then current practice of dumping garbage on open land or in water or incinerating it, fouling the air and still leaving piles of ash for subsequent disposal.[8] It soon became a model for municipalities around the county. Vincenz's method and the leading role that the Fresno site played in popularizing the trench and compaction method of disposal provided the rationale for the listing of the site as a National Historic Landmark.

The designation of the Fresno site grew out of a conscious effort to "broaden the scope" of the National Historic Landmark program. The move for designation began in the year prior to the first administration of George W. Bush but then became a hot potato because of the administration's stance on a whole host of environmental issues.[9] The National Park Service worked with Professor Martin V. Melosi, director of the Institute for Public History at the University of Houston and a leading historian of municipal sanitation and infrastructure, to carry out the research that led to the nomination of the Fresno Sanitary Landfill as a National Historic Landmark.[10] Melosi succeeded in moving the NHL program into new and uncharted landmark territory—into an area that he had helped develop as a field of historical inquiry.[11] The effort seems entirely salutary, for at its base the handling of garbage is a fundamental and telling aspect of human history. Coming to terms historically with sites such as the Fresno landfill has tremendous possibilities not only for historical insight but also for helping us focus on our ongoing relationship to natural resources, waste, and the environment. It is difficult to survey the history of such a site without moving our perspective forward to contemplate our own piles of garbage and our own systems of disposal.

Still, for some the designation of the Fresno landfill seemed evidence of preservation run amok—it simply didn't fit commonly held notions of preservation and its link to the canon of nationalism or aesthetic accomplishment. Paul Rogers wrote in the *San Jose Mercury News*, "Other presidents have honored Pearl Harbor, Alcatraz and Martin Luther King's birthplace as national historic landmarks. Now the Bush administration has added its own hallowed place: a garbage dump in Fresno."[12] Despite the merits of the designation, the criticism of Interior Secretary Gale Norton prompted her to quickly backtrack, seeking to dump the dump by "temporarily" rescinding the historical designation. Residents of Fresno were not at all sure they wanted to be known nationally for their dump. Environmentalists seized upon the designation as an ironic tribute to an administration with decidedly questionable commitments to the

environment that had decided to designate a dump as a historic site rather than protect remaining stands of giant sequoia trees or coastlines eyed for oil drilling.

What was even more controversial about the designation was the fact that the Fresno site had for years accepted battery acid from a local manufacturer, medical wastes from hospitals, and other toxic substances. The designers of the Fresno Sanitary Landfill had certainly not anticipated that decomposition of garbage would eventually create dangerous levels of methane gas that would migrate off of the site or that volatile organic chemicals would turn up in the region's groundwater. In 1987, the EPA ordered the closure of the Fresno landfill. In 1989, the EPA placed the property on the National Priorities List of Superfund sites, among the most dangerously polluted sites in the country. The site was then cleaned up by the EPA at a cost of $9.5 million. Equipment to collect and flare methane gas was installed, and a geomembrane liner and 4 to 5 feet of additional soil was placed over the entire trash mound to prevent water runoff from polluting the area. Still, much political theater was made possible by the fact that at a time when the Bush administration was withdrawing from international environmental treaties it was designating as a National Historic Landmark a landfill that had been a Superfund cleanup site.[13]

Secretary Norton announced the rescinding of the Fresno designation on August 28, 2001. September 11 turned attention to other political matters, and in its aftermath Norton never executed the written memo to rescind her designation. Today the Fresno Sanitary Landfill still occupies a spot on the National Historic Landmarks list.

The Need to Engage Superfund Sites Historically

What I would like to consider is the extent to which the landmark designation has been disseminated to a broad public. Public awareness of the site history was clearly spurred when the designation debate played out in newspapers and on television in August 2001, but interest seems to have quickly passed after September 11. What I find most striking is the fact that the public authorities who control the site have made no effort to share its history with the thousands of people who now visit the site every week. In 2002, Fresno built a 350-acre regional sports park in the area, including the landfill itself. The new park has five playgrounds, six softball fields, and seven soccer fields (fig. 11.4). The Web site for the city parks calls the area an "environmentally conscious facility, which includes integration of a former landfill site." There are also hiking trails and a "hilltop overlook."[14]

But for people using those trails or surveying the scene from the overlook, there is nothing on the site— no marker, no brochure, no historical photographs, and no personal interpretations—that presents the significant history of the Fresno Sanitary Landfill. There is nothing that points out that the "hilltop overlook" occupies an eminence created with 7.9 million cubic yards[15] of people's garbage deposited over a period of half a century. There is no design engagement with, or historical interpretation of, the various human processes that either polluted or cleaned up the site. No one is drawn into a consideration of where the piles of Gatorade bottles and soda cans that collect in the sports park trash receptacles are going to end up. Expanding the canon of National Landmarks seems all very well and good; however, we should ask why there is not room in a $25-million budget for a sports park to disseminate the site's rich history and to encourage reflection about the process and politics of garbage and human relationships to natural resources and the environment (fig. 11.5).

11.4. Aerial view of the Fresno Sports Park with the capped Sanitary Landfill at right. Photograph, c. 2003. City of Fresno.

As a Superfund site, the Fresno Sanitary Landfill today has engaged in precisely the sort of cultural and historical amnesia that has become such a common element of other toxic cleanup sites. The public should not have to read scholarly journals or back issues of local newspapers to engage the history of a site that is so ripe for interpretation. The site should have been designed,

11.5. View across Sports Park ball field with Fresno Sanitary Landfill rising in the background.
Photograph by author, 2010.

marked, and interpreted in a way that made the history of the "overlook" mound more palpable. Modern sports parks today often have fitness trails—mile-long walking or running courses that connect fifteen to twenty exercise stations with apparatus and instruction signs for completing various exercises. These systems provide a framework for individual exercise and health.[16] At Fresno a similar system with a path and individual interpretative stations that explored the history of the landfill, and the site reclamation could provide a framework for the social exercise of citizenship, for civic and public health education. Signs atop the "outlook" could declare that you are now standing on a pile of 7.9 million cubic yards of trash. Information could be provided about the amount of waste generated by the average household today and where that garbage ends up today. Another sign or station might explore the public health danger of the toxic pollution caused by the landfill before it was contained and cleaned up. Another sign could describe the remediation technology that permitted the site to be used as a sports park; it could explain the methane being flared off at the site today. Working more directly with traces of the site's history could begin to constitute a politics of place in Fresno whereby people would understand the history of waste while being encouraged to think about their own levy on the land and its resources. This is a project on which historians, designers, and ecologists, as well as planners, could productively collaborate.

Historians and designers certainly have a stake in environmental cleanup, in confronting the many threats posed by polluted, toxic environments. However, beyond this broad citizenship interest, it seems that we can quite productively bring to bear the methods and insights of our disciplines to better confront the challenges of toxic waste sites. A key ideal of many Superfund and brownfield reclamation projects is not only to mitigate environmental problems but to recycle or reuse abandoned sites that are often already tied into existing transportation and utility infrastructures. I would argue that these sites are also tied into an infrastructure of community history and memory;[17] exploring such a perspective offers tremendous potential to engage the work of citizens, communities, and agencies working for site reclamation and renewal.

As in the case of the Fresno designation, the idea of establishing some alignment between historic preservation and environmentally toxic sites might appear fraught with difficulty. The EPA's health and environmental goal is to remove or contain toxic substances in a way that seems very much at odds with preservationists' efforts to develop site-specific narratives of place and to engage people directly in the material dimensions of history on a site. Preservationists aim to recognize, frame, and chronicle the material traces of history in the landscape. Preservation work often focuses on restoration and renovation. In projects of adaptive reuse preservationists aim to find new uses for buildings and sites that take the place of the obsolete uses that they were originally designed for. People charged with the cleanup of toxic sites aim to eradicate or at least to neutralize the accumulations of the past. The initial effort is of course to eradicate pollution, but the buildings and landscapes tied to the pollution are often casualties of the process. This opposition between preservation and remediation seems quite unfortunate.

As we think about the political and citizenship dimensions of designing with and interpreting history on Superfund sites, it is important to keep in mind that there is a long tradition of political calculus accompanying historic preservation projects. In 1850, in one of the earliest acts of public preservation in the United States, the New York State Legislature purchased Washington's Revolutionary War headquarters at Newburgh, New York. The committee of the legislature argued that the physical properties of buildings and landscapes made their associated histories especially tangible, capable of "transmit[ting] to our children a knowledge of the virtues of the fathers of the republic." The committee declared: "If our love of country is excited when we read the biography of our revolutionary heroes, or the history of revolutionary events, how much more will the flame of patriotism burn in our bosoms when we tread the ground where was shed the blood of our fathers, or when we move among the scenes where were conceived and consummated their noble achievements."[18] In the 1850s, preservation of this headquarters seemed especially important. Here, in 1783, Washington stemmed a rising revolt among his own troops, who were organizing to march on the Congress because they had not been paid for their military service. The preservationists had a very clear political purpose; they wanted to diffuse portraits of nationalism and the memory of Washington's leadership to defuse the growing tensions over slavery. They wrote, "It will be good for our citizens in these days of political collisions, in there days of political demagoguism: it will be good for them in these days when we hear the sound of disunion reiterated from every part of the Country; in all future time occasionally to chasten their minds by reviewing the history of our revolutionary struggle."[19]

The preservation of the headquarters was more successful than the political agenda that prompted it. Nevertheless, this early preservation campaign revealed that

11.6. Central Chemical Company EPA Superfund site, Hagerstown, Maryland. Photographs 2003. UVA School of Architecture.

ideals of politics and citizenship often complemented the curatorial zeal that seemed to stand at the center of the preservation movement. It is this effort to make use of sites in framing a politics of place that can usefully be adapted to the cleanup and redevelopment of toxic sites.

Site Stewardship: Cultivating a Politics of Place in Hagerstown

Scholarly and public interest in industrial heritage has spurred the development of industrial history and increased the sophistication with which we are able to scrutinize the dynamic relationship between people, technology, buildings, sites, and the broader economy. Observers, drawing on the work of historians of technology and historians of labor and industry, are able to engage industrial sites historically with a fairly high degree of rigor. Using the historical methods of industrial, labor, and environmental history, it is possible to come to terms on these sites with the important inter-

section between resources, labor, technology, and the environment to understand precisely how industries operated in buildings and on the land as well as within broader systems of transport, environment, finance, and consumption.[20] Today these same methods can be used to better come to terms with the architectural, cultural, economic, and environmental history of polluted industrial sites. The history of many American communities is inextricably linked to the industries that help explain a central part of their very existence. The industrial landscape has great potential in helping people take measure of local and regional history. This is the case whether the sites are polluted or not.

In 2003, my colleague Julie Bargmann and I and our students in the School of Architecture at the University of Virginia explored ways of drawing upon the methods and framework of industrial history in narrating the history of, and designing reuse proposals for, a Superfund site in Hagerstown, Maryland. We undertook a yearlong project that focused on Hagerstown's Central Chemical Superfund site (fig. 11.6). The work of our course

11.7. Site reused as wildlife and bird habitat with abandoned buildings adapted as viewing platforms. Gretchen Kelly Giumarro, designer, 2003. UVA School of Architecture.

11.8. Site reused as a city park that manages and remediates storm water and gray water from the adjacent neighborhoods. Brian Gerich, designer, 2003. UVA School of Architecture.

looked at systems such as industrial and environmental flows both on the site and in the surrounding region. It quickly became apparent that Superfund sites could usefully be approached both historically and in terms of their future redevelopment in a broader context. Just as the original industrial development relied on adjacent industries, workers drawn from the town, and the structure of transportation and investment, revealing these connections lays the basis for a more transparent approach to the future possibilities and limitation of redevelopment. An approach that builds on and cultivates a cultural, historical, and geographical perspective seems best calibrated to raise the most important questions about future redevelopment. Many of the places with Superfund sites are dealing with pervasive deindustrialization. An analysis of the history of Superfund sites can give citizens an important framework for coming to grips with the broader economic trends that continue to shape their communities.

An additional advantage of an emphasis on keeping, identifying, interpreting, and reusing major elements of a Superfund site's former industrial occupation is that it promotes a more gradual, incremental approach to the site that will tend to cultivate mixed-use scenarios for reuse. The redesign is more likely to breed some complexity as the future program is adjusted and integrated with existing buildings and spaces. Redesign efforts that focus on the reuse of existing industrial structures on the site tend to encourage a more interesting set of designs that envision complex, multiuse, chronologically disparate approaches to redevelopment. This sort of redesign is quite likely to be more useful to a variety of stakeholders in the surrounding community. Our students'

designs for the Central Chemical site took seriously the existing buildings and the varying levels of pollution across the site. This work contrasted with the penchant for single-use redevelopment schemes that place a soccer field, a warehouse district, or a new shopping center on reclaimed sites. It was precisely the varied and mixed-use palette of our proposals that prompted the greatest enthusiasm from Hagerstown's residents, who had been struggling through the process of envisioning the future of the Central Chemical Company site. Here adaptive reuse went beyond preservation's interest in finding new uses for existing buildings and sites; it actually set out to foster environmental stewardship and to enrich the lives of citizens engaged in both site remediation and subsequent site reuse.

As our project developed, we had the opportunity to present our histories and our designs to many people in the community. It was readily apparent that important forms of social capital were created through a process that helped people see their Superfund sites and their communities in palpable historical terms. As a Superfund site and its broader community come into focus historically, people's understandings and attachments to them tend to strengthen. We provided guidebooks, exhibition posters, and a Web site that explored aspects of Hagerstown's industrial and architectural history. At the Central Chemical site, knowing that in the 1950s the firm began manufacturing the pesticide DDT and that it dumped batches into a pond on the site that drained into Antietam Creek and then the Potomac River helps delineate the bounds of the problem. Historical understanding and connection paves the way toward a more informed public involvement and stewardship of the site and the future of the

community. By grounding the cleanup in public histori-cal understanding, remediation is not simply the province of experts seeking detachment from an angry or scared citizenry. Rather, it is a process grounded in some clarity about both history and future possibilities.

History is one important element in constituting a politics of place. It is the historical perspective that fore-grounds the dynamic of human agency and lets people move more or less seamlessly from an understanding of historical agency on a particular site to a deeper con-ception of their own actions as citizens. In the case of Superfund sites, a design that reveals the process of environmental remediation constitutes another impor-tant venue for strengthening the public understanding and ongoing stewardship that these sites require. What Julie Bargmann and I have done is to encourage design and interpretative strategies that will bring people into a more profound understanding of polluted sites. We have proposed first using industrial site histories to help people better understand the issues raised by such sites. These can take the form of discussions in public meet-ings, Web sites, information brochures, exhibitions, guided tours of sites, and site markers.

We have also suggested that designers incorporate the traces of history into the designs for the reuse of these sites in order to preserve a palpable venue for ongoing site interpretation. Students in our Hagerstown studio project developed especially creative ways of incorporating the physical traces of the industrial pro-duction and environmental remediation into their design proposals for the reuse of the Central Chemical site. Gretchen Kelly Giumarro designed a project that she termed "Industrial Nesting." It was founded on the idea

that DDT not only fouled the Central Chemical site, but it also inhibited the absorption of calcium by various spe-cies of birds, leading them to lay weak-shelled eggs, and drastically reduced the reproduction rates of bald eagles, ospreys, and peregrine falcons. Giumarro proposed a diverse bird habitat for the site. Rather than removing the buildings from the site, she proposed that the build-ings, with their link to the history of industry and pol-lution on the site, be converted into bird perches and blinds for birdwatchers (fig. 11.7). Other buildings were also to be converted into educational and recreational centers. This "redemptive" design proposal maintained the site history, giving it a meaning and significance far greater than if the site were simply developed as a bird habitat with no connection to the buildings, landscapes, or history of Central Chemical. Brian Gerich drew inspi-ration from another aspect of Central Chemical's history of pollution—the fact that its water runoff polluted local streams. He developed a phased plan whereby the site would take on a larger and larger role in gathering neigh-borhood storm water and filtering it as the remediation process advanced (fig. 11.8). Buildings on the site would provide incubator spaces for companies doing research in ecological technologies. Kent Dougherty designed a sports park which, rather than hiding the history of local contamination, actually used the biopiles and quar-ries developed during site remediation and gave them a new use as a foundation for a skateboard, in-line skat-ing, and biking park. Dougherty's design departed from the usual approach of flattening the site for redevelop-ment and removing the traces of remediation (figs. 11.9 and 11.10). Instead, the landforms created during remediation were simply given a new use, interpreted

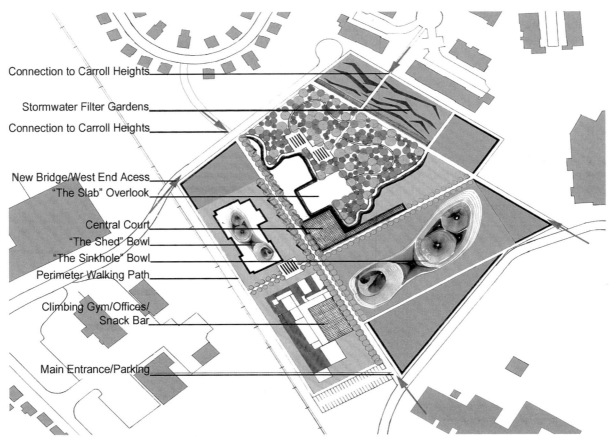

Connection to Carroll Heights

Stormwater Filter Gardens
Connection to Carroll Heights

New Bridge/West End Acess
"The Slab" Overlook

Central Court
"The Shed" Bowl
"The Sinkhole" Bowl
Perimeter Walking Path

Climbing Gym/Offices/
Snack Bar

Main Entrance/Parking

ABOVE

11.9. Site reused as an extreme sports park that connects to neighborhoods and teaches visitors about the remediation process. Kent Dougherty, designer, 2003. UVA School of Architecture.

BELOW

11.10. Site reused as an extreme sports park with direct connection to neighborhoods, permitting visitors to witness and explore the site's remediation. Kent Dougherty, designer, 2003. UVA School of Architecture.

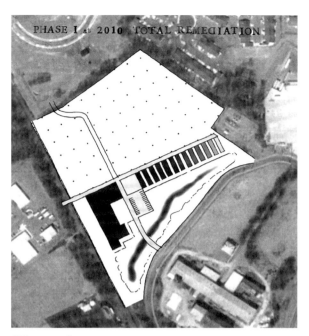

Phase I

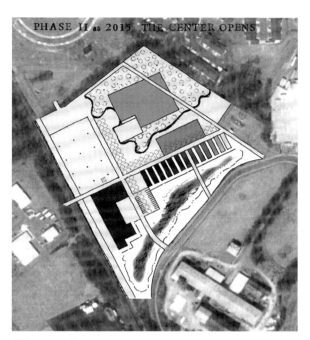

Phase II

through signs and exhibits. Cara Ruppert designed an "EcoLab Park" where, as remediation progressed, a center for studying urban ecology and pollution, a laboratory, a library, and an educational building would be established in the old Central Chemical structures (fig. 11.11). Historical exhibits in those buildings would convey the full site history in palpable terms—represented by the reused buildings. The site would also take a hand in storm water filtering, reversing the history of pollution on the site. Ben Spencer envisioned mixed uses for Central Chemical buildings and grounds, including agriculture, wildlife habitat, a renewable energy plant, a recycling center, and a public market (fig. 11.12). Sarah Trautvetter designed a dynamic landscape that envisioned the gradual return of people to the Central Chemical site—this time as a cultural center and outdoor theater. As the site was cleaned, the fences would be moved further into the park and the spectacle of performance in the park would go from "standing room only," observing the remediation process from afar, to full audience participation in cultural events (fig. 11.13). The strength of these proposals resided in part in their cultivation of a history and a politics of place rooted in the specific buildings and landscapes and associations of the Central Chemical plant. Such engagements were largely absent from the earlier redevelopment proposals, which like the treatment of the Fresno site completely ignored the power and possibilities embedded in the historic landscape, and open to interpretation by historians, ecologists, designers, and local residents.

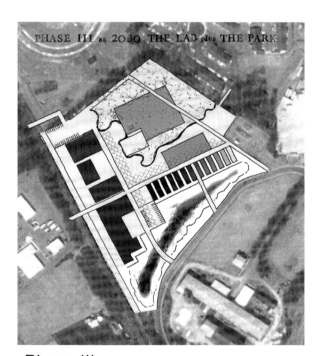

Phase III

11.11. Site reused as a laboratory for testing ecological systems and remediation techniques. The laboratory expands over the site as the site is cleaned. Cara Ruppert, designer, 2003. UVA School of Architecture.

11.12. *Site reused as a farm for production of local foods. Public access to the site would expand as remediation proceeds. Ben Spencer, designer, 2003.* UVA School of Architecture.

Many of the Central Chemical projects included remediation as part of the site history that was framed and made visible. In going public with site histories we can foster a firmer foundation for citizens struggling to envision the future shape and operations of their community—visions that are best informed by a more profound understanding of the intricate connections between human knowledge, values, and power and the actual form of settled human landscape. In this sense, while working toward novel ends, we work within the older political framework of preservation evident in the campaign to preserve Washington's Headquarters. The mid-nineteenth-century preservationists promoted an understanding of place that was historical; however, in their view its importance rested in no small part on motivating future political action by citizens who derived some of their politics and understanding of the world from tangible encounters with what Dolores Hayden has termed "the power of place."[21] For historians, preservationists, designers, and the public such projects can spur an important dialogue that links insights about the past with visions for the future.

Advocating Place

Our approach to industrial sites and the effort to use site interpretation to make citizens more aware and engaged in pressing issues related to the future form and nature of community life is part of the broader effort to come to terms historically with everyday landscapes. This process would not have been possible without the sustained commitment on the part of a generation of historians to grapple with the form and meaning of everyday landscapes. In this sense I very much appreciate Joseph Amato's advocacy of local histories in his recent book

Rethinking Home: A Case for Writing Local History. Amato argues that

> local historians provide a passionate attachment to concrete places in an age when home and place, locale and landscape, are in a state of great mutation. This tension provides the basis for an ever-deepening conversation. . . . [Local history] awakens a passion for understanding the compass of local action. In this way, local history serves the intelligence that frees the energy of local people to work in the dimensions of the possible. Committed to understanding the present and the changes that characterize it, local history proves a golden asset for all vital people of a place.[22]

It galvanizes citizenship.

The serious efforts to understand the form and history of the everyday landscape on Superfund sites gives us an ideal venue for working with a broad popular public. History is no longer something set apart, detached, captured in studies of the houses of a wealthy elite who could command the services of famous architects. We can now begin to take seriously the everyday places where most people live, work, and visit.[23] The challenge is getting the insights out of the academy and disseminated in more public and popular venues—in designs for the renewal of Superfund sites, in historic districts, in guidebooks of neighborhood history and architecture, in internet-based audio tours, on Web sites that feature the Superfund remediation process for specific localities, in museum exhibitions, in secondary school curricula that focus on local history and architecture, and in popular journalism and lectures. Lots of good work has been done in this regard. Approaching toxic sites as places of culture and memory is a politically important and intellectually vital project that should be expanded.

11.13. Site reused as a cultural center and outdoor theater. Remediation itself is treated as a performance, with the public gradually drawn into the site as it is cleansed of its toxic chemical wastes. Sarah Trautvetter, designer, 2003. UVA School of Architecture.

Notes

CHAPTER ONE

Introduction

1. Carleton Knight III, "Philip Johnson Sounds Off," *Historic Preservation*, 38 (Sept./Oct. 1986): 34.
2. *Washington Post*, Mar. 7, 1987.
3. *New York Times*, Nov. 29, 1985.
4. Knight, "Philip Johnson Sounds Off," 34, 36.
5. See Irwin Altman and Setha Low, ed., *Place Attachment* (New York: Plenum Publishing, 1992); Tony Hiss, *The Experience of Place* (New York: Random House, 1991); Ned Kaufman, "Places of Historical, Cultural, and Social Value: Identification and Protection, Part I," *Environmental Law in New York* 12 (Nov. 2001): 211–12, 224–33; Ned Kaufman, *Place, Race, and Story: Essays on the Past and Future of Historic Preservation* (New York: Routledge, 2009).
6. For an excellent and concise overview of the development of historic preservation in the United States, see Mike Wallace, "Preserving the Past: A History of Historic Preservation in the United States," in Mike Wallace, *Mickey Mouse History and Other Essays on American Memory* (Philadelphia: Temple University Press, 1996), 178–210; and Mike Wallace, "Preservation Revisited," in Mike Wallace, *Mickey Mouse History*, 224–37; see also Charles B. Hosmer, Jr., *The Presence of the Past: A History of the Preservation Movement in the United States Before Williamsburg* (New York: Putnam, 1965); Charles B. Hosmer Jr., *Preservation Comes of Age: From Williamsburg to the National Trust, 1926–1949*, 2 vols. (Charlottesville: University Press of Virginia, 1981); for an excellent critique of the pitfalls of a preservation movement steeped in the canon of architectural aesthetics, see Richard Longstreth, "Architectural History and the Practice of Historic Preservation in the United States," *Journal of the Society of Architectural Historians* 58 (Sept. 1999): 326–333.
7. David Lowenthal, *The Past Is a Foreign Country* (Cambridge: Cambridge University Press, 1985); Michael Kamen, *Mystic Chords of Memory: The Transformation of Tradition in American Culture* (New York: Knopf, 1991).
8. See, for example, Jeffrey Blustein, *The Moral Demands of Memory* (Cambridge: Cambridge University Press, 2008), or Christopher Duerksen and Richard J. Roddewig,

Takings Law in Plain English (Washington, D.C.: National Trust for Historic Preservation, 1994).
9. William J. Murtagh, *Keeping Time: The History and Theory of Preservation in America* (Hoboken, N.J.: Wiley, 2006), esp. focuses on the changing dynamic of private and public initiative in historic preservation.
10. See, for example, Hosmer, *The Presence of the Past*, which points to the 1850 preservation of the Hasbrouck House used as Washington's Headquarters, in Newburgh, New York, followed shortly by the preservation of Mt. Vernon, as the start of the preservation movement in the United States.
11. *New York Times*, Dec. 24, 1986.
12. Kevin Melchionne, "Living in Glass Houses: Domesticity, Interior Decoration, and Environmental Aesthetics," *Journal of Aesthetics and Art Criticism* 56 (Spring 1998): 191–200; Alice Friedman, *Women and the Making of the Modern House: A Social and Architectural History* (New York: Abrams, 1998), 126–159.
13. Knight, "Philip Johnson Sounds Off," 38.
14. *New York Times*, July 16, 1987.
15. A biographical contribution to this genre is Richard Cahan, *They All Fall Down: Richard Nickel's Struggle to Save America's Architecture* (Washington, D.C., Preservation Press, 1994); see also the illuminating discussion of demolition in Neil Harris, *Building Lives: Constructing Rites and Passages* (New Haven: Yale University Press, 1999); for the urban framework of destruction and preservation, see both Max Page, *The Creative Destruction of Manhattan, 1900–1940* (Chicago: University of Chicago Press, 1999), and Michael Holleran, *Boston's "Changeful Times": Origins of Preservation and Planning in America* (Baltimore: Johns Hopkins University Press, 1998).
16. See Robert M. Fogelson, *Downtown: Its Rise and Fall, 1880–1950* (New Haven: Yale University Press, 2001), esp. chap. 7, "Inventing Blight: Downtown and the Origins of Urban Redevelopment," 317–380.
17. Page, *The Creative Destruction of Manhattan*, 111–143.
18. Norman Tyler, *Historic Preservation: An Introduction to its History, Principles, and Practice* (New York: Norton, 2000); Robert E. Stipe, *A Richer Heritage: Historic Preservation in the Twenty-First Century* (Chapel Hill: University of North

Carolina Press, 2003); see also, Paul Spencer Byard, *The Architecture of Additions: Design and Regulation* (New York: Norton, 1998).

19. For a useful discussion of public history and commemoration, see Dolores Hayden, *The Power of Place: Urban Landscapes as Public History* (Cambridge: MIT Press, 1995); Kirk Savage, *Standing Soldiers, Kneeling Slaves: Race, War, and Monument in Nineteenth-Century America* (Princeton: Princeton University Press, 1997); Ivan Karp, Christine Mullen Kreamer, and Steven D. Lavine, eds., *Museums and Communities: The Politics of Public Culture* (Washington, D.C.: Smithsonian Institution Press, 1992); Casey Nelson Blake, ed., *The Arts of Democracy: Art, Public Culture, and the State* (Philadelphia: University of Pennsylvania Press, 2007); David Glassberg, "Public History and the Study of Memory," *Public Historian* 18 (Spring 1996): 7–23; Lowenthal, *The Past Is a Foreign Country*; James W. Loewen, *Lies Across America: What Our Historic Sites Get Wrong* (New York: New Press, 1999).

CHAPTER TWO

Patriotism in Place

1. See, for example, Charles B. Hosmer, Jr., *The Presence of the Past: A History of the Preservation Movement in the United States Before Williamsburg* (New York: Putnam, 1965), which points to the 1850 preservation of the Hasbrouck House used as Washington's Headquarters, in Newburgh, N.Y., followed shortly by the preservation of Mt. Vernon, as the start of the preservation movement in the United States.

2. Michael G. Kammen, *Mystic Chords of Memory: The Transformation of Tradition in American Culture* (New York: Knopf, 1991), esp. part I; Michael Wallace, "Preserving the Past: A History of Historic Preservation in the United States," in Mike Wallace, *Mickey Mouse History and Other Essays on American Memory* (Philadelphia: Temple University Press, 1996), 178–210; Sarah J. Purcell, *Sealed with Blood: War, Sacrifice, and Memory in Revolutionary America* (Philadelphia: University of Pennsylvania Press, 2002); on relative disinterest in historic preservation in the early nineteenth century, see Norman Tyler, Ted J. Ligibel, and Ilene R. Tyler, *Historic Preservation: An Introduction to Its History, Principles, and Practice* (New York: Norton, 2009), 12.

3. *Columbian Centinel*, Aug. 28, 1824, reprinted in Edgar Ewing Brandon, ed., *Lafayette, Guest of the Nation: A Contemporary Account of the Triumphal Tour of General Lafayette, Through the United States in 1824–1825 as Reported by the Local Newspapers* (Oxford, Ohio: Oxford Historical Press, 1950), vol. 1, 108.

4. Sylvia Neely, "The Politics of Liberty in the Old World and the New: Lafayette's Return to America in 1824," *Journal of the Early Republic* 6 (Summer 1986): 151–171; on patriotism in the preservation movement in the United States, see Hosmer, *The Presence of the Past*, 264; on the importance of the Revolution's ideals in creating political and social unity, see Purcell, *Sealed with Blood*.

5. Harold Kirker, *The Architecture of Charles Bulfinch* (Cambridge: Harvard University Press, 1969), 232–233; Charles A. Place, *Charles Bulfinch, Architect and Citizen* (Boston: Houghton Mifflin, 1925), 124–125; Walter Muir Whitehill, *Boston: A Topographical History* (Cambridge: Harvard University Press, 1959; 1968), 42–43; Abram English Brown, *Faneuil Hall and Faneuil Hall Market* (Boston, 1900).

6. Charlene Mires, *Independence Hall in American Memory* (Philadelphia: University of Pennsylvania Press, 2002), 66.

7. Stanley J. Idzerda, ed., *Lafayette, Hero of Two Worlds: The Art and Pageantry of His Farewell Tour of America, 1824–1825* (Flushing, N.Y.: Queens Museum, 1989); Anne C. Loveland, *Emblem of Liberty: The Image of Lafayette in the American Mind* (Baton Rouge: Louisiana State University Press, 1971); Marian Klamkin, *The Return of Lafayette, 1824–1825* (New York: Scribner, 1975); Fred Somkin, *Unquiet Eagle: Memory and Desire in the Idea of American Freedom, 1815–1860* (Ithaca: Cornell University Press, 1967), 131–174.

8. *The Order of Exercises in the Chapel of Transylvania University: A Collection of Original Pieces in Honour of the Arrival of General Lafayette . . .* (Lexington, Ky., 1825), 8, quoted in Somkin, *Unquiet Eagle,* 167.

9. *Cahawba Press and Alabama Intelligencer*, April 9, 1825, reprinted in Edgar Ewing Brandon, ed. and comp., *A Pilgrimage of Liberty: A Contemporary Account of the Triumphal Tour of General Lafayette Through the Southern and Western States in 1825, as Reported by the Local Newspapers* (Athens, Ohio: Lawhead Press, 1944), 151.

10. *New London Gazette*, Aug. 25, 1824, reprinted in *New-York American*, Sept. 9, 1824, 78.

11. Somkin, *Unquiet Eagle,* 137–139; Loveland, *Emblem of Liberty,* 52–60.

12. *New-York American*, Sept. 9, 1824, reprinted in Brandon, ed., *Lafayette, Guest of the Nation,* 1:185–186.

13. *American,* Aug. 24, 1824, reprinted in Brandon, ed., *Lafayette, Guest of the Nation,* 1:86–87.

14. Marc H. Miller, "Lafayette's Farewell Tour and American Art," in Idzerda, ed., *Lafayette, Hero of Two Worlds*, 145.

15. *Daily Advertiser*, Sept. 20, 1824, reprinted in Brandon, ed., *Lafayette, Guest of the Nation,* 1:241.

16. *Commercial Advertiser,* Aug. 24, 1824, reprinted in Brandon, ed., *Lafayette, Guest of the Nation,* 1:66.

17. *Pennsylvania Intelligencer*, Feb. 4, 1825, reprinted in Brandon, ed., *Lafayette, Guest of the Nation,* 3:237.

18. In the 1850s the tent was placed for safekeeping and display in the Patent Office Building, then displayed at the Centennial Exposition in Philadelphia in 1876. See Karal Ann Marling, *George Washington Slept Here: Colonial Revivals and American Culture, 1876–1976* (Cambridge: Harvard University Press, 1988), 25–27.

19. *Concord Gazette and Middlesex Yeoman*, Sept. 4, 1824, and *Columbian Centinel,* Sept. 1, 1824, reprinted in Brandon, ed., *Lafayette, Guest of the Nation,* 1:160, 177.

20. *Concord Gazette and Middlesex Yeoman,* Sept. 4, 1824, reprinted in Brandon, ed., *Lafayette, Guest of the Nation,* 1:160.

21. *Columbian Centinel*, Sept. 8, 1824, reprinted in Brandon, ed., *Lafayette, Guest of the Nation,* 1:158.

22. Keith H. Basso, *Wisdom Sits in Places: Landscape and Language Among the Western Apache* (Albuquerque: University of New Mexico Press, 1996), offers an important reflection on the meaning of place, narrative, and social coherence in the context of a different cultural system.

23. Quoted in Sarah J. Purcell, "Commemoration, Public Art, and the Changing Meaning of the Bunker Hill Monument," *The Public Historian* 25 (Spring 2003): 62.

24. *Columbian Centinel*, Aug. 28, 1824, reprinted in Brandon, ed., *Lafayette, Guest of the Nation,* 1:117.

25. Daniel Webster's circular letter of 1823, quoted in George Washington Warren, *The History of the Bunker Hill Monument Association During the First Century of the United States of America* (Boston: James R. Osgood, 1877), 41.

26. George Edward Ellis, *Sketches of Bunker Hill Battle and Monument: With Illustrative Documents* (Charlestown: C. P. Emmons, 1843).
27. Helen Mar Pierce Gallagher, *Robert Mills, Architect of the Washington Monument* (New York: Columbia University Press, 1935), 98–104, 204–207.
28. Ellis, *Sketches of Bunker Hill Battle and Monument*, 162.
29. Horatio Greenough, *The Travels, Observations, and Experience of a Yankee Stonecutter* (New York: Putnam, 1852), 37, quoted in Purcell, *Sealed with Blood,* 201.
30. Warren, *The History of the Bunker Hill Monument Association*; William Wilder Wheildon, *Memoir of Solomon Willard, Architect and Superintendent of the Bunker Hill Monument* (Boston: Bunker Hill Monument Association, 1865); National Park Service, *Documents Relating to the Organization and Purpose of the Bunker Hill Monument Association and to the Construction of the Bunker Hill Monument, 1823–1846,* 2 vols. (Denver: National Park Service, 1982); see esp. vol. 1, 75–78.
31. Ellis, *Sketches of Bunker Hill Battle and Monument*, 156.
32. *The Works of Daniel Webster*, 7th ed. (Boston: Little, Brown, 1853), vol. 1, 61, 62, 78.
33. *Richmond Enquirer*, Oct. 26, 1824, reprinted in Brandon, ed., *Lafayette, Guest of the Nation*, 3:37.
34. *Portsmouth and Norfolk Herald*, Oct. 25, 1824, reprinted in Brandon, ed., *Lafayette, Guest of the Nation*, 3:53.
35. *Journals of the Continental Congress*, Oct. 29, 1781, vol. 3, 682.
37. Auguste Levasseur, *Lafayette in America in 1824 and 1825* (orig. pub. in French in 1829) trans. Alan R. Hoffman (Manchester, N. H.: Lafayette Press, 2006), 199.
38. *Portsmouth and Norfolk Herald*, Oct. 25, 1824, reprinted in Brandon, ed., *Lafayette, Guest of the Nation*, 3:58.
39. Levasseur, *Lafayette in America in 1824 and 1825*, 199, 204.
40. Levasseur, *Lafayette in America in 1824 and 1825*, 205–212.
41. Robert D. Ward, *An Account of General La Fayette's Visit to Virginia in the Years 1824–'25* (Richmond: West, Johnson & Co., 1881), 28, 37.
42. Levasseur, *Lafayette in America in 1824 and 1825*, 201–202.
43. *Memoirs of General Lafayette. With An Account of His Visit to America and of His Reception by the People of the United States, from His Arrival, August 15th, to the Celebration at York-town, October 19th, 1824* (Boston: E. G. House, 1824), 254.
44. American State Papers, House of Representatives, 25th Cong., 2nd Sess., Military Affairs, vol. 7, p. 907, no. 770. "On the expediency of carrying into effect the resolutions of the Congress of the Confederation for Erecting Monuments to the General Officers of the Revolutionary Army, and a marble column at York-Town, Virginia."
45. http://www.nps.gov/york/historyculture/vicmon03.htm
46. National Park Service, "Outline of Development, Colonial National Monument, Yorktown, Virginia," 1933, http://www.nps.gov/history/history/park_histories/index.htm#c.
47. *New York Commercial Advertiser*, Sept. 27, 1824, reprinted in Brandon, ed., *Lafayette, Guest of the Nation*, 2:36–37.
48. *United States Gazette*, Oct. 1, 1824, reprinted in Brandon, ed., *Lafayette, Guest of the Nation*, 2:72, 73, 77.
49. Charlene Mires, *Independence Hall in American Memory* (Philadelphia: University of Pennsylvania Press, 2002), provides an excellent overview of the changing form, meaning, and value of Independence Hall; Edward M. Riley, "The Independence Hall Group," *Transactions of the American Philosophical Society*, new series, 43 (1953): 7–42; Haviland's 1831 report is quoted in Riley, "The

Independence Hall Group," 34; see also Constance M. Greiff, *Independence: The Creation of a National Park* (Philadelphia: University of Pennsylvania Press, 1987), 35–36.
50. *Richmond Enquirer*, Oct. 26, 1824, reprinted in Brandon, ed., *Lafayette, Guest of the Nation*, 3:66.
51. *Raleigh Register*, Mar. 1, 1825, reprinted in Brandon, ed. and comp., *A Pilgrimage of Liberty*, 22.
52. *Commercial Advertiser*, Sept. 24, 1824, reprinted in Brandon, ed., *Lafayette, Guest of the Nation*, 2:19.
53. *Maryland Republican*, Dec. 21 and 28, 1824, reprinted in Brandon, ed., *Lafayette, Guest of the Nation*, 3:203.
54. *Virginia Herald*, Nov. 27, 1824, reprinted in Brandon, ed., *Lafayette, Guest of the Nation*, 3:144.
55. *Southern Chronicle*, Mar. 19, 1825, reprinted in Brandon, ed. and comp., *A Pilgrimage of Liberty*, 47.
56. *Frederick Intelligencer*, Jan. 1, 1825, reprinted in Brandon, ed., *Lafayette, Guest of the Nation*, 3:221.
57. *Illinois Gazette*, May 14, 1825, reprinted in Brandon, ed. and comp., *A Pilgrimage of Liberty*, 226.
58. *Washington Gazette*, Oct. 14, 1824, reprinted in Brandon, ed., *Lafayette, Guest of the Nation*, 3:24.
59. *Columbian Centinel*, Aug. 28, 1824, reprinted in Brandon, ed., *Lafayette, Guest of the Nation*, 1:108.
60. *Journal* [Poughkeepsie], Sept. 22, 1824, reprinted in Brandon, ed., *Lafayette, Guest of the Nation*, 1:224.
61. *Daily Advertiser* [Albany], Sept. 20, 1824, reprinted in Brandon, ed., *Lafayette, Guest of the Nation*, 1:241.
62. *Commercial Advertiser*, Aug. 17, 1824, reprinted in Brandon, ed., *Lafayette, Guest of the Nation*, 1:39.
63. *Niles Register* 27 (1824): 102, reprinted in Brandon, ed., *Lafayette, Guest of the Nation*, 2:122.
64. *Raleigh Register*, Mar. 11, 1825, reprinted in Brandon, ed. and comp., *A Pilgrimage of Liberty*, 22.
65. *Mississippi Gazette*, April 23, 1825, reprinted in Brandon, ed. and comp., *A Pilgrimage of Liberty*, 206.
66. *The Reporter*, June 6, 1825, reprinted in Brandon, ed. and comp., *A Pilgrimage of Liberty*, 361–362.
67. *Savannah Georgian*, Mar. 19, 1825, reprinted in Brandon, ed. and comp., *A Pilgrimage of Liberty*, 111.
68. *United States Gazette*, Sept. 27 and 30, 1824; see also Mires, *Independence Hall in American Memory*, 67–73.
69. *United States Gazette*, Sept. 27, 1824.
70. *The True American*, Oct. 2, 1824, reprinted in Brandon, ed., *Lafayette, Guest of the Nation*, 2:40.
71. *Commercial Advertiser*, Sept. 24, 1824, reprinted in Brandon, ed., *Lafayette, Guest of the Nation*, 2:20.
72. Thomas Jefferson to Pierre Charles L'Enfant, April 1791, quoted in H. Paul Caemmerer, *The Life of Pierre Charles L'Enfant* (Washington, D.C.: National Republic Publishing Co., 1950), 149.
73. *United States Gazette*, Oct. 14, 1824.
74. "Architecture in the United States," *American Journal of Science and Arts* 17 (January 1830): 107, 263.
75. Marc H. Miller, "Lafayette's Farewell Tour and American Art," 116–121.
76. Purcell, *Sealed with Blood*, 181–186.
77. Purcell, *Sealed with Blood*, 164–169.
78. "Architecture In The United States," *American Journal of Science and Arts*, 107.

CHAPTER THREE

Captured by Context

1. Michael Holleran, "Roots in Boston, Branches in Planning and Parks," in Max Page and Randall Mason, eds., *Giving

Preservation a History: Histories of Historic Preservation in the United States (New York: Routledge, 2004), 90–96; see also Michael Holleran, *Boston's "Changeful Times": Origins of Preservation and Planning in America* (Baltimore: Johns Hopkins University Press, 1998).

2. Robert R. Weyeneth, "Ancestral Architecture: The Early Preservation Movement in Charleston," in Page and Mason, eds., *Giving Preservation a History*, 257–281; for a critical reading of design issues in the Charleston Historic District, see James Hare, "Exaggerated Reverence for the Past: The Challenge of Design Review in the Charleston Historic District Design," in David Ames and Richard Wagner, *Design & Historic Preservation* (Newark: University of Delaware Press, 2009), 43–60.

3. Chris Wilson, *The Myth of Santa Fe: Creating a Modern Regional Tradition* (Albuquerque: University of New Mexico Press, 1997), esp. 252–253.

4. William J. Murtagh, *Keeping Time: The History and Theory of Preservation in America* (Hoboken, N.J.: Wiley, 2006), 87–98. On strategies of design compatibility, see Norman Tyler, Ted J. Ligibel, and Ilene R. Tyler, *Historic Preservation: An Introduction to Its History, Principles, and Practice* (New York: Norton, 2009), 107; see also Daniel Bluestone, "Detroit's City Beautiful and the Problem of Commerce," *Journal of the Society of Architectural Historians* 47 (Sept. 1988): 245–262.

5. *The Athens Charter for the Restoration of Historic Monuments* (Athens: International Congress of Architects and Technicians of Historic Monuments, 1931), n.p.

6. Australia ICOMOS, *The Burra Charter: The Australia ICOMOS Charter for Places of Cultural Significance* (Burwood, Austral.: Australia ICOMOS, 2000), 3–4.

7. International Council on Monuments and Sites, World Heritage List Report, "Monticello and the University of Virginia in Charlottesville," Dec. 29, 1986, 2.

8. Richard Guy Wilson, ed., *Thomas Jefferson's Academical Village: The Creation of an Architectural Masterpiece* (Charlottesville: Bayly Art Museum of the University of Virginia, 1993); Richard Guy Wilson and Sara A. Butler, *The Campus Guide: University of Virginia* (New York: Princeton Architectural Press, 1999).

9. Enrollment numbers are available in the annual catalogs of the University.

10. Virginius Dabney, *Mr. Jefferson's University: A History* (Charlottesville: University Press of Virginia, 1981), 26.

11. Philip Alexander Bruce, *History of the University of Virginia, 1819–1919*, 5 vols. (New York: Macmillan, 1920–1922), vol. 4, 54.

12. Fiske Kimball, "Jefferson the Architect," *University of Virginia Journal of Engineering* 6 (May 1926): 164; I appreciate Joseph Lahendro sharing this quotation with me. Paul Venable Turner, *Campus: an America Planning Tradition* (Cambridge: MIT Press, 1984).

13. See Lydia Mattice Brandt, "Variations on Mount Vernon: Replicas of an Icon as Vehicles for American Memory" (masters thesis, Department of Architectural History, University of Virginia, 2006); Lydia Mattice Brandt, "Re-creating Mount Vernon: The Virginia Building at the 1893 Chicago World's Columbian Exposition," *Winterthur Portfolio* 43 (Spring 2009): 79–114.

14. Governor J. L. Kemper to J. E. Peyton, Oct. 9, 1876, in Governor James L. Kemper, Correspondence, letter books, 1874–1875, Library of Virginia, Richmond.

15. Governor Kemper's Address to the Legislature republished in the *Norfolk Virginian*, Dec. 2, 1875.

16. Ibid.

17. Virginia did not build a pavilion at the Centennial. Moreover, out of respect for the legislature's decision Governor Kemper refused even to issue an executive proclamation declaring a Virginia Day at the Centennial. Governor J. L. Kemper to J. E. Peyton, Oct. 9, 1876, in Governor James L. Kemper, Correspondence, letter books, 1874–1875, Library of Virginia, Richmond.

18. William M. Thornton, "Report of the Faculty to the Rector and Visitors," Oct. 31, 1895, Minutes of the General Faculty, 14 (Sept. 15, 1895–June 15, 1899): 106–111, Special Collections, University of Virginia Library.

19. Faculty Resolution submitted to the Board of Visitors, Nov. 4, 1895, Minutes of the General Faculty, 14 (Sept. 15, 1895–June 15, 1899): 122, Special Collections, University of Virginia Library.

20. William R. Mead to Dr. A. H. Buckmaster, Nov. 5, 1895, in Proctor's Records, RG-5/3, box 22, "Misc Correspondence and Vouchers of the Bursar," Special Collections, University of Virginia Library.

21. W.M.T. [William M. Thornton], "The Work of Restoration," *Alumni Bulletin* 2 (Feb. 1896): 134–135.

22. William M. Thornton, "Report of the Faculty to the Rector and Visitors," Oct. 31, 1895, Minutes of the General Faculty, 14 (Sept. 15, 1895–June 15, 1899): 110, Special Collections, University of Virginia Library.

23. Francis H. Smith, "The Rotunda," *Alumni Bulletin* 2 (Nov. 1895): 85.

24. "The University of Virginia: A Plea for Its Restoration," n.d., (c. 1895-1896), in "Law Building," University of Virginia President's Papers, RG-2/1/2.471 Subseries I, box 15, Special Collections, University of Virginia Library.

25. Stanford White, "The Buildings of the University of Virginia," *Corks & Curls* 11 (1898): 127.

26. *College Topics*, Nov. 9, 1895.

27. William Mynn Thornton, Chairman of the Faculty, Committee on Faculty Report, May 1893, Faculty Chairman's letter book, vol. 21, 551, Special Collections, University of Virginia Library.

28. William M. Thornton, "Physical Culture at the University of Virginia," *Alumni Bulletin of the University of Virginia* 1 (July 1894): 24–28.

29. John Kevan Peebles, "Thos. Jefferson Architect," *Alumni Bulletin of the University of Virginia* 1 (Nov. 1894): 68–74; also, John Kevan Peebles, "Thomas Jefferson, Architect," *American Architect and Building News* 47 (Jan. 19, 1895): 29–30.

30. Peebles, "Thos. Jefferson Architect," 74.

31. Jeffrey L. Hantman, "Brooks Hall at the University of Virginia: Unraveling the Mystery," *Magazine of Albemarle County History* 47 (1989): 62–92.

32. See James C. Southall, *Opening of the Lewis Brooks Museum at the University of Virginia, June 27th 1878. Address on Man's Age in the World* (Richmond: University of Virginia Board of Visitors, 1878), 7–8.

33. *Jeffersonian*, Jan. 9, 1878.

34. Quoted in Southall, *Opening of the Lewis Brooks Museum*, 9.

35. Peebles, "Thos. Jefferson Architect," 74.

36. Bruce, *History of the University of Virginia* vol. 3, 170.

37. University of Virginia Board of Visitors Minutes, June 29, 1892, Special Collections, University of Virginia Library.

38. Albemarle County Deed Book, 117, p. 338; the deed involved the sale of land by A. C. Chancellor to Saint Anthony Alumni Association; the deed book, located in the Albemarle County Courthouse, Charlottesville, Virginia.

39. Stanford White to Robert Robertson, Supt. Buildings & Grounds, July 20, 1896, and Stanford White to W. C. N. Randolph, Chairman Board of Visitors, April 3, 1896, Buildings and Grounds Collection, RG-5/5, box 1, "McKim, Mead & White Correspondence," Special Collections, University of Virginia Library.

40. Henry-Russell Hitchcock, *Architecture: Nineteenth and Twentieth Centuries* (Baltimore: Penguin, 1958), 598; Paul Spencer Byard, *The Architecture of Additions: Design and Regulation* (New York: Norton, 1998); see also Richard Guy Wilson, "Jefferson's Lawn: Perceptions, Interpretations, Meanings," in Wilson, ed., *Thomas Jefferson's Academical Village*, 47–72.

41. Stanford White to William M. Thornton, Feb. 26, 1896, Buildings and Grounds Collection, RG-5/5, box 1, "McKim, Mead & White Correspondence," Special Collections, University of Virginia Library.

42 McKim, Mead & White to William M. Thornton, Mar. 11, 1896, Chairman of the Faculty, RG-19, #21 letter book, Jan. 1896 to Mar. 1897.

43. Warren H. Manning to Edwin A. Alderman, Feb. 5, 1909, President's Papers, RG-2/1/2.471 Subseries I, box 6, Special Collections, University of Virginia Library.

44. Warren H. Manning, "Report to Accompany a Plan for the University of Virginia, Charlottesville, VA.," Oct. 8, 1908, President's Papers, RG-2/1/2.471 Subseries I, box 6, Special Collections, University of Virginia Library.

45 McKim, Mead & White to Edwin A. Alderman, June 12, 1906, President's Papers, RG-2/1/2.471 Subseries I, box 6, "Buildings and Grounds President's House," Special Collections, University of Virginia Library.

46. K. Edward Lay, *The Architecture of Jefferson Country: Charlottesville and Albemarle County, Virginia* (Charlottesville: University Press of Virginia, 2000), 157.

47 *College Topics*, Jan. 26, 1910, and May 24, 1911, and Ludlow & Peabody [William Orr Ludlow and Charles Samuel Peabody] to Edwin A. Alderman, Aug. 31, 1911, President's Papers, "Dawson's Row," RG-2/1/2.471 Subseries I, box 8, Special Collections, University of Virginia Library.

48. Secretary of the University to Walter Dabney Blair, May 16, 1921, President's Papers, RG-2/1/2.472 Subseries VI, box 5, "Buildings and Grounds: Gymnasium," Special Collections, University of Virginia Library.

49. Edwin A. Alderman to Walter D. Blair, May 24, 1921, and May 20, 1921, President's Papers, RG-2/1/2.472 Subseries VI, box 5, "Buildings and Grounds: Gymnasium," Special Collections, University of Virginia Library; for earlier discussion of Virginia graduates designing university buildings, see Edwin A. Alderman to Charles Samuel Peabody, April 1912, President's Papers, RG-2/1/2.471 Subseries I, box 9, "Education," Special Collections, University of Virginia Library.

50. Walter Dabney Blair to Edwin A. Alderman, May 19, 1921, President's Papers, RG-2/1/2.472 Subseries VI, box 5, "Buildings and Grounds: Gymnasium," Special Collections, University of Virginia Library.

51. Walter Dabney Blair to William A. Lambeth, May 20, 1921, President's Papers, RG-2/1/2.472 Subseries VI, box 5, "Buildings and Grounds: Gymnasium," Special Collections, University of Virginia Library.

52. Fiske Kimball to William A. Lambeth, Feb. 10, 1928, President's Papers, RG-2/1/2.472 Subseries VII, box 6, "Dormitories (2)," Special Collections, University of Virginia Library.

53. Ibid.

54. Fiske Kimball to Edwin A. Alderman, Mar. 5, 1928, President's Papers, RG-2/1/2.472 Subseries VII, box 6, "Dormitories (2)," Special Collections, University of Virginia Library.

55. See press release about New Library and PWA Grant, President's Papers, RG-2/1/2.49, box 7, "Library," Special Collections, University of Virginia Library.

56. Harry Clemons to Nathaniel L. Goodrich, Librarian, Dartmouth College, June 20, 1932, Papers of the University Librarian, RG-12/1/1.681, box 3, "Office Administrative Files 1927–1956," Special Collections, University of Virginia Library.

57. Werner K. Sensbach to Ulrich Franzen, Mar. 15, 1974, and Werner K. Sensbach, "Library Expansion, Memorandum of Meeting," Jan. 31, 1974, and Mar. 8, 1974, President's Papers, RG-2/1/3.791 Special Records, box 1, "Special Committee: Undergraduate Library, 1972–1976," Special Collections, University of Virginia Library.

58. This is the assessment of Carroll William Westfall, who is actually quite sympathetic to the continuation of classical designs in contexts like the University of Virginia, see Carroll William Westfall, "Why the Orders Belong in Studio," *Journal of Architectural Education* 61 (May 2008): 96–97.

59. Robert E. Lee Taylor to James H. Corbitt, Aug. 31, 1944, President's Papers, RG-2/1/2.541, box 1a, "Building Program 1943–1944," Special Collections, University of Virginia Library.

60 Lewis A. Coffin, Jr., to Professor Robert K. Gooch, Oct. 29, 1947, President's Papers, RG-2/1/2.541, box 1a, "Building Program 1947," Special Collections, University of Virginia Library.

61. Lewis A. Coffin, Jr., to Colgate Darden, Jan. 21, 1948, President's Papers, RG-2/1/2.541, box 1a, "Building Program 1948," Special Collections, University of Virginia Library.

62 Jesse W. Beans to Vincent Shea, June 20, 1951, President's Papers, RG-2/1/2.581, box 28, "Physics," Special Collections, University of Virginia Library.

63. Minutes of the Meeting of the Art Commission, Mar. 26, 1952, Governor John S. Battle Papers, box 57, Executive Departments, 1950–1954, "Art Commission Minutes," Library of Virginia, Richmond.

64. Minutes of the University of Virginia Board of Visitors, April 11, 1952, p. 233, Special Collections, University of Virginia Library.

65. Theodore J. Young to Colgate Darden Jr., May 27, 1952, RG-2/1/2.591, President's Papers, box 5, 1952, "Physics Building—1952," Special Collections, University of Virginia Library.

66 Minutes of the Meeting of the Art Commission, Nov. 13, .1959, Governor J. Lindsay Almond, Jr., Executive Papers, 1958–1962, box 8, "Art Commission," Library of Virginia, Richmond,

67. Minutes of the Meeting of the Art Commission, Oct. 2, 1959, Governor J. Lindsay Almond, Jr., Executive Papers, 1958–1962, box 8 "Art Commission," Library of Virginia, Richmond.

68. M. E. Kayhoe, "Memorandum of Telephone Conversation with Mr. Ballou, on October 26, 1959," Physical Plant A & E Services Papers, Project Files, 1958–1979, RG-31/1/1.851, box 24, "Life Sciences Building (Gilmer Hall) Correspondence File #1," Special Collections, University of Virginia Library.

69. Alfred Burger to M. E. Kayhoe, Aug. 6, 1962, RG-31/1/1.851, box 10, "#2 Chemistry Committee," Special Collections, University of Virginia Library.

70. Vincent Shea to Stainback and Scribner, April 29, 1963, RG-31/1/1.851, box 10, "Contract Stainback and Scribner," Special Collections, University of Virginia Library.

71. Stephen Bernard James, "Louis I. Kahn at the University of Virginia: The Unbuilt Chemistry Building" (master of architectural history thesis, University of Virginia, May 1999).

72. Edgar F. Shannon, Jr., to Louis I Kahn, Nov. 19, 1962, RG-31/1/1.851, box 11, "#2 Chemistry Building (Kahn)," Special Collections, University of Virginia Library; see

also "The building is cold, forbidding and prison like in appearance," in Chemistry Building Committee, "Memorandum of Meeting Held 1 November 1962," RG-31/1/1.851, box 10, "#2 Chemistry Committee," Special Collections, University of Virginia Library.

73. Louis I. Kahn to Edgar Shannon, Jr., Nov. 27, 1962, President's Papers, RG-2/1/2.661, box 7, Special Collections, University of Virginia Library.

74 Minutes of the Board of Visitors Buildings and Grounds Committee, April 19, 1963, Board of Visitors Committee Records, RG-1/1/3, box 11, "Buildings and Grounds Committee Minutes," Special Collections, University of Virginia Library; Bernard Mayo, William Zuk, Charles Woltz, and Thomas K. Fitz Patrick to Edgar F. Shannon, Jr., April 19, 1963, RG-31/1/1.851, box 10, "Contract Stainback & Scribner," Special Collections, University of Virginia Library.

75. Sasaki, Dawson, DeMay Associates, Inc., *The University of Virginia Development Plan*, August 1965.

76. Richard P. Dober, executive director, Sasaki, to M. E. Kayhoe, Jan. 7, 1963, President's Papers, RG-2/2/2.661, box 8, "Committee on Master Plan 1962–1963," Special Collections, University of Virginia Library.

77. Minutes of the Meeting of the Art Commission, Dec. 20, 1965, Governor Albertis S. Harrison, Jr., Papers, box 90, Correspondence, 1963–1965, "Art Commission," Library of Virginia, Richmond.

78. Minutes of the Board of Visitors Buildings and Grounds Committee, Oct. 1, 1971, Board of Visitors Committee Records, RG-1/1/3, box 11, "Buildings and Grounds Committee Minutes," Special Collections, University of Virginia Library.

79. "Memorandum of meeting held Nov. 2 and 3, 1965, in Watertown, Massachusetts," Physical Plant A & E Services Papers, Project Files, 1958–1979, box 4, "Committee: Architecture-Library Building," Special Collections, University of Virginia Library.

80. J. Norwood Bosserman to Werner K. Sensbach, Sept. 22, 1967, Physical Plant A & E Services Papers, Project Files, 1958–1979, box 5, "#3 Architecture Library 9/1/67 to 6/30/68," Special Collections, University of Virginia Library.

81. Frank W. Rogers to Edgar Shannon, April 17, 1967, Board of Visitors Committee Records, RG-1/1/3, box 11, "Buildings and Grounds Committee Correspondence (1)," Special Collections, University of Virginia Library.

82. Hardy C. Dillard to Frank W. Rogers, Jan. 16, 1967, President's Papers, RG-2/1/2.701, box 28, "Law-General 1966–1967," Special Collections, University of Virginia Library.

83. Frank E. Hartman to Eggers and Higgins, April 2, 1949, President's Papers, RG-2/1/2.561, box 4, "Site Plans 1949," Special Collections, University of Virginia Library; Eggers and Higgins, "Report on Revisions to Master Site Plan," April 5, 1949, President's Papers, RG-2/1/2.561, box 4, "Site Plans 1949," Special Collections, University of Virginia Library; for later version of same concern, see Minutes of the Board of Visitors Buildings and Grounds Committee, Jan. 23, 1974, Board of Visitors Committee Records, RG-1/1/3, box 11, "Buildings and Grounds Committee Minutes," Special Collections, University of Virginia Library.

84. Hardy C. Dillard to Frank W. Rogers, Jan. 16, 1967, President's Papers, RG-2/1/2.701, box 28, "Law-General 1966–1967," Special Collections, University of Virginia Library.

85. Frank W. Rogers to Weldon Cooper, Mar. 11, 1966, Board of Visitors Committee Records, RG-1/1/3, box 11, "Buildings

and Ground Committee General Correspondence 1959–1971," Special Collections, University of Virginia Library.

86. Edgar Shannon to Thomas K. Fitz Patrick, April 4, 1967, President's Papers, RG-2/1/2.701, box 11, "Committee Architectural Advisory, 1966–1967," Special Collections, University of Virginia Library.

87. Hugh Stubbins & Associates, Inc., Architects, Cambridge, Massachusetts, "Master Plan for School of Law, Judge Advocate General's School, Graduate School of Business Administration and Coordinate Facilities," c. 1967, President's Papers, RG-2/1/2.711, box 14, "Special Committee—Law & Graduate Business Complex, Copeley Hill," Special Collections, University of Virginia Library.

88. Minutes, General Committee Meeting for School of Law and GSBA Complex, Feb. 28, 1968, President's Papers, RG-2/1/2.711, box 14, "Special Committee—Law & Graduate Business Complex, Copeley Hill," Special Collections, University of Virginia Library.

89. School of Education Building Meeting Memorandum, May 17, 1967, Physical Plant A & E Services, Project Files, RG-31/1/1.851, 1958–1979, box 33, "Education Building, July 1966–January 1971," Special Collections, University of Virginia Library.

90. Minutes of the Virginia Art Commission, May 5, 1961, in A. Edwin Kendrew to M. E. Kayhoe, May 12, 1961, President's Papers, RG-2/1/2.651, box 6, "Buildings and Grounds Planning Department," Special Collections, University of Virginia.

91. Minutes of the Committee on the Future of the University, 1965–1968, RG-20/18/2.751, Special Collections, University of Virginia Library.

92. W. Davidson Call to T. Braxton Woody, July 8, 1968, Material on Admission of Women, T. Braxton Woody, ms. 1982-A, box 1, "Alumni Replies," Special Collections, University of Virginia Library.

93. Bill Lyle to T. Braxton Woody, June 28, 1968, Material on Admission of Women, T. Braxton Woody, ms. 1982-A, box 1, "Alumni Replies," Special Collections, University of Virginia Library.

94. Kenneth Suskin to T. Braxton Woody, Sept. 12, 1968, Material on Admission of Women, T. Braxton Woody, ms. 1982-A, box 1, "Alumni Replies," Special Collections, University of Virginia Library.

95. Minutes of the University of Virginia Board of Visitors, April 11, 1952, p. 233, Special Collections, University of Virginia Library.

96. Frederick Doveton Nichols, "The Rotunda: Once More the Center of the University," *University of Virginia Alumni News*, March 1955, 5; "projected restoration of the Rotunda to its original Jeffersonian plan" is the language of the Board of Visitors Minutes, Dec. 17, 1955, p. 438, Special Collections, University of Virginia Library.

97. Frederick D. Nichols, *Phoenix in Virginia*, university pamphlet, c. 1955; see also Elizabeth Wilkerson, "Mr. Jefferson's Rotunda: A Return to the Original," *Alumni News*, Jan./Feb. 1976.

98. Francis L. Berkeley, "Frederick Doveton Nichols, 1911–1995," manuscript in Francis L. Berkeley, Jr., Papers, mss. 12747-b, -c, -d, box 4, Special Collections, University of Virginia Library.

99. Minutes of the Meeting of the Art Commission, Feb. 11, 1955, Governor Thomas B. Stanley Papers, 1954–1958, box 7, "Art Commission Minutes," Library of Virginia, Richmond.

100. Board of Visitors Minutes, Feb. 12, 1955, p. 395, Special Collections, University of Virginia Library.

101. Frederick Doveton Nichols, "Jeffersonian Buildings and Grounds Case Statement," unpublished manuscript,

October 1985, Nichols Papers, Special Collections, University of Virginia Library.

102. *Washington Post*, Sept. 22, 1973; see also *Richmond Times Dispatch*, Mar. 16, 1966; *Cavalier Daily*, April 10 and 19, 1974.

103. *New York Times*, Nov. 9, 1976.

104. Vincent Scully, Jr., "Seaside and New Haven," in Andrés Duany and Elizabeth Plater-Zyberk, *Towns and Town-Making Principles* (New York: Rizzoli, 1990), 17–20.

105. Robert A. M. Stern, "Something Borrowed, Something New," *Horizon* (Dec. 1977): 52.

106. Robert A. M. Stern, *New Directions in American Architecture* (New York: George Braziller, 1969), 31.

107. As both a designer and a theorist Robert Venturi also played a major role in reorienting architectural practice away from High Modernism. His 1966 book *Complexity and Contradiction in Architecture* demonstrated a vital interest in the sweep of architectural history and in the application of historical precedent. Venturi's exploration of architecture's power of symbolism and representation and its key signifying elements helped reinvigorate a serious-minded focus on how a sense of continuity between the past and the present could be better cultivated in contemporary architecture. At the same time, historic district design controls gathered new ground and fostered an ideal of aesthetic harmony, which now increasingly informed the ways in which architects approached their projects in traditional settings. Neil Levine, "Robert Venturi and 'The Return of Historicism,'thin;" in Christopher Mead, ed., *The Architecture of Robert Venturi* (Albuquerque: University of New Mexico Press, 1989), 45–67; Nikolaus Pevsner, "The Return of Historicism," *Journal of the Royal Institute of British Architects* 68 (1961): 230–240. See Robert Venturi, *Complexity and Contradiction in Architecture* (New York: Museum of Modern Art, 1966).

108. *Washington Post*, Sept. 6, 1986; in 2004 the university demolished Stern's Observatory Hill Dining Hall and replaced it with a larger but far less accomplished structure by Dagit-Saylor (2005); see also Alison K. Hoagland, "Ironic Historicism: Postmodernism and Historic Preservation," in David Ames and Richard Wagner, *Design & Historic Preservation* (Newark: University of Delaware Press, 2009), 113–144.

109. Memorandum from James C. Wheat III to Board of Visitors, "Architectural Design Policy and the Groundswalk," Oct. 8, 1998, Board of Visitors Buildings and Grounds Committee, Board of Visitors Committee Records, RG-1/1/3, box 15, "Buildings and Grounds Committee Correspondence," Special Collections, University of Virginia Library.

110. *Business Wire*, Nov. 8, 2006.

111. *Washington Post*, Nov. 10, 2006; since I teach at the University of Virginia, I need to acknowledge my own professional entry into the arguments described here, starting in the year 2005.

112. The letter is reproduced in "Open Letter to the Board of Visitors, the University Administration, and the University Community," Sept. 7, 2005, *Lunch: Trespass* 1 (2006): 18 (UVA School of Architecture student publication).

113. Carroll William Westfall, "Why the Orders Belong in Studio," *Journal of Architectural Education* 61 (May 2008): 95–107.

CHAPTER FOUR

Dutch Homesteads in Modern Brooklyn

1. David Lowenthal, *The Past Is a Foreign Country* (Cambridge: Cambridge University Press, 1985), 399.

2. Michael Kammen, *Mystic Chords of Memory: The Transformation of Tradition in American Culture* (New York: Knopf, 1991), 259; a similar approach is incisively followed in Michael Wallace, "Reflections on the History of Historic Preservation," in Susan Porter Benson, Stephen Brier, and Roy Rosenzweig, eds., *Presenting the Past: Essays on History and the Public* (Philadelphia: Temple University Press, 1986), 165–199; see also Michael H. Frisch, "The Memory of History," in *Presenting the Past*, 5–17; David W. Blight, "'For Something Beyond the Battlefield': Frederick Douglass and the Memory of the Civil War," *Journal of American History* 75 (Mar. 1989): 1156–1178.

3. Randall Mason, *The Once and Future New York: Historic Preservation and the Modern City* (Minneapolis: University of Minnesota Press, 2009), xxv; Mason coins the alluring term "memory infrastructure" to describe this process.

4. Nedda C. Allbray, *Flatbush: The Heart of Brooklyn* (Charleston, S.C.: Arcadia Publishing, 2004), 10, 120–121.

5. John J. Snyder, [Preservation] Committee Report, Flatbush Taxpayers Association, December 1909, Brooklyn Historical Society.

6. Benjamin F. Thompson, *History of Long Island* (New York: E. French, 1839), 461.

7. Thomas M. Strong, *The History of the Town of Flatbush, In Kings County, Long Island* (New York: Thomas R. Mercein, Jr., 1842), 54, 177.

8. For exploration of these developments, see Kevin Stayton, *Dutch by Design: Tradition and Change in Two Historic Brooklyn Houses* (New York: Brooklyn Museum/Phaidon, 1990), esp. 75–88; Aram Harutunian, "The Dutch-American Vernacular Style of Architecture," in *The Dutch and America* (Los Angeles: UCLA Publication Services, 1982), 9–19; Roderic H. Blackburn and Ruth Piwonka, *Remembrance of Patria: Dutch Arts and Culture in Colonial America, 1609–1776* (Albany: Albany Institute of History and Art, 1988), 117–118; Clifford W. Zink, "Dutch Framed Houses in New York and New Jersey," *Winterthur Portfolio* 22 (Winter 1987): 265–294; on the relation of vernacular and high-style forms, see also Dell Upton, "Vernacular Architecture in Eighteenth-Century Virginia," *Winterthur Portfolio* 17 (Summer/Autumn, 1982): 95–119.

9. Strong, *The History of the Town of Flatbush*, 176.

10 Joseph Downs, "The Greek Revival in the United States," *Metropolitan Museum of Art Bulletin*, n.s. 2 (Jan. 1944): 173–176.

11. Kings County Deeds, Liber 24, p. 452, July 8, 1828.

12. *The Wealth and Biography of the Wealthy Citizens of the City of New York* (New York: Sun Printing Office, 1846), 7.

13. See Flatbush Assessment Rolls, 1858–1880, Municipal Reference Library, New York City.

14. For a discussion of a similar suburban transition, see Tamara Plakins Thornton, *Cultivating Gentlemen: The Meaning of Country Life Among the Boston Elite, 1785–1860* (New Haven: Yale University Press, 1989).

15. Henry Stiles, *The Civil, Political, Professional, and Ecclesiastical History and the Commercial and Industrial Record of the County of Kings and the City of Brooklyn, N.Y. from 1683 to 1884*, 3 vols. (New York: W. W. Munsell & Co., 1884), vol. 1, pp. 352, 362; vol. 3, p. 1299.

16. Andrew Jackson Downing, *The Architecture of Country Houses* (New York: D. Appleton & Co., 1850), design xxxi, pp. 338–340; Flatbush Assessment Roll, 1858, Town Records of Kings County, New York City Municipal Archives.

17. See Gwendolyn Wright, *Moralism and the Model Home: Domestic Architecture and Cultural Conflict in Chicago, 1873–1913* (Chicago: University of Chicago Press, 1980); Clifford Edward Clark, Jr., *The American Family Home,*

1800–1960 (Chapel Hill: University of North Carolina Press, 1986), 3–71.

18. David Schuyler, *Apostle of Taste: Andrew Jackson Downing, 1815–1852* (Baltimore: Johns Hopkins University Press, 1996).

19. See Joseph T. Butler, *Washington Irving's Sunnyside* (Tarrytown, N.Y., 1974); W. Barksdale Maynard, "'Best, Lowliest Style!' The Early-Nineteenth-Century Rediscovery of American Colonial Architecture," *Journal of the Society of Architectural Historians* 59 (Sept. 2000): 351–352.

20. Gertrude Lefferts Vanderbilt, *The Social History of Flatbush* (New York: D. Appleton and Company, 1881), 5–6, 9.

21. Ibid., 59, 60, 62.

22. *Brooklyn Citizen*, Jan. 22, 1916.

23 Strong, *The History of the Town of Flatbush*, 176.

24. *New York Times*, Aug. 1, 1938; Manuscript Census, Kings County, New York, U.S. Census of Population, in National Archives Microfilm Collection, 1870: Ditmas, *Historic Homesteads*.

25. Flatbush Township Census Records, 1850.

26. John Vanderbilt Will, Kings County Probate Court, Liber 6, p. 313, June 11, 1842.

27. John Vanderbilt Will, Kings County Probate Court, Liber 2, p. 226, May 15, 1812.

28. Gertrude Lefferts Vanderbilt, *The Lefferts Family, Written for My Brother's Children by Their Aunt* (Flatbush, N.Y., 1897), 20.

29. For discussion of the rising circulation of real estate as a form of commodity, see Elizabeth Blackmar, *Manhattan for Rent, 1785–1850* (Ithaca: Cornell University Press, 1989), 161, 251; see also William John McLaughlin, "Dutch Rural New York: Community, Economy, and Family in Colonial Flatbush," (Ph.D. dissertation, Columbia University, 1981), 57.

30. John C. Vanderveer Will, Liber 9, p. 215, Probate Records, Kings County Courthouse.

31 Henry A. Meyer, *Vanderveer Park: Reminiscences of Its Growth* (Brooklyn: Robert L. Stillson, 1901).

32 *Brooklyn Gazette*, April 9, 1898.

33. Marc Linder and Lawrence S. Zacharias, *Of Cabbages and Kings County: Agriculture and the Formation of Modern Brooklyn* (Iowa City: University of Iowa Press, 1999), 31, 91, 127, 156, 157, 178, 203, 219, 223, 246.

34. *New York Times*, Oct. 9, 1910.

35. Susan Catin Will, Kings County Probate Court, Liber 9, p. 142, February 26, 1844. This was a form of protection from commercial engagements outside of Flatbush that Matthew Clarkson also apparently sought in the 1840s when he deeded his real estate to his farmer brother-in-law, who then deeded it to Matthew's children in the 1860s.

36. *Brooklyn Daily Eagle*, Dec. 8, 1915.

37. Flatbush Township Census, 1845, New York City Municipal Archives.

38. Vanderbilt, *The Social History of Flatbush*, 228.

39. *Brooklyn Daily Eagle*, Dec. 19, 1915.

40. Vanderbilt, *The Social History of Flatbush*, 229.

41. U.S. Census, 1880, 1900, 1910; New York State Census, 1905, Kings County Courthouse, Brooklyn, New York.

42. *Brooklyn Daily Eagle*, Sept. 28, 1911.

43. New York State Census, 1905.

44. New York State Census, 1915, Kings County Courthouse, Brooklyn, New York.

45. "Ditmas House Another Landmark in Flatbush Soon to Be Removed," n.d., c. 1915–1916, clippings file. Brooklyn Historical Society.

46. *Brooklyn Daily Eagle*, Sept. 30, 1931.

47. At his death in 1914, Ditmas controlled numerous residential lots and properties in the neighborhood around the old farmhouse; see John H. Ditmas, Final Account, Probate Records, Kings County Courthouse, June 14, 1915.

48. McLaughlin, "Dutch Rural New York," 42–49; Strong, *The History of the Town of Flatbush*, 11; Allbray, *Flatbush*, 11–15.

49. *Brooklyn Daily Eagle*, April 8, 1906.

50. For twentieth-century development, see Columbia University, Graduate School of Architecture, Planning and Preservation, Historic Preservation Division, *Flatbush: Architecture and Urban Development from Dutch Settlement to Commercial Strip* (New York; privately printed Columbia University, 1990).

51. Charles A. Ditmas, "Report of the Historical Committee," *Flatbush Magazine* 6 (Mar. 1928): 3.

52. Ditmas, *Historic Homesteads*, 15.

53. Charles B. Hosmer, Jr., *The Presence of the Past* (New York: Putnam, 1965), 131–132.

54. Hosmer, *The Presence of the Past*, charts this transition in interest from an organization such as the Mount Vernon Ladies Association, founded in 1856, to one like the Society for the Preservation of New England Antiquities, founded in 1910; James M. Lindgren, "'A Spirit That Fires the Imagination': Historic Preservation and Cultural Regeneration in Virginia and New England, 1850–1950," in Max Page and Randall Mason, eds., *Giving Preservation a History: Histories of Historic Preservation in the United States* (New York: Routledge, 2004), 107–127; see also John S. Patterson, "From Battle Ground to Pleasure Ground: Gettysburg as a Historic Site," in Warren Leon and Roy Rosenzweig, eds., *History Museums in the United States: A Critical Assessment*, (Urbana: University of Illinois Press, 1989), 128–157.

55. Vanderbilt, *The Social History of Flatbush*, 5–6.

56. Alice P. Kenney, "Neglected Heritage: Hudson Valley Dutch Material Culture," *Winterthur Portfolio* 20 (Spring 1985): 54; Mrs. John King Van Rensselaer, *The Goede Vrouw of Mana-ha-ta at Home and in Society, 1609–1760* (New York: Scribner, 1898), pp. vi–vii.

57. Annual Reports of Minutes of the Flatbush Taxpayers Association, Brooklyn Historical Society.

58. Barbara Welter, "The Cult of True Womanhood, 1820–1860," *American Quarterly* 18 (Summer 1966): 131–175; Nancy F. Cott, *The Bonds of Womanhood: 'Woman's Sphere' in New England, 1780–1835* (New Haven: Yale University Press, 1977), chap. 2; Linda Kerber, "Separate Spheres, Female Worlds, Woman's Place: The Rhetoric of Women's History," *Journal of American History* 75 (June 1988): 9–39.

59. Charles A. Ditmas to Mrs. Russell Sage, undated letter, c. 1910, Kings County Historical Society Papers, Brooklyn Historical Society.

60. Charles A. Ditmas, "Historic Flatbush," manuscript, c. 1910, Kings County Historical Society Papers, Brooklyn Historical Society.

61 John J. Snyder, [Preservation Report], Flatbush Taxpayers' Association, June 1906, Flatbush Taxpayers' Association Records, Brooklyn Historical Society.

62. Ditmas, *Historic Homesteads*, 73.

63. *Flatbush News*, Jan. 11, 1908.

64. John J. Snyder, [Preservation Report], Flatbush Taxpayers' Association, June 1906.

65. *Brooklyn Daily Eagle*, Mar. 8, 1911.

66. Franklin W. Hooper to John J. Snyder, Jr., May 11, 1911; Olmsted Brothers to Franklin W. Hooper, May 8, 1911, Flatbush Taxpayers' Association Papers, Brooklyn Historical Society.

67. *Flatbush News*, July 27, 1911.

68. Building Department Records, Block 5187, Lot 1, Brooklyn Municipal Building.

69. *Brooklyn Daily Eagle*, Sept. 12, 1911.

70. Edmund D. Fisher, *Flatbush: Past & Present* (Brooklyn: Midwood Club, 1902), 87.

71. Wright, *Moralism and the Model Home*; Clark, *The American Family Home*.

72. *Brooklyn Daily Eagle*, April 2, 1903.

73. Columbia University, Graduate School of Architecture, *Flatbush: Architecture and Urban Development from Dutch Settlement to Commercial Strip*, 42–47; Allbray, *Flatbush*, 137–149.

74. *New York Times*, Nov. 17, 1912.

75. *Brooklyn Daily Eagle*, April 2. 1903.

76. *New York Times*, Dec. 28, 1905.

77. New York Secretary of State, *Report of the Secretary of State of the Enumeration of Inhabitants of the State* 1915 and 1925 (Albany, N.Y.: J. B. Lyon Co., 1916, 1926).

78. Minutes of the Flatbush Taxpayers' Association, Dec. 2, 1909.

79. "Among the Club-Houses," unidentified scrapbook clipping, Brooklyn Historical Society; see also *New York Times*, Nov. 11, 1894; Allbray. *Flatbush*, 135.

80. Gunnison, *Flatbush of To-Day*, 62.

81. Mildred Stapley, "The Old Dutch Houses of Flatbush," *Country Life in America*, October 1, 1911, 59–61, 90, 92, 94.

82. *Brooklyn Daily Eagle*, Sept. 28, 1911.

83 Charles A. Ditmas to Atlantic, Gulf & Pacific Co., January 16, 1917, Kings County Historical Society Papers, Brooklyn Historical Society.

84. *New York Times*, Nov. 27, 1934; United States Department of Commerce, Thirteenth Census of the United States, Manuscript Returns, Brooklyn Enumeration District No. 1019, Sheet 7 A; *New York Times*, Feb. 11, 1904.

85. New York State Census for Kings County, 1915, in the Kings County Supreme Court Building.

86. For exploration of issues of urban social identity, see John F. Kasson, *Rudeness and Civility: Manners in Nineteenth-Century Urban America* (New York: Hill & Wang, 1990), 93.

87. Candidates for Historical Society membership were proposed by one member and seconded by another; they then filled out an application that was dominated by a lengthy recording of an applicant's genealogy. In connection with a Columbia University professor, William H. Kilpatrick, the society undertook the translation of Flatbush church records. The society also sponsored numerous lectures that focused on colonial and Revolutionary War subjects. Papers of the Kings County Historical Society, Brooklyn Historical Society.

88. See Thomas Andrew Denenberg, *Wallace Nutting and the Invention of Old America* (New Haven: Yale University Press, 2003).

89. *Brooklyn Daily Eagle*, Nov. 21, 1915.

90. Louis Lefferts Downs to Alfred T. White, Sept. 29, 1916; Alfred T. White to W. H. Fox, Sept. 30, 1916; W. H. Fox to Alfred T. White, Oct. 3, 1916.

91. *Museums of the Brooklyn Institute of Arts and Sciences Report for the Year 1905* (Brooklyn, 1906), 40; *Museums of the Brooklyn Institute of Arts and Sciences Report for the Year 1906* (Brooklyn, 1907), 46.

92. See Elizabeth Stillinger, *The Antiquers* (New York: Knopf, 1980), 215–221; Wendy Kaplan, "R. T. H. Halsey: An Ideology of Collecting American Decorative Arts," *Winterthur Portfolio* 17 (Spring 1982): 43–53; Henry Watson Kent and Florence N. Levy, *Catalogue of an exhibition of American Paintings, Furniture, Silver, and Other Objects of Art, MDCXXV–MDCCCXXV* (New York: Metropolitan Museum, 1909).

93. Kaplan, "R. T. H. Halsey," 45–46; Hosmer, *The Presence of the Past*, 216–218.

94. "Minutes of the Brooklyn Institute of Arts and Science," vol. 12, pp. 72, 75, 99; "List of Purchases of Early American Furniture, from 1914 through 1918," Director's Papers, "Furniture," file 370, Brooklyn Museum Archives; Dianne H. Pilgrim, "The Period Room: An Illusion of the Past," in Donald C. Peirce and Hope Alswang, *American Interiors, New England to the South* (New York: Universe Books, 1983), 2–3; Dianne H. Pilgrim, "Inherited from the Past: The American Period Room," *American Art Journal* 10 (May 1978): 4–23; see also *Museums of the Brooklyn Institute of Arts and Sciences [Annual] Report*, (1915–1920).

95. *Town and Country Life*, Sept. 16, 1905, 20.

96. *New York Times*, Mar. 18, 1906.

97. On Pratt gift, see Luke Vincent Lockwood to William H. Fox, April 16, 1914; on preservation and display, see Luke Vincent Lockwood to Elizabeth Haynes, Mar. 5, 1934, Decorative Arts Division, Brooklyn Museum.

98. Minutes of the Old Dutch House Preservation Committee, April 2, 1917, privately published; *Brooklyn Daily Eagle*, February, 25, 1918.

99. *Brooklyn Daily Eagle*, Oct. 8 and 19, 1916; *New York Times*, July 9, 1916.

100. Raymond Ingersoll to F. A. M. Burrell, Oct. 17, 1917.

101. Luke Vincent Lockwood to William H. Fox, May 18, 1920, Decorative Arts Commission, Brooklyn Museum.

102. *New York Times*, June 25, 1915.

103. Annette Stott, *Holland Mania: The Unknown Dutch Period in American Art and Culture* (Woodstock, N.Y.: Overlook Press, 1998), 78–100, 152–183; *Wallace Nutting and the Invention of Old America*, 87, 88, 193; Stillinger, *The Antiquers*, x–xv; Kaplan, "R. T. H. Halsey," 43–53; William Bertholet Rhoads, *The Colonial Revival* (New York: Garland Publishing, 1977).

104. *Brooklyn Daily Eagle*, Jan. 18, 1918.

105. *Brooklyn Daily Eagle*, Nov. 21, 1915, Dec. 19, 1917; on the process of segregation in preservation, see Lowenthal, *The Past Is a Foreign Country*, 404–405.

106. J. B. Jackson, "The Necessity for Ruins," in *The Necessity for Ruins* (Amherst: University of Massachusetts Press, 1980), 101–102; Daniel Abramson explores some of this same terrain in a useful essay, "Make History, Not Memory: History's Critique of Memory," in *Harvard Design Magazine* (Fall 1999): 78–83.

107. *New York Times*, Feb. 24, 1932.

108. *New York Times*, Feb. 24, 1932, June 10, 1932, and Dec. 7, 1932.

CHAPTER FIVE

Conservation on the Hudson

1. Randall Mason, *The Once and Future New York: Historic Preservation and the Modern City* (Minneapolis: University of Minnesota Press, 2009), 9–19.

2. David Harmon, Francis P. McManamon, and Dwight T. Pitcaithley, eds., *The Antiquities Act: A Century of American Archaeology, Historic Preservation, and Nature Conservation* (Tucson: University of Arizona Press, 2006), 1–34, 267–285.

3. The National Parks Act, 1916, August 25, 1916. [H.R. 15522]

4. William Cronon, "The Trouble with Wilderness; or, Getting Back to the Wrong Nature," in William Cronon, ed., *Uncommon Ground: Rethinking the Human Place in Nature* (New York: Norton, 1995), 69–90; see also Roderick Nash, "The Value of Wilderness," *Environmental Review* 3 (1977): 14–25.

5. Carolyn Merchant, *American Environmental History: An Introduction* (New York: Columbia University Press, 2007), 134–156; Philip Pregill and Nancy Volkman, *Landscapes in History* (New York: Wiley, 1999), 653–671.

6. *New York Times*, Mar. 5, 1898; see Geological Survey of New Jersey, *Annual Report of the State Geologist for the Year 1897* (Trenton: John L. Murphy Publishing Co., 1898), 150.

7. *New York Daily Tribune*, May 30, 1898.

8. Arthur P. Abbott, *The Greatest Park in the World, Palisades Interstate Park: Its Purpose, History, and Achievement* (New York: Historian Publishing Co., 1914), 7.

9. *New York Times*, Mar. 5, 1898.

10. Chapter 170 of the New York Legislature Session Laws for 1900.

11. *Nyack Evening Journal*, Mar. 17, 1902; *Rockland County Times*, Mar. 15 and April 19, 1902, and April 8, 1905.

12. *New York Daily Tribune*, Oct. 14, 1894;

13. On historic preservation and resistance to modern capitalism, see Mike Wallace, "Preserving the Past: A History of Historic Preservation in the United States," and "Preservation Revisited," in Mike Wallace, *Mickey Mouse History and Other Essays on American Memory* (Philadelphia: Temple University Press, 1996), 178–210, 224–237; see also Karal Ann Marling, *George Washington Slept Here: Colonial Revivals and American Culture, 1876–1976* (Cambridge: Harvard University Press, 1988), 83–84.

14. Andrew Carnegie, "Wealth," *North American Review* 148 (June 1889): 653–664; see also David Nasaw, "The Gospels of Andrew Carnegie," chap. 20 in David Nasaw, *Andrew Carnegie* (New York: Penguin, 2006), 343–360.

15. Mason, *The Once and Future New York*, esp. xxv–xxviii.

16. *New York Times*, Mar. 5, 1898.

17. Thomas Cole, "Essay on American Scenery," *American Monthly Magazine* 1 (January 1836): 1–12; see also Alan Wallach, "Thomas Cole's 'River in the Catskills' as Antipastoralism," *Art Bulletin* 84 (June 2002): 339–341.

18. George Perkins Marsh, *Man and Nature; or, Physical Geography as Modified by Human Action* (New York: Scribner, 1864); David Lowenthal, *George Perkins Marsh: Prophet of Conservation* (Seattle: University of Washington Press, 2000); Marcus Hall, *Earth Repair: A Transatlantic History of Environmental Restoration* (Charlottesville: University of Virginia Press, 2005).

19. Marsh, *Man and Nature*, 43.

20. Marsh, *Man and Nature*, 235.

21. Frances F. Dunwell, *The Hudson River Highlands* (New York: Columbia University Press, 1991), 139–140; Robert O. Binnewies, *Palisades: 100,000 Acres in 100 Years* (New York: Fordham University Press, 2001), 7–8.

22. Philip G. Terrie, *Contested Terrain: A New History of Nature and People in the Adirondacks* (Syracuse, N.Y.: Syracuse University Press, 1997), 102, 115.

23. Dunwell, *The Hudson River Highlands*, 138, 143.

24. Raymond J. O'Brien, *American Sublime: Landscape and Scenery of the Lower Hudson Valley* (New York: Columbia University Press, 1981), 237, 244.

25. *New York Daily Tribune*, June 4, 1899.

26. *New York Daily Tribune,* June 25, 1899.

27. *New York Evening Post*, Feb. 5, 1894.

28. For discussion of this development in Boston, see Henry C. Binford, *The First Suburbs: Residential Communities on the Boston Periphery, 1815–1860* (Chicago: University of Chicago Press, 1985), 31–41, 202–204, 222, 229.

29. William H. Appleton to William E. Dodge, June 19, 1894, box 44, George W. Perkins Papers, Manuscript Division, Butler Library, Columbia University, New York City.

30. William E. Dodge to John Smock, Oct. 12, 1894, box 44, Perkins Papers.

31. *New York Times*, Oct. 8, 1895.

32. Resolutions of the Palisades Protective Association, July 12, 1894, box 44, Perkins Papers.

33. William E. Dodge to Charles Eliot Norton, July 18, 1894; William E. Dodge to Frederick Law Olmsted, July 23, 1894, box 44, Perkins Papers.

34. Olmsted quoted in *New York Daily Tribune*, Oct. 14, 1894.

35. Cleveland H. Dodge to John D. Rockefeller, May 18, 1906, Rockefeller Family Papers, Record Group 2, box 125, folder 1116, Rockefeller Archives, Tarrytown, New York.

36. *New York Evening Post*, Jan. 22, 1901.

37. *New York Times*, July 10, 1900.

38. *Acts of the One Hundred and Nineteenth Legislature of the State of New Jersey, and Fifty-First Under the New Constitution* (Camden, N.J.: F. F. Patterson, 1895), chap. xxviii.

39. *Annual Report of the Riparian Commissioners of the State of New Jersey, for the Year 1895, with Accompanying Documents* (Trenton, N.J.: John L. Marphy Publishing Co., 1896), 8; *Acts of the State of New Jersey, 1898)*, chap. 191.

40. William C. Spencer to Cleveland H. Dodge, Feb. 5, 1895, box 44, Perkins Papers.

41. Corporations Ledger Book, Liber 31, p. 138, Office of Public Records of Hudson County, Jersey City, New Jersey.

42. *Newark Evening News*, Mar. 20, 1895.

43. David Schuyler, *The New Urban Landscape* (Baltimore, Johns Hopkins University Press, 1986), 174–178.

44. J. James R. Croes to William E. Dodge, Mar. 27, 1896, box 44, Perkins Papers.

45. J. James R. Croes to William E. Dodge, April 8, 1896, box 44, Perkins Papers.

46. See John T. Fry, Secretary of Navy Department, to John A. T. Hall, chairman, Committee on Military Affairs, House of Representatives, Dec. 18 and 27, 1897, Records of the U.S. House of Representatives, 55th Cong., Record Group 233, box 95, National Archives, Washington, D.C.; *New York Times*, Feb. 20, 1896; *New York Times*, Dec. 15, 1895; see also Binnewies, *Palisades*, 10.

47. *Newark Evening News*, Feb. 19, 1896, April 24, 1896, and Feb. 4, 1898.

48. William E. Dodge to Frederick Law Olmsted, July 23, 1894, box 44, Perkins Papers.

49. *Newark Evening News*, Feb. 22, 1896.

50. *Newark Evening News*, Feb. 22, 1896.

51. *New York Evening Post*, Sept. 23, 1897.

52. *Sixth Annual Report of the American Scenic and Historic Preservation Society* (New York, 1901), 15.

53. A. D. F. Hamlin, "The Preservation of Historic Sites and Buildings in Europe," Jan. 15, 1902, box 6, American Scenic and Historic Preservation Society Archives (hereafter, ASHPS).

54. Edward Hagaman Hall to Reverend Howard Duffield, April 26, 1905; Reverend Howard Duffield to Edward Hagaman Hall, April 29, 1905; box 8, ASHPS.

55. *Annual Report of the American Scenic and Historic Preservation Society* (New York, 1907).

56. Edward Hagaman Hall to Reverend Howard Duffield, April 26, 1905, box 8, ASHPS.

57. *New York Evening Post*, Mar. 18, 1901; *Newark Evening Post*, Nov. 19, 1897.

58. W. Allen Butler to Edward H. Hall, Dec. 18, 1900, box 6, ASHPS.

59. *Hackensack Evening Record*, Mar. 1, 1901.

60. Theodore Roosevelt, "Governor's Message," Jan. 3, 1900, in *Documents of the State of New York, 123rd Sess., 1900* (Albany: James B. Lyon, 1900), 52–53.

61. Binnewies, *Palisades*, 17, states that there were several versions of the New Jersey bill and that the power of condemnation was hotly contested. According to Binnewies, it was the lobbying of the Women's Clubs that helped retain the public power of condemnation in the bill.

62. *New York Evening Post*, April 4, 1900.

63. John A. Garraty, *Right-Hand Man: The Life of George W. Perkins* (New York: Harper & Bro., 1960), 83; see United States Manuscript Census Returns, New York State, 1900, enumeration district 1048, sheet 9.

64. *New York Evening Post*, Jan. 22, 1901; *New York Evening Sun*, April 25, 1901.

65. George W. Perkins, "Memorandum for the New York State Palisades Park Commission," October 18, 1900, box 44, Perkins Papers.

66. George W. Perkins, [Plan of Operation], c. 1900, box 44, Perkins Papers.

67. Frederick S. Lamb to George W. Perkins, Oct. 16, 1900, and Dec. 3, 1900, and George W. Perkins to Edward H. Hall, Dec. 5, 1900, box 44, Perkins Papers; Charles R. Lamb to George W. Perkins, June 15, 1903, George W. Perkins to Charles R. Lamb, July 3, 1903, and George W. Perkins to Edward H. Hall, Nov. 26, 1904, box 45, Perkins Papers.

68. Elizabeth B. Vermilye to George W. Perkins, July [24–25], 1900, box 44, Perkins Papers; *New York Times*, May 4, 1900.

69. George W. Perkins to Elizabeth B. Vermilye, July 26, 1900, and Elizabeth B. Vermilye to George W. Perkins, July 28, 1900, box 44, Perkins Papers.

70. League for the Preservation of the Palisades, "An Appeal for the Palisades," Aug. 1900; George W. Perkins to S. Wood McClave, Sept. 12, 1900, box 44, Perkins Papers.

71. Elizabeth B. Vermilye to George W. Perkins, Jan. 9, 1901, George W. Perkins to Elizabeth B. Vermilye, Jan. 17, 1901, and Elizabeth B. Vermilye to George W. Perkins, Jan. 24, 1901, box 44, Perkins Papers.

72. Elizabeth B. Vermilye to George W. Perkins, May 12, 1901, and George W. Perkins to Elizabeth B. Vermilye, May 14, 1901, box 44, Perkins Papers; S. Wood McClave to George W. Perkins, February 21, 1902, and George W. Perkins to S. Wood McClave, Feb. 27 1902, box 45, Perkins Papers. The league also published an illustrated booklet emphasizing the role of women in Palisades preservation and on the 1899 study commission; see League for the Preservation of the Palisades, *How the Palisades Were Saved* (New York: n.p., 1905).

73. Bergen County, New Jersey, Deed Book, vol. 13, p. 168, Feb. 12, 1891, Bergen Country Courthouse, Hackensack, N.J.

74. "Carpenter Brothers Bradstreet Credit Report," box 44, Perkins Papers.

75. United States Manuscript Census Return, New York State, 1900, enumeration district 113, sheet 30.

76. George W. Carpenter to George W. Perkins, Oct. 5, 1900, box 44, Perkins Papers.

77. George W. Perkins to George W. Carpenter, Oct. 24, 1900, box 44, Perkins Papers.

78. "Minutes of the Commissioners of the Palisades Interstate Park," Dec. 3, 1900, box 44, Perkins Papers.

79. [Carpenter Brothers Memorandum of Agreement], December 1900, box 44, Perkins Papers.

80. Frances F. Dunwell, *The Hudson River Highlands* (New York: Columbia University Press, 1991), 117; Ron Chernow, *House of Morgan: An American Banking Dynasty and the Rise of Modern Finance* (New York: Atlantic Monthly Press, 1990), 32, 52; United States Manuscript Census Returns, New York State, 1900, enumeration district 16, sheet 4; *New York Times*, July 1, 1894.

81. *The Commercial*, Jan. 9, 1901; see also *New York Tribune Illustrated Supplement*, January 6, 1901.

82. "Governor's Message, Jan. 2, 1901," *Journal of the Senate of the State of New York at Their One Hundred and Twenty-Fourth Session* (Albany: James B. Lyon, 1901), 31–32.

83. George W. Perkins to J. P. Morgan, May 14, 1901, box 44, Perkins Papers.

84. Minutes of the American Scenic and Historic Preservation Society, Jan. 23 1905; George F. Kunz to J. Pierpont Morgan, Jan. 24, 1905; J. Pierpont Morgan to George F. Kunz, January 25, 1905, box 8, ASHPS.

85. *Nyack Evening Journal*, Mar. 8 1906.

86 *Nyack Evening Journal*, Mar. 10, 1898.

87. *Nyack Evening Journal*, Mar. 22, 1898.

88. *Nyack Evening Journal*, Jan. 29, and Mar. 30, 1906.

89. United States Manuscript Census Returns, New York State, 1910, enumeration district 96, sheet 15.

90. "James P. McQuaide," in Arthur S. Tompkins, ed., *Historical Record to the Close of the Nineteenth Century of Rockland County, New York* (Nyack, N.Y.: Van Deusen & Joyce, 1902), 154–155; United States Manuscript Census Returns, New York State, 1900, enumeration district 61, sheets 9 and 10; "Arthur C. Tucker and James P. McQuaide, Respondents v. The Mack Paving Company of New York, Appellant," in Marcus T. Hun, Reporter, *Reports of Cases Heard And Determined in the Appellate Division of the Supreme Court of the State of New York*, vol. 61 (Albany: J. B. Lyon, 1901), 521–528.

91. *Nyack Evening Journal*, Feb. 25, 1902.

92. *Rockland County Times*, Mar. 15, 1902.

93. James P. McQuaide to John D. Rockefeller, Jr., Mar. 3, 14 and 21, 1902; John D. Rockefeller, Jr., to James P. McQuaide, Mar. 18, 1902; John D. Rockefeller, Jr., to Timothy L. Woodruff, Mar. 18, 1902; Timothy L. Woodruff to John D. Rockefeller, Jr., Mar. 19, 24, and 26, 1902; John D. Rockefeller to Benjamin B. Odell, Mar. 31, 1902; Record Group 2, box 125, folder 1116, Rockefeller Archives, Pocantico Hills, New York.

94. *Rockland County Times*, April 19, 1902; *New York Times*, April 3, 1902; *Nyack Evening Star*, Feb. 25, and April 16, 1902.

95. James R. McQuaide to John D. Rockefeller, Jr., Mar. 28, 1902, Record Group 2, box 125, folder 1116, Rockefeller Archives, Pocantico Hills, N.Y.

96. *Nyack Evening Journal*, April 3, 1902; *New York Times*, April 3, 1902; New York State, *Public Papers of Benjamin B. Odell, Jr., Governor for 1902* (Albany: J. B. Lyon, 1907), 201–202.

97. *Nyack Evening Star*, April 15, 1902.

98. *Rockland County Times*, April 19, 1902.

99. *New York Times*, Jan. 14, 1906.

100. *New York Times*, July 12, 1933.

101. George F. Kunz, "On the Preservation of the Scenic Beauty in the Conservation of the National Resources of the States," May 1908, box 10, ASHPS Papers; see also George F. Kunz, "The Economic Value of Public Parks and Scenic Preservation," *Scientific Monthly* 16 (April 1923): 374–380.

102. Starr J. Murphy to Timothy L. Woodruff, Mar. 10, 1906, Record Group 2, box 125, folder 1116, Rockefeller Archives, Pocantico Hills, New York.

103. *Nyack Evening Journal*, June 4, 1906.

104. Michael G. Kammen, *Mystic Chords of Memory*, (New York: Knopf, 1991), 44–45.

105. J. DuPratt White to George Perkins, Dec. 24, 1903, box 45, Perkins Papers; see John Brisben Walker "The Wonders of New York 1903–1909," *Cosmopolitan* 36 (Dec. 1903) 143–160.

106. George W. Perkins to the Editor of the *Trenton* [N.J.] *Times*, Oct. 6, 1909, box 45; George W. Perkins to General Stewart L. Woodford, June 21, 1909, box 28, Perkins Papers.

107. Kammen, *Mystic Chords of Memory*, 246–247; Karal Ann Marling, *George Washington Slept Here: Colonial Revivals and American Culture, 1876–1976* (Cambridge: Harvard University Press, 1988), 201–221.

108. "Dedication of Palisades Interstate Park," in Edward Hagaman Hall, ed., *The Hudson-Fulton Celebration: The Fourth Annual Report of the Hudson-Fulton Celebration Commission to the Legislature of the State of New York* (Albany: J. B. Lyon, 1910), 393–412.

109. George W. Perkins to Theodore Roosevelt, Feb. 25, 1909, box 45, Perkins Papers; Perkins dedication address reproduced in *Tenth Annual Report of the Commissioners of the Palisades Interstate Park* (Albany: J. B. Lyon, 1910), 8.

110. *Tenth Annual Report of the Commissioners of the Palisades Interstate Park* (Albany: J. B. Lyon, 1910), 8; "Hamilton McKown Twombly," *National Cyclopedia of American Biography* (New York: James T. White & Co., 1943), vol. 30, p. 17.

111. Marjorie W. Brown, *Arden House: A Living Expression of the Harriman Family* (New York: Columbia University Press, 1981), 11–16; George Kennan, *E. H. Harriman, A Biography* (Boston: Houghton Mifflin, 1922).

112. Helen M. Gould to John D. Rockefeller, Dec. 29, 1909; John D. Rockefeller to Andrew Carnegie, December 23, 1909; Andrew Carnegie to John D. Rockefeller, December 28, 1909, Record Group 2, box 125, folder 1116, Rockefeller Archives, Pocantino, N.Y.

113. *Standard Union*, Jan. 9, 1910, and Nov. 6, 1910.

114. George W. Perkins to Woodrow Wilson, April 4, 1912, box 46, Perkins Papers.

115. Charles P. Heydt to George W. Perkins, May 12, 1911, box 45, Perkins Papers.

116. John D. Rockefeller, Jr., to George W. Perkins, Dec. 5, 1912; George W. Perkins to John D. Rockefeller, Dec. 6, 1912, Record Group 2, box 125, folder 1116, Rockefeller Archives, Pocantico Hills, N.Y.; see also Mary W. Harriman to George W. Perkins, July 23, 1912; George W. Perkins to Mary W. Harriman, July 24, 1912; box 46, Perkins Papers.

117. J. DuPratt White to George W. Perkins, April 16, 1912, box 46, Perkins Papers.

118. *Nyack Evening Journal*, Mar. 8, 1906.

119. George Perkins to John D. Rockefeller, Jr., June 2, 1915; Record Group 2, box 125, folder 1116, Rockefeller Archives.

120. "Wilson P. Foss," *Southeastern New York. A History of the Counties of Ulster, Dutchess, Orange, Rockland, and Putnam*, ed. Louise Hasbrouck Zimm (New York: Lewis Historical Publishing Co., 1946), vol. 3, 458–465; *Rockland County Times*, Mar. 17, 1904, September 27, 1930.

121. *New York Evening Post*, May 2, 1896, and August 27, 1914; *New York Times*, Aug. 16, 1914; George W. Perkins to L. H. Smith, September 1, 1914; George W. Perkins to Mrs. Hoyle Tomkies, Aug. 26, 1914; J. DuPratt White to George W. Perkins, August [c. 20], 1914, box 47, Perkins Papers.

122. Nancy Wynne Newhall, *Contribution to the Heritage of Every American: The Conservation Activities of John D. Rockefeller, Jr.* (New York: Knopf, 1957); Steven C. Wheatley, "Rockefeller, John D., Jr.," *American National Biography* 18 (1999): 697–700; *http://archive.rockefeller. edu/bio/jdrjr.php;* Matthew M. Palus, "Authenticity, Legitimation, and Twentieth-Century Tourism: The John D. Rockefeller, Jr., Carriage Roads, Acadia National Park, Maine," in Paul A. Shackel, *Myth, Memory, and the Making of the American Landscape* (Gainesville: University Press of Florida, 2001), 179–196.

CHAPTER SIX

The Arch and the Neighborhood

1. Charles B. Hosmer, Jr., *Preservation Comes of Age: From Williamsburg to the National Trust, 1926–1949* (Charlottesville: University Press of Virginia, 1981), 626–649; for a confirming preservationist critique, see Richard W. Longstreth, [Book Review of Hosmer's *Preservation Comes of Age*], *Winterthur Portfolio* 17 (Winter 1982): 293; J. Meredith Neil, [Book Review of Hosmer's *Preservation Comes of Age*], *American Historical Review* 88 (October 1983): 1100; see also Charles E. Peterson, "Before the Arch: Some Early Architects and Engineers on the St. Louis Riverfront," in David Ames and Richard Wagner, *Design and Historic Preservation* (Newark: University of Delaware Press, 2009), 161–176; Joseph Heathcott and Máire Agnes Murphy, "Corridors of Flight, Zones of Renewal: Industry, Planning, and Policy in the Making of Metropolitan St. Louis, 1940–1980," *Journal of Urban History* 31 (Jan. 2005), 151–189.

2. Section 1 of the Historic Sites Act of 1935, 49 Stat. 666; 16 U.S.C. 461–467.

3. Hosmer, *Preservation Comes of Age*, 626.

4. "Extract from Draft of Minutes of Executive Session, Advisory Board, National Park Service, October 28, 29, 1937," Records of the National Park Service (hereafter NPS), National Historic Sites, Jefferson National Expansion Memorial, Record Group 79, box 2639, National Archives, Washington, D.C.

5. Sharon A. Brown, *Administrative History Jefferson National Expansion Memorial National Historic Site, Part I* (Washington, D.C.: United States Department of Interior, 1984), chap. 1, p. 16 [internet pagination]; on the range of motivations for the project, see also Regina M. Bellavia and Gregg Bleam, *Cultural Landscape Report for Jefferson National Expansion Memorial, St. Louis, Missouri* (Washington, D.C., National Park Service, 1996), 14–16.

6. See Daniel Bluestone, "Academics in Tennis Shoes: Historic Preservation and the Academy," *Journal of the Society of Architectural Historians* 58 (Sept. 1999): 300–307.

7. Charles Peterson's 1933 guidelines are reproduced in "The Historic American Building Survey Continued," *Journal of the Society of Architectural Historians* 16 (Oct. 1957), 57.

8. Brown, *Administrative History Jefferson National Expansion Memorial*, chap. 1, p. 2 [internet pagination].

9. Civic League of Saint Louis, *A City Plan for Saint Louis: Reports of the Several Committees Appointed by the Executive Board of the Civic League to Draft a City Plan* (St. Louis: Woodward & Tiernan, 1907), 72–75.

10. For a similar discussion of City Beautiful, see Daniel Bluestone, "Detroit's City Beautiful and the Problem

of Commerce," *Journal of the Society of Architectural Historians* 47 (Sept. 1988): 245–262.

11. Harland Bartholomew, *A Plan for the Central River Front, St. Louis, Missouri* (St. Louis: City Plan Commission, 1928), 2, 6, 7, 28–34.

12. Civic Improvement League, *Report of the Open Air Playgrounds Committee, Civic Improvement League, 1903* (St. Louis: Civic Improvement League, 1903), 5, 19.

13. Civic League of Saint Louis, *Billboard Advertising in St. Louis* (St. Louis: Civic League, 1910), 7.

14. Civic League of St. Louis, *A Year of Civic Effort: Addresses and Reports at the Annual Meeting* (St. Louis: Civic League of St. Louis, 1907), 45–46.

15. For a history of the St. Louis pageant, see David Glassberg, *American Historical Pageantry: The Uses of Tradition in the Early Twentieth Century* (Chapel Hill: University of North Carolina Press, 1990), 159–199; Donald Bright Oster, "Nights of Fantasy: The St. Louis Pageant and Masque of 1914," *Bulletin of the Missouri Historical Society* 31 (April 1975): 175–205.

16. "Minutes of the United States Territorial Expansion Commission, 19 December 1934," typed transcript, 41–43, Jefferson National Expansion Memorial Association Papers, Jefferson National Expansion Memorial Historic Site Archives, St. Louis, Missouri.

17. The site is mapped in Sanborn Map Company, *Insurance Maps of Vincennes, Indiana* (New York: Sanborn Map Company, 1927), map 9.

18. Edwin C. Bearss, *George Rogers Clark Memorial: Historic Structures Report Historical Data* (Washington, D.C.: United States Department of the Interior, 1970).

19. *New York Times*, Sept. 4, 1933.

20. "Minutes of the United States Territorial Expansion Commission," 2–3.

21. Michael Kammen, *Mystic Chords of Memory: The Transformation of Tradition in American Culture* (New York: Knopf, 1991), 444–480; Hal Rothman, *Preserving Different Pasts: The American National Monuments* (Urbana: University of Illinois Press, 1989).

22. "Minutes of the United States Territorial Expansion Commission," 31 48, 52, 56.

23. "Minutes of the United States Territorial Expansion Commission," 8–9.

24. United States Territorial Expansion Commission, *Reports Approved by the Executive Committee of the United States Commission at its Meeting in St. Louis on April 13, 1935* (St. Louis: The Commission, 1935), no pagination.

25. John L. Nagle, "Report on United States Territorial Expansion Memorial at St. Louis, Missouri," Aug. 20, 1935, Records of the NPS, National Historic Sites, Jefferson National Expansion Memorial, Record Group 79, box 2632.

26. United States Executive Order 7253, Dec. 21, 1935, reprinted in Clifford L. Lord, ed., *Presidential Executive Orders* (New York: Books, Inc., 1944), 616.

27. W. F. Pfeiffer to Harold L. Ickes, Dec. 21, 1935; Paul O. Peters to Harold L. Ickes, Dec. 21, 1935; W. H. Gage Glue Company to Interior Department, Sept. 21, 1935; St. Louis Coffee & Spice Mills to Harold L. Ickes, Dec. 21, 1935; G. S. Robins & Company to Harold L. Ickes, Dec. 21, 1935; W. E. Beckman to Harold L. Ickes, Dec. 21, 1935; Julius Johnson to President Franklin D. Roosevelt, Dec. 22, 1922; Records of the NPS, National Historic Sites, Jefferson National Expansion Memorial, Record Group 79, box 2632.

28. Brown, *Administrative History Jefferson National Expansion Memorial*, chap. 2, 13–14 [internet pagination].

29. Charles E. Peterson, "A Museum of American Architecture," July 1936, Records of the NPS, National Historic Sites, Jefferson National Expansion Memorial, Record Group 79, box 2633; see also Charles E. Peterson, "Museum of Modern Architecture: A Proposed Institution of Research and Public Education," *Octagon: A Journal of the American Institute of Architects* 8 (Nov. 1936): 12–13; Peterson, "Before the Arch," 167–169.

30. Charles E. Peterson to Edward C. Kemper, Sept. 26, 1936, Records of the NPS National Historic Sites, Jefferson National Expansion Memorial, Record Group 79, box 2633.

31. Charles E. Peterson to John L. Nagle, May 11, 1937, Records of the NPS, National Historic Sites, Jefferson National Expansion Memorial, Record Group 79, box 2634; Charles E. Peterson to John L. Nagle, Nov. 12, 1936, Records of the NPS, National Historic Sites, Jefferson National Expansion Memorial, Record Group 79, box 2633.

32. Charles E. Peterson, "A Museum of American Architecture," July 1936, Records of the NPS, National Historic Sites, Jefferson National Expansion Memorial, Record Group 79, box 2633.

33. Charles E. Peterson to John L. Nagle, Oct. 28, 1936, Records of the NPS, National Historic Sites, Jefferson National Expansion Memorial, Record Group 79, box 2633; *St. Louis Daily Globe-Democrat*, Nov. 28, 1936, and Mar. 23, 1941; *St. Louis Post-Dispatch*, June 1, 1941; John Albury Bryan, "Iron in St. Louis Architecture Between 1800 and 1900," 1961, paper in files of Historic Sites Division, U.S. Department of the Interior.

34. John L. Nagle to Charles E. Peterson, Dec. 3, 1936, Records of the NPS, National Historic Sites, Jefferson National Expansion Memorial, Record Group 79, box 2633.

35. Thomas E. Tallmadge to John L. Nagle, Dec. 28, 1936, Records of the NPS, National Historic Sites, Jefferson National Expansion Memorial, Record Group 79, box 2633; See also Brown, *Administrative History Jefferson National Expansion Memorial* chap. 2, p. 11–12 [internet pagination unclear]; and Bellavia and Bleam, *Cultural Landscape Report for Jefferson National Expansion Memorial*, 18, which both treat Tallmadge's report at length as a key in the Park Service's sweeping clearance on the site. Neither Brown nor Bellavia and Bleam discuss the fact that Nagle had pushed Tallmadge to alter his early support for a broad preservation program as part of Nagle's effort to keep the project focused on the commemorative program outlined in President Roosevelt's executive order.

36. John L. Nagle to Director of the National Park Service, Dec. 8, 1936, Records of the NPS, National Historic Sites, Jefferson National Expansion Memorial, Record Group 79, box 2633.

37. Ned J. Burns to Charles E. Peterson, Feb. 11, 1937, Records of the NPS, National Historic Sites, Jefferson National Expansion Memorial, Record Group 79, box 2633.

38. Hosmer, *Preservation Comes of Age*, 633.

39. Charles E. Peterson to John L. Nagle, Oct. 28, 1936, Records of the NPS, National Historic Sites, Jefferson National Expansion Memorial, Record Group 79, box 2633.

40. See Jefferson National Expansion Memorial Association, "An Architectural Competition for a Memorial to Thomas Jefferson and the Pioneers to Whom We Owe Our National Expansion," [c. Oct. 1935]; John G. Lonsdale to Arno B. Cammerer, May 29, 1935, Records of the NPS, National Historic Sites, Jefferson National Expansion Memorial, Record Group 79, box 2632.

41. John L. Nagle, "The Essentially National Aspects of the Jefferson National Expansion Memorial," Mar. 16, 1938,

Speech to the North Side Kiwanis Club of St. Louis, broadcast over station WIL, Records of the NPS, National Historic Sites, Jefferson National Expansion Memorial, Record Group 79, box 2636.

42. Hermon C. Bumpus, Herbert E. Bolton,. Archibald M. McCrea to Arno B. Cammerer, Sept. 2, 1937, Records of the NPS, National Historic Sites, Jefferson National Expansion Memorial, Record Group 79, box 2635; see "Hermon C. Bumpus," *National Cyclopedia of American Biography, Being the History of the United States* (New York: James T. White & Co., 1945), vol. 32, p. 331–332; in 1940, Bumpus received the Cornelius Amory Pugsley Gold Medal given by the American Scenic and Historic Preservation Society, for his educational work in national parks.

43. Hermon C. Bumpus to John L. Nagle, Oct. 2, 1937, Records of the NPS, National Historic Sites, Jefferson National Expansion Memorial, Record Group 79, box 2635.

44. John L. Nagle to Hermon C. Bumpus, Oct. 6, 1937, Records of the NPS, National Historic Sites, Jefferson National Expansion Memorial, Record Group 79, box 2635.

45. Hermon C. Bumpus to Acting Secretary of the Interior, Nov. 10, 1939; John L. Nagle, "Memorandum for the Director," Nov. 13, 1939, Records of the NPS, National Historic Sites, Jefferson National Expansion Memorial, Record Group 79, box 2637.

46. Hosmer, *Preservation Comes of Age*, 643; see also Brown, *Administrative History Jefferson National Expansion Memorial*, chap. 2, p. 35 [internet pagination].

47. Daniel Bluestone, "Civic and Aesthetic Reserve: Ammi B. Young's 1850's Federal Custom House Designs," *Winterthur Portfolio* 25 (Summer/Autumn, 1990), 131–156.

48. Perry T. Rathbone to Julian C. Spotts, Jan. 17, 1941, Records of the NPS, National Historic Sites, Jefferson National Expansion Memorial, Record Group 79, box 2656.

49. *St. Louis Post-Dispatch*, Jan. 20, 22, and 23, 1941; *St. Louis Globe-Democrat*, Jan. 19 and 20, 1941; Laura Inglis to National Park Service, Jan. 17, 1941, Julius Polk, Jr., to Harold L. Ickes, Jan. 20, 1941, and Nelle J. Krabbe to Julian C. Spotts, Jan. 21, 1941, Records of the NPS, National Historic Sites, Jefferson National Expansion Memorial, Record Group 79, box 2656.

50. Julius Polk, Jr., to Harold L. Ickes, Jan. 20, 1941, Records of the NPS, National Historic Sites, Jefferson National Expansion Memorial, Record Group 79, box 2656; W. Rufus Jackson [St. Louis postmaster] to John L. Nagle, Feb. 18, 1938, reprinted in *St. Louis Post-Dispatch*, Jan. 21, 1941.

51. Daniel Cox Fahey, Jr., to Fount Rothwell, Sept. 14, 1936, Records of the NPS, National Historic Sites, Jefferson National Expansion Memorial, Record Group 79, box 2633; "Report of the Museum Committee Meeting, January [1938], 28–29, at St. Louis," Feb. 1, 1938, Records of the NPS, National Historic Sites, Jefferson National Expansion Memorial, Record Group 79, box 2659; Charles E. Peterson, "Memorandum for Mr. Nagle—The Old St. Louis Custom House," Aug. 9, 1940, Records of the NPS, National Historic Sites, Jefferson National Expansion Memorial, Record Group 79, box 2656.

52. Charles E. Peterson to Julian C. Spotts, Nov. 20, 1940, Records of the NPS, National Historic Sites, Jefferson National Expansion Memorial, Record Group 79, box 2656.

53. Newton B. Drury, "Memorandum for Mr. Demary," Dec. 13, 1940, Records of the NPS, National Historic Sites, Jefferson National Expansion Memorial, Record

Group 79, box 2656; "Statement of National Park Service Position Regarding Demolition of Old Custom House," Jan. 23, 1941, Records of the NPS, National Historic Sites, Jefferson National Expansion Memorial, Record Group 79, box 2641.

54. Ronald F. Lee to Newton B. Drury, Feb. 4, 1941, Records of the NPS, National Historic Sites, Jefferson National Expansion Memorial, Record Group 79, box 2642.

55. Brown, *Administrative History Jefferson National Expansion Memorial*, chap. 3, p. 12 [internet pagination].

56. *St. Louis Daily Globe-Democrat*, Mar. 23, 1941.

57. Roy E. Appleman, "Review and Comment, Byan Prospectus for Museum of Western Architecture, Jefferson National Expansion Memorial," Dec. 17, 1956, NPS, JNEM Files, box 3.

58. *St. Louis Daily Globe-Democrat*, Jan. 23, and April 3, 1947.

59. John A Kouwenhoven to Conrad L. Wirth, Oct. 6, 1958, Jackson E. Price to John A. Kouwenhoven, Oct. 20, 1958, Thomas C. Vint to Albert Simons, April 24, 1958, and M. H. Harvey to Conrad L. Wirth, July 25, 1958, NPS, JNEM Files, box 3.

60. Harold L. Ickes to John L. Cochran, Aug. 1, 1936, Records of the NPS, National Historic Sites, Jefferson National Expansion Memorial, Record Group 79, box 2633.

61. *St. Louis Post-Dispatch*, July 9, and Oct. 10, 1939.

62. *St. Louis Star-Times*, June 25, 1940.

63. *St. Louis Star-Times*, May 2, 1938.

64. Charles W. Porter, "The Purpose and Theme of the Jefferson National Expansion Memorial Project, St. Louis, Missouri, Together with Comments on the Proper Scope of the National Park Service's National Historic Site Project at that Place," Feb. 27, 1944, Records of the NPS, National Historic Sites, Jefferson National Expansion Memorial, Record Group 79, box 2647.

65. John A. Bryan to Julian C. Spotts, Feb. 1, 1945, Records of the NPS, National Historic Sites, Jefferson National Expansion Memorial, Record Group 79, box 2653; see also Porter, "The Purpose and Theme of the Jefferson National Expansion Memorial Project."

66. Newton B. Drury to Mr. Tilden, Feb. 19, 1945, Records of the NPS, National Historic Sites, Jefferson National Expansion Memorial, Record Group 79, box 2653; Bellavia and Bleam, *Cultural Landscape Report for Jefferson National Expansion Memorial*, 25–28.

67. John L. Nagle to Hermon C. Bumpus, Feb. 24, 1938, Records of the NPS, National Historic Sites, Jefferson National Expansion Memorial, Record Group 79, box 2636.

68. See Alvin Stauffer and Thomas A. Pitkin, "Historical Problems Raised by the Executive Order Authorizing the Jefferson National Expansion Memorial, St. Louis," April 11, 1939, NPS, JNEM Files, box 3; Porter, "The Purpose and Theme of the Jefferson National Expansion Memorial Project"; the inaccuracies of the executive order were raised earlier by opponents of the memorial as reason to reject the project—see Washington Post, Sept. 22, 1936.

69. "Temporary Exhibit Plan, National Expansion Room, Jefferson National Expansion Memorial," April 1942, Records of the NPS, National Historic Sites, Jefferson National Expansion Memorial, Record Group 79, box 2658.

70. Julian C. Spotts, "Concept of the Memorial, Together with Comments on Dr. Porter's Report of November, 27, 1944," Feb. 6, 1945, Records of the NPS, National Historic Sites, Jefferson National Expansion Memorial, Record Group 79, box 2653.

71. Julian C. Spotts, "Memorandum for the Director [Newton B. Drury]," Feb. 9, 1945, and Ned J. Burns [Note on

Spott's Memo], Feb. 1945, Records of the NPS, National Historic Sites, Jefferson National Expansion Memorial, Record Group 79, box 2653.

72. On the competition and its context, see: Hélène Lipstadt, "Co-Making the Modern Monument: The Jefferson National Expansion Memorial Competition and Saarinen's Gateway Arch," in Eric Mumford, ed., *Modern Architecture in St. Louis: Washington University and Postwar American Architecture, 1948–1973* (Chicago: University of Chicago Press, 2004), 5–25.

73. Jefferson National Expansion Memorial Association, *Architectural Competition for the Jefferson National Expansion Memorial Program, St. Louis, Missouri, 1947*, Records of the NPS, National Historic Sites, Jefferson National Expansion Memorial, Record Group 79, box 2641; for Park Service collaboration on the prospectus, see, for example, Newton B. Drury to Luther Ely Smith, Feb. 26, 1946, Records of the NPS, National Historic Sites, Jefferson National Expansion Memorial, Record Group 79, box 2653.

74. Richard Knight, *Saarinen's Quest: A Memoir* (San Francisco: William Stout Publishers, 2008), 38–40; Hélène Lipstadt, "The Gateway Arch, Designing America's First Modern Monument," in Eeva-Liisa Pelkonen and Donald Albrecht, editors, *Eero Saarinen: Shaping the Future* (New Haven: Yale University Press, 2006), 222–229; Lipstadt, "Co-Making the Modern Monument," 5–25; Antonio Román, *Eero Saarinen: An Architecture of Multiplicity* (London: Laurence King Publishing, 2002), 124–141; "audacious" assessment in *New York Times*, April 26, 1953.

75. Jefferson National Expansion Memorial Association, *Architectural Competition*; on interest in Williamsburg-like reconstruction and the tour of inspection to Williamsburg by city officials, see *St. Louis Star-Times*, Feb. 17, 1947.

76. Saarinen quoted in *St. Louis Post-Dispatch*, Mar. 7, 1948; see also Aline B. Louchheim's review in *New York Times*, Feb. 29, 1948.

77. *St. Louis Star-Times*, Feb. 19, 1948.

78. See Lipstadt, "Co-Making the Modern Monument," 17, 19; Mary McLeod, "The Battle for the Monument: The Vietnam Veterans Memorial," in Hélène Lipstadt, *The Experimental Tradition* (New York: Architectural League of New York, 1989), 115–137.

79. Bellavia and Bleam, *Cultural Landscape Report for Jefferson National Expansion Memorial*, 48, 53, 64.

80. Charles E. Peterson, "Before the Arch," 161.

81. The list maintained by the NPS contains a limited number of historic places in the United States that are considered "exception places." In 2008 the Missouri list included only thirty-six sites besides the Gateway Arch.

82. "Statement by Walter Metcalfe, Dr. Peter Raven, and Dr. Robert Archibald Concerning the St. Louis Riverfront and the Grounds of the Gateway Arch," May 8, 2008, Danforth Foundation, St. Louis, Missouri.

83. *St. Louis Post-Dispatch*, May 18, 2008.

CHAPTER SEVEN

Preservation and Destruction in Chicago

1. *Chicago Tribune*, April 26, 1856.

2. See, for example: William J. Murtagh, *Keeping Time: The History and Theory of Preservation in America* (Pittstown, N.J.: Main Street Press, 1988), 62–64.

3. Such a reading has recently been exemplified in the work of Randall Mason, *The Once and Future New York: Historic Preservation and the Modern City* (Minneapolis: University of Minnesota Press, 2009), and Vincent Leszynski Michael, "Preserving the Future: Historic Districts in New York and Chicago in the Late 20th Century" Ph.D. dissertation, Department of Art History, University of Illinois–Chicago Circle, 2007.

4. Daniel Bluestone, "Preservation and Renewal in Post–World War II Chicago," *Journal of Architectural Education*, 47 (May 1994): 210–223; Theodore W. Hild, "The Demolition of the Garrick Theater and the Birth of the Preservation Movement in Chicago," *Illinois Historical Journal* 88 (Summer 1995): 78–100; Richard Cahan, *They All Fall Down: Richard Nickel's Struggle to Save America's Architecture* (New York: Wiley, 1994); Michael, "Preserving the Future."

5. *Chicago Tribune*, June 13, 1855.

6. *Chicago Tribune*, May 7, 1906.

7. *Chicago Tribune*, Jan. 31, 1868.

8. *Chicago Tribune*, Mar. 19, 1875.

9. *Chicago Tribune*, Sept. 18, 1872.

10. *Chicago Tribune*, May 7, 1906.

11. Vincent Michael, "Chicago Water Tower & Pumping Station," in Alice Sinkevitch, ed., *AIA Guide to Chicago* (New York: Harcourt Brace, 1993), 107–108.

12. *Chicago Tribune*, June 21, 1911.

13. *Chicago Tribune*, Oct. 1 and 9, 1910; June 21, and Aug. 3, 1911; Mar. 7, 1926; July 29, 1926; February 27, 1949.

14. *Chicago Tribune*, May 6, 7, and 29, 1928; Mar. 13, 1929.

15. Editorial reprinted in *Chicago Tribune*, May 18, 1928.

16. *Chicago Tribune*, April 20, 1924.

17. *Chicago Tribune*, May 6, 1928.

18. *Chicago Tribune*, June 30, 1928.

19. *Chicago Tribune*, April 10, 1935.

20. Quoted in Mayor Edward J. Kelly to City Council of Chicago, Nov. 8, 1937, in *Journal of the Proceedings of the City Council of the City of Chicago, Illinois, for the Council Year 1937–1938* (Chicago: Fred Klein Co., 1938), 4725.

21. Mayor Edward J. Kelly to City Council of Chicago, April 15, 1936, in *Journal of the Proceedings of the City Council of the City of Chicago . . . 1935–1936* (Chicago: Fred Klein Co., 1936), 1588.

22. *Journal of the Proceedings of the City Council of the City of Chicago . . . 1936–1937* (Chicago: Fred Klein Co., 1937), 3654–3656.

23. *Chicago Tribune*, Aug. 13, 1899.

24. Mayor Edward J. Kelly to City Council of Chicago, Jan. 25, 1937, in *Journal of the Proceedings of the City Council of the City of Chicago . . . 1936–1937*, 3140.

25. Mayor Edward J. Kelly to City Council of Chicago, Nov. 24, 1937, in *Journal of the Proceedings of the City Council of the City of Chicago . . . 1937–1938*, 4780–4784.

26. Mayor Edward J. Kelly quoted in *Journal of the Proceedings of the of the City Council of the City of Chicago 1936–1937*, 3451.

27. *Chicago Tribune*, Nov. 18, 1932.

28. See Robert Bruegmann, "The Marquette Building and the Myth of the Chicago School," *Threshold*, No. 5/6 (Fall 1991): 7–18; Robert Bruegmann, "Myth of the Chicago School," in Charles Waldheim and Katerina Ray, eds., *Chicago Architecture: Histories, Revisions, Alternatives* (Chicago: University of Chicago Press, 2005): 15–29; Daniel Bluestone, *Constructing Chicago* (New Haven: Yale University Press, 1991), 105–151.

29. *Industrial Chicago* (Chicago: Goodspeed Publishing, 1891), vol. 1, p. 168.

30. *Chicago Tribune*, Mar. 29, 1925.

31. H. Laurence Miller, Jr., "On the 'Chicago School of Economics'," *Journal of Political Economy* 70 (Feb. 1962), 70–71.

32 *Chicago Tribune*, Sept. 22, 1912.

33. *Chicago Tribune*, June 28, 1914, also in 1914 the *Chicago Tribune* published a photograph of Maher's Stevenson House on Sheridan Road labeling it "an interesting example of the Chicago School of Residential Architecture"; see *Chicago Tribune*, July 5, 1914.

34. *Chicago Tribune*, Sept. 13, 1938.

35. Bruegmann, "Myth of the Chicago School."

36. Museum of Modern Art, "*Early Modern Architecture, Chicago 1870–1910*" [typescript catalog], (New York: Museum of Modern Art, 1933).

37. *Chicago Tribune*, June 20, 1933.

38. Hugh Morrison, *Louis Sullivan, Prophet of Modern Architecture* (New York: Museum of Modern Art and W. W. Norton, 1935), 270.

39. Sigfried Giedion, *Space, Time, and Architecture: The Growth of a New Tradition* (Cambridge: Harvard University Press, 1941); Carl Condit, *The Rise of the Skyscraper* (Chicago: University of Chicago Press, 1952); Carl Condit, *The Chicago School of Architecture: A History of Commercial and Public Buildings in the City Area, 1875-1925* (Chicago: University of Chicago Press, 1964); see also Reyner Banham, "A Walk in The Loop," *Chicago* 2 (Spring 1965): 24–28; Bluestone, *Constructing Chicago*, 106–108.

40. "The Shrinking Giant," *Newsweek*, Dec. 8, 1958, 76.

41. Raymond A. Mohl, "Race and Housing in the Postwar City: An Explosive History," *Journal of the Illinois State Historical Society* 94 (Spring 2001): 8–30; Amanda Irene Seligman, "'Apologies to Dracula, Werewolf, Frankenstein': White Homeowners and Blockbusters in Postwar Chicago," *Journal of the Illinois State Historical Society* 94 (Spring 2001): 70–95.

42. "An Encroaching Menace," *Life Magazine* April 11, 1955, 125–134.

43. "A New Rage to Reconstruct Central Chicago," *Architectural Forum*, 116 (May 1962): 114–115.

44. "The Chicago School," *Inland Architect* 1 (Oct. 1957): 15–16.

45. "The Chicago School," *Inland Architect* 1 (October 1957): 15–16.

46. Edward C. Logelin, "This Is Chicago Dynamic," *Inland Architect* 1 (October 1957): 9–10.

47. *Chicago Tribune*, Oct. 31, 1957.

48. Quoted in *Chicago Sun-Times*, Oct. 30, 1957.

49. *Chicago Sun-Times*, Oct. 31, 1957.

50. "Forum of Formidables," *Inland Architect* 1 (April 1958): 14–17.

51. George E. Danforth, "Mies van der Rohe," *Inland Architect* 7 (November 1963): 6.

52. *Chicago Tribune*, Mar. 19, 1957.

53. See Frederick T. Aschman to Van Allen Bradley, Jan. 11, 1956, and Thomas B. Stauffer, "Round Robin [memorandum]," April 24, 1956, Leon Despres Papers, box 40, Chicago Historical Society.

54. *Chicago Tribune*, Mar. 2, 1957.

55. *Chicago Tribune*, Mar. 2, 1957.

56. *Hyde Park Herald*, Dec. 25, 1957.

57. *Chicago Tribune*, July 18, and Aug. 19, 1957.

58. Hyde Park-Kenwood Community Conference, "Questions and Suggestions of Kenwood Block Groups on Urban Renewal Planning," Feb. 1956, Housing and Home Finance Agency Record, Urban Renewal Demonstration Case Files, Record Group 207, box 17, National Archives, Washington, D.C.

59. See Margaret M. Myerson, "Urban Redevelopment in Hyde Park" master's thesis, Department of Political Science, University of Chicago, March 1959; Peter H. Rossi and Robert H. Dentler, *The Politics of Urban Renewal* (New York: Free Press of Glencoe, 1961); on opposition, see Margery Frisbie, *An Alley in Chicago: The Ministry of a City Priest* (Kansas City, Mo.: Sheed & Ward, 1991), 94–110; John H. Sengstacke, "Are We Telling the Urban Renewal Story?" in *Renewing Chicago in the 60's* (Chicago: Metropolitan Center for Neighborhood Renewal, 1961): 55–61; *Chicago Tribune*, Jan. 31, 1957.

60. Brochure for the University Apartments, I. M. Pei, architect; Ruth Moore Papers, box 4, Chicago Historical Society.

61. *Chicago Tribune*, July 23, 1960.

62. Hyde Park-Kenwood Community Conference, *Segments of the Past* (Chicago: The Conference, 1962), n. p.

63. Ruth Moore, "A Second Life for Landmarks," *Chicago* 2 (Spring 1965): 28–31.

64. Historic American Buildings Survey Records, Library of Congress, Washington, D.C.

65. *Chicago Tribune*, Feb. 23, and May 28, 1964.

66. See Cahan, *They All Fall Down*. 139–141. Nickel also asserted that he lacked money to preserve the house; see *Chicago Tribune*, Feb. 23, 1964.

67. *Chicago Tribune*, Aug. 27, 1964.

68. Thomas B. Stauffer to Mr. Burch, Nov. 27, 1955; Thomas Stauffer to Jack Ringer, Jan. 3, 1967; box 1, Chicago Heritage Committee; Thomas Stauffer to Judge Augustine Bowe, June 20, 1962, box 2, Chicago Heritage Committee.

69. Earl H. Reed, "The Triangle Look—An Architectural Portrait," in *4th Annual Old Town Holiday, Art Fair* (Chicago: Menomonee Club, 1953), 37, 39.

70. Jessie Scott Blouke to William Heyer, Oct. 8, 1963, OTTA Papers.

71. Pierre Blouke, Pres., OTTA, to Triangle Members, May 1955, OTTA Papers.

72. *Chicago Tribune*, May 22, 1930.

73. *Chicago Tribune*, Dec. 7, 1930.

74. Earl H. Reed, "Report on the Historic American Buildings Survey in Northern Illinois to the Chicago Chapter of the American Institute of Architects," June 16, 1936, entry 7, State Organization Files, 1933-56, box 5 (Illinois), RG 515, National Archives, quoted in Lisa Pfueller Davidson and Martin J. Perschler, "The Historic American Buildings Survey During the New Deal Era: Documenting "a Complete Resume of the Builders' Art," *CRM* 1 (Fall 2003): 55; "Reed, Earl Howell, Jr.," *Who's Who in Chicago and Vicinity* (Chicago: A. N. Marquis Co., 1936), 832–833.

75. *Chicago Tribune*, June 10, 1954.

76. *Chicago Tribune*, Mar. 7, 1954.

77. Seymour Goldstein and Doe Goldstein, "Old Town Architecture," *16th Annual Old Town Holiday, Art Fair* (Chicago: Menomonee Club, 1965), 84.

78. John A. Holabird, Jr., "Old Town Architecture," *15th Annual Town Old Holiday, Art Fair* (Chicago: Menomonee Club, 1964), 4-7.

79. Herman Kogan, "A Sense of History, More or Less," *10th Annual Old Town Holiday, Art Fair* (Chicago: Menomonee Club, 1959), 55, 57, 59.

80. Walter Lister, Jr., "Old Town," *11th Annual Old Town Holiday, Art Fair* (Chicago: Menomonee Club, 1960), 28.

81 Walter Lister, Jr., "Old Town," 30.

82. *Chicago Tribune*, Nov. 19, and May 13, 1954; June 13, 1965.

83. *Chicago Tribune*, Aug. 31, 1961.

84. Both the 1961 and 1964 references are from Old Town Triangle Board of Directors to Triangle Residents, April 28, 1964, OTTA Papers.

85. Mid-North Neighborhood Association, "The Image of Mid-North," 1961, LCPA, Mid-North Neighborhood

Association, box 1, Special Collections and Archives, DePaul University Library, Chicago, Illinois.

86. *Chicago Tribune*, Jan. 29, 1959; Mar. 17, 1960; Dec. 6, 1964.

87. Urban Renewal Administration, Housing and Home Finance Agency, *Twenty Questions and Answers on Urban Renewal* (Washington, D.C.: U.S. Government Printing Office, Feb. 1963).

88. Barbara Snow, ed., "Preservation and Urban Renewal: Is Coexistence Possible?" *Antiques* 84 (Oct. 1963), 442-453.

89. Providence City Plan Commission, *College Hill. A Demonstration Study of Historic Area Renewal* (Providence: Sentry Offset Service, 1959), v; Urban Renewal Administration, Housing and Home Finance Agency, *Historic Preservation Through Urban Renewal* (Washington, D.C.: U.S. Government Printing Office, Jan. 1963).

90. Providence City Plan Commission, *College Hill*; Chicago Department of Urban Renewal, *A Preliminary Study: Preserving the Architectural Character of a Neighborhood* (Chicago: Department of Urban Renewal, 1964).

91. For examples of this view, see Sara Little, "Don't Chain Yourself to the Past," *House Beautiful* Feb. 1952, 66–72, 134; Joseph Mason, "Good Houses Never Die," *Good Housekeeping* July 1950, 84–86; "This MODERN House Is 150 Years Old," *House Beautiful* Nov. 1950, 236–239; Cynthia Kellogg, "Modern House with a Past," *New York Times Magazine*, Jan. 24, 1960, 50–51; "Today's Transitional Houses," *House & Garden*, Oct. 1954, 174–179.

92. Earl H. Reed to Preservation Officers/Circular Letter, Sept. 26, 1956, Committee on Historic Resources, box 1948–1969, AIA Archives, Washington, D.C.

93. "Pullman Building to Go but Its Legends Will Linger," *Sun Times*, Oct. 9, 1955.

94. Historic American Buildings Survey Records, Library of Congress, Washington, D.C.; *Chicago Tribune*, June 19, 1958; Jan. 12, 1959; August 22, 1958; Jan. 31, 1965; Feb. 14, Oct. 3, and May 15, 1965.

95. Leonard S. Eisenberg [Manager, Arthur Rubloff & Co.] to Georgie Anne Geyer, Dec. 8, 1961, box 1, Chicago Heritage Committee; see Georgie Anne Geyer, "Razing of Historic Buildings Brings City World Stigma," *Chicago Daily News*, Dec. 6, 1961

96. Hild, "The Demolition of the Garrick Theater and the Birth of the Preservation Movement in Chicago," 78–100.

97. Cahan, *They All Fall Down*, 103–119.

98. Mies's position quoted in *Chicago Sun-Times*, June 14, 1960; Corbusier quoted in "Corbu and Stauffer Comment on Garrick Theatre," *Progressive Architecture* 42 (June, 1961): 208.

99. *Chicago Sun-Times*, June 9, 11, 13, 14, and 18, 1960.

100. Richard Nickel to Edward D. Stone, May 10, 1960, box 1, RN Papers, Chicago Historical Society.

101. Quoted in Elinor Rickey, "What Chicago Could Be Proud Of," *Harper's Magazine*, December 1961, 34–39.

102. See letter to the editor, *Chicago Sun-Times*, May 17, 1960.

103. Richard H. Howland to David B. Wallerstein, June 28, 1960, in National Trust Library, University of Maryland, College Park. The owners had already rejected pleas from the National Trust for Historic Preservation to renovate the building and attract new tenants at higher rents. Richard H. Howland, president of the Trust, insisted that their idea came not from "mere antiquarians suggesting that the building be preserved intact as an architectural monument" but rather from "realists in today's world."

104. *The People of the State of Illinois on the Relation of Marbro Corporation and Atlas Wrecking Company, Plaintiffs-Appellants, v. George L. Ramsey, Commissioner of Buildings of the City of Chicago, Defendants; Appellate Court of Illinois, First District, Second Division; 28 Ill. App. 2d 252; 171 N.E. 2d 246; 1960 Ill. App.*

105. See Cahan, *They All Fall Down*.

106. Ruth Moore, "Architectural Art in Razed Buildings to Be Saved for Future," *Chicago Sun-Times*, Sept. 25, 1960.

107. Dorothy Johnson, "Handbook for Structural Cannibalism," *Chicago* 3 (Winter, 1966): 53–54.

108. Thomas J. Schlereth, "The City as Artifact," in James R. Grossman, Ann Durkin Keating, and Janice L. Reiff, eds. *Encyclopedia of Chicago* (Chicago: University of Chicago Press, 2004), 288.

109. Norman Ross, "Chicago Is Destroying Architectural Heritage," *Inland Architect* 6 (Sept. 1962): 6; similar sentiments expressed in *Chicago Sun-Times*, Nov. 27, 1964.

110. Ruth Moore, "The Citizens Are Learning," *Inland Architect* 4 (April 1961): 9.

111. Richard Nickel to John Vinci, June 21, 1960, box 2, RN Papers, Chicago Historical Society.

112. *Chicago Tribune*, Nov. 20, 1960.

113. *Chicago Tribune*, Oct. 4 and 8, 1962; Aug. 15, 1963; May 14, 1964.

114. *Chicago Tribune*, Mar. 17, 1963.

115. Ruth Moore, "A City Reborn," *Chicago Sun-Times*, Oct. 14, 1958.

116. *Chicago Tribune*, Jan. 25, 1895; see also Bluestone, *Constructing Chicago*, 174.

117. Noble W. Lee to Thomas B. Stauffer, Mar. 11, 1963; Thomas B. Stauffer to Noble W. Lee, Mar. 12, and April 2, 1963, box 1, Chicago Heritage Committee; David Norris to Richard Nickel, Dec. 29, 1961, box 1, Richard Nickel Papers, Chicago Historical Society.

118. *Chicago Tribune*, May 25, 1968, and Feb. 27, 1969

119. See Vincent Scully, *American Architecture and Urbanism* (New York: Praeger, 1969).

120. "News Press Release from the Office of Senator Paul H. Douglas," July 10, 1961, in National Trust Library, University of Maryland, College Park.

121. Earl H. Reed to David D. Henry, Mar. 6, 1961; Thomas B. Stauffer to Richard J. Daley, Mar. 6, 1961; Ben Weese to Editor of the *Chicago Sun-Times*, Oct. 5, 1961; Minutes of the Chicago Heritage Committee, Sept. 7, 1961, box 1, Chicago Heritage Committee Papers; see also *Chicago Tribune*, June 22, 1961; *Chicago Sun-Times*, Feb. 14, 1961, and Sept. 14, 1961.

122. *Chicago Sun-Times*, Oct. 31, 1957.

123. Carl Condit, "Opinion of the People, letter to editor," *Chicago Sun-Times*, Sept. 23, 1960; Richard Nickel wrote to the developers of the Cable Building site and complimented them on the design of the new building, Richard Nickel to Ray Henson, Continental Assurance Co., Feb. 12, 1962, box 2, Richard Nickel Papers, Chicago Historical Society..

124. Ben Weese, "The Republic Building," *Inland Architect* 4 (Dec. 1960): 9.

125. Rand, McNally & Company, *Guide to Chicago and Environs* (Chicago: Rand, McNally, 1927); Arthur Muschenheim, *A Guide to Chicago Architecture* (Chicago: Skidmore, Ownigs & Merrill, 1962); Art Institute of Chicago, *A Selective Guide to Chicago Architecture* (Chicago: Art Institute, 1963).

126. Richard Nickel to Samuel A. Lichtmann, Nov. 9, 1962; Richard Nickel to Thomas Stauffer, June 17, 1962; Thomas Stauffer to Judge Augustine Bowe, Chair Commission of Chicago Architectural Landmarks, June 20, 1962; Tom Stauffer to Prof. Condit, Nov. 18, 1962; Carl Condit to Thomas Stauffer, Nov. 29, 1962, box 2, Chicago Heritage Committee.

127. *Chicago Tribune*, Feb. 21, 1969.

CHAPTER EIGHT
Chicago's Mecca Flat Blues

1. For a discussion, see Daniel Bluestone, "Academics in Tennis Shoes: Historic Preservation and the Academy," *Journal of the Society of Architectural Historians* 58 (Sept. 1999): 300–307; see also Patricia Mooney-Melvin, "Professional Historians and 'Destiny's Gate,'" *Public Historian* 17 (Summer 1995), 9–24; Richard Cahan, *They All Fall Down: Richard Nickel's Struggle to Save America's Architecture* (Washington, D.C.: Preservation Press, 1994); Daniel Bluestone, "Preservation and Renewal in Post-World War II Chicago," *Journal of Architectural Education* 47 (May 1994): 210–223; Theodore W. Hild, "The Demolition of the Garrick Theater and the Birth of the Preservation Movement in Chicago," Illinois *Historical Journal* 188 (1995): 79–100.

2. William H. Jordy, "The Commercial Style and the 'Chicago School,'" *Perspectives in American History* 1 (1967): 390–400; focusing on the work of a single yet prolific firm, architectural historian Robert Bruegmann offers a more nuanced and insightful view of Chicago architecture and urbanism in his book. *The Architects and the City: Holabird and Roche of Chicago, 1880–1918* (Chicago: University of Chicago Press, 1997); see also essays collected in *Chicago Architecture, 1872–1922: Birth of a Metropolis.* ed. John Zukowsky (Munich: Prestel-Verlag, 1987); a fine exception to the relative dearth of serious treatments of the Chicago apartment is Neil Harris, *Chicago Apartments: A Century of Lakefront Luxury* (New York: Acanthus Press, 2004).

3. *Industrial Chicago: The Building Interests* (Chicago: Good-speed Publishing Company, 1891), 1:240.

4. Carroll William Westfall, "Chicago's Better Tall Apartment Buildings, 1871–1923," *Architectura* 21 (Jan. 1992): 178; see also Westfall, "From Home to Towers: A Century of Chicago's Best Hotels and Tall Apartment Buildings," in *Chicago Architecture, 1872–1922*, 266–289.

5. *Chicago Tribune*, March 3, 1905.

6. Elizabeth C. Cromley, *Alone Together: A History of New York's Early Apartments* (Ithaca, N.Y.: Cornell University Press, 1990); Gwendolyn Wright, *Building the Dream: A Social History of Housing in America* (New York: Pantheon, 1981), 96–113, 135–151.

7. *Chicago Tribune*, Sept. 12, 1891; see also the building note in *Industrial Chicago* 1:591–592, and Carl W. Condit, *The Chicago School of Architecture: A History of Commercial and Public Building in the Chicago Area, 1875–1925* (Chicago: University of Chicago Press, 1964), 156–157.

8. Westfall, "Chicago's Better Tall Apartment Buildings," 184.

9. Apartment house advertisements championing "exclusive" suburban areas often appeared in the *Chicago Tribune*. For example, advertisements for Chicago's Pattington Apartments declared, "This beautiful property is located in the exclusive residence section of the north shore" (*Chicago Tribune*, Mar. 17, 1905). Advertisements for a Clarendon Avenue apartment declared that its apartments were "overlooking large private lawns" of adjacent single-family residences (*Chicago Tribune*, April 21, 1907).

10. *Chicago Tribune*, Sept. 12, 1891.

11. In 1898, upon completing the Richmond Court Apartments in the Boston suburb of Brookline, Ralph Adams Cram and Bertram Grosvenor Goodhue declared that the courtyard plan was "quite unusual in this country, though frequently found abroad." With the "effect of a large English Manor," Richmond Court took on the "qualities of strength, dignity and repose, while the court is not forced into fulfilling the ignominious function of a mere light well." Quoted in Douglass Shand Tucci, *Built in Boston: City and Suburb, 1800–1950* (Boston: New York Graphic Society, 1978), 118–119.

12. E. S. Hanson, "As the Editor Sees It," *Apartment House* 1 (Jan. 1911): 18.

13. Herbert Croly, "Some Apartment Houses in Chicago," *Architectural Record* 21 (Feb. 1907): 119–130.

14. "The 'Mecca' Hotel," advertisement, published on the back of McNally & Company's *Standard Map of the Columbian Exposition and City of Chicago* (Chicago: Rand McNally & Company, 1893), refers to the balconies as "promenade balconies." Copy in Chicago Historical Society.

15. *Chicago Tribune*, July 15, 1888.

16. *Chicago Tribune*, Sept. 12, 1891.

17. Daniel Bluestone, *Constructing Chicago* (New Haven: Yale University Press, 1991), 105–51.

18. Johann Friedrich Geist, *Arcades: The History of a Building Type* (Cambridge: M.I.T Press, 1983), 3–114.

19. Cromley, *Alone Together*, 48, 55, 61, 129, 145, 148, 164, 195, 200; Elizabeth Hawes, *New York, New York: How the Apartment House Transformed the Life of the City (1869–1930)* (New York: Knopf, 1993), 134–135, 161–167; Iain C. Taylor, "The Insanitary Housing Question and Tenement Dwellings in Nineteenth-Century in Liverpool," in *Multi-Storey Living: The British Working-Class*, ed. Anthony Sutcliffe (London: Croom Helm, 1974), 41–87; Devereux Bowly, Jr., The *Poorhouse: Subsidized Housing in Chicago, 1895–1976* (Carbondale, Ill: Southern Illinois University Press, 1978), 1–4; Cristina Cocchioni and Mario De Grassi, *La Casa Popolare a Roma* (Rome: Kappa 1984); Johann Friedrich Geist and Klaus Kurvers, *Das Berliner Mietshaus, 1862–1945* (Munich: Prestel, 1984).

20. *Chicago Tribune*, Aug. 21, 1892; *Economist* June 15, 1901, 775.

21. "Synopsis of Building News," *Inland Architect and News Record* 20 (Dec. 1892), 58; Condit, *The Chicago School of Architecture*, 157–158; see also C. W. Westfall, "The Civilized 2800 Block on Pine Grove Av.," *Inland Architect* 18 (July 1974), 13–18; the Sanborn Fire Insurance Map for 1894 records only foundations for the Brewster, suggesting that it was still incomplete in 1894; the Blue Book does not record residents until 1897.

22. Frank A. Randall, *History of the Development of Building Construction in Chicago* (Urbana, Ill.: University of Illinois Press, 1949), 298.

23. Glen E. Holt and Dominic A. Pacyga, *Chicago: A Historical Guide to the Neighborhoods: The Loop and South Side* (Chicago: Chicago Historical Society, 1979), 49–57.

24. "Flats for the Armour Mission," *Inland Architect and Builder 8* (Jan. 1887): 101.

25. Harper Leech and John Charles Carroll, *Armour and His Times* (New York: D. Appleton & Co., 1938), 211–212.

26. *Chicago Tribune*, Sept. 12, 1891, and April 21, 1901, "The 'Mecca' Hotel" advertisement (see n. 14); Cook County Deed Books, Chicago, Illinois.

27. Manuscript Population Schedule, Twelfth Census of the United States, 1900, Chicago, Cook County, Illinois, enumeration district 84.

28. Allan H. Spear, *Black Chicago: The Making of a Negro Ghetto, 1890–1920* (Chicago: University of Chicago Press, 1967); Thomas Lee Philpott, *The Slum and the Ghetto: Immigrants, Blacks, and Reformers in Chicago, 1880–1930* (New York: Oxford University Press, 1978).

29. Manuscript Population Schedule, Thirteenth Census of the United States, 1910, Chicago, Cook County, Illinois, enumeration district 214.

30. *Chicago Tribune*, April 8, 1911, and Feb. 2, 1912; see "Franklin T. Pember," in *History and Biography of*

Washington County and the Town of Queensbury, New York, with Historical Notes on the Various Towns, ed. Gresham Publishing Co. (Richmond, Ind.: Gresham Publishing, 1894), 287–291.

31. Commission on Chicago landmarks, *Black Metropolis Historic District* (Chicago: Commission on Chicago Landmarks, 1994), 45.

32. Advertisements capture the transition of the Mecca from white to black; see *Chicago Tribune*, April 9, 1911, and *Chicago Defender*, May 11, 1912. On racial transition in the Black Belt, see *Black Metropolis Historic District*, 45.

33. Philpott, *The Slum and the Ghetto*, 177–179; *Chicago Tribune*, July 29, 1919; Chicago Commission on Race Relations, *The Negro in Chicago. A Study of Race Relations and a Race Riot* (Chicago: University of Chicago Press, 1922).

34. Accounts vary on when the first black tenants moved into the Mecca; based on advertisements, it seems clearly to have happened between 1911 and 1912; *Life* magazine reported in 1951 that the first blacks moved in "by 1912"; see "The Mecca: Chicago's Showiest Apartment Has Given Up All but the Ghost," *Life*, Nov. 19, 1951, 133; *Harper's* quoted a tenant in 1950 as saying that in 1917 "white people hadn't been gone so long"; see John Bartlow Martin, "The Strangest Place in Chicago," *Harper's Magazine* 201 (December 1950): 89.

35. Manuscript Population Schedule, Fourteenth Census of the United States, 1920, Chicago, Cook County, Illinois, enumeration district 84.

36. *Black Metropolis Historic District*, 5–6.

37. *Chicago Tribune*, Mar. 29, 1943.

38. Gwendolyn Brooks, *In the Mecca* (New York: Harper & Row, 1968), 5–31.

39. Irene Macauley, *The Heritage of Illinois Institute of Technology* (Chicago: Illinois Institute of Technology, 1978), 36.

40. Macauley, *Heritage of Illinois Institute of Technology*, 39–40.

41. "A Sketch of James D. Cunningham, Head of Republic Flow Meters," in Philip Hampson, *The Road to Success* (Chicago: Chicago Tribune Company, 1953), 37–39.

42. James Cunningham Report to the Board of Trustees, May 17, 1937, in Armour Institute of Technology Board of Trustees Minutes, 1934–1940; this report and other manuscripts cited are located, unless stated otherwise, in the Illinois Institute of Technology Archives, Paul V. Calvin Library, Illinois Institute of Technology, Chicago.

43. Bowly, The *Poorhouse*, 27–32; Arnold R. Hirsch, *Making the Second Ghetto: Race and Housing in Chicago, 1940–1960* (New York: Cambridge University Press, 1983).

44. Minutes of Annual Meeting of the Board of Trustees, Oct. 11, 1937, in Armour Institute of Technology Board of Trustees Minutes, 1934–1940.

45. Henry T. Heald, "President's Report, for the Year Ended August 31, 1940," in Illinois Institute of Technology Board of Trustees Minutes, vol. 1, 1940–1941.

46. See, for example, Illinois Institute of Technology, Minutes of the Special Meeting of the Board of Trustees, July 9, 1943, Illinois Institute of Technology Board of Trustees Minutes, vol. 2, 1942–1943.

47. Buildings and Grounds Committee Minutes, May 17, 1944, Board of Trustees of Illinois Institute of Technology, 1943–1947, box HB 12; see similar concern in original campus proposal, in James Cunningham Report to the Board of Trustees, May 17, 1937, in Armour Institute of Technology Board of Trustees Minutes, 1934–1940.

48. James Cunningham Report to the Board of Trustees, May 17, 1937, in Armour Institute of Technology Board of Trustees Minutes, 1934–1940.

49. Illinois Institute of Technology, Executive Committee of the Board of Trustees, Minutes of Meeting, Sept. 24, 1941, box HB 4, 1941–1944.

50. Metropolitan Housing Council, "The Case of the Mecca Building," *Housing News* 2 (Aug. 1942): 1–2; typescript newsletter in Board of Trustees of Illinois Institute of Technology, box HB 2; see also City Council of Chicago, Committee on Housing, "Report of the Subcommittee to Investigate Housing Among Colored People," *Journal of the Proceedings of the City Council of Chicago*, June 19, 1941, 4982–4987; Hirsch, *Making the Second Ghetto*, 20, 22.

51 Newton C. Farr to Henry T. Heald, July 31, 1942, and Henry T. Heald to Newton C. Farr, July 31, 1942, Board of Trustees of Illinois Institute of Technology, box HB 2.

52 *Chicago Defender*, May 1, 1943.

53. *Chicago Defender*, May 15, 1943.

54. *Chicago Defender*, May 15, 1943; Newton Farr, "Report on the Mecca," Minutes of the Regular Meeting of the Board of Trustees, Illinois Institute of Technology, April 12, 1943.

55. *Chicago Defender*, June 5, 1943; draft of "Petition for Mandamus," Board of Trustees of Illinois Institute of Technology, box HB 2.

56. Illinois Institute of Technology to the Tenants of the Mecca Building, May 1943, Board of Trustees of Illinois Institute of Technology, box HB 2.

57. Illinois Institute of Technology, Minutes of the Special Meeting of the Board of Trustees, July 9, 1943, and Aug. 9, 1943, Illinois Institute of Technology Board of Trustees Minutes, vol. 2, 1942–1943; "Black Belt" reference is from James Cunningham Report to the Board of Trustees, May 17, 1937, in Armour Institute of Technology Board of Trustees Minutes, 1934–1940.

58. "Additional Considerations Which Should be Given Weight by the War Department in Determining Acceptable Bid," Board of Trustees of Illinois Institute of Technology, box HB 1.

59. Henry T. Heald To Henry L. Stimson, Sept. 7, 1943; Henry T. Heald to Sydney G. McAllister, Sept. 6, 1943, in box HB 1.

60. Henry T. Heald, *Reclaiming Chicago's Blighted Areas* (Chicago: Metropolitan Housing Council, 1946), Metropolitan Housing Council pamphlet without pagination located in Chicago Historical Society.

61. Wilford G. Winholtz to Members of the Chicago Land Clearance Commission, Jan. 26, 1948, South Side Planning Board Files, July 1947 to April 1950, Board of Trustees of Illinois Institute of Technology, box HB 12.

62. Henry T. Heald to Chicago Housing Authority, Oct. 4, 1944, in Minutes of the Illinois Institute of Technology, Buildings and Grounds Committee, Oct. 4, 1944, Board of Trustees Buildings and Grounds Committee, 1943–1947, box HB 12.

63. Bowly, *The Poorhouse*, 61–65

64. Kevin Harrington, "Order, Space, Proportion—Mies's Curriculum at IIT," in *Mies van der Rohe: Architect as Educator, Catalog for Exhibition, June 6–July 12, 1986* (Chicago: Illinois Institute of Technology, 1968), 49–68.

65. Skidmore, Owings & Merrill, Architects, "Outline of Preliminary Report, Illinois Institute of Technology Housing Report," c. 1945; see also Illinois Institute of Technology, Buildings and Grounds Committee, Oct. 4, 1944, Board of Trustees Buildings and Grounds Committee, 1943–1947, box HB 12.

66. "Illinois Tech Replans 16 City Blocks," *Architectural Forum* 85 (Sept. 1946): 102–103.

67. SOM, "Outline of Preliminary Report, Illinois Institute of Technology Housing Report," c. 1945; Illinois Institute of Technology, Building and Grounds Committee Minutes, 1943–1955, box HB 12.

68. SOM, "Outline of Preliminary Report."

69. See Oscar C. Brown to Milton Mumford, Feb. 9, 1948, and Wilford C. Winholtz to Oscar C. Brown, Feb. 13, 1948, President Henry T. Heald Papers, South Side Planning Board Files, box HB 63; Oscar C. Brown, *Some Facts and Factors on Housing for Negroes in Chicago* (Chicago: Oscar C. Brown Corporation, 1953), Oscar C. Brown Corporation pamphlet, no pagination, located in Chicago Historical Society.

70. Buildings and Grounds Committee of the Board of Trustees Minutes, Feb. 17, 1950, in Illinois Institute of Technology, Buildings and Grounds Committee Minutes, 1943–1955.

71. *Chicago Tribune*, May 23, 1950.

72. Quoted in *Chicago Daily News*, Aug. 14, 1951.

73. *Journal of the Proceedings of the City Council of Chicago*, Mar. 24, 1950, 5998, and Oct. 25, 1950, 7057.

74. *Chicago Defender*, May 27, 1950.

75. *Chicago Tribune*, May 23, 1950.

76. See ibid.; "The Mecca's End," *Newsweek* Jan. 14, 1952, 23–24.

77. "The Mecca's End," 23–24; *Chicago Sun Times*, Dec. 30, 1951.

78. Martin, "The Strangest Place in Chicago," 86–97.

79. Martin, "The Strangest Place in Chicago," 86.

80. Quoted in "The Mecca's End," 24.

81. "The Mecca, Chicago's Showiest Apartment Has Given Up All but the Ghost," 133.

82. Jim Hurlbut, "WMAQ Radio Script, June 6, 1950," President Henry T. Heald Papers, box HB 40.

83. Kevin Harrington, "S. R. Crown Hall," in *AIA Guide to Chicago*, ed. Alice Sinkevitch (San Diego, 1993), 376–377; Commission on Chicago Landmarks, *S. R. Crown Hall, Illinois Institute of Technology, 3360 S. State St., Preliminary Staff Summary of Information* (Chicago: Commission on Chicago Landmarks, 1996).

84. Eero Saarinen, quoted in Macauley, *The Heritage of Illinois Institute of Technology*, 78.

85. Bluestone, "Preservation and Renewal in Post-World War II Chicago."

CHAPTER NINE

A Virginia Courthouse Square

1. *New York Times*, Nov. 1, 2, 3, 6, 7, 8, and 10 1998. See Thomas Jefferson Foundation, "Report of the Research Committee on Thomas Jefferson and Sally Hemings," January 2000, *http://www.monticello.org/plantation/hemingscontro/hemings_report.html;* see also Annette Gordon-Reed, *Thomas Jefferson and Sally Hemings: An American Controversy* (Charlottesville: University Press of Virginia, 1997); and Annette Gordon-Reed, *The Hemingses of Monticello: An American Family* (New York: Norton, 2008).

2. J. B. Jackson, "Several American Landscapes," in Ervin H. Zube, *Landscapes: Selected Writings of J. B. Jackson* (Amherst: University of Massachusetts Press, 1970), 43.

3. Joseph S. Wood, *The New England Village* (Baltimore: Johns Hopkins University Press, 1997), 1–8; see also Joseph S. Wood and M. Steinitz, "A World We Have Gained: House, Common, and Village in New England," *Journal of Historical Geography* 18 (1992): 105–120; Dona Brown, *Inventing New England: Regional Tourism in the Nineteenth-Century* (Washington, D.C.: Smithsonian Institution Press, 1995); William Butler, "Another City upon a Hill: Litchfield, Connecticut, and the Colonial Revival," in Alan Axelrod, ed., *The Colonial Revival in America* (New York: Norton 1985), 15–51; Martyn Bowden, "Invented Tradition and Academic Convention in Geographical Thought About New England," *GeoJournal* 26 (Feb. 1992): 187–194.

4. Patricia Mooney-Melvin, "Harnessing the Romance of the Past: Preservation, Tourism, and History," *Public Historian* 13 (Spring 1991): 35–48; Richard J. Roddewig, "Selling America's Heritage . . . Without Selling Out," *Preservation Forum* 2 (Fall 1988): 2–7; Peter H. Brink, "Heritage Tourism in the U.S.A.: Grassroots Efforts to Combine Preservation and Tourism, *APT Bulletin* 29 (1998), 59–63;

5. Martha Norkunas, *The Politics of Public Memory: Tourism, History, and Ethnicity in Monterey, California* (Albany: State University of New York Press, 1993).

6 An excellent essay on editing layers of history in Virginia, dealing with Jamestown and the Shenandoah National Park, is Audrey J. Horning, "Of Saints and Sinners: Mythic Landscapes of the Old and New South," in Paul A. Shackel, ed., *Myth, Memory, and the Making of the American Landscape* (Gainesville: University Press of Florida, 2001), 21–46.

7. PMA Planners & Architects and Graham Landscape Architecture, *The Historic Court Square Enhancement Plan Prepared for the City of Charlottesville, Virginia* (Newport News, Va., 2000), 5.

8. PMA, *Historic Court Square*, 1, 3.

9. Michele H. Bogart, *Public Sculpture and the Civic Ideal in New York City, 1890–1930* (Chicago: University of Chicago Press, 1989), 55–59; William H. Wilson, *The City Beautiful Movement* (Baltimore: Johns Hopkins University Press, 1989); Daniel Bluestone, "Detroit's City Beautiful and the Problem of Commerce," *Journal of the Society of Architectural Historians* 47 (Sept. 1988), 245–262.

10. *Daily Progress*, Nov. 10, 1908; see A. Robert Kuhlthau and Harry W. Webb, "Sculpture in and Around Charlottesville: Confederate Memorials," *Magazine of Albemarle County History* 48 (1990): 1–57.

11. *Daily Progress*, April 22, 1907.

12. *Daily Progress*, Aug. 25, 1908.

13. *Daily Progress*, Jan. 1, 1909.

14. *Daily Progress*, Aug. 25, 1908.

15. *Daily Progress*, Jan. 12, 1909.

16. *Daily Progress*, Jan. 9, 1909.

17. Kirk Savage, *Standing Soldiers, Kneeling Slaves* (Princeton: Princeton University Press, 1997), 162–208.

18. Savage, *Standing Soldiers.*

19. *Program of Order of Procession—Confederate Monument Unveiling: Wednesday, May 5, 1909*, pamphlet, Charlottesville-Albemarle Historical Collection, Jefferson-Madison Regional Library, Charlottesville, Va.

20. Homer Richerd, ed., *Memorial History of the John Bowie Strange Camp, United Confederate Veterans* (Charlottesville: Michie Co., 1920), 51.

21. Thirteenth Census of the United States, 1910, Charlottesville enumeration schedules.

22. The names and racial composition of residents around Court Square is gathered from Charlottesville city directories and the United States Population Census returns, both of which give names and designate race in the early twentieth century.

23. Minutes of the Albemarle County Board of Supervisors, Mar. 18, 1914; located in the Albemarle County Clerk's Office.

24. *Daily Progress*, Mar. 19, 1914.

25. James Alexander, *Early Charlottesville: Recollections of James Alexander, 1828–1874* (Charlottesville, Va.: Michie Co., 1963), 5.

26. This account is developed using United States Census records, Charlottesville city directories, and Charlottesville land deeds and tax records.

27. *Daily Progress*, Dec. 9, 1916.

28. *Daily Progress*, July 6, 1918.

29. *Daily Progress*, Feb. 13, 1919.

30. Paul Goodloe McIntire to Edwin A. Alderman, June 10, 1918, and Edwin A. Alderman to Paul Goodloe McIntire, June 4, 1918, RG-2/1/2.472 Subseries IV, box 2, Special Collections, University of Virginia Library.

31. Paul Goodloe McIntire to W. O. Watson, Mar. 27, 1919, RG-2/1/2.472 Subseries IV, box 2, Special Collections, University of Virginia Library.

32. Anson Phelps Stokes to Edwin A. Alderman, Feb. 20, 1919, RG-2/1/2.472 Subseries III, box 2, and Edwin A. Alderman to Paul Goodloe McIntire, Mar. 4, 1919, RG-1001, Alderman Papers, Special Collections, University of Virginia Library.

33. William R. Wilkerson and William G. Shenkir, *Paul G. McIntire: Businessman and Philanthropist* (Charlottesville: McIntire School of Commerce Foundation, 1988), 29–30.

34. *The Unveiling of the Lewis-Clark Statue at Midway Park in the City of Charlottesville, Virginia, November Twenty-One, Nineteen Hundred Nineteen*, ed. W. M. Forrest, (Charlottesville: City of Charlottesville, 1919), 10.

35. *Daily Progress*, Jan. 21, 1926.

36. *Washington Herald*, May 9, 1920.

37. *Daily Progress*, Feb. 13, 1919.

38. *Daily Progress*, Feb. 13, 1919.

39. W. O. Watson to Paul Goodloe McIntire, Oct. 16, 1917, Albemarle Charlottesville Historical Society (hereafter ACHS).

40. *Daily Progress*, Oct. 19, 1921.

41. Savage, *Standing Soldiers*, 133, 150, 196.

42. W. O. Watson to Charles Keck, Oct. 7, 1920, and Charles Keck to W. O. Watson, Oct. 8, 1920, ACHS; *Daily Progress*, Nov. 16, 1966.

43. L. M. Bowman to Charles Keck, July 16, 1921, L. M. Bowman to Charles Keck, Nov. 3, 1920, and Paul Goodloe McIntire to W. O. Watson, telegram, July 1916, ACHS.

44. *Daily Progress*, Oct. 19, 1921.

45. *Daily Progress*, Mar. 28, 1921.

46. See Albemarle County Minute Book, vol. 15, Nov. 6, 1855, 240–241; Albemarle County Board of Supervisors Minutes (1872–1882), July 29, 1874, 103; Nov. 19, 1878, 223–224; Albemarle County Board of Supervisors Minutes (1892–1900), Sept. 30, 1892, 27, and April 25, 1895, 102.

47. Albemarle County Board of Supervisors Minutes, April 29 and Aug. 17, 1921.

48. *Daily Progress*, May 4, 1921.

49. *Daily Progress*, April 4, 1921.

50. *Daily Progress*, Feb. 20 and 25 and April 22, 1907.

51. *Daily Progress*, April 11, 1907.

52. *Daily Progress*, Mar. 12, 1906.

53. *Daily Progress*, Nov. 29, 1927.

54. *Daily Progress*, April 4, 1921.

55. *Daily Progress*, Oct. 28, 1924.

56. *Daily Progress*, July 15 and 16, 1924.

57. For a fuller discussion, see Daniel Bluestone, "Charlottesville Skyscrapers, 1919–1929: Ego, Imagination, and Modern Form in a Historic Landscape," *Magazine of Albemarle County History* 66 (2008): 1–34.

58. *Daily Progress*, Oct. 28, 1924.

59. *Hill's Charlottesville City Directory, 1931* (Richmond: Hill Directory Co., 1931), 41.

60. *Daily Progress*, April 8, 1924.

61. K. Edward Lay, *The Architecture of Jefferson Country: Charlottesville and Albemarle County, Virginia* (Charlottesville: University Press of Virginia, 2000), 157–158.

62. *Daily Progress*, June 16, 1937.

63. Albemarle County Board of Supervisors Minutes (1934–1943), (Feb. 17, 1938), 234, and (Mar. 2, 1938), 236.

64. *Daily Progress*, Mar. 12, 1938.

65. Albemarle County Board of Supervisors Minutes (1934–1943), (May 18, 1938), 254.

66. Albemarle County Board of Supervisors Minutes (1934–1943), (May 18, 1938), 253.

67. For R. C. Vandegrift, architect, see *Daily Progress*, July 27, 1901; for fire, see *Daily Progress*, Feb. 22, 1932; for Peyton purchase, see Charlottesville City Deed Book, vol. 89, p. 200; for additional information, see "Francis Bradley Peyton Junior Last Will and Testament," Charlottesville City Will Book, vol. 9, pp. 263–268, Office of the Clerk of the Circuit Court, Charlottesville, Va. The apartments were converted to offices after Peyton's death in 1962. See also Howard Newlon, *A People Called: The University Baptist Church and Its Predecessor, High Street Baptist, Charlottesville, Virginia, 1900–2000* (Charlottesville, Va.: University Baptist Church, 2000). Aaron Wunsch encouraged me to pursue the High Street Baptist Church conversion.

68. *Daily Progress*, Oct. 5, 1938.

69. Albemarle County Board of Supervisors Minutes (1934–1943), (May 18, 1938), 256.

70. *Daily Progress*, Oct. 5, 1938.

71 Marc Leepson, *Saving Monticello: The Levy Family's Epic Quest to Rescue the House That Jefferson Built* (New York: Free Press, 2001).

72. *Daily Progress*, Sept. 13, 1938.

73 *Daily Progress*, Nov. 4, 1938.

74. *Daily Progress*, Nov. 4, 1938.

75. *Daily Progress*, Nov. 4, 1938.

76. *Daily Progress*, Aug. 2, 1938.

77. *Daily Progress*, Aug. 5, 1938.

78. http://www.vahistory.org/massive.resistance/timeline.html.

79. *Daily Progress*, June 11, 1960.

80. *Daily Progress*, June 11, 1960, esp. letter to editor from Francis H. Fife, "Slum Problem Solution"; see also the transcript of Mayor Thomas J. Michie's radio address on urban renewal, *Daily Progress*, June 10, 1960.

81. James Robert Saunders, *Urban Renewal and the End of Black Culture in Charlottesville, Virginia: An Oral History of Vinegar Hill* (Jefferson, N.C.: McFarland, 1988).

82. *Daily Progress*, June 10, 1960.

83. *Daily Progress*, June 15, 1960.

84. See, for example, Robert M. Fogelson, *Downtown: Its Rise and Fall, 1880–1950* (New Haven: Yale University Press, 2001); Kevin Fox Gotham, "A City Without Slums: Urban Renewal, Public Housing, and Downtown Revitalization in Kansas City, Missouri," *American Journal of Economics and Sociology* 60 (Jan. 2001): 286–316.

85. Mary Jones's story is assembled from United States Census records, Charlottesville city directories, and the records of the Vinegar Hill urban renewal, ACHS.

CHAPTER TEN

Drive-By History

1. See Marguerite S. Shaffer, "A Nation on Wheels," chap. 4 in Marguerite S. Shaffer, *See America First: Tourism and National Identity, 1880–1940* (Washington, D.C.:

Smithsonian Institution Press, 2001), 130–168; John A. Jakle, *The Tourist: Travel in Twentieth-Century North America* (Lincoln: University of Nebraska Press, 1985), 120–145.

2. *Los Angeles Times*, Sept. 16, 1923.

3. William E. Carson to Newspaper Editors, Nov. 8, 1929, Virginia State Library, Archives Division, Publications Branch, "Highway Historical Markers Records, 1928–1968, Correspondence," box 10.

4. *New York Times*, Dec. 22, 1929.

5. Timothy Davis, "Mount Vernon Memorial Highway: Changing Conceptions of an American Commemorative Landscape," in Joachim Wolschke-Bulmahn, ed., *Places of Commemoration: Search for Identity and Landscape Design* (Washington, D.C.: Dumbarton Oaks Research Library and Collection, 2001), 131–184.

6. William M. E. Rachal, "Historical Markers on Virginia Highways," c. 1941, Virginia State Library, Archives Division, Publications Branch, "Highway Historical Markers, Records, 1928–1968, Correspondence," box 2.

7. James M. Lindgren, *Preserving the Old Dominion: Historic Preservation and Virginia Traditionalism* (Charlottesville: University of Virginia Press, 1993).

8. See Henry S. Randall, *The Life of Thomas Jefferson*, 3 vols. (New York: Derby & Jackson, 1858), vol. 1, 336–337.

9. Edward S. Jouett to Mrs. Frederick Page, c. June 1910, quoted in *Daily Progress*, June 6, 1910.

10. *Daily Progress*, June 3, 1910.

11. *Acts and Joint Resolutions of the General Assembly of the State of Virginia, Session Which Commenced at the State Capitol on Wednesday, January 13, 1926* (Richmond: Davis Bottom, Superintendent of Public Printing, 1926), chap. 169, approved March 17, 1926, 307.

12. Walter W. Ristow, "American Road Maps and Guides," *Scientific American* 62 (May 1946): 397–406; Warren J. Belasco, *Americans on the Road: From Autocamp to Motel, 1910–1945* (Cambridge: MIT Press, 1979).

13. *Washington Post*, June 15, 1924.

14. Virginia Historic Highway Association, *Virginia Historic Shrines and Scenic Attractions Accessible by Virginia Historic Highway Tour Officially Designated by the General Assembly of Virginia* (Lynchburg, Va.: J. P. Bell Co., 1928); "Junius P. Fishburn," *History of Virginia*, vol. 6, *Virginia Biography* (Chicago: American Historical Society, 1924), 455.

15. *Minutes of Meetings of the State Conservation and Development Commission, July 16, 1926–Dec. 31, 1927*, May 5, 1927, Virginia State Library, Archives Division.

16. Mrs. T. A. Cordry, *The Story of the Marking of the Santa Fe Trail by the Daughters of the American Revolution in Kansas and the State of Kansas* (Topeka, Kans.: Crane & Company, 1915); *New York Times*, July 11, 1909.

17. See Marguerite S. Shaffer, "A Nation on Wheels," chap. 4 in Shaffer, *See America First*, 130–168; Jakle, *The Tourist*, 120–145; Michael Kammen, *Mystic Chords of Memory: The Transformation of Tradition in American Culture* (New York: Knopf, 1991), 274–276; Drake Hokanson, *The Lincoln Highway: Main Street Across America* (Iowa City: University of Iowa Press, 1988); see also Multiple Property Resource Nomination to National Register of Historic Places, "The Commemorative Markers Placed by the United Daughters of the Confederacy on the Jefferson Davis Highway in Virginia, 1913–1947."

18. State Commission on Conservation and Development, *Minute Books and Programs of* Meetings, 1926–1933, 10 vols., vol. Oct. 15, 1926–Dec. 31, 1927, Oct. 15, 1926, Virginia State Library, Archives Division (hereafter VSL Archives).

19. Daniel J. Boorstin, *The Image: A Guide to Pseudo-Events in America* (New York: Harper & Row, 1961), 112.

20. W. E. Carson to C. J. Millard, Mar. 9, 1928, "Conservation and Development, Miscellaneous," box 10.

21. State Commission on Conservation and Development, *Minute Books and Programs of Meetings, 1926–1933*, vol. Oct. 15, 1926–Dec. 31, 1927, July 27, 1927, VSL Archives.

22. *Minutes of Meetings of the Conservation and Development Commission of Virginia, Jan.–Dec. 1928*, Jan. 20, 1928.

23. Judge A. C. Carson to Governor Harry F. Byrd, July 14, 1927, Executive Papers, Governor Harry Flood Byrd, box 8, VSL Archives.

24. "Memorandum: The Organization and Operation of the Conservation and Development Commission, May 2, 1927." State Commission on Conservation and Development, *Minute Books and Programs of Meetings, 1926–1933*, vol. Oct. 15, 1926–Dec. 31 1927, May 5, 1927, VSL Archives.

25. William J. Showalter quoted in William E. Carson (chairman, State Commission on Conservation and Development), *Conservation and Development in Virginia: Outline of the Work of the Virginia State Commission on Conservation and Development, January 1930 to December, 1933* (Richmond: Division of Purchase and Printing, 1934), 3.

26. William E. Carson to Newspaper Editors, Nov. 8, 1929, "Highway Historical Markers Records, 1928–1968, Correspondence," Publications Branch, box 2, VSL Archives.

27. William E. Carson to Newspaper Editors, Nov. 8, 1929, Division of History Papers, box 10, VSL Archives; Carson, *Conservation and Development in Virginia*, 7.

28. "A Publicity Program for the Development of the State of Virginia," in State Commission on Conservation and Development, *Minute Books and Programs of Meetings, 1926–1933*, vol. Oct. 15, 1926–Dec. 31. 1927, Nov. 22, 1927, VSL Archives.

29. *American Motorist*, April 1928, 54.

30. F. E. Turin, Manager of the Advertising Board of Norfolk-Portsmouth Chamber of Commerce, to Harry F. Byrd, April 30, 1928, "Conservation and Development, Miscellaneous," Division of History Papers, box 10, VSL Archives.

31. State Commission on Conservation and Development, Division of History and Archaeology [H. J. Eckenrode, director; Colonel Bryan Conrad, asst. director], *Key to Inscriptions on Virginia Highway Historical Markers* (Richmond: Division of Purchase and Printing, 1929), 3.

32. "Memorandum of Dr. H. J. Eckenrode Relating to the Work of the Division of Archaeology and History and the Placing of Historical Markers, January 1927," in State Commission on Conservation and Development, *Minute Books and Programs of Meetings, 1926–1933*, vol. Oct. 15, 1926–Dec. 31 1927, VSL Archives.

33. Ibid.

34. D. S. Freeman to Eckenrode, Sept. 7, 1927, Department of Conservation and Development, Division of History Papers, Correspondence, 1927–1950, box 10, VSL Archives.

35. Board Authorized to Place Suitable Monuments or Markers on, at, or in Places of Historic Interest Located in the Commonwealth, Act 1922, chap. 127, page 210.

36. Gov. Harry F. Byrd to Mrs. W. W. Sale, Mar. 12, 1927, Executive Papers, Governor Harry Flood Byrd, box 5, "Battlefield Markers Commission," VSL Archives.

37. Wm. Byrd to E. O. Fippin, Aug. 26 1927, Department of Conservation and Development, Division of History Papers, Correspondence, 1927–1950, box 5, VSL Archives.

38. Carson to Eckenrode, Dec. 9, 1927, Eckenrode to Carson, Dec. 10, 1927, and Carson to Eckenrode, Dec. 28, 1927, Department of Conservation and Development, Division of History Papers, Correspondence, 1927–1950, box 10, VSL Archives.

39. Carson to Eckenrode, Nov. 6, 1929, Department of Conservation and Development, Division of History Papers, Correspondence, 1927–1950, box 10, VSL Archives.

40. "Bringing History to the Motorist on Virginia's Well-Marked Highways," *Highway Magazine* 23 (June 1932): 123–125.

41. *Key to Inscriptions on Virginia Highway Markers.*

42. Eckenrode to Will C. Barnes, U.S. Geographic Board, July 22, 1929, Department of Conservation and Development, Division of History Papers, Correspondence, 1927–1950, box 1, VSL Archives; see also Eckenrode to G. R. Michaels, Sept. 8, 1930, Department of Conservation and Development, Division of History Papers, Correspondence, 1927–1950, box 6, VSL Archives.

43. Mary H. Mitchell, *Hollywood Cemetery: The History of a Southern Shrine* (Richmond: Virginia State Library, 1985), 3; *Washington Post*, Nov. 19, 1903; *New York Times*, July 3, 1858.

44. William E. Carson to Herbert Hoover, Jan. 28, 1929; William E. Carson to Harry F. Byrd, Jan. 21 and 28, 1929, in Executive Papers, Gov. Harry Flood Byrd, "Conservation and Development, Miscellaneous," box 10, VSL Archives.

45. Gaines M. Foster, *Ghosts of the Confederacy: Defeat, the Lost Cause, and the Emergence of the New South, 1865 to 1913* (New York: Oxford University Press, 1987); see also Kirk Savage, *Standing Soldiers, Kneeling Slaves: Race, War, and Monument in Nineteenth-Century America* (Princeton: Princeton University Press, 1997).

46. Eckenrode to Carson, July 8, 1931, Department of Conservation and Development, Division of History Papers, Correspondence, 1927–1950, box 10, VSL Archives.

47. Charles H. L. Johnston to Harry Byrd, July 9, 1927, Department of Conservation and Development, Division of History Papers, Correspondence, 1927–1950, box 5, VSL Archives.

48. Carson to Byrd, Sept. 10, 1927, Governor Harry Byrd Papers, box 10, VSL Archives.

49. "Memorandum of Dr. H. J. Eckenrode Relating to the Work of the Division of Archaeology and History and the Placing of Historical Markers, January 1927," in State Commission on Conservation and Development, *Minute Books and Programs of Meetings, 1926–1933*, vol. Oct. 15, 1926–Dec. 31 1927, VSL Archives.

50. Mrs. H. F. Lewis [Board for the Erection of Historical Markers in Virginia] to Mrs. Randolph, Sept. 27, 1927, Department of Conservation and Development, Division of History Papers, Correspondence, 1927–1950, box 5, VSL Archives.

51. Eckenrode to Carson, Jan. 5 and 26, 1931, and Carson to Eckenrode, Jan. 27, 1931, Department of Conservation and Development, Division of History Papers, Correspondence, 1927–1950, box 10, VSL Archives.

52. Fairfax Harrison to Eckenrode, Dec. 4, 1927, Eckenrode to Harrison, Dec. 5 1927, Fairfax Harrison to Eckenrode, Dec. 23, 1927, Eckenrode to Fairfax Harrison, June 18, 1928, Harrison to Eckenrode, June 19, 1928, Eckenrode to Harrison, July 18, 1928, Eckenrode to Harrison, July 19, 1928, and Harrison to Eckenrode, July 3, 1929, Department of Conservation and Development, Division of History Papers, Correspondence, 1927–1950, box 11, VSL Archives.

53. "Memorandum of Dr. H. J. Eckenrode Relating to the Work of the Division of Archaeology and History and the Placing of Historical Markers, January 1927," in State Commission on Conservation and Development, *Minute Books and Programs of Meetings, 1926–1933*, vol. Oct. 15, 1926–Dec. 31, 1927, VSL Archives.

54. A. S. Johnson to H. J. Eckenrode, May 30, 1929, A. S. Johnson to Eckenrode, May 1, 1929, Eckenrode to Johnson, May 16, 1929, and Eckenrode to Johnson, June 1, 1929; Department of Conservation and Development, Division of History Papers, Correspondence, 1927–1950, box 5, VSL Archives. The construction date is now generally believed to be about 1680. Robert Cohaniss to H. J. Eckenrode, Dec. 9, 1930, Department of Convservation and Development, Division of History papers, Correspondence, 1927–1950, box 2, VSL Archives.

55. Eggleston to Eckenrode, July 3, 1929, and Eckenrode to Eggleston July 5, 1929; see also Eggleston to Eckenrode, Dec. 4, 1928, and Eckenrode to Dr. J. D. Eggleston, Hampden-Sydney, Va., Mar. 11, 1927; Archives and Records Division, Department of Conservation and Development, Division of History Papers, Correspondence, 1927–1950, box 3, VSL Archives.

56. Eckenrode to Dr. Douglas S. Freeman, Sept. 16, 1928, Department of Conservation and Development, Division of History Papers, Correspondence, 1927–1950, box 10, "WE Carson, 1928," VSL Archives.

57. Eckenrode to Carson, Dec. 30, 1927, Department of Conservation and Development, Division of History Papers, Correspondence, 1927–1950, box 10, "WE Carson, 1927," VSL Archives.

58. Hamilton J. Eckenrode, "The Direct Method of History Teaching," c. December 1930, Virginia State Library, Archives and Records Division, Department of Conservation and Development, Division of History Papers, Correspondence, 1927–1950, box 1, VSL Archives.

59. Eckenrode to Dr. W. A. R. Goodwin, Jan. 25, 1933, Department of Conservation and Development, Division of History Papers, box 10, VSL Archives.

60 Eckenrode, "The Direct Method of History Teaching."

61 Eckenrode to Mr. Jay W. Johns, "Ash Lawn" Charlottesville, Va., Mar. 16, 1938, Department of Conservation and Development, Division of History Papers, Correspondence, 1927–1950, box 5, VSL Archives.

62. For a provocatively insightful reading of the shallowness of highway marker programs, see Robin W. Winks, "A Public Historiography," *Public Historian* 14 (Summer 1992): 93–105; and James B. Jones, Jr., "Register Listing and Roadside Historic Markers in Tennessee: A Study of Two Public History Programs," *Public Historian* 10 (Summer 1988): 19–30.

CHAPTER ELEVEN

Toxic Memory

1. See William J. Murtagh, "Rehabilitation and Adaptive Use," in William J. Murtagh, *Keeping Time: The History and Theory of Preservation in America* (New York: Wiley, 2006), 99–106.

2. On the politics of place, see Daniel Kemmis, *Community and the Politics of Place* (Norman: University of Oklahoma Press, 1990); Keith H. Basso, *Wisdom Sits in Places: Landscape and Language Among the Western Apache* (Albuquerque: University of New Mexico Press, 1996); Ned Kaufman, "Places of Historical, Cultural, and Social

Value: Identification and Protection, Part I," *Environmental Law in New York* 12 (Nov. 2001): 211–233.

3. Charles Eliot Norton, "The Lack of Old Homes in America," *Scribner's Magazine*, May 1889: 638.

4. Charles Eliot Norton, "The Lack of Old Homes in America," 638.

5. Kemmis, *Community and the Politics of Place*.

6. Martin V. Melosi, "The Fresno Sanitary Landfill in an American Cultural Context," *Public Historian* 24 (Summer 2002): 17–35.

7. Mike Wallace, "Preserving the Past: A History of Historic Preservation in the United States," in Mike Wallace, *Mickey Mouse History and Other Essays on American Memory* (Philadelphia: Temple University Press, 1996), 178–210; Mike Wallace, "Preservation Revisited," in Mike Wallace, *Mickey Mouse History*, 224–237; Daniel Bluestone, "Academics in Tennis Shoes: Historic Preservation and the Academy," *Journal of the Society of Architectural Historians* 58 (Sept. 1999): 300–307.

8. Martin V. Melosi and the National Park Service, "Fresno Sanitary Landfill," National Historic Landmark Nomination, National Park Service, August 2000.

9. Melosi, "The Fresno Sanitary Landfill in an American Cultural Context," 21–22.

10. Melosi not only did the research for the landmark designation of the Fresno Sanitary landfill; his 2002 article in the *Public Historian* is the basis for this chronicle of the controversy surrounding the designation of the Fresno Sanitary Landfill as a National Historic Landmark. All details of this account can be found in Melosi's article unless cited otherwise.

11. See Martin Melosi, *The Sanitary City: Urban Infrastructure in America from Colonial Times to the Present* (2000).

12. Paul Rogers, "Leaky Trash Site Chosen as National Treasure," *San Jose Mercury News*, August 28, 2001, quoted in Melosi, "The Fresno Sanitary Landfill in an American Cultural Context," 19.

13. Ibid.; and Mark Grossi, "Dump Cleanup Inspected," *Fresno Bee*, March 19, 2005.

14. http://www.fresno.gov/parks-rec/parkdisplay.asp?RecNo=117.

15. Melosi, "Fresno Sanitary Landfill," National Historic Landmark Nomination.

16. On fitness trails, see Douglas N. Knudson, "Park Trails for Fitness," http://www.ces.purdue.edu/extmedia/FNR/FNR-106.html.

17. Randall Mason, "Historic Preservation, Public Memory, and the Making of Modern New York City," in Max Page and Randall Mason, *Giving Preservation a History: Histories of Historic Preservation in the United States* (New York: Routledge, 2004), 143–157.

18. Richard Caldwell, *A True History of the Acquisition of Washington's Headquarters at Newburgh, by the State of New York* (Middletown, N.Y.: Stivers, Slauson & Boyd, 1887), 21.

19. Caldwell, *A True History*, 21.

20. The work of environmental historian William Cronon, *Nature's Metropolis: Chicago and the Great West* (New York: Norton, 1991), exemplifies this sort of historical perspective.

21. Dolores Hayden, *The Power of Place: Urban Landscapes as Public History* (Cambridge: MIT Press, 1995).

22. Joseph A. Amato, *Rethinking Home: A Case for Writing Local History* (Berkeley: University of California Press, 2002), 186.

23 For an illuminating discussion of this approach, see: Ned Kaufman, *Place, Race, and Story: Essays on the Past and Future of Historic Preservation* (New York: Routledge, 2009).

Index

[Page numbers in italic refer to captions. Page numbers preceded by "C" refer to color section.]